THE BEST OF
FoxTrot

Other FoxTrot Books by Bill Amend

FoxTrot
Pass the Loot
Black Bart Says Draw
Eight Yards, Down and Out
Bury My Heart at Fun-Fun Mountain
Say Hello to Cactus Flats
May the Force Be with Us, Please
Take Us to Your Mall
The Return of the Lone Iguana
At Least This Place Sells T-shirts
Come Closer, Roger, There's a Mosquito on Your Nose
Welcome to Jasorassic Park
I'm Flying, Jack . . . I Mean, Roger
Think iFruity
Death by Field Trip
Encyclopedias Brown and White
His Code Name Was The Fox
Your Momma Thinks Square Roots Are Vegetables
Who's Up for Some Bonding?
Am I a Mutant or What!
Orlando Bloom Has Ruined Everything
My Hot Dog Went Out, Can I Have Another?
How Come I'm Always Luigi?
Houston, You Have a Problem
And When She Opened the Closet, All the Clothes Were Polyester
Math, Science, and Unix Underpants
FoxTrot Sundaes

Anthologies

FoxTrot: The Works
FoxTrot en masse
Enormously FoxTrot
Wildly FoxTrot
FoxTrot Beyond a Doubt
Camp FoxTrot
Assorted FoxTrot
FoxTrot: Assembled with Care
FoxTrotius Maximus
Jam-Packed FoxTrot
Wrapped-Up FoxTrot

THE BEST OF

FoxTrot

Volume One

by Bill Amend

Andrews McMeel
Publishing, LLC

Kansas City • Sydney • London

FoxTrot is distributed internationally by Universal Uclick.

The Best of FoxTrot © 2010 by Bill Amend. All rights reserved. Printed in China. No part of this book may be used or reproduced in any manner whatsoever without written permission except in the case of reprints in the context of reviews. For information, write Andrews McMeel Publishing, LLC, an Andrews McMeel Universal company, 1130 Walnut Street, Kansas City, Missouri 64106.

10 11 12 13 14 SDB 10 9 8 7 6 5 4 3 2 1

ISBN: 978-0-7407-7733-2

Library of Congress Control Number: 2009929504

www.andrewsmcmeel.com

www.foxtrot.com

Introduction

As miracles go, my being signed by Universal Press Syndicate in the fall of 1987 to do a daily comic strip wasn't on par with, say, the parting of the Red Sea, or walking on water or anything, but I'm pretty sure it still met the minimum definition. From the point of view of anyone who knew me, it certainly must have seemed like one.

I was twenty-five at the time and living with my parents with no clear career path. While I had drawn lots of cartoons for fun and for school publications over the years, my résumé wasn't what you'd think a syndicate would be looking for. I'd never had a comic strip published (actually, in high school I had one published, which they then told me would be my last). I'd taken one art class in college—basic drawing—and received a B-minus. I'd contributed plenty of single-panel editorial cartoons to my college newspaper, but those had minimal dialogue, no story lines, and no recurring characters. I'd majored in physics, which gave me practice at drawing ramps and blocks and sine waves, but not much more than that. My only real professional art experience was that I'd worked for two months after graduation as an assistant assistant assistant animator in San Francisco before the small commercial studio realized just how unqualified I was.

All I had going for me were these photocopied batches of something called "FoxTrot" that I'd been putting together off and on for two years. But I guess Universal was just insanely good at spotting potential cartoon talent. Or just plain insane. Whatever the reason, they signed me to a twenty-year deal, and in April 1988 I went from unpublished nobody to published somebody. Well, realistically I was still a nobody, but at least I felt like a somebody.

Unlike a lot of comics, FoxTrot didn't really have much of a concept to it, other than being about a family. What set it apart from the scads of other family strips already in print, or at least what I hoped set it apart, was the irreverent and contemporary sensibility I tried to bring to it. Peter was a bossy older brother who loved Bruce Springsteen. Paige was a shopaholic freshman prone to screaming who loathed her two siblings. And Jason was the MENSA-candidate Terminator robot of annoying little brothers. I took the oft-used staples of clueless Dad and sensible Mom to extremes, with Roger destroying computers simply by turning them on and Andy preparing meals that were so healthy they were lethal. And I made the family pet an iguana. None of it was genius, but it seemed to work okay.

5

Not every newspaper leaped at the chance to run FoxTrot, but enough did that I was able to make a living from the get-go with just the strip, and gradually my client list grew. When Berke Breathed retired Bloom County, I picked up a lot of papers, and then years later I gained many more when Gary Larson and Bill Watterson called it quits. Bill Watterson was nice enough to contribute a foreword to my first book, which no doubt influenced about 99 percent of its sales. Because that first book sold well, I was able to sustain a publishing program that captured every strip I wrote in both black-and-white smaller collections and larger anthologies with colored Sundays. (This would prove to be a huge headache in later years every time I accidentally repeated a joke and people would e-mail me, but I guess there are far worse headaches a cartoonist could have.)

What excites me about the opportunity to do this two-volume "Best of" collection is not only can I showcase the strips I'm most proud of (and conveniently hide my many clunkers), but it allows a nice overview of the first twenty years of the strip. While the characters in FoxTrot haven't aged, this cartoonist certainly has, and so has the world we live in. It's fun to see the gradual evolution of my writing style and art style, and the changes in our culture's technologies and trends and interests all in one place.

In the early years, with very few things in the strip set in stone, I was free to let my characters go off in any funny or interesting direction that occurred to me. I tried my hand at more weighty subjects, introduced new characters, and generally experimented to see what worked and what didn't. In later years, with the strip fairly well established with readers, I was far less free to roam randomly. The characters' personalities and traits were largely set and their quirks explored. Fans had expectations they wanted me to meet. Whereas before it had been about taking the strip to wherever the humor was, now it was more about finding ways to bring the humor to the strip. Basically it meant I had to work harder if I wanted FoxTrot to stay funny and fresh and surprising.

With this collection, we've divided the first twenty years of FoxTrot in half, with volume one containing roughly the first decade and volume two the second. The chronology is maintained as much as possible while still keeping story lines and Sundays neatly laid out. I've added annotations in the margins with some strips. I'm sure some would wish there were more, but I was concerned they'd become too distracting if I'd gone crazy with them. If in the future I think of any important notes I left out, I'll try to post them on my Web site so you can write them in yourself.

Because defining what constitutes the "best" is so subjective, I'm sure I've left out strips that were favorites to some. Winnowing down seven thousand strips to just under seventeen hundred was an inelegant task, and I hope you'll forgive any horrific omissions.

A quick note about the Sundays: Since many of the older strips weren't stored digitally and had to be restored from old film separations, I apologize if the colors don't look entirely perfect. My publisher did an amazing job given what they had to work from. I also opted to leave out the intro toss-away panels that were part of my older Sundays so all the strips would share a common format and to maximize the number of strips I could include.

Finally, I want to thank everyone at Universal and Andrews McMeel for their many years of editorial, sales, and personal support, especially syndicate editors extraordinaire Greg Melvin, John Glynn, Sue Roush, Jake Morrissey, Alan McDermott, and Lee Salem, and book editors par excellence Dorothy O'Brien, Erin Friedrich, and Stephanie Bennett. I also want to thank the hundreds of newspaper editors who have allowed me to be a part of their comics pages for so long. And most especially, love and thanks to my family—Keeta, Maddie, William, Mom, Dad, Rich, Nicole, Mark—for their patience with me and the weirdness that comes with this job. Even without the aforementioned miracle of having my cartoons syndicated, I'd still be blessed.

Bill Amend
June 2010

April 10, 1988

My first published strip. Photo-shop hadn't been invented yet, so including these photos was a minor nightmare.

May 1, 1988

The final panel originally had Paige saying, "pinch in the butt," but my syndicate was nervous about a new cartoonist using such strong language.

9

This was the first strip in my first submission to the syndicate. I like that it ended up as my first published daily.

April 11, 1988

April 12, 1988

It's probably not best to introduce a character as an offscreen voice, but I think this introduction of Paige works pretty well.

April 13, 1988

My girlfriend at the time's last name was Stephen. I was trying to score points, obviously. I guess it worked, as her last name is now Amend.

April 14, 1988

Paige was introduced with no visuals. Here, Peter is introduced with no dialogue.

April 15, 1988

April 16, 1988

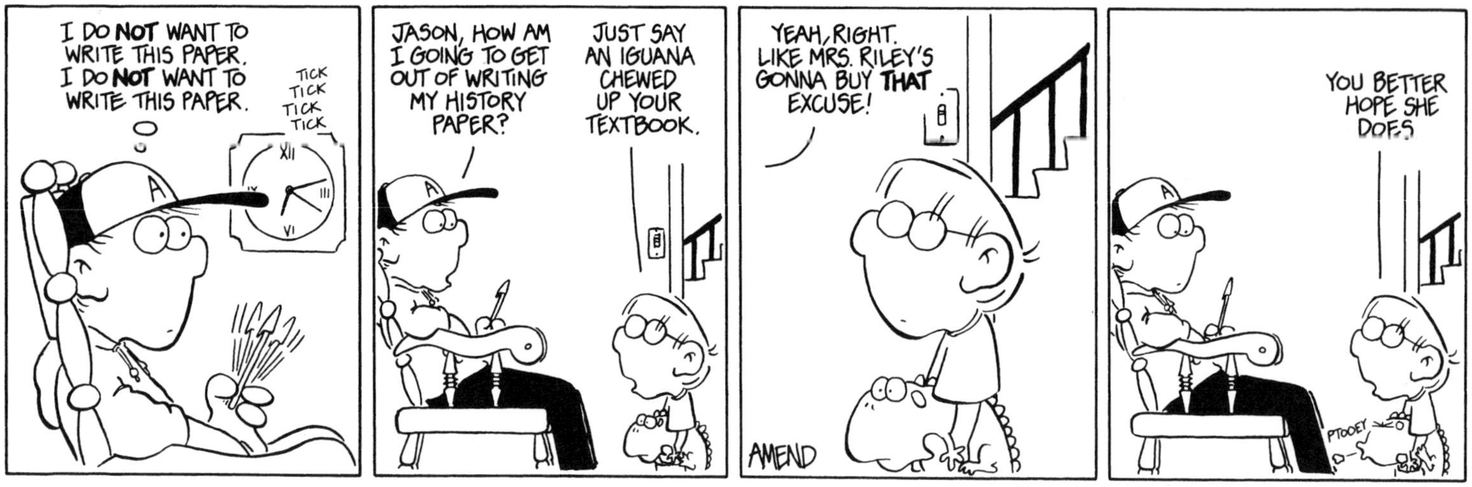
I DO **NOT** WANT TO WRITE THIS PAPER. I DO **NOT** WANT TO WRITE THIS PAPER.
TICK TICK TICK TICK
JASON, HOW AM I GOING TO GET OUT OF WRITING MY HISTORY PAPER?
JUST SAY AN IGUANA CHEWED UP YOUR TEXTBOOK.
YEAH, RIGHT. LIKE MRS. RILEY'S GONNA BUY **THAT** EXCUSE!
AMEND
YOU BETTER HOPE SHE DOES
PTOOEY

April 18, 1988

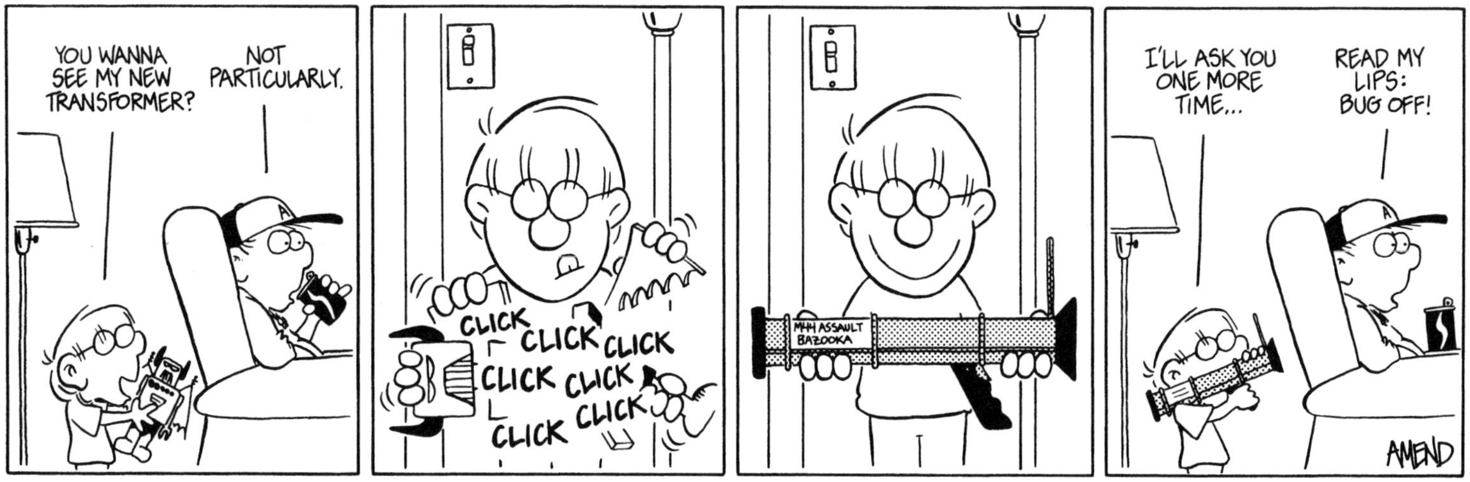
YOU WANNA SEE MY NEW TRANSFORMER?
NOT PARTICULARLY.
CLICK CLICK CLICK CLICK CLICK CLICK CLICK
M-44 ASSAULT BAZOOKA
I'LL ASK YOU ONE MORE TIME...
READ MY LIPS: BUG OFF!
AMEND

April 20, 1988

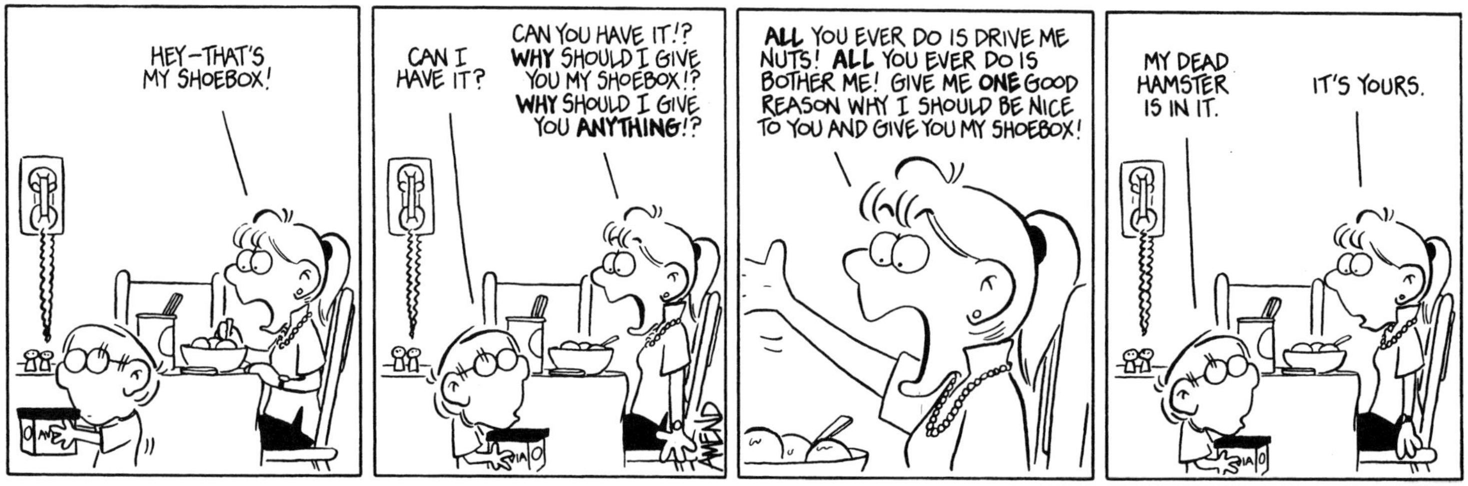
HEY–THAT'S MY SHOEBOX!
CAN I HAVE IT?
CAN YOU HAVE IT!? **WHY** SHOULD I GIVE YOU MY SHOEBOX!? **WHY** SHOULD I GIVE YOU **ANYTHING**!?
AMEND
ALL YOU EVER DO IS DRIVE ME NUTS! **ALL** YOU EVER DO IS BOTHER ME! GIVE ME **ONE** GOOD REASON WHY I SHOULD BE NICE TO YOU AND GIVE YOU MY SHOEBOX!
MY DEAD HAMSTER IS IN IT.
IT'S YOURS.

April 23, 1988

April 25, 1988

I'm pretty sure I swiped this joke from something *Lost in Space*'s June Lockhart once told me. It's a long story.

April 27, 1988

April 28, 1988

13

May 3, 1988

My sister's bedroom was next to mine. Strips like this were pretty easy to write.

May 5, 1988

My first of many fake newspaper headlines. Paulina was a *Sports Illustrated* swimsuit model back in the late '80s.

14

May 6, 1988

May 7, 1988

May 30, 1988

The moment right before disaster is usually the funniest.

July 18, 1988

Peter is channeling my own facial hair woes here.

May 23, 1988

I'm not quite sure what I was thinking when I drew this girl's hair. Hey, it was the '80s.

May 24, 1988

Pre-Internet I had to go to the library to research what a motorcycle cop's uniform might look like. I guess I could have just run some red lights.

May 25, 1988

I actually got to meet Springsteen about ten years ago. I wisely chose to restrain my inner Peter.

May 26, 1988

May 27, 1988

May 28, 1988

I liked this little guy, but I realized Jason was already Paige's personal demon, so this was his only appearance.

June 3, 1988

June 4, 1988

June 7, 1988

18

June 13, 1988

June 14, 1988

I grew up in the San Francisco area, hence the poster.

June 15, 1988

I'm told that real iguanas shouldn't eat mealworms. Fortunately, Quincy is a cartoon iguana.

June 16, 1988

I like letting the reader imagine the chaos. Plus, it's easy to draw.

June 17, 1988

20

June 18, 1988

The first of a bunch of Paige and Pierre strips I did over the years. I always wish I'd drawn them better.

July 17, 1988

August 14, 1988

21

I didn't have a daughter when I wrote these. In hindsight I underplayed the agony.

July 4, 1988

July 5, 1988

22

July 6, 1988

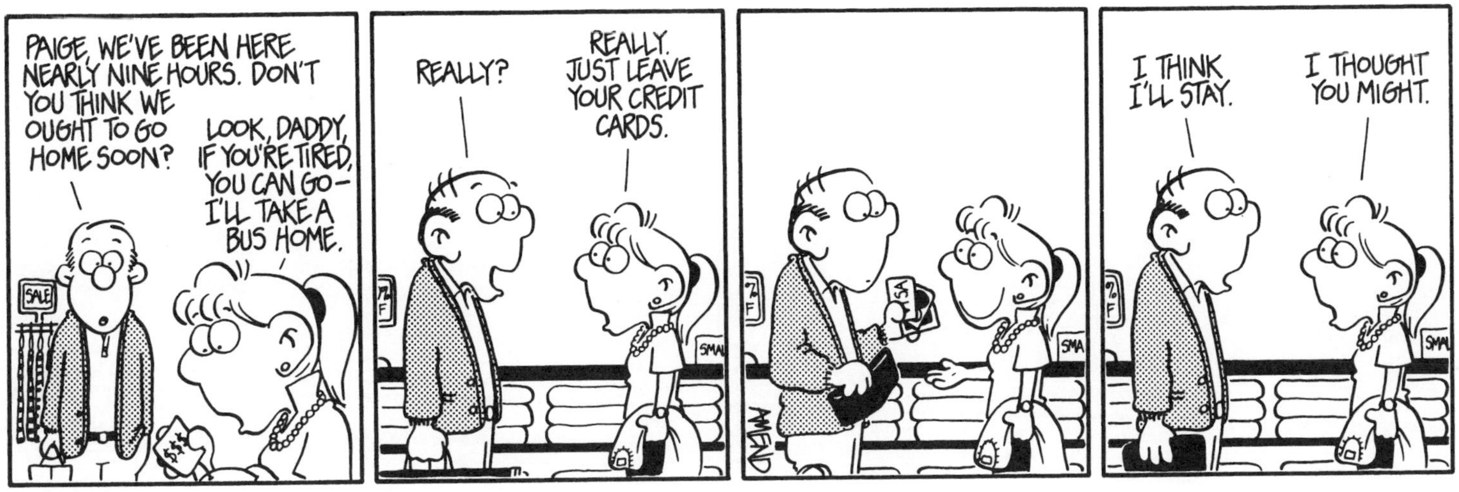
PAIGE, WE'VE BEEN HERE NEARLY NINE HOURS. DON'T YOU THINK WE OUGHT TO GO HOME SOON?
LOOK, DADDY, IF YOU'RE TIRED, YOU CAN GO– I'LL TAKE A BUS HOME.
SALE
REALLY?
REALLY. JUST LEAVE YOUR CREDIT CARDS.
AMEND
I THINK I'LL STAY.
I THOUGHT YOU MIGHT.

July 7, 1988

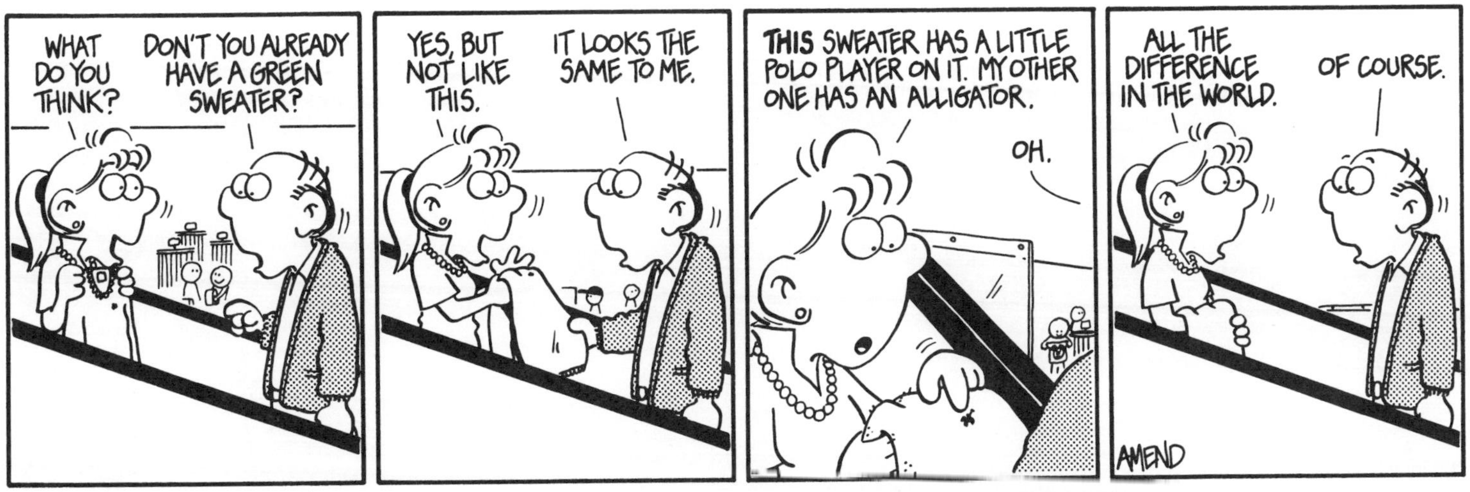
WHAT DO YOU THINK?
DON'T YOU ALREADY HAVE A GREEN SWEATER?
YES, BUT NOT LIKE THIS.
IT LOOKS THE SAME TO ME.
THIS SWEATER HAS A LITTLE POLO PLAYER ON IT. MY OTHER ONE HAS AN ALLIGATOR.
OH.
ALL THE DIFFERENCE IN THE WORLD.
OF COURSE.
AMEND

July 8, 1988

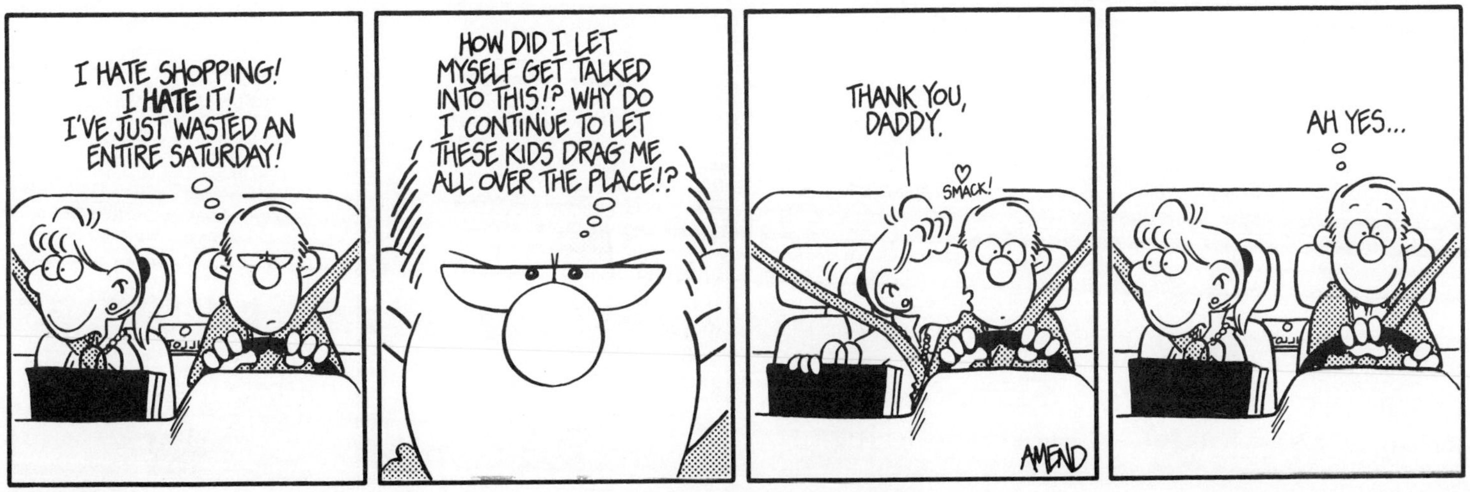
I HATE SHOPPING! I HATE IT! I'VE JUST WASTED AN ENTIRE SATURDAY!
HOW DID I LET MYSELF GET TALKED INTO THIS!? WHY DO I CONTINUE TO LET THESE KIDS DRAG ME ALL OVER THE PLACE!?
THANK YOU, DADDY.
SMACK!
AMEND
AH YES...

July 9, 1988

After about six months, I decided to give Peter a steady girlfriend.

September 20, 1988

Having Denise be blind seemed like an interesting break from the usual stuff you find in comic strips.

September 21, 1988

September 22, 1988

September 26, 1988

September 27, 1988

September 30, 1988

25

October 3, 1988

October 4, 1988

As I recall, my mother's sister called my mom to congratulate me on my engagement after this strip ran. Oops.

26

October 5, 1988

October 6, 1988

The movie I made my senior year in high school was just about this dangerous.

October 7, 1988

October 8, 1988

I was really proud of myself for thinking this one up.

July 26, 1988

I'd gotten a fair number of complaints that readers couldn't tell Paige and Andy apart, so I gave Mrs. Fox a haircut.

October 14, 1988

28

October 15, 1988

October 26, 1988

October 27, 1988

October 28, 1988

December 5, 1988

December 6, 1988

30

December 7, 1988

December 8, 1988

December 9, 1988

There's a brazenness about Denise that I find appealing.

December 10, 1988

This was the first storyline with a Jason/Quincy costume. It proved to be a good device for getting Quincy in the strip more often.

February 6, 1989

I spent hours flip-flopping between "Iguanoman" and "Iguanaman." In the end I decided "Iguano" sounded nerdier.

February 7, 1989

February 8, 1989

February 9, 1989

February 10, 1989

February 11, 1989

33

A newspaper client asked me to address teen drinking and drug use in the strip. In a rare moment of accommodation, I did these.

March 6, 1989

March 7, 1989

It still boggles my mind that newspapers actually ran some of these.

March 8, 1989

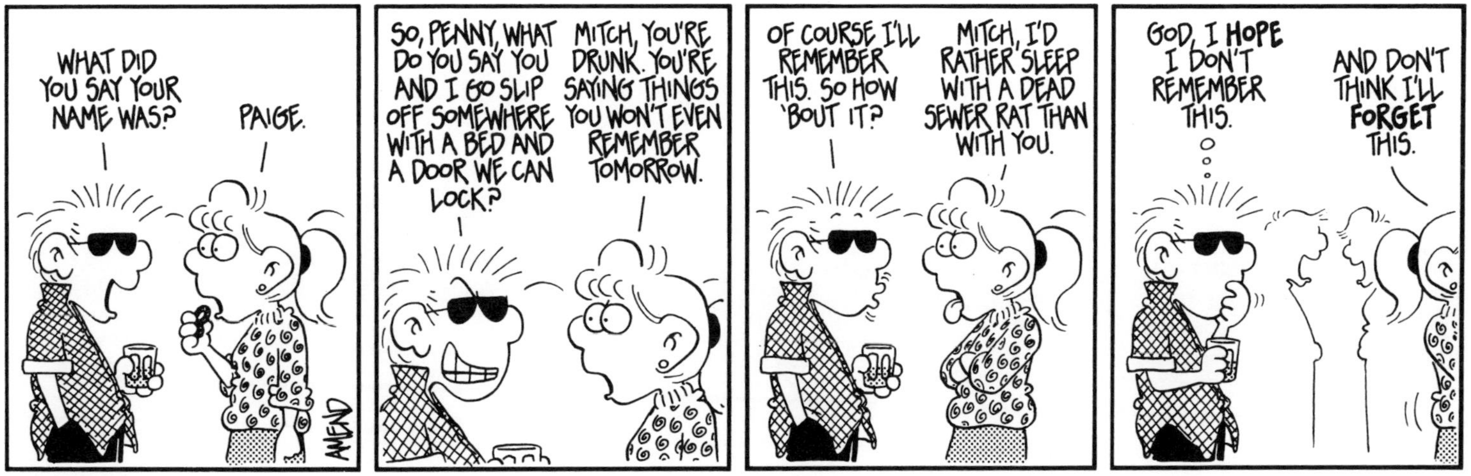
WHAT DID YOU SAY YOUR NAME WAS?
PAIGE.
SO, PENNY, WHAT DO YOU SAY YOU AND I GO SLIP OFF SOMEWHERE WITH A BED AND A DOOR WE CAN LOCK?
MITCH, YOU'RE DRUNK. YOU'RE SAYING THINGS YOU WON'T EVEN REMEMBER TOMORROW.
OF COURSE I'LL REMEMBER THIS. SO HOW 'BOUT IT?
MITCH, I'D RATHER SLEEP WITH A DEAD SEWER RAT THAN WITH YOU.
GOD, I **HOPE** I DON'T REMEMBER THIS.
AND DON'T THINK I'LL **FORGET** THIS.

March 9, 1989

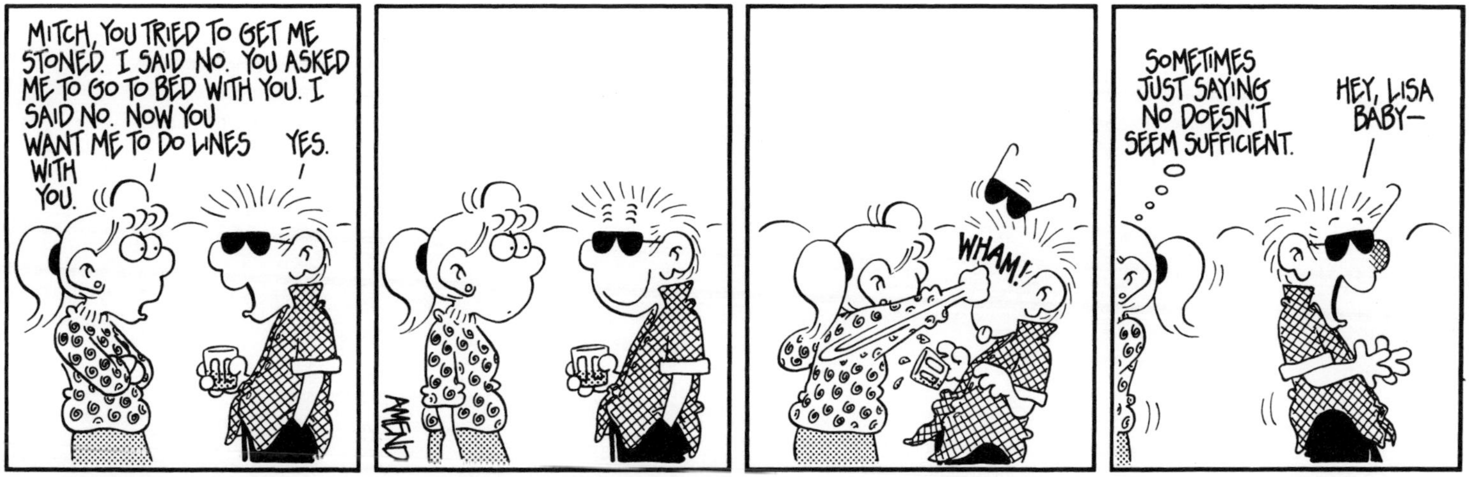
MITCH, YOU TRIED TO GET ME STONED. I SAID NO. YOU ASKED ME TO GO TO BED WITH YOU. I SAID NO. NOW YOU WANT ME TO DO LINES WITH YOU.
YES.
WHAM!
SOMETIMES JUST SAYING NO DOESN'T SEEM SUFFICIENT.
HEY, LISA BABY—

March 10, 1989

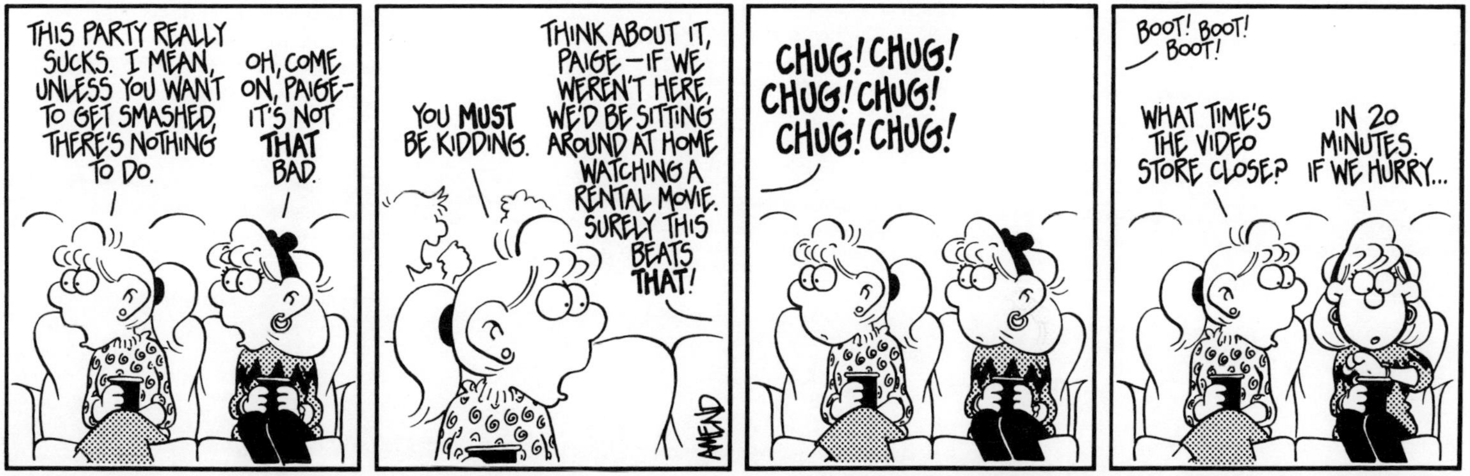
THIS PARTY REALLY SUCKS. I MEAN, UNLESS YOU WANT TO GET SMASHED, THERE'S NOTHING TO DO.
OH, COME ON, PAIGE- IT'S NOT **THAT** BAD.
YOU **MUST** BE KIDDING.
THINK ABOUT IT, PAIGE—IF WE WEREN'T HERE, WE'D BE SITTING AROUND AT HOME WATCHING A RENTAL MOVIE. SURELY THIS BEATS **THAT**!
CHUG! CHUG! CHUG! CHUG! CHUG! CHUG!
BOOT! BOOT! BOOT!
WHAT TIME'S THE VIDEO STORE CLOSE?
IN 20 MINUTES. IF WE HURRY...

March 11, 1989

April 3, 1989

By freak chance, two years after these ran, my wife and I ate at a restaurant by the same name on our honeymoon.

April 4, 1989

April 5, 1989

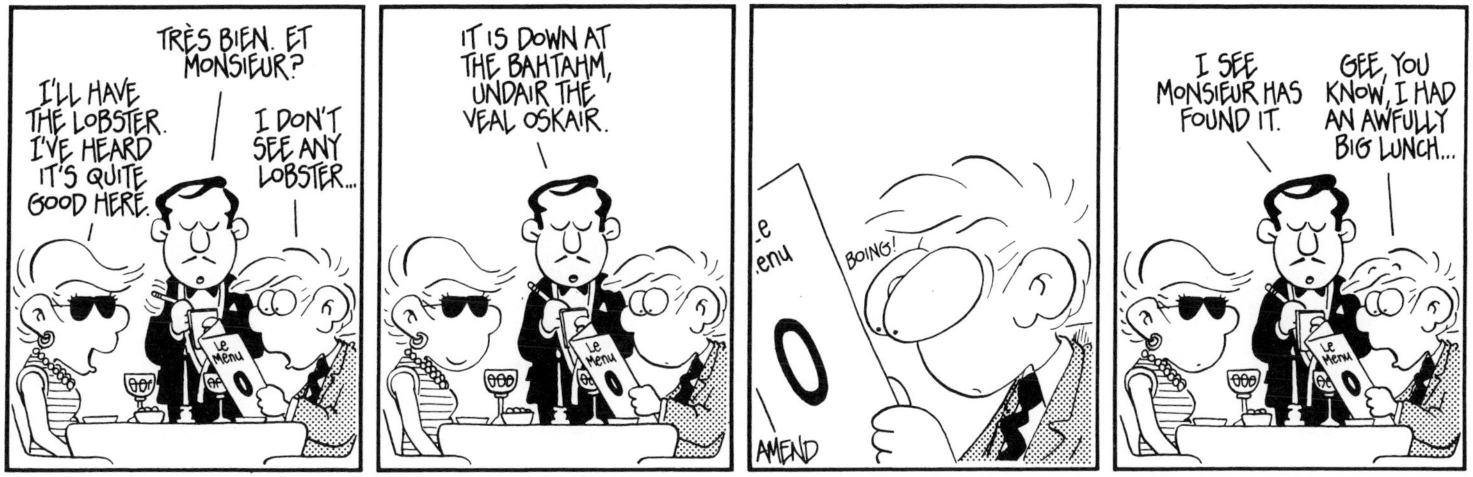
I'LL HAVE THE LOBSTER. I'VE HEARD IT'S QUITE GOOD HERE.
TRÈS BIEN. ET MONSIEUR?
I DON'T SEE ANY LOBSTER...
Le Menu
IT IS DOWN AT THE BAHTAHM, UNDAIR THE VEAL OSKAIR.
BOING!
AMEND
I SEE MONSIEUR HAS FOUND IT.
GEE, YOU KNOW, I HAD AN AWFULLY BIG LUNCH...

April 6, 1989

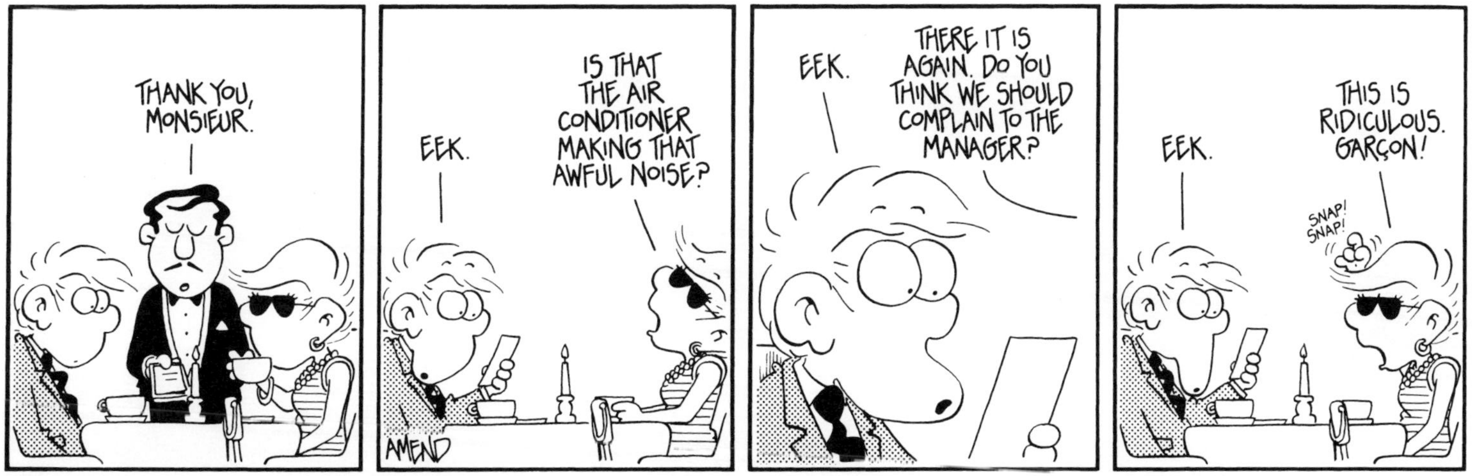
THANK YOU, MONSIEUR.
EEK.
IS THAT THE AIR CONDITIONER MAKING THAT AWFUL NOISE?
AMEND
EEK.
THERE IT IS AGAIN. DO YOU THINK WE SHOULD COMPLAIN TO THE MANAGER?
EEK.
THIS IS RIDICULOUS. GARÇON!
SNAP! SNAP!

April 7, 1989

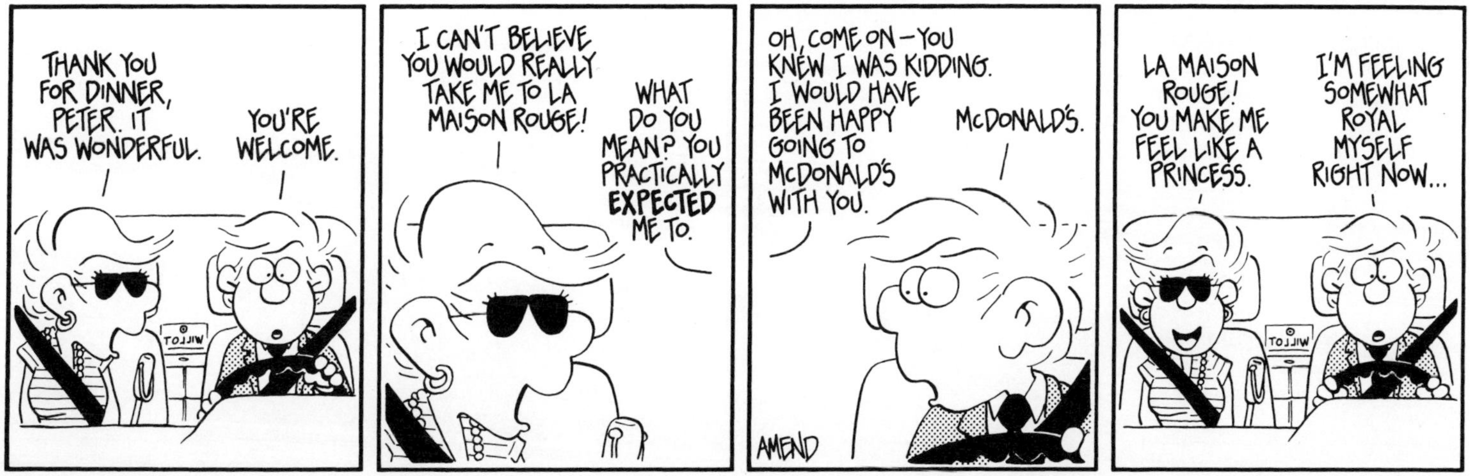
THANK YOU FOR DINNER, PETER. IT WAS WONDERFUL.
YOU'RE WELCOME.
I CAN'T BELIEVE YOU WOULD REALLY TAKE ME TO LA MAISON ROUGE!
WHAT DO YOU MEAN? YOU PRACTICALLY **EXPECTED** ME TO.
OH, COME ON—YOU KNEW I WAS KIDDING. I WOULD HAVE BEEN HAPPY GOING TO McDONALD'S WITH YOU.
McDONALD'S.
AMEND
LA MAISON ROUGE! YOU MAKE ME FEEL LIKE A PRINCESS.
I'M FEELING SOMEWHAT ROYAL MYSELF RIGHT NOW...

April 8, 1989

In reviewing the strips for this book, I've noticed that Jason has a thing for leeches. What that means, I don't know.

April 24, 1989

Not quite sure why Paige's and Jason's shirts switched colors from the previous day.

April 25, 1989

38

April 26, 1989

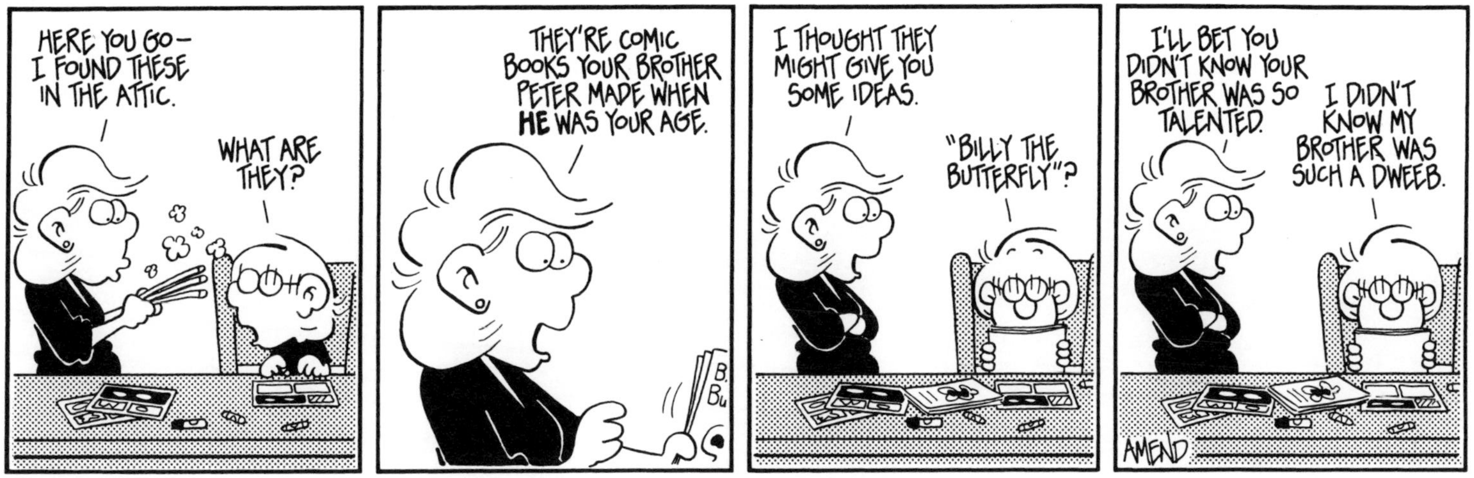
HERE YOU GO—I FOUND THESE IN THE ATTIC.
WHAT ARE THEY?
THEY'RE COMIC BOOKS YOUR BROTHER PETER MADE WHEN **HE** WAS YOUR AGE.
I THOUGHT THEY MIGHT GIVE YOU SOME IDEAS.
"BILLY THE BUTTERFLY"?
I'LL BET YOU DIDN'T KNOW YOUR BROTHER WAS SO TALENTED.
I DIDN'T KNOW MY BROTHER WAS SUCH A DWEEB.
AMEND

April 27, 1989

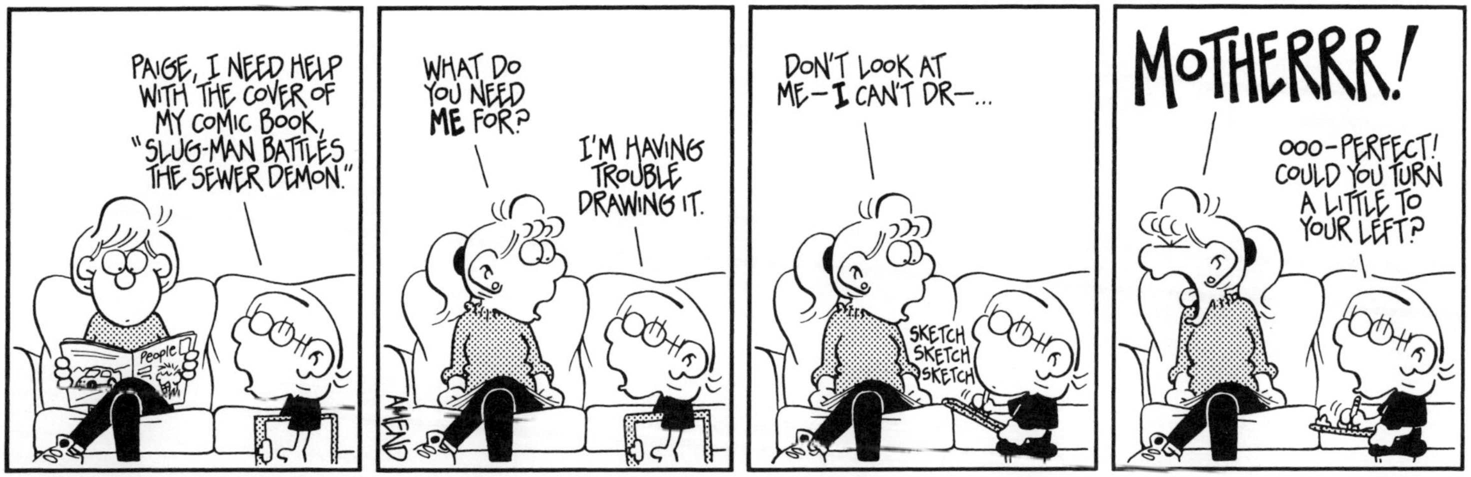
PAIGE, I NEED HELP WITH THE COVER OF MY COMIC BOOK, "SLUG-MAN BATTLES THE SEWER DEMON."
People
WHAT DO YOU NEED **ME** FOR?
I'M HAVING TROUBLE DRAWING IT.
AMEND
DON'T LOOK AT ME—**I** CAN'T DR—...
SKETCH SKETCH SKETCH
MOTHERRR!
OOO—PERFECT! COULD YOU TURN A LITTLE TO YOUR LEFT?

April 28, 1989

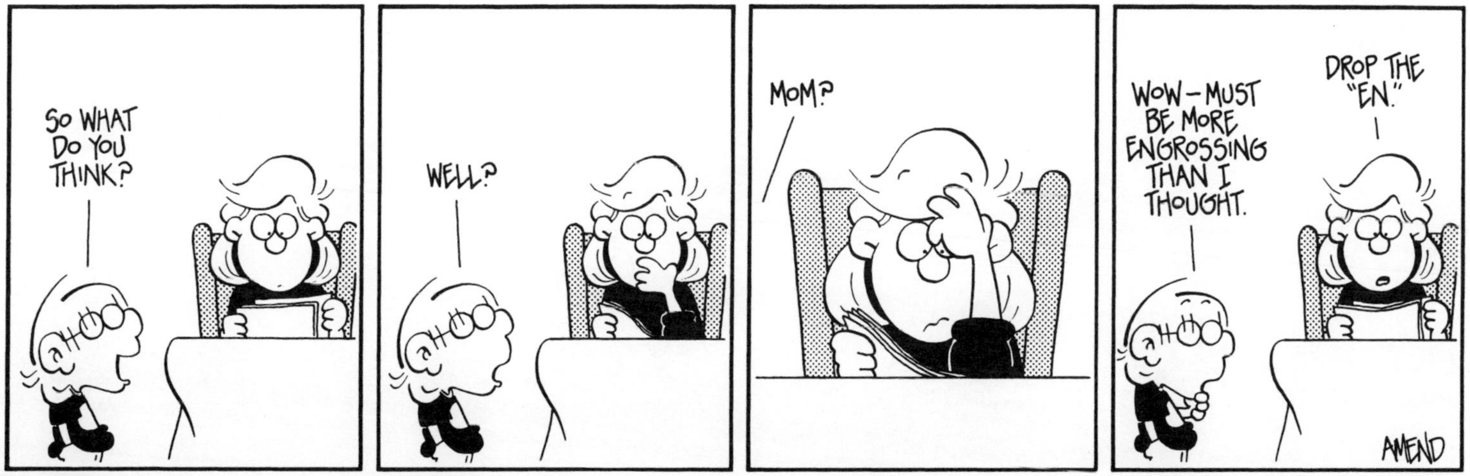
SO WHAT DO YOU THINK?
WELL?
MOM?
WOW—MUST BE MORE ENGROSSING THAN I THOUGHT.
DROP THE "EN."
AMEND

April 29, 1989

I didn't have an iguana when I was Jason's age, but I did have destructive younger siblings.

May 1, 1989

May 5, 1989

May 6, 1989

Trying to draw an accurate Apollo rocket in the days before Google Images was a huge pain.

October 16, 1988

Either that kitchen table is really high, or I drew Paige unusually short.

November 27, 1988

41

May 15, 1989

May 16, 1989

It's always fun to give a jerky character the same last name as your editor.

42

May 17, 1989

May 18, 1989

May 19, 1989

Coyote Point refers to an actual make-out spot near where I grew up.

May 20, 1989

Jason's first foray into geeky movie attire.

June 19, 1989

June 20, 1989

44

June 21, 1989

June 22, 1989

When I first started dating my wife, she and her sisters were on the news dressed in *Star Trek* costumes. I feel for Paige here.

June 23, 1989

June 24, 1989

July 23, 1989

A rare attempt at stretching my art a little in the third and fourth panels.

September 3, 1989

September 14, 1989

September 15, 1989

Any time you can work a word like "pus" into your strip counts as a win.

April 23, 1990

47

November 6, 1989

November 7, 1989

48

November 8, 1989

November 9, 1989

November 10, 1989

November 11, 1989

49

I don't remember much of what I learned in elementary school, but I do remember making papier-mâché dinosaurs.

October 11, 1989

October 13, 1989

For the record, my strip does not condone the killing of baby triceratops.

October 14, 1989

November 24, 1989

May 15, 1990

A takeoff on the old Folgers coffee commercials.

July 25, 1990

You've still got Marcus and Quincy, Jason. Don't be sad.

January 7, 1990

January 14, 1990

The lettering in panel two
has a nice look.

February 12, 1990

February 14, 1990

Apologies for not hyphenat-
ing "Spider-Man."

February 17, 1990

January 15, 1990

I'm pretty sure I just quoted one of my old physics assignments here.

January 16, 1990

The teacher is based on one of my college professors. He's since shaved off the beard.

54

January 17, 1990

January 18, 1990

January 19, 1990

January 20, 1990

Admit it, suction cup leeches
would be cool.

January 29, 1990

January 30, 1990

January 31, 1990

February 1, 1990

February 2, 1990

February 3, 1990

February 19, 1990

Yes, kids, once upon a time color was optional.

February 20, 1990

58

February 21, 1990

Computer specs have, um, changed a little over the years.

February 22, 1990

February 23, 1990

I did the computer text with my super-fancy dot matrix printer. Ooooo.

February 24, 1990

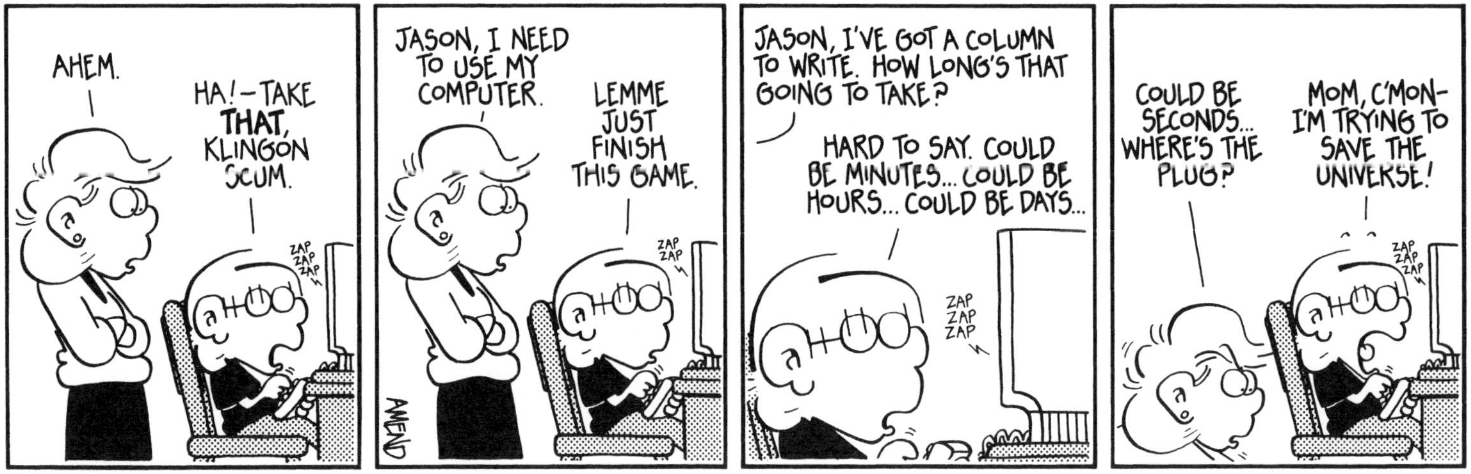
AHEM.
HA! - TAKE THAT, KLINGON SCUM.
ZAP ZAP ZAP
JASON, I NEED TO USE MY COMPUTER.
LEMME JUST FINISH THIS GAME.
ZAP ZAP
AMEND
JASON, I'VE GOT A COLUMN TO WRITE. HOW LONG'S THAT GOING TO TAKE?
HARD TO SAY. COULD BE MINUTES... COULD BE HOURS... COULD BE DAYS...
ZAP ZAP ZAP
COULD BE SECONDS... WHERE'S THE PLUG?
MOM, C'MON- I'M TRYING TO SAVE THE UNIVERSE!
ZAP ZAP ZAP

March 5, 1990

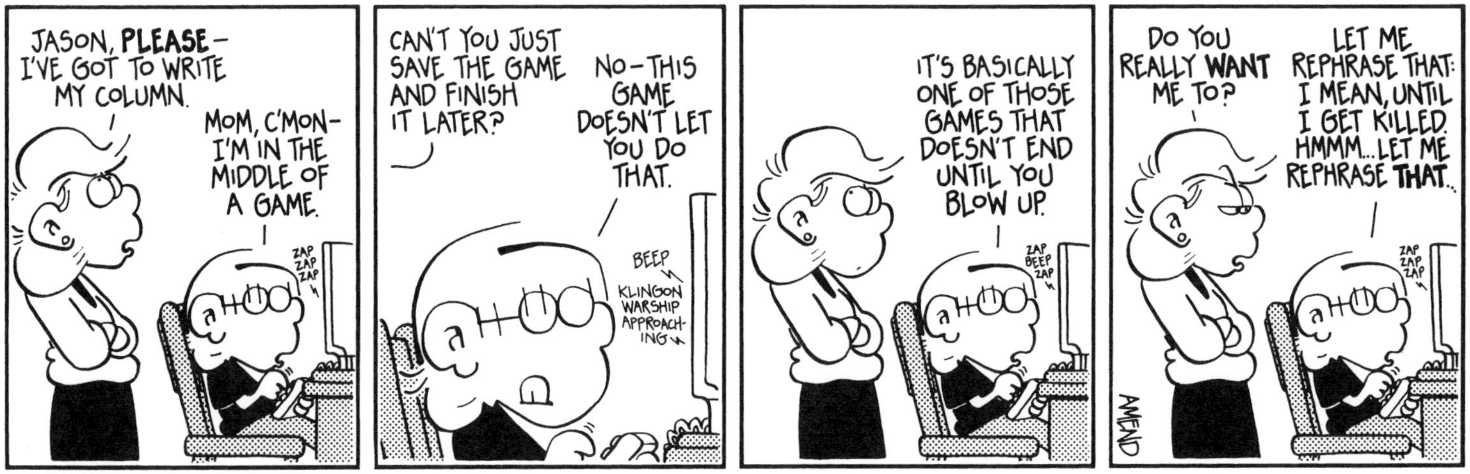
JASON, PLEASE - I'VE GOT TO WRITE MY COLUMN.
MOM, C'MON- I'M IN THE MIDDLE OF A GAME.
ZAP ZAP ZAP
CAN'T YOU JUST SAVE THE GAME AND FINISH IT LATER?
NO-THIS GAME DOESN'T LET YOU DO THAT.
BEEP
KLINGON WARSHIP APPROACHING
IT'S BASICALLY ONE OF THOSE GAMES THAT DOESN'T END UNTIL YOU BLOW UP.
ZAP BEEP ZAP
DO YOU REALLY WANT ME TO?
LET ME REPHRASE THAT: I MEAN, UNTIL I GET KILLED. HMMM... LET ME REPHRASE THAT...
ZAP ZAP ZAP
AMEND

March 6, 1990

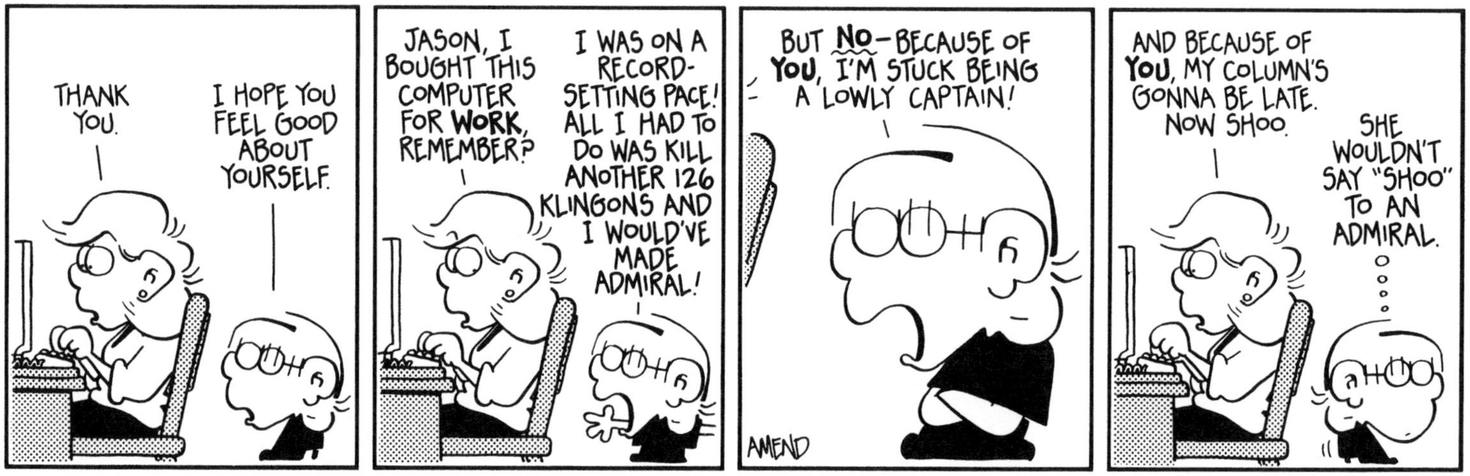
THANK YOU.
I HOPE YOU FEEL GOOD ABOUT YOURSELF.
JASON, I BOUGHT THIS COMPUTER FOR WORK, REMEMBER?
I WAS ON A RECORD-SETTING PACE! ALL I HAD TO DO WAS KILL ANOTHER 126 KLINGONS AND I WOULD'VE MADE ADMIRAL!
BUT NO - BECAUSE OF YOU, I'M STUCK BEING A LOWLY CAPTAIN!
AMEND
AND BECAUSE OF YOU, MY COLUMN'S GONNA BE LATE. NOW SHOO.
SHE WOULDN'T SAY "SHOO" TO AN ADMIRAL.

March 7, 1990

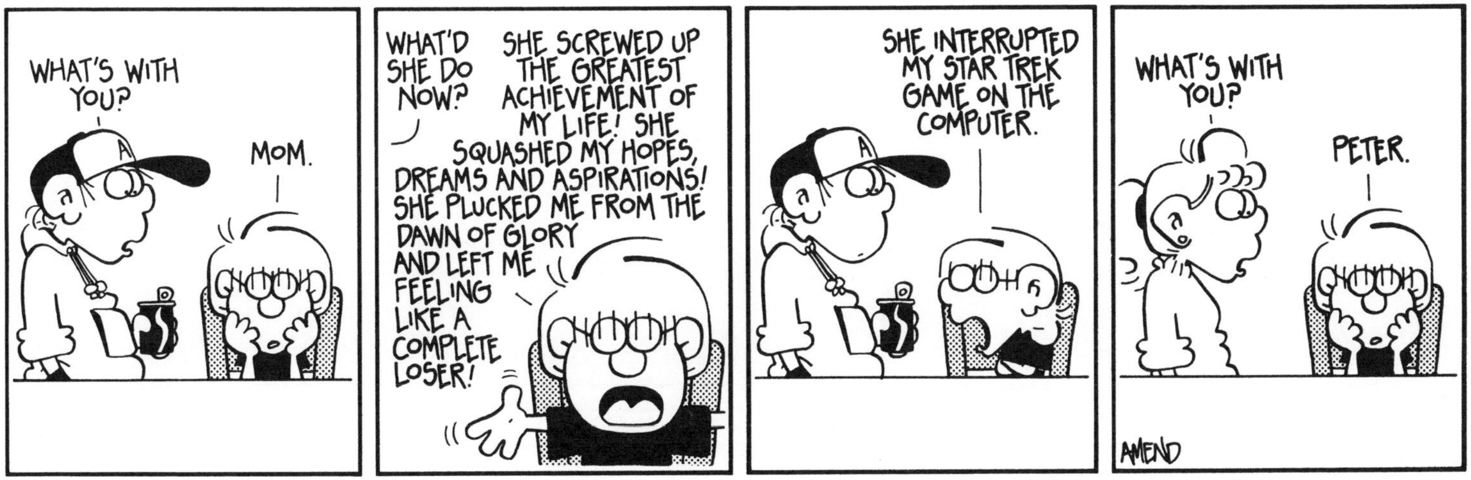
WHAT'S WITH YOU?
MOM.
WHAT'D SHE DO NOW?
SHE SCREWED UP THE GREATEST ACHIEVEMENT OF MY LIFE! SHE SQUASHED MY HOPES, DREAMS AND ASPIRATIONS! SHE PLUCKED ME FROM THE DAWN OF GLORY AND LEFT ME FEELING LIKE A COMPLETE LOSER!
SHE INTERRUPTED MY STAR TREK GAME ON THE COMPUTER.
WHAT'S WITH YOU?
PETER.
AMEND
March 8, 1990

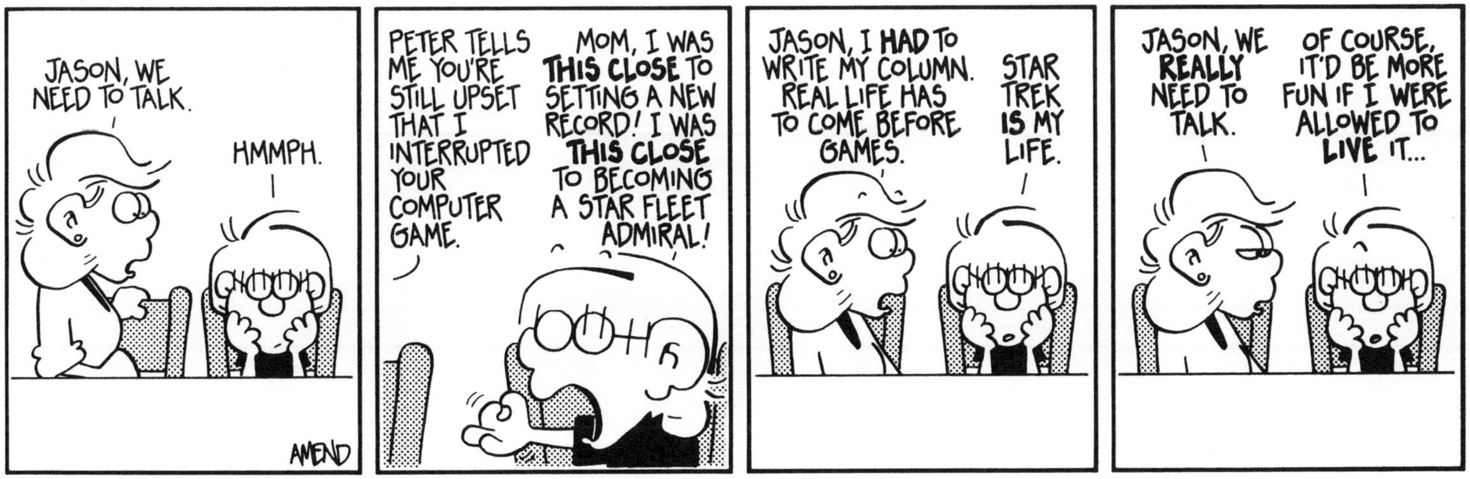
JASON, WE NEED TO TALK.
HMMPH.
AMEND
PETER TELLS ME YOU'RE STILL UPSET THAT I INTERRUPTED YOUR COMPUTER GAME.
MOM, I WAS **THIS CLOSE** TO SETTING A NEW RECORD! I WAS **THIS CLOSE** TO BECOMING A STAR FLEET ADMIRAL!
JASON, I **HAD** TO WRITE MY COLUMN. REAL LIFE HAS TO COME BEFORE GAMES.
STAR TREK **IS** MY LIFE.
JASON, WE **REALLY** NEED TO TALK.
OF COURSE, IT'D BE MORE FUN IF I **WERE** ALLOWED TO **LIVE** IT...
March 9, 1990

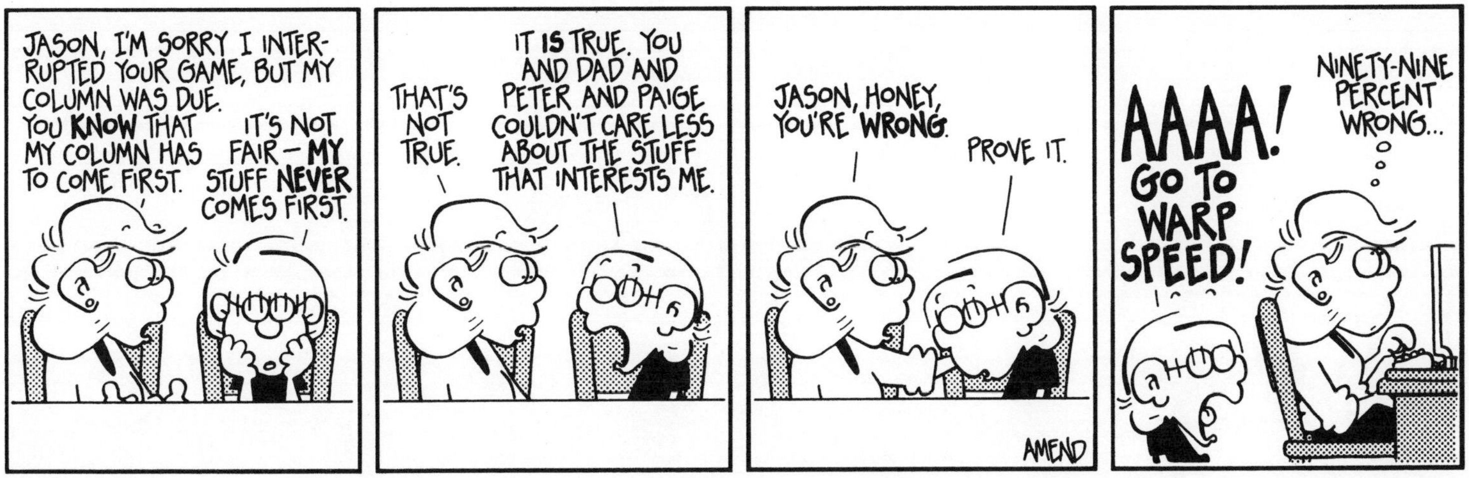
JASON, I'M SORRY I INTERRUPTED YOUR GAME, BUT MY COLUMN WAS DUE. YOU **KNOW** THAT MY COLUMN HAS TO COME FIRST.
IT'S NOT FAIR—**MY** STUFF **NEVER** COMES FIRST.
THAT'S NOT TRUE.
IT **IS** TRUE. YOU AND DAD AND PETER AND PAIGE COULDN'T CARE LESS ABOUT THE STUFF THAT INTERESTS ME.
JASON, HONEY, YOU'RE **WRONG**.
PROVE IT.
AMEND
AAAA! GO TO WARP SPEED!
NINETY-NINE PERCENT WRONG...
March 10, 1990

April 30, 1990

I usually avoid birthdays in the strip since the characters don't age. I liked this story line, though.

May 1, 1990

62

May 2, 1990

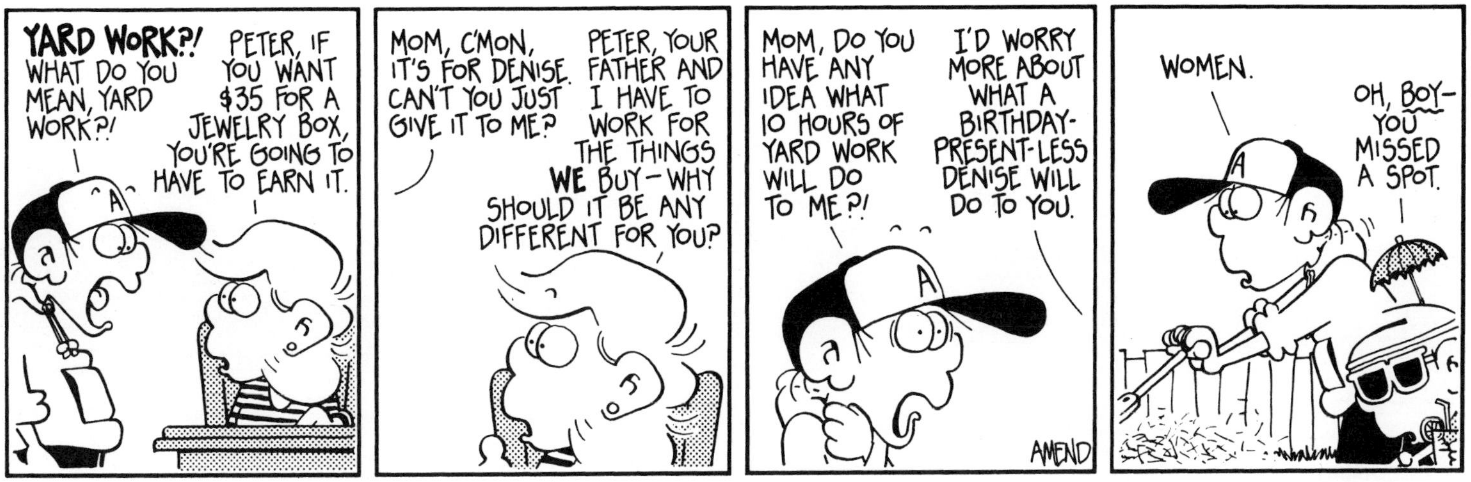
YARD WORK?! WHAT DO YOU MEAN, YARD WORK?!
PETER, IF YOU WANT $35 FOR A JEWELRY BOX, YOU'RE GOING TO HAVE TO EARN IT.
MOM, C'MON, IT'S FOR DENISE. CAN'T YOU JUST GIVE IT TO ME?
PETER, YOUR FATHER AND I HAVE TO WORK FOR THE THINGS WE BUY—WHY SHOULD IT BE ANY DIFFERENT FOR YOU?
MOM, DO YOU HAVE ANY IDEA WHAT 10 HOURS OF YARD WORK WILL DO TO ME?!
I'D WORRY MORE ABOUT WHAT A BIRTHDAY-PRESENT-LESS DENISE WILL DO TO YOU.
AMEND
WOMEN.
OH, BOY—YOU MISSED A SPOT.

May 3, 1990

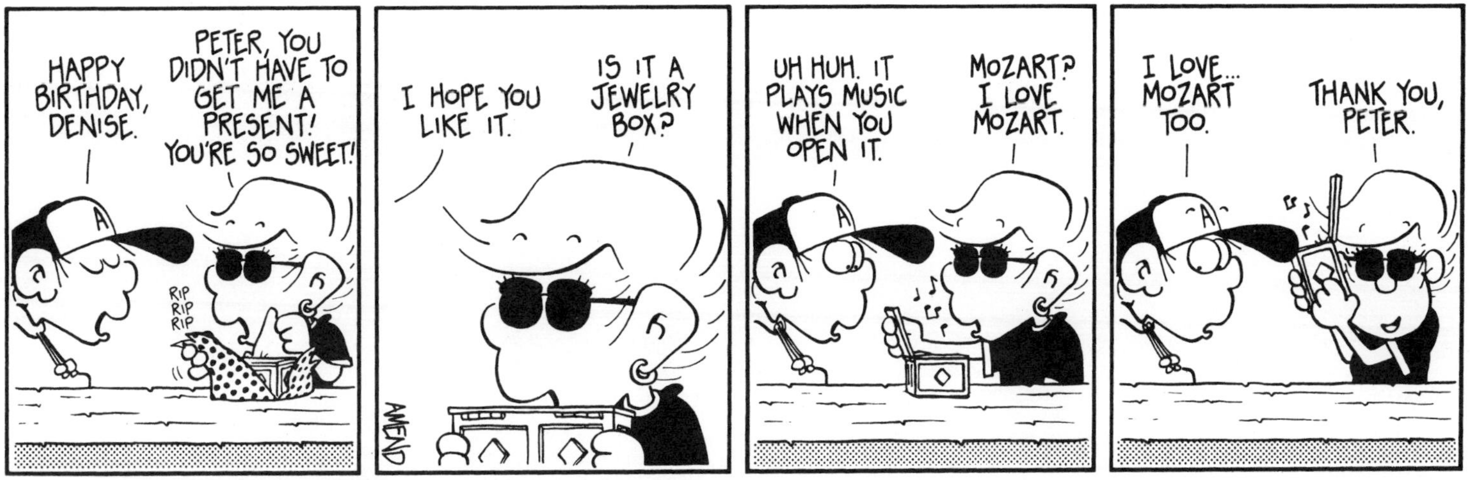
HAPPY BIRTHDAY, DENISE.
PETER, YOU DIDN'T HAVE TO GET ME A PRESENT! YOU'RE SO SWEET!
RIP RIP RIP
I HOPE YOU LIKE IT.
IS IT A JEWELRY BOX?
AMEND
UH HUH. IT PLAYS MUSIC WHEN YOU OPEN IT.
MOZART? I LOVE MOZART.
I LOVE... MOZART TOO.
THANK YOU, PETER.

May 4, 1990

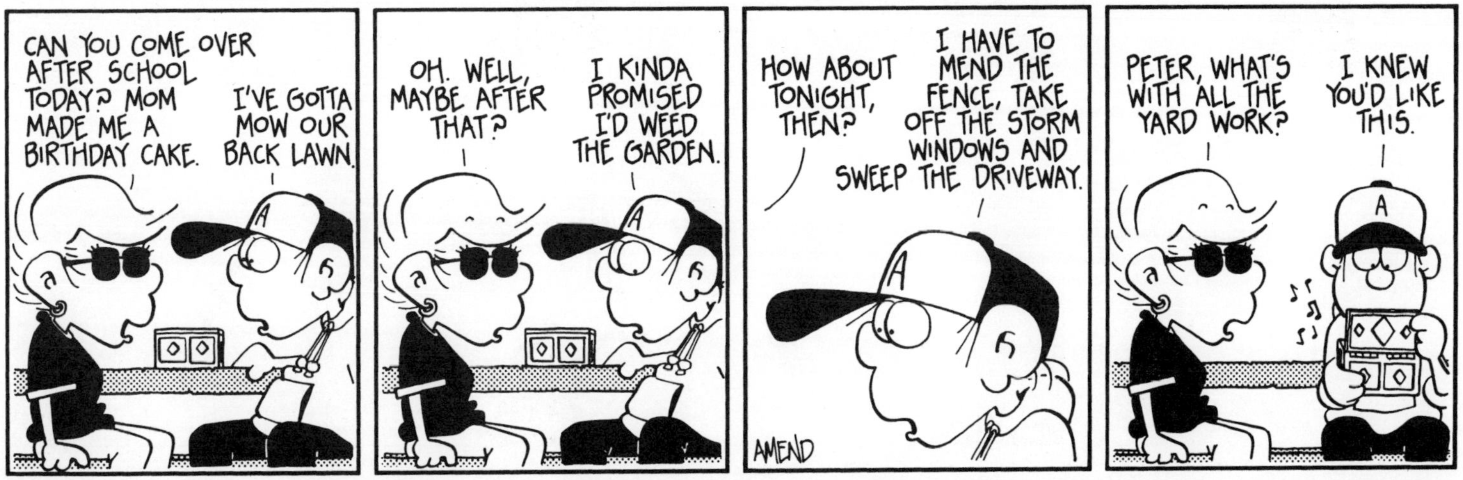
CAN YOU COME OVER AFTER SCHOOL TODAY? MOM MADE ME A BIRTHDAY CAKE.
I'VE GOTTA MOW OUR BACK LAWN.
OH. WELL, MAYBE AFTER THAT?
I KINDA PROMISED I'D WEED THE GARDEN.
HOW ABOUT TONIGHT, THEN?
I HAVE TO MEND THE FENCE, TAKE OFF THE STORM WINDOWS AND SWEEP THE DRIVEWAY.
AMEND
PETER, WHAT'S WITH ALL THE YARD WORK?
I KNEW YOU'D LIKE THIS.

May 5, 1990

I think Pierre's hair took longer to ink than the rest of the strip combined.

February 11, 1990

The sound effects might be funnier than the joke here.

April 15, 1990

64

See, kids? You, too, can draw Paige!

November 20, 1990

After having Quincy chew up *Star Trek* figures, this seemed only fair.

April 22, 1991

June 11, 1991

May 26, 1990

I mercifully left out the "Paige shops for a suitable dress in two hours" sequence.

May 29, 1990

May 30, 1990

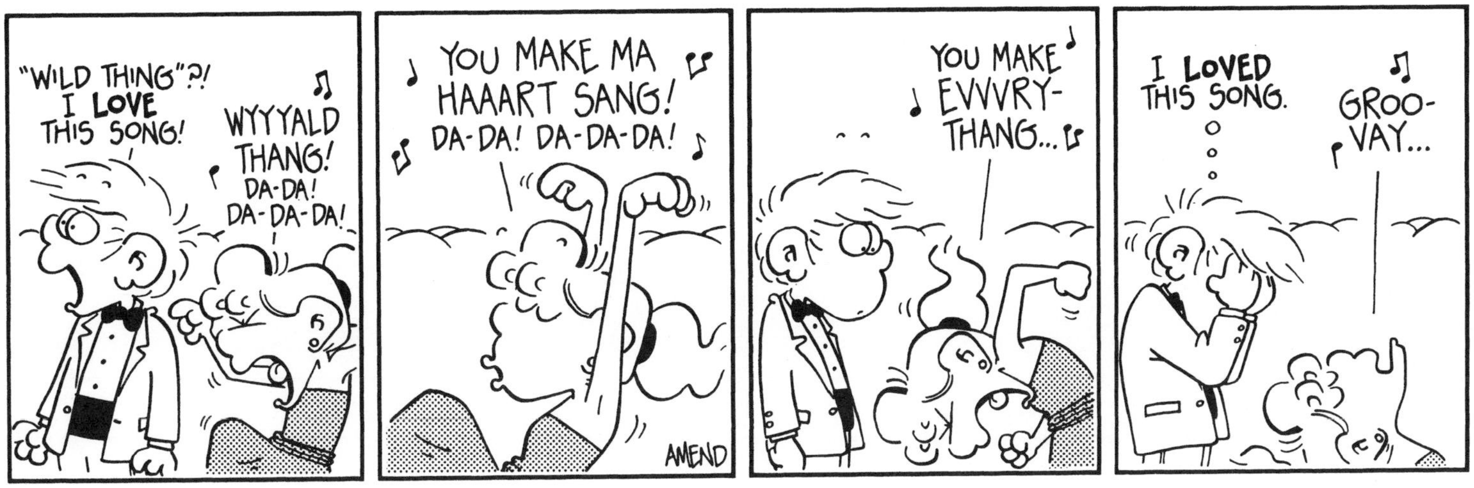
"WILD THING"?! I **LOVE** THIS SONG!
WYYYALD THANG! DA-DA! DA-DA-DA!
YOU MAKE MA HAAART SANG! DA-DA! DA-DA-DA!
YOU MAKE EVVVRY-THANG...
I **LOVED** THIS SONG.
GROO-VAY...
AMEND

May 31, 1990

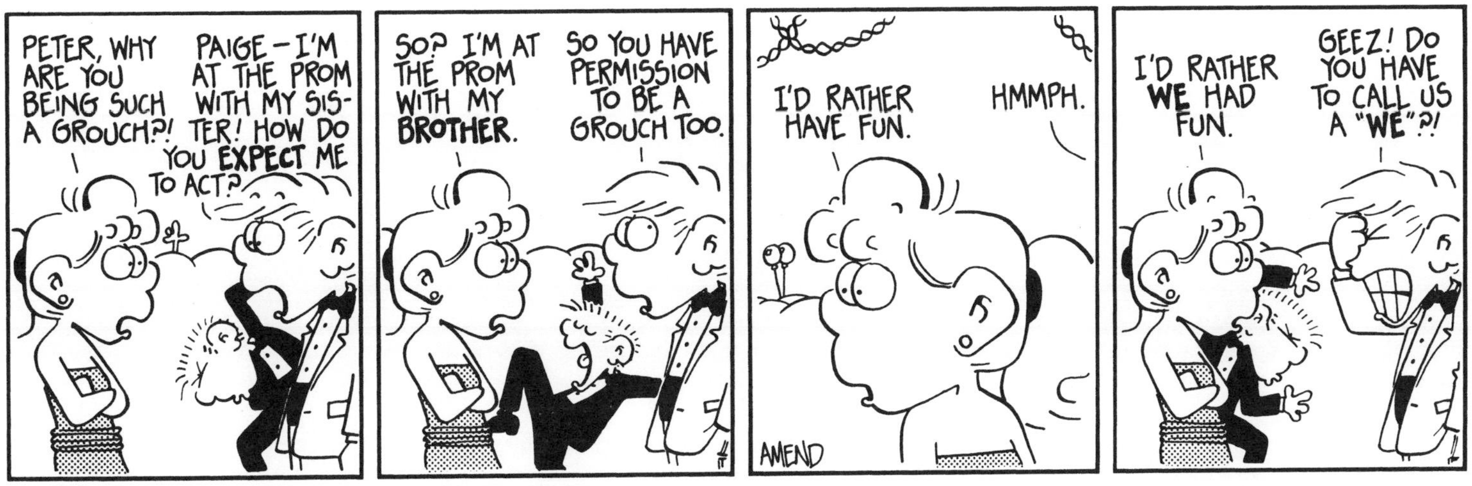
PETER, WHY ARE YOU BEING SUCH A GROUCH?!
PAIGE—I'M AT THE PROM WITH MY SISTER! HOW DO YOU **EXPECT** ME TO ACT?
SO? I'M AT THE PROM WITH MY **BROTHER**.
SO YOU HAVE PERMISSION TO BE A GROUCH TOO.
I'D RATHER HAVE FUN.
HMMPH.
AMEND
I'D RATHER **WE** HAD FUN.
GEEZ! DO YOU HAVE TO CALL US A "**WE**"?!

June 1, 1990

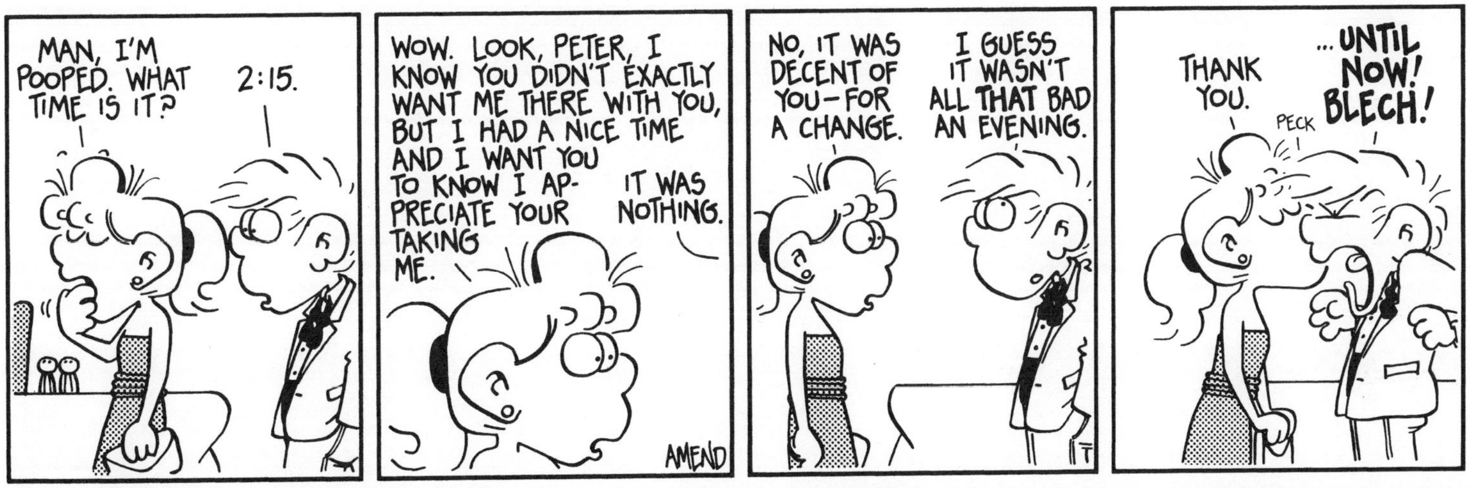
MAN, I'M POOPED. WHAT TIME IS IT?
2:15.
WOW. LOOK, PETER, I KNOW YOU DIDN'T EXACTLY WANT ME THERE WITH YOU, BUT I HAD A NICE TIME AND I WANT YOU TO KNOW I APPRECIATE YOUR TAKING ME.
IT WAS NOTHING.
AMEND
NO, IT WAS DECENT OF YOU—FOR A CHANGE.
I GUESS IT WASN'T ALL **THAT** BAD AN EVENING.
THANK YOU.
PECK
...**UNTIL NOW! BLECH!**

June 2, 1990

When I was fourteen I made an elaborate haunted house in our basement. I didn't start in June, but that's only because I didn't think to.

June 4, 1990

June 5, 1990

June 6, 1990

68

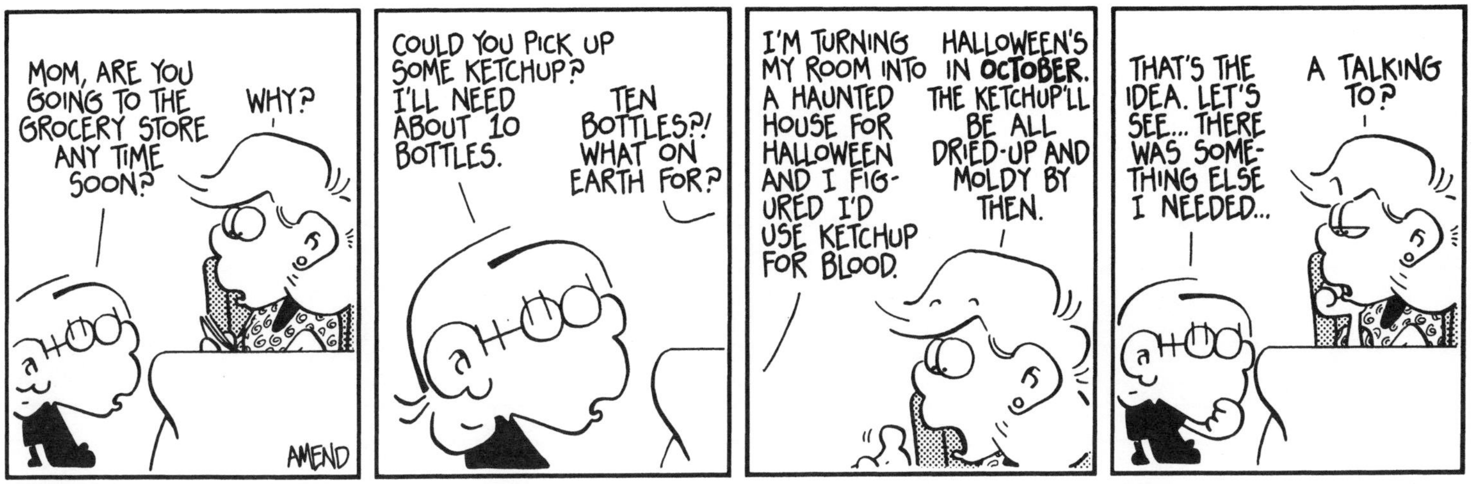
MOM, ARE YOU GOING TO THE GROCERY STORE ANY TIME SOON?
WHY?
COULD YOU PICK UP SOME KETCHUP? I'LL NEED ABOUT 10 BOTTLES.
TEN BOTTLES?! WHAT ON EARTH FOR?
I'M TURNING MY ROOM INTO A HAUNTED HOUSE FOR HALLOWEEN AND I FIGURED I'D USE KETCHUP FOR BLOOD.
HALLOWEEN'S IN **OCTOBER**. THE KETCHUP'LL BE ALL DRIED-UP AND MOLDY BY THEN.
THAT'S THE IDEA. LET'S SEE... THERE WAS SOMETHING ELSE I NEEDED...
A TALKING TO?
AMEND

June 7, 1990

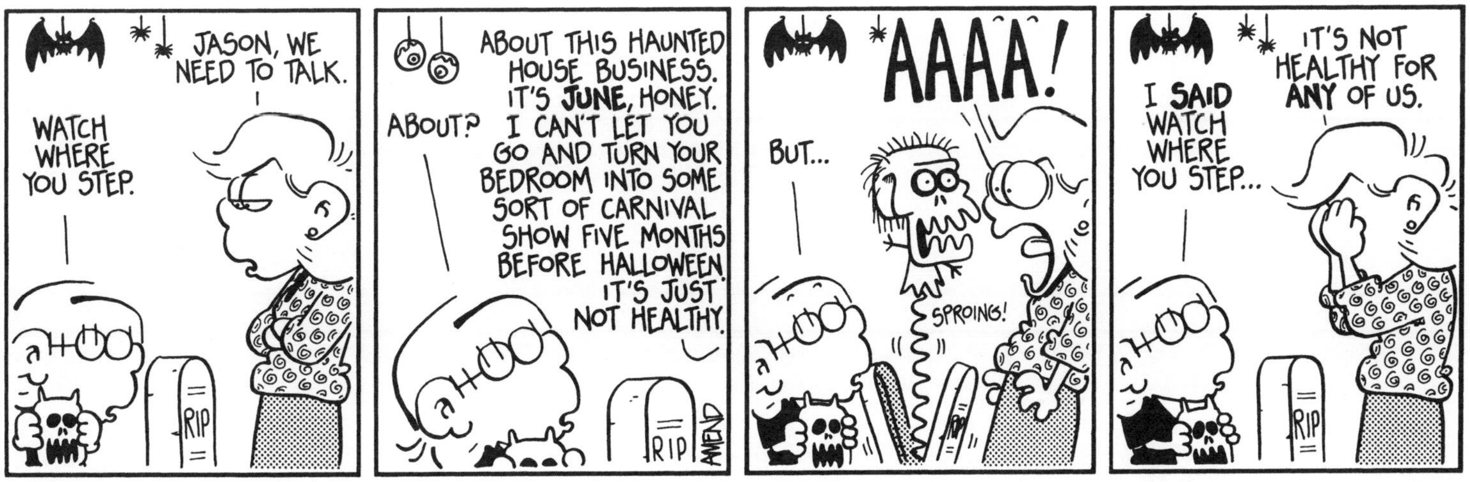
JASON, WE NEED TO TALK.
WATCH WHERE YOU STEP.
RIP
ABOUT?
ABOUT THIS HAUNTED HOUSE BUSINESS. IT'S **JUNE**, HONEY. I CAN'T LET YOU GO AND TURN YOUR BEDROOM INTO SOME SORT OF CARNIVAL SHOW FIVE MONTHS BEFORE HALLOWEEN. IT'S JUST NOT HEALTHY.
RIP
AMEND
BUT...
AAAA!
SPROING!
I **SAID** WATCH WHERE YOU STEP...
IT'S NOT HEALTHY FOR **ANY** OF US.
RIP

June 8, 1990

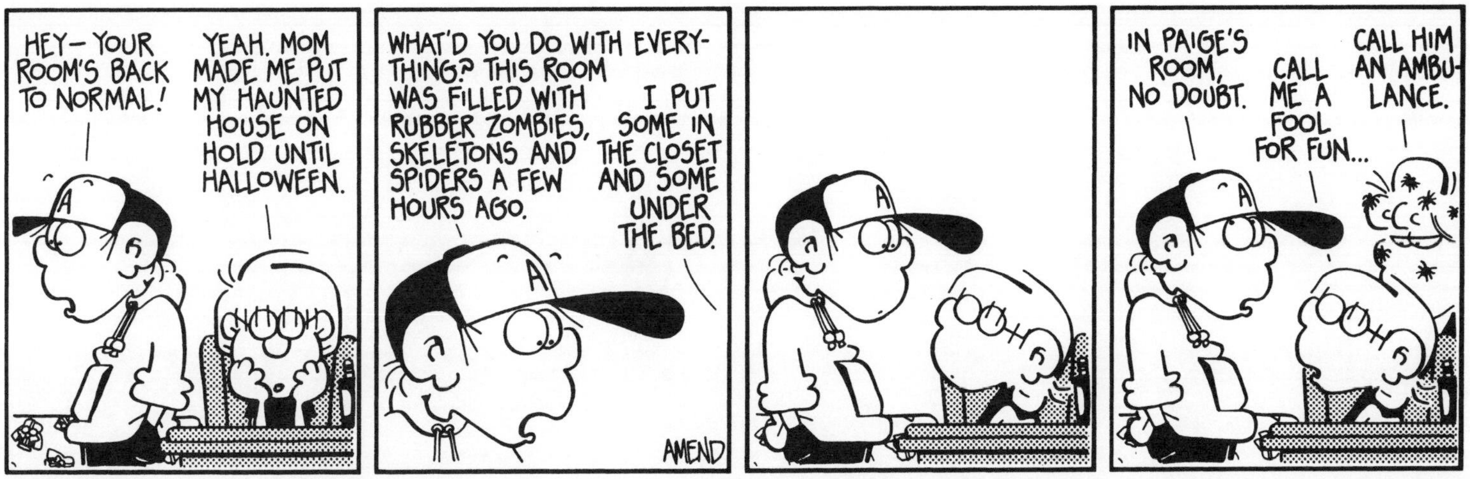
HEY— YOUR ROOM'S BACK TO NORMAL!
YEAH. MOM MADE ME PUT MY HAUNTED HOUSE ON HOLD UNTIL HALLOWEEN.
WHAT'D YOU DO WITH EVERYTHING? THIS ROOM WAS FILLED WITH RUBBER ZOMBIES, SKELETONS AND SPIDERS A FEW HOURS AGO.
I PUT SOME IN THE CLOSET AND SOME UNDER THE BED.
AMEND
IN PAIGE'S ROOM, NO DOUBT.
CALL ME A FOOL FOR FUN...
CALL HIM AN AMBULANCE.

June 9, 1990

July 9, 1990

Pay no attention to Skip's vanishing forehead.

July 10, 1990

July 11, 1990

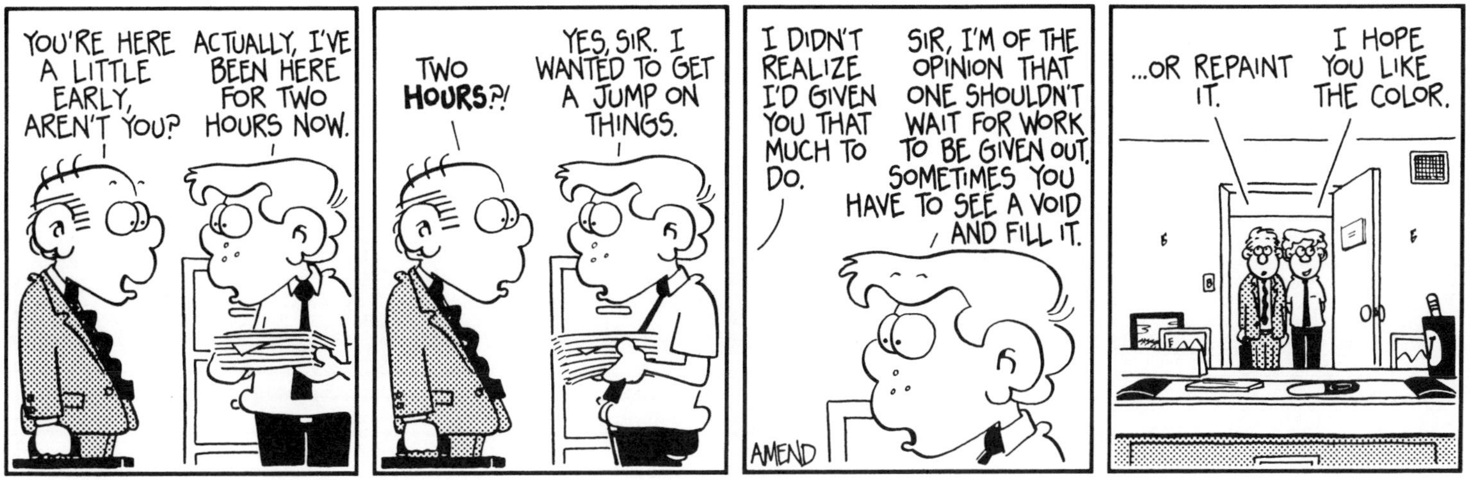
YOU'RE HERE A LITTLE EARLY, AREN'T YOU?
ACTUALLY, I'VE BEEN HERE FOR TWO HOURS NOW.
TWO **HOURS**?!
YES, SIR. I WANTED TO GET A JUMP ON THINGS.
I DIDN'T REALIZE I'D GIVEN YOU THAT MUCH TO DO.
SIR, I'M OF THE OPINION THAT ONE SHOULDN'T WAIT FOR WORK TO BE GIVEN OUT. SOMETIMES YOU HAVE TO SEE A VOID AND FILL IT.
AMEND
...OR REPAINT IT.
I HOPE YOU LIKE THE COLOR.

July 12, 1990

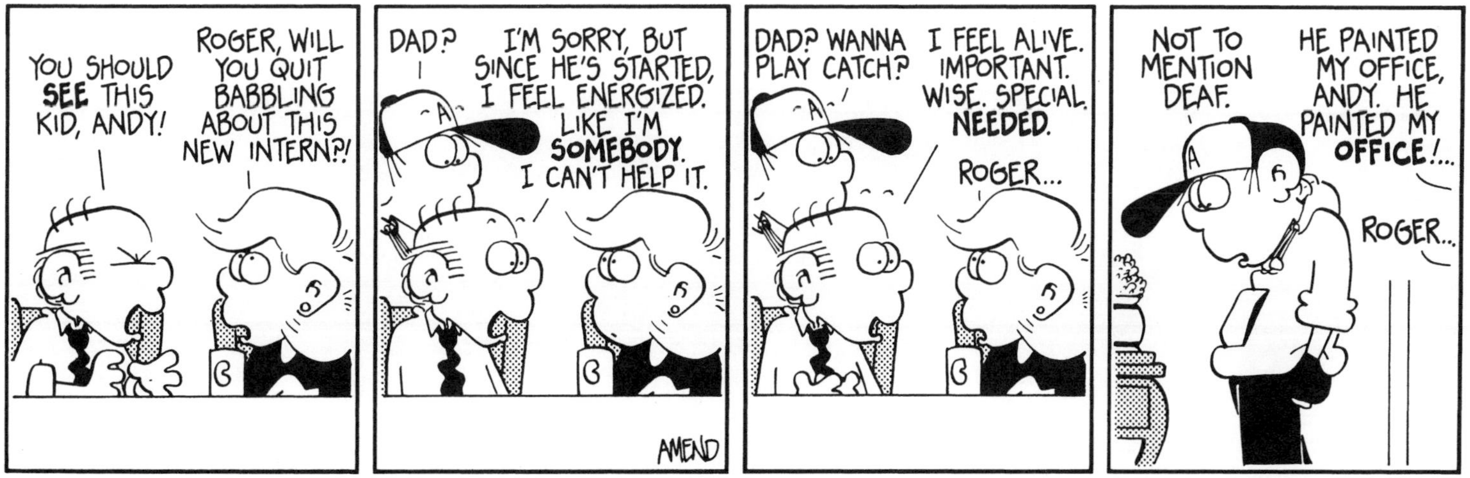
YOU SHOULD **SEE** THIS KID, ANDY!
ROGER, WILL YOU QUIT BABBLING ABOUT THIS NEW INTERN?!
DAD?
I'M SORRY, BUT SINCE HE'S STARTED, I FEEL ENERGIZED. LIKE I'M **SOMEBODY**. I CAN'T HELP IT.
AMEND
DAD? WANNA PLAY CATCH?
I FEEL ALIVE. IMPORTANT. WISE. SPECIAL. **NEEDED**.
ROGER...
NOT TO MENTION DEAF.
HE PAINTED MY OFFICE, ANDY. HE PAINTED MY **OFFICE**!...
ROGER...

July 13, 1990

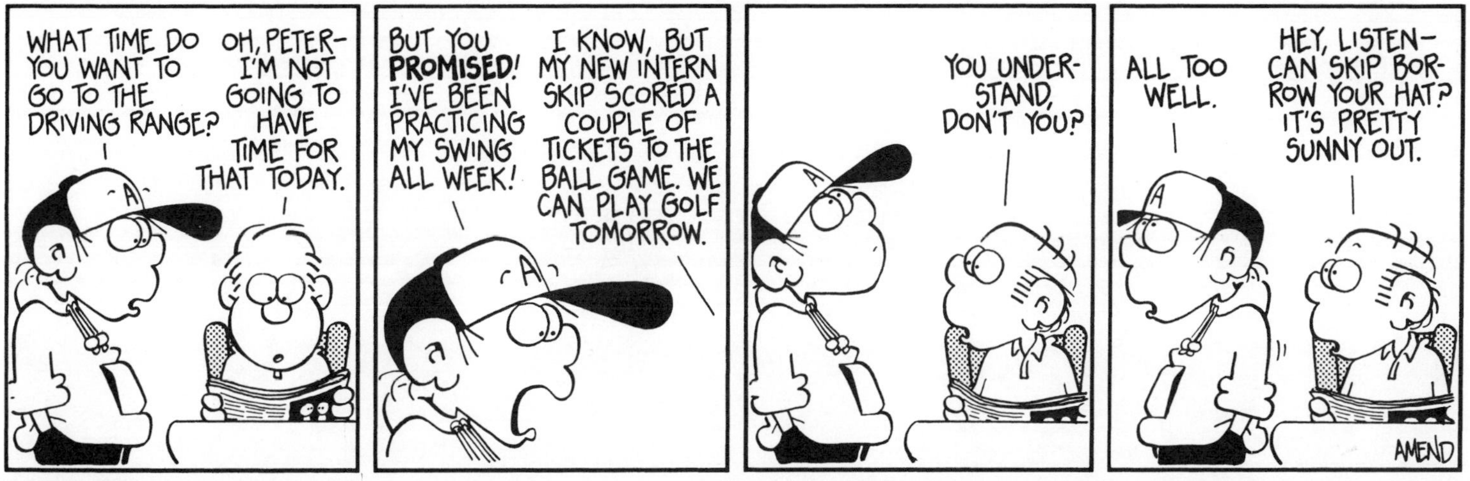
WHAT TIME DO YOU WANT TO GO TO THE DRIVING RANGE?
OH, PETER- I'M NOT GOING TO HAVE TIME FOR THAT TODAY.
BUT YOU **PROMISED**! I'VE BEEN PRACTICING MY SWING ALL WEEK!
I KNOW, BUT MY NEW INTERN SKIP SCORED A COUPLE OF TICKETS TO THE BALL GAME. WE CAN PLAY GOLF TOMORROW.
YOU UNDER-STAND, DON'T YOU?
ALL TOO WELL.
HEY, LISTEN- CAN SKIP BOR-ROW YOUR HAT? IT'S PRETTY SUNNY OUT.
AMEND

July 14, 1990

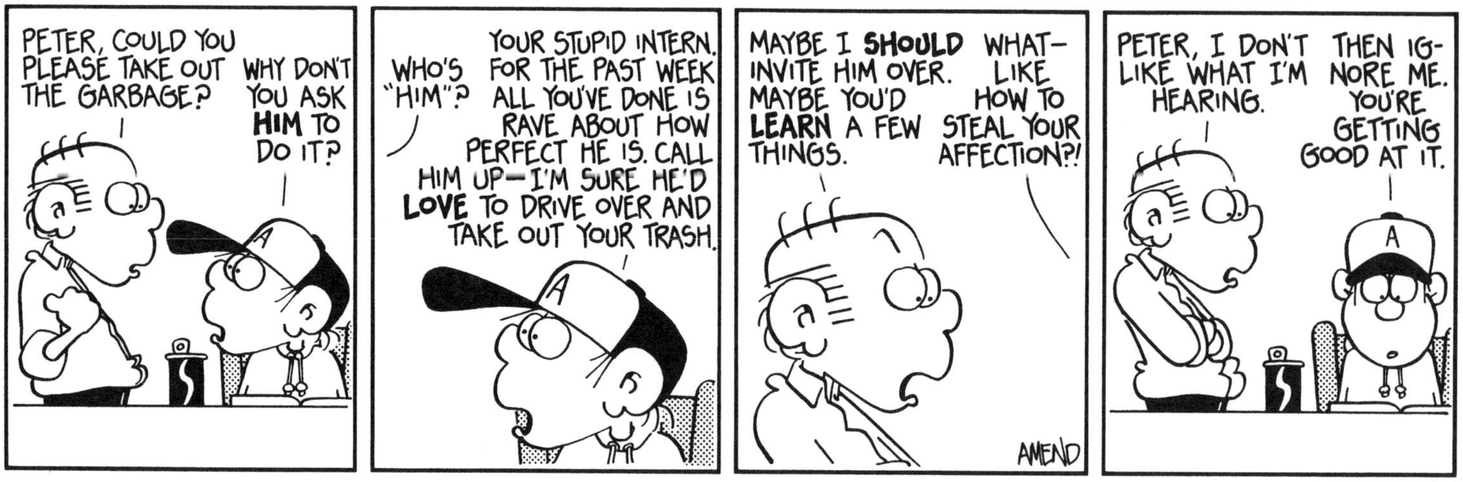

PETER, COULD YOU PLEASE TAKE OUT THE GARBAGE?
WHY DON'T YOU ASK **HIM** TO DO IT?
WHO'S "HIM"?
YOUR STUPID INTERN. FOR THE PAST WEEK ALL YOU'VE DONE IS RAVE ABOUT HOW PERFECT HE IS. CALL HIM UP—I'M SURE HE'D **LOVE** TO DRIVE OVER AND TAKE OUT YOUR TRASH.
MAYBE I **SHOULD** INVITE HIM OVER. MAYBE YOU'D **LEARN** A FEW THINGS.
WHAT–LIKE HOW TO STEAL YOUR AFFECTION?!
AMEND
PETER, I DON'T LIKE WHAT I'M HEARING.
THEN IGNORE ME. YOU'RE GETTING GOOD AT IT.

July 16, 1990

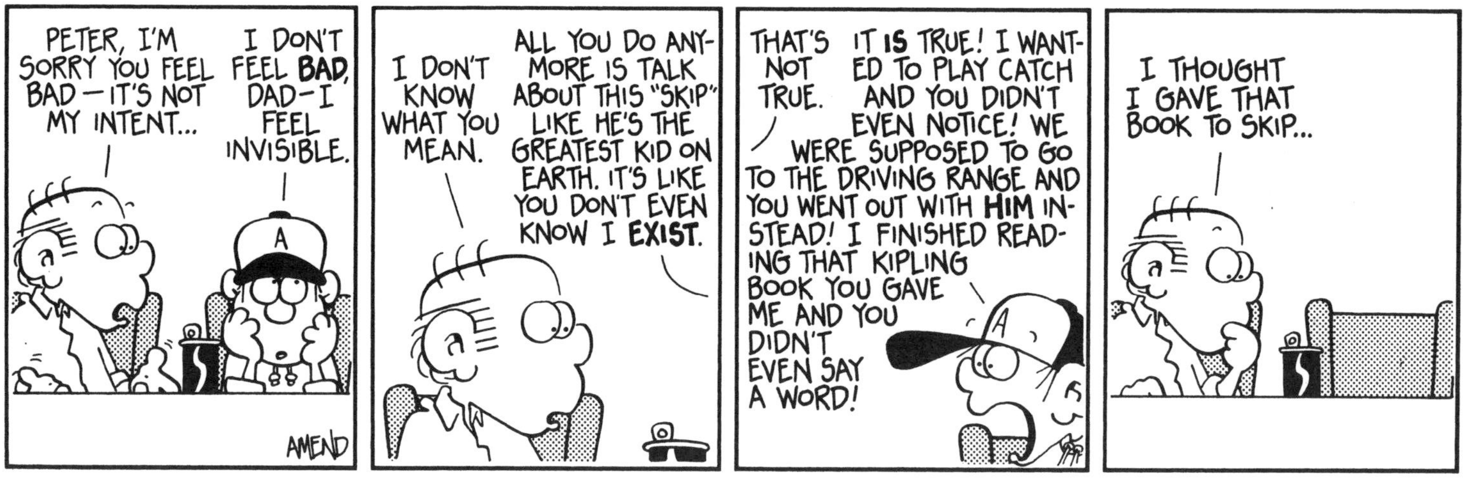

PETER, I'M SORRY YOU FEEL BAD—IT'S NOT MY INTENT...
I DON'T FEEL **BAD**, DAD—I FEEL INVISIBLE.
AMEND
I DON'T KNOW WHAT YOU MEAN.
ALL YOU DO ANYMORE IS TALK ABOUT THIS "SKIP" LIKE HE'S THE GREATEST KID ON EARTH. IT'S LIKE YOU DON'T EVEN KNOW I **EXIST**.
THAT'S NOT TRUE.
IT **IS** TRUE! I WANTED TO PLAY CATCH AND YOU DIDN'T EVEN NOTICE! WE WERE SUPPOSED TO GO TO THE DRIVING RANGE AND YOU WENT OUT WITH **HIM** INSTEAD! I FINISHED READING THAT KIPLING BOOK YOU GAVE ME AND YOU DIDN'T EVEN SAY A WORD!
I THOUGHT I GAVE THAT BOOK TO SKIP...

July 17, 1990

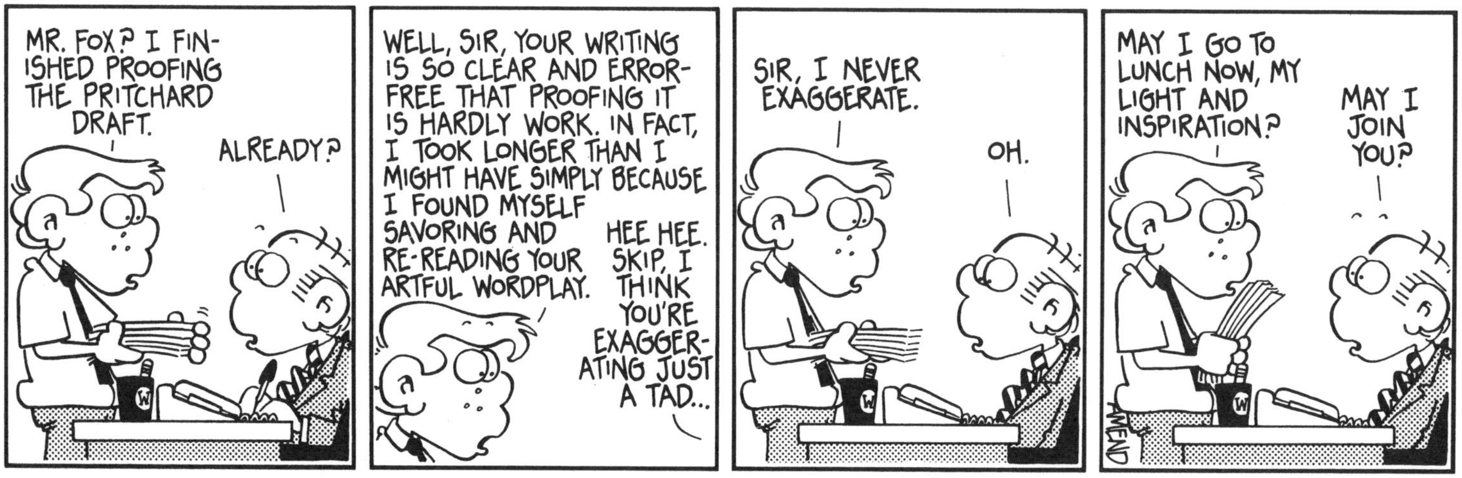

MR. FOX? I FINISHED PROOFING THE PRITCHARD DRAFT.
ALREADY?
WELL, SIR, YOUR WRITING IS SO CLEAR AND ERROR-FREE THAT PROOFING IT IS HARDLY WORK. IN FACT, I TOOK LONGER THAN I MIGHT HAVE SIMPLY BECAUSE I FOUND MYSELF SAVORING AND RE-READING YOUR ARTFUL WORDPLAY.
HEE HEE. SKIP, I THINK YOU'RE EXAGGERATING JUST A TAD...
SIR, I NEVER EXAGGERATE.
OH.
MAY I GO TO LUNCH NOW, MY LIGHT AND INSPIRATION?
MAY I JOIN YOU?
AMEND

July 18, 1990

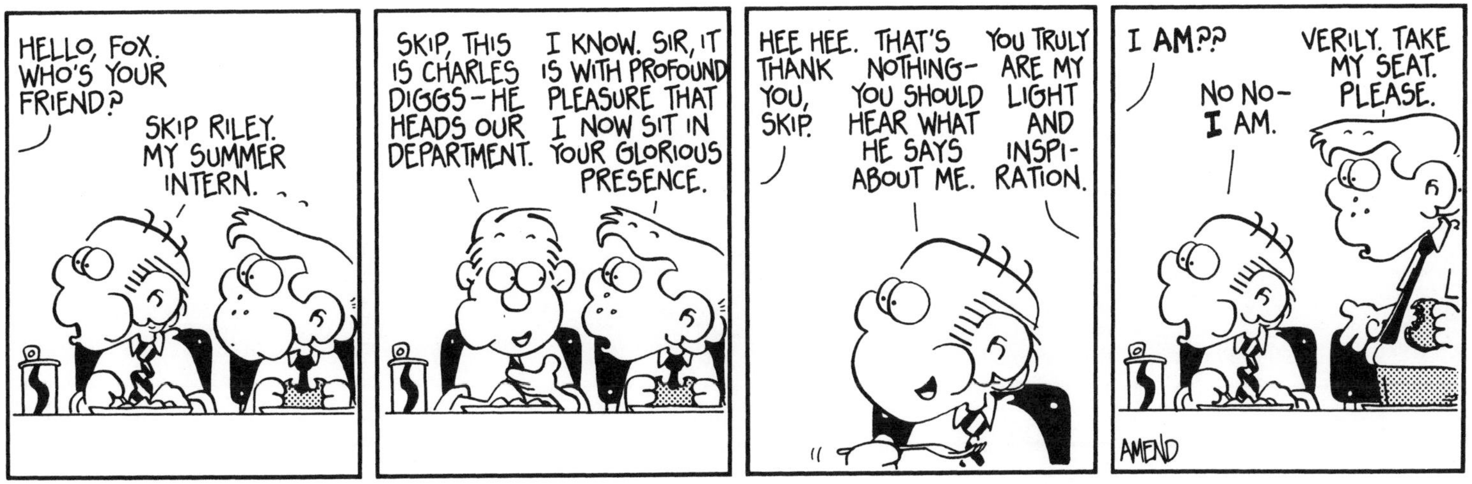
HELLO, FOX. WHO'S YOUR FRIEND?
SKIP RILEY. MY SUMMER INTERN.
SKIP, THIS IS CHARLES DIGGS—HE HEADS OUR DEPARTMENT.
I KNOW. SIR, IT IS WITH PROFOUND PLEASURE THAT I NOW SIT IN YOUR GLORIOUS PRESENCE.
HEE HEE. THANK YOU, SKIP.
THAT'S NOTHING— YOU SHOULD HEAR WHAT HE SAYS ABOUT ME.
YOU TRULY ARE MY LIGHT AND INSPIRATION.
I AM??
NO NO— I AM.
VERILY. TAKE MY SEAT. PLEASE.
AMEND
July 19, 1990

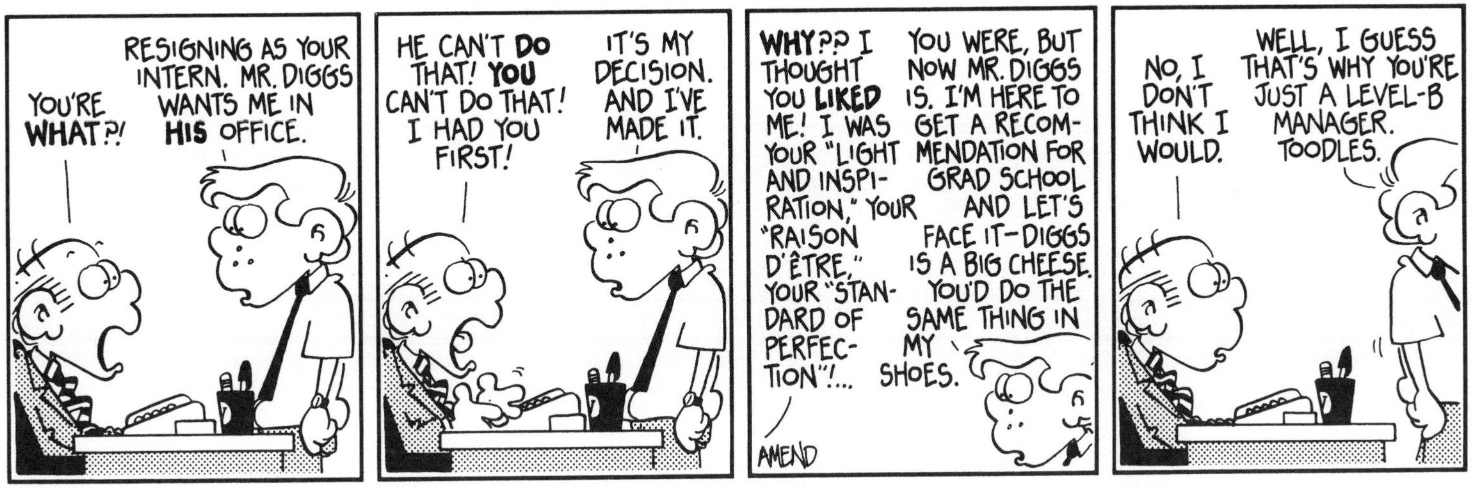
YOU'RE WHAT?!
RESIGNING AS YOUR INTERN. MR. DIGGS WANTS ME IN HIS OFFICE.
HE CAN'T DO THAT! YOU CAN'T DO THAT! I HAD YOU FIRST!
IT'S MY DECISION. AND I'VE MADE IT.
WHY?? I THOUGHT YOU LIKED ME! I WAS YOUR "LIGHT AND INSPIRATION," YOUR "RAISON D'ÊTRE," YOUR "STANDARD OF PERFECTION"!...
YOU WERE, BUT NOW MR. DIGGS IS. I'M HERE TO GET A RECOMMENDATION FOR GRAD SCHOOL AND LET'S FACE IT—DIGGS IS A BIG CHEESE. YOU'D DO THE SAME THING IN MY SHOES.
AMEND
NO, I DON'T THINK I WOULD.
WELL, I GUESS THAT'S WHY YOU'RE JUST A LEVEL-B MANAGER. TOODLES.
July 20, 1990

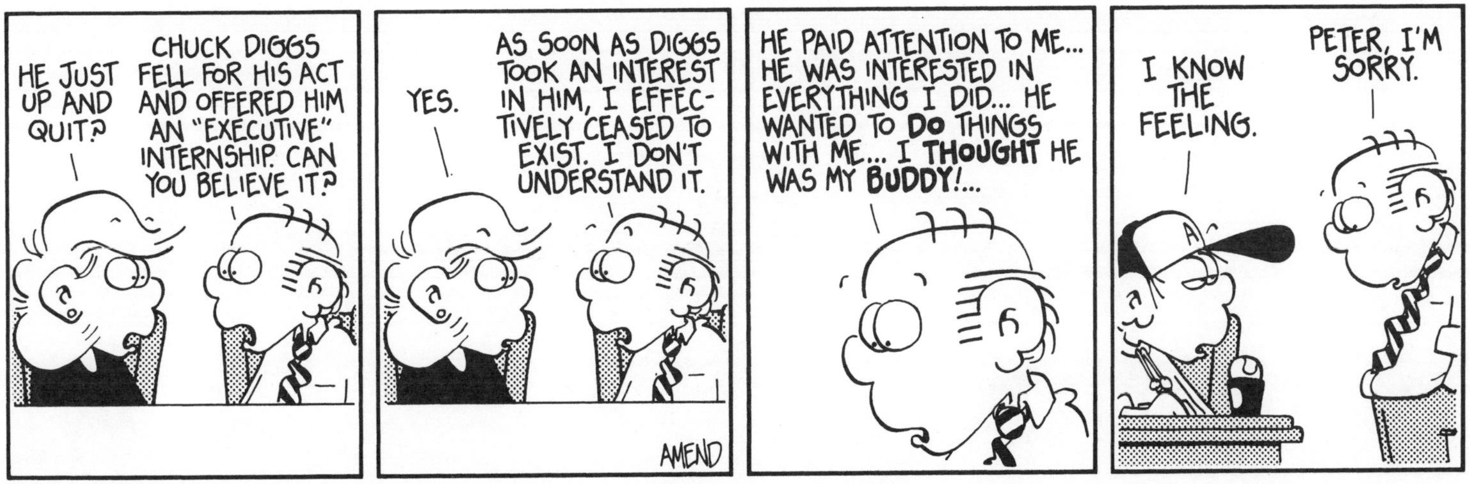
HE JUST UP AND QUIT?
CHUCK DIGGS FELL FOR HIS ACT AND OFFERED HIM AN "EXECUTIVE" INTERNSHIP. CAN YOU BELIEVE IT?
YES.
AS SOON AS DIGGS TOOK AN INTEREST IN HIM, I EFFECTIVELY CEASED TO EXIST. I DON'T UNDERSTAND IT.
AMEND
HE PAID ATTENTION TO ME... HE WAS INTERESTED IN EVERYTHING I DID... HE WANTED TO DO THINGS WITH ME... I THOUGHT HE WAS MY BUDDY!...
I KNOW THE FEELING.
PETER, I'M SORRY.
July 21, 1990

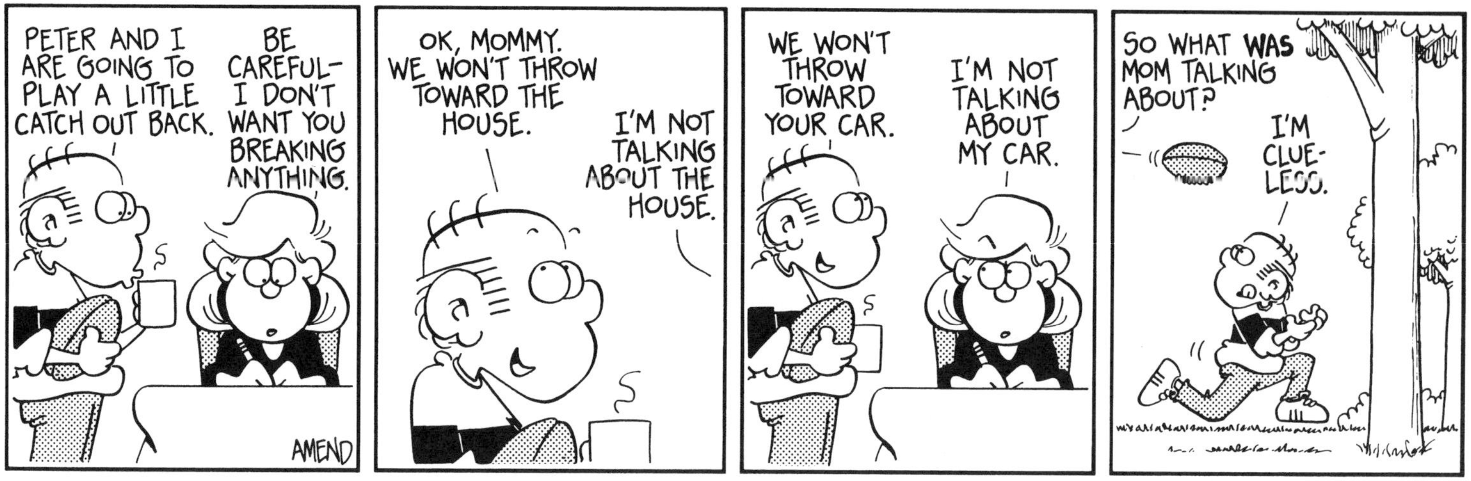
PETER AND I ARE GOING TO PLAY A LITTLE CATCH OUT BACK.
BE CAREFUL- I DON'T WANT YOU BREAKING ANYTHING.
AMEND
OK, MOMMY. WE WON'T THROW TOWARD THE HOUSE.
I'M NOT TALKING ABOUT THE HOUSE.
WE WON'T THROW TOWARD YOUR CAR.
I'M NOT TALKING ABOUT MY CAR.
SO WHAT **WAS** MOM TALKING ABOUT?
I'M CLUE-LESS.

August 21, 1990

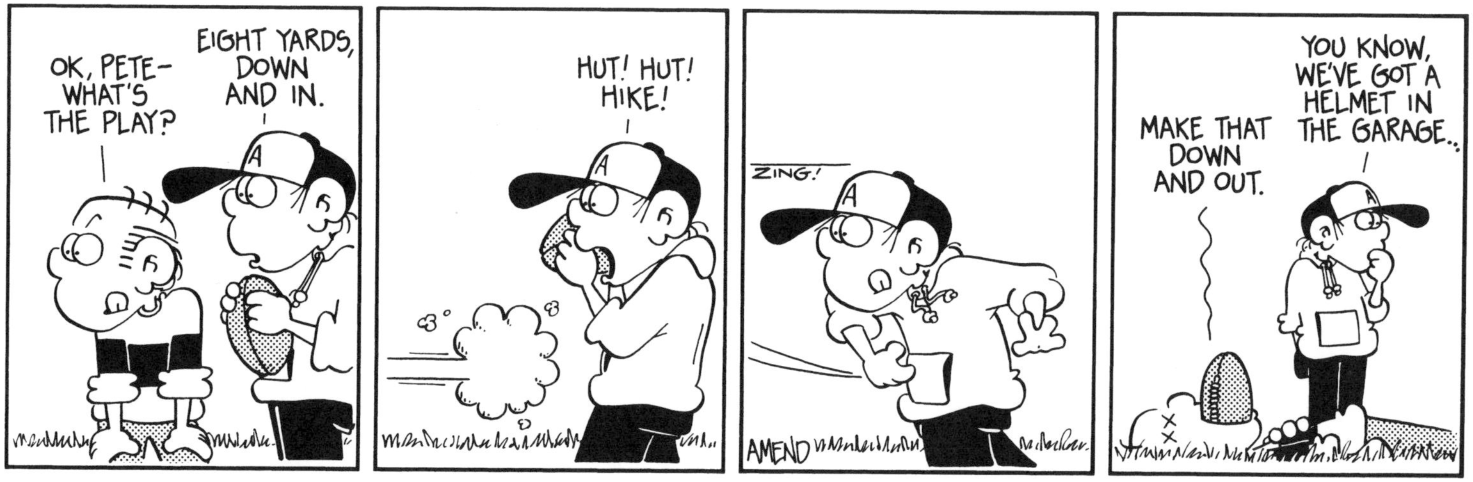
OK, PETE- WHAT'S THE PLAY?
EIGHT YARDS, DOWN AND IN.
HUT! HUT! HIKE!
ZING!
AMEND
MAKE THAT DOWN AND OUT.
YOU KNOW, WE'VE GOT A HELMET IN THE GARAGE...

August 22, 1990

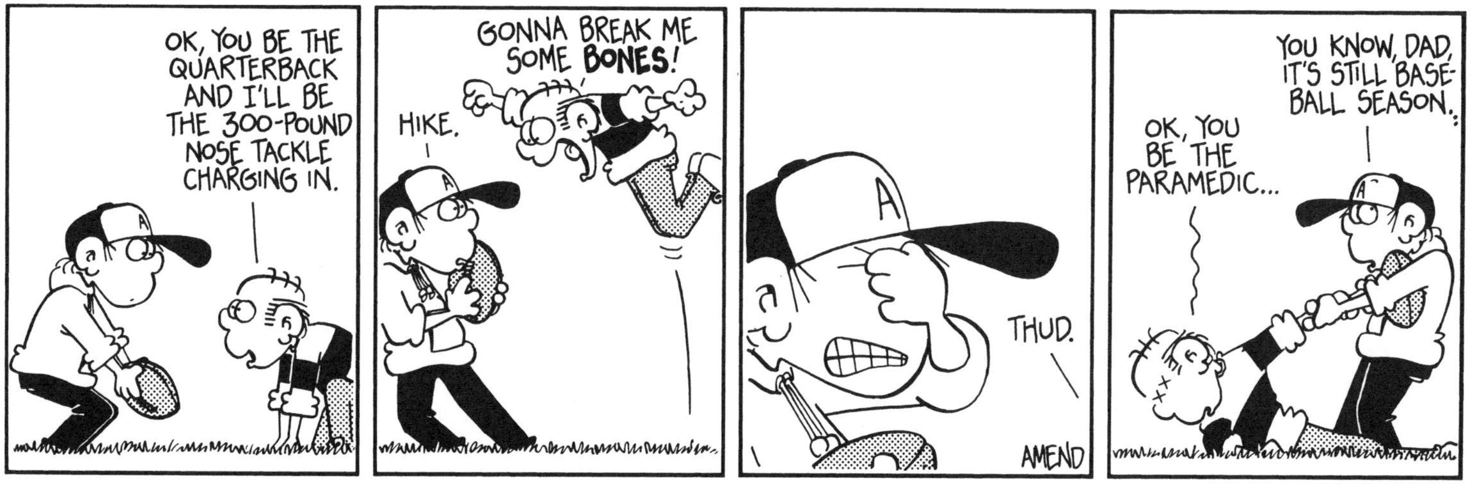
OK, YOU BE THE QUARTERBACK AND I'LL BE THE 300-POUND NOSE TACKLE CHARGING IN.
HIKE.
GONNA BREAK ME SOME **BONES**!
THUD.
AMEND
OK, YOU BE THE PARAMEDIC...
YOU KNOW, DAD, IT'S STILL BASE-BALL SEASON...

August 23, 1990

August 24, 1990

August 25, 1990

This is certainly the story of *my* athletic life.

July 5, 1991

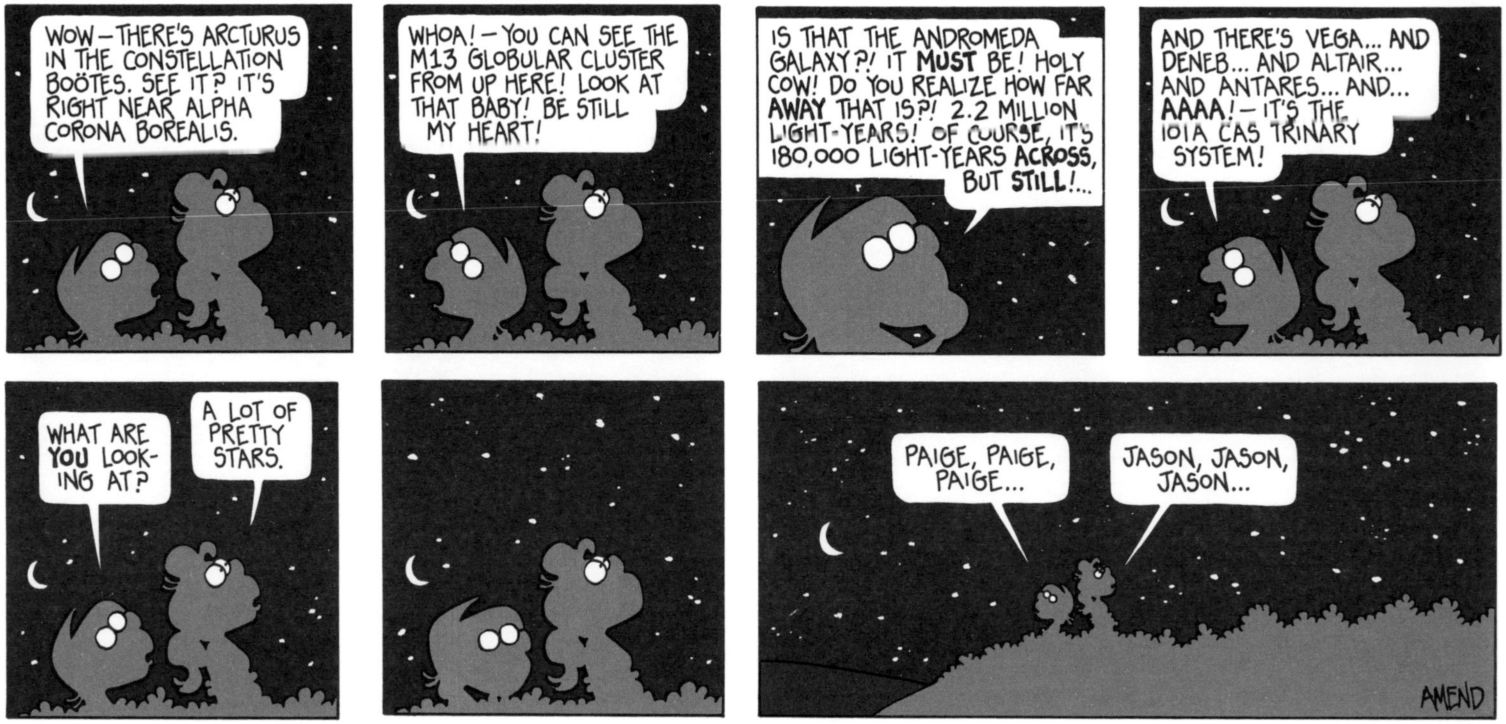
WOW—THERE'S ARCTURUS IN THE CONSTELLATION BOÖTES. SEE IT? IT'S RIGHT NEAR ALPHA CORONA BOREALIS.
WHOA!—YOU CAN SEE THE M13 GLOBULAR CLUSTER FROM UP HERE! LOOK AT THAT BABY! BE STILL MY HEART!
IS THAT THE ANDROMEDA GALAXY?! IT MUST BE! HOLY COW! DO YOU REALIZE HOW FAR AWAY THAT IS?! 2.2 MILLION LIGHT-YEARS! OF COURSE, IT'S 180,000 LIGHT-YEARS ACROSS, BUT STILL!...
AND THERE'S VEGA... AND DENEB... AND ALTAIR... AND ANTARES... AND... AAAA!—IT'S THE 101A CAS TRINARY SYSTEM!
WHAT ARE YOU LOOKING AT?
A LOT OF PRETTY STARS.
PAIGE, PAIGE, PAIGE...
JASON, JASON, JASON...
AMEND

August 12, 1990

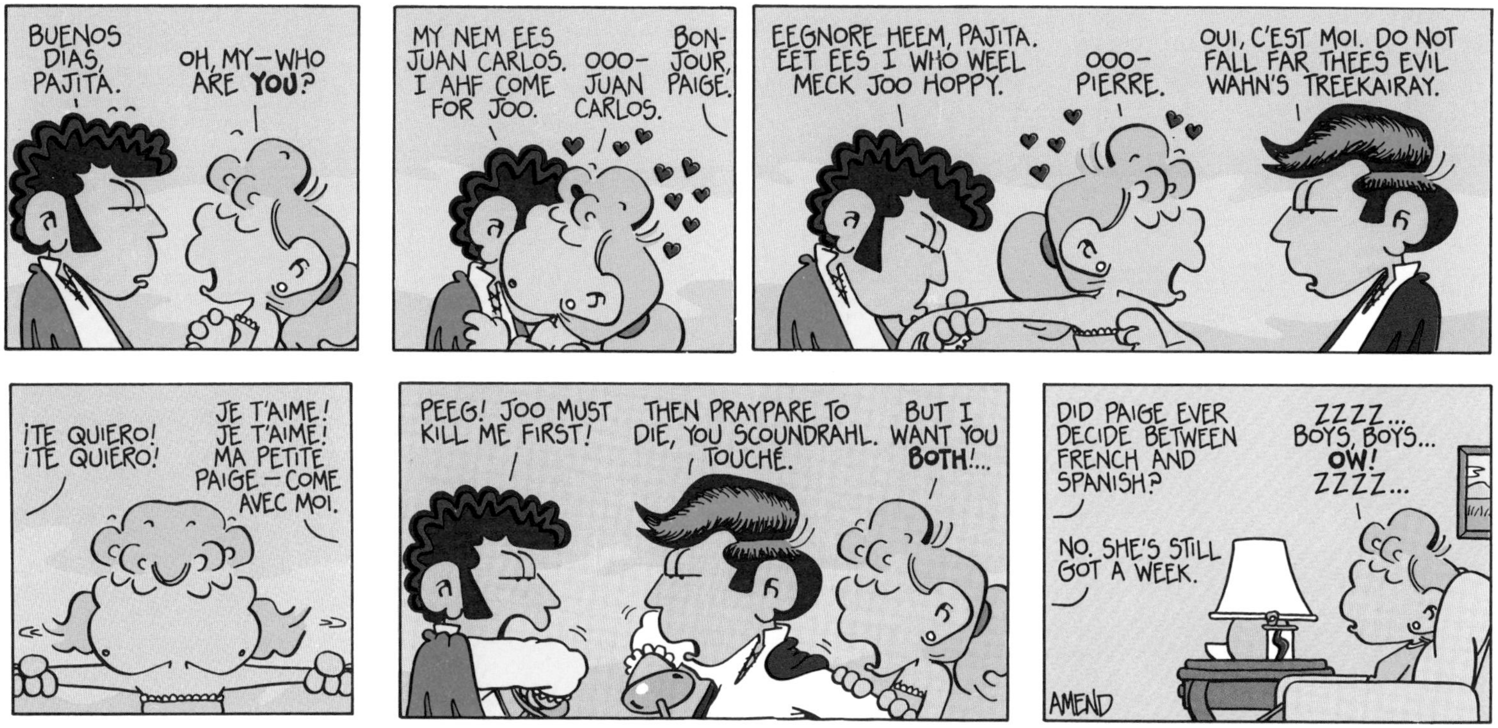
BUENOS DIAS, PAJITA.
OH, MY—WHO ARE YOU?
MY NEM EES JUAN CARLOS. I AHF COME FOR JOO.
OOO—JUAN CARLOS.
BON-JOUR, PAIGE.
EEGNORE HEEM, PAJITA. EET EES I WHO WEEL MECK JOO HOPPY.
OOO—PIERRE.
OUI, C'EST MOI. DO NOT FALL FAR THEES EVIL WAHN'S TREEKAIRAY.
¡TE QUIERO! ¡TE QUIERO!
JE T'AIME! JE T'AIME! MA PETITE PAIGE—COME AVEC MOI.
PEEG! JOO MUST KILL ME FIRST!
THEN PRAYPARE TO DIE, YOU SCOUNDRAHL. TOUCHÉ.
BUT I WANT YOU BOTH!...
DID PAIGE EVER DECIDE BETWEEN FRENCH AND SPANISH?
ZZZZ... BOYS, BOYS... OW! ZZZZ...
NO. SHE'S STILL GOT A WEEK.
AMEND

August 26, 1990

I always thought Jason's optometrist should've given Paige kickbacks.

October 7, 1990

Home movies of us hanging up stockings were a Christmas tradition. I don't recall any aliens, though.

December 23, 1990

September 24, 1990

September 25, 1990

September 26, 1990

September 27, 1990

September 28, 1990

September 29, 1990

79

October 22, 1990

October 23, 1990

October 24, 1990

This last panel still makes me laugh. I know, I'm weird.

October 25, 1990

October 26, 1990

October 27, 1990

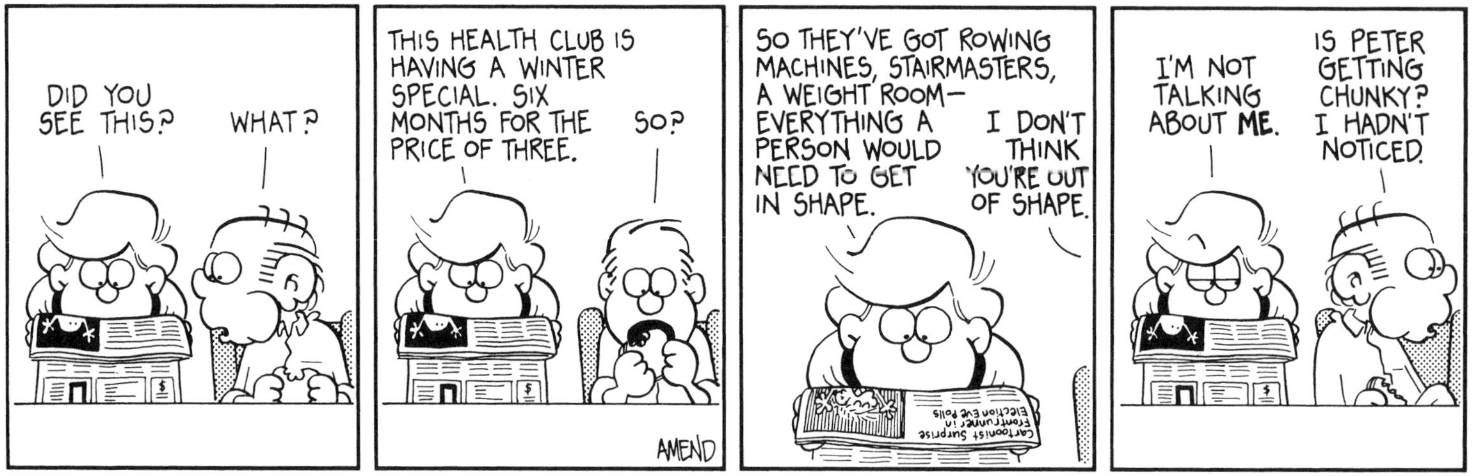
DID YOU SEE THIS?
WHAT?
THIS HEALTH CLUB IS HAVING A WINTER SPECIAL. SIX MONTHS FOR THE PRICE OF THREE.
SO?
SO THEY'VE GOT ROWING MACHINES, STAIRMASTERS, A WEIGHT ROOM— EVERYTHING A PERSON WOULD NEED TO GET IN SHAPE.
I DON'T THINK YOU'RE OUT OF SHAPE.
I'M NOT TALKING ABOUT **ME**.
IS PETER GETTING CHUNKY? I HADN'T NOTICED.
AMEND

November 5, 1990

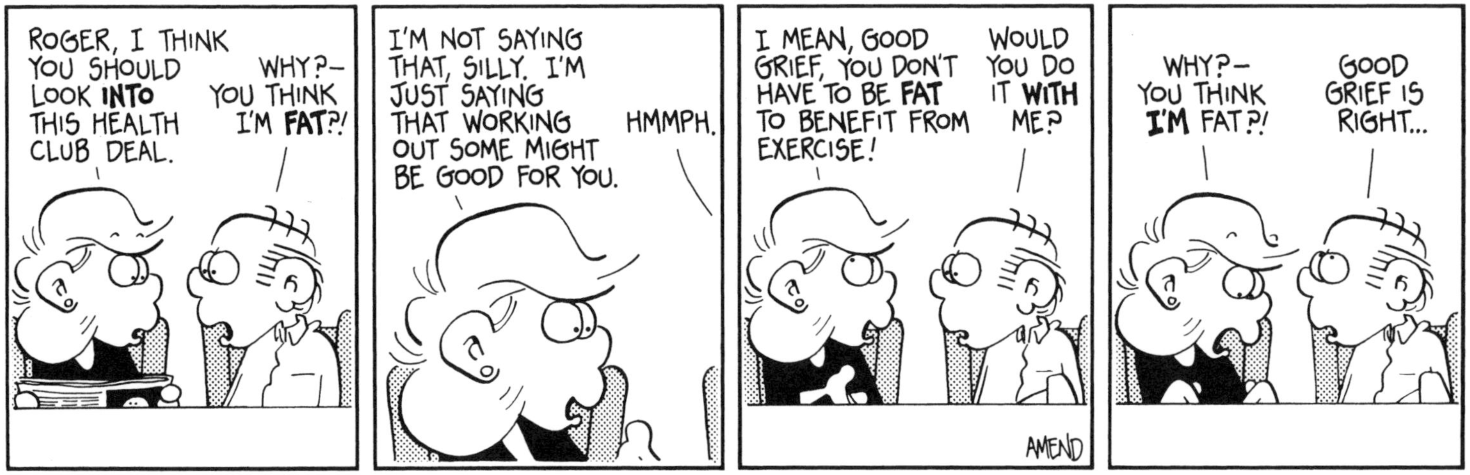
ROGER, I THINK YOU SHOULD LOOK **INTO** THIS HEALTH CLUB DEAL.
WHY?— YOU THINK I'M **FAT**?!
I'M NOT SAYING THAT, SILLY. I'M JUST SAYING THAT WORKING OUT SOME MIGHT BE GOOD FOR YOU.
HMMPH.
I MEAN, GOOD GRIEF, YOU DON'T HAVE TO BE **FAT** TO BENEFIT FROM EXERCISE!
WOULD YOU DO IT **WITH** ME?
WHY?— YOU THINK **I'M** FAT?!
GOOD GRIEF IS RIGHT...
AMEND

November 6, 1990

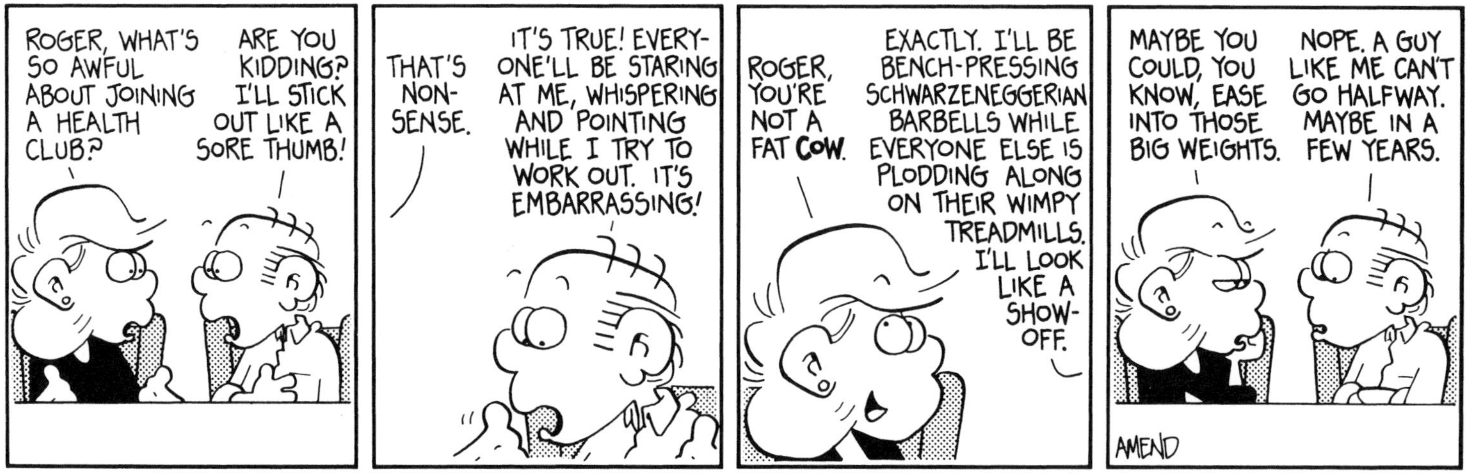
ROGER, WHAT'S SO AWFUL ABOUT JOINING A HEALTH CLUB?
ARE YOU KIDDING? I'LL STICK OUT LIKE A SORE THUMB!
THAT'S NON-SENSE.
IT'S TRUE! EVERY-ONE'LL BE STARING AT ME, WHISPERING AND POINTING WHILE I TRY TO WORK OUT. IT'S EMBARRASSING!
ROGER, YOU'RE NOT A FAT **COW**.
EXACTLY. I'LL BE BENCH-PRESSING SCHWARZENEGGERIAN BARBELLS WHILE EVERYONE ELSE IS PLODDING ALONG ON THEIR WIMPY TREADMILLS. I'LL LOOK LIKE A SHOW-OFF.
MAYBE YOU COULD, YOU KNOW, EASE INTO THOSE BIG WEIGHTS.
NOPE. A GUY LIKE ME CAN'T GO HALFWAY. MAYBE IN A FEW YEARS.
AMEND

November 7, 1990

November 8, 1990

November 9, 1990

November 10, 1990

November 12, 1990

I wasn't yet married at the time, so this was probably close to my actual morning diet.

November 13, 1990

84

November 14, 1990

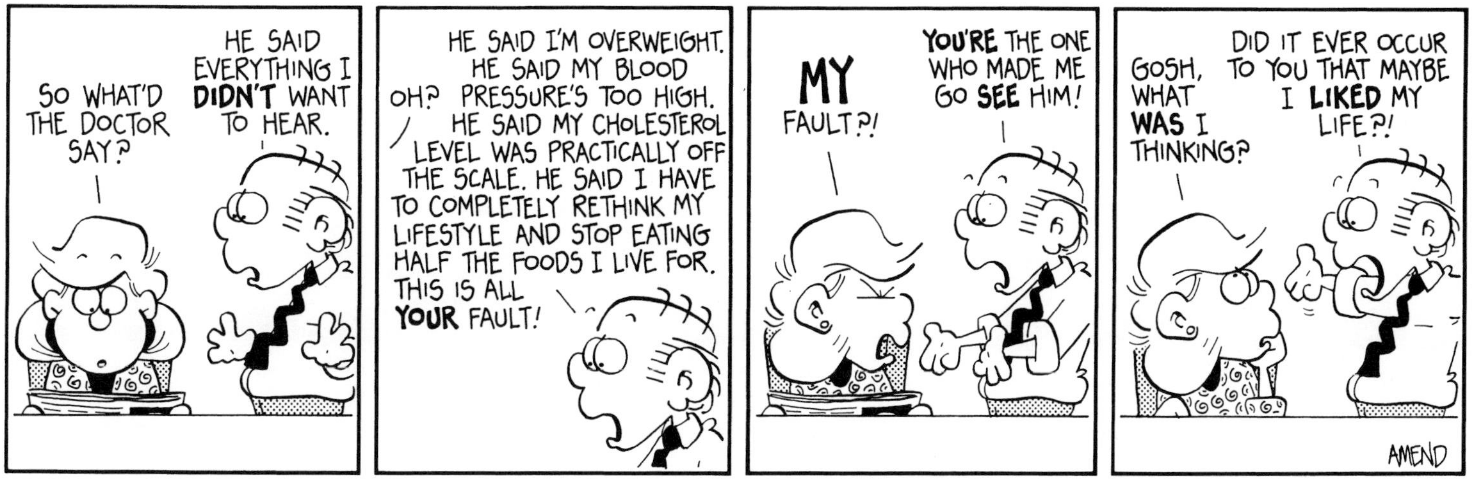
SO WHAT'D THE DOCTOR SAY?
HE SAID EVERYTHING I **DIDN'T** WANT TO HEAR.
OH?
HE SAID I'M OVERWEIGHT. HE SAID MY BLOOD PRESSURE'S TOO HIGH. HE SAID MY CHOLESTEROL LEVEL WAS PRACTICALLY OFF THE SCALE. HE SAID I HAVE TO COMPLETELY RETHINK MY LIFESTYLE AND STOP EATING HALF THE FOODS I LIVE FOR. THIS IS ALL **YOUR** FAULT!
MY FAULT?!
YOU'RE THE ONE WHO MADE ME GO **SEE** HIM!
GOSH, WHAT **WAS** I THINKING?
DID IT EVER OCCUR TO YOU THAT MAYBE I **LIKED** MY LIFE?!
AMEND

November 15, 1990

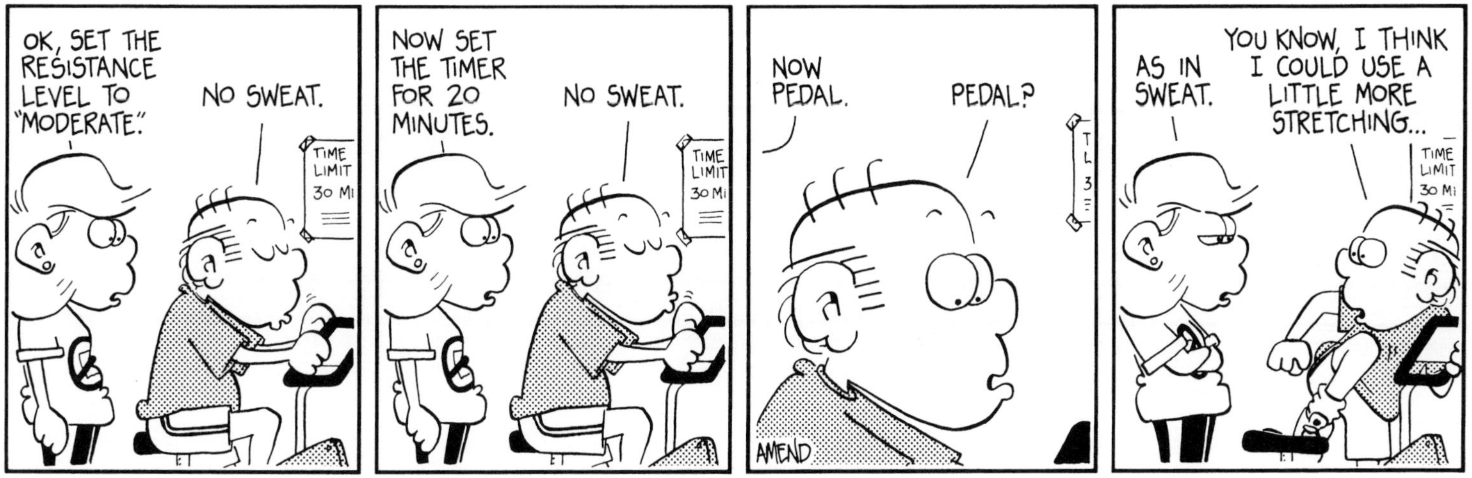
OK, SET THE RESISTANCE LEVEL TO "MODERATE."
NO SWEAT.
TIME LIMIT 30 MI
NOW SET THE TIMER FOR 20 MINUTES.
NO SWEAT.
TIME LIMIT 30 MI
NOW PEDAL.
PEDAL?
AMEND
AS IN SWEAT.
YOU KNOW, I THINK I COULD USE A LITTLE MORE STRETCHING...
TIME LIMIT 30 MI

November 16, 1990

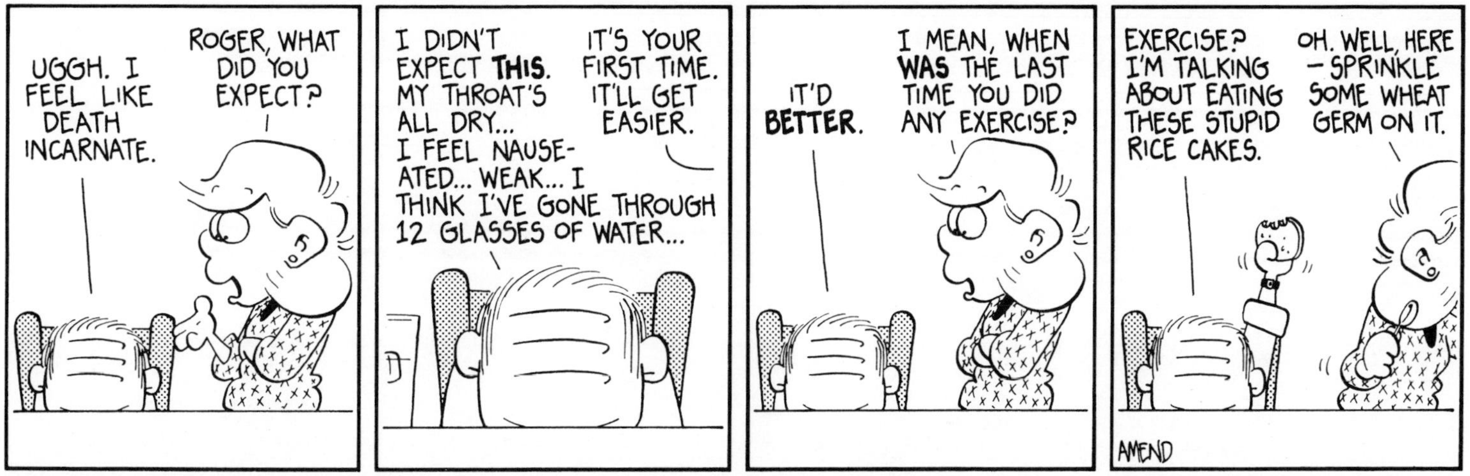
UGGH. I FEEL LIKE DEATH INCARNATE.
ROGER, WHAT DID YOU EXPECT?
I DIDN'T EXPECT **THIS**. MY THROAT'S ALL DRY... I FEEL NAUSEATED... WEAK... I THINK I'VE GONE THROUGH 12 GLASSES OF WATER...
IT'S YOUR FIRST TIME. IT'LL GET EASIER.
IT'D **BETTER**.
I MEAN, WHEN **WAS** THE LAST TIME YOU DID ANY EXERCISE?
EXERCISE? I'M TALKING ABOUT EATING THESE STUPID RICE CAKES.
OH. WELL, HERE — SPRINKLE SOME WHEAT GERM ON IT.
AMEND

November 17, 1990

January 28, 1991

January 29, 1991

January 30, 1991

I might have exaggerated the terrain here just a little.

January 31, 1991

February 1, 1991

February 2, 1991

I've never established where the Foxes live. This put them near an NBA city, though.

February 4, 1991

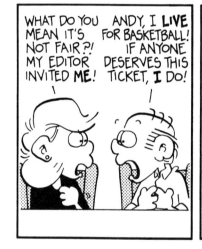

February 5, 1991

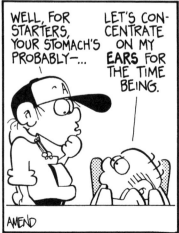

February 6, 1991

February 7, 1991

February 8, 1991

February 9, 1991

March 25, 1991

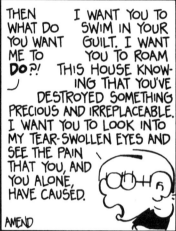

March 26, 1991

I liked the idea of Peter being afraid of Jason.

March 27, 1991

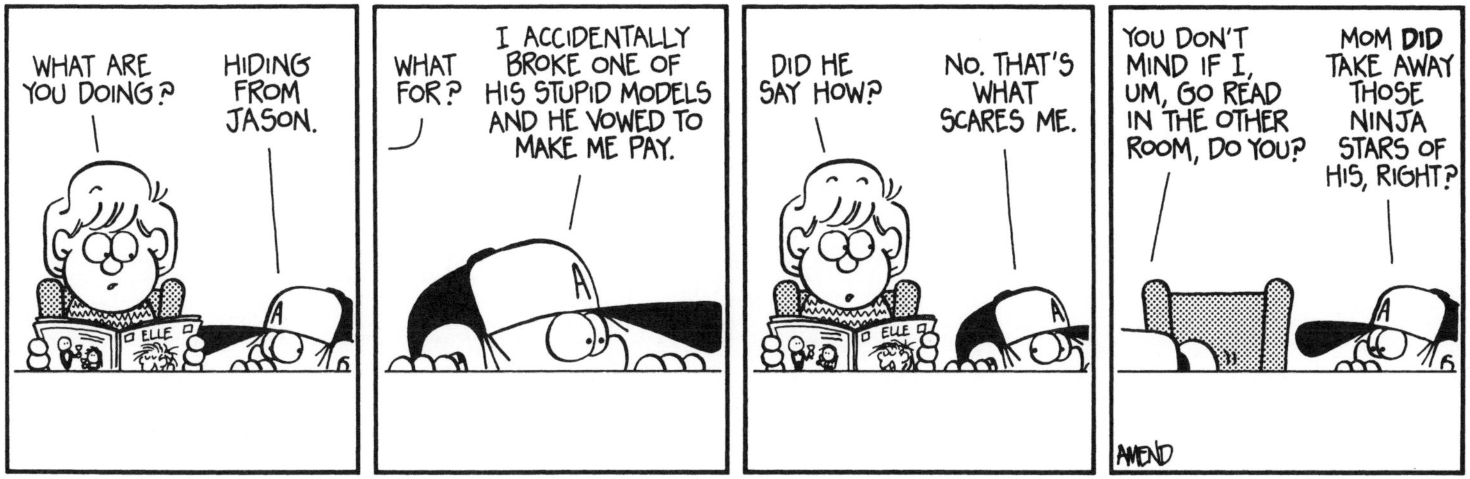
WHAT ARE YOU DOING?
HIDING FROM JASON.
WHAT FOR?
I ACCIDENTALLY BROKE ONE OF HIS STUPID MODELS AND HE VOWED TO MAKE ME PAY.
DID HE SAY HOW?
NO. THAT'S WHAT SCARES ME.
YOU DON'T MIND IF I, UM, GO READ IN THE OTHER ROOM, DO YOU?
MOM **DID** TAKE AWAY THOSE NINJA STARS OF HIS, RIGHT?
AMEND

March 28, 1991

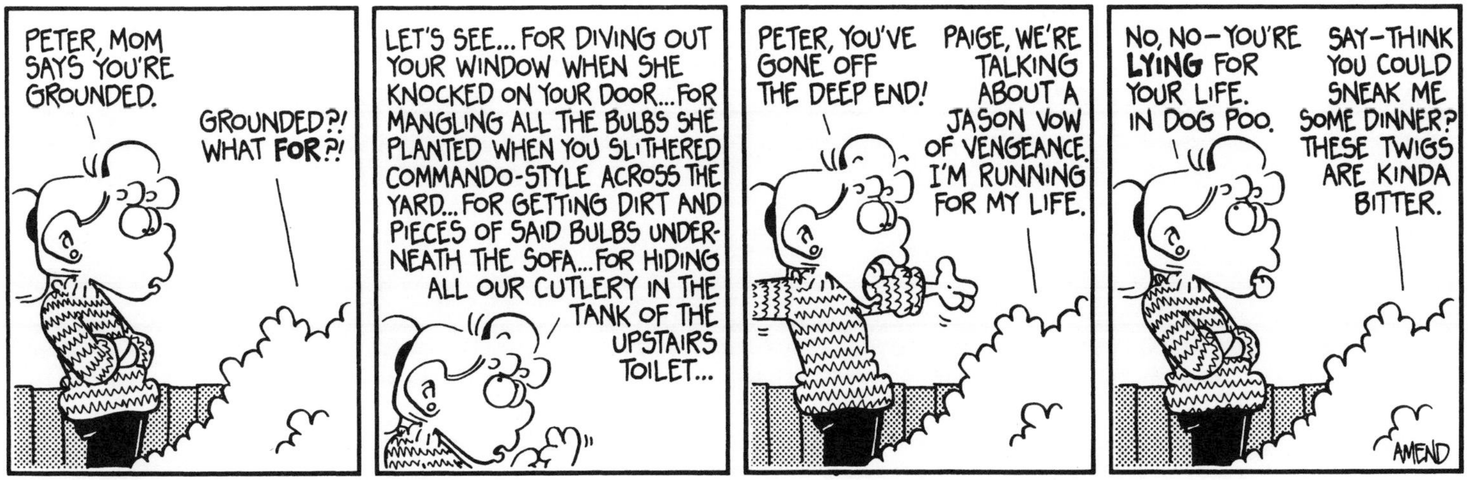
PETER, MOM SAYS YOU'RE GROUNDED.
GROUNDED?! WHAT **FOR**?!
LET'S SEE... FOR DIVING OUT YOUR WINDOW WHEN SHE KNOCKED ON YOUR DOOR... FOR MANGLING ALL THE BULBS SHE PLANTED WHEN YOU SLITHERED COMMANDO-STYLE ACROSS THE YARD... FOR GETTING DIRT AND PIECES OF SAID BULBS UNDERNEATH THE SOFA... FOR HIDING ALL OUR CUTLERY IN THE TANK OF THE UPSTAIRS TOILET...
PETER, YOU'VE GONE OFF THE DEEP END!
PAIGE, WE'RE TALKING ABOUT A JASON VOW OF VENGEANCE. I'M RUNNING FOR MY LIFE.
NO, NO—YOU'RE **LYING** FOR YOUR LIFE. IN DOG POO.
SAY—THINK YOU COULD SNEAK ME SOME DINNER? THESE TWIGS ARE KINDA BITTER.
AMEND

March 29, 1991

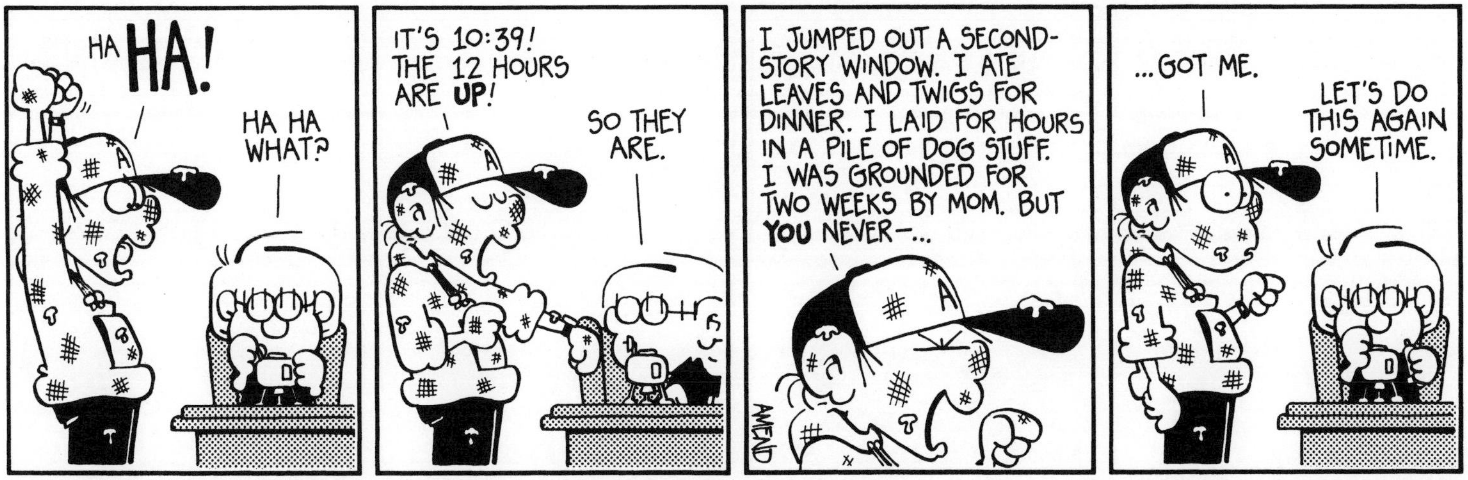
HA **HA!**
HA HA WHAT?
IT'S 10:39! THE 12 HOURS ARE **UP**!
SO THEY ARE.
I JUMPED OUT A SECOND-STORY WINDOW. I ATE LEAVES AND TWIGS FOR DINNER. I LAID FOR HOURS IN A PILE OF DOG STUFF. I WAS GROUNDED FOR TWO WEEKS BY MOM. BUT **YOU** NEVER—...
AMEND
...GOT ME.
LET'S DO THIS AGAIN SOMETIME.

March 30, 1991

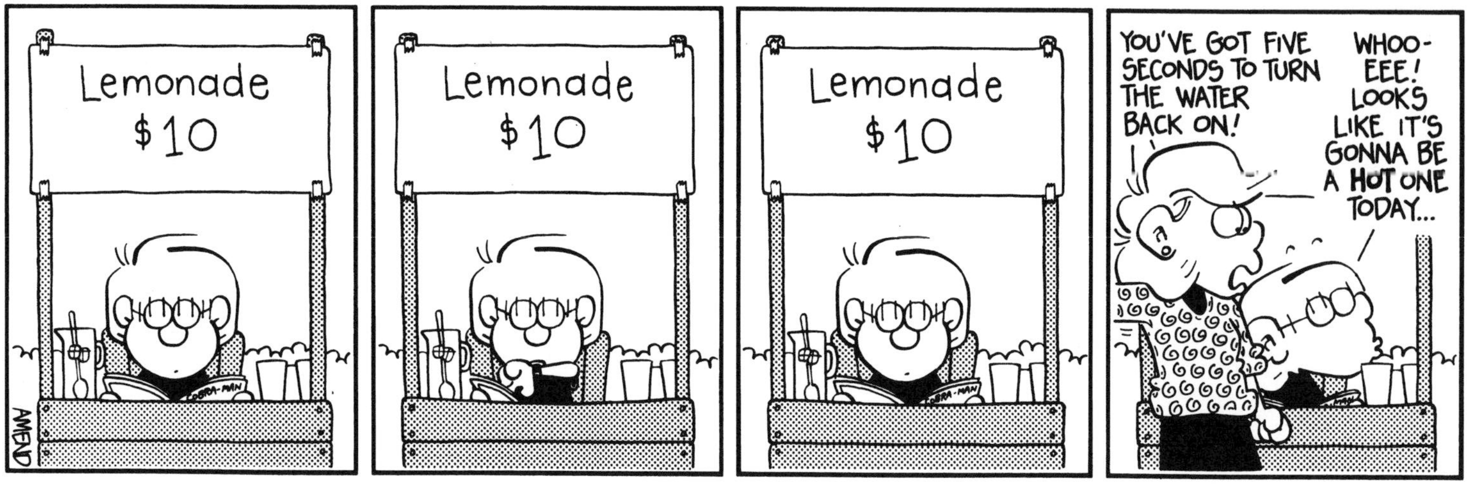
Lemonade $10
AMEND
Lemonade $10
Lemonade $10
YOU'VE GOT FIVE SECONDS TO TURN THE WATER BACK ON!
WHOO-EEE! LOOKS LIKE IT'S GONNA BE A **HOT** ONE TODAY...

April 29, 1991

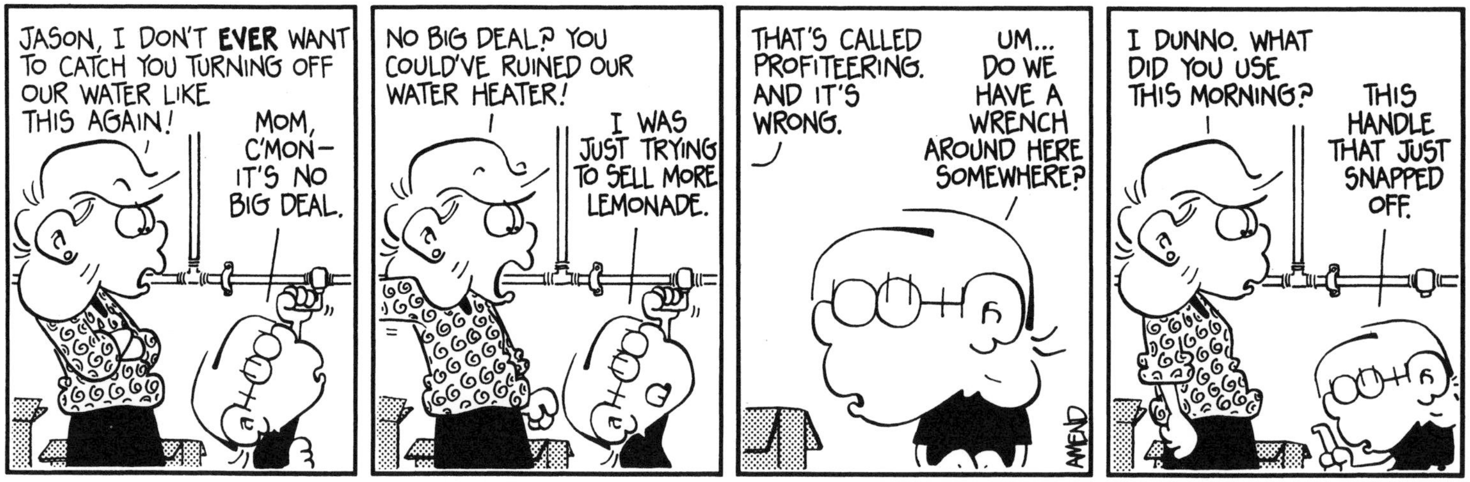
JASON, I DON'T **EVER** WANT TO CATCH YOU TURNING OFF OUR WATER LIKE THIS AGAIN!
MOM, C'MON– IT'S NO BIG DEAL.
NO BIG DEAL?! YOU COULD'VE RUINED OUR WATER HEATER!
I WAS JUST TRYING TO SELL MORE LEMONADE.
THAT'S CALLED PROFITEERING. AND IT'S WRONG.
UM... DO WE HAVE A WRENCH AROUND HERE SOMEWHERE?
AMEND
I DUNNO. WHAT DID YOU USE THIS MORNING?
THIS HANDLE THAT JUST SNAPPED OFF.

April 30, 1991

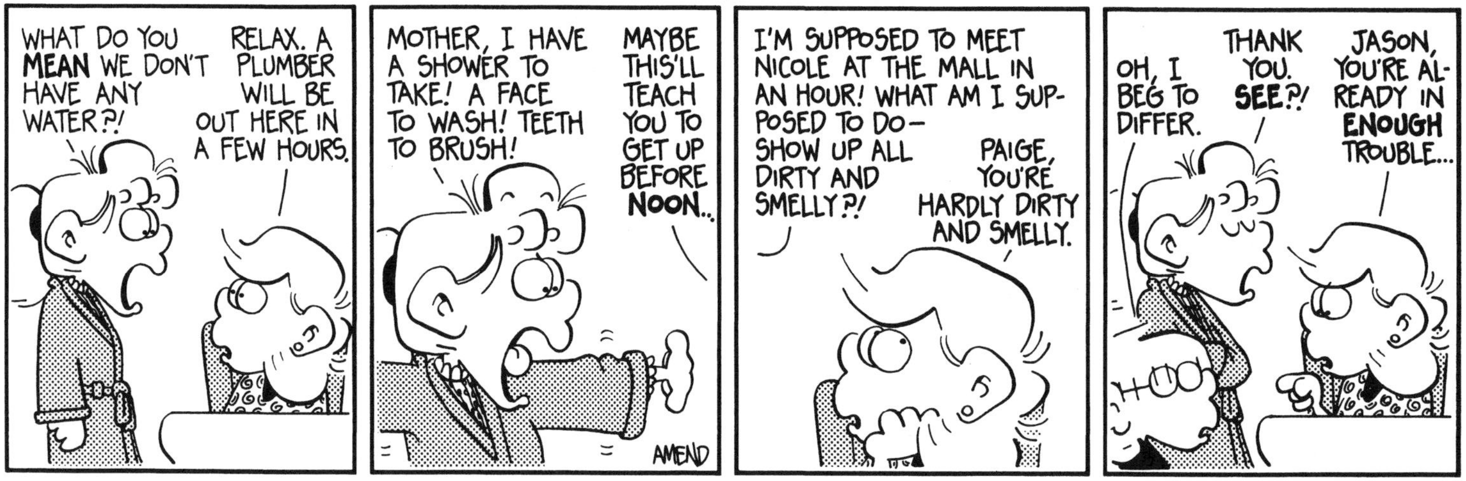
WHAT DO YOU **MEAN** WE DON'T HAVE ANY WATER?!
RELAX. A PLUMBER WILL BE OUT HERE IN A FEW HOURS.
MOTHER, I HAVE A SHOWER TO TAKE! A FACE TO WASH! TEETH TO BRUSH!
MAYBE THIS'LL TEACH YOU TO GET UP BEFORE **NOON**...
AMEND
I'M SUPPOSED TO MEET NICOLE AT THE MALL IN AN HOUR! WHAT AM I SUPPOSED TO DO– SHOW UP ALL DIRTY AND SMELLY?!
PAIGE, YOU'RE HARDLY DIRTY AND SMELLY.
OH, I BEG TO DIFFER.
THANK YOU. **SEE?!**
JASON, YOU'RE ALREADY IN **ENOUGH** TROUBLE...

May 1, 1991

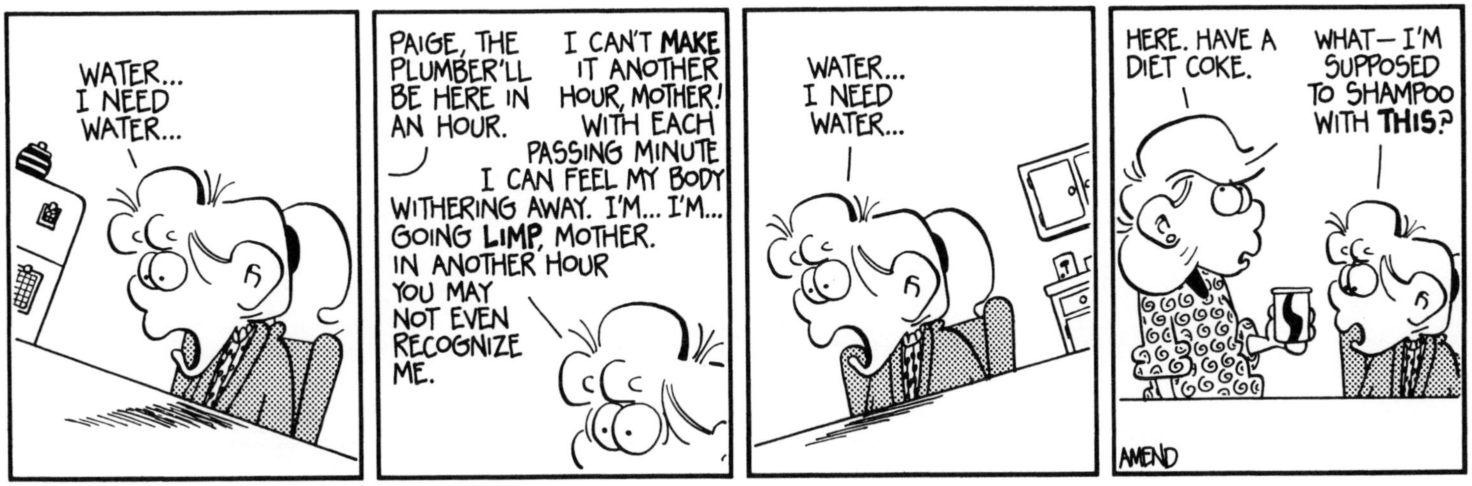
WATER... I NEED WATER...
PAIGE, THE PLUMBER'LL BE HERE IN AN HOUR.
I CAN'T **MAKE** IT ANOTHER HOUR, MOTHER! WITH EACH PASSING MINUTE I CAN FEEL MY BODY WITHERING AWAY. I'M... I'M... GOING **LIMP**, MOTHER. IN ANOTHER HOUR YOU MAY NOT EVEN RECOGNIZE ME.
WATER... I NEED WATER...
HERE. HAVE A DIET COKE.
WHAT— I'M SUPPOSED TO SHAMPOO WITH **THIS**?
AMEND

May 2, 1991

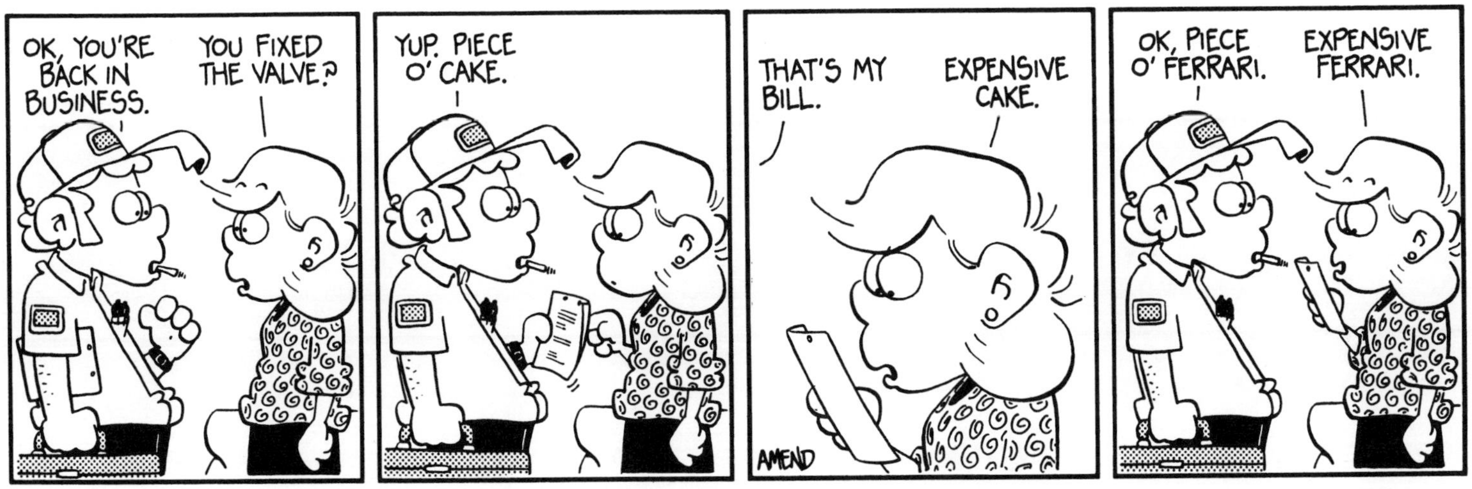
OK, YOU'RE BACK IN BUSINESS.
YOU FIXED THE VALVE?
YUP. PIECE O' CAKE.
THAT'S MY BILL.
EXPENSIVE CAKE.
AMEND
OK, PIECE O' FERRARI.
EXPENSIVE FERRARI.

May 3, 1991

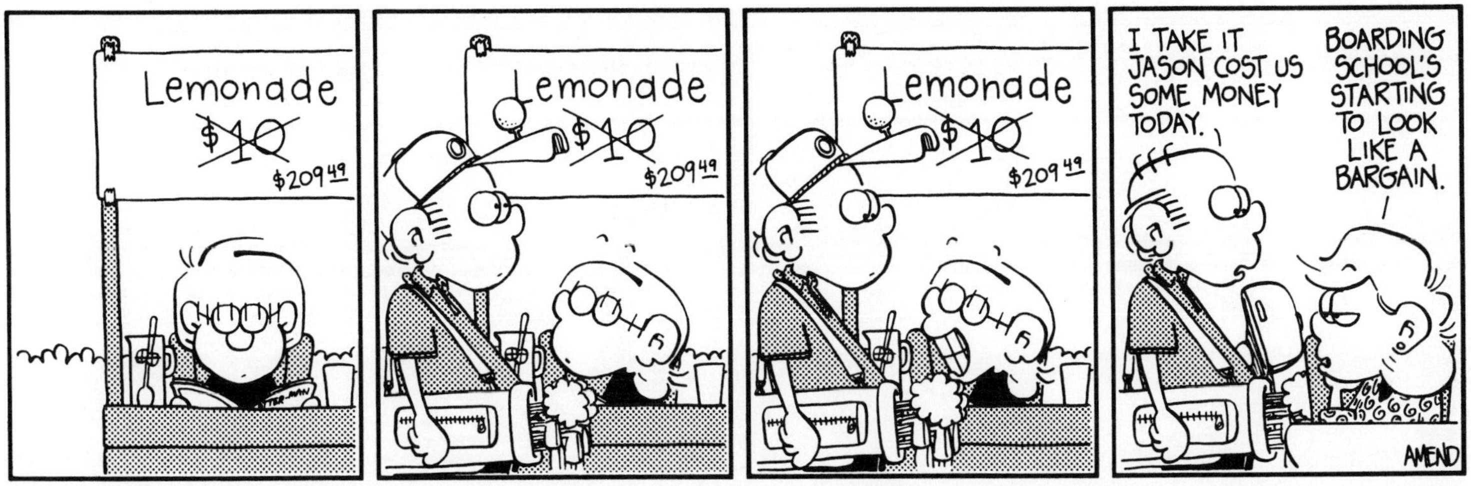
Lemonade
$10
$209.49
I TAKE IT JASON COST US SOME MONEY TODAY.
BOARDING SCHOOL'S STARTING TO LOOK LIKE A BARGAIN.
AMEND

May 4, 1991

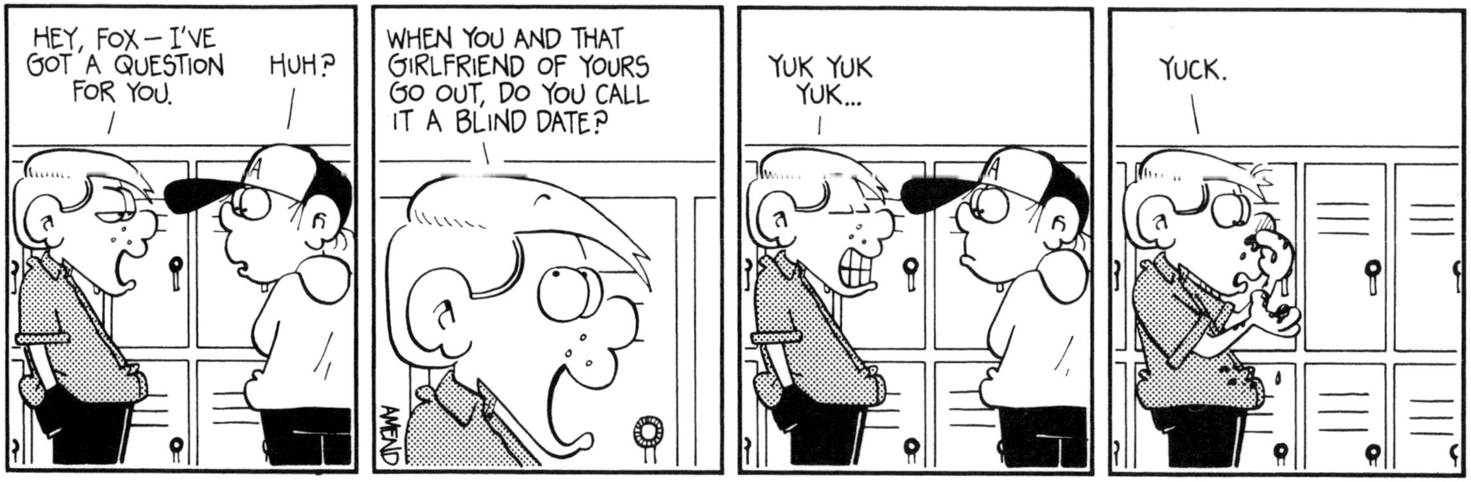
HEY, FOX – I'VE GOT A QUESTION FOR YOU.
HUH?
WHEN YOU AND THAT GIRLFRIEND OF YOURS GO OUT, DO YOU CALL IT A BLIND DATE?
AMEND
YUK YUK YUK...
YUCK.

June 3, 1991

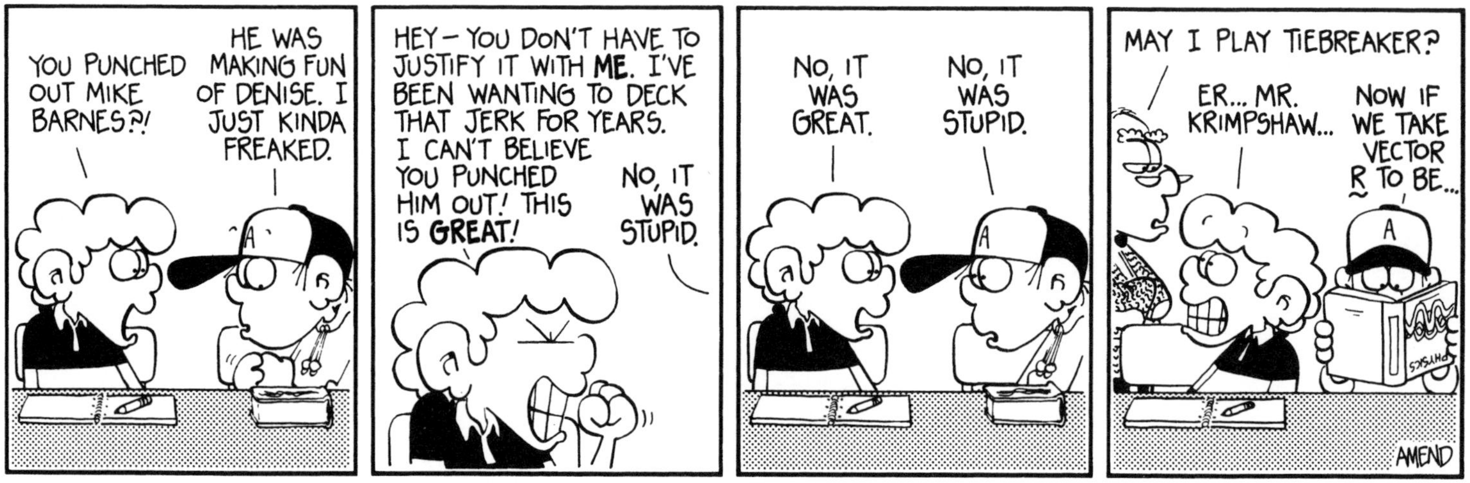
YOU PUNCHED OUT MIKE BARNES?!
HE WAS MAKING FUN OF DENISE. I JUST KINDA FREAKED.
HEY – YOU DON'T HAVE TO JUSTIFY IT WITH **ME**. I'VE BEEN WANTING TO DECK THAT JERK FOR YEARS. I CAN'T BELIEVE YOU PUNCHED HIM OUT! THIS IS **GREAT**!
NO, IT WAS STUPID.
NO, IT WAS GREAT.
NO, IT WAS STUPID.
MAY I PLAY TIEBREAKER?
ER... MR. KRIMPSHAW...
NOW IF WE TAKE VECTOR R TO BE...
AMEND

June 4, 1991

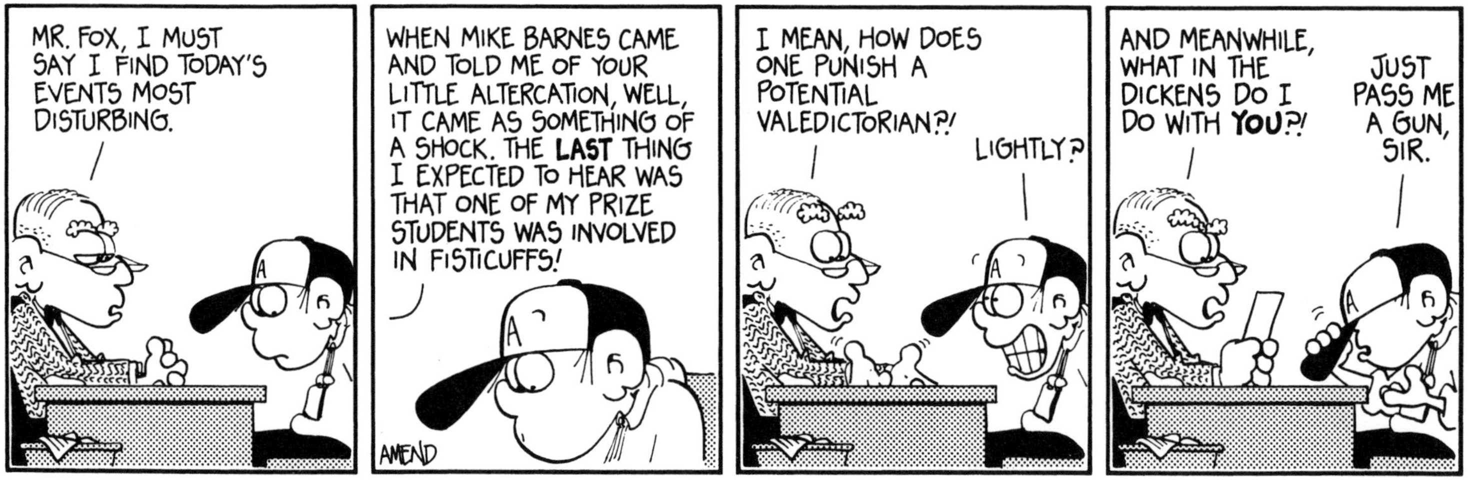
MR. FOX, I MUST SAY I FIND TODAY'S EVENTS MOST DISTURBING.
WHEN MIKE BARNES CAME AND TOLD ME OF YOUR LITTLE ALTERCATION, WELL, IT CAME AS SOMETHING OF A SHOCK. THE **LAST** THING I EXPECTED TO HEAR WAS THAT ONE OF MY PRIZE STUDENTS WAS INVOLVED IN FISTICUFFS!
AMEND
I MEAN, HOW DOES ONE PUNISH A POTENTIAL VALEDICTORIAN?!
LIGHTLY?
AND MEANWHILE, WHAT IN THE DICKENS DO I DO WITH **YOU**?!
JUST PASS ME A GUN, SIR.

June 5, 1991

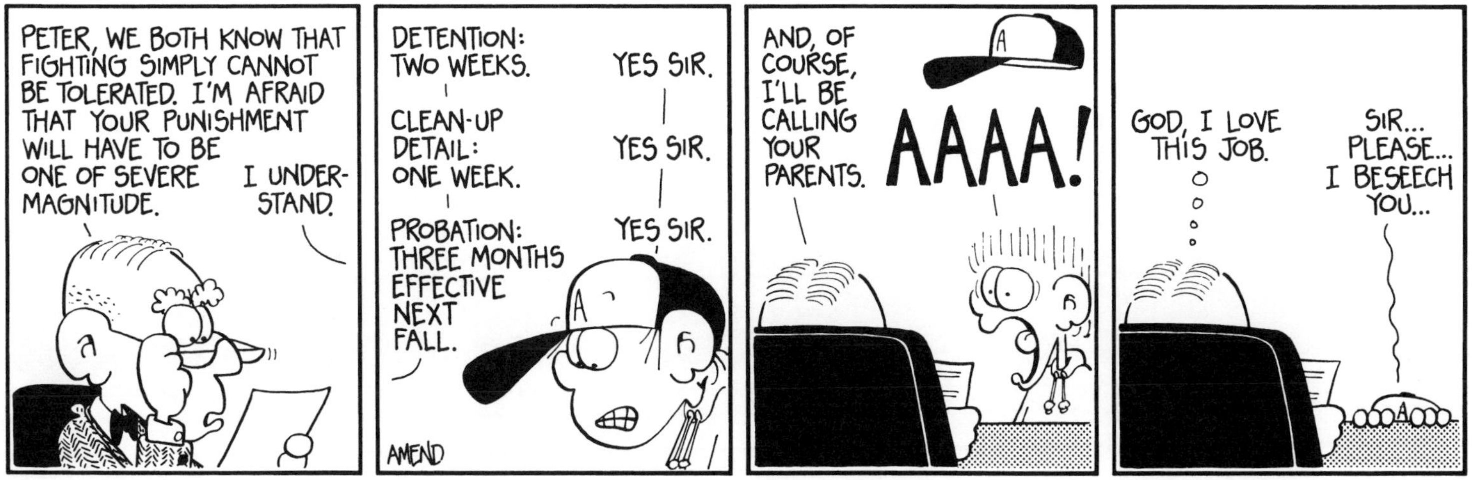
PETER, WE BOTH KNOW THAT FIGHTING SIMPLY CANNOT BE TOLERATED. I'M AFRAID THAT YOUR PUNISHMENT WILL HAVE TO BE ONE OF SEVERE MAGNITUDE.
I UNDERSTAND.
DETENTION: TWO WEEKS.
YES SIR.
CLEAN-UP DETAIL: ONE WEEK.
YES SIR.
PROBATION: THREE MONTHS EFFECTIVE NEXT FALL.
YES SIR.
AMEND
AND, OF COURSE, I'LL BE CALLING YOUR PARENTS.
AAAA!
GOD, I LOVE THIS JOB.
SIR... PLEASE... I BESEECH YOU...

June 6, 1991

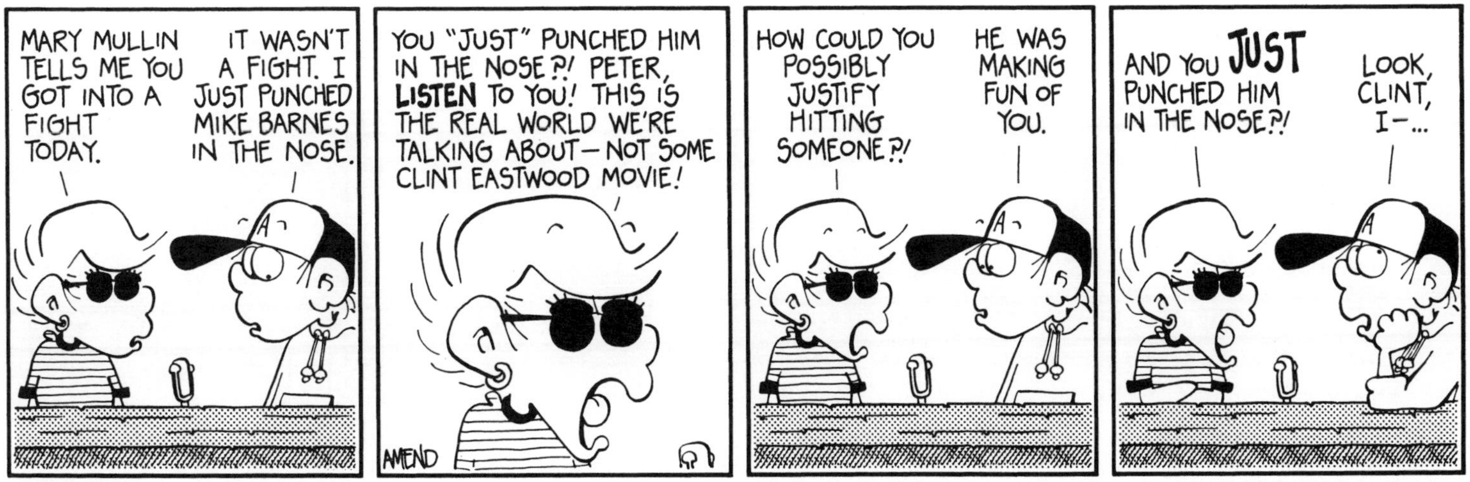
MARY MULLIN TELLS ME YOU GOT INTO A FIGHT TODAY.
IT WASN'T A FIGHT. I JUST PUNCHED MIKE BARNES IN THE NOSE.
YOU "JUST" PUNCHED HIM IN THE NOSE?! PETER, LISTEN TO YOU! THIS IS THE REAL WORLD WE'RE TALKING ABOUT—NOT SOME CLINT EASTWOOD MOVIE!
AMEND
HOW COULD YOU POSSIBLY JUSTIFY HITTING SOMEONE?!
HE WAS MAKING FUN OF YOU.
AND YOU JUST PUNCHED HIM IN THE NOSE?!
LOOK, CLINT, I—...

June 7, 1991

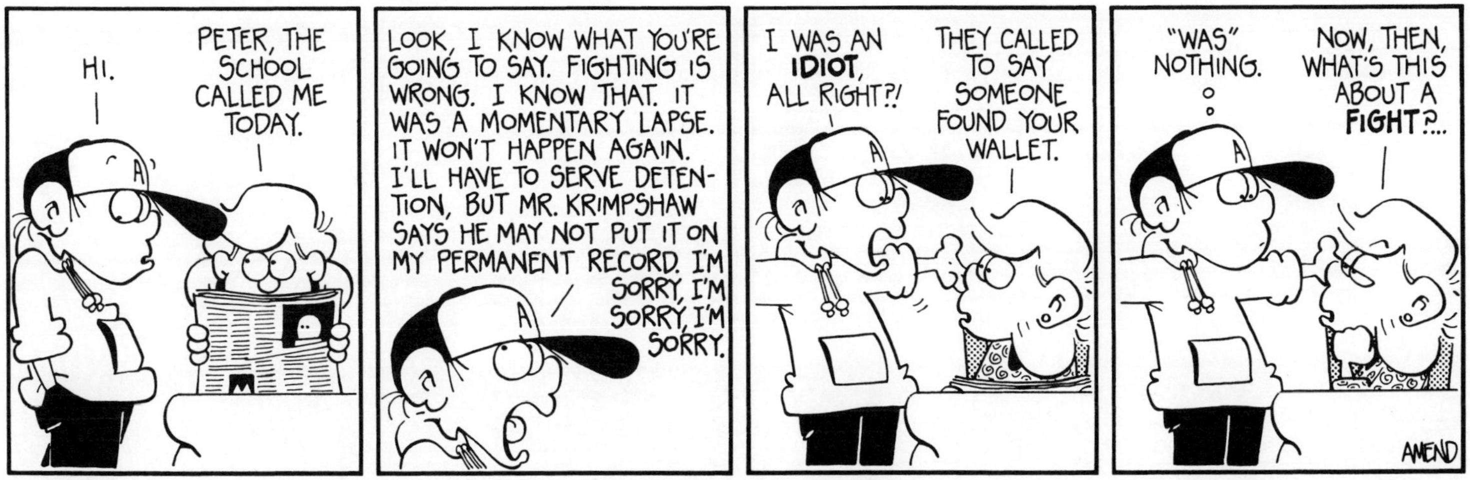
HI.
PETER, THE SCHOOL CALLED ME TODAY.
LOOK, I KNOW WHAT YOU'RE GOING TO SAY. FIGHTING IS WRONG. I KNOW THAT. IT WAS A MOMENTARY LAPSE. IT WON'T HAPPEN AGAIN. I'LL HAVE TO SERVE DETENTION, BUT MR. KRIMPSHAW SAYS HE MAY NOT PUT IT ON MY PERMANENT RECORD. I'M SORRY, I'M SORRY, I'M SORRY.
I WAS AN IDIOT, ALL RIGHT?!
THEY CALLED TO SAY SOMEONE FOUND YOUR WALLET.
"WAS" NOTHING.
NOW, THEN, WHAT'S THIS ABOUT A FIGHT?...
AMEND

June 8, 1991

Inventing the Fun-Fun empire of parks and resorts is one of my prouder achievements.

June 17, 1991

June 18, 1991

June 19, 1991

96

June 20, 1991

June 21, 1991

In reality, my wife loves roller coasters. This would be more like if I dragged her to BlizzCon.

June 22, 1991

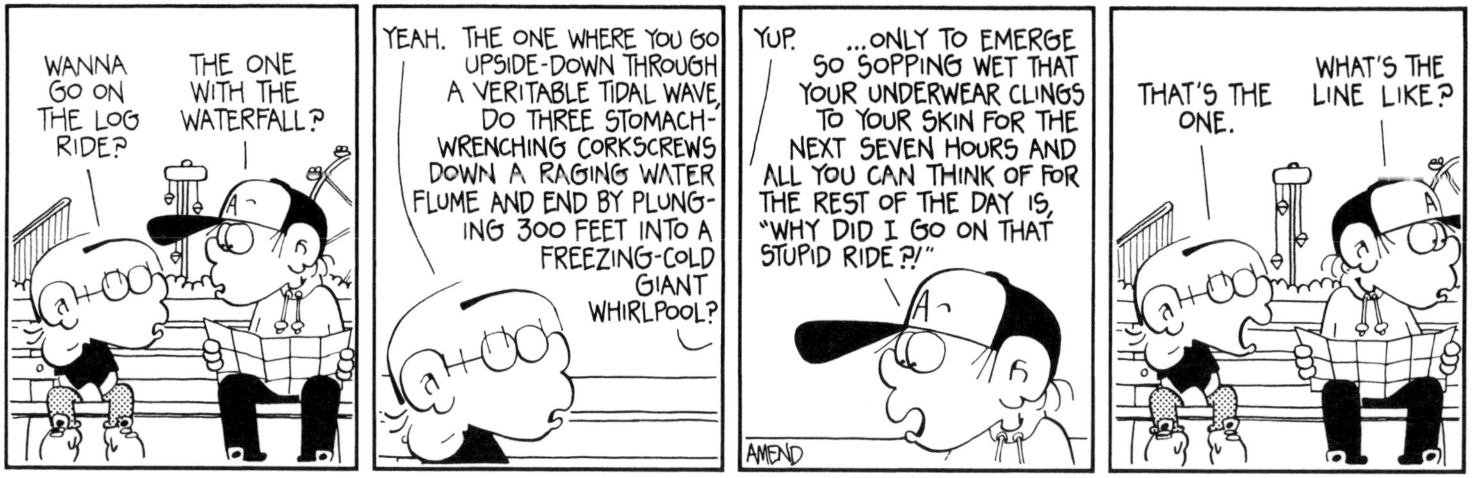
WANNA GO ON THE LOG RIDE?
THE ONE WITH THE WATERFALL?
YEAH. THE ONE WHERE YOU GO UPSIDE-DOWN THROUGH A VERITABLE TIDAL WAVE, DO THREE STOMACH-WRENCHING CORKSCREWS DOWN A RAGING WATER FLUME AND END BY PLUNGING 300 FEET INTO A FREEZING-COLD GIANT WHIRLPOOL?
YUP.
...ONLY TO EMERGE SO SOPPING WET THAT YOUR UNDERWEAR CLINGS TO YOUR SKIN FOR THE NEXT SEVEN HOURS AND ALL YOU CAN THINK OF FOR THE REST OF THE DAY IS, "WHY DID I GO ON THAT STUPID RIDE?!"
AMEND
THAT'S THE ONE.
WHAT'S THE LINE LIKE?

June 24, 1991

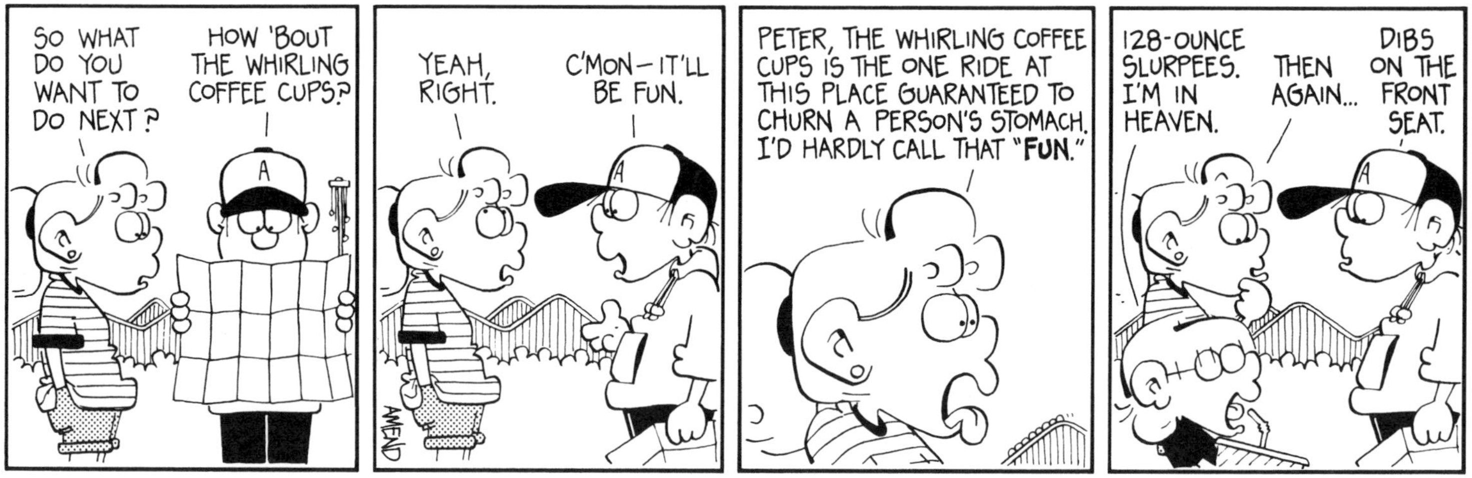
SO WHAT DO YOU WANT TO DO NEXT?
HOW 'BOUT THE WHIRLING COFFEE CUPS?
YEAH, RIGHT.
C'MON– IT'LL BE FUN.
AMEND
PETER, THE WHIRLING COFFEE CUPS IS THE ONE RIDE AT THIS PLACE GUARANTEED TO CHURN A PERSON'S STOMACH. I'D HARDLY CALL THAT "FUN."
128-OUNCE SLURPEES. I'M IN HEAVEN.
THEN AGAIN...
DIBS ON THE FRONT SEAT.

June 25, 1991

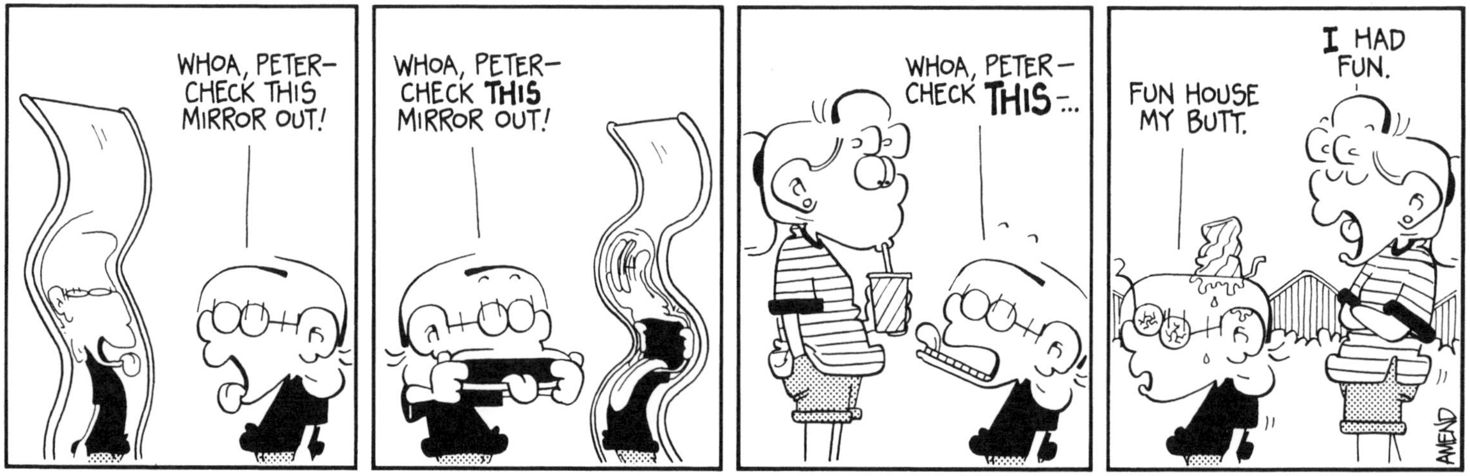
WHOA, PETER– CHECK THIS MIRROR OUT!
WHOA, PETER– CHECK THIS MIRROR OUT!
WHOA, PETER– CHECK THIS-...
FUN HOUSE MY BUTT.
I HAD FUN.
AMEND

June 26, 1991

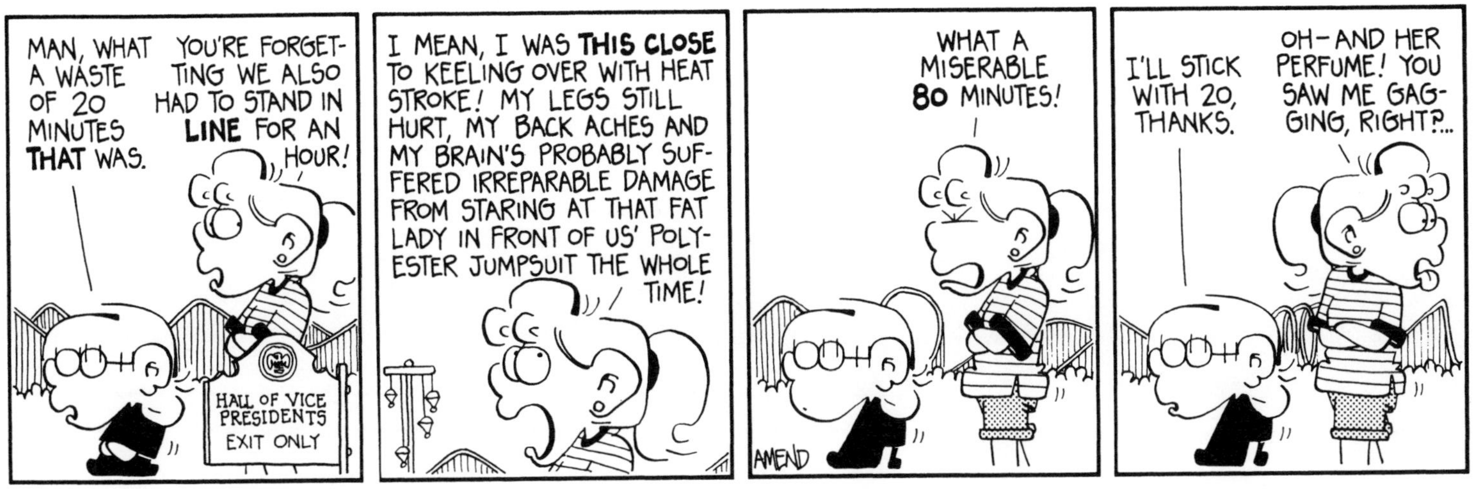
MAN, WHAT A WASTE OF 20 MINUTES **THAT** WAS.
YOU'RE FORGETTING WE ALSO HAD TO STAND IN **LINE** FOR AN HOUR!
HALL OF VICE PRESIDENTS
EXIT ONLY
I MEAN, I WAS **THIS CLOSE** TO KEELING OVER WITH HEAT STROKE! MY LEGS STILL HURT, MY BACK ACHES AND MY BRAIN'S PROBABLY SUFFERED IRREPARABLE DAMAGE FROM STARING AT THAT FAT LADY IN FRONT OF US' POLYESTER JUMPSUIT THE WHOLE TIME!
WHAT A MISERABLE **80** MINUTES!
I'LL STICK WITH 20, THANKS.
OH–AND HER PERFUME! YOU SAW ME GAGGING, RIGHT?...

June 27, 1991

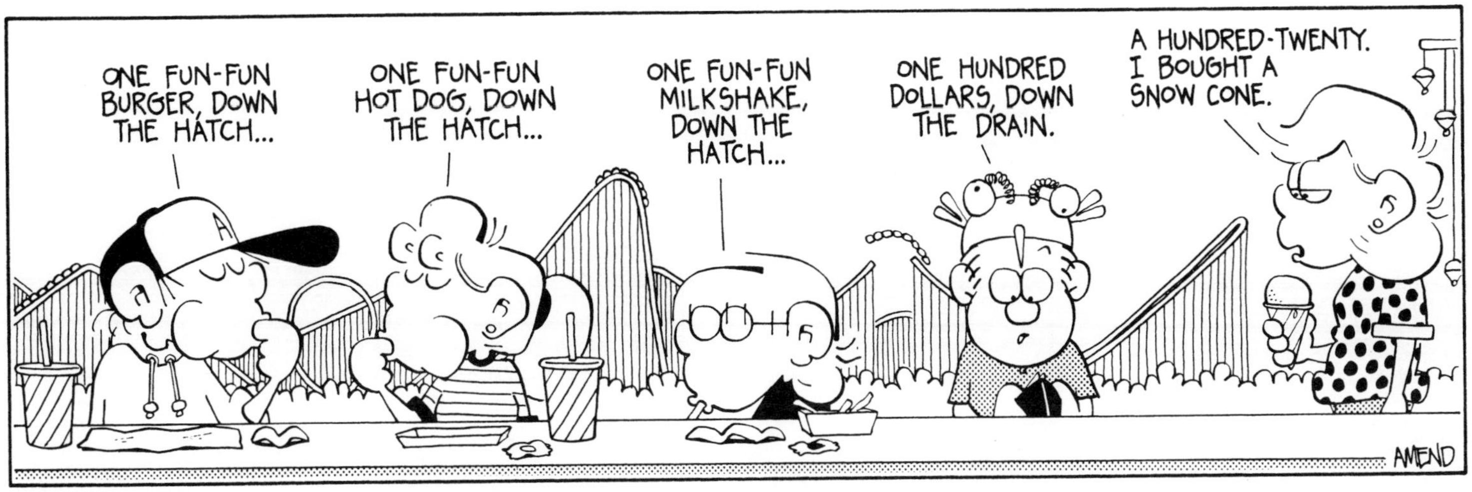
ONE FUN-FUN BURGER, DOWN THE HATCH...
ONE FUN-FUN HOT DOG, DOWN THE HATCH...
ONE FUN-FUN MILKSHAKE, DOWN THE HATCH...
ONE HUNDRED DOLLARS, DOWN THE DRAIN.
A HUNDRED-TWENTY. I BOUGHT A SNOW CONE.

June 28, 1991

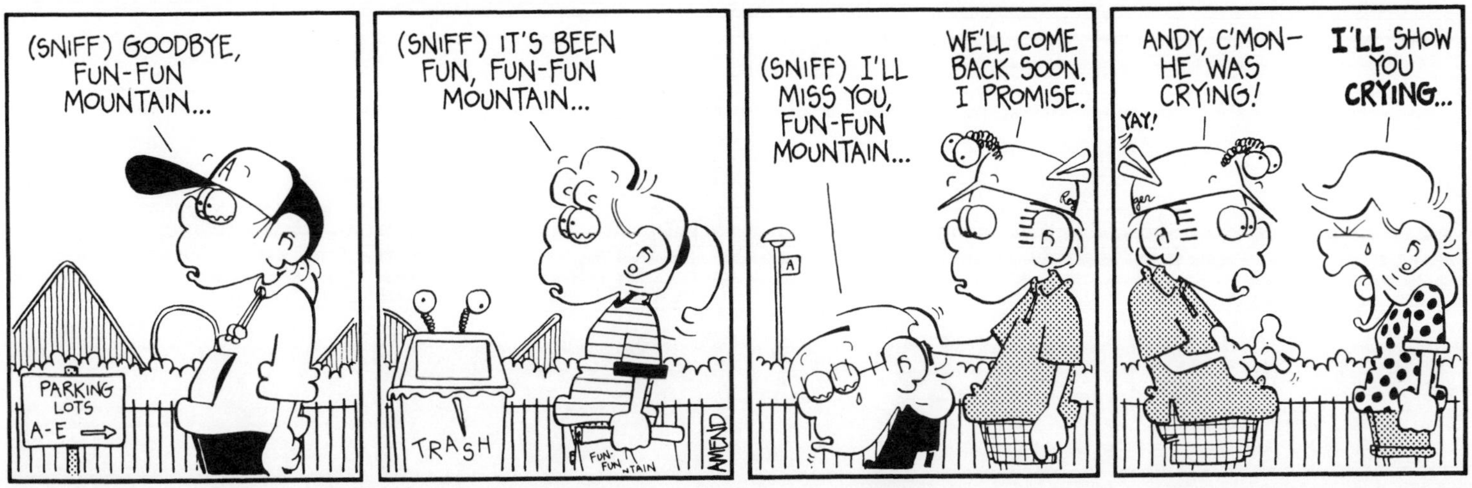
(SNIFF) GOODBYE, FUN-FUN MOUNTAIN...
PARKING LOTS A-E
(SNIFF) IT'S BEEN FUN, FUN-FUN MOUNTAIN...
TRASH
(SNIFF) I'LL MISS YOU, FUN-FUN MOUNTAIN...
WE'LL COME BACK SOON. I PROMISE.
YAY!
ANDY, C'MON– HE WAS CRYING!
I'LL SHOW YOU **CRYING**...

June 29, 1991

July 15, 1991

These strips were fun to do. Figuring out Paige's handwriting style was the hardest part.

July 16, 1991

100

July 17, 1991

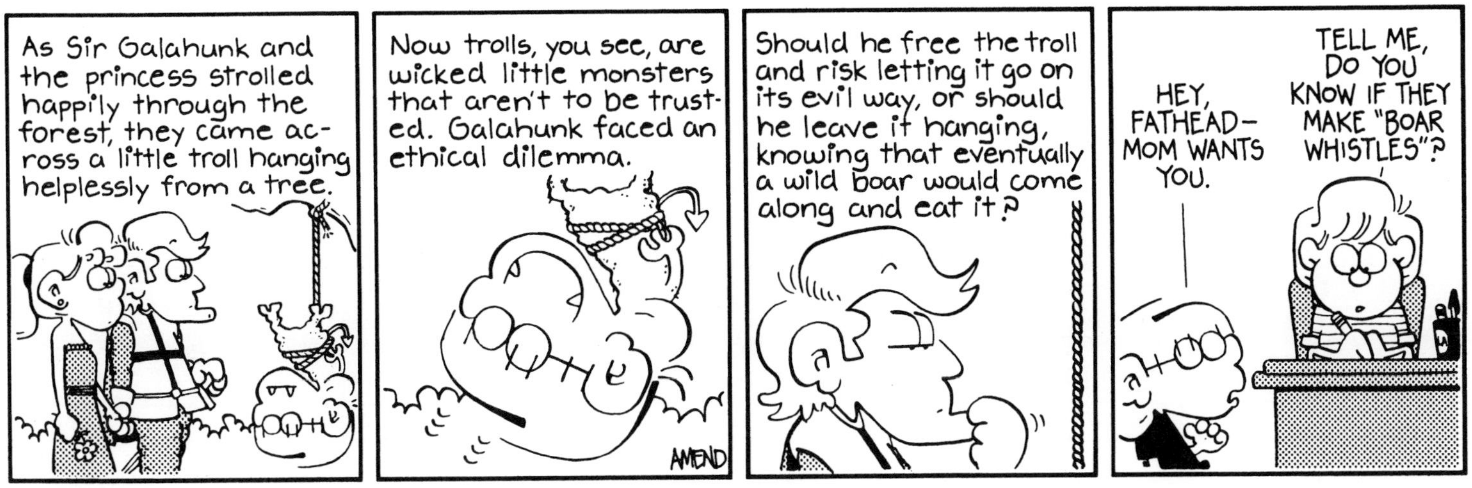
As Sir Galahunk and the princess strolled happily through the forest, they came across a little troll hanging helplessly from a tree.
Now trolls, you see, are wicked little monsters that aren't to be trusted. Galahunk faced an ethical dilemma.
AMEND
Should he free the troll and risk letting it go on its evil way, or should he leave it hanging, knowing that eventually a wild boar would come along and eat it?
HEY, FATHEAD– MOM WANTS YOU.
TELL ME, DO YOU KNOW IF THEY MAKE "BOAR WHISTLES"?
July 18, 1991

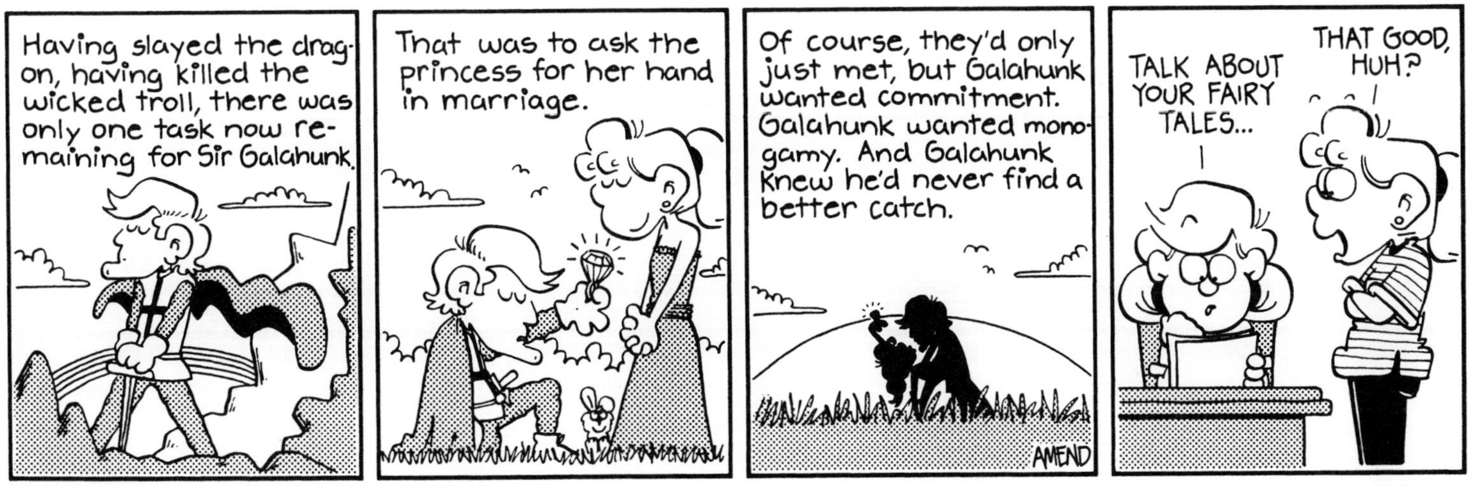
Having slayed the dragon, having killed the wicked troll, there was only one task now remaining for Sir Galahunk.
That was to ask the princess for her hand in marriage.
Of course, they'd only just met, but Galahunk wanted commitment. Galahunk wanted monogamy. And Galahunk knew he'd never find a better catch.
AMEND
TALK ABOUT YOUR FAIRY TALES...
THAT GOOD, HUH?
July 19, 1991

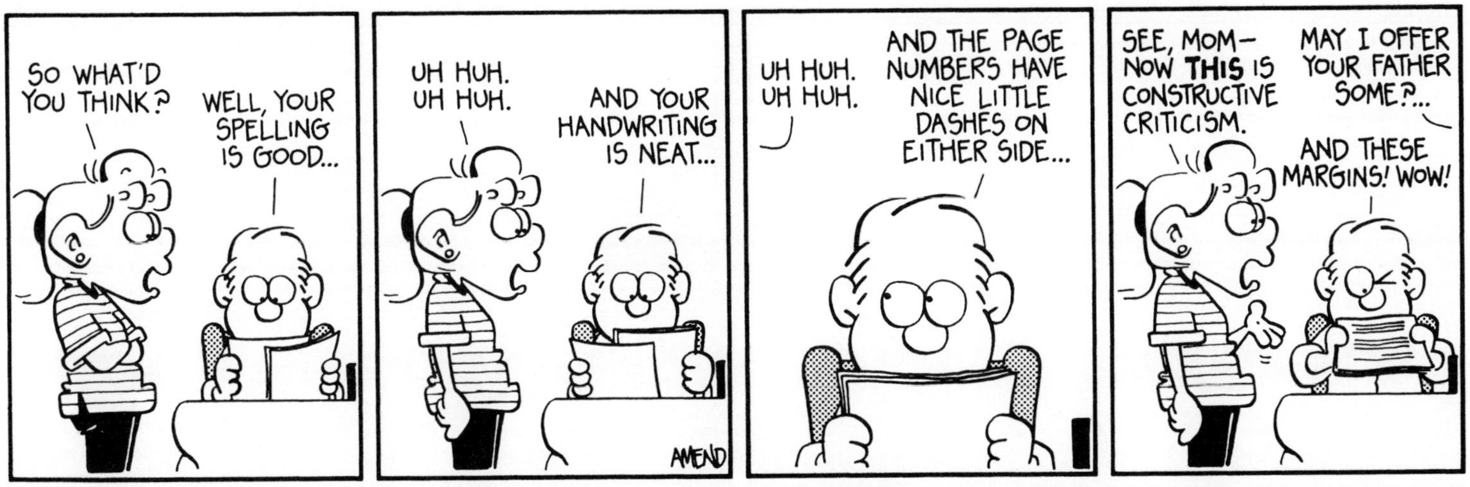
SO WHAT'D YOU THINK?
WELL, YOUR SPELLING IS GOOD...
UH HUH. UH HUH.
AND YOUR HANDWRITING IS NEAT...
AMEND
UH HUH. UH HUH.
AND THE PAGE NUMBERS HAVE NICE LITTLE DASHES ON EITHER SIDE...
SEE, MOM– NOW THIS IS CONSTRUCTIVE CRITICISM.
MAY I OFFER YOUR FATHER SOME?...
AND THESE MARGINS! WOW!
July 20, 1991

I almost used this Ho-Ho line as a book title, as I recall.

August 2, 1991

February 28, 1992

March 6, 1992

Hard to argue with the Catwoman angle.

I'm not sure I want to know what earns someone a "Golden Gallows Award."

October 21, 1991

October 22, 1991

October 23, 1991

October 24, 1991

October 25, 1991

October 26, 1991

I didn't know Bil Keane very well when I did these. Fortunately, he liked them.

March 9, 1992

March 10, 1992

106

March 11, 1992

WHAT'S THIS SUPPOSED TO BE? THAT'S THE GHOST "IDA KNOW" EXITING JEFFY'S BODY.

SEE, THE GHOST TOOK OVER HIS BEING AND MADE HIM GO ON A PSYCHOTIC RAMPAGE CHASING THE DOG AROUND THE HOUSE WITH AN AX. SEE HOW THE DOTTED LINE WEAVES ALL OVER THE PLACE?

AND YOU EXPECT THE GUY WHO DOES "FAMILY CIRCUS" TO **USE** THIS?! HE WOULDN'T HAVE TO PAY FOR IT.

DON'T BE SO SURE. YOU KNOW, MAYBE IT'D BE FUNNIER IF HE CHASED HIS MOM...

March 12, 1992

I DON'T GET IT. WELL, SEE, AFTER THE BLACK WIDOW BITES DOLLY, THE FATHER SETS IT FREE, SAYING, "AT LEAST **ONE** WILL LIVE."

I STILL DON'T GET IT. WHAT DO YOU MEAN? I JUST **EXPLAINED** IT TO YOU!

I JUST DON'T THINK IT'S FUNNY. OK?!

IT'S SUPPOSED TO BE **TOUCHING!**

March 13, 1992

It's very touching, Jason.
Don't listen to your sister.

WELL, YOU'LL BE RELIEVED TO KNOW I'VE STOPPED TRYING TO DRAW "FAMILY CIRCUS" CARTOONS. HALLELUJAH.

I JUST HAD TOO MANY GOOD IDEAS. THIS BIL KEANE GUY WOULD HAVE TO GO ON VACATION EVERY OTHER WEEK JUST TO MAKE ROOM FOR ME. IT'S TOO MUCH TO ASK. I MEAN, AFTER ALL, HE DID **CREATE** THE THING. NOPE, TIME TO MOVE ON. TO WHAT?

I FIGURE I'LL GO AFTER ONE OF THOSE STRIPS WHERE THE ORIGINAL CREATOR DIED A MILLION YEARS AGO. SINCE THEY'RE ALREADY BEING DRAWN BY REPLACEMENT ARTISTS, WHAT'S TO STOP ME FROM REPLACING **THEM?** JASON, WHAT'S WRONG WITH JUST CREATING A **NEW** COMIC STRIP?

I'VE NARROWED THE CANDIDATES DOWN TO 20... I SAID, WHAT'S WRONG WITH A **NEW** COMIC STRIP?!

March 14, 1992

I'm not sure this show was superhugely popular, but I really, really liked it.

March 30, 1992

Apparently the DVD versions leave out the eye-patched "Old Indy."

March 31, 1992

April 1, 1992

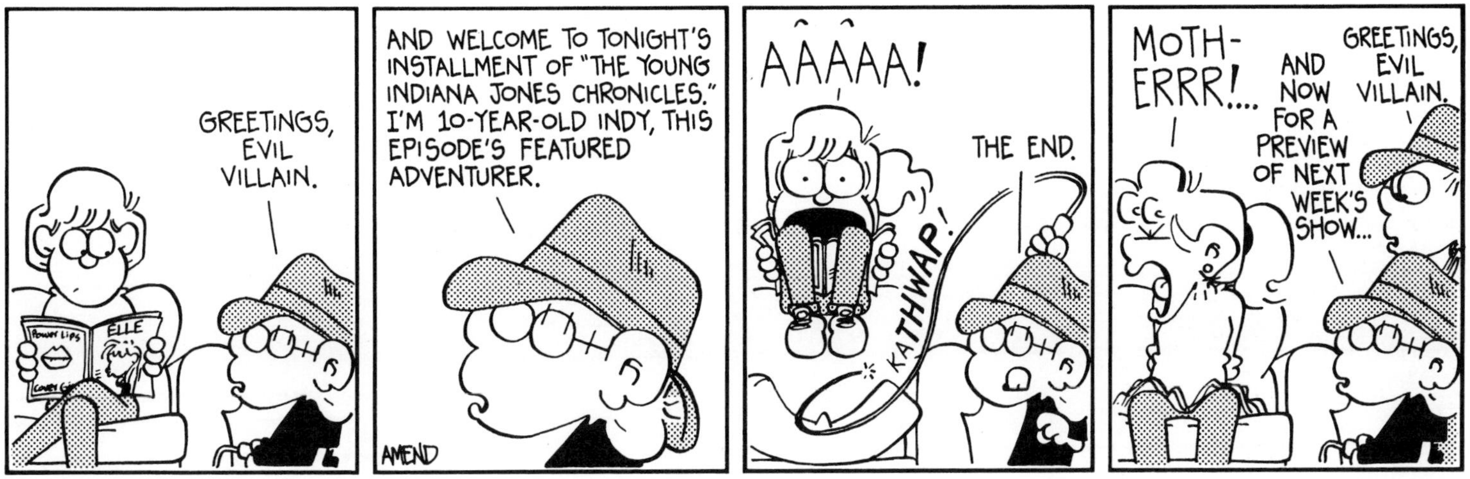
GREETINGS, EVIL VILLAIN.
ELLE
AND WELCOME TO TONIGHT'S INSTALLMENT OF "THE YOUNG INDIANA JONES CHRONICLES." I'M 10-YEAR-OLD INDY, THIS EPISODE'S FEATURED ADVENTURER.
AMEND
AAAAA!
THE END.
KATHWAP!
MOTH-ERRR!...
AND NOW FOR A PREVIEW OF NEXT WEEK'S SHOW...
GREETINGS, EVIL VILLAIN.

April 2, 1992

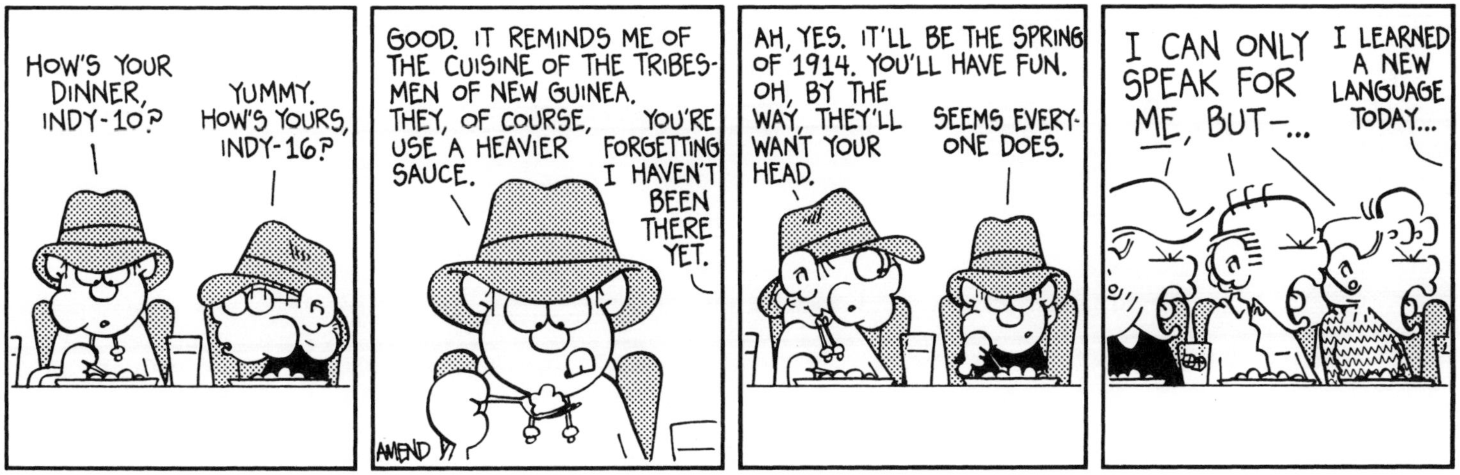
HOW'S YOUR DINNER, INDY-10?
YUMMY. HOW'S YOURS, INDY-16?
GOOD. IT REMINDS ME OF THE CUISINE OF THE TRIBESMEN OF NEW GUINEA. THEY, OF COURSE, USE A HEAVIER SAUCE.
YOU'RE FORGETTING I HAVEN'T BEEN THERE YET.
AMEND
AH, YES. IT'LL BE THE SPRING OF 1914. YOU'LL HAVE FUN. OH, BY THE WAY, THEY'LL WANT YOUR HEAD.
SEEMS EVERYONE DOES.
I CAN ONLY SPEAK FOR ME, BUT—...
I LEARNED A NEW LANGUAGE TODAY...

April 3, 1992

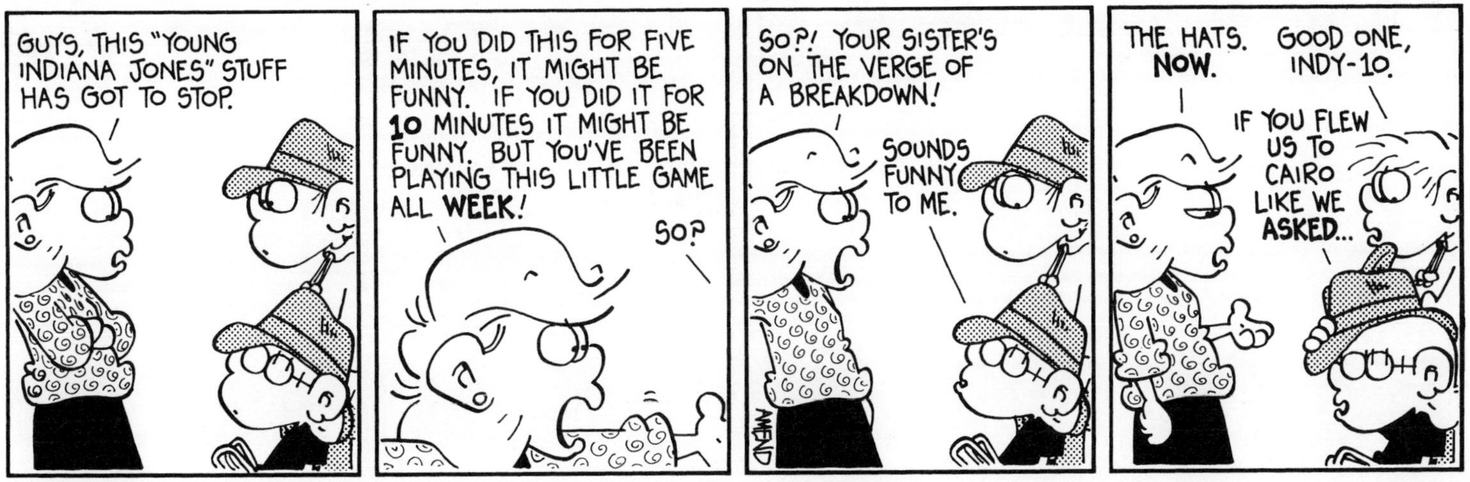
GUYS, THIS "YOUNG INDIANA JONES" STUFF HAS GOT TO STOP.
IF YOU DID THIS FOR FIVE MINUTES, IT MIGHT BE FUNNY. IF YOU DID IT FOR 10 MINUTES IT MIGHT BE FUNNY. BUT YOU'VE BEEN PLAYING THIS LITTLE GAME ALL WEEK!
SO?
SO?! YOUR SISTER'S ON THE VERGE OF A BREAKDOWN!
SOUNDS FUNNY TO ME.
AMEND
THE HATS. NOW.
GOOD ONE, INDY-10.
IF YOU FLEW US TO CAIRO LIKE WE ASKED...

April 4, 1992

My first Sunday with dialogue balloons. Not sure why I didn't start using them sooner.

January 5, 1992

Clearly, I should have been a poet.

February 9, 1992

110

April 5, 1992

I wish I could do Slug Man strips more often. They're lots of fun to draw.

May 17, 1992

To illustrate Jason speaking in a lower voice, I lowered his jaw.

April 13, 1992

April 14, 1992

April 15, 1992

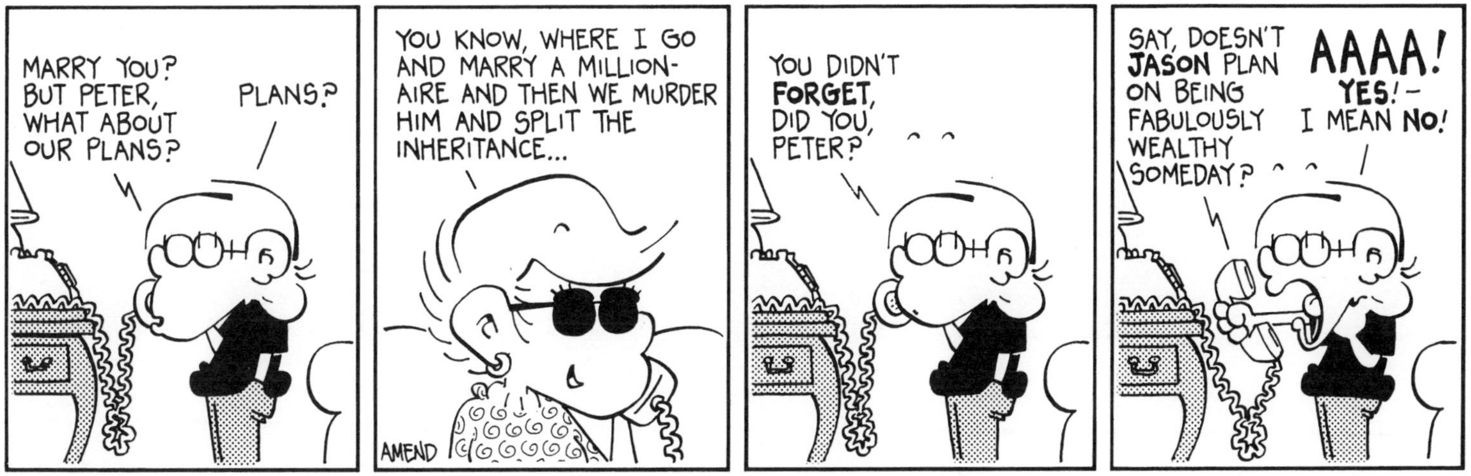
MARRY YOU? BUT PETER, WHAT ABOUT OUR PLANS?
PLANS?
YOU KNOW, WHERE I GO AND MARRY A MILLIONAIRE AND THEN WE MURDER HIM AND SPLIT THE INHERITANCE...
AMEND
YOU DIDN'T **FORGET**, DID YOU, PETER?
SAY, DOESN'T **JASON** PLAN ON BEING FABULOUSLY WEALTHY SOMEDAY?
AAAA! **YES**! – I MEAN **NO**!

April 16, 1992

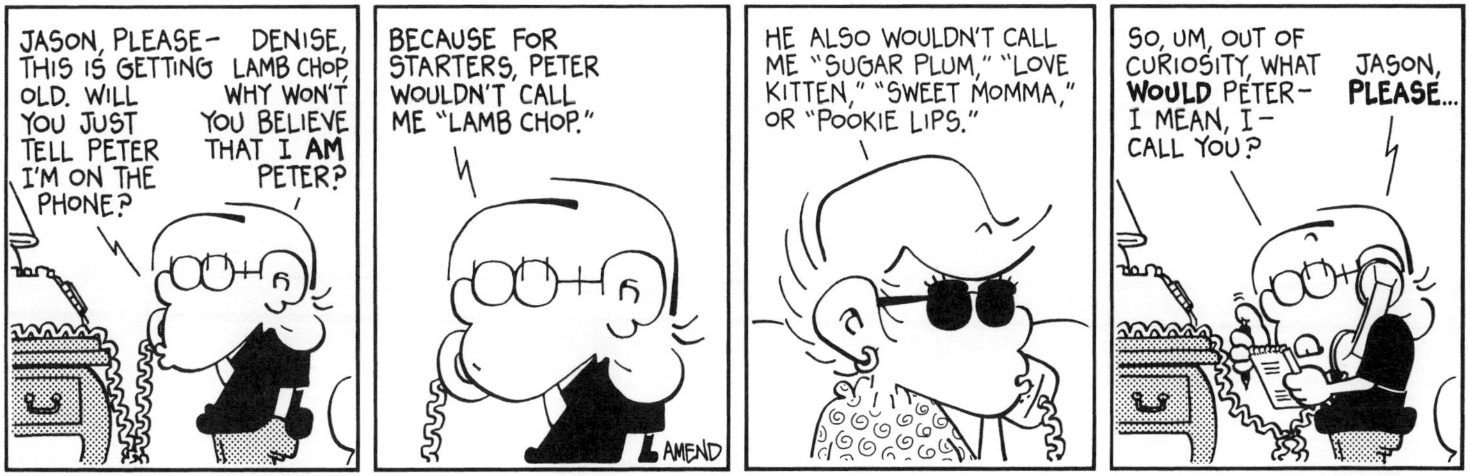
JASON, PLEASE– THIS IS GETTING OLD. WILL YOU JUST TELL PETER I'M ON THE PHONE?
DENISE, LAMB CHOP, WHY WON'T YOU BELIEVE THAT I **AM** PETER?
BECAUSE FOR STARTERS, PETER WOULDN'T CALL ME "LAMB CHOP."
AMEND
HE ALSO WOULDN'T CALL ME "SUGAR PLUM," "LOVE KITTEN," "SWEET MOMMA," OR "POOKIE LIPS."
SO, UM, OUT OF CURIOSITY, WHAT **WOULD** PETER– I MEAN, I– CALL YOU?
JASON, **PLEASE**...

April 17, 1992

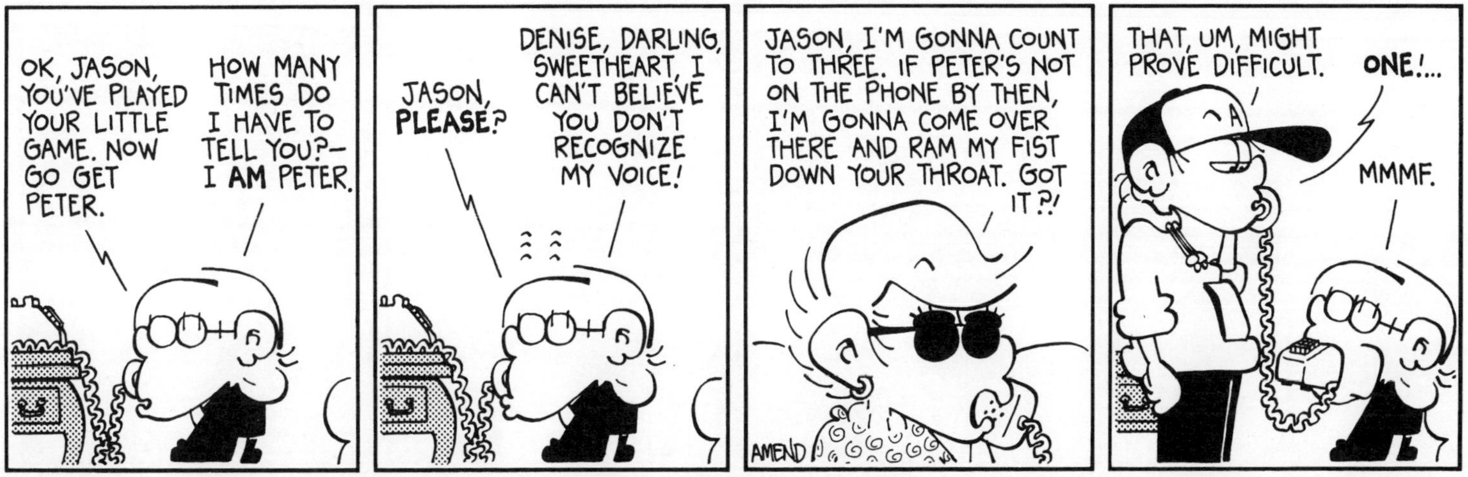
OK, JASON, YOU'VE PLAYED YOUR LITTLE GAME. NOW GO GET PETER.
HOW MANY TIMES DO I HAVE TO TELL YOU?– I **AM** PETER.
JASON, **PLEASE**?
DENISE, DARLING, SWEETHEART, I CAN'T BELIEVE YOU DON'T RECOGNIZE MY VOICE!
JASON, I'M GONNA COUNT TO THREE. IF PETER'S NOT ON THE PHONE BY THEN, I'M GONNA COME OVER THERE AND RAM MY FIST DOWN YOUR THROAT. GOT IT?!
AMEND
THAT, UM, MIGHT PROVE DIFFICULT.
ONE!...
MMMF.

April 18, 1992

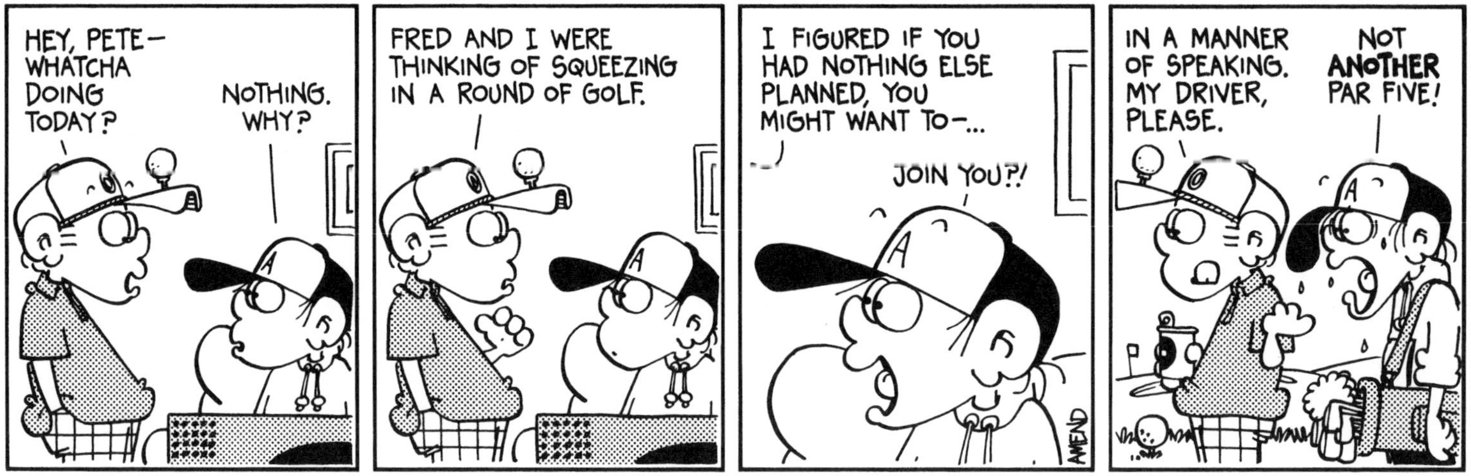
HEY, PETE—
WHATCHA DOING TODAY?
NOTHING. WHY?
FRED AND I WERE THINKING OF SQUEEZING IN A ROUND OF GOLF.
I FIGURED IF YOU HAD NOTHING ELSE PLANNED, YOU MIGHT WANT TO—...
JOIN YOU?!
IN A MANNER OF SPEAKING. MY DRIVER, PLEASE.
NOT ANOTHER PAR FIVE!
AMEND
June 8, 1992

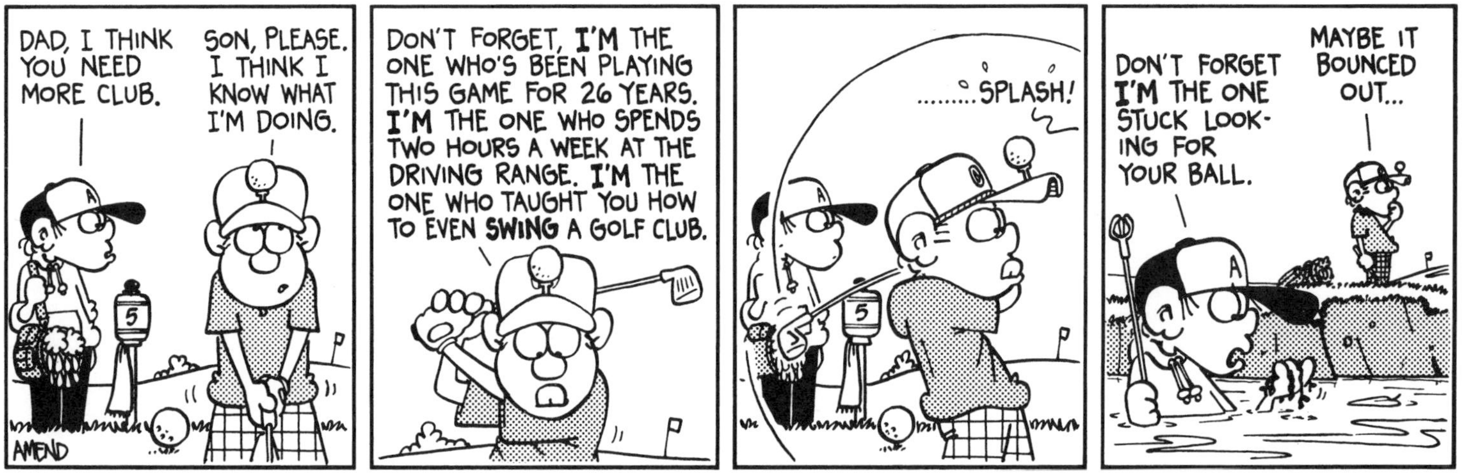
DAD, I THINK YOU NEED MORE CLUB.
SON, PLEASE. I THINK I KNOW WHAT I'M DOING.
5
AMEND
DON'T FORGET, I'M THE ONE WHO'S BEEN PLAYING THIS GAME FOR 26 YEARS. I'M THE ONE WHO SPENDS TWO HOURS A WEEK AT THE DRIVING RANGE. I'M THE ONE WHO TAUGHT YOU HOW TO EVEN SWING A GOLF CLUB.
........SPLASH!
5
DON'T FORGET I'M THE ONE STUCK LOOK-ING FOR YOUR BALL.
MAYBE IT BOUNCED OUT...
June 9, 1992

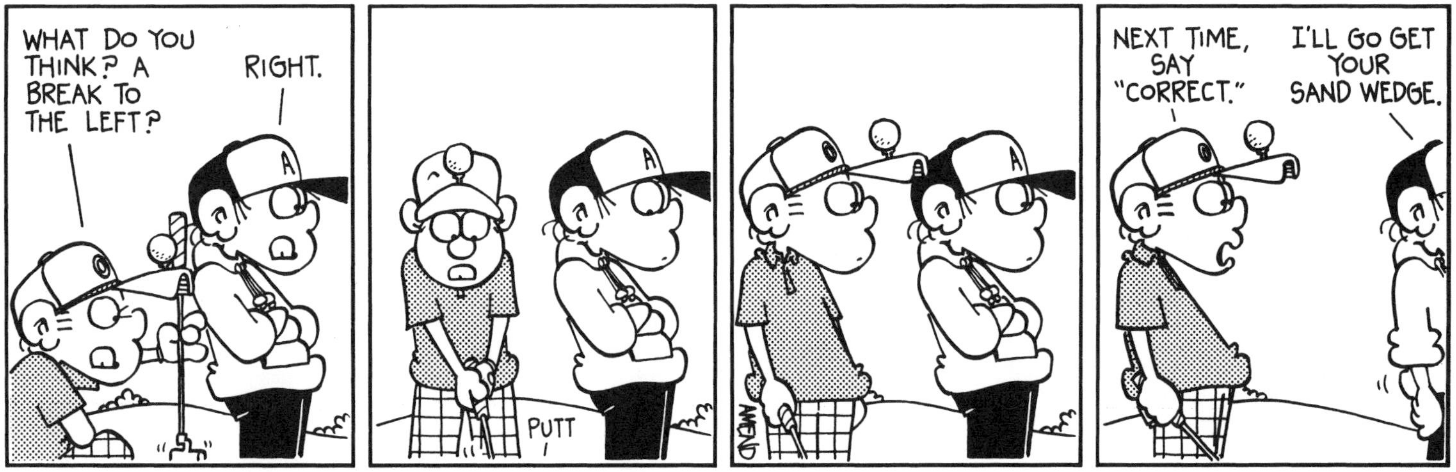
WHAT DO YOU THINK? A BREAK TO THE LEFT?
RIGHT.
PUTT
AMEND
NEXT TIME, SAY "CORRECT."
I'LL GO GET YOUR SAND WEDGE.
June 10, 1992

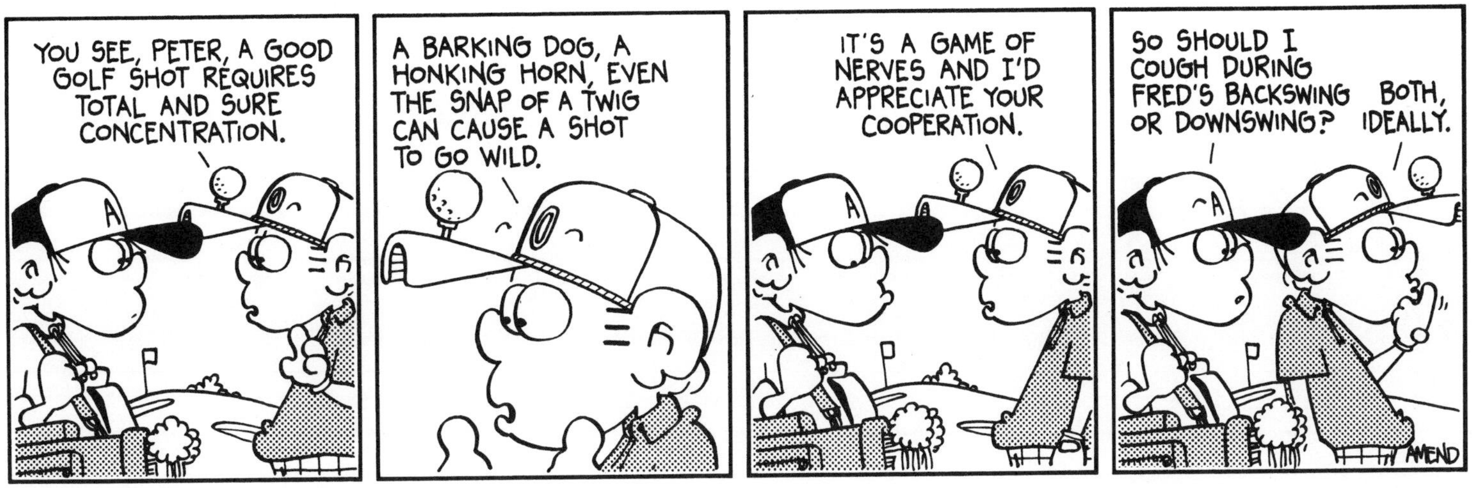
YOU SEE, PETER, A GOOD GOLF SHOT REQUIRES TOTAL AND SURE CONCENTRATION.
A BARKING DOG, A HONKING HORN, EVEN THE SNAP OF A TWIG CAN CAUSE A SHOT TO GO WILD.
IT'S A GAME OF NERVES AND I'D APPRECIATE YOUR COOPERATION.
SO SHOULD I COUGH DURING FRED'S BACKSWING OR DOWNSWING?
BOTH, IDEALLY.
AMEND

June 11, 1992

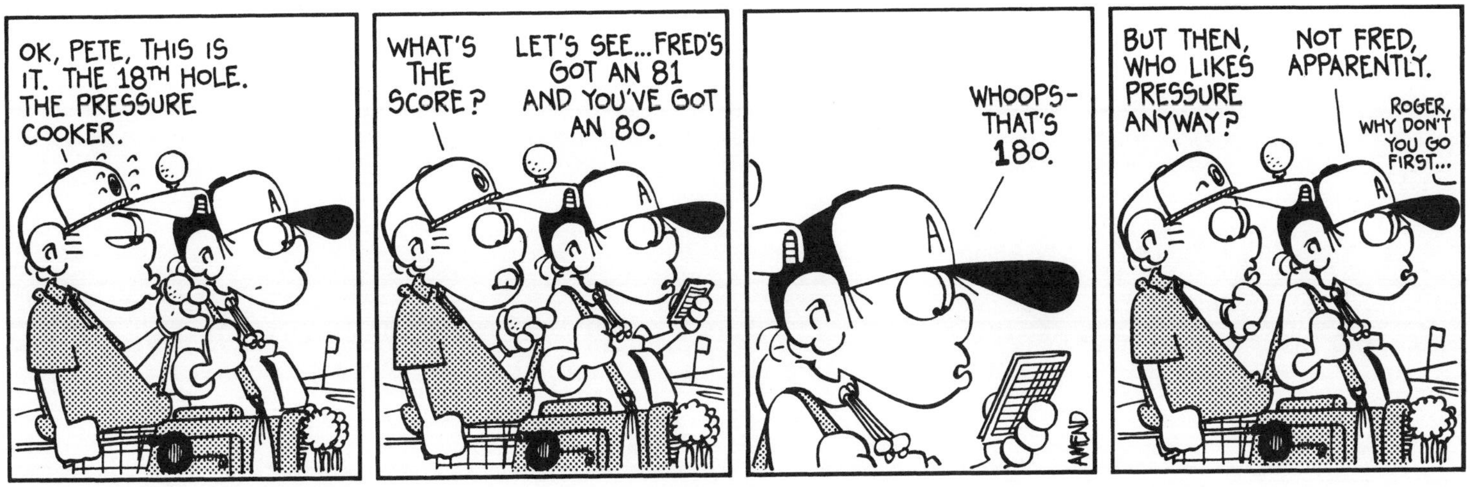
OK, PETE, THIS IS IT. THE 18TH HOLE. THE PRESSURE COOKER.
WHAT'S THE SCORE?
LET'S SEE... FRED'S GOT AN 81 AND YOU'VE GOT AN 80.
WHOOPS- THAT'S 180.
AMEND
BUT THEN, WHO LIKES PRESSURE ANYWAY?
NOT FRED, APPARENTLY.
ROGER, WHY DON'T YOU GO FIRST...

June 12, 1992

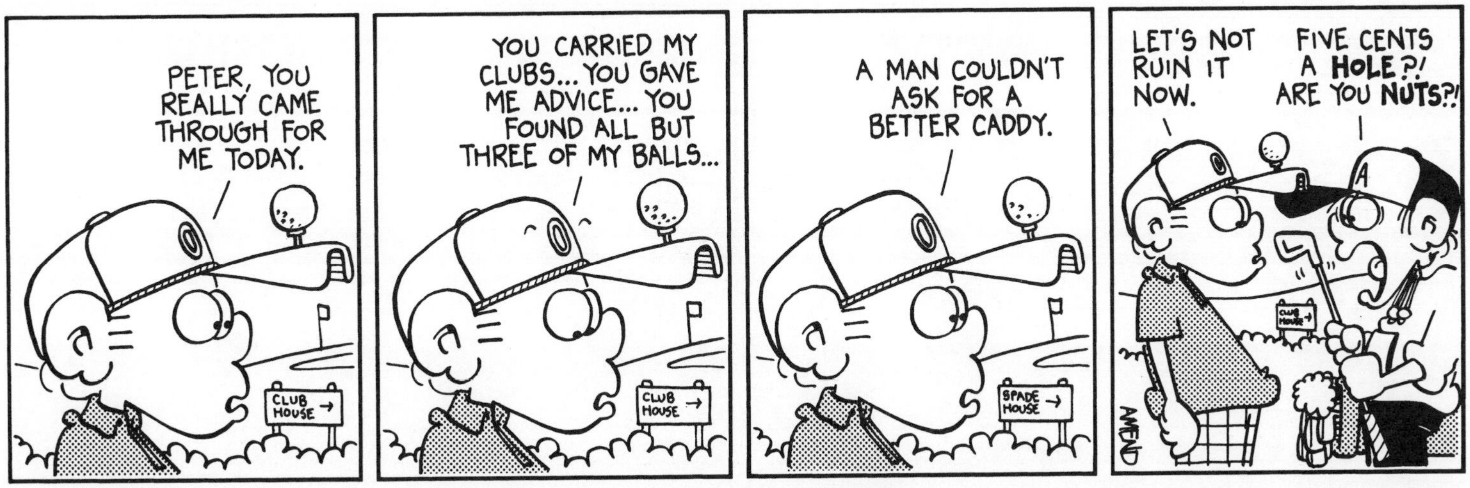
PETER, YOU REALLY CAME THROUGH FOR ME TODAY.
CLUB HOUSE →
YOU CARRIED MY CLUBS... YOU GAVE ME ADVICE... YOU FOUND ALL BUT THREE OF MY BALLS...
CLUB HOUSE →
A MAN COULDN'T ASK FOR A BETTER CADDY.
SPADE HOUSE →
LET'S NOT RUIN IT NOW.
FIVE CENTS A **HOLE**?! ARE YOU **NUTS**?!
AMEND

June 13, 1992

I wanted to upgrade the family gaming console, so I came up with this story line to get rid of the old one.

June 22, 1992

June 23, 1992

116

June 24, 1992

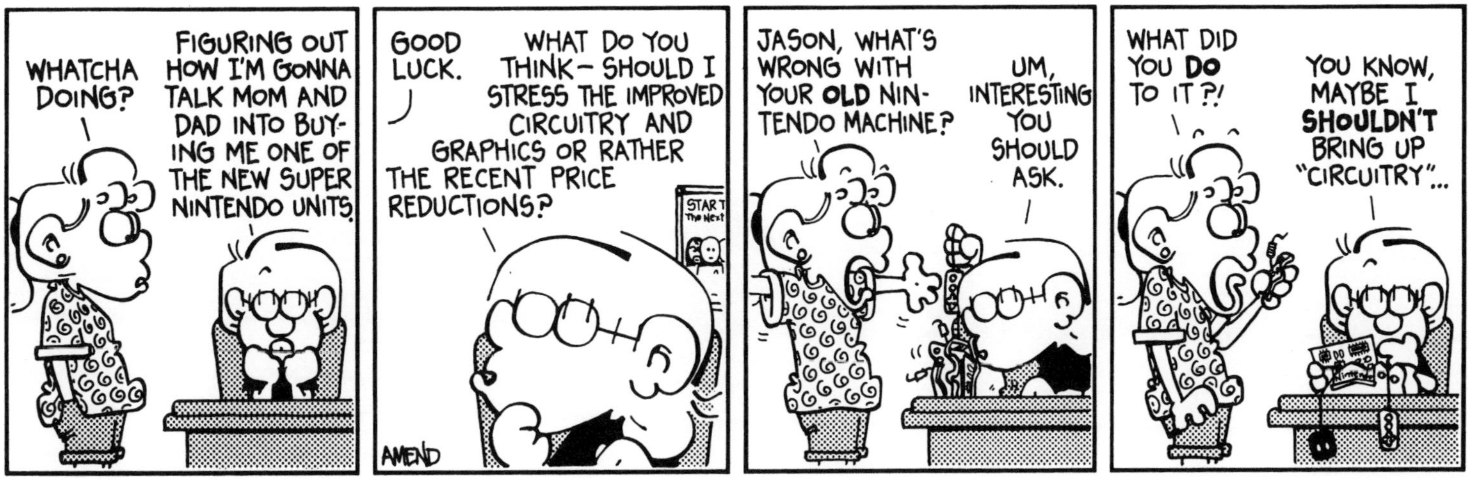
WHATCHA DOING?
FIGURING OUT HOW I'M GONNA TALK MOM AND DAD INTO BUYING ME ONE OF THE NEW SUPER NINTENDO UNITS.
GOOD LUCK.
WHAT DO YOU THINK— SHOULD I STRESS THE IMPROVED CIRCUITRY AND GRAPHICS OR RATHER THE RECENT PRICE REDUCTIONS?
AMEND
JASON, WHAT'S WRONG WITH YOUR OLD NINTENDO MACHINE?
UM, INTERESTING YOU SHOULD ASK.
WHAT DID YOU DO TO IT?!
YOU KNOW, MAYBE I SHOULDN'T BRING UP "CIRCUITRY"...

June 25, 1992

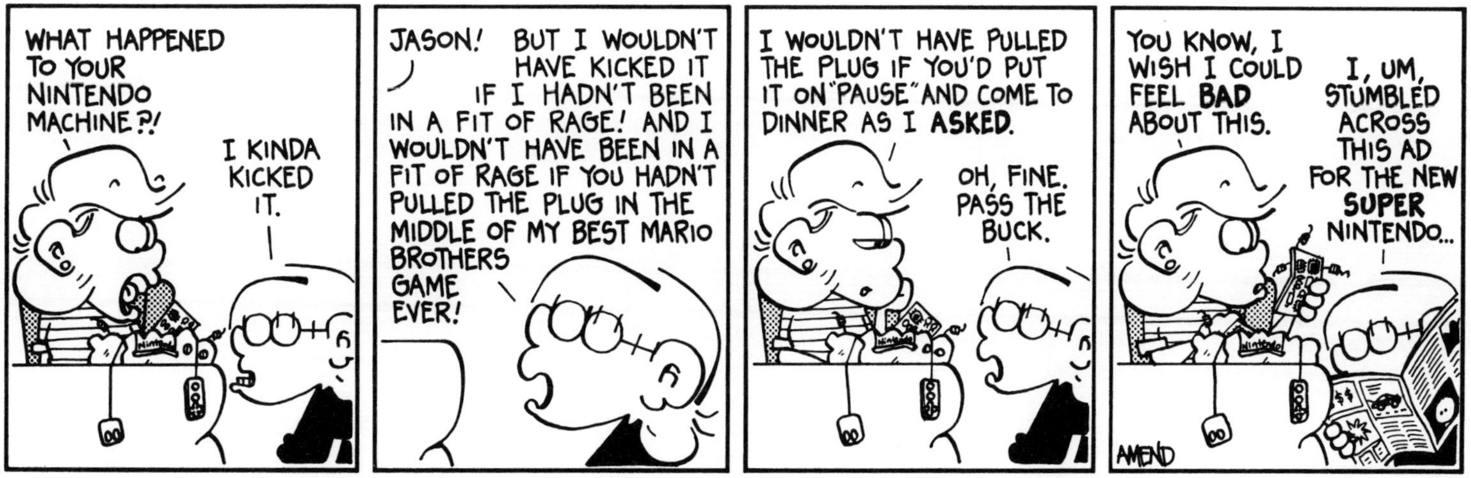
WHAT HAPPENED TO YOUR NINTENDO MACHINE?!
I KINDA KICKED IT.
JASON!
BUT I WOULDN'T HAVE KICKED IT IF I HADN'T BEEN IN A FIT OF RAGE! AND I WOULDN'T HAVE BEEN IN A FIT OF RAGE IF YOU HADN'T PULLED THE PLUG IN THE MIDDLE OF MY BEST MARIO BROTHERS GAME EVER!
I WOULDN'T HAVE PULLED THE PLUG IF YOU'D PUT IT ON "PAUSE" AND COME TO DINNER AS I ASKED.
OH, FINE. PASS THE BUCK.
YOU KNOW, I WISH I COULD FEEL BAD ABOUT THIS.
I, UM, STUMBLED ACROSS THIS AD FOR THE NEW SUPER NINTENDO...
AMEND

June 26, 1992

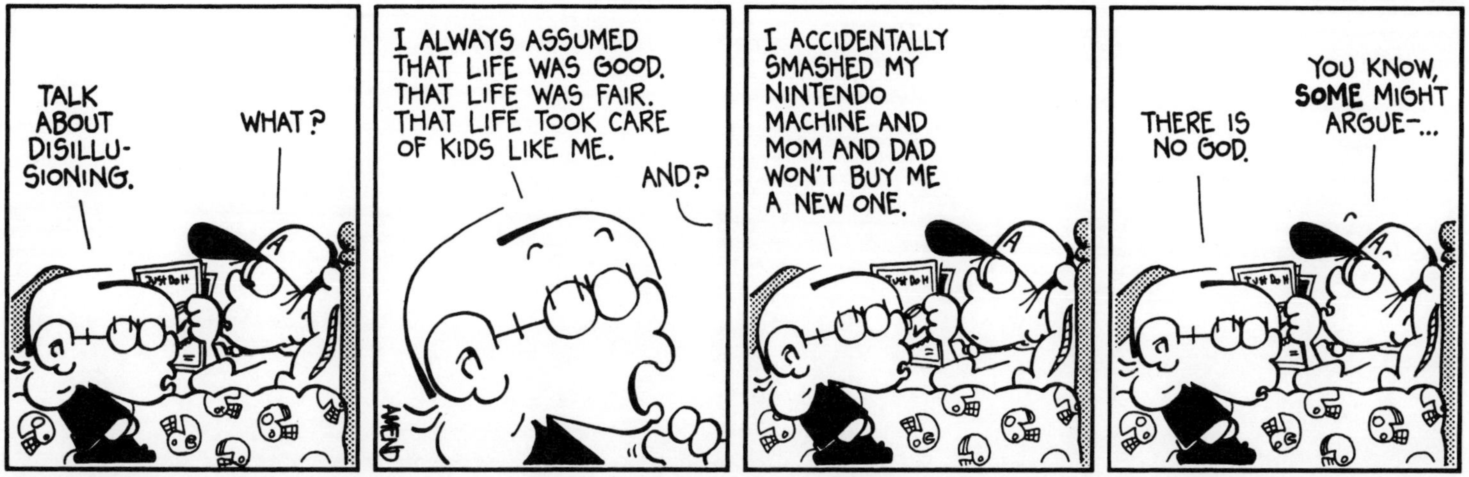
TALK ABOUT DISILLUSIONING.
WHAT?
I ALWAYS ASSUMED THAT LIFE WAS GOOD. THAT LIFE WAS FAIR. THAT LIFE TOOK CARE OF KIDS LIKE ME.
AND?
AMEND
I ACCIDENTALLY SMASHED MY NINTENDO MACHINE AND MOM AND DAD WON'T BUY ME A NEW ONE.
THERE IS NO GOD.
YOU KNOW, SOME MIGHT ARGUE—...

June 27, 1992

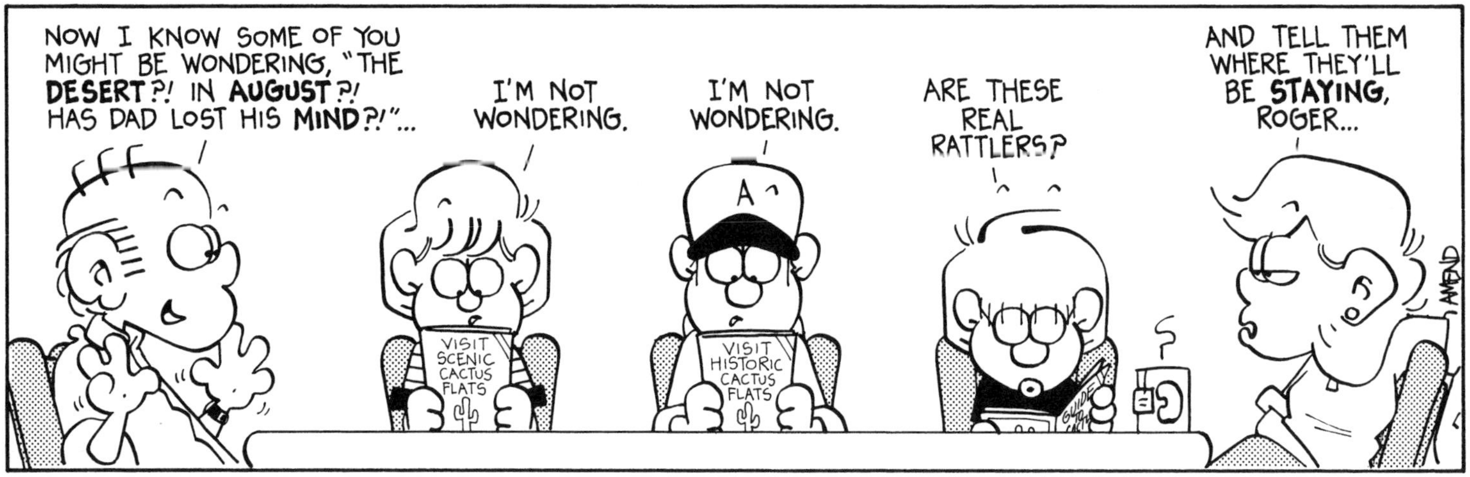
NOW I KNOW SOME OF YOU MIGHT BE WONDERING, "THE **DESERT**?! IN **AUGUST**?! HAS DAD LOST HIS **MIND**?!"...
I'M NOT WONDERING.
I'M NOT WONDERING.
ARE THESE REAL RATTLERS?
AND TELL THEM WHERE THEY'LL BE **STAYING**, ROGER...
VISIT SCENIC CACTUS FLATS
VISIT HISTORIC CACTUS FLATS
AMEND

August 3, 1992

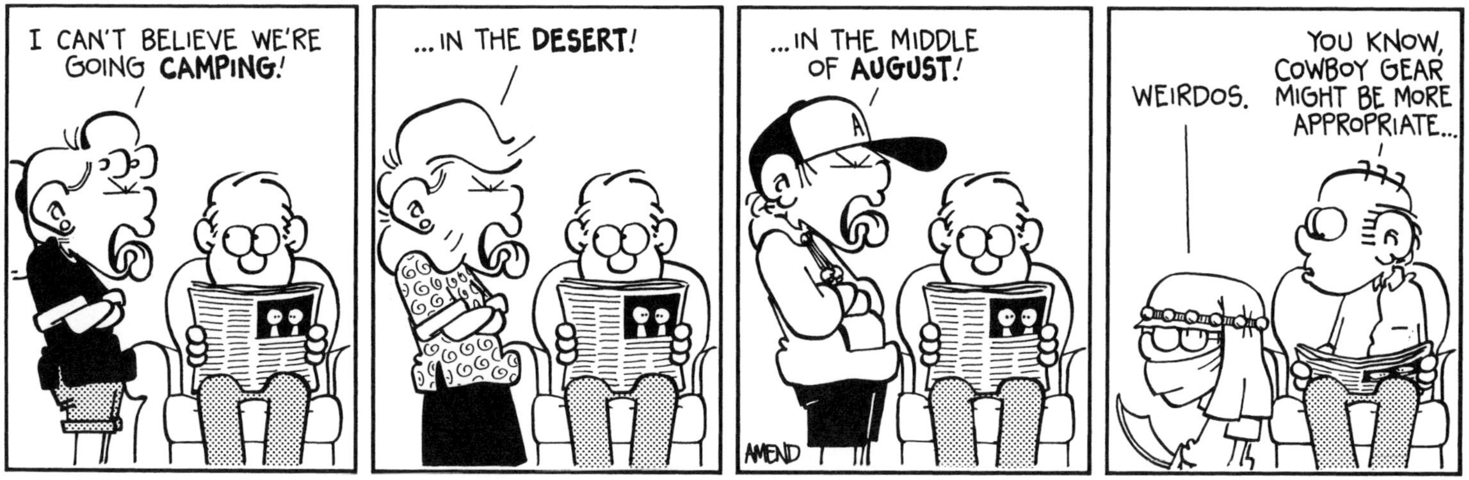
I CAN'T BELIEVE WE'RE GOING **CAMPING**!
...IN THE **DESERT**!
...IN THE MIDDLE OF **AUGUST**!
WEIRDOS.
YOU KNOW, COWBOY GEAR MIGHT BE MORE APPROPRIATE...
AMEND

August 4, 1992

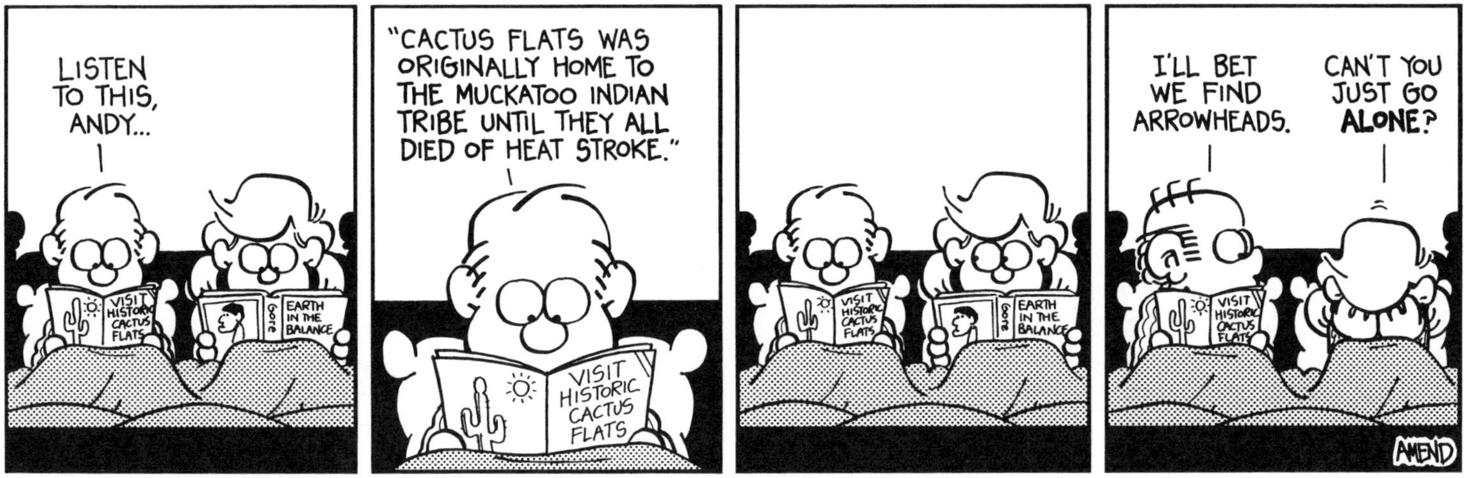
LISTEN TO THIS, ANDY...
"CACTUS FLATS WAS ORIGINALLY HOME TO THE MUCKATOO INDIAN TRIBE UNTIL THEY ALL DIED OF HEAT STROKE."
VISIT HISTORIC CACTUS FLATS
EARTH IN THE BALANCE
Gore
I'LL BET WE FIND ARROWHEADS.
CAN'T YOU JUST GO **ALONE**?
AMEND

August 5, 1992

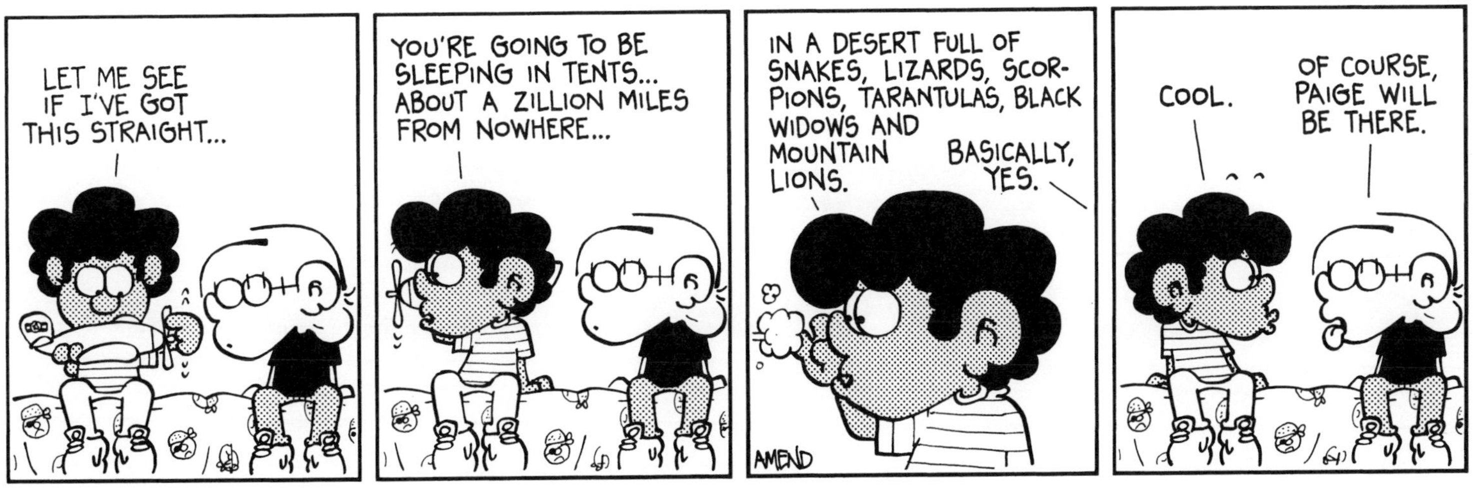
LET ME SEE IF I'VE GOT THIS STRAIGHT...
YOU'RE GOING TO BE SLEEPING IN TENTS... ABOUT A ZILLION MILES FROM NOWHERE...
IN A DESERT FULL OF SNAKES, LIZARDS, SCORPIONS, TARANTULAS, BLACK WIDOWS AND MOUNTAIN LIONS.
BASICALLY, YES.
AMEND
COOL.
OF COURSE, PAIGE WILL BE THERE.

August 6, 1992

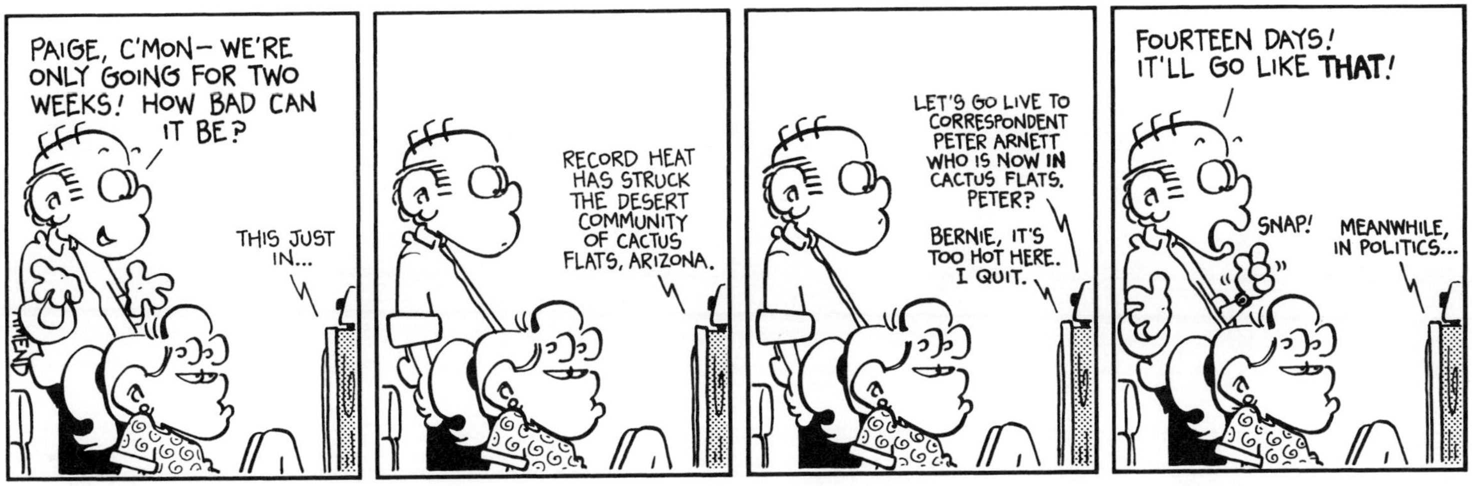
PAIGE, C'MON– WE'RE ONLY GOING FOR TWO WEEKS! HOW BAD CAN IT BE?
THIS JUST IN...
AMEND
RECORD HEAT HAS STRUCK THE DESERT COMMUNITY OF CACTUS FLATS, ARIZONA.
LET'S GO LIVE TO CORRESPONDENT PETER ARNETT WHO IS NOW IN CACTUS FLATS. PETER?
BERNIE, IT'S TOO HOT HERE. I QUIT.
FOURTEEN DAYS! IT'LL GO LIKE **THAT**!
SNAP!
MEANWHILE, IN POLITICS...

August 7, 1992

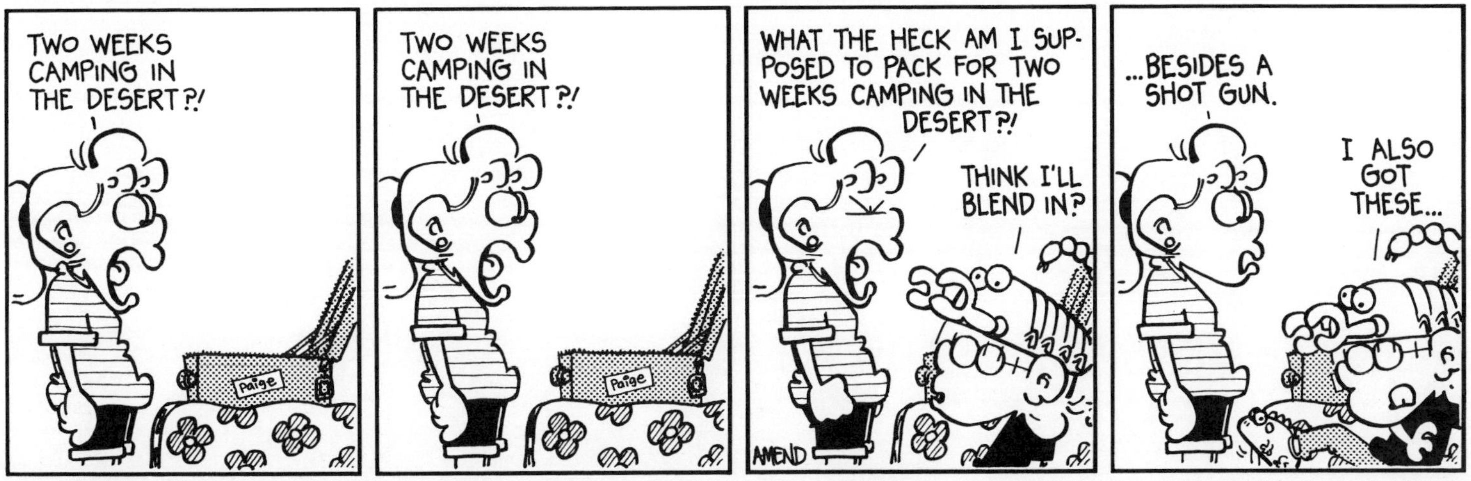
TWO WEEKS CAMPING IN THE DESERT?!
Paige
TWO WEEKS CAMPING IN THE DESERT?!
Paige
WHAT THE HECK AM I SUPPOSED TO PACK FOR TWO WEEKS CAMPING IN THE DESERT?!
THINK I'LL BLEND IN?
AMEND
...BESIDES A SHOT GUN.
I ALSO GOT THESE...

August 8, 1992

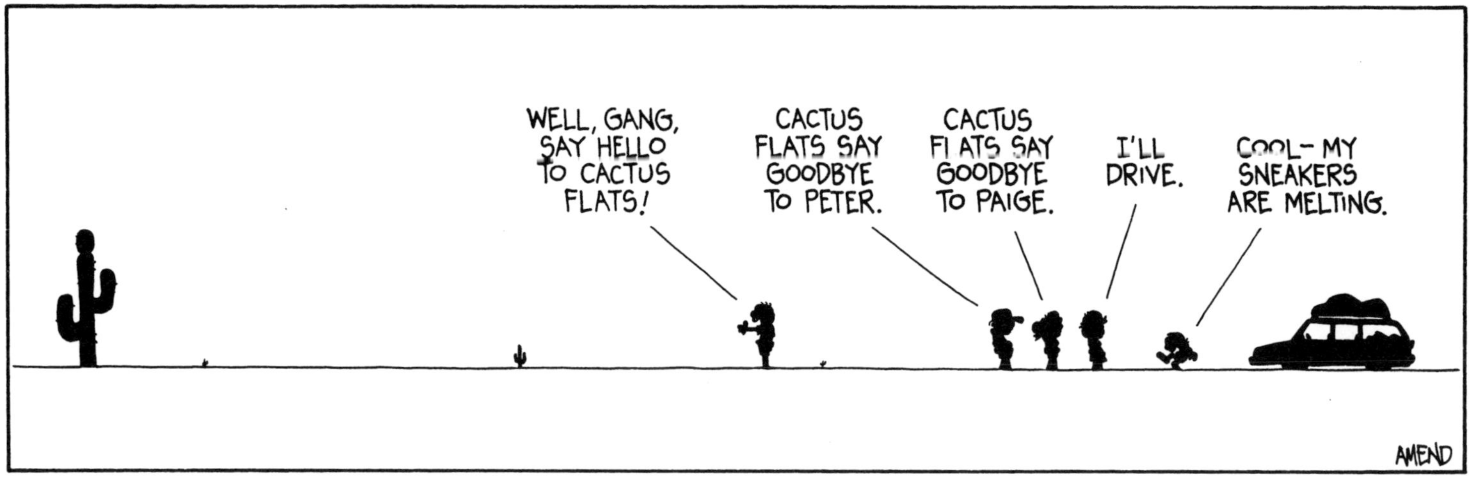
WELL, GANG, SAY HELLO TO CACTUS FLATS!
CACTUS FLATS SAY GOODBYE TO PETER.
CACTUS FLATS SAY GOODBYE TO PAIGE.
I'LL DRIVE.
COOL– MY SNEAKERS ARE MELTING.
AMEND

August 10, 1992

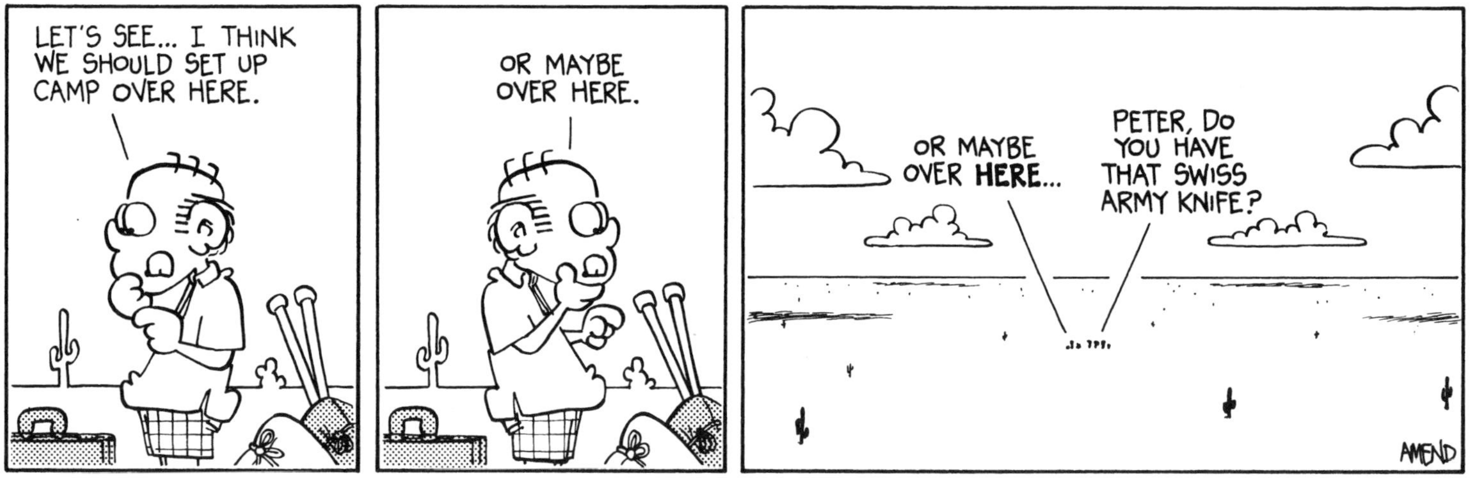
LET'S SEE... I THINK WE SHOULD SET UP CAMP OVER HERE.
OR MAYBE OVER HERE.
OR MAYBE OVER **HERE**...
PETER, DO YOU HAVE THAT SWISS ARMY KNIFE?
AMEND

August 11, 1992

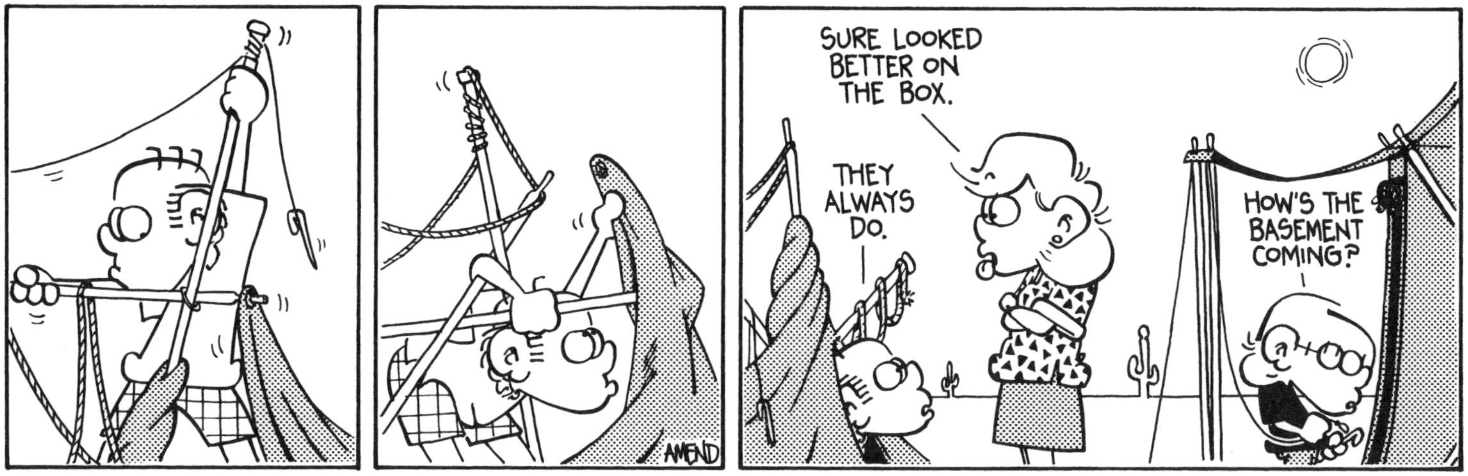
AMEND
SURE LOOKED BETTER ON THE BOX.
THEY ALWAYS DO.
HOW'S THE BASEMENT COMING?

August 12, 1992

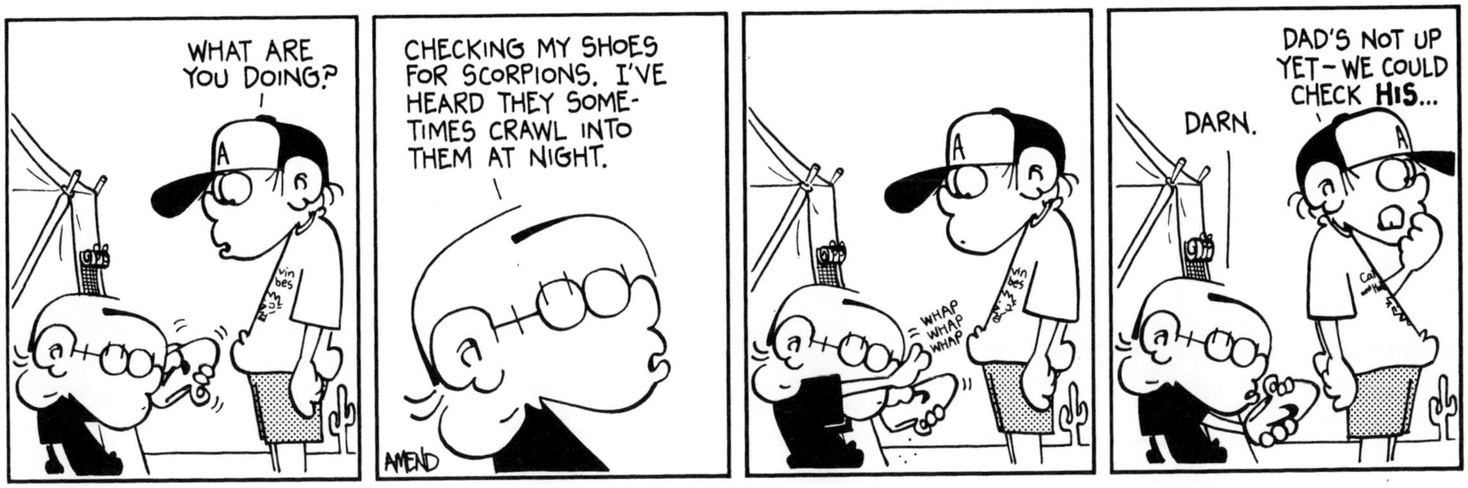
WHAT ARE YOU DOING?
CHECKING MY SHOES FOR SCORPIONS. I'VE HEARD THEY SOMETIMES CRAWL INTO THEM AT NIGHT.
WHAP WHAP WHAP
DARN.
DAD'S NOT UP YET–WE COULD CHECK **HIS**...
AMEND

August 13, 1992

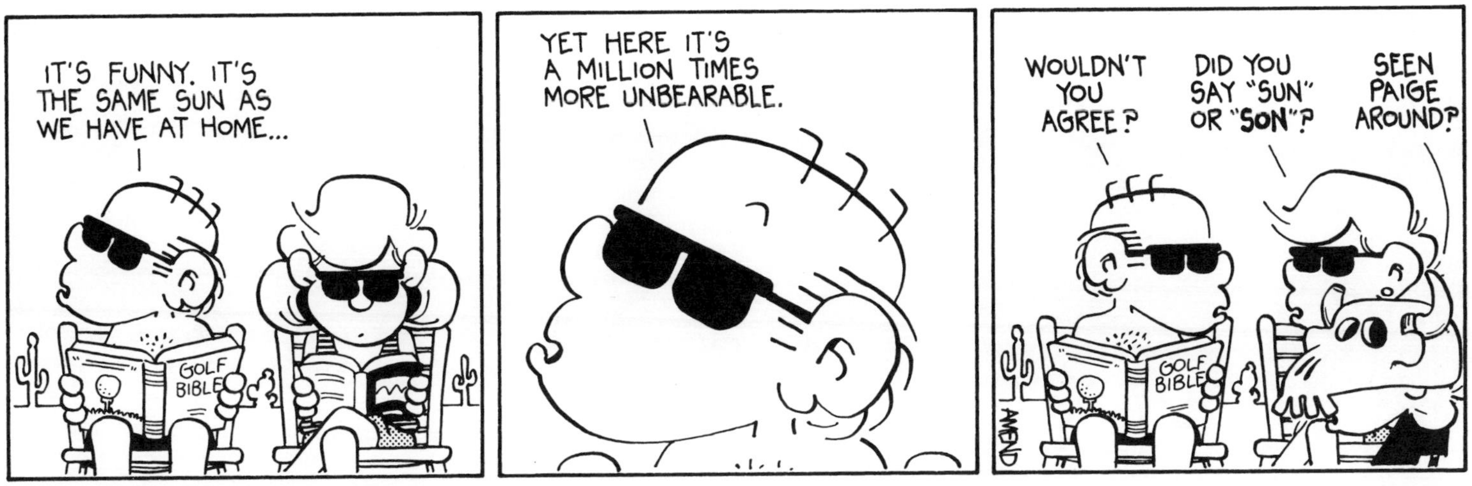
IT'S FUNNY. IT'S THE SAME SUN AS WE HAVE AT HOME...
GOLF BIBLE
YET HERE IT'S A MILLION TIMES MORE UNBEARABLE.
WOULDN'T YOU AGREE?
DID YOU SAY "SUN" OR "**SON**"?
SEEN PAIGE AROUND?
GOLF BIBLE
AMEND

August 14, 1992

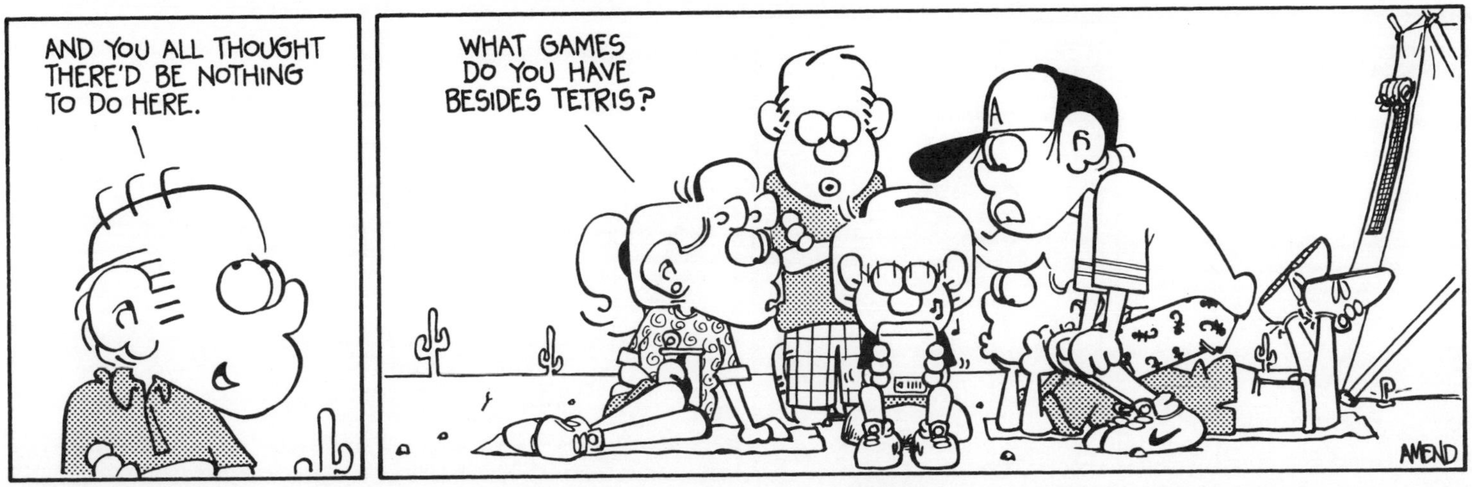
AND YOU ALL THOUGHT THERE'D BE NOTHING TO DO HERE.
WHAT GAMES DO YOU HAVE BESIDES TETRIS?
AMEND

August 15, 1992

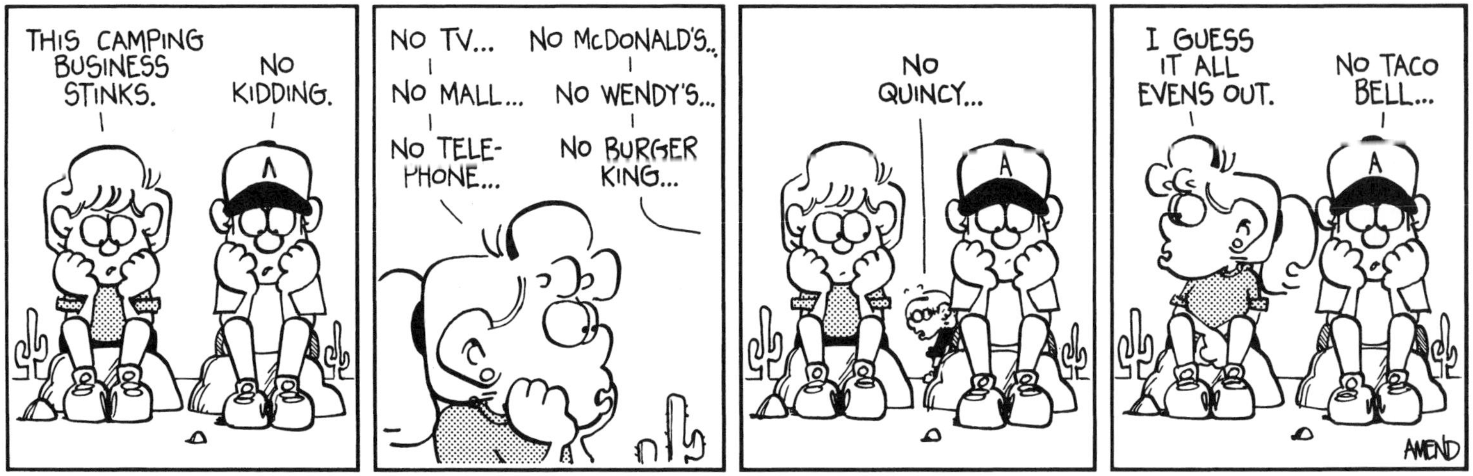
THIS CAMPING BUSINESS STINKS.
NO KIDDING.
NO TV...
NO MALL...
NO TELE-PHONE...
NO McDONALD'S...
NO WENDY'S...
NO BURGER KING...
NO QUINCY...
I GUESS IT ALL EVENS OUT.
NO TACO BELL...
AMEND

August 17, 1992

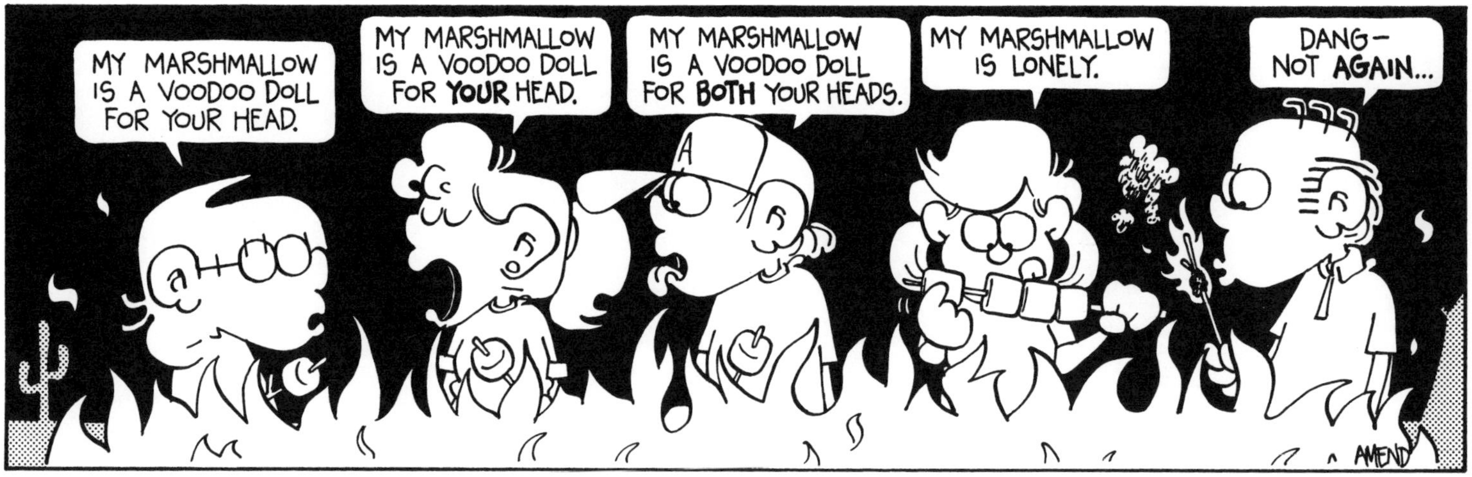
MY MARSHMALLOW IS A VOODOO DOLL FOR YOUR HEAD.
MY MARSHMALLOW IS A VOODOO DOLL FOR **YOUR** HEAD.
MY MARSHMALLOW IS A VOODOO DOLL FOR **BOTH** YOUR HEADS.
MY MARSHMALLOW IS LONELY.
DANG— NOT **AGAIN**...
AMEND

August 18, 1992

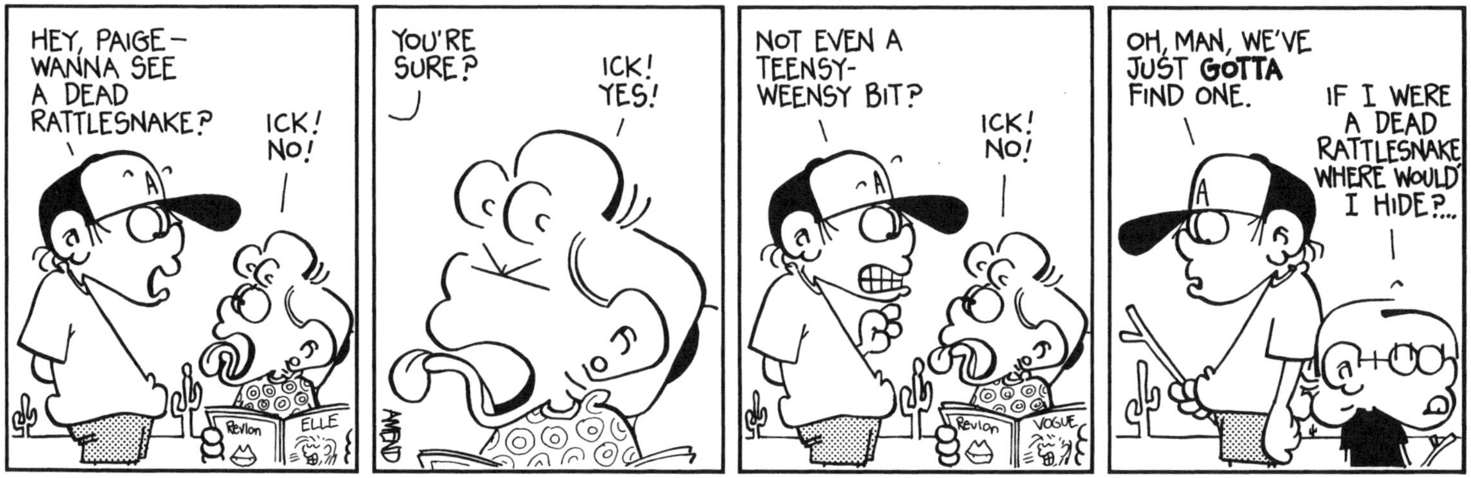
HEY, PAIGE— WANNA SEE A DEAD RATTLESNAKE?
ICK! NO!
Revlon
ELLE
YOU'RE SURE?
ICK! YES!
AMEND
NOT EVEN A TEENSY-WEENSY BIT?
ICK! NO!
Revlon
VOGUE
OH, MAN, WE'VE JUST **GOTTA** FIND ONE.
IF I WERE A DEAD RATTLESNAKE WHERE WOULD I HIDE?...

August 19, 1992

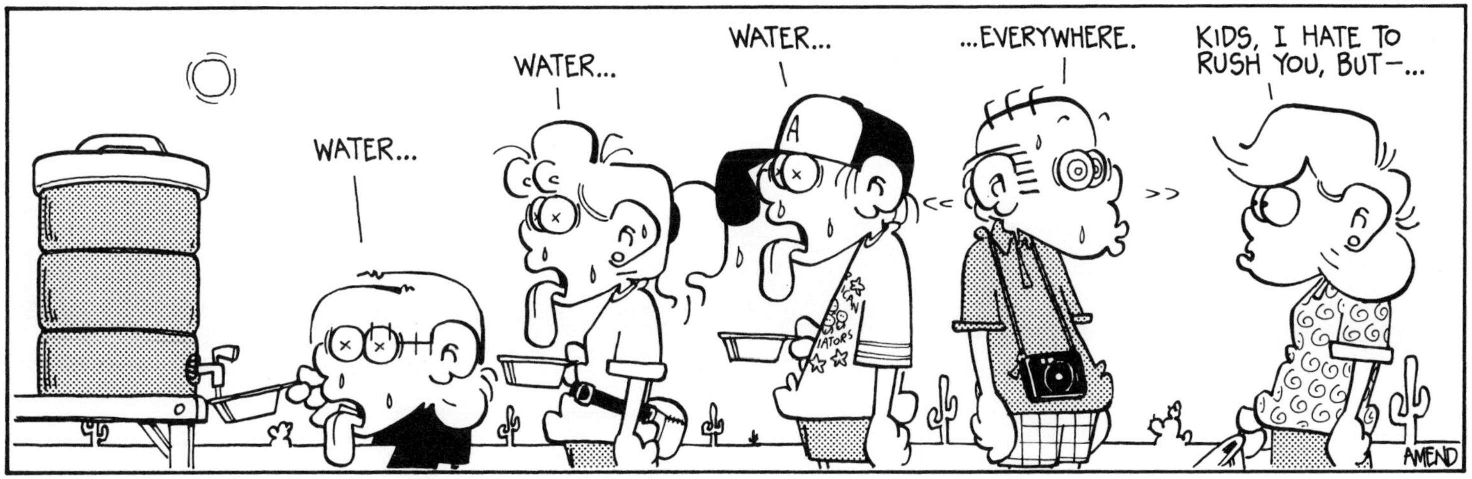
WATER...
WATER...
WATER...
...EVERYWHERE.
KIDS, I HATE TO RUSH YOU, BUT—...
AMEND

August 20, 1992

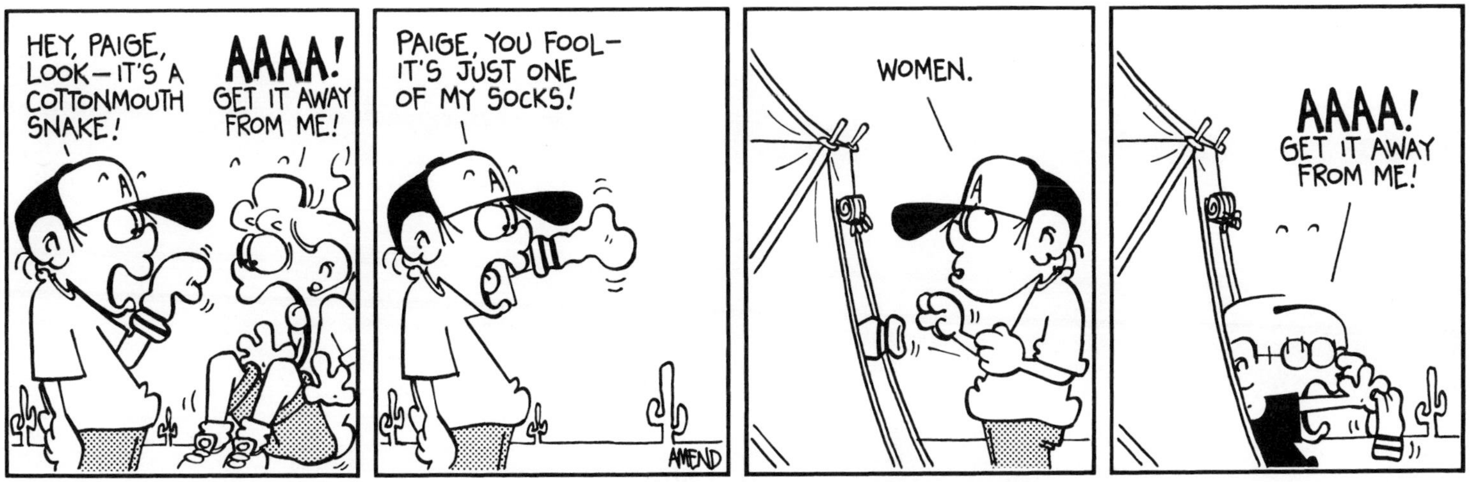
HEY, PAIGE, LOOK—IT'S A COTTONMOUTH SNAKE!
AAAA! GET IT AWAY FROM ME!
PAIGE, YOU FOOL—IT'S JUST ONE OF MY SOCKS!
AMEND
WOMEN.
AAAA! GET IT AWAY FROM ME!

August 21, 1992

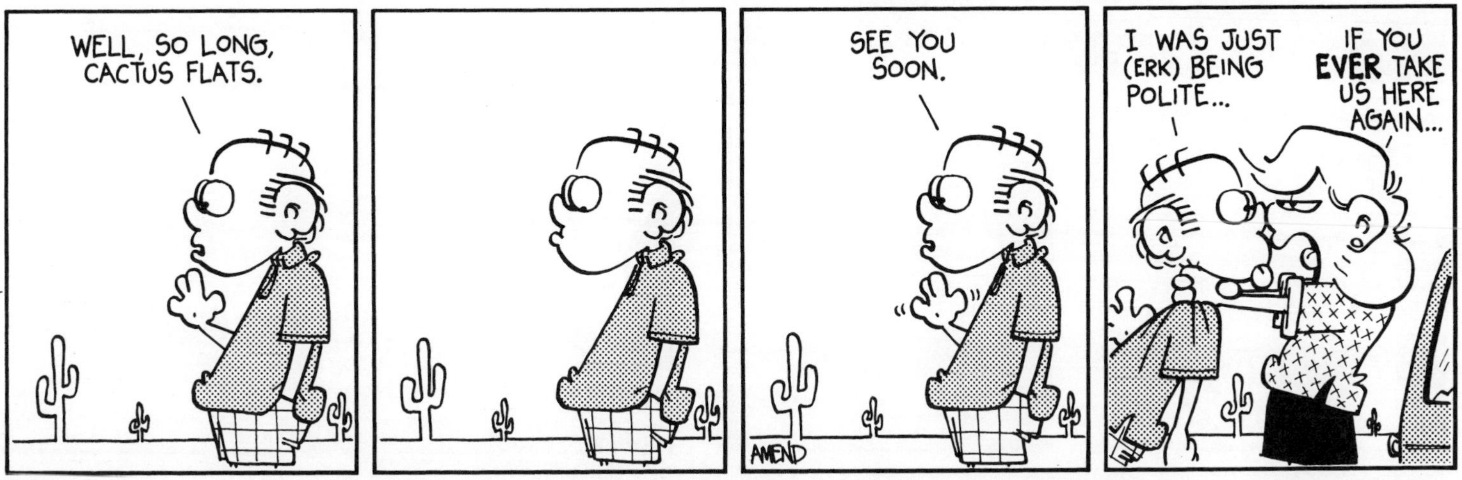
WELL, SO LONG, CACTUS FLATS.
SEE YOU SOON.
AMEND
I WAS JUST (ERK) BEING POLITE...
IF YOU EVER TAKE US HERE AGAIN...

August 22, 1992

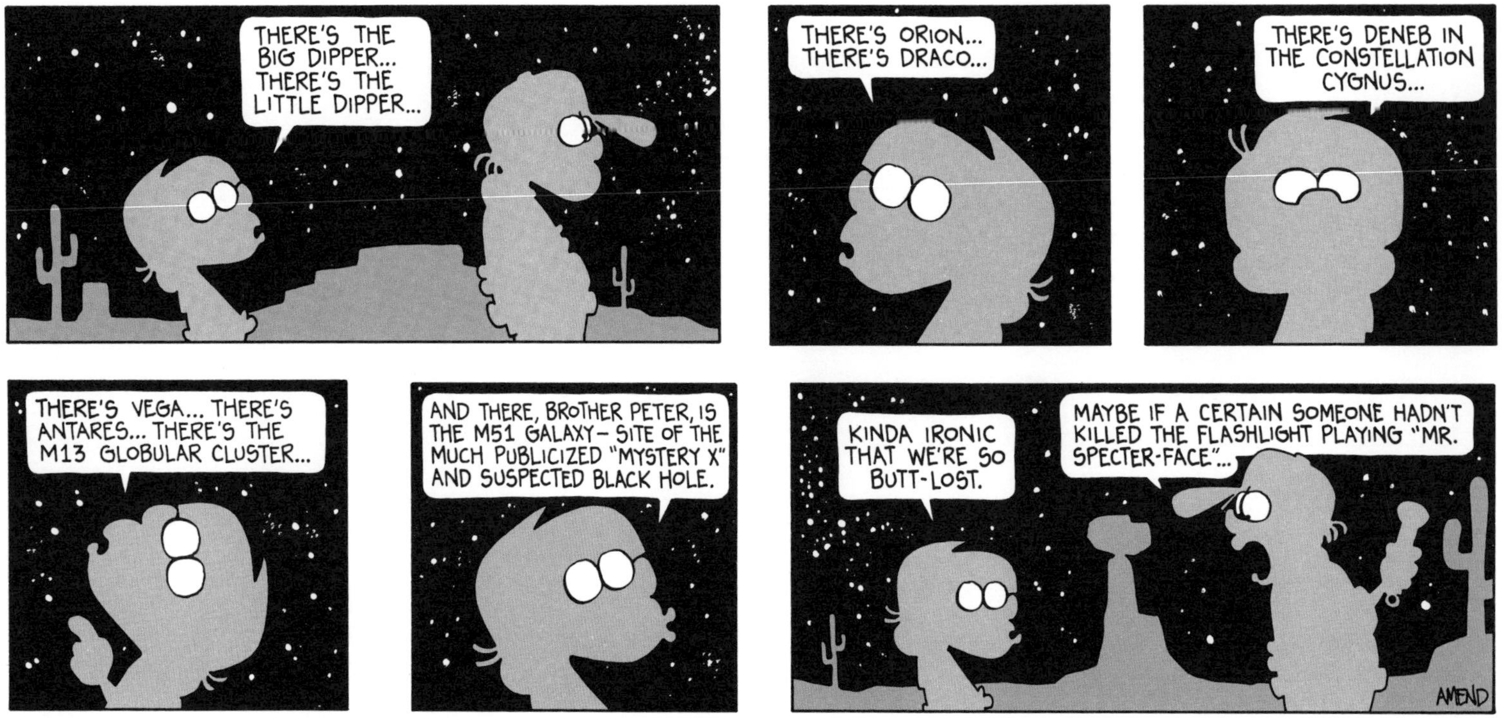
THERE'S THE BIG DIPPER... THERE'S THE LITTLE DIPPER...
THERE'S ORION... THERE'S DRACO...
THERE'S DENEB IN THE CONSTELLATION CYGNUS...
THERE'S VEGA... THERE'S ANTARES... THERE'S THE M13 GLOBULAR CLUSTER...
AND THERE, BROTHER PETER, IS THE M51 GALAXY– SITE OF THE MUCH PUBLICIZED "MYSTERY X" AND SUSPECTED BLACK HOLE.
KINDA IRONIC THAT WE'RE SO BUTT-LOST.
MAYBE IF A CERTAIN SOMEONE HADN'T KILLED THE FLASHLIGHT PLAYING "MR. SPECTER-FACE"...
AMEND

August 16, 1992

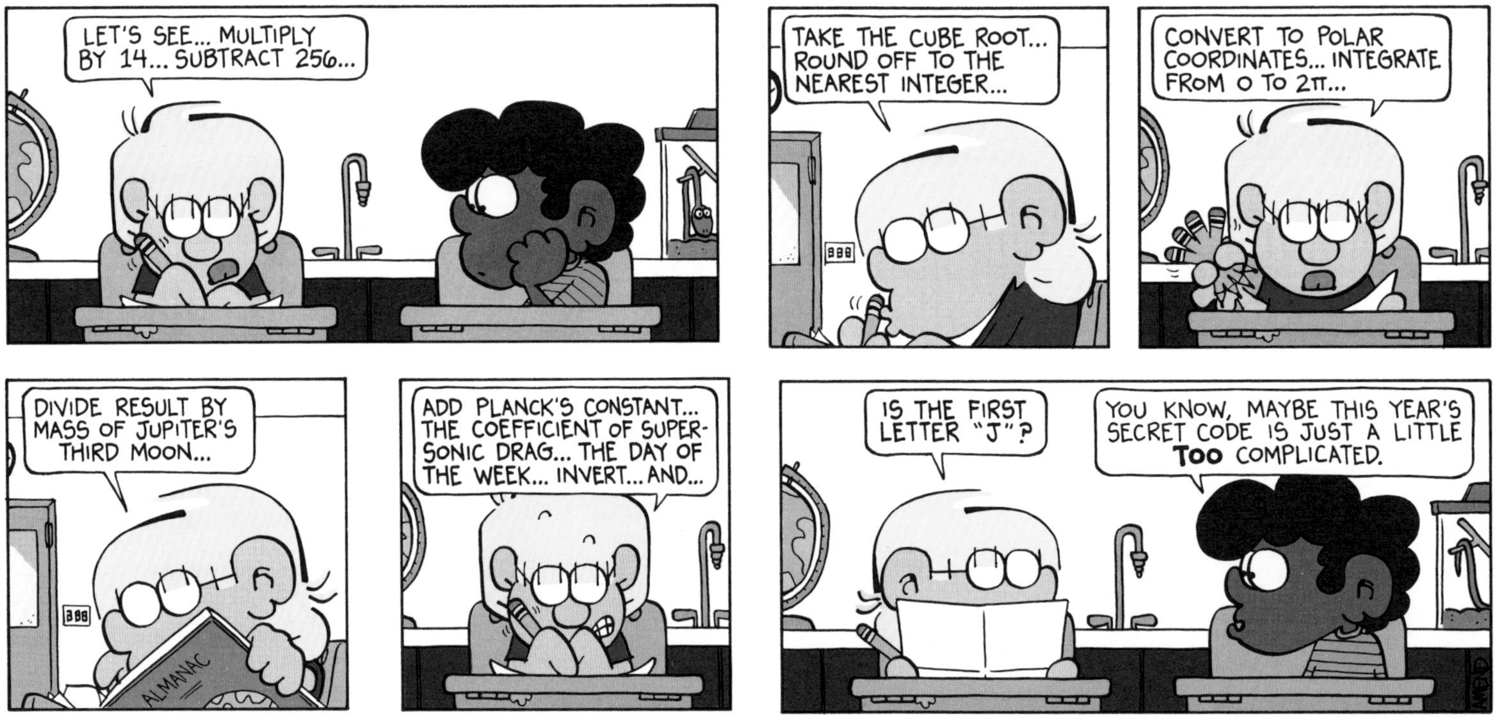
LET'S SEE... MULTIPLY BY 14... SUBTRACT 256...
TAKE THE CUBE ROOT... ROUND OFF TO THE NEAREST INTEGER...
CONVERT TO POLAR COORDINATES... INTEGRATE FROM 0 TO 2π...
DIVIDE RESULT BY MASS OF JUPITER'S THIRD MOON...
ALMANAC
ADD PLANCK'S CONSTANT... THE COEFFICIENT OF SUPER-SONIC DRAG... THE DAY OF THE WEEK... INVERT... AND...
IS THE FIRST LETTER "J"?
YOU KNOW, MAYBE THIS YEAR'S SECRET CODE IS JUST A LITTLE **TOO** COMPLICATED.
AMEND

September 6, 1992

July 3, 1992

The stuff in the third panel is made up, but it has a nice plausibility.

November 11, 1992

November 26, 1992

125

Hey, we cartoonists have to think about these things.

October 5, 1992

October 6, 1992

126

October 7, 1992

October 8, 1992

October 9, 1992

October 10, 1992

December 1, 1992

December 2, 1992

128

December 4, 1992

December 5, 1992

December 8, 1992

December 9, 1992

129

WHAT'S IN THE BAGS?

CHRISTMAS LIGHTS, ANDY.

EVER SINCE I WAS A LITTLE KID I'VE DREAMED OF HAVING ONE OF THOSE HOUSES WITH THE BILLIONS OF LIGHTS AND THE ROBOT SANTAS.

WELL, I'VE GOT THE LIGHTS AND I'VE GOT THE DESIRE. NOW ALL I NEED TO DO IS GET MY BUTT UP ON THAT ICY ROOF.

OF COURSE, YOU PICK THE WEEK WHEN I'M OUT OF TUMS.

WE'VE GOT A 220-VOLT OUTLET, RIGHT?

AMEND

December 14, 1992

ROGER, WHAT KIND OF CHRISTMAS LIGHTS **ARE** THESE?!

AH, YOU ALREADY NOTICE A DIFFERENCE.

PRESENTING THE NOËL-BLASTER SERIES 250XB OUTDOOR HOLIDAY LIGHT STRING. EACH 250-FOOT CABLE FEATURES OVER 500 60-WATT HALOGEN BULBS SEALED IN COLORFUL AND AIRTIGHT PLASTIC HOUSINGS.

Noël-Blaster 250XB

GUARANTEED TO WAKE UP THE NEIGHBORS.

FIRE TRUCKS HAVE A WAY OF DOING THAT, YES.

WHAT DO YOU SUPPOSE THEY MEAN BY "CERTIFIED ELECTRICIAN"?

AMEND

December 15, 1992

PETER, I WANT YOU TO GO HELP YOUR FATHER HANG ALL THOSE CHRISTMAS LIGHTS OUTSIDE.

WHAT?!

MOM, IT'S LIKE A ZILLION BELOW OUT THERE! WHY DO **I** HAVE TO DO IT?! WHY NOT JASON?! WHY NOT PAIGE?! WHY NOT YOU?!

WHY DOES IT HAVE TO BE **ME**?!

BECAUSE YOU KNOW CPR.

WHY ARE THE LIGHTS DIMMING?

AMEND

December 16, 1992

December 17, 1992

December 18, 1992

December 19, 1992

I wouldn't mind a set of those fake teeth for Halloween.

January 3, 1993

Was I really an Apple fanboy during their Quadra years? Wow.

January 17, 1993

132

November 27, 1992

June 24, 1993

July 28, 1993

Pretty sure I wrote this after a paper canceled me for using the word "hell."

January 24, 1993

(A) This was fun to draw, and
(B) I want this kite.

April 4, 1993

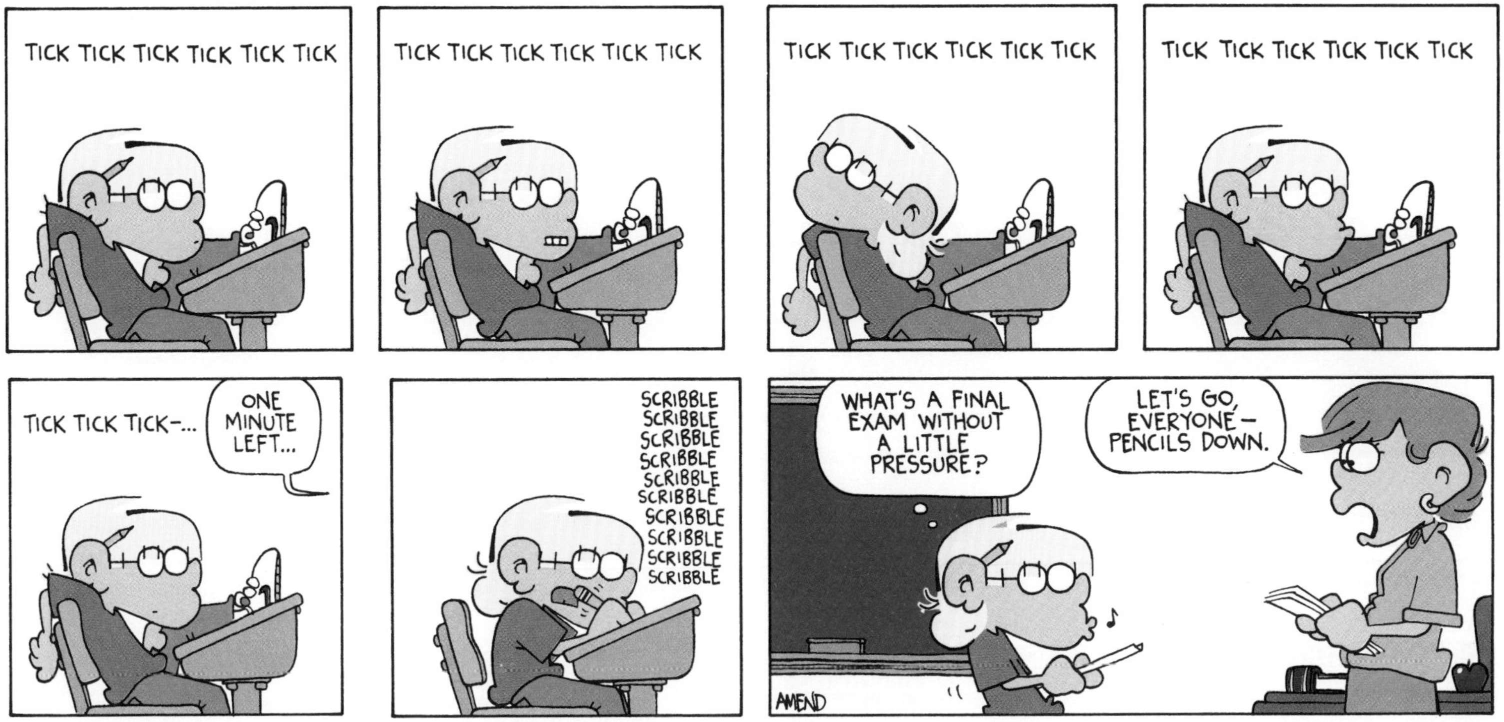
TICK TICK TICK TICK TICK TICK
TICK TICK TICK TICK TICK TICK
TICK TICK TICK TICK TICK TICK
TICK TICK TICK TICK TICK TICK
TICK TICK TICK–...
ONE MINUTE LEFT...
SCRIBBLE SCRIBBLE SCRIBBLE SCRIBBLE SCRIBBLE SCRIBBLE SCRIBBLE SCRIBBLE SCRIBBLE SCRIBBLE
WHAT'S A FINAL EXAM WITHOUT A LITTLE PRESSURE?
LET'S GO, EVERYONE – PENCILS DOWN.
AMEND

June 6, 1993

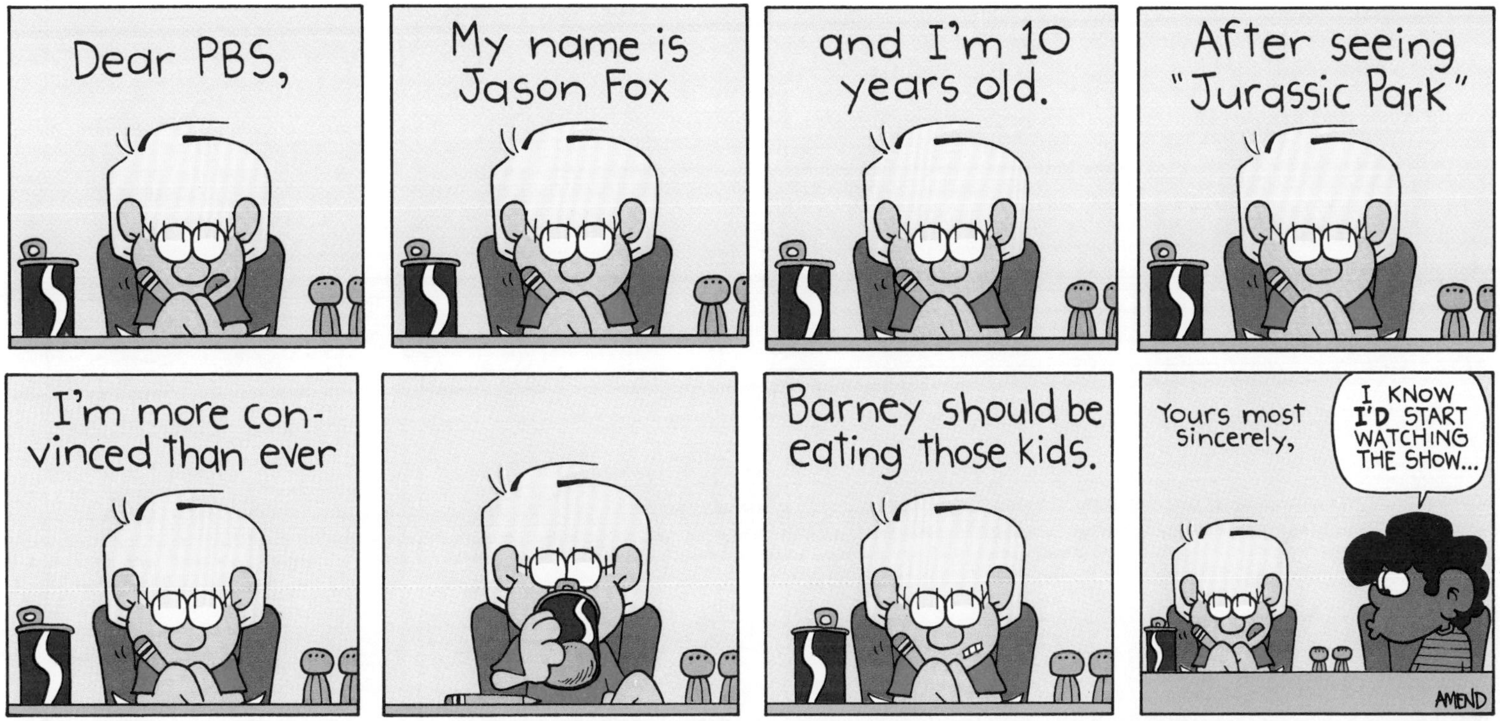
Dear PBS,
My name is Jason Fox
and I'm 10 years old.
After seeing "Jurassic Park"
I'm more con-vinced than ever
Barney should be eating those kids.
Yours most Sincerely,
I KNOW **I'D** START WATCHING THE SHOW...
AMEND

June 13, 1993

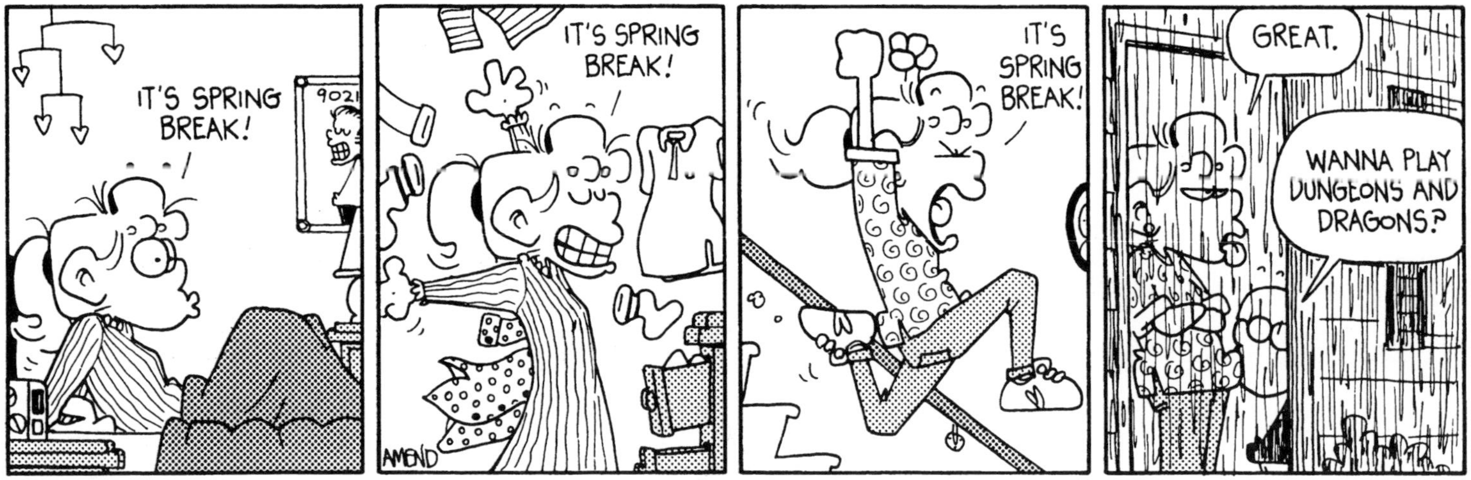
IT'S SPRING BREAK!
IT'S SPRING BREAK!
AMEND
IT'S SPRING BREAK!
GREAT.
WANNA PLAY DUNGEONS AND DRAGONS?

March 22, 1993

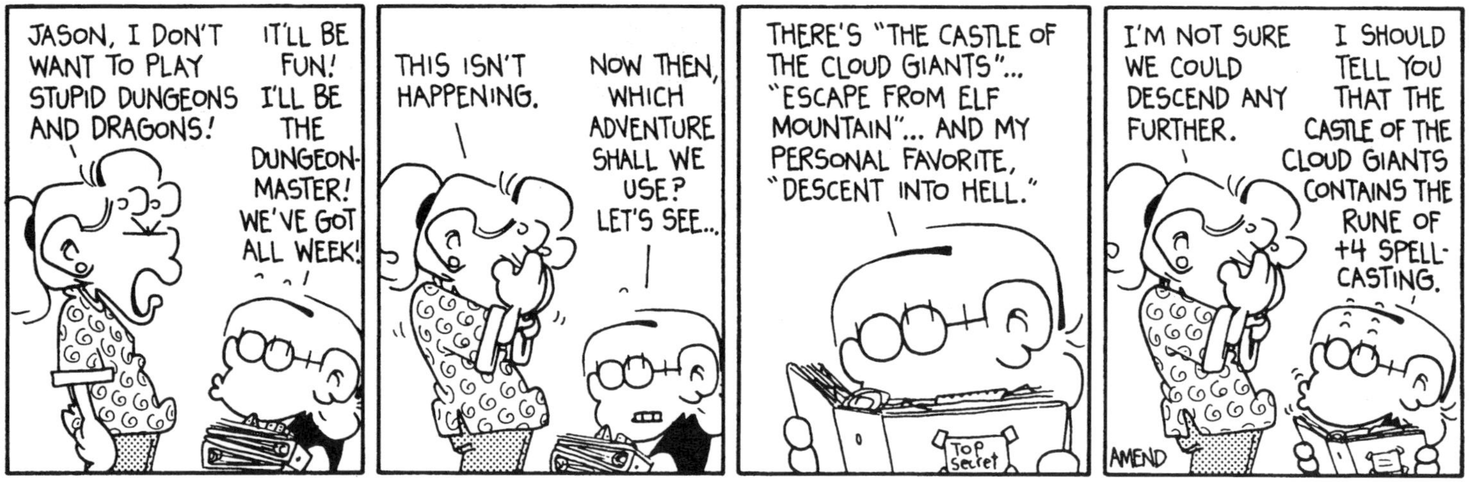
JASON, I DON'T WANT TO PLAY STUPID DUNGEONS AND DRAGONS!
IT'LL BE FUN! I'LL BE THE DUNGEON-MASTER! WE'VE GOT ALL WEEK!
THIS ISN'T HAPPENING.
NOW THEN, WHICH ADVENTURE SHALL WE USE? LET'S SEE...
THERE'S "THE CASTLE OF THE CLOUD GIANTS"... "ESCAPE FROM ELF MOUNTAIN"... AND MY PERSONAL FAVORITE, "DESCENT INTO HELL."
Top Secret
I'M NOT SURE WE COULD DESCEND ANY FURTHER.
I SHOULD TELL YOU THAT THE CASTLE OF THE CLOUD GIANTS CONTAINS THE RUNE OF +4 SPELL-CASTING.
AMEND

March 23, 1993

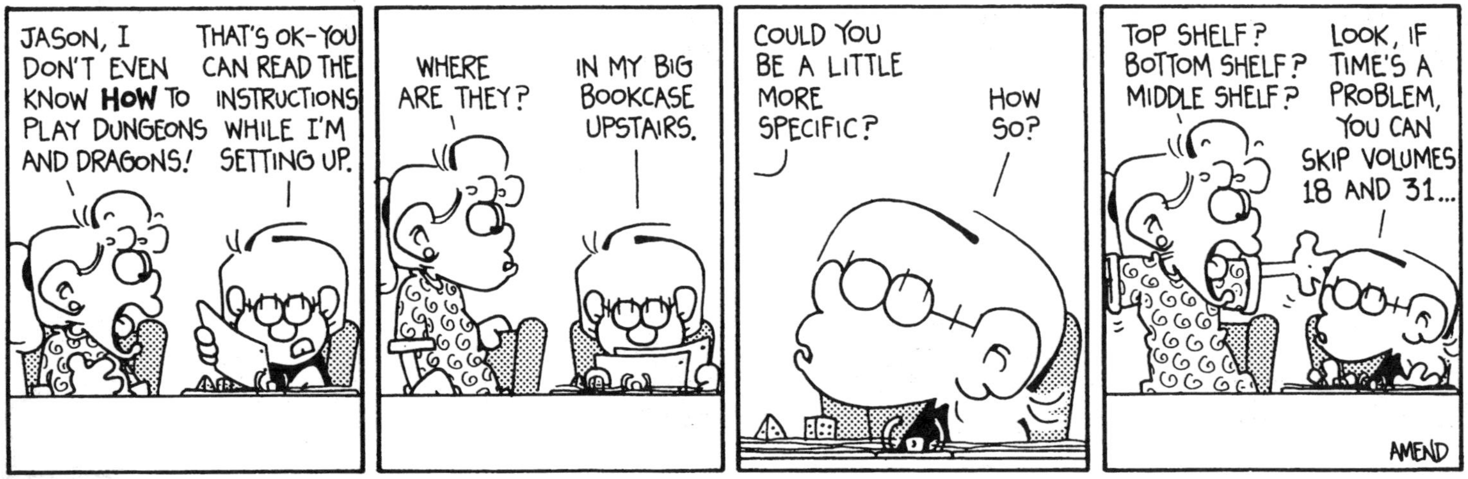
JASON, I DON'T EVEN KNOW **HOW** TO PLAY DUNGEONS AND DRAGONS!
THAT'S OK-YOU CAN READ THE INSTRUCTIONS WHILE I'M SETTING UP.
WHERE ARE THEY?
IN MY BIG BOOKCASE UPSTAIRS.
COULD YOU BE A LITTLE MORE SPECIFIC?
HOW SO?
TOP SHELF? BOTTOM SHELF? MIDDLE SHELF?
LOOK, IF TIME'S A PROBLEM, YOU CAN SKIP VOLUMES 18 AND 31...
AMEND

March 24, 1993

March 25, 1993

About a week after this strip ran, I received a very nice phone call from David Copperfield. I still don't know how he got my number. Magic?

March 26, 1993

I think just about every D&D game I played in high school devolved into something like this.

March 27, 1993

137

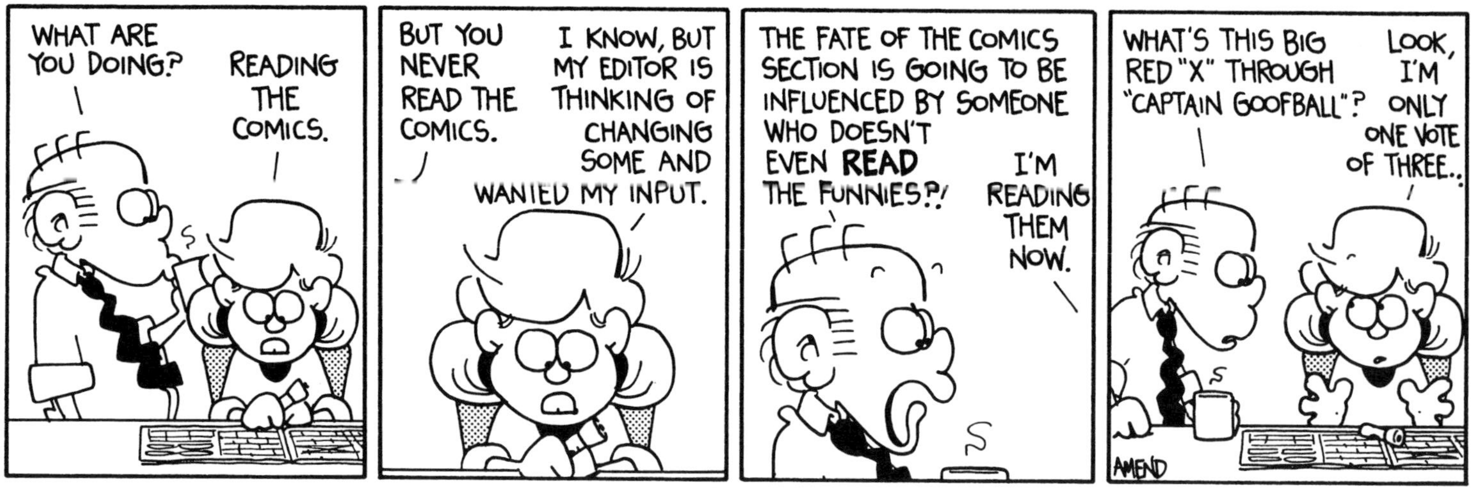
WHAT ARE YOU DOING?
READING THE COMICS.
BUT YOU NEVER READ THE COMICS.
I KNOW, BUT MY EDITOR IS THINKING OF CHANGING SOME AND WANTED MY INPUT.
THE FATE OF THE COMICS SECTION IS GOING TO BE INFLUENCED BY SOMEONE WHO DOESN'T EVEN **READ** THE FUNNIES?!
I'M READING THEM NOW.
WHAT'S THIS BIG RED "X" THROUGH "CAPTAIN GOOFBALL"?
LOOK, I'M ONLY ONE VOTE OF THREE..
AMEND

April 12, 1993

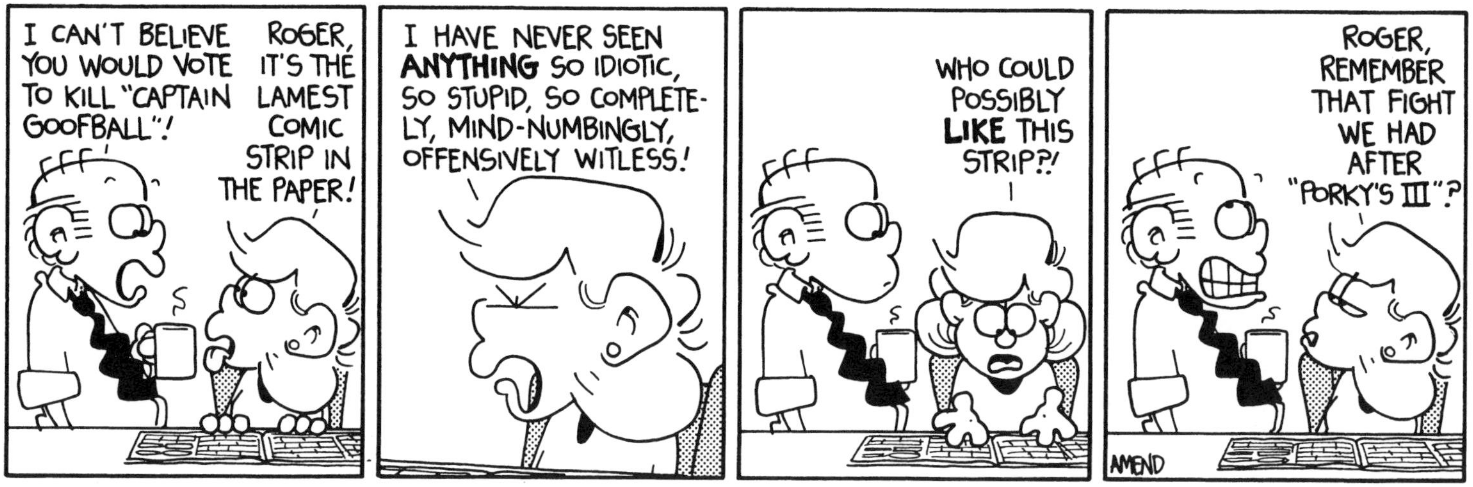
I CAN'T BELIEVE YOU WOULD VOTE TO KILL "CAPTAIN GOOFBALL"!
ROGER, IT'S THE LAMEST COMIC STRIP IN THE PAPER!
I HAVE NEVER SEEN **ANYTHING** SO IDIOTIC, SO STUPID, SO COMPLETE-LY, MIND-NUMBINGLY, OFFENSIVELY WITLESS!
WHO COULD POSSIBLY **LIKE** THIS STRIP?!
ROGER, REMEMBER THAT FIGHT WE HAD AFTER "PORKY'S III"?
AMEND

April 13, 1993

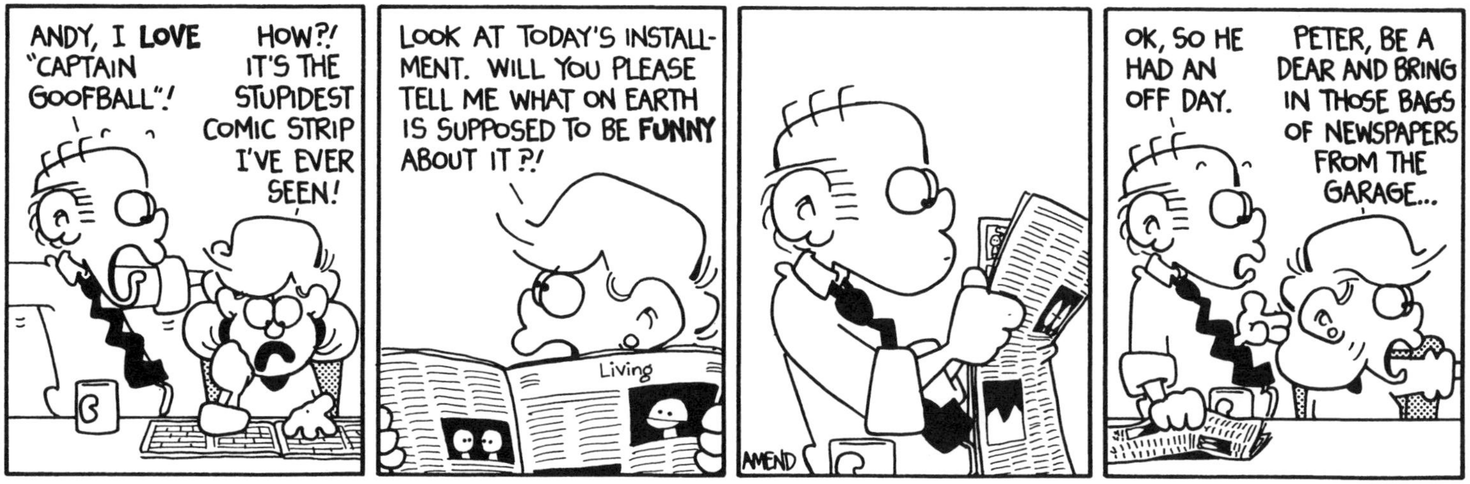
ANDY, I **LOVE** "CAPTAIN GOOFBALL"!
HOW?! IT'S THE STUPIDEST COMIC STRIP I'VE EVER SEEN!
LOOK AT TODAY'S INSTALL-MENT. WILL YOU PLEASE TELL ME WHAT ON EARTH IS SUPPOSED TO BE **FUNNY** ABOUT IT?!
Living
AMEND
OK, SO HE HAD AN OFF DAY.
PETER, BE A DEAR AND BRING IN THOSE BAGS OF NEWSPAPERS FROM THE GARAGE...

April 14, 1993

HMMPH.

WELL, I GUESS THAT ABOUT DOES IT.

FOUR WEEKS OF "CAPTAIN GOOFBALL" COMIC STRIPS AND NOT A FUNNY ONE IN THE BATCH. I THINK I'VE PROVEN MY POINT. I'M GOING TO VOTE TO CANCEL IT.

ANDY, YOU CAN'T JUDGE "CAPTAIN GOOFBALL" ON A DAY-TO-DAY BASIS, OR EVEN A MONTH-TO-MONTH ONE! YOU HAVE TO LOOK AT THE BROADER BODY OF WORK!

HOW BROAD?

WHEN I WAS 13, THE STRIP WAS A RIOT.

AND JUST AS **YOU** ARE NO LONGER **13**...

AMEND

April 15, 1993

OK, SO MAYBE "CAPTAIN GOOFBALL" **HAS** GOTTEN KINDA STUPID OVER THE YEARS. SO WHAT?

SO WHAT?!

ANDY, I GREW **UP** WITH THIS COMIC STRIP! READING "CAPTAIN GOOFBALL" ON SUNDAYS WAS ONE OF THE HIGHLIGHTS OF MY CHILD-HOOD! YOU **CAN'T** VOTE TO CANCEL IT!

I MEAN, THAT STRIP MADE ME LAUGH MY HEAD OFF WHEN I WAS A KID.

MAYBE TODAY'S KIDS WOULD LIKE A CHANCE TO LAUGH **THEIR** HEADS OFF.

BUT KIDS TODAY DON'T EVEN **READ** NEWSPAPERS!

CALL THIS A HUNCH, BUT—...

AMEND

April 16, 1993

WHATCHA READING?

THIS NEW COMIC STRIP. IT REPLACED DUMB OL' "CAPTAIN GOOFBALL."

"CAPTAIN GOOFBALL" WAS NOT **DUMB!**

AT LEAST, NOT 30 YEARS AGO WHEN IT REALLY MATTERED.

...TO ME.

HEE HEE HEE— THIS IS PRETTY FUNNY.

AMEND

April 17, 1993

Usually Jason is an exaggeration of me; however, in this case I think I was more excited for this movie than he was.

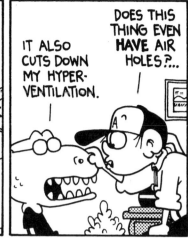

June 7, 1993

June 8, 1993

June 9, 1993

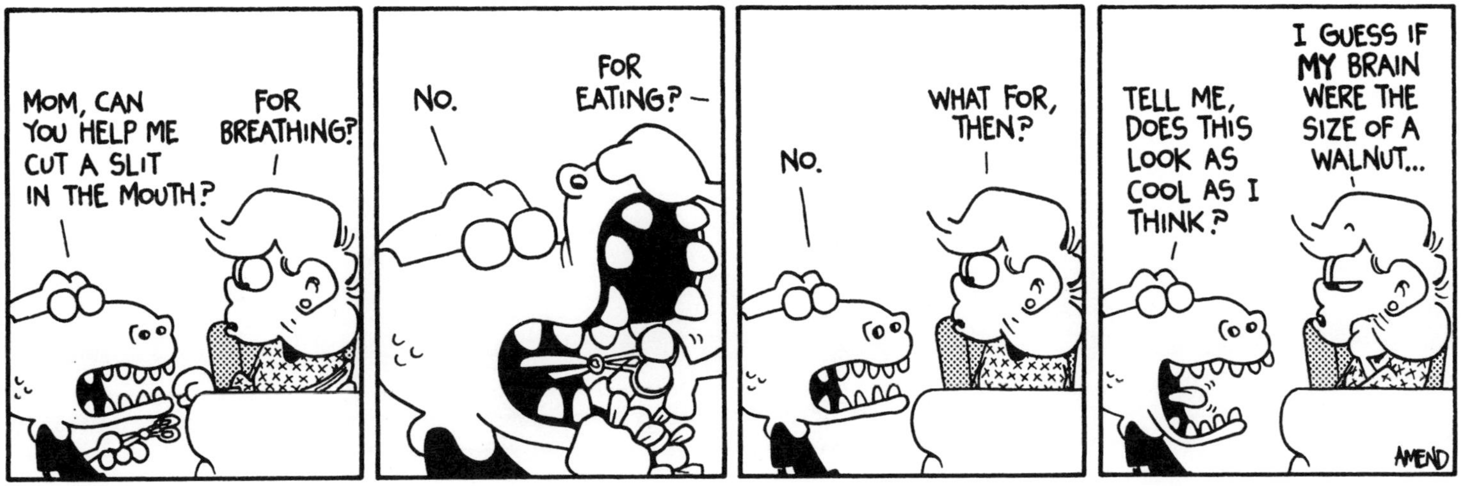
MOM, CAN YOU HELP ME CUT A SLIT IN THE MOUTH?
FOR BREATHING?
NO.
FOR EATING? —
NO.
WHAT FOR, THEN?
TELL ME, DOES THIS LOOK AS COOL AS I THINK?
I GUESS IF MY BRAIN WERE THE SIZE OF A WALNUT...
AMEND
June 10, 1993

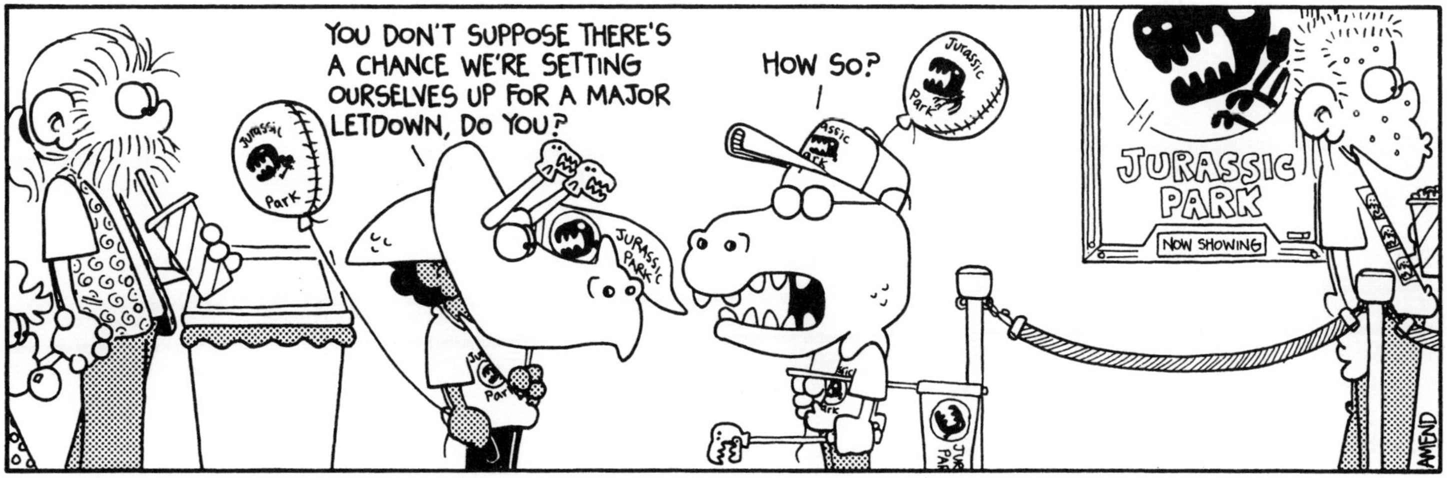
YOU DON'T SUPPOSE THERE'S A CHANCE WE'RE SETTING OURSELVES UP FOR A MAJOR LETDOWN, DO YOU?
HOW SO?
JURASSIC PARK
NOW SHOWING
AMEND
June 11, 1993

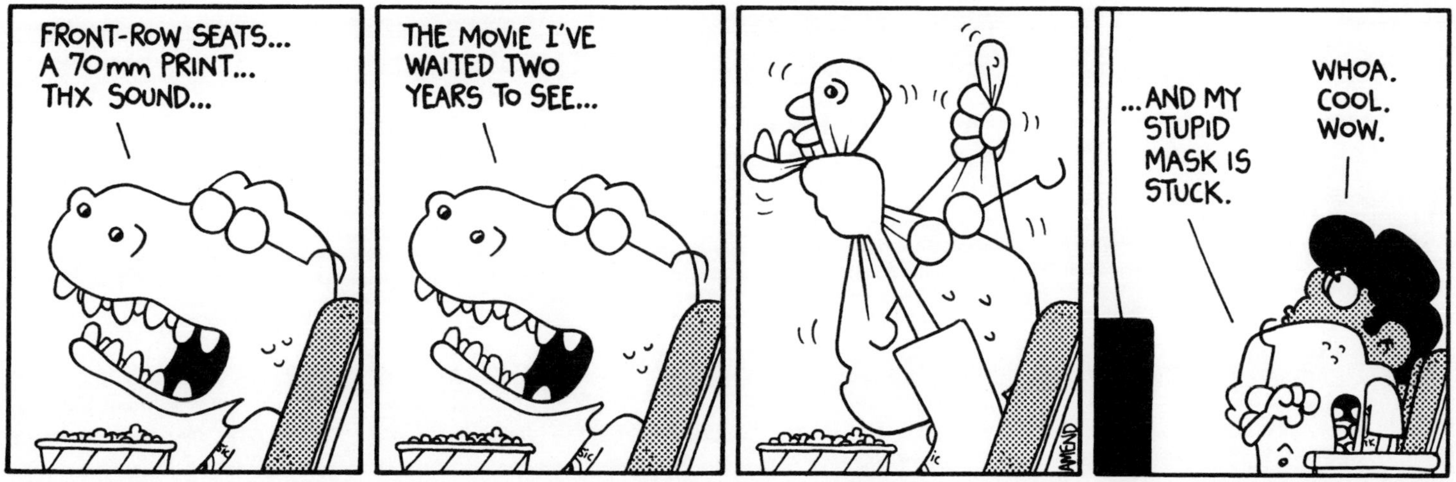
FRONT-ROW SEATS... A 70mm PRINT... THX SOUND...
THE MOVIE I'VE WAITED TWO YEARS TO SEE...
...AND MY STUPID MASK IS STUCK.
WHOA. COOL. WOW.
AMEND
June 12, 1993

August 27, 1993

Harlan Ellison included this strip in a book of his. Very flattering.

October 5, 1993

October 18, 1993

142

September 12, 1993

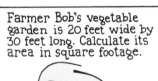  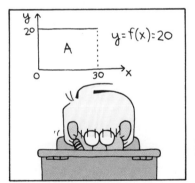 

September 19, 1993

It's been almost seventeen years now, and I still get e-mails about this strip.

September 20, 1993

September 21, 1993

144

September 22, 1993

September 23, 1993

Feel free to repeat this experiment. It should work.

September 24, 1993

September 25, 1993

October 10, 1993

I lived near Boston as a kid. I mean Baston.

December 5, 1993

WOW! I CAN'T BELIEVE DAD GOT ME A BEAVIS STOCKING!

I CAN'T BELIEVE DAD GOT ME A BUTT-HEAD ONE!

HUH-HUH HUH-HUH M HUH HNNGH M HNNGH HUH M HUH-HUH-HUH M HUH-HUH HUH-HUH M HUH HNNGH HUH HUH-HUH HUH HUH M HUH HNNGH HUH M HUH-HUH

THEY CAN'T BELIEVE IT?!?

THE WOMAN AT THE STORE SAID THEY WERE QUITE THE RAGE.

LET ME SHOW YOU RAGE.

I read that Mike Judge, who created *Beavis and Butt-Head,* was also a physics major. We're taking over!

MOM, I HAVE TO WRITE AN ESSAY ON "MACBETH" AND I THOUGHT MAYBE YOU COULD HELP ME WITH IT.

"MACBETH"? YOU'RE STUDYING "MACBETH"?

"IS THIS A DAGGER WHICH I SEE BEFORE ME, THE HANDLE TOWARD MY HAND?... I GO, AND IT IS DONE; THE BELL INVITES ME. HEAR IT NOT, DUNCAN; FOR IT IS A KNELL THAT SUMMONS THEE TO HEAVEN OR TO HELL!"

THAT "MACBETH"?

I KEEP FORGETTING YOU WERE AN ENGLISH MAJOR.

ACT I. SCENE I.— AN OPEN PLACE. THUNDER AND LIGHTNING. ENTER THREE WITCHES...

HEY, PETER — TRIVIA TIME. WHAT'S THE CAPITAL OF BELGIUM?

UM, BRUSSELS.

NORWAY? OSLO. ITALY? ROME. SWITZERLAND? BERN. THE CZECH REPUBLIC? PRAGUE.

ARE YOU SURE??

DEFINITELY.

HOMEWORK'S DONE.

WHAT'S "PROG"?

February 14, 1994

February 15, 1994

February 16, 1994

MOM, WHAT'S WRONG?

OH, I'M JUST FLOUNDERING IN ONE OF MY USUAL PARENTAL DILEMMAS.

A FEW DAYS AGO, I STUMBLED ACROSS A VALENTINE'S DAY CARD THAT JASON HAD WRITTEN TO SOME GIRL AT HIS SCHOOL NAMED GRETCHEN. IT WAS, SHALL WE SAY, OF A ROMANTIC NATURE.

JASON?! THIS IS JASON?!

ANYWAY, I'M DYING TO FIND OUT MORE ABOUT THIS GIRL, BUT I DON'T DARE TELL HIM THAT I—...

JASON AND GRETCHEN, SITTIN' IN A TREE...

...KNOW.

February 17, 1994

WHO TOLD YOU ABOUT GRETCHEN?

JASON, SWEETIE, I SAW THE VALENTINE'S DAY CARD YOU MADE FOR HER.

IT'S PRETTY OBVIOUS THAT YOU LIKE HER A LOT, AND I JUST WANT YOU TO KNOW THAT IT'S OK. NO ONE IS GOING TO MAKE FUN OF YOU.

I JUST WISH YOU'D TELL US ABOUT HER.

WELL, SHE HAS THIS GREAT WAY OF EATING MICE...

DID YOU SAY MICE?

ARE WE ALLOWED TO MAKE FUN OF GRETCHEN?

February 18, 1994

GRETCHEN'S A SNAKE?!

SHE'S MISS O'MALLEY'S BOA CONSTRICTOR.

YOU MADE THAT VALENTINE'S DAY CARD FOR A SNAKE?!

WHO'D YOU THINK IT WAS FOR?

WELL, FOR STARTERS, A GIRL.

EEW! GROSS! ICK! WHAT KIND OF A WEIRDO DO YOU THINK I AM?!

DON'T ASK.

WOULD IT BE OK IF MARCUS AND I BUILT AN ANDROID THIS WEEKEND?

February 19, 1994

149

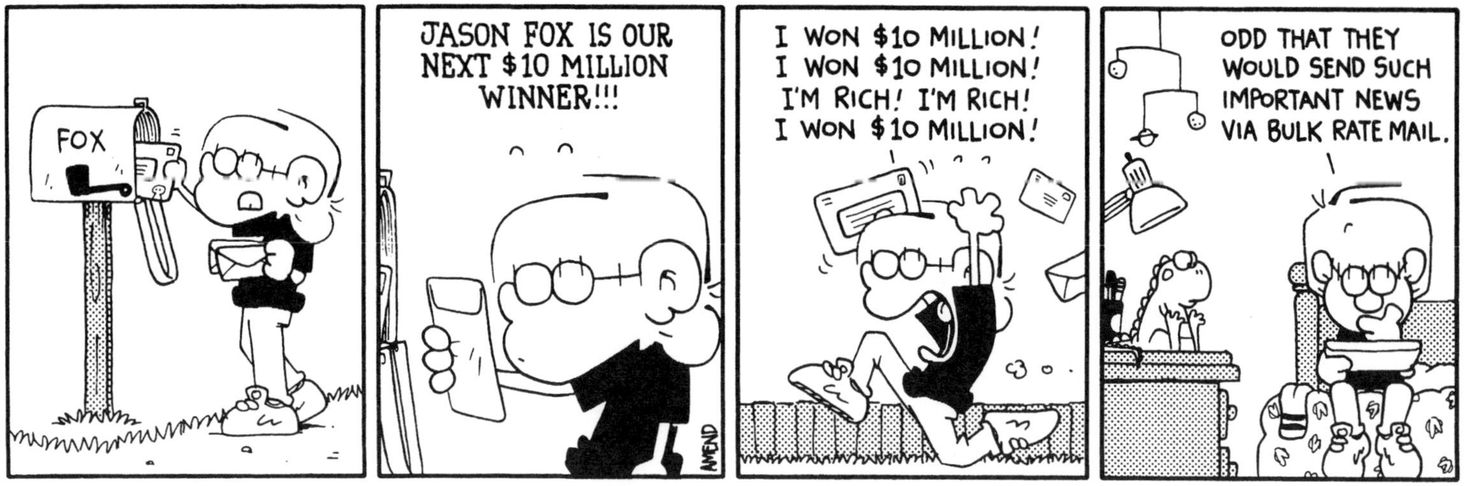
FOX
JASON FOX IS OUR NEXT $10 MILLION WINNER!!!
I WON $10 MILLION! I WON $10 MILLION! I'M RICH! I'M RICH! I WON $10 MILLION!
ODD THAT THEY WOULD SEND SUCH IMPORTANT NEWS VIA BULK RATE MAIL.
AMEND

February 28, 1994

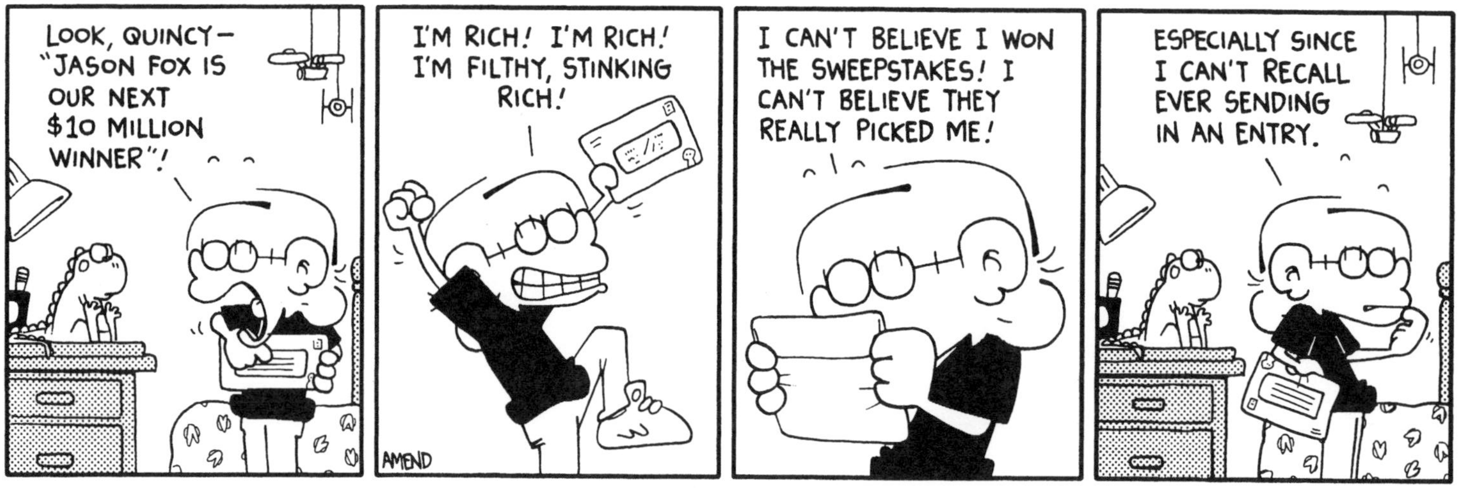
LOOK, QUINCY– "JASON FOX IS OUR NEXT $10 MILLION WINNER"!
I'M RICH! I'M RICH! I'M FILTHY, STINKING RICH!
I CAN'T BELIEVE I WON THE SWEEPSTAKES! I CAN'T BELIEVE THEY REALLY PICKED ME!
ESPECIALLY SINCE I CAN'T RECALL EVER SENDING IN AN ENTRY.
AMEND

March 1, 1994

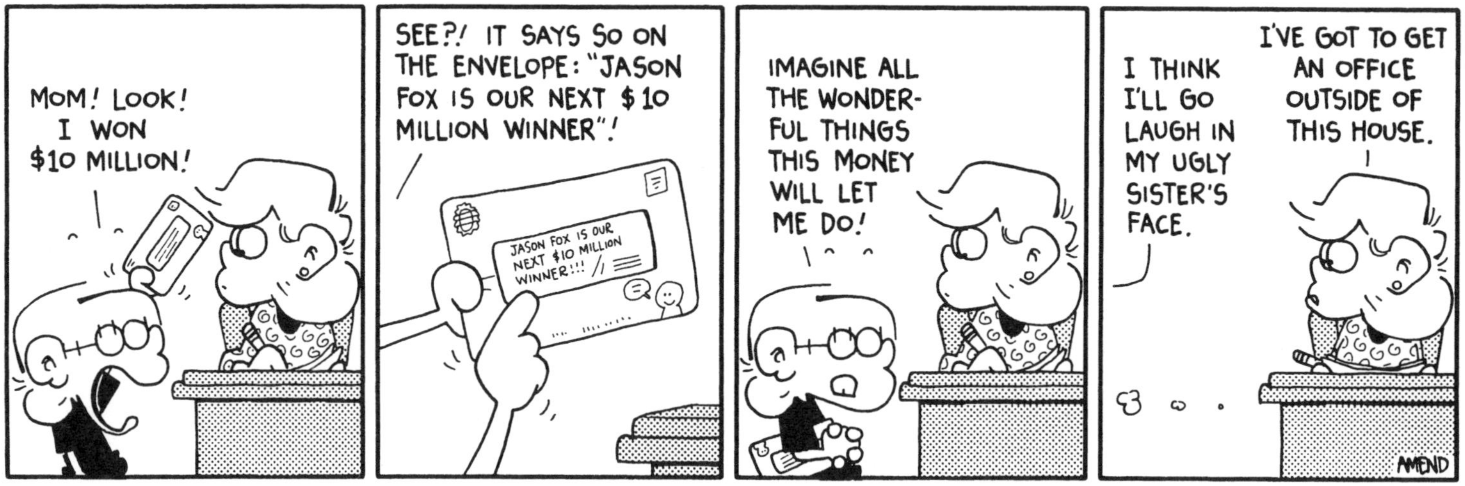
MOM! LOOK! I WON $10 MILLION!
SEE?! IT SAYS SO ON THE ENVELOPE: "JASON FOX IS OUR NEXT $10 MILLION WINNER"!
JASON FOX IS OUR NEXT $10 MILLION WINNER!!!
IMAGINE ALL THE WONDERFUL THINGS THIS MONEY WILL LET ME DO!
I THINK I'LL GO LAUGH IN MY UGLY SISTER'S FACE.
I'VE GOT TO GET AN OFFICE OUTSIDE OF THIS HOUSE.
AMEND

March 2, 1994

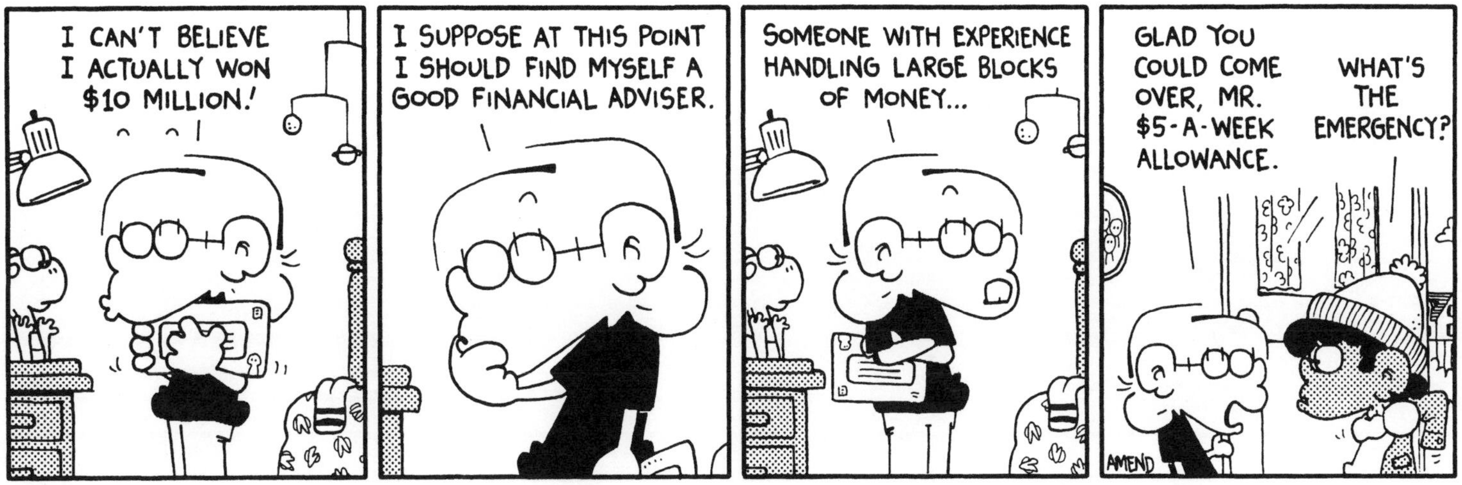
I CAN'T BELIEVE I ACTUALLY WON $10 MILLION!
I SUPPOSE AT THIS POINT I SHOULD FIND MYSELF A GOOD FINANCIAL ADVISER.
SOMEONE WITH EXPERIENCE HANDLING LARGE BLOCKS OF MONEY...
GLAD YOU COULD COME OVER, MR. $5-A-WEEK ALLOWANCE.
WHAT'S THE EMERGENCY?
AMEND

March 3, 1994

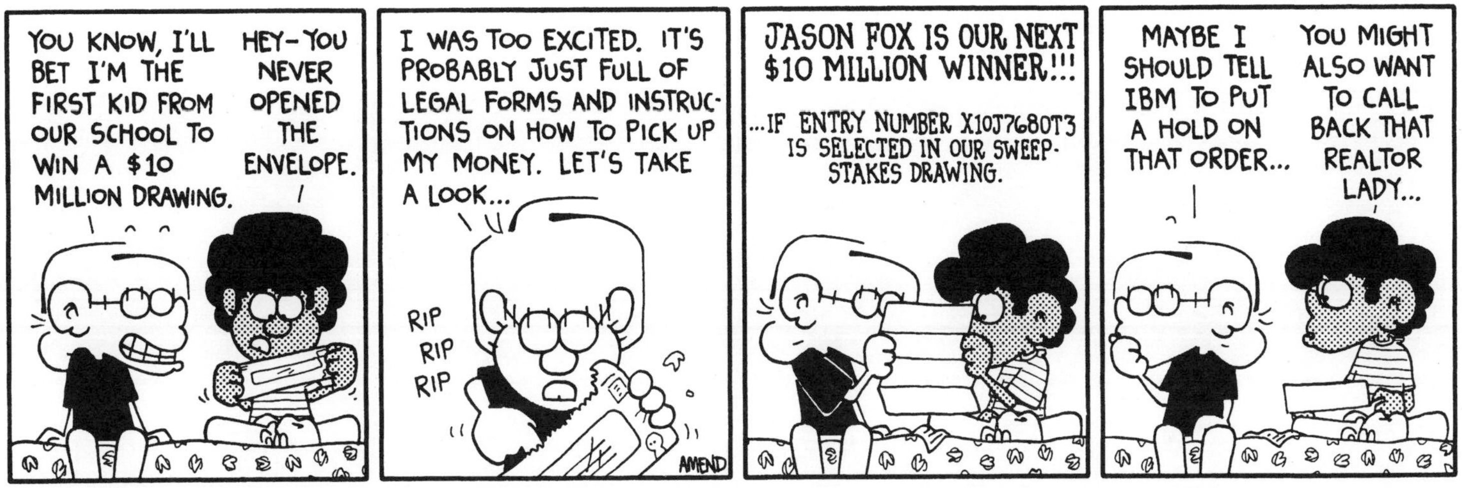
YOU KNOW, I'LL BET I'M THE FIRST KID FROM OUR SCHOOL TO WIN A $10 MILLION DRAWING.
HEY—YOU NEVER OPENED THE ENVELOPE.
I WAS TOO EXCITED. IT'S PROBABLY JUST FULL OF LEGAL FORMS AND INSTRUCTIONS ON HOW TO PICK UP MY MONEY. LET'S TAKE A LOOK...
RIP RIP RIP
AMEND
JASON FOX IS OUR NEXT $10 MILLION WINNER!!!
...IF ENTRY NUMBER X10J7680T3 IS SELECTED IN OUR SWEEPSTAKES DRAWING.
MAYBE I SHOULD TELL IBM TO PUT A HOLD ON THAT ORDER...
YOU MIGHT ALSO WANT TO CALL BACK THAT REALTOR LADY...

March 4, 1994

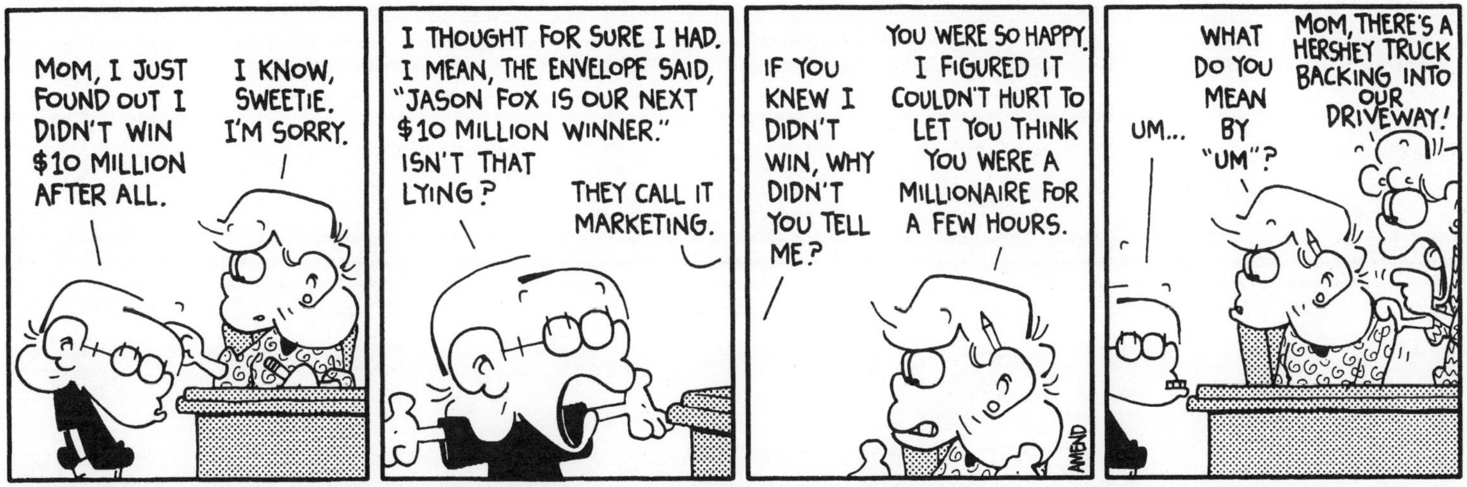
MOM, I JUST FOUND OUT I DIDN'T WIN $10 MILLION AFTER ALL.
I KNOW, SWEETIE. I'M SORRY.
I THOUGHT FOR SURE I HAD. I MEAN, THE ENVELOPE SAID, "JASON FOX IS OUR NEXT $10 MILLION WINNER." ISN'T THAT LYING?
THEY CALL IT MARKETING.
IF YOU KNEW I DIDN'T WIN, WHY DIDN'T YOU TELL ME?
YOU WERE SO HAPPY. I FIGURED IT COULDN'T HURT TO LET YOU THINK YOU WERE A MILLIONAIRE FOR A FEW HOURS.
AMEND
UM...
WHAT DO YOU MEAN BY "UM"?
MOM, THERE'S A HERSHEY TRUCK BACKING INTO OUR DRIVEWAY!

March 5, 1994

February 25, 1994

Hugh Andrews now runs Andrews McMeel Publishing. Obviously Jason's prank didn't harm his career.

March 22, 1994

April 1, 1994

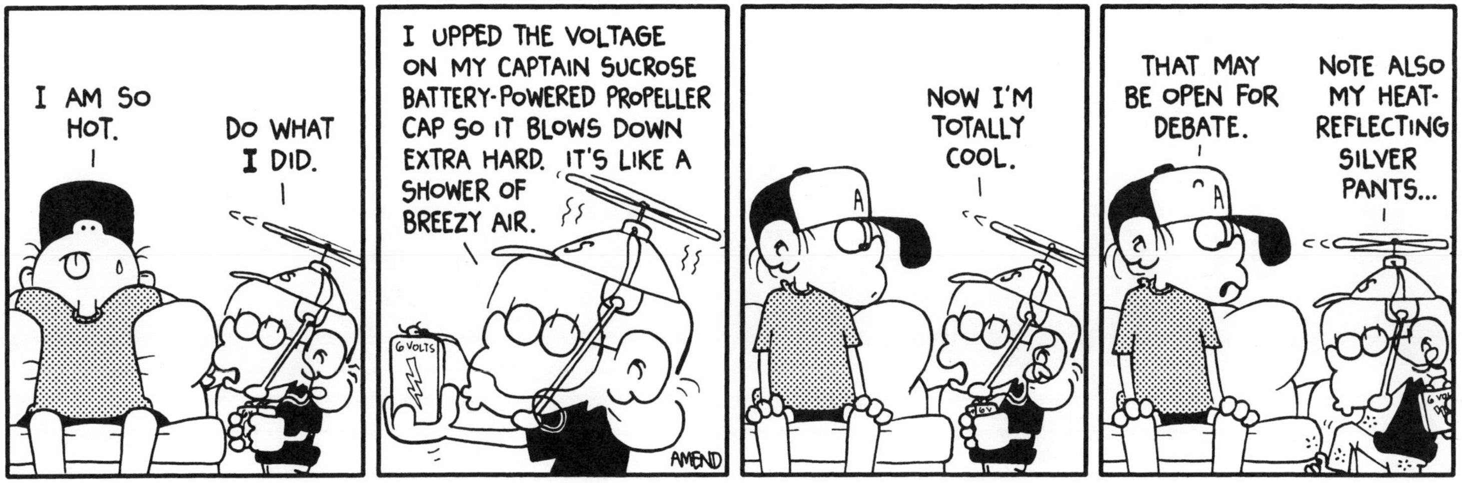
I AM SO HOT.
DO WHAT I DID.
I UPPED THE VOLTAGE ON MY CAPTAIN SUCROSE BATTERY-POWERED PROPELLER CAP SO IT BLOWS DOWN EXTRA HARD. IT'S LIKE A SHOWER OF BREEZY AIR.
6 VOLTS
NOW I'M TOTALLY COOL.
THAT MAY BE OPEN FOR DEBATE.
NOTE ALSO MY HEAT-REFLECTING SILVER PANTS...
AMEND

July 7, 1994

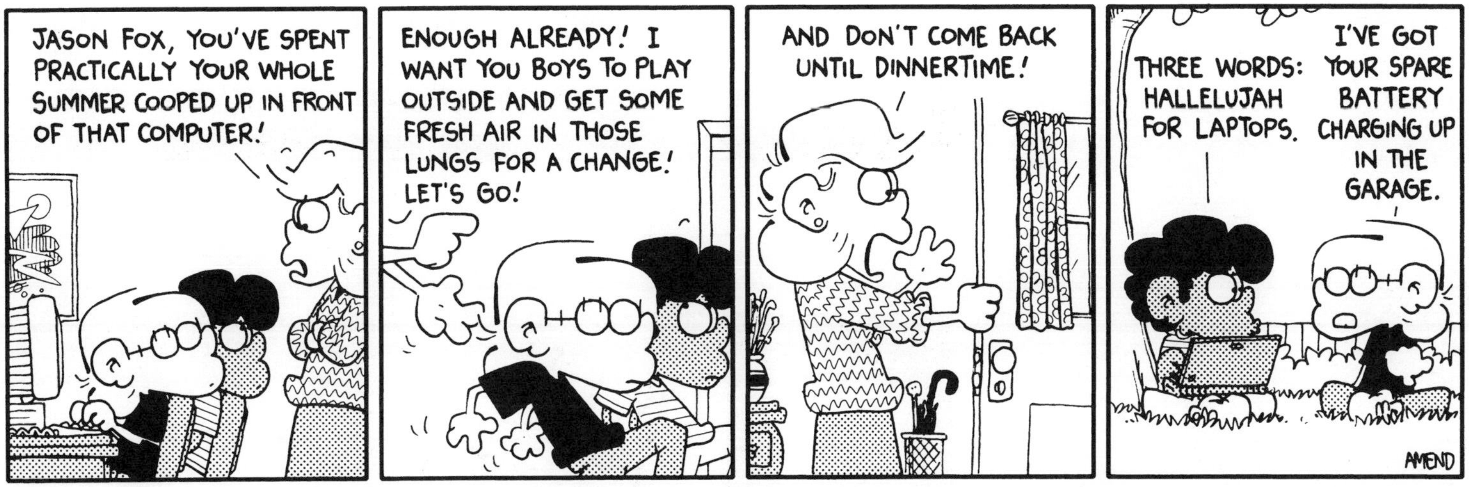
JASON FOX, YOU'VE SPENT PRACTICALLY YOUR WHOLE SUMMER COOPED UP IN FRONT OF THAT COMPUTER!
ENOUGH ALREADY! I WANT YOU BOYS TO PLAY OUTSIDE AND GET SOME FRESH AIR IN THOSE LUNGS FOR A CHANGE! LET'S GO!
AND DON'T COME BACK UNTIL DINNERTIME!
THREE WORDS: HALLELUJAH FOR LAPTOPS.
I'VE GOT YOUR SPARE BATTERY CHARGING UP IN THE GARAGE.
AMEND

August 23, 1994

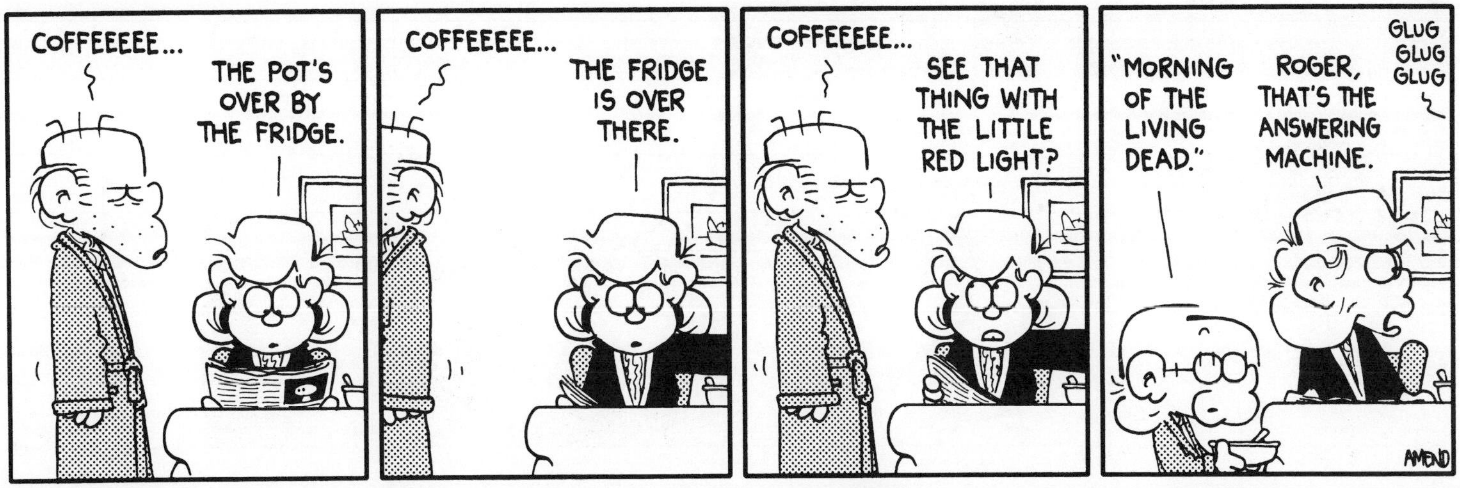
COFFEEEEE...
THE POT'S OVER BY THE FRIDGE.
COFFEEEEE...
THE FRIDGE IS OVER THERE.
COFFEEEEE...
SEE THAT THING WITH THE LITTLE RED LIGHT?
"MORNING OF THE LIVING DEAD."
ROGER, THAT'S THE ANSWERING MACHINE.
GLUG GLUG GLUG
AMEND

November 10, 1994

Unlike Peter, I didn't start drinking coffee until college, but I've definitely made up for the late start.

March 27, 1994

May 1, 1994

May 8, 1994

This ran on Mother's Day when my wife was pregnant with our first child.

June 12, 1994

I love how the alien helmets are built to accommodate ponytails.

155

April 18, 1994

J. D. Parker was my computer science professor in college.

April 19, 1994

April 20, 1994

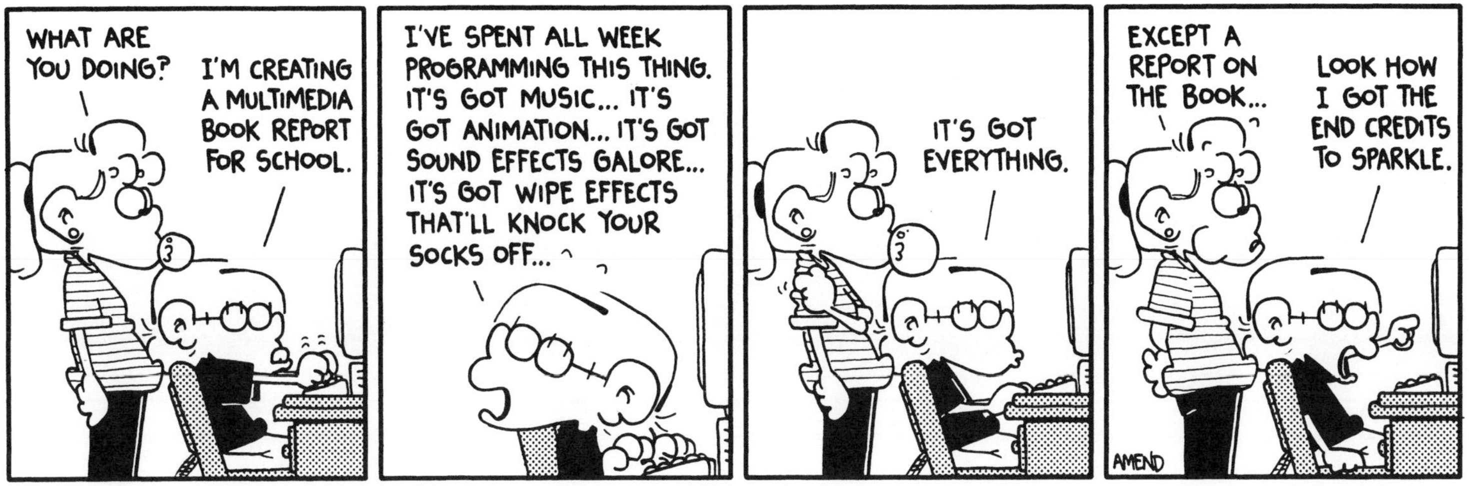
WHAT ARE YOU DOING?
I'M CREATING A MULTIMEDIA BOOK REPORT FOR SCHOOL.
I'VE SPENT ALL WEEK PROGRAMMING THIS THING. IT'S GOT MUSIC... IT'S GOT ANIMATION... IT'S GOT SOUND EFFECTS GALORE... IT'S GOT WIPE EFFECTS THAT'LL KNOCK YOUR SOCKS OFF...
IT'S GOT EVERYTHING.
EXCEPT A REPORT ON THE BOOK...
LOOK HOW I GOT THE END CREDITS TO SPARKLE.
AMEND
April 21, 1994

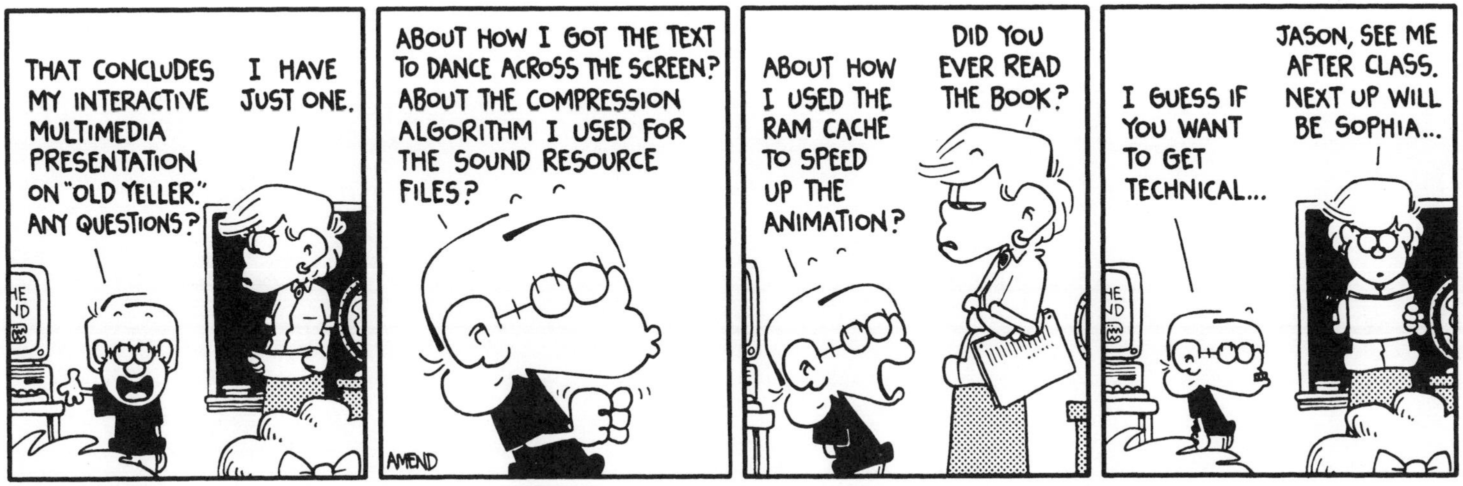
THAT CONCLUDES MY INTERACTIVE MULTIMEDIA PRESENTATION ON "OLD YELLER." ANY QUESTIONS?
I HAVE JUST ONE.
ABOUT HOW I GOT THE TEXT TO DANCE ACROSS THE SCREEN? ABOUT THE COMPRESSION ALGORITHM I USED FOR THE SOUND RESOURCE FILES?
ABOUT HOW I USED THE RAM CACHE TO SPEED UP THE ANIMATION?
DID YOU EVER READ THE BOOK?
I GUESS IF YOU WANT TO GET TECHNICAL...
JASON, SEE ME AFTER CLASS. NEXT UP WILL BE SOPHIA...
AMEND
April 22, 1994

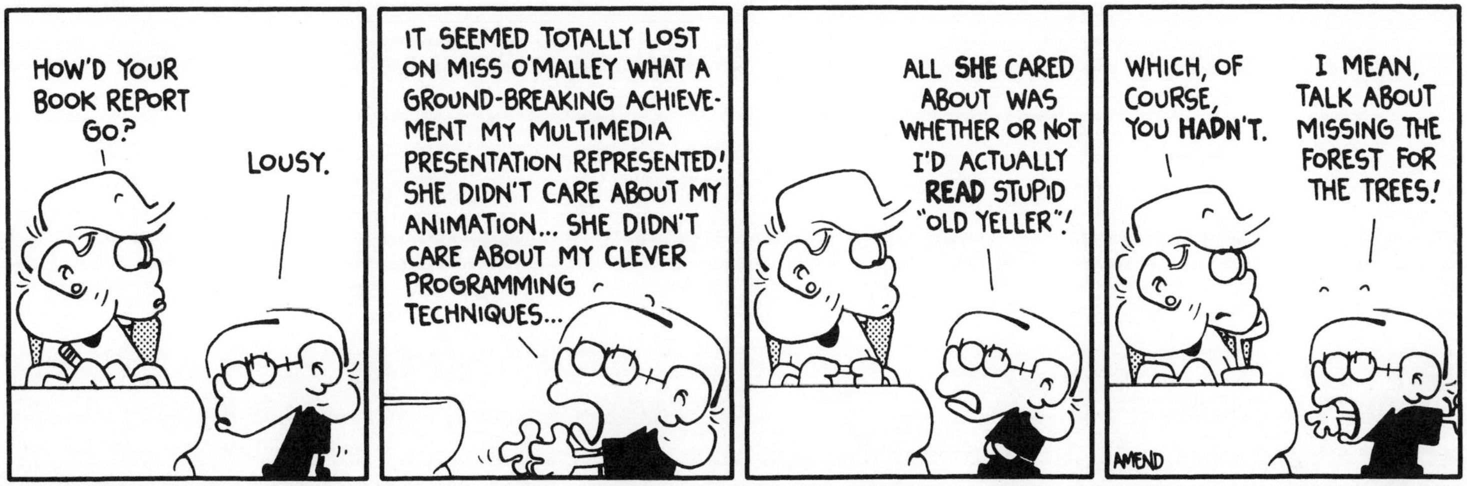
HOW'D YOUR BOOK REPORT GO?
LOUSY.
IT SEEMED TOTALLY LOST ON MISS O'MALLEY WHAT A GROUND-BREAKING ACHIEVEMENT MY MULTIMEDIA PRESENTATION REPRESENTED! SHE DIDN'T CARE ABOUT MY ANIMATION... SHE DIDN'T CARE ABOUT MY CLEVER PROGRAMMING TECHNIQUES...
ALL **SHE** CARED ABOUT WAS WHETHER OR NOT I'D ACTUALLY **READ** STUPID "OLD YELLER"!
WHICH, OF COURSE, YOU **HADN'T**.
I MEAN, TALK ABOUT MISSING THE FOREST FOR THE TREES!
AMEND
April 23, 1994

May 9, 1994

May 10, 1994

Paige is, by design, perpetually boyfriendless, but I thought a little brush with romance wouldn't hurt her.

May 11, 1994

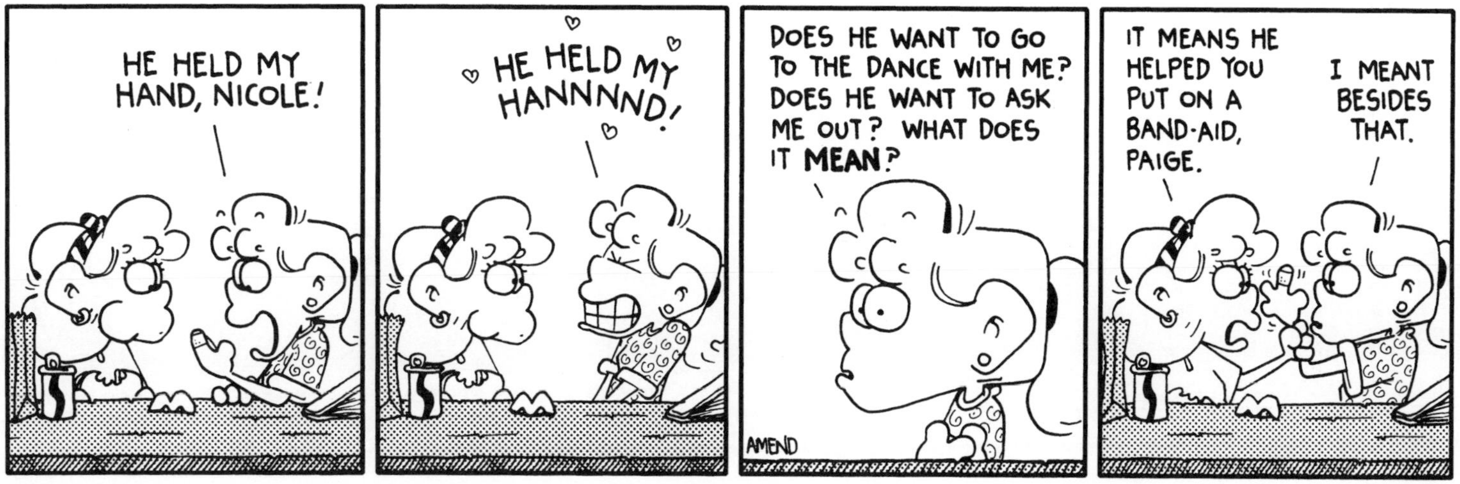
HE HELD MY HAND, NICOLE!
HE HELD MY HANNNND!
DOES HE WANT TO GO TO THE DANCE WITH ME? DOES HE WANT TO ASK ME OUT? WHAT DOES IT **MEAN**?
AMEND
IT MEANS HE HELPED YOU PUT ON A BAND-AID, PAIGE.
I MEANT BESIDES THAT.

May 12, 1994

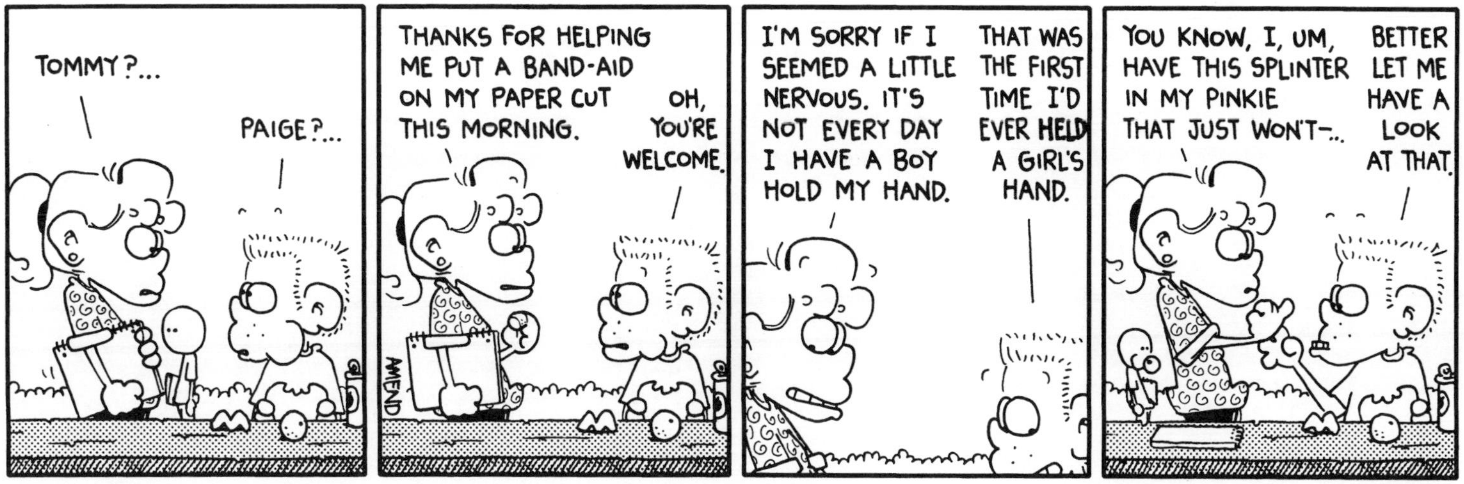
TOMMY?...
PAIGE?...
THANKS FOR HELPING ME PUT A BAND-AID ON MY PAPER CUT THIS MORNING.
OH, YOU'RE WELCOME.
AMEND
I'M SORRY IF I SEEMED A LITTLE NERVOUS. IT'S NOT EVERY DAY I HAVE A BOY HOLD MY HAND.
THAT WAS THE FIRST TIME I'D EVER **HELD** A GIRL'S HAND.
YOU KNOW, I, UM, HAVE THIS SPLINTER IN MY PINKIE THAT JUST WON'T-..
BETTER LET ME HAVE A LOOK AT THAT.

May 13, 1994

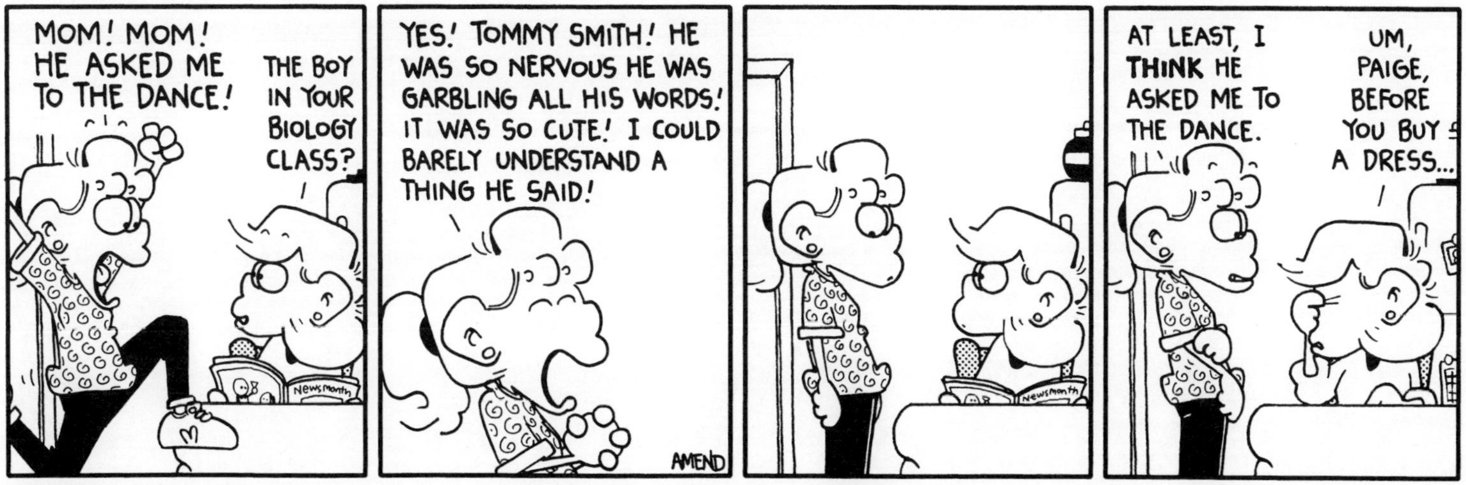
MOM! MOM! HE ASKED ME TO THE DANCE!
THE BOY IN YOUR BIOLOGY CLASS?
YES! TOMMY SMITH! HE WAS SO NERVOUS HE WAS GARBLING ALL HIS WORDS! IT WAS SO CUTE! I COULD BARELY UNDERSTAND A THING HE SAID!
AMEND
AT LEAST, I **THINK** HE ASKED ME TO THE DANCE.
UM, PAIGE, BEFORE YOU BUY A DRESS...

May 14, 1994

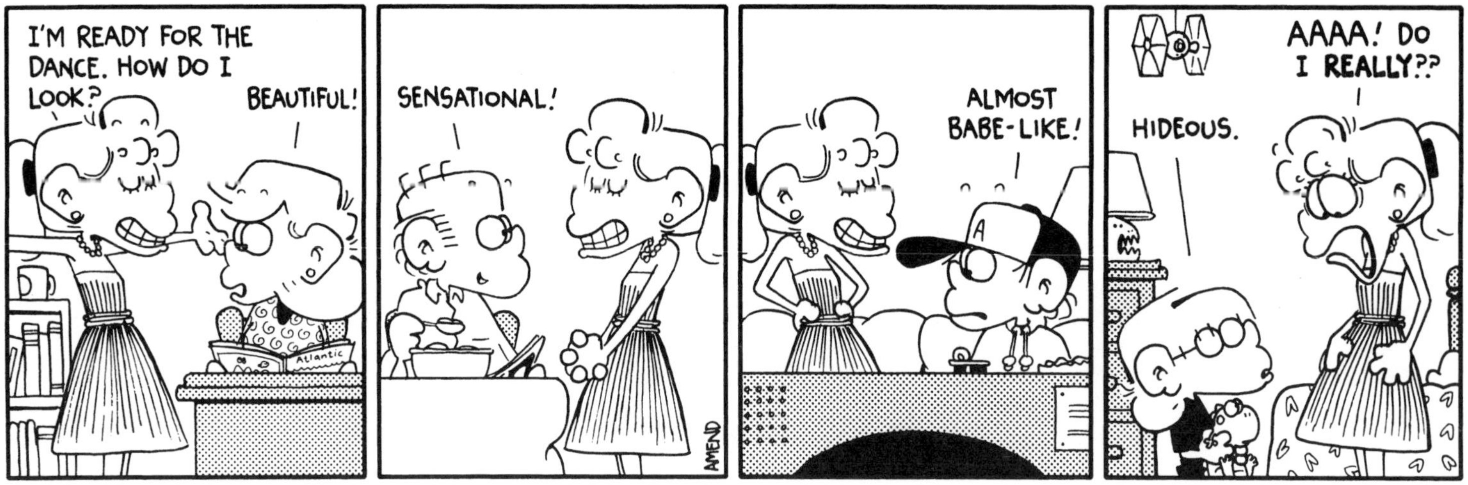
I'M READY FOR THE DANCE. HOW DO I LOOK?
BEAUTIFUL!
Atlantic
SENSATIONAL!
AMEND
ALMOST BABE-LIKE!
HIDEOUS.
AAAA! DO I **REALLY**??

May 16, 1994

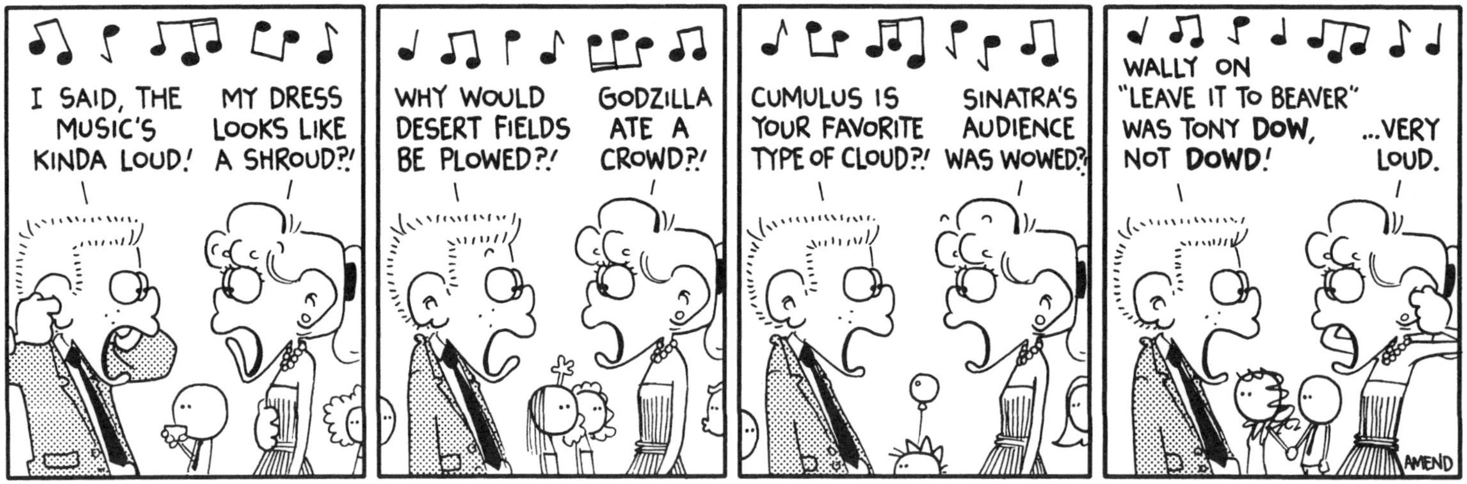
I SAID, THE MUSIC'S KINDA LOUD!
MY DRESS LOOKS LIKE A SHROUD?!
WHY WOULD DESERT FIELDS BE PLOWED?!
GODZILLA ATE A CROWD?!
CUMULUS IS YOUR FAVORITE TYPE OF CLOUD?!
SINATRA'S AUDIENCE WAS WOWED?!
WALLY ON "LEAVE IT TO BEAVER" WAS TONY **DOW**, NOT **DOWD**!
...VERY LOUD.
AMEND

May 17, 1994

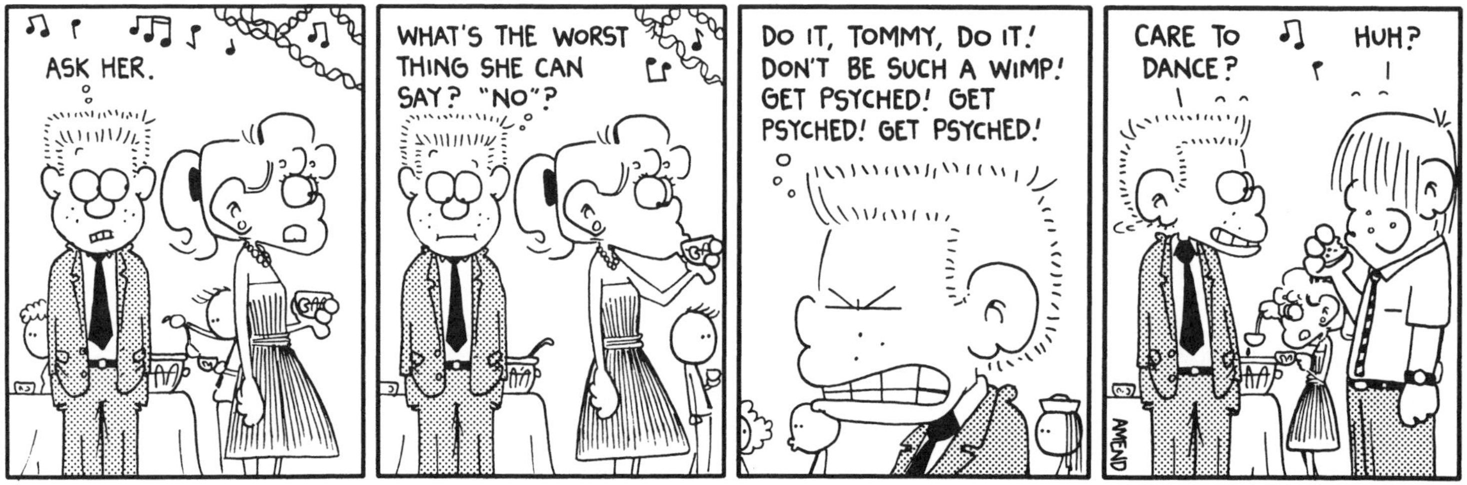
ASK HER.
WHAT'S THE WORST THING SHE CAN SAY? "NO"?
DO IT, TOMMY, DO IT! DON'T BE SUCH A WIMP! GET PSYCHED! GET PSYCHED! GET PSYCHED!
AMEND
CARE TO DANCE?
HUH?

May 18, 1994

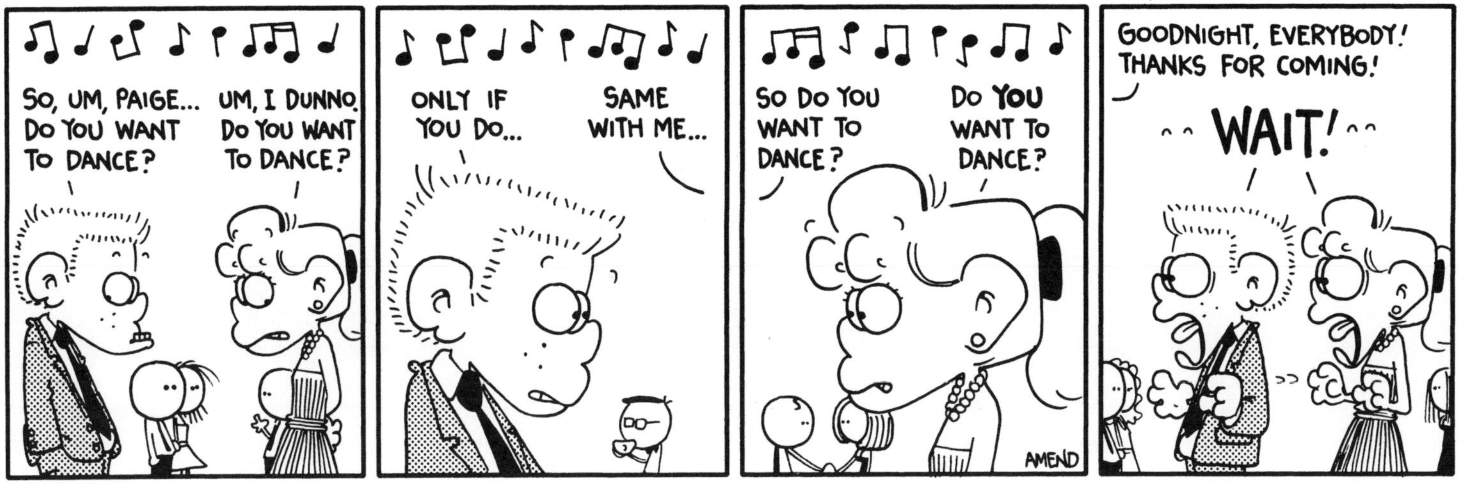
SO, UM, PAIGE... DO YOU WANT TO DANCE?
UM, I DUNNO. DO YOU WANT TO DANCE?
ONLY IF YOU DO...
SAME WITH ME...
SO DO YOU WANT TO DANCE?
DO **YOU** WANT TO DANCE?
AMEND
GOODNIGHT, EVERYBODY! THANKS FOR COMING!
WAIT!

May 19, 1994

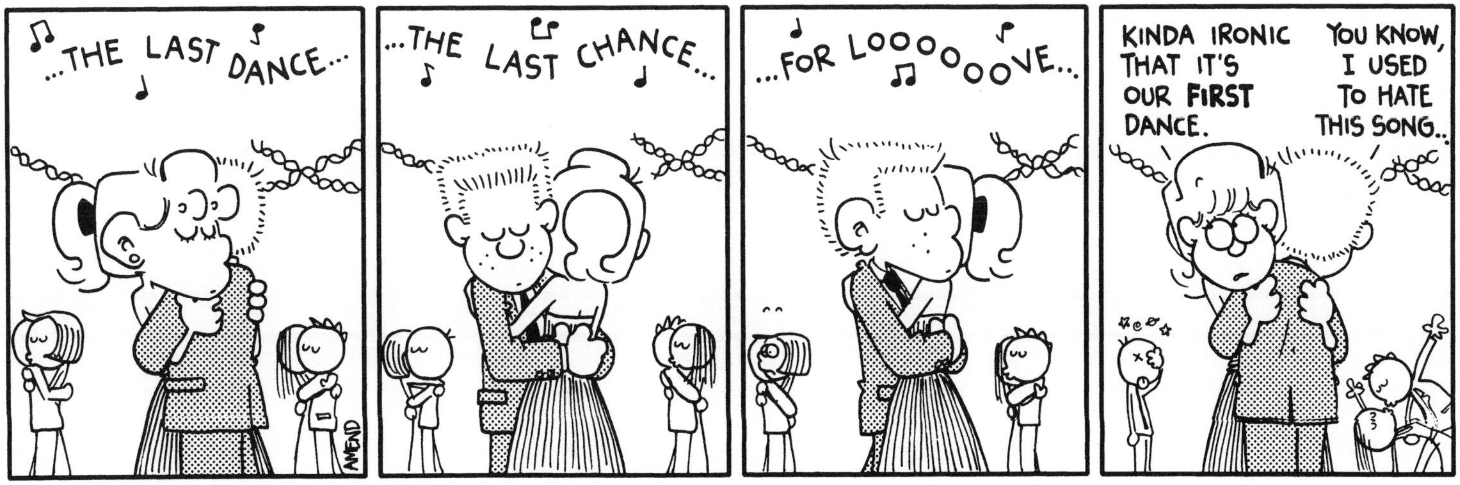
...THE LAST DANCE...
AMEND
...THE LAST CHANCE...
...FOR LOOOOOOOVE...
KINDA IRONIC THAT IT'S OUR **FIRST** DANCE.
YOU KNOW, I USED TO HATE THIS SONG...

May 20, 1994

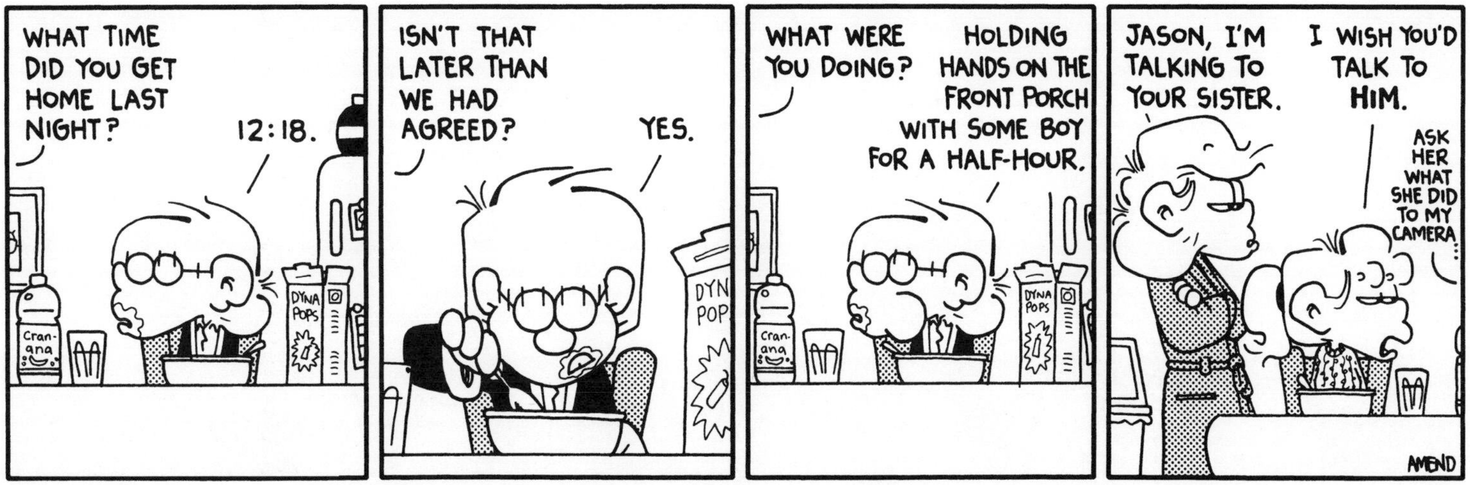
WHAT TIME DID YOU GET HOME LAST NIGHT?
12:18.
ISN'T THAT LATER THAN WE HAD AGREED?
YES.
WHAT WERE YOU DOING?
HOLDING HANDS ON THE FRONT PORCH WITH SOME BOY FOR A HALF-HOUR.
JASON, I'M TALKING TO YOUR SISTER.
I WISH YOU'D TALK TO **HIM**.
ASK HER WHAT SHE DID TO MY CAMERA...
AMEND

May 21, 1994

I wrote these strips as I prepared to face my own ten-year college reunion.

May 23, 1994

May 24, 1994

May 25, 1994

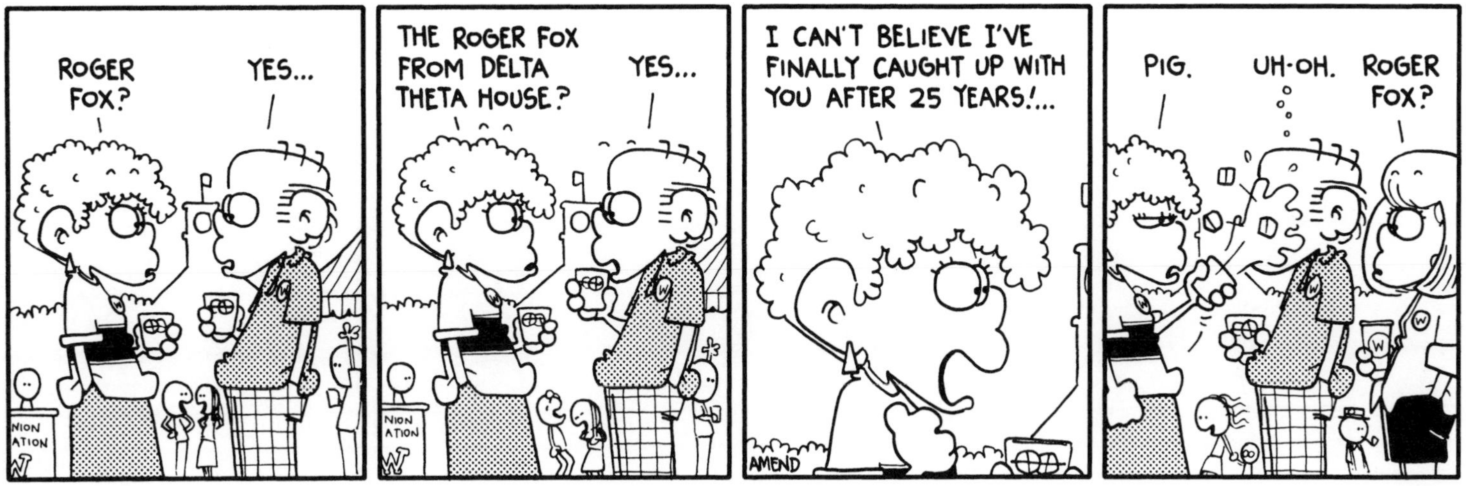
ROGER FOX?
YES...
THE ROGER FOX FROM DELTA THETA HOUSE?
YES...
I CAN'T BELIEVE I'VE FINALLY CAUGHT UP WITH YOU AFTER 25 YEARS!...
PIG.
UH-OH.
ROGER FOX?

May 26, 1994

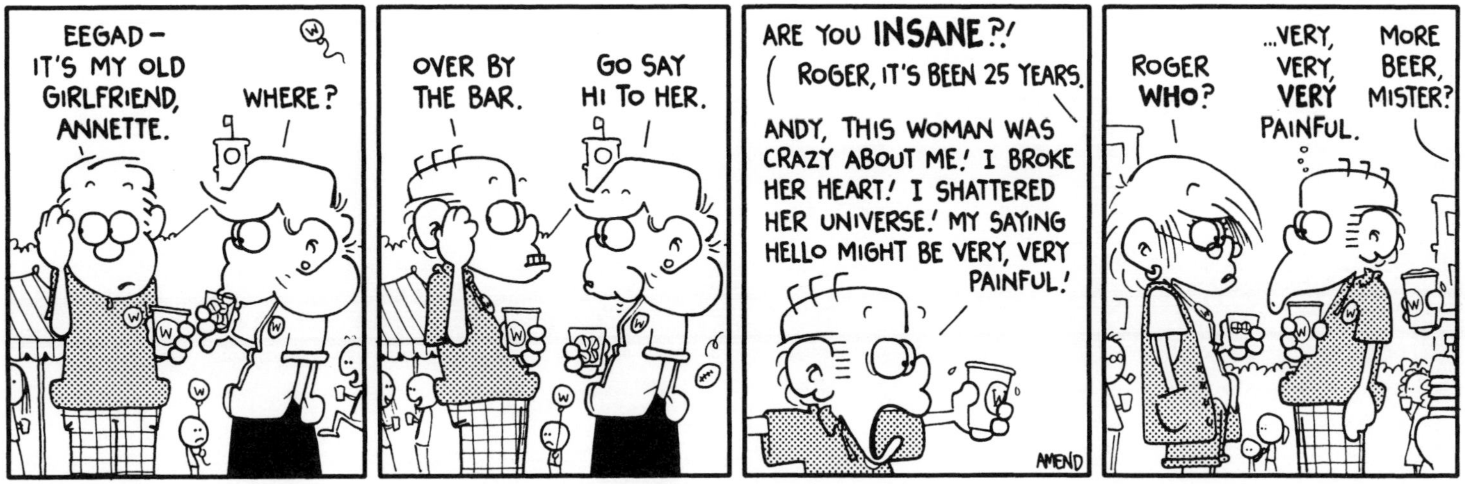
EEGAD– IT'S MY OLD GIRLFRIEND, ANNETTE.
WHERE?
OVER BY THE BAR.
GO SAY HI TO HER.
ARE YOU **INSANE**?!
ROGER, IT'S BEEN 25 YEARS.
ANDY, THIS WOMAN WAS CRAZY ABOUT ME! I BROKE HER HEART! I SHATTERED HER UNIVERSE! MY SAYING HELLO MIGHT BE VERY, VERY PAINFUL!
ROGER **WHO**?
...VERY, VERY, **VERY** PAINFUL.
MORE BEER, MISTER?

May 27, 1994

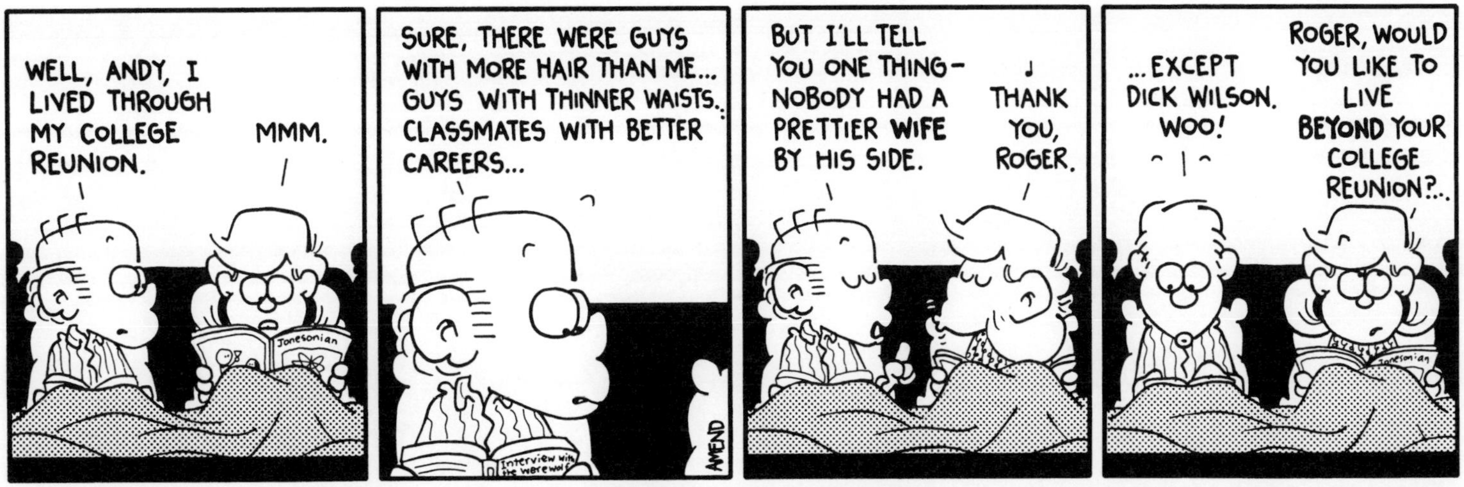
WELL, ANDY, I LIVED THROUGH MY COLLEGE REUNION.
MMM.
SURE, THERE WERE GUYS WITH MORE HAIR THAN ME... GUYS WITH THINNER WAISTS... CLASSMATES WITH BETTER CAREERS...
BUT I'LL TELL YOU ONE THING– NOBODY HAD A PRETTIER **WIFE** BY HIS SIDE.
THANK YOU, ROGER.
...EXCEPT DICK WILSON. WOO!
ROGER, WOULD YOU LIKE TO LIVE **BEYOND** YOUR COLLEGE REUNION?..

May 28, 1994

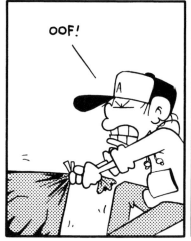

November 30, 1994

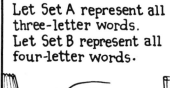

December 14, 1994

December 27, 1994

July 10, 1994

August 21, 1994

Jason was not happy that I wouldn't let him wear a Spider-Man mask in this strip. I needed readers to know who he was.

Blink Blink Blink

SNQRZZZZz

Blink Blink Blink

SNQRZZZZz

WHUMP!

DROOOOOOOL...

I'VE GOT TO STOP CHEWING GUM WHEN I READ.

I FOUND A CROWBAR.

September 11, 1994

Gray Wolf

Bengal Tiger

California Condor

Black Rhino

Humpback Whale

Peter Fox

SPOT THE **MOST** ENDANGERED SPECIES.

PAIGE, YOU LEFT YOUR DIARY OUT ON YOUR DRESSER — OF **COURSE** I'M GONNA READ IT!

I COULD'VE SWORN IT WAS UNDER HER MATTRESS..

October 2, 1994

166

WELCOME TO COMPUNET.

YOU HAVE 65,031 WAITING MESSAGES.

MAYBE SETTING MY USERNAME TO "FABIO" WASN'T SUCH A HOT IDEA.

DIANE@NASA.GOV WISHES TO CHAT.
↳ LUCILLE@OSU.EDU WISHES TO CHAT.
↳ JOYCE@UPS.COM WISHES TO CHAT.

Back in the early days of home Internet use, you generally used a service like AOL or CompuServe as a gateway.

September 28, 1994

THIS COMPUNET IS REALLY COOL.

NERD.

YOU CAN ACCESS THE INTERNET...   NERD.

YOU CAN CHAT WITH FAMOUS CARTOONISTS...   NERD.

YOU CAN READ BACK-ISSUE ARTICLES FROM MODEL ROCKETRY MAGAZINE...   NERD.

THEY'VE EVEN GOT AN ONLINE MALL WHERE YOU CAN GO SHOPPING.

NERDETTE.

GO FIND OUT WHAT MOM'S CREDIT LIMIT IS.

September 29, 1994

JASON, WILL YOU PLEASE TURN OFF THE MODEM? I NEED TO USE THE TELEPHONE.

BUT I'M RIGHT IN THE MIDDLE OF A DOWNLOAD!

COMPUNET JUST STARTED CARRYING BLACK BANSHEE COMIC BOOK PREVIEWS. I'M DOWNLOADING THE FIRST THREE PAGES OF NEXT MONTH'S ISSUE.

HOW LONG WILL THAT TAKE?

WELL, LET'S SEE... I STARTED AT ABOUT 4:15...

HOW'S MIDNIGHT SOUND?

JASON, ARE YOU FAMILIAR WITH A LITTLE THING CALLED A PHONE JACK?

September 30, 1994

167

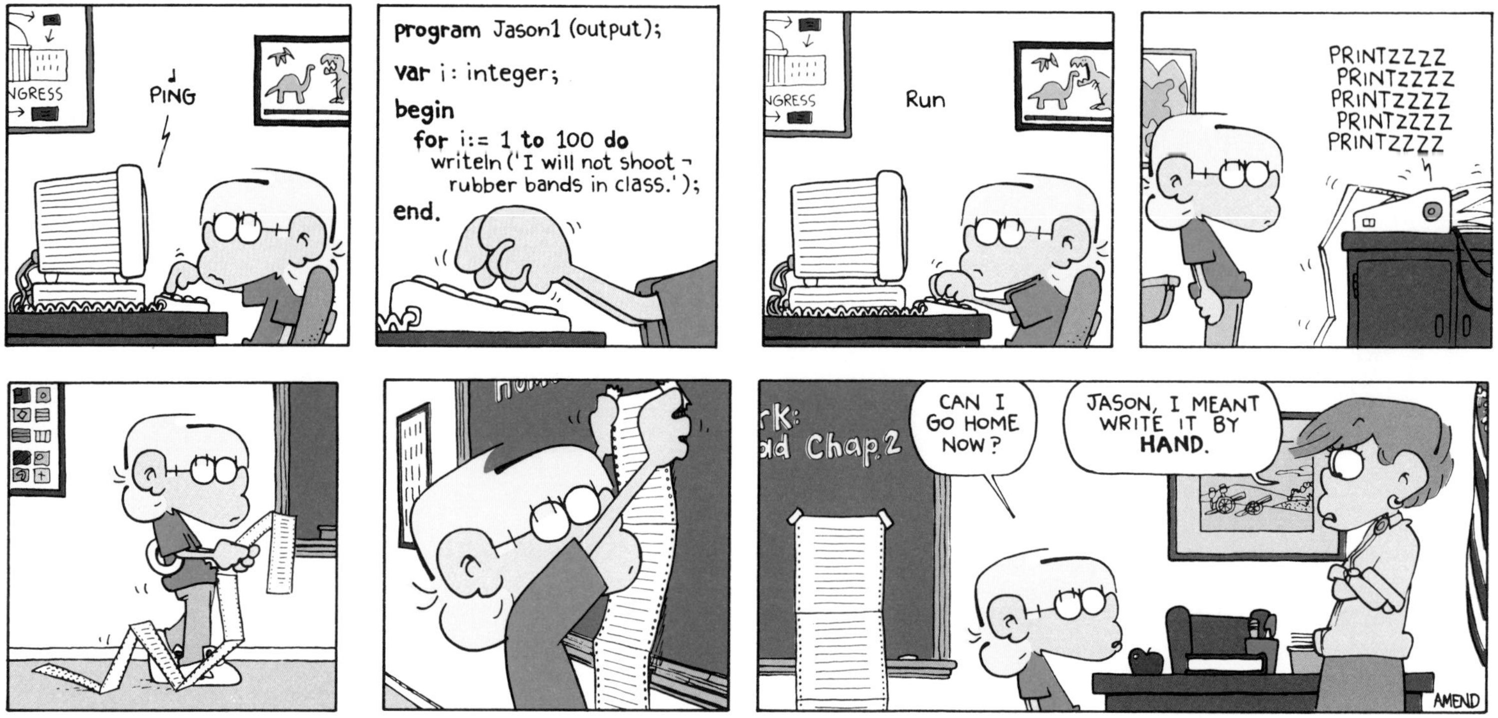
PING
program Jason1 (output);
var i : integer;
begin
for i:= 1 to 100 do
writeln ('I will not shoot rubber bands in class.');
end.
Run
PRINTZZZZ
PRINTZZZZ
PRINTZZZZ
PRINTZZZZ
PRINTZZZZ
CAN I GO HOME NOW?
JASON, I MEANT WRITE IT BY **HAND**.
AMEND

September 18, 1994

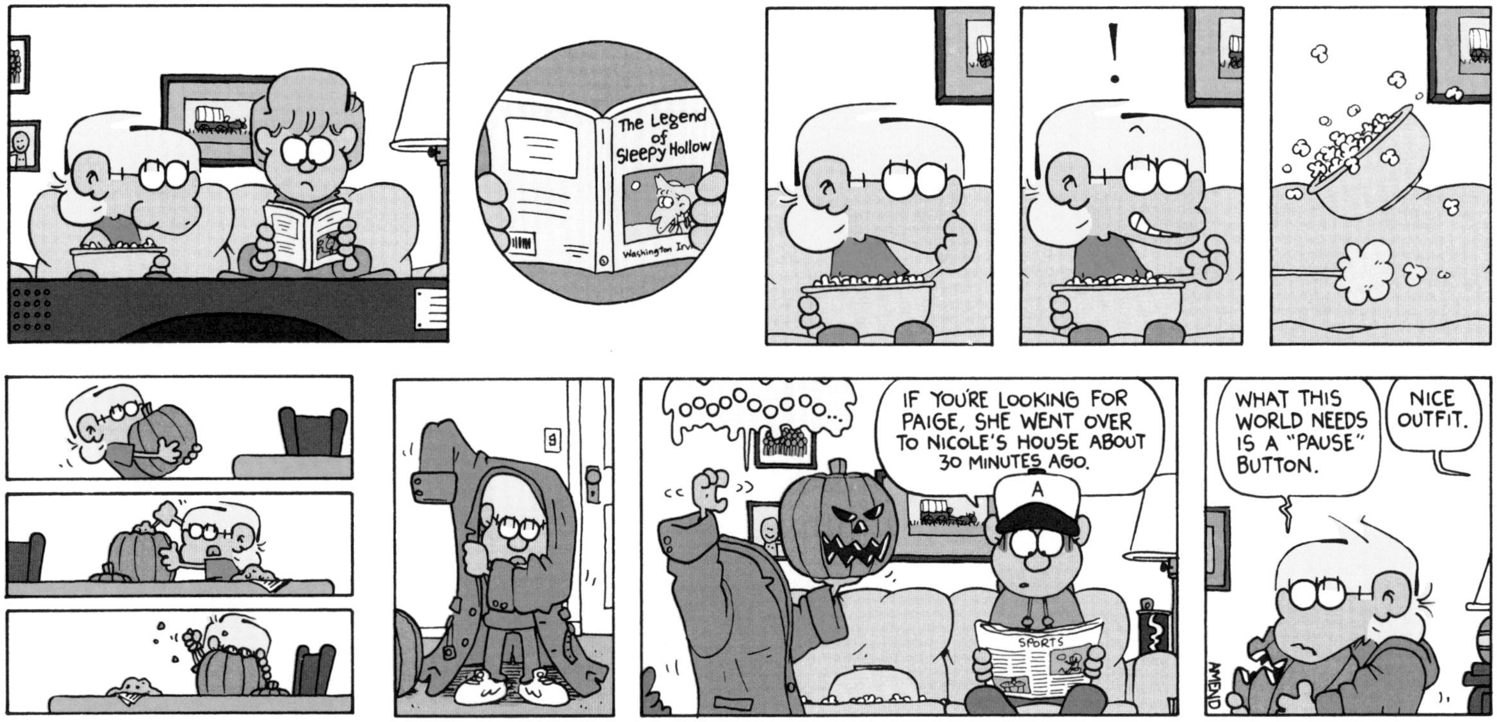
The Legend of Sleepy Hollow
!
oooooooooo...
IF YOU'RE LOOKING FOR PAIGE, SHE WENT OVER TO NICOLE'S HOUSE ABOUT 30 MINUTES AGO.
SPORTS
WHAT THIS WORLD NEEDS IS A "PAUSE" BUTTON.
NICE OUTFIT.
AMEND

October 30, 1994

November 6, 1994

I'm usually lousy at caricatures, but I thought these *Star Trek* dolls turned out pretty well.

December 4, 1994

I hated that *The Far Side*® was ending, but I loved that it gave me an excuse to do these. I also hate that my publisher is making me put a ® in that last sentence.

October 17, 1994

October 18, 1994

October 19, 1994

October 20, 1994

October 21, 1994

October 22, 1994

October 24, 1994

October 27, 1994

October 28, 1994

MOM, IS IT OK IF I STAY OVER AT NICOLE'S?

PAIGE, NO.

YOU HAVEN'T FINISHED YOUR HOMEWORK... YOUR ROOM IS A MESS... YOU PROMISED YOU'D HELP ME WITH DINNER...

BESIDES, TONIGHT IS A SCHOOL NIGHT.

ACTUALLY, I MEANT FOR THE WEEK.

THE WEEK??

GUESS WHAT MOVIE OPENS IN 5,526 MINUTES.

November 14, 1994

THAT'S ONE DOG-EARRED MAGAZINE.

IT'S THE CINEMAFANGIQUE "STAR TREK: GENERATIONS" PREVIEW ISSUE. I READ IT EVERY DAY AFTER SCHOOL.

IT'S GOT ALL THESE AMAZING BEHIND-THE-SCENES PHOTOS! HERE'S BRENT "DATA" SPINER GETTING HIS HAIR COMBED... HERE'S WORF SITTING IN BEVERLY CRUSHER'S DIRECTOR'S CHAIR... HERE'S PATRICK STEWART EATING A BAGEL BETWEEN SHOTS... I THINK IT'S POPPYSEED.

ISN'T THIS JUST THE COOLEST STUFF YOU'VE EVER SEEN IN YOUR LIFE, DAD?! ISN'T IT?! ISN'T IT?! ISN'T IT?!

I BELIEVE WHAT WE HAVE HERE IS A "STAR TREK: GENERATIONS" GAP.

HERE'S WILLIAM SHATNER TYING HIS SHOES...

November 15, 1994

PETER! PETER! I DID IT!

I MEMORIZED THE ENTIRE KLINGON DICTIONARY! 191 PAGES AND I KNOW IT ALL! I'M GONNA BE THE BEST KLINGON IN THE THEATER FRIDAY, I KNOW IT!

ASK ME SOMETHING! ANYTHING! I KNOW ALL 1,400 WORDS!

WHY??

"QATLH." C'MON— GIMME SOMETHING HARD...

November 16, 1994

I had to run out and buy *The Klingon Dictionary* just for this strip.

173

November 17, 1994

November 18, 1994

November 19, 1994

Discovering *The X-Files* that first season was pure nerdy bliss.

January 6, 1995

January 26, 1995

January 27, 1995

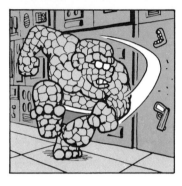

"Researching" this strip at the comic book store was the best part.

April 2, 1995

April 30, 1995

176

RUNNING SHOES...

OVERCOAT...

IGUANA.

MOTH-ERRR!

HOW TO REALLY DRESS FOR SUCCESS.

January 30, 1995

GREETINGS. I AM IGUANOMAN.

JASON, YOU ARE SO WEIRD.

I COME FROM A GALAXY FAR, FAR AWAY, BUT I SEEM TO HAVE MADE A WRONG TURN SOMEWHERE.

COULD YOU POSSIBLY DIRECT ME TO THE PLANET EARTH?

THIS IS EARTH, YOU GEEK!

RIGHT. AND I SUPPOSE YOU'RE GOING TO TELL ME YOU'RE HUMAN.

ACTUALLY, I'M ON THE VERGE OF GOING APE.

January 31, 1995

GREETINGS, EARTHLING. WHAT'S FOR DINNER?

ZITI NEFERTITI.

WHAT'S THAT?

OH, JUST A LITTLE SOMETHING I MADE UP. IT'S PASTA TUBES STUFFED WITH MASHED EGGPLANT AND GREEN OLIVES.

I WAS AFRAID OF THIS. MY DIGESTIVE TRACT IS INCOMPATIBLE WITH YOUR HUMANOID DIET. I WILL REQUIRE ALTERNATIVE SUSTENANCE.

SUCH AS?

I BELIEVE YOU EARTHLINGS CALL THEM "HO HO'S."

JASON, MUST WE GO THROUGH THIS EVERY OTHER DAY?

February 1, 1995

February 2, 1995

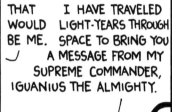

February 3, 1995

February 4, 1995

February 13, 1995

February 14, 1995

I have no idea what his pendant thing is. I think I imagined it was a bag of dirt from some famous outdoor theater.

February 15, 1995

February 16, 1995

February 17, 1995

February 18, 1995

February 20, 1995

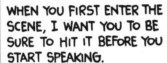
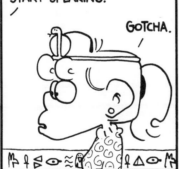

February 21, 1995

February 22, 1995

181

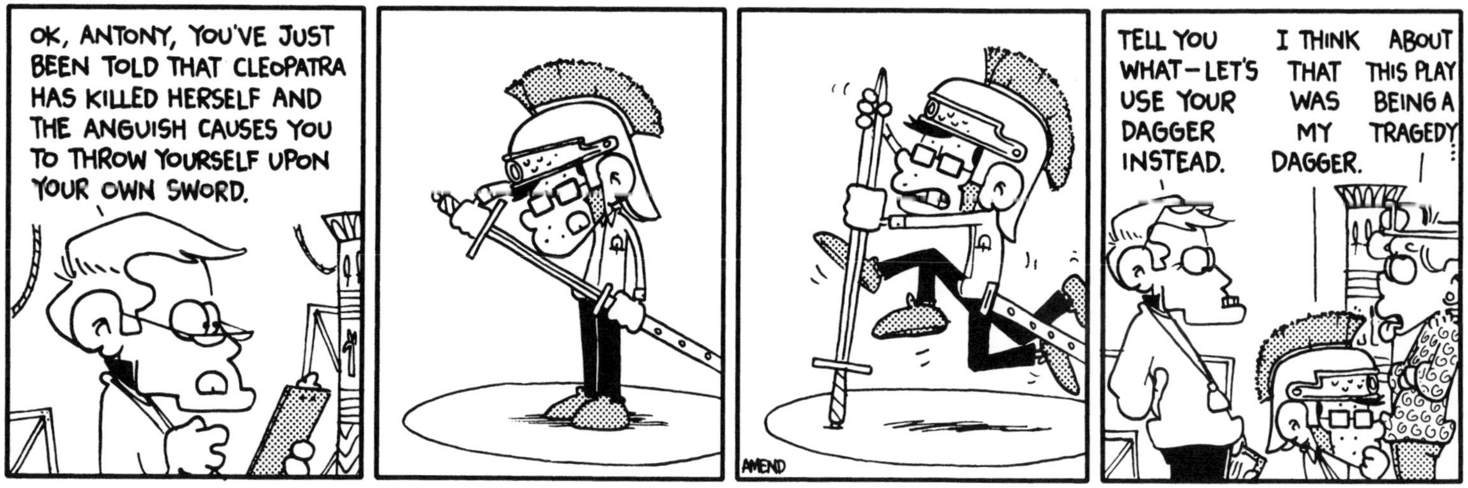
OK, ANTONY, YOU'VE JUST BEEN TOLD THAT CLEOPATRA HAS KILLED HERSELF AND THE ANGUISH CAUSES YOU TO THROW YOURSELF UPON YOUR OWN SWORD.
TELL YOU WHAT–LET'S USE YOUR DAGGER INSTEAD.
I THINK THAT WAS MY DAGGER.
ABOUT THIS PLAY BEING A TRAGEDY...

February 23, 1995

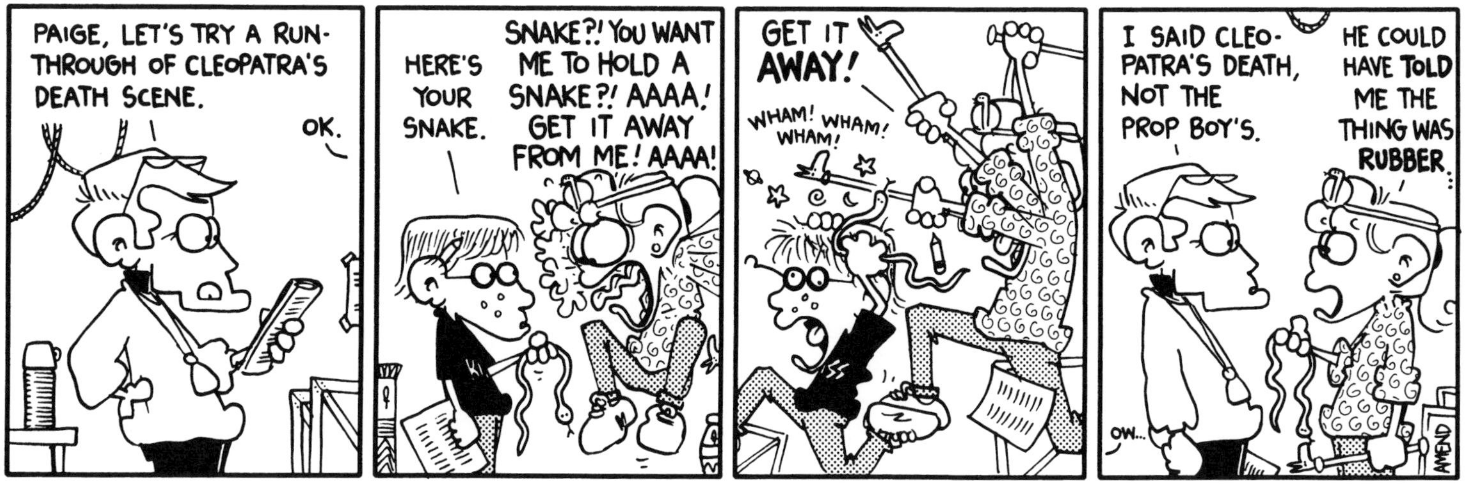
PAIGE, LET'S TRY A RUN-THROUGH OF CLEOPATRA'S DEATH SCENE.
OK.
HERE'S YOUR SNAKE.
SNAKE?! YOU WANT ME TO HOLD A SNAKE?! AAAA! GET IT AWAY FROM ME! AAAA!
GET IT AWAY!
WHAM! WHAM! WHAM!
I SAID CLEO-PATRA'S DEATH, NOT THE PROP BOY'S.
HE COULD HAVE TOLD ME THE THING WAS RUBBER.
OW...

February 24, 1995

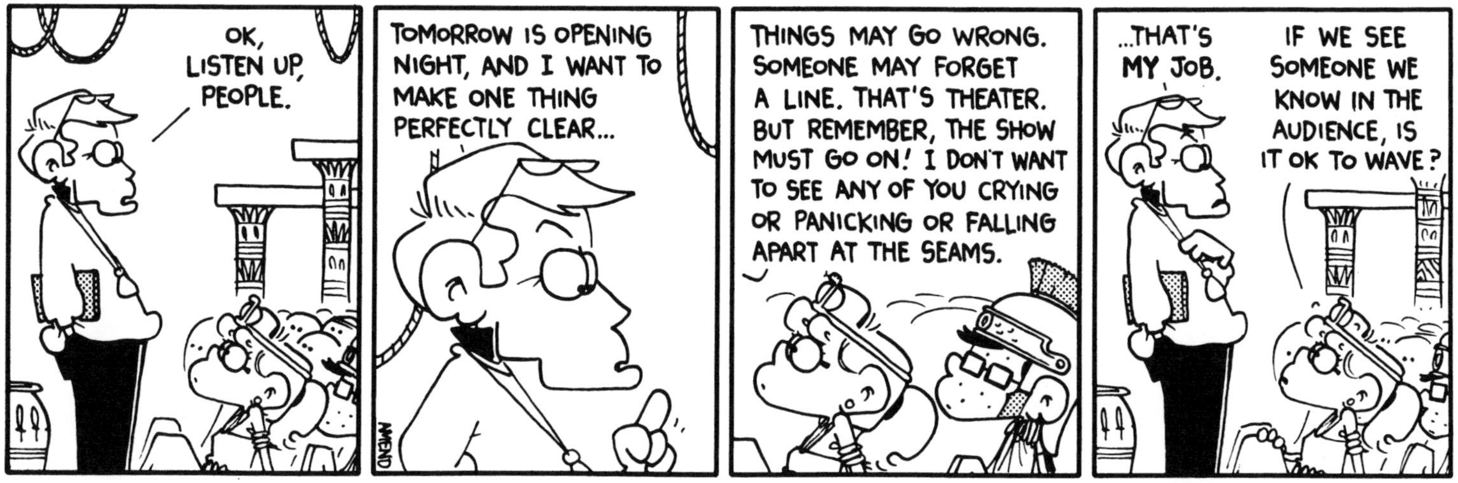
OK, LISTEN UP, PEOPLE.
TOMORROW IS OPENING NIGHT, AND I WANT TO MAKE ONE THING PERFECTLY CLEAR...
THINGS MAY GO WRONG. SOMEONE MAY FORGET A LINE. THAT'S THEATER. BUT REMEMBER, THE SHOW MUST GO ON! I DON'T WANT TO SEE ANY OF YOU CRYING OR PANICKING OR FALLING APART AT THE SEAMS.
...THAT'S MY JOB.
IF WE SEE SOMEONE WE KNOW IN THE AUDIENCE, IS IT OK TO WAVE?

February 25, 1995

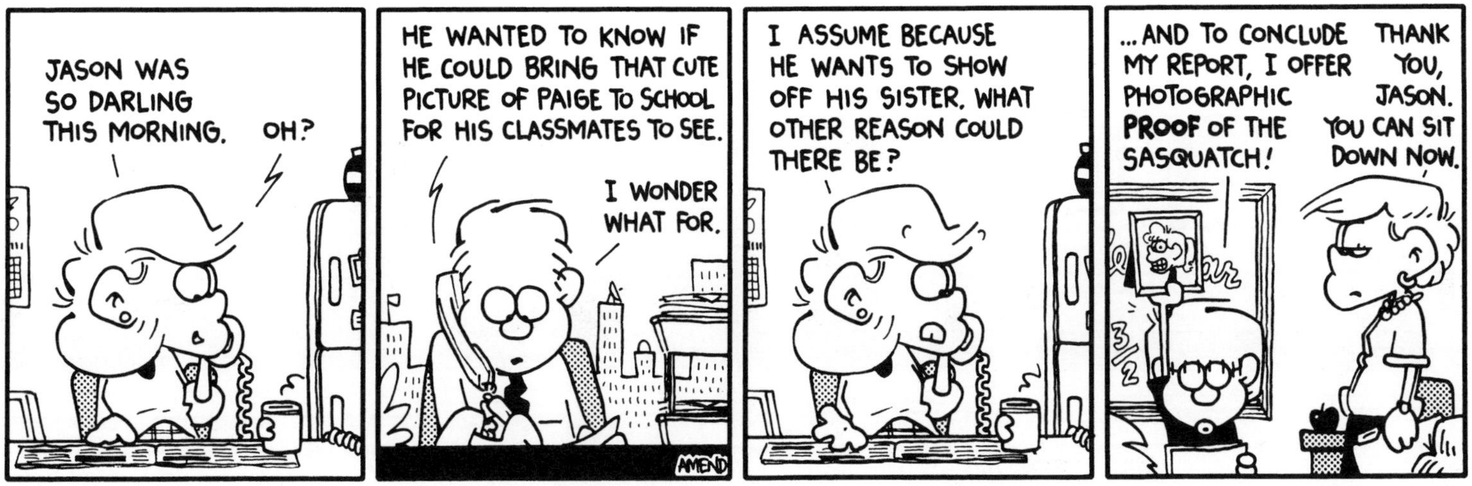
JASON WAS SO DARLING THIS MORNING.
OH?
HE WANTED TO KNOW IF HE COULD BRING THAT CUTE PICTURE OF PAIGE TO SCHOOL FOR HIS CLASSMATES TO SEE.
I WONDER WHAT FOR.
I ASSUME BECAUSE HE WANTS TO SHOW OFF HIS SISTER. WHAT OTHER REASON COULD THERE BE?
...AND TO CONCLUDE MY REPORT, I OFFER PHOTOGRAPHIC **PROOF** OF THE SASQUATCH!
THANK YOU, JASON. YOU CAN SIT DOWN NOW.
AMEND

February 8, 1995

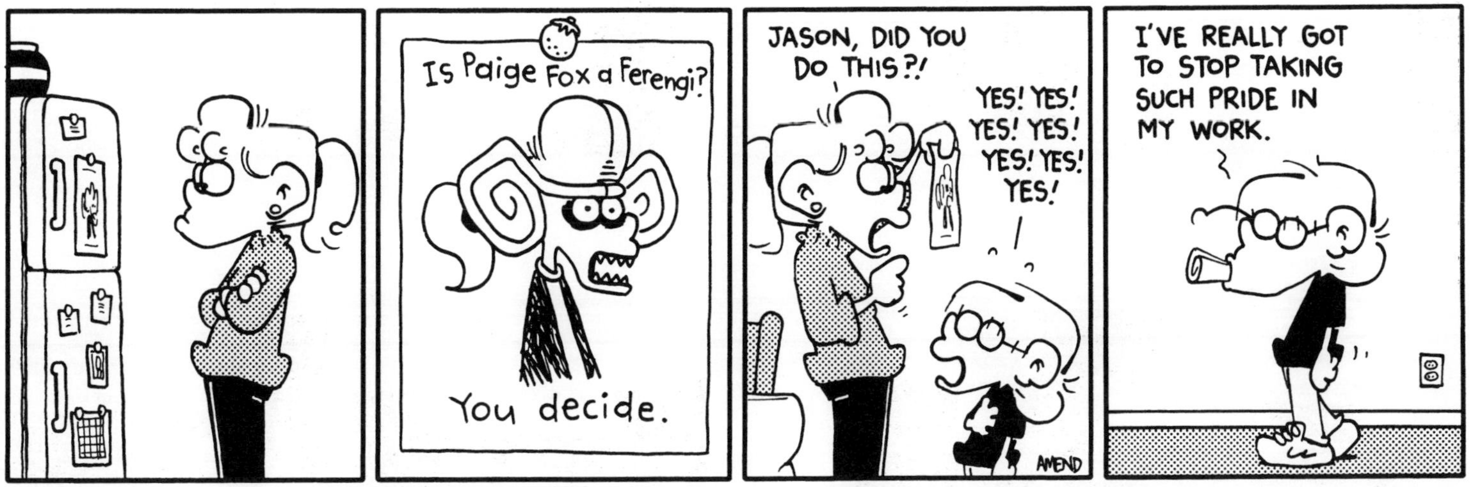
Is Paige Fox a Ferengi?
You decide.
JASON, DID YOU DO THIS?!
YES! YES! YES! YES! YES! YES! YES!
AMEND
I'VE REALLY GOT TO STOP TAKING SUCH PRIDE IN MY WORK.

March 21, 1995

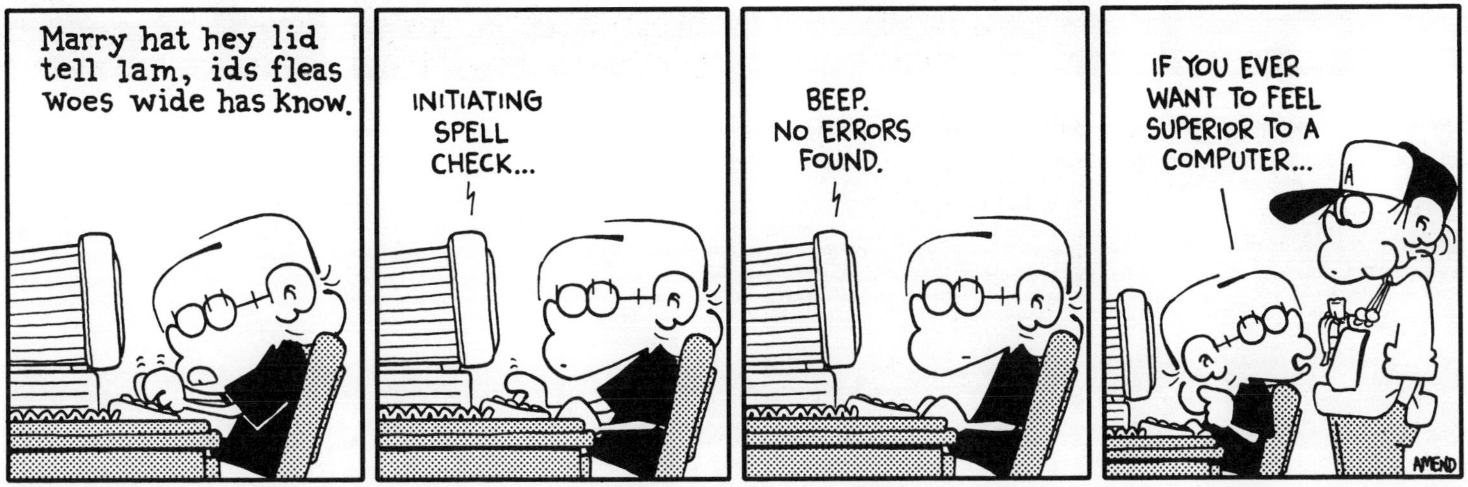
Marry hat hey lid tell lam, ids fleas woes wide has know.
INITIATING SPELL CHECK...
BEEP. NO ERRORS FOUND.
IF YOU EVER WANT TO FEEL SUPERIOR TO A COMPUTER...
AMEND

May 22, 1995

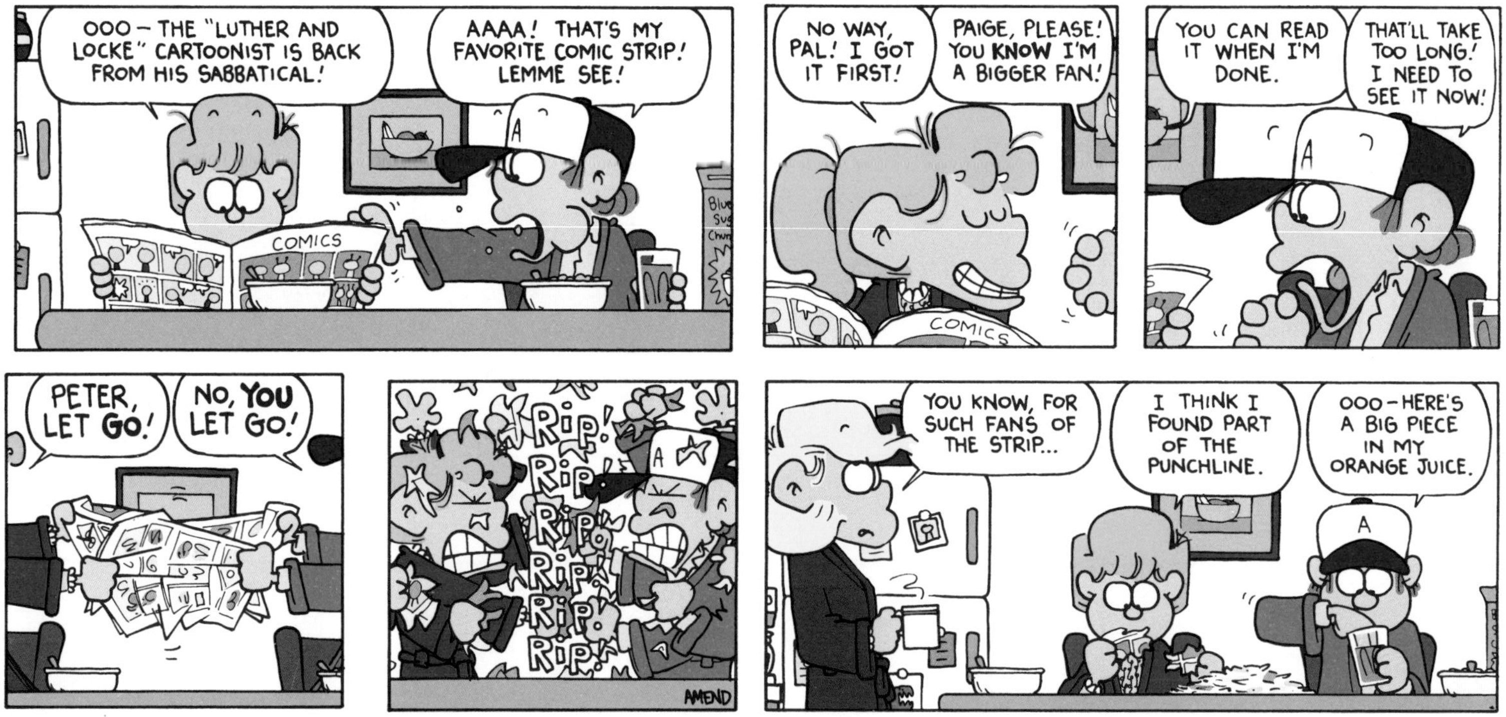
OOO – THE "LUTHER AND LOCKE" CARTOONIST IS BACK FROM HIS SABBATICAL!
AAAA! THAT'S MY FAVORITE COMIC STRIP! LEMME SEE!
COMICS
NO WAY, PAL! I GOT IT FIRST!
PAIGE, PLEASE! YOU KNOW I'M A BIGGER FAN!
COMICS
YOU CAN READ IT WHEN I'M DONE.
THAT'LL TAKE TOO LONG! I NEED TO SEE IT NOW!
PETER, LET GO!
NO, YOU LET GO!
RIP! RIP! RIP! RIP! RIP! RIP!
AMEND
YOU KNOW, FOR SUCH FANS OF THE STRIP...
I THINK I FOUND PART OF THE PUNCHLINE.
OOO – HERE'S A BIG PIECE IN MY ORANGE JUICE.

January 1, 1995

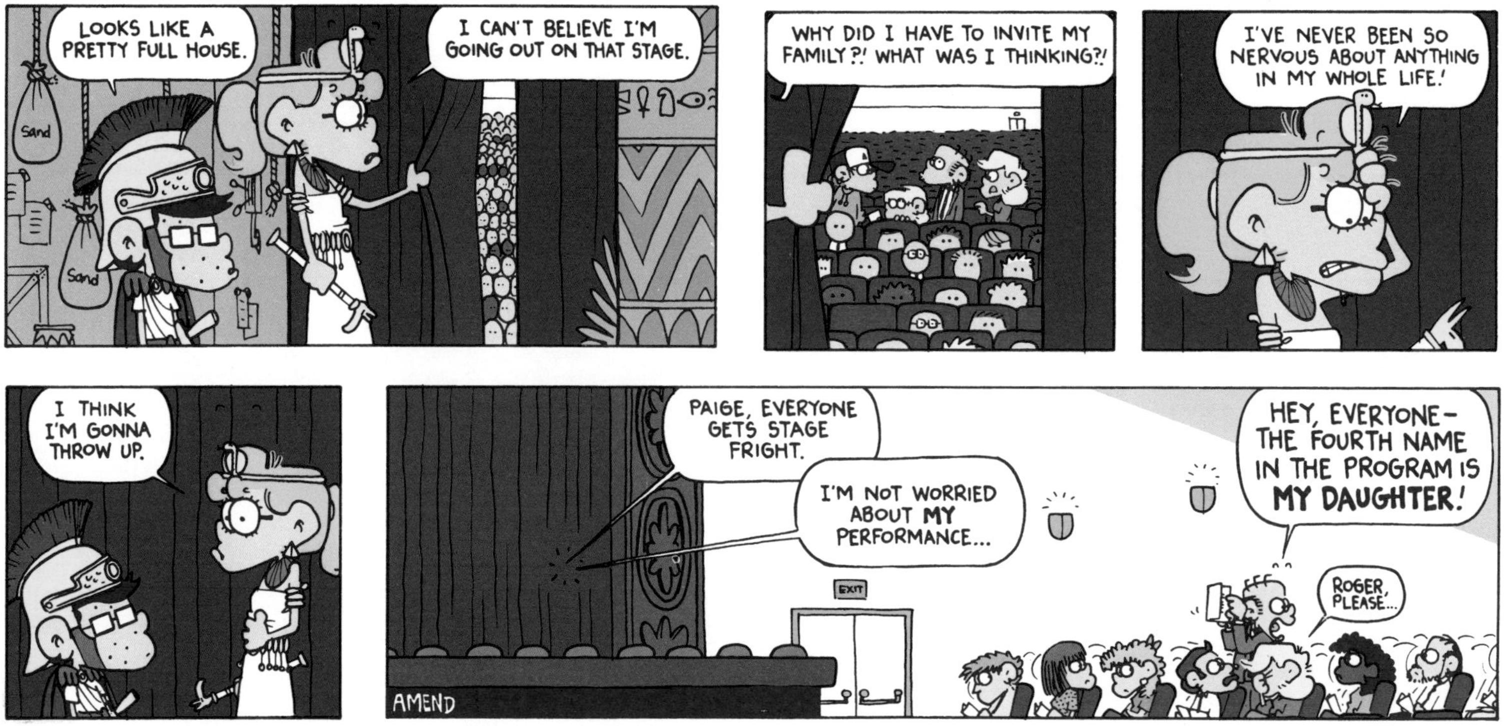
LOOKS LIKE A PRETTY FULL HOUSE.
I CAN'T BELIEVE I'M GOING OUT ON THAT STAGE.
Sand
Sand
WHY DID I HAVE TO INVITE MY FAMILY?! WHAT WAS I THINKING?!
I'VE NEVER BEEN SO NERVOUS ABOUT ANYTHING IN MY WHOLE LIFE!
I THINK I'M GONNA THROW UP.
PAIGE, EVERYONE GETS STAGE FRIGHT.
I'M NOT WORRIED ABOUT MY PERFORMANCE...
EXIT
HEY, EVERYONE – THE FOURTH NAME IN THE PROGRAM IS MY DAUGHTER!
ROGER, PLEASE...
AMEND

February 26, 1995

May 23, 1995

I've been known to try to re-create this sandwich in real life.

June 19, 1995

November 29, 1995

185

My daughter was about ten months old at this point, so I figured I'd work in some baby jokes.

PAIGE, DO YOU REMEMBER MARGARET O'DELL FROM MY BOOK CLUB?

THE WEIRD, PREGNANT LADY?

WELL, SHE'S NO LONGER PREGNANT. SHE WANTED TO KNOW IF YOU COULD BABY-SIT FOR HER TOMORROW NIGHT.

HOW OLD'S THE KID?

HER DAUGHTER'S NINE MONTHS. SHE ALSO WANTED TO KNOW HOW MUCH YOU CHARGE.

LET'S SEE... NINE MONTHS IS 15 MONTHS UNDER TWO YEARS, INVERT THAT, ADD ONE AND MULTIPLY BY THE BASE RATE.

YOU KNOW, FOR SOMEONE WHO CLAIMS A "B-" IS THE BEST SHE CAN DO IN MATH...

...DIVIDE BY THE GIRL COEFFICIENT OF 1.05, ADD 50 CENTS FOR SHORT NOTICE, ROUND TO TWO DECIMAL PLACES...

June 26, 1995

HI, THERE! YOU MUST BE LITTLE KATHERINE!

UM, IT'S "KATHERINE." WITH A "K."

THAT'S WHAT I SAID.

NO, YOU SAID "CATHERINE" WITH A "C." I COULD TELL.

HOLD ON — I'LL BE RIGHT BACK.

HI, THERE! YOU MUST BE THE LITTLE GIRL WHO'S GOING TO NEED MASSIVE THERAPY IN 12 YEARS!

OK, THE VIDEO CAMERA I HID IN THIS DOLL SHOULD PROVE I'M RIGHT...

June 27, 1995

OK, PAIGE, HERE ARE MY GROUND RULES...

IF THERE'S AN ACCIDENT, I WANT YOU TO CALL ME. IF SHE EATS SOMETHING SHE SHOULDN'T, I WANT YOU TO CALL ME. IF SHE CRIES FOR MORE THAN A MINUTE, I WANT YOU TO CALL ME. IF SHE SNEEZES, I WANT YOU TO CALL ME. IF SHE WETS HER DIAPER, I WANT YOU TO CALL ME. IF SHE **DOESN'T** WET HER DIAPER, I WANT YOU TO CALL ME.

THE REST ARE ON THIS LIST.

OOPS! I ALMOST FORGOT— HERE'S THE NUMBER WHERE I'LL BE.

DANG.

186

June 28, 1995

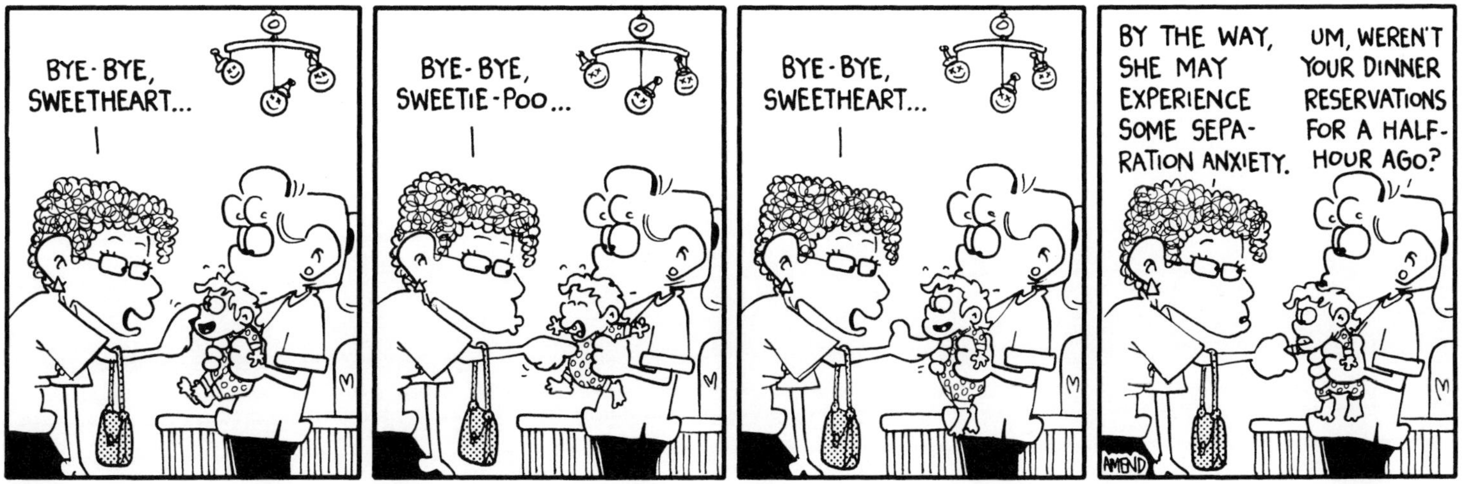
BYE-BYE, SWEETHEART...
BYE-BYE, SWEETIE-POO...
BYE-BYE, SWEETHEART...
BY THE WAY, SHE MAY EXPERIENCE SOME SEPA-RATION ANXIETY.
UM, WEREN'T YOUR DINNER RESERVATIONS FOR A HALF-HOUR AGO?
AMEND

June 29, 1995

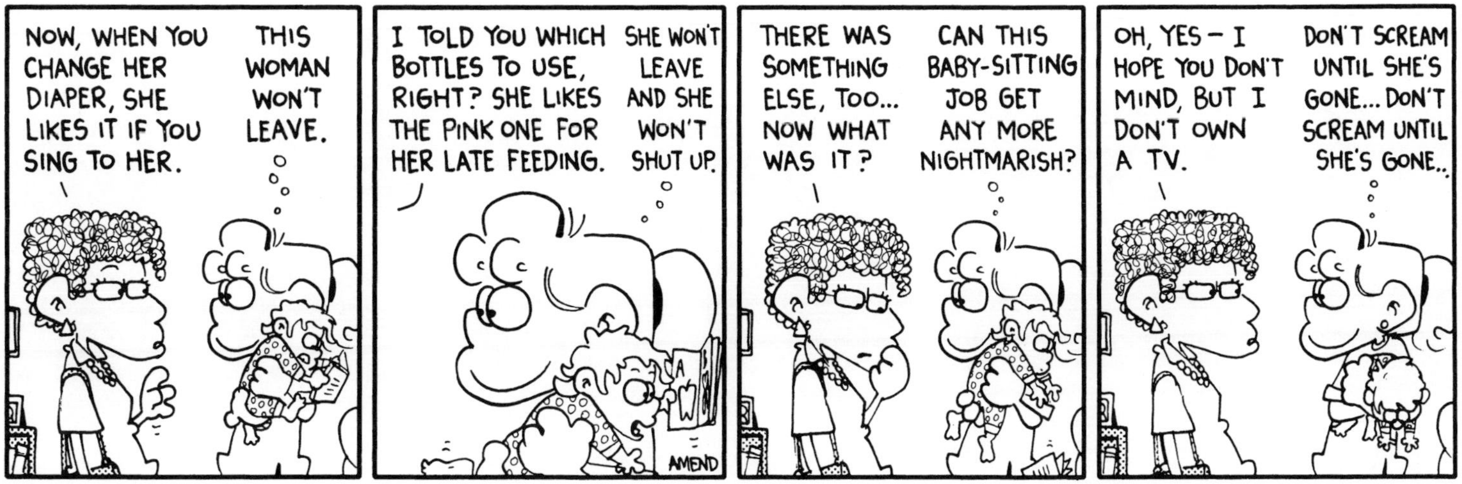
NOW, WHEN YOU CHANGE HER DIAPER, SHE LIKES IT IF YOU SING TO HER.
THIS WOMAN WON'T LEAVE.
I TOLD YOU WHICH BOTTLES TO USE, RIGHT? SHE LIKES THE PINK ONE FOR HER LATE FEEDING.
SHE WON'T LEAVE AND SHE WON'T SHUT UP.
AMEND
THERE WAS SOMETHING ELSE, TOO... NOW WHAT WAS IT?
CAN THIS BABY-SITTING JOB GET ANY MORE NIGHTMARISH?
OH, YES – I HOPE YOU DON'T MIND, BUT I DON'T OWN A TV.
DON'T SCREAM UNTIL SHE'S GONE... DON'T SCREAM UNTIL SHE'S GONE...

June 30, 1995

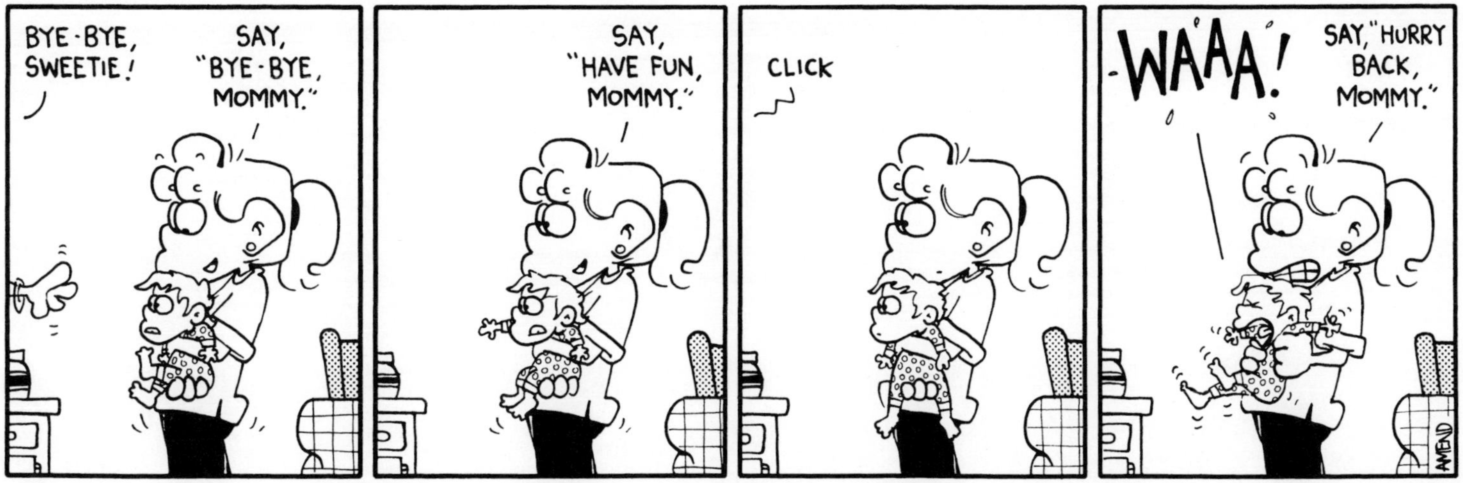
BYE-BYE, SWEETIE!
SAY, "BYE-BYE, MOMMY."
SAY, "HAVE FUN, MOMMY."
CLICK
WAAA!
SAY, "HURRY BACK, MOMMY."
AMEND

July 1, 1995

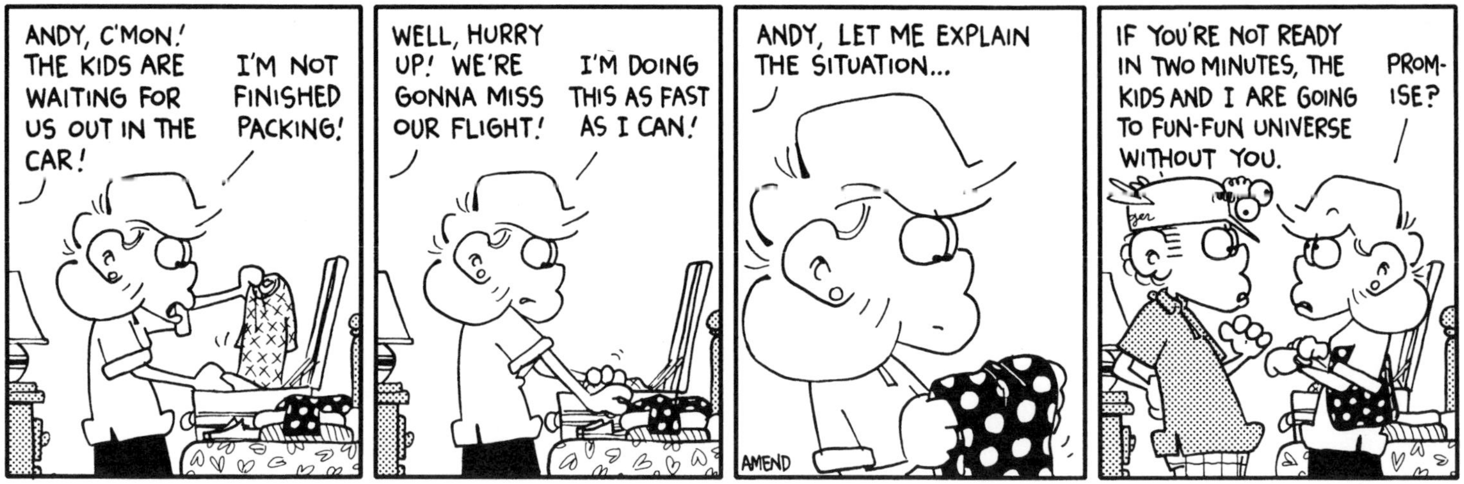
ANDY, C'MON! THE KIDS ARE WAITING FOR US OUT IN THE CAR!
I'M NOT FINISHED PACKING!
WELL, HURRY UP! WE'RE GONNA MISS OUR FLIGHT!
I'M DOING THIS AS FAST AS I CAN!
ANDY, LET ME EXPLAIN THE SITUATION...
AMEND
IF YOU'RE NOT READY IN TWO MINUTES, THE KIDS AND I ARE GOING TO FUN-FUN UNIVERSE WITHOUT YOU.
PROMISE?

August 21, 1995

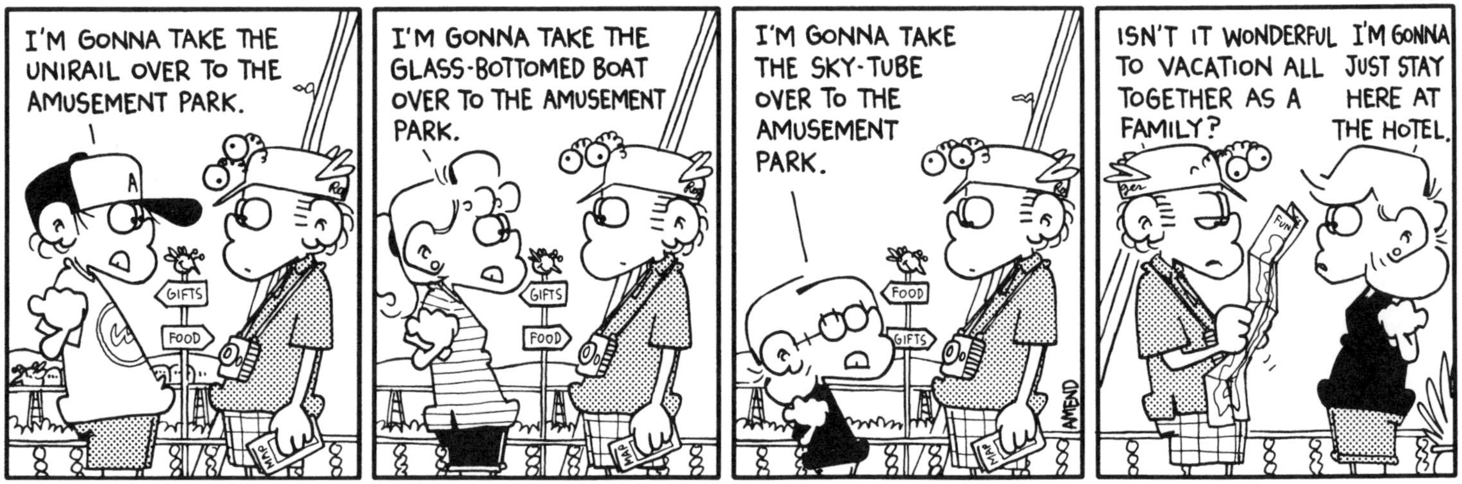
I'M GONNA TAKE THE UNIRAIL OVER TO THE AMUSEMENT PARK.
GIFTS
FOOD
I'M GONNA TAKE THE GLASS-BOTTOMED BOAT OVER TO THE AMUSEMENT PARK.
GIFTS
FOOD
I'M GONNA TAKE THE SKY-TUBE OVER TO THE AMUSEMENT PARK.
FOOD
GIFTS
AMEND
ISN'T IT WONDERFUL TO VACATION ALL TOGETHER AS A FAMILY?
I'M GONNA JUST STAY HERE AT THE HOTEL.

August 26, 1995

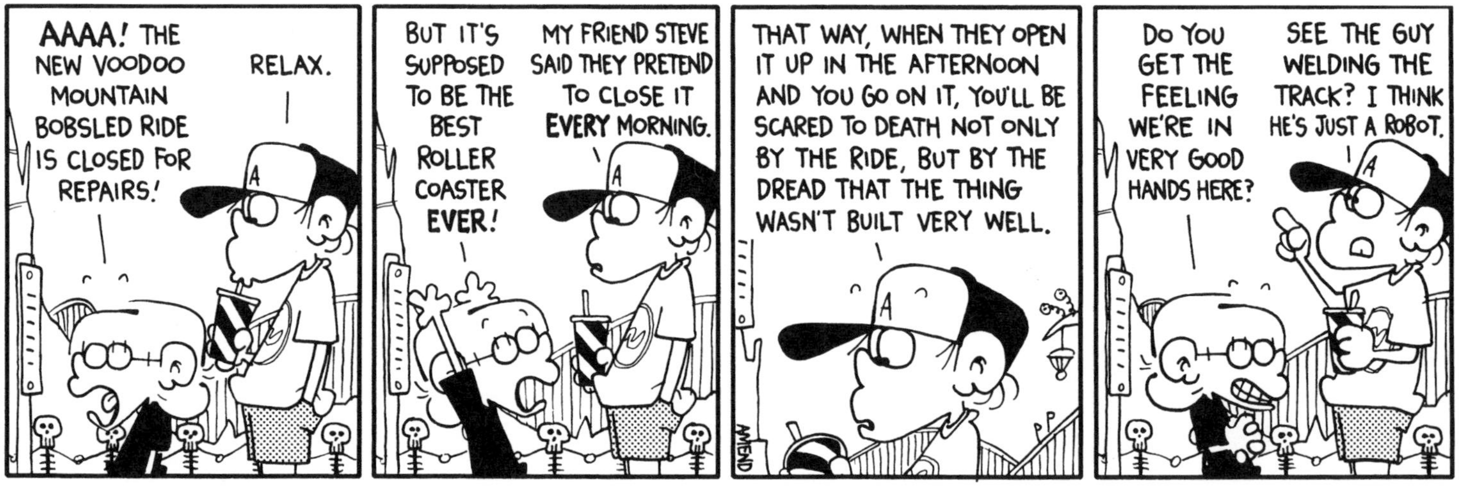
AAAA! THE NEW VOODOO MOUNTAIN BOBSLED RIDE IS CLOSED FOR REPAIRS!
RELAX.
BUT IT'S SUPPOSED TO BE THE BEST ROLLER COASTER EVER!
MY FRIEND STEVE SAID THEY PRETEND TO CLOSE IT EVERY MORNING.
THAT WAY, WHEN THEY OPEN IT UP IN THE AFTERNOON AND YOU GO ON IT, YOU'LL BE SCARED TO DEATH NOT ONLY BY THE RIDE, BUT BY THE DREAD THAT THE THING WASN'T BUILT VERY WELL.
AMEND
DO YOU GET THE FEELING WE'RE IN VERY GOOD HANDS HERE?
SEE THE GUY WELDING THE TRACK? I THINK HE'S JUST A ROBOT.

August 28, 1995

August 30, 1995

August 31, 1995

Sometimes I think I don't exaggerate enough.

September 2, 1995

September 5, 1995

September 6, 1995

 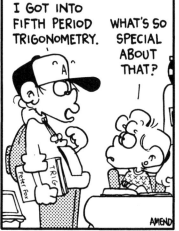  

September 7, 1995

September 24, 1995

I'm pretty sure *MythBusters* debunked this. Oh well.

October 1, 1995

October 2, 1995

October 3, 1995

October 4, 1995

October 5, 1995

I decided it was time to give Jason a rival. Enter Eileen Jacobson.

October 6, 1995

October 7, 1995

October 9, 1995

October 12, 1995

194

October 16, 1995

October 17, 1995

October 19, 1995

October 21, 1995

December 1, 1995

December 2, 1995

January 3, 1996

October 29, 1995

I doubt Jason would be *worse* than some TV executives.

February 18, 1996

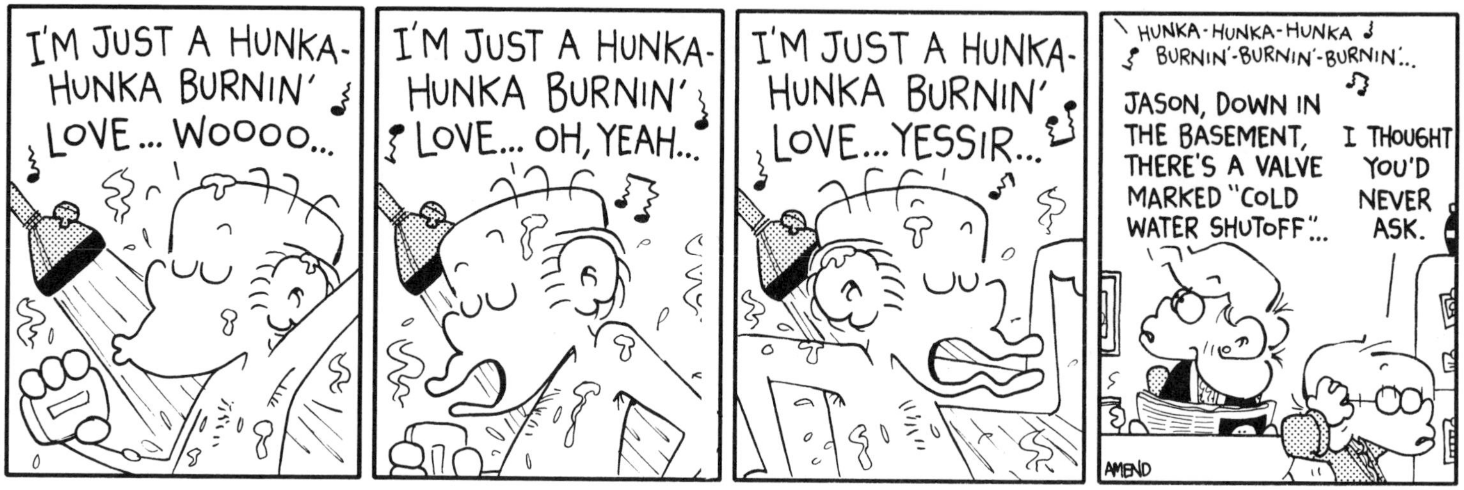

I'M JUST A HUNKA-HUNKA BURNIN' LOVE... WOOOO...
I'M JUST A HUNKA-HUNKA BURNIN' LOVE... OH, YEAH...
I'M JUST A HUNKA-HUNKA BURNIN' LOVE... YESSIR...
HUNKA-HUNKA-HUNKA BURNIN'-BURNIN'-BURNIN'...
JASON, DOWN IN THE BASEMENT, THERE'S A VALVE MARKED "COLD WATER SHUTOFF"...
I THOUGHT YOU'D NEVER ASK.
AMEND

January 12, 1996

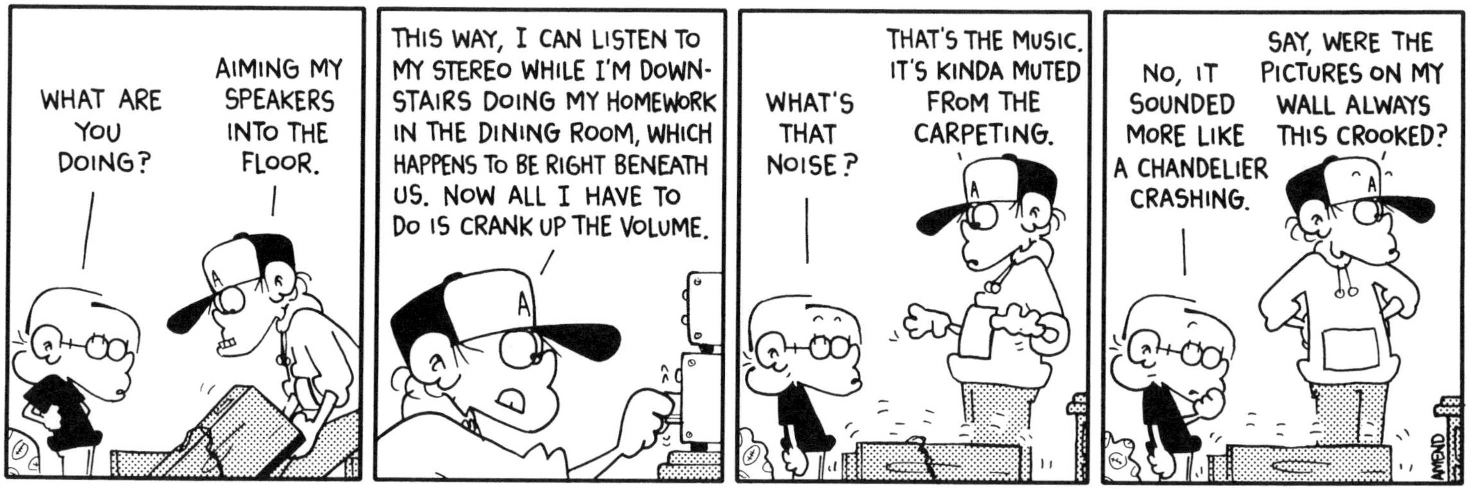

WHAT ARE YOU DOING?
AIMING MY SPEAKERS INTO THE FLOOR.
THIS WAY, I CAN LISTEN TO MY STEREO WHILE I'M DOWNSTAIRS DOING MY HOMEWORK IN THE DINING ROOM, WHICH HAPPENS TO BE RIGHT BENEATH US. NOW ALL I HAVE TO DO IS CRANK UP THE VOLUME.
WHAT'S THAT NOISE?
THAT'S THE MUSIC. IT'S KINDA MUTED FROM THE CARPETING.
NO, IT SOUNDED MORE LIKE A CHANDELIER CRASHING.
SAY, WERE THE PICTURES ON MY WALL ALWAYS THIS CROOKED?
AMEND

January 17, 1996

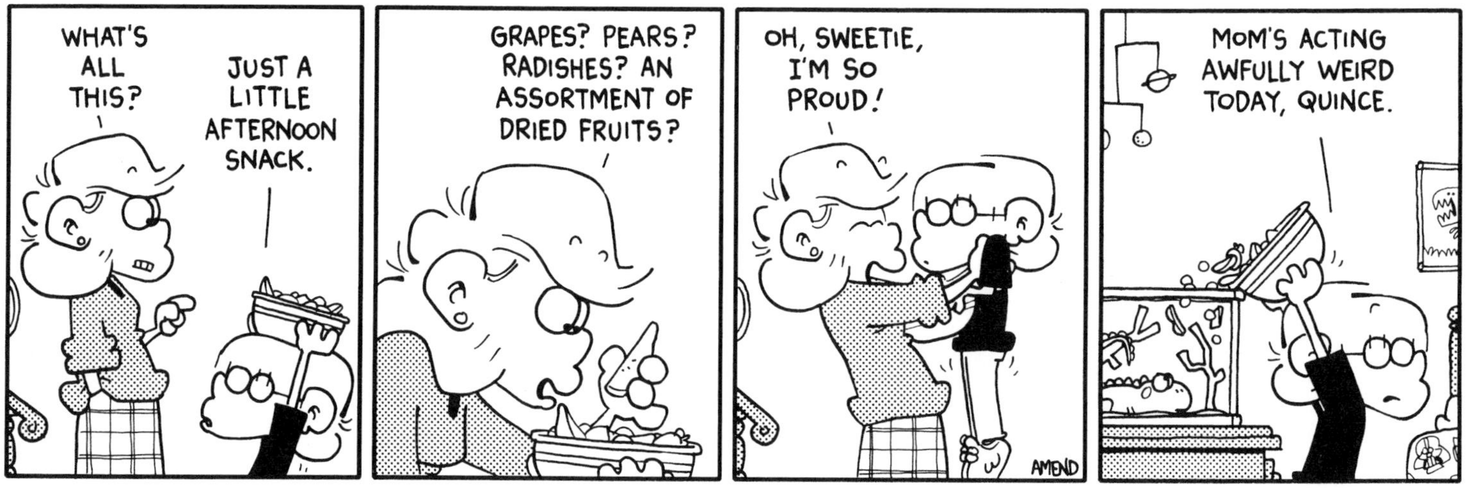

WHAT'S ALL THIS?
JUST A LITTLE AFTERNOON SNACK.
GRAPES? PEARS? RADISHES? AN ASSORTMENT OF DRIED FRUITS?
OH, SWEETIE, I'M SO PROUD!
AMEND
MOM'S ACTING AWFULLY WEIRD TODAY, QUINCE.

January 18, 1996

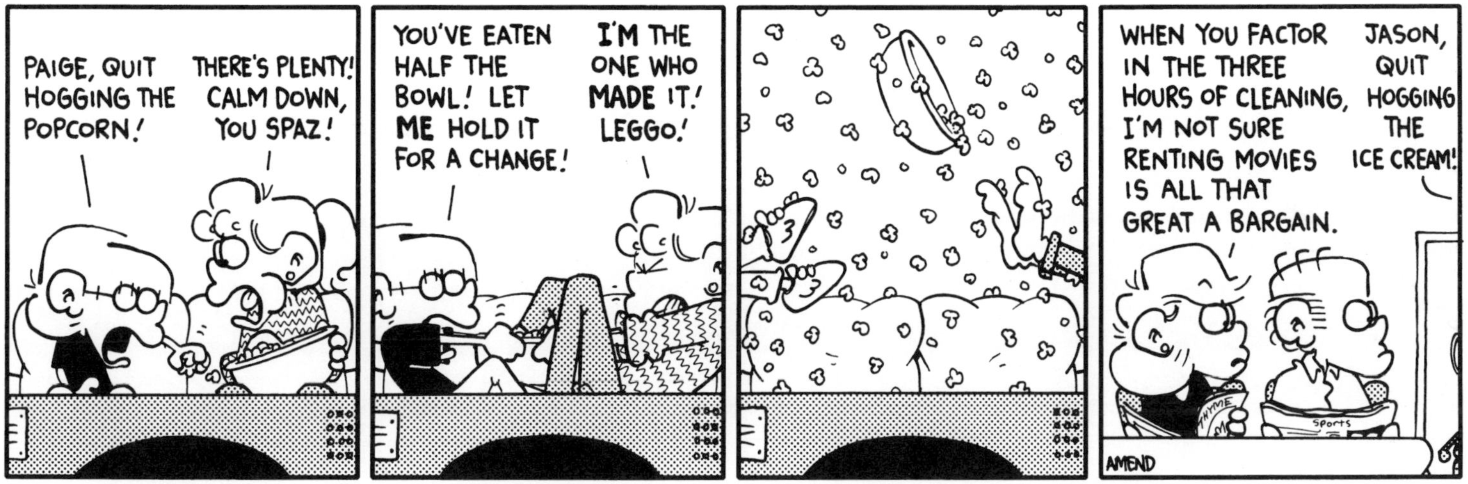
PAIGE, QUIT HOGGING THE POPCORN!
THERE'S PLENTY! CALM DOWN, YOU SPAZ!
YOU'VE EATEN HALF THE BOWL! LET ME HOLD IT FOR A CHANGE!
I'M THE ONE WHO MADE IT! LEGGO!
WHEN YOU FACTOR IN THE THREE HOURS OF CLEANING, I'M NOT SURE RENTING MOVIES IS ALL THAT GREAT A BARGAIN.
JASON, QUIT HOGGING THE ICE CREAM!
Sports
AMEND

February 16, 1996

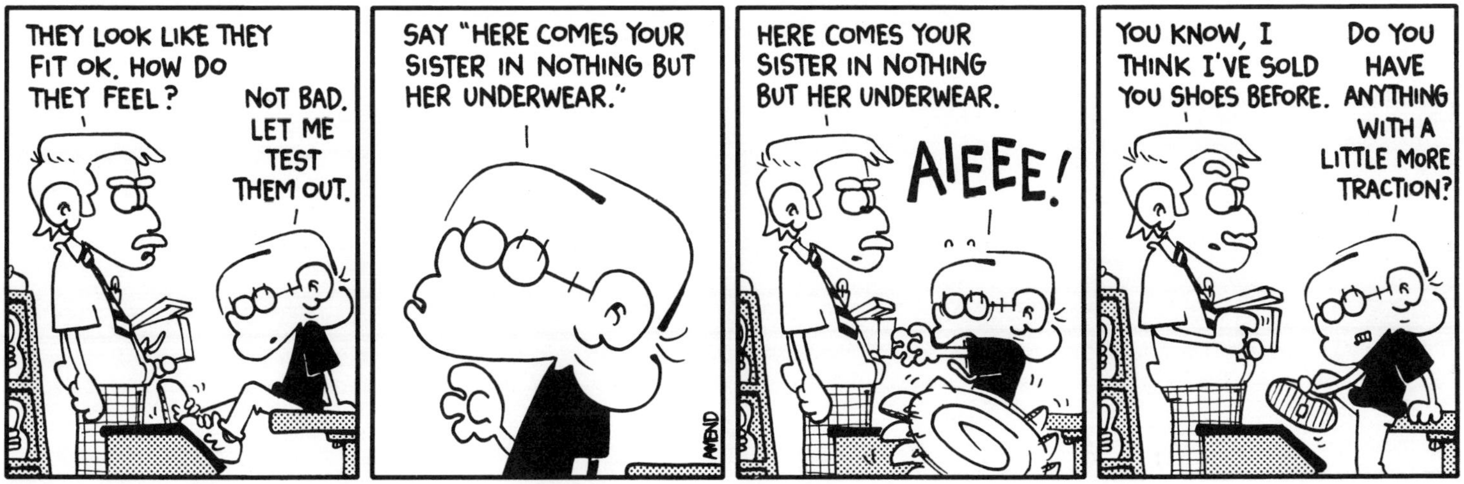
THEY LOOK LIKE THEY FIT OK. HOW DO THEY FEEL?
NOT BAD. LET ME TEST THEM OUT.
SAY "HERE COMES YOUR SISTER IN NOTHING BUT HER UNDERWEAR."
AMEND
HERE COMES YOUR SISTER IN NOTHING BUT HER UNDERWEAR.
AIEEE!
YOU KNOW, I THINK I'VE SOLD YOU SHOES BEFORE.
DO YOU HAVE ANYTHING WITH A LITTLE MORE TRACTION?

March 1, 1996

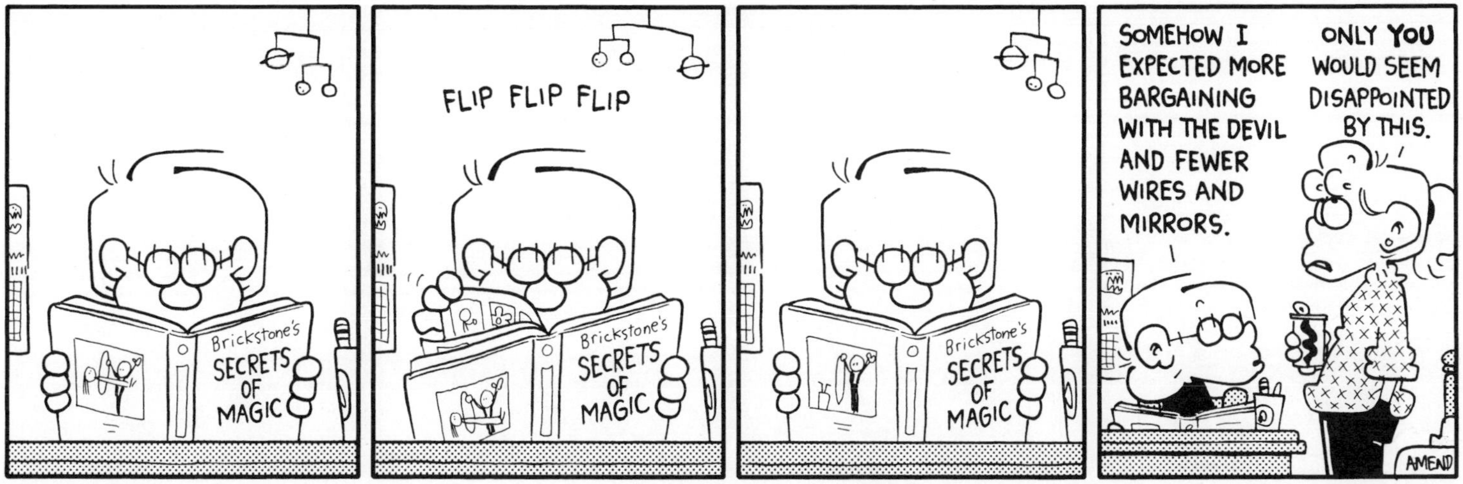
Brickstone's SECRETS OF MAGIC
FLIP FLIP FLIP
Brickstone's SECRETS OF MAGIC
Brickstone's SECRETS OF MAGIC
SOMEHOW I EXPECTED MORE BARGAINING WITH THE DEVIL AND FEWER WIRES AND MIRRORS.
ONLY YOU WOULD SEEM DISAPPOINTED BY THIS.
AMEND

April 25, 1996

Sometimes, I come up with characters that make me question my sanity.

Panel 1:
I **REALLY** DO NOT WANT TO GO TO WORK THIS WEEK.
WHY'S THAT?

Panel 2:
PEMBROOK'S BRINGING IN SOME EFFICIENCY CONSULTANT TO TRY TO SQUEEZE EVEN MORE SAVINGS OUT OF MY DEPARTMENT. IT'S GOING TO BE A NIGHTMARE, I CAN TELL.
HAVE YOU MET THIS PERSON?

Panel 3:
FRED DID. HE SAID SHE WAS SOME SORT OF BIGWIG.
WELL, THAT'S EXCITING. AT LEAST YOU KNOW SHE'LL HAVE SOME GOOD IDEAS.

Panel 4:
NO, NO, I SAID SHE WEARS A BIG WIG.
GREAT.
MEDIUM-TIP PENS?! DO YOU THINK INK GROWS ON TREES?!

January 29, 1996

Panel 1:
MR. FOX, YOUR SUPERIORS BROUGHT ME IN THIS WEEK TO HELP INCREASE YOUR DEPARTMENT'S EFFICIENCY.

Panel 2:
BUDGETS ARE TIGHT, AND WASTE WILL NO LONGER BE TOLERATED.

Panel 3:
SO ENOUGH CHIT-CHAT. LET'S GET TO WORK.

Panel 4:
ITEM ONE: THIS PERFECTLY GOOD PAPER CLIP I FOUND IN YOUR TRASH.
BARB, ANY CHANCE I'VE GOT A MEETING TO GO TO?

January 30, 1996

Panel 1:
MR. FOX, WHAT'S THIS?!
UM, A PENCIL?

Panel 2:
IT'S A Nº 2½ PENCIL, TO BE PRECISE. I FOUND IT ON YOUR DESK.
I LIKE Nº 2½ PENCILS. SO WHAT?

Panel 3:
MR. FOX, I'VE CHECKED AND NO ONE ELSE IN THIS DEPARTMENT USES Nº 2½ PENCILS. EFFICIENCY DEMANDS THAT ALL PENCILS IN THIS OFFICE BE THE SAME AND PURCHASED IN BULK. YOUR LITTLE PENCIL INDULGENCE IS UNNECESSARILY COSTING THIS COMPANY PENNIES EACH MONTH. **PENNIES!**

Panel 4:
LET'S PICK THIS UP LATER. YOUR BOSS IS TREATING ME TO LUNCH AT THE RITZ IN 10 MINUTES.
ABOUT YOUR "ONE PAPER CUP FOR THE WEEK" POLICY...

January 31, 1996

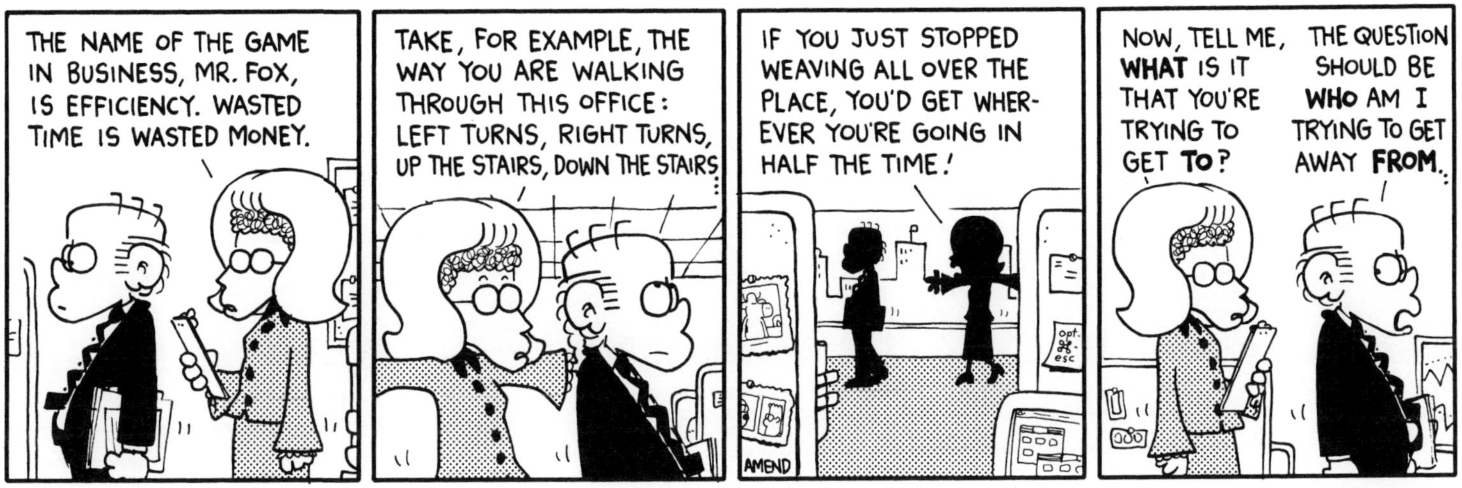
THE NAME OF THE GAME IN BUSINESS, MR. FOX, IS EFFICIENCY. WASTED TIME IS WASTED MONEY.
TAKE, FOR EXAMPLE, THE WAY YOU ARE WALKING THROUGH THIS OFFICE: LEFT TURNS, RIGHT TURNS, UP THE STAIRS, DOWN THE STAIRS
IF YOU JUST STOPPED WEAVING ALL OVER THE PLACE, YOU'D GET WHEREVER YOU'RE GOING IN HALF THE TIME!
opt. ⌘ esc
AMEND
NOW, TELL ME, WHAT IS IT THAT YOU'RE TRYING TO GET TO?
THE QUESTION SHOULD BE WHO AM I TRYING TO GET AWAY FROM.

February 1, 1996

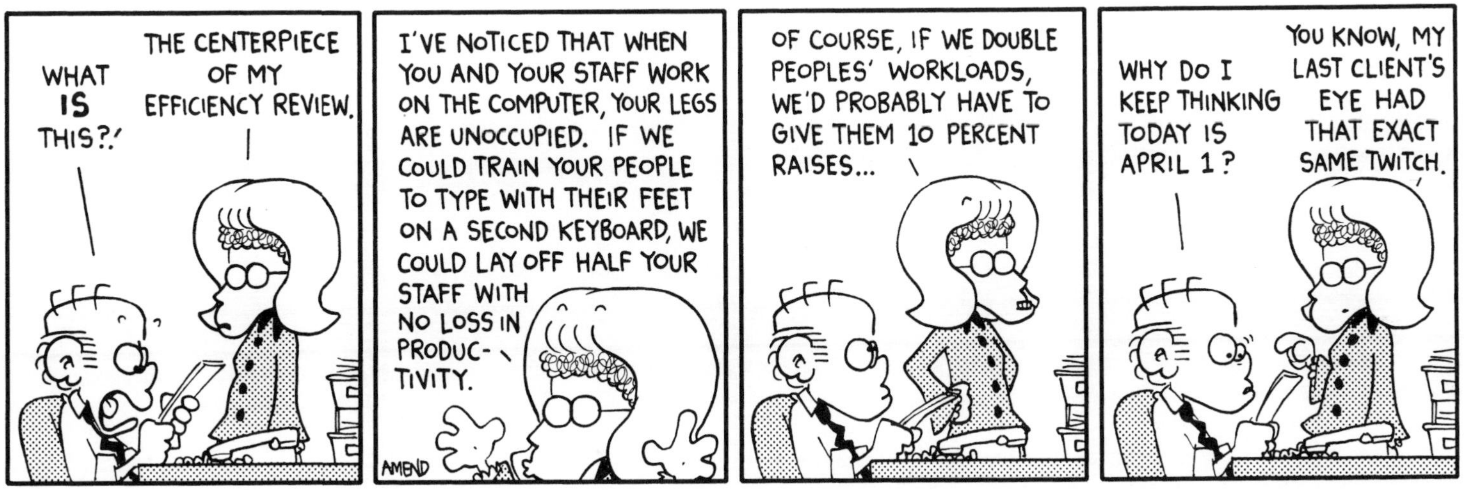
WHAT IS THIS?!
THE CENTERPIECE OF MY EFFICIENCY REVIEW.
I'VE NOTICED THAT WHEN YOU AND YOUR STAFF WORK ON THE COMPUTER, YOUR LEGS ARE UNOCCUPIED. IF WE COULD TRAIN YOUR PEOPLE TO TYPE WITH THEIR FEET ON A SECOND KEYBOARD, WE COULD LAY OFF HALF YOUR STAFF WITH NO LOSS IN PRODUCTIVITY.
AMEND
OF COURSE, IF WE DOUBLE PEOPLES' WORKLOADS, WE'D PROBABLY HAVE TO GIVE THEM 10 PERCENT RAISES...
WHY DO I KEEP THINKING TODAY IS APRIL 1?
YOU KNOW, MY LAST CLIENT'S EYE HAD THAT EXACT SAME TWITCH.

February 2, 1996

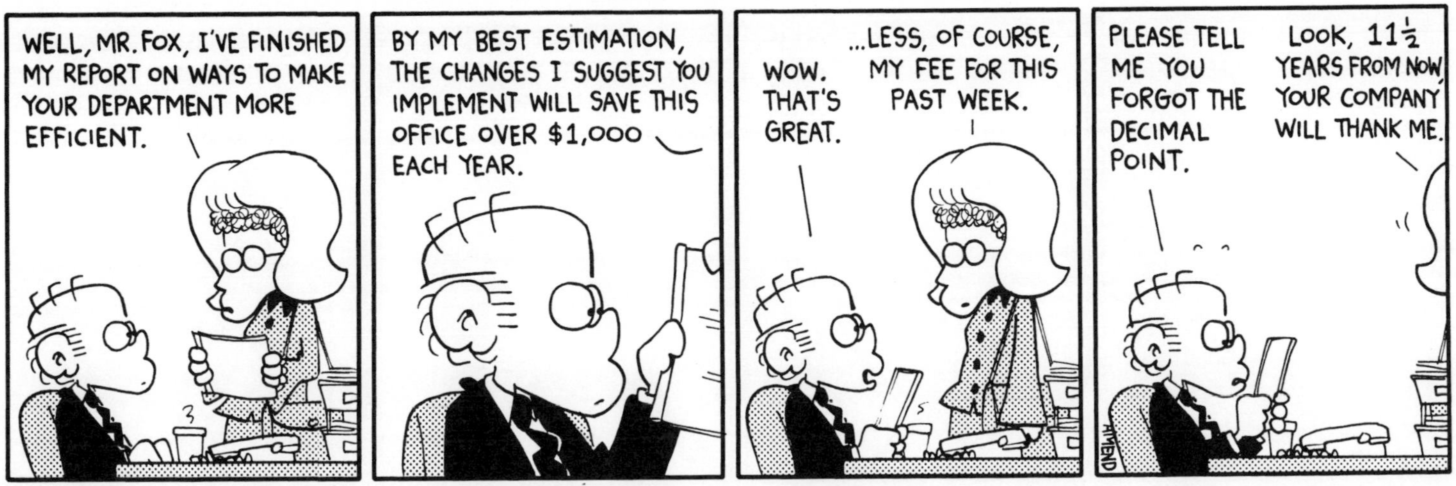
WELL, MR. FOX, I'VE FINISHED MY REPORT ON WAYS TO MAKE YOUR DEPARTMENT MORE EFFICIENT.
BY MY BEST ESTIMATION, THE CHANGES I SUGGEST YOU IMPLEMENT WILL SAVE THIS OFFICE OVER $1,000 EACH YEAR.
WOW. THAT'S GREAT.
...LESS, OF COURSE, MY FEE FOR THIS PAST WEEK.
PLEASE TELL ME YOU FORGOT THE DECIMAL POINT.
LOOK, 11½ YEARS FROM NOW, YOUR COMPANY WILL THANK ME.
AMEND

February 3, 1996

For a few years in the '90s cigars were all the rage.

March 4, 1996

March 5, 1996

202

March 6, 1996

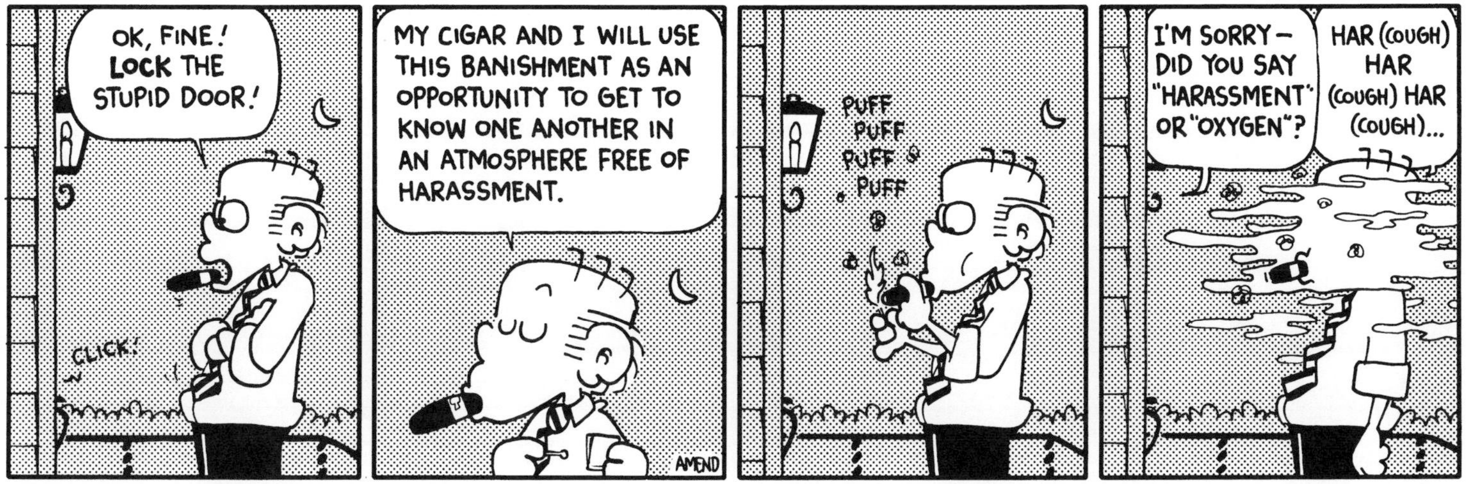
OK, FINE! LOCK THE STUPID DOOR!
CLICK!
MY CIGAR AND I WILL USE THIS BANISHMENT AS AN OPPORTUNITY TO GET TO KNOW ONE ANOTHER IN AN ATMOSPHERE FREE OF HARASSMENT.
AMEND
PUFF PUFF PUFF PUFF
I'M SORRY— DID YOU SAY "HARASSMENT" OR "OXYGEN"?
HAR (COUGH) HAR (COUGH) HAR (COUGH)...
March 7, 1996

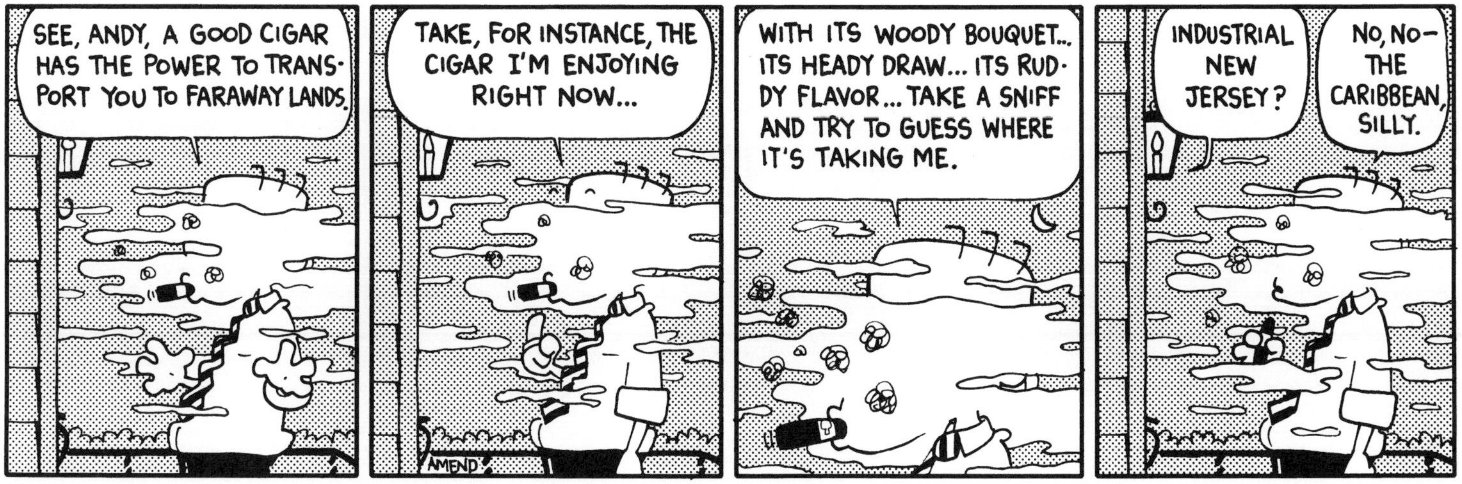
SEE, ANDY, A GOOD CIGAR HAS THE POWER TO TRANSPORT YOU TO FARAWAY LANDS.
TAKE, FOR INSTANCE, THE CIGAR I'M ENJOYING RIGHT NOW...
AMEND
WITH ITS WOODY BOUQUET... ITS HEADY DRAW... ITS RUDDY FLAVOR... TAKE A SNIFF AND TRY TO GUESS WHERE IT'S TAKING ME.
INDUSTRIAL NEW JERSEY?
NO, NO— THE CARIBBEAN, SILLY.
March 8, 1996

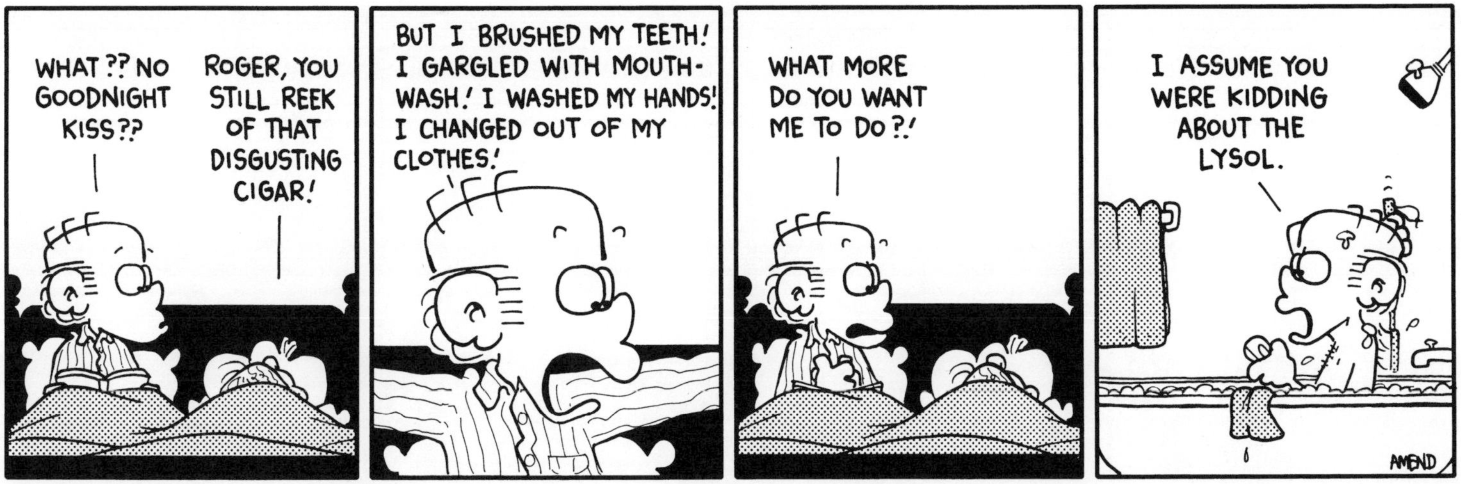
WHAT?? NO GOODNIGHT KISS??
ROGER, YOU STILL REEK OF THAT DISGUSTING CIGAR!
BUT I BRUSHED MY TEETH! I GARGLED WITH MOUTHWASH! I WASHED MY HANDS! I CHANGED OUT OF MY CLOTHES!
WHAT MORE DO YOU WANT ME TO DO?!
I ASSUME YOU WERE KIDDING ABOUT THE LYSOL.
AMEND
March 9, 1996

Since the characters don't age, things like the length of Peter and Denise's relationship prove tricky.

March 11, 1996

March 12, 1996

March 13, 1996

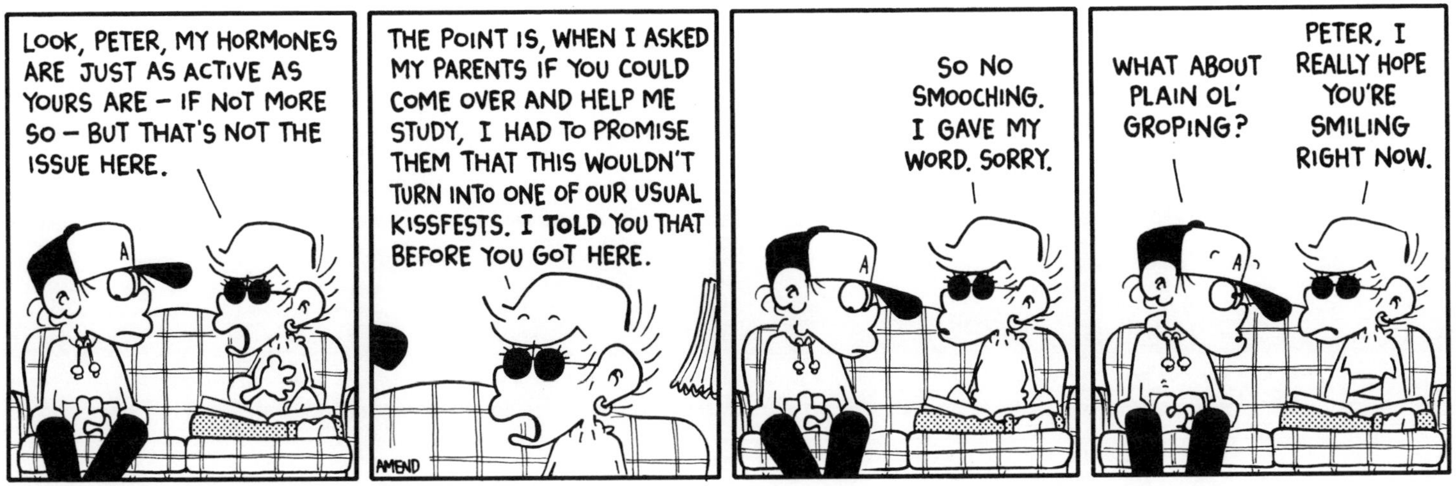
LOOK, PETER, MY HORMONES ARE JUST AS ACTIVE AS YOURS ARE – IF NOT MORE SO – BUT THAT'S NOT THE ISSUE HERE.
THE POINT IS, WHEN I ASKED MY PARENTS IF YOU COULD COME OVER AND HELP ME STUDY, I HAD TO PROMISE THEM THAT THIS WOULDN'T TURN INTO ONE OF OUR USUAL KISSFESTS. I **TOLD** YOU THAT BEFORE YOU GOT HERE.
AMEND
SO NO SMOOCHING. I GAVE MY WORD. SORRY.
WHAT ABOUT PLAIN OL' GROPING?
PETER, I REALLY HOPE YOU'RE SMILING RIGHT NOW.

March 14, 1996

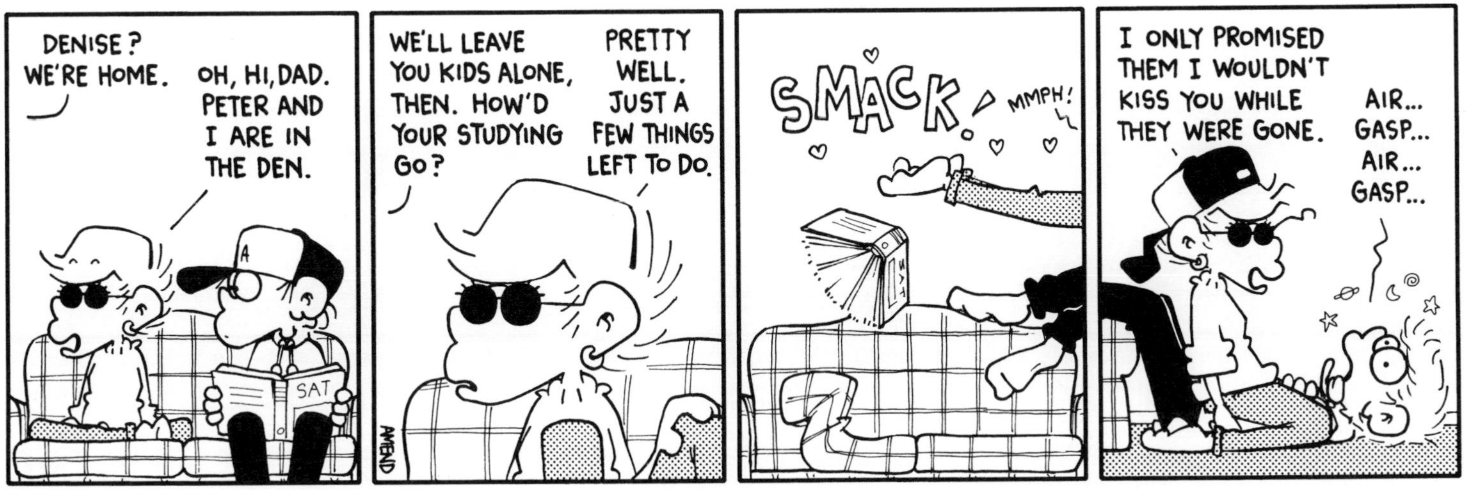
DENISE? WE'RE HOME.
OH, HI, DAD. PETER AND I ARE IN THE DEN.
SAT
WE'LL LEAVE YOU KIDS ALONE, THEN. HOW'D YOUR STUDYING GO?
PRETTY WELL. JUST A FEW THINGS LEFT TO DO.
AMEND
SMACK!
MMPH!
I ONLY PROMISED THEM I WOULDN'T KISS YOU WHILE THEY WERE GONE.
AIR... GASP... AIR... GASP...

March 15, 1996

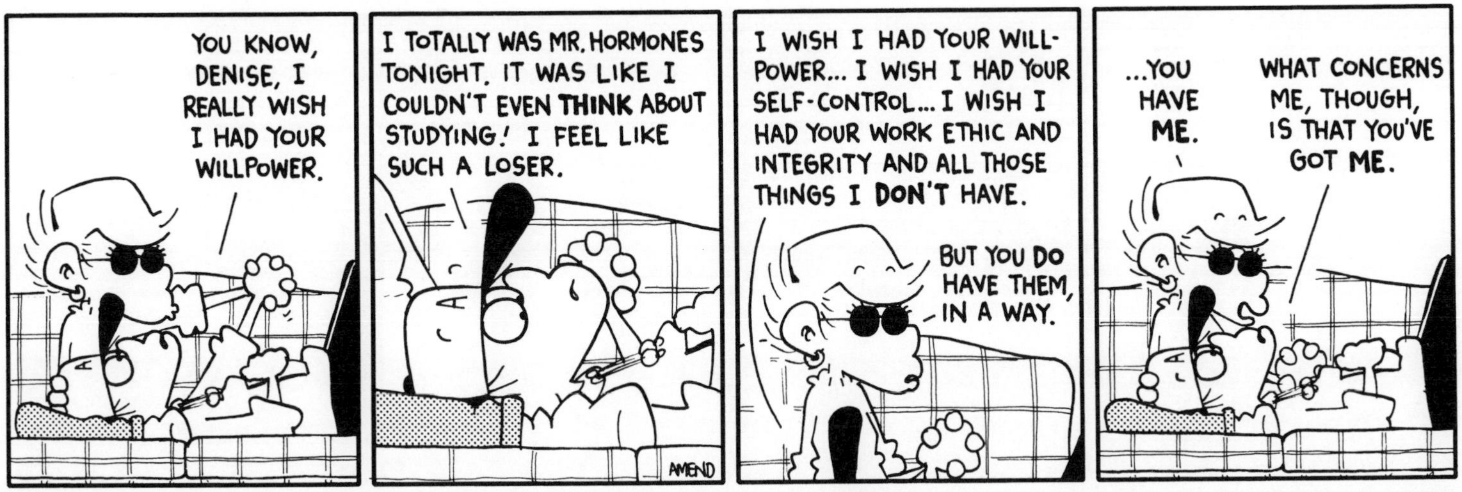
YOU KNOW, DENISE, I REALLY WISH I HAD YOUR WILLPOWER.
I TOTALLY WAS MR. HORMONES TONIGHT. IT WAS LIKE I COULDN'T EVEN **THINK** ABOUT STUDYING! I FEEL LIKE SUCH A LOSER.
AMEND
I WISH I HAD YOUR WILL-POWER... I WISH I HAD YOUR SELF-CONTROL... I WISH I HAD YOUR WORK ETHIC AND INTEGRITY AND ALL THOSE THINGS I **DON'T** HAVE.
BUT YOU **DO** HAVE THEM, IN A WAY.
...YOU HAVE **ME**.
WHAT CONCERNS ME, THOUGH, IS THAT YOU'VE GOT **ME**.

March 16, 1996

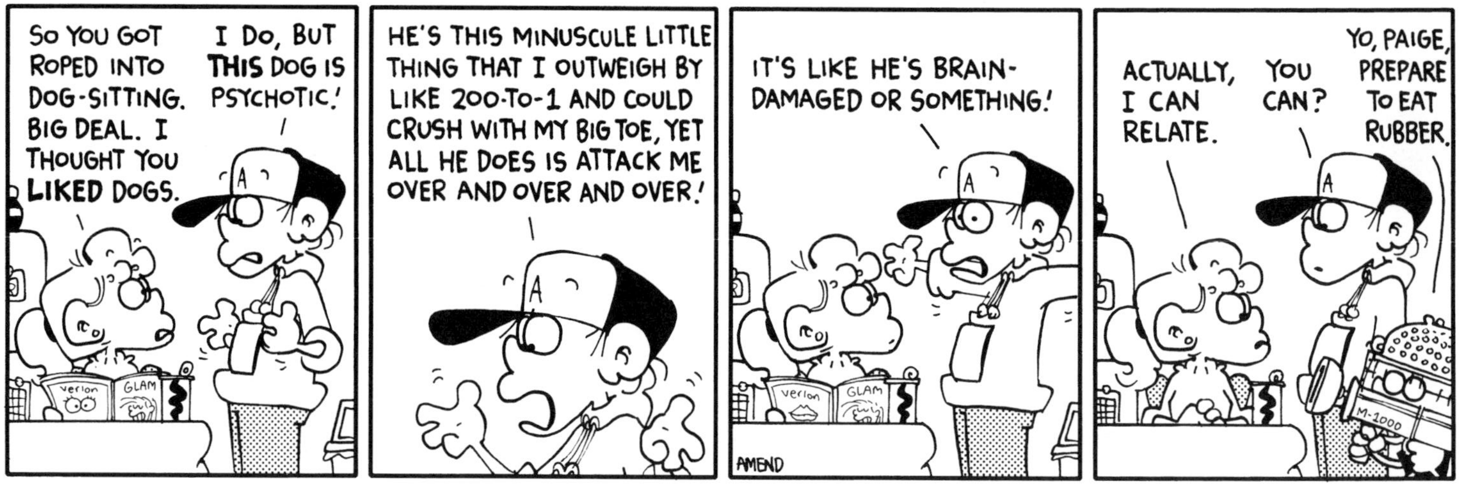
SO YOU GOT ROPED INTO DOG-SITTING. BIG DEAL. I THOUGHT YOU LIKED DOGS.
I DO, BUT THIS DOG IS PSYCHOTIC!
Verlon
GLAM
HE'S THIS MINUSCULE LITTLE THING THAT I OUTWEIGH BY LIKE 200-TO-1 AND COULD CRUSH WITH MY BIG TOE, YET ALL HE DOES IS ATTACK ME OVER AND OVER AND OVER!
IT'S LIKE HE'S BRAIN-DAMAGED OR SOMETHING!
AMEND
ACTUALLY, I CAN RELATE.
YOU CAN?
YO, PAIGE, PREPARE TO EAT RUBBER.
M-2000

March 25, 1996

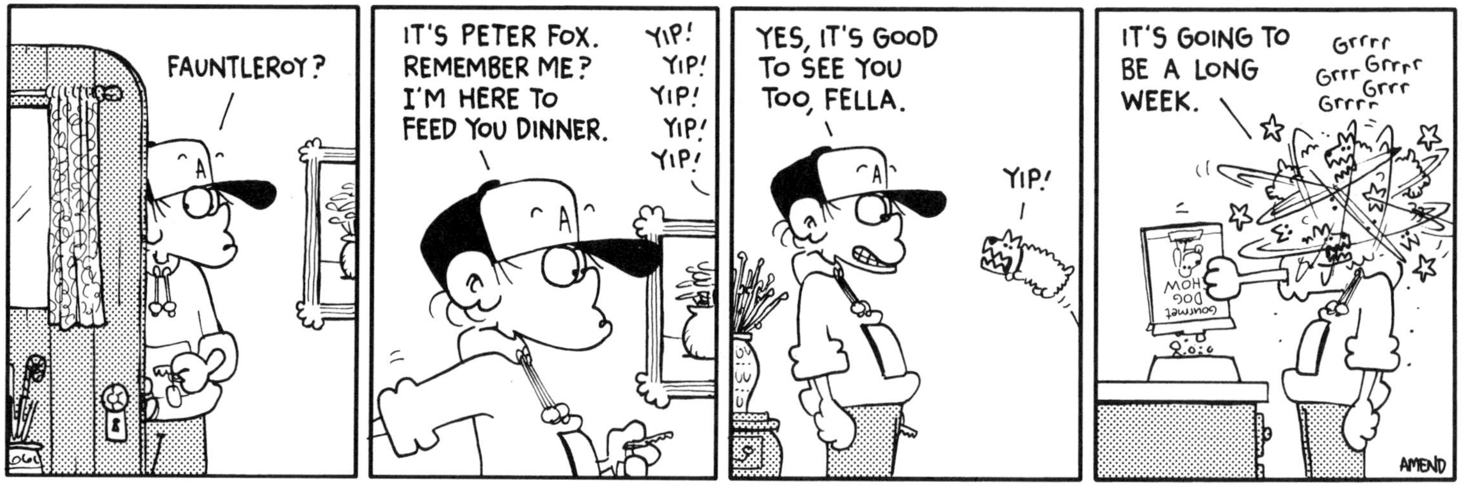
FAUNTLEROY?
IT'S PETER FOX. REMEMBER ME? I'M HERE TO FEED YOU DINNER.
YIP! YIP! YIP! YIP! YIP!
YES, IT'S GOOD TO SEE YOU TOO, FELLA.
YIP!
IT'S GOING TO BE A LONG WEEK.
Grrrr Grrr Grrrr Grrr Grrrr
AMEND

March 26, 1996

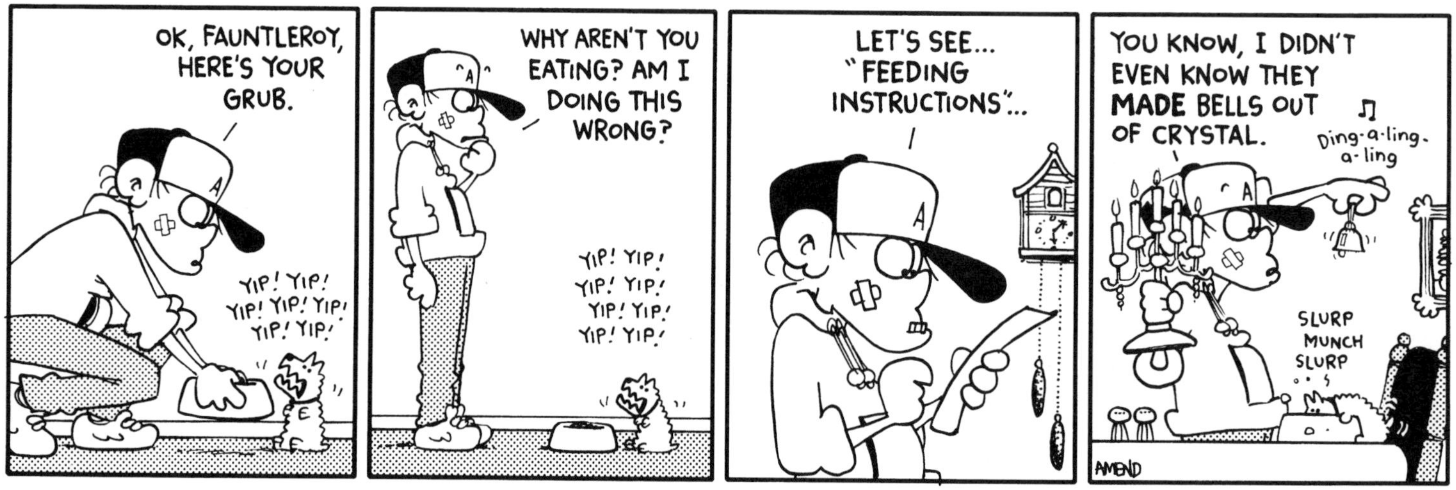
OK, FAUNTLEROY, HERE'S YOUR GRUB.
YIP! YIP! YIP! YIP! YIP! YIP! YIP!
WHY AREN'T YOU EATING? AM I DOING THIS WRONG?
YIP! YIP! YIP! YIP! YIP! YIP! YIP! YIP!
LET'S SEE... "FEEDING INSTRUCTIONS"...
YOU KNOW, I DIDN'T EVEN KNOW THEY MADE BELLS OUT OF CRYSTAL.
Ding-a-ling-a-ling
SLURP MUNCH SLURP
AMEND

March 27, 1996

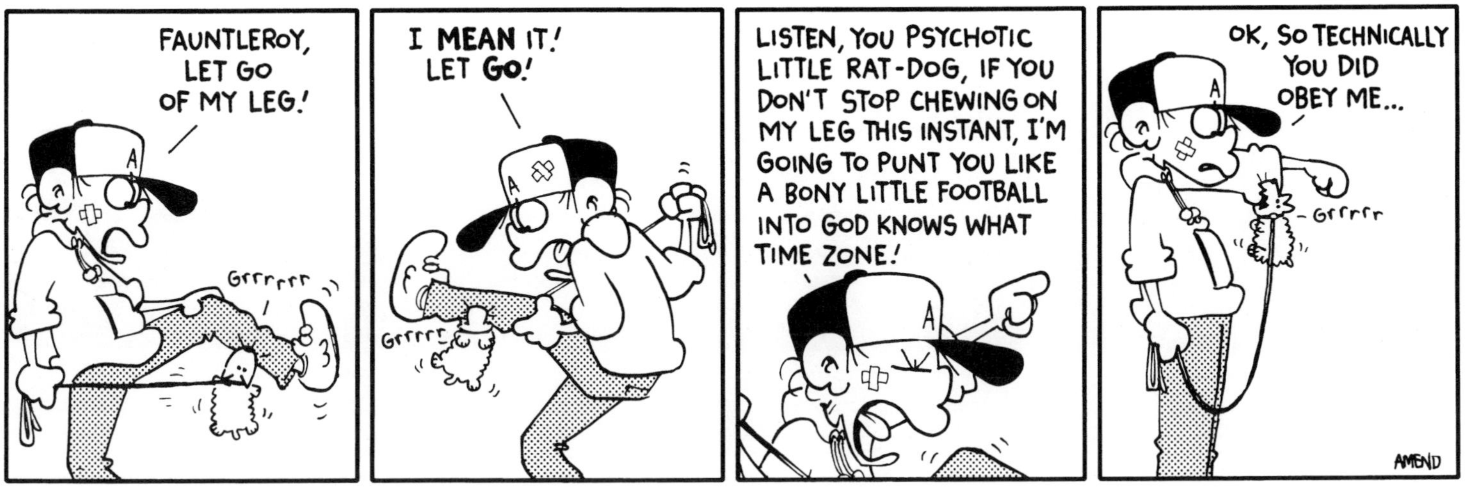
FAUNTLEROY, LET GO OF MY LEG!
Grrrrrr
I MEAN IT! LET GO!
Grrrr
LISTEN, YOU PSYCHOTIC LITTLE RAT-DOG, IF YOU DON'T STOP CHEWING ON MY LEG THIS INSTANT, I'M GOING TO PUNT YOU LIKE A BONY LITTLE FOOTBALL INTO GOD KNOWS WHAT TIME ZONE!
OK, SO TECHNICALLY YOU DID OBEY ME...
Grrrr
AMEND

March 28, 1996

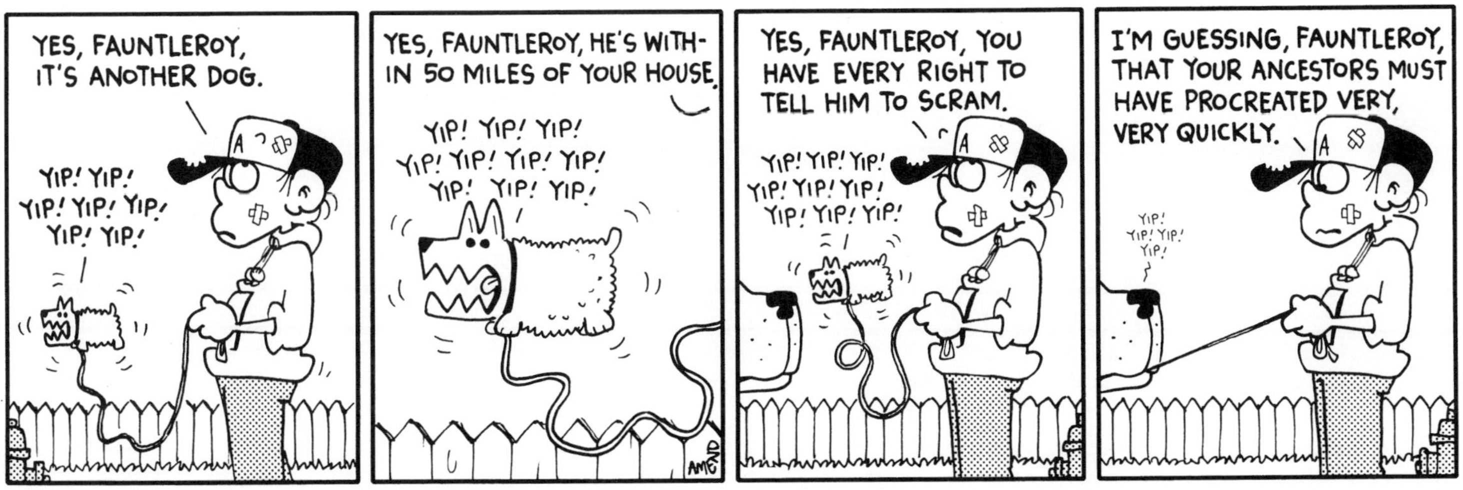
YES, FAUNTLEROY, IT'S ANOTHER DOG.
YIP! YIP! YIP! YIP! YIP! YIP! YIP!
YES, FAUNTLEROY, HE'S WITHIN 50 MILES OF YOUR HOUSE.
YIP! YIP! YIP! YIP! YIP! YIP! YIP! YIP! YIP! YIP!
YES, FAUNTLEROY, YOU HAVE EVERY RIGHT TO TELL HIM TO SCRAM.
YIP! YIP! YIP! YIP! YIP! YIP! YIP! YIP! YIP!
I'M GUESSING, FAUNTLEROY, THAT YOUR ANCESTORS MUST HAVE PROCREATED VERY, VERY QUICKLY.
YIP! YIP! YIP! YIP!
AMEND

March 29, 1996

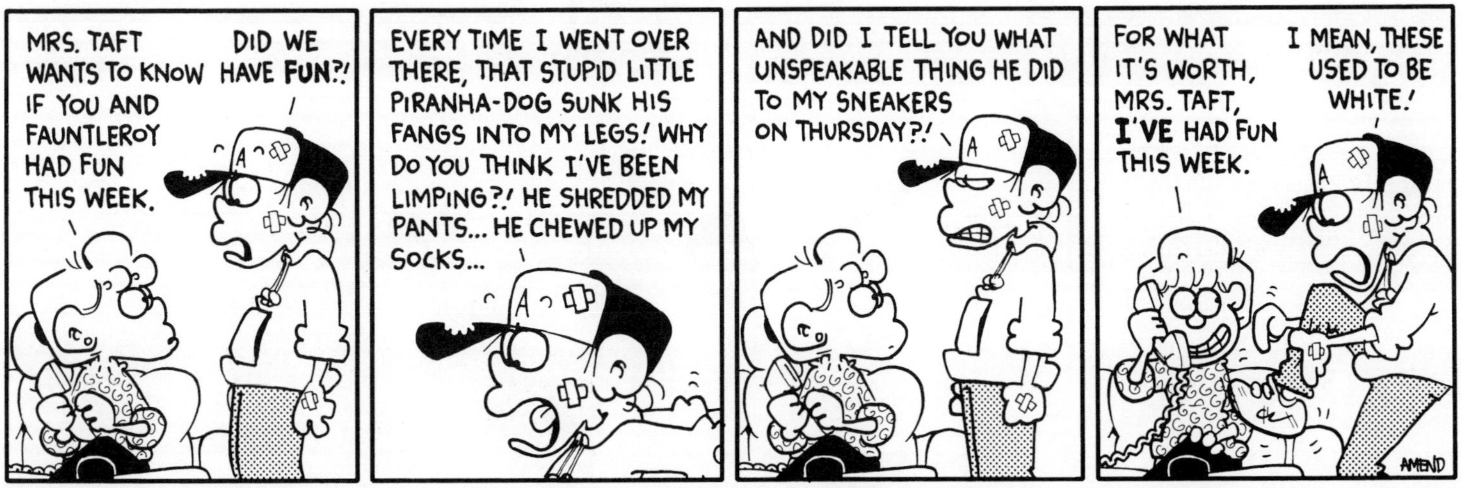
MRS. TAFT WANTS TO KNOW IF YOU AND FAUNTLEROY HAD FUN THIS WEEK.
DID WE HAVE FUN?!
EVERY TIME I WENT OVER THERE, THAT STUPID LITTLE PIRANHA-DOG SUNK HIS FANGS INTO MY LEGS! WHY DO YOU THINK I'VE BEEN LIMPING?! HE SHREDDED MY PANTS... HE CHEWED UP MY SOCKS...
AND DID I TELL YOU WHAT UNSPEAKABLE THING HE DID TO MY SNEAKERS ON THURSDAY?!
FOR WHAT IT'S WORTH, MRS. TAFT, I'VE HAD FUN THIS WEEK.
I MEAN, THESE USED TO BE WHITE!
AMEND

March 30, 1996

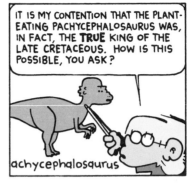
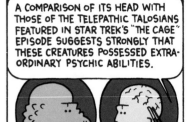

Stephen Jay Gould came and gave a lecture when I was in college, and I spent the whole hour drawing cartoons. So sad.

April 14, 1996

208

May 12, 1996

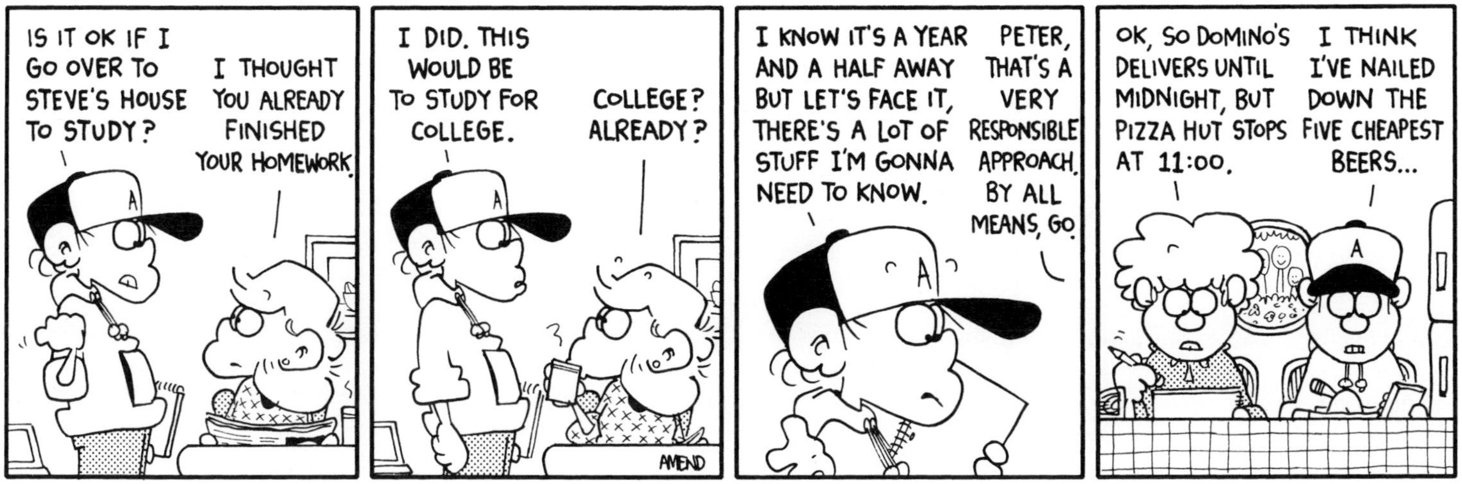
IS IT OK IF I GO OVER TO STEVE'S HOUSE TO STUDY?
I THOUGHT YOU ALREADY FINISHED YOUR HOMEWORK.
I DID. THIS WOULD BE TO STUDY FOR COLLEGE.
COLLEGE? ALREADY?
I KNOW IT'S A YEAR AND A HALF AWAY BUT LET'S FACE IT, THERE'S A LOT OF STUFF I'M GONNA NEED TO KNOW.
PETER, THAT'S A VERY RESPONSIBLE APPROACH. BY ALL MEANS, GO.
OK, SO DOMINO'S DELIVERS UNTIL MIDNIGHT, BUT PIZZA HUT STOPS AT 11:00.
I THINK I'VE NAILED DOWN THE FIVE CHEAPEST BEERS...
AMEND

May 1, 1996

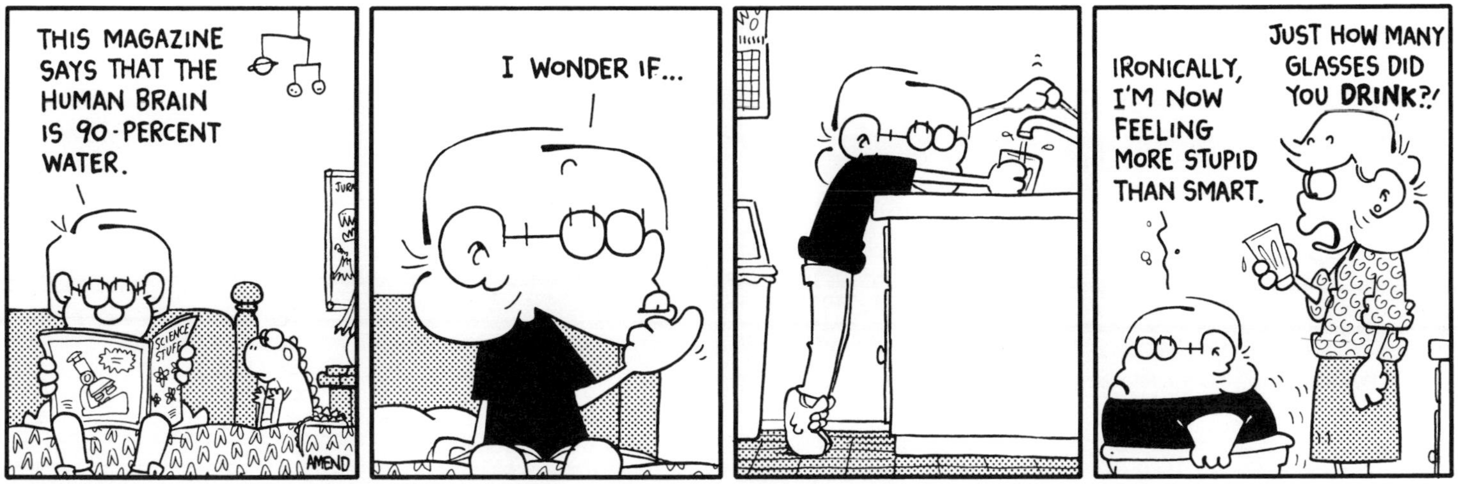
THIS MAGAZINE SAYS THAT THE HUMAN BRAIN IS 90-PERCENT WATER.
SCIENCE STUFF
AMEND
I WONDER IF...
IRONICALLY, I'M NOW FEELING MORE STUPID THAN SMART.
JUST HOW MANY GLASSES DID YOU **DRINK**?!

May 23, 1996

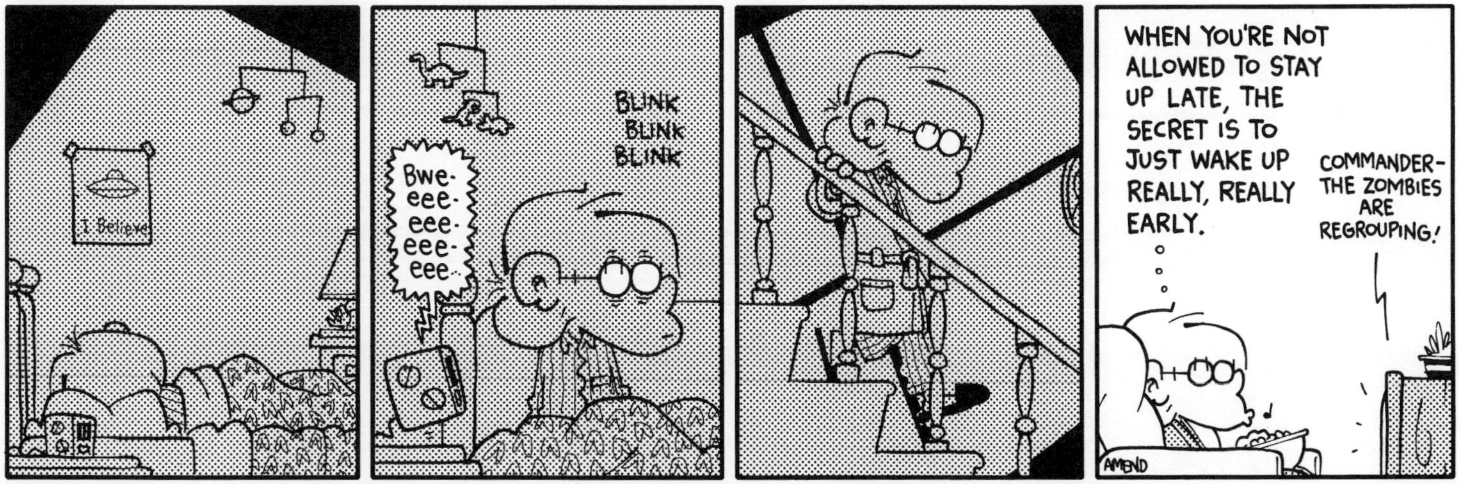
I Believe
Bwe-eee-eee-eee-eee...
BLINK BLINK BLINK
WHEN YOU'RE NOT ALLOWED TO STAY UP LATE, THE SECRET IS TO JUST WAKE UP REALLY, REALLY EARLY.
COMMANDER-THE ZOMBIES ARE REGROUPING!
AMEND

June 14, 1996

MOM! MOM! PAIGE GOT A 91 ON HER MATH FINAL!

I HEARD.

I WAS HER TUTOR! I HELPED HER DO IT! SHE DOUBTED SHE COULD GET AN "A," BUT SHE STUDIED AND STUDIED AND SHE DID!

THINK ABOUT WHAT THIS MEANS!

THAT IF YOU WORK HARD ENOUGH, YOU CAN ACCOMPLISH ALMOST ANYTHING?

NO, NO— IT MEANS SHE OWES ME $10.

I KEEP FORGETTING, THAT'S YOUR "MONEY" SMILE.

June 3, 1996

TEN DOLLARS, QUINCY! THINK ABOUT HOW MUCH MONEY THIS IS!

A WHOPPING 40 QUARTERS... 100 DIMES... 200 NICKELS... 1,000 PENNIES...

AND, DARE I COMPUTE IT?...

ANY IDEA WHY OUR SON WANTED THE EXCHANGE RATE FOR THE TURKISH LIRA?

NO, AND IF HE DOESN'T STOP THAT SQUEALING SOON...

June 4, 1996

IF I TAKE THE $10 THAT PAIGE PAID ME, PLUS THE $3.82 I HAD HIDDEN UNDER MY MATTRESS...

...AND CONVERT IT FROM U.S. DOLLARS TO TURKISH LIRA...

GOOD LORD, I'M A MILLIONAIRE.

June 5, 1996

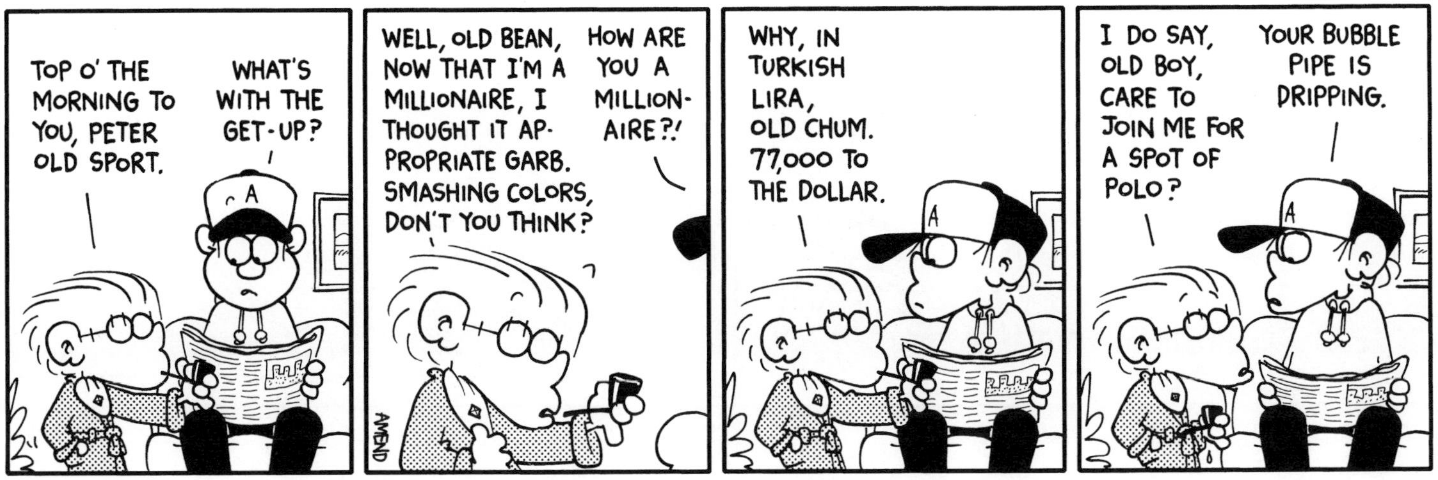
TOP O' THE MORNING TO YOU, PETER OLD SPORT.
WHAT'S WITH THE GET-UP?
WELL, OLD BEAN, NOW THAT I'M A MILLIONAIRE, I THOUGHT IT AP-PROPRIATE GARB. SMASHING COLORS, DON'T YOU THINK?
HOW ARE YOU A MILLION-AIRE?!
WHY, IN TURKISH LIRA, OLD CHUM. 77,000 TO THE DOLLAR.
I DO SAY, OLD BOY, CARE TO JOIN ME FOR A SPOT OF POLO?
YOUR BUBBLE PIPE IS DRIPPING.

June 6, 1996

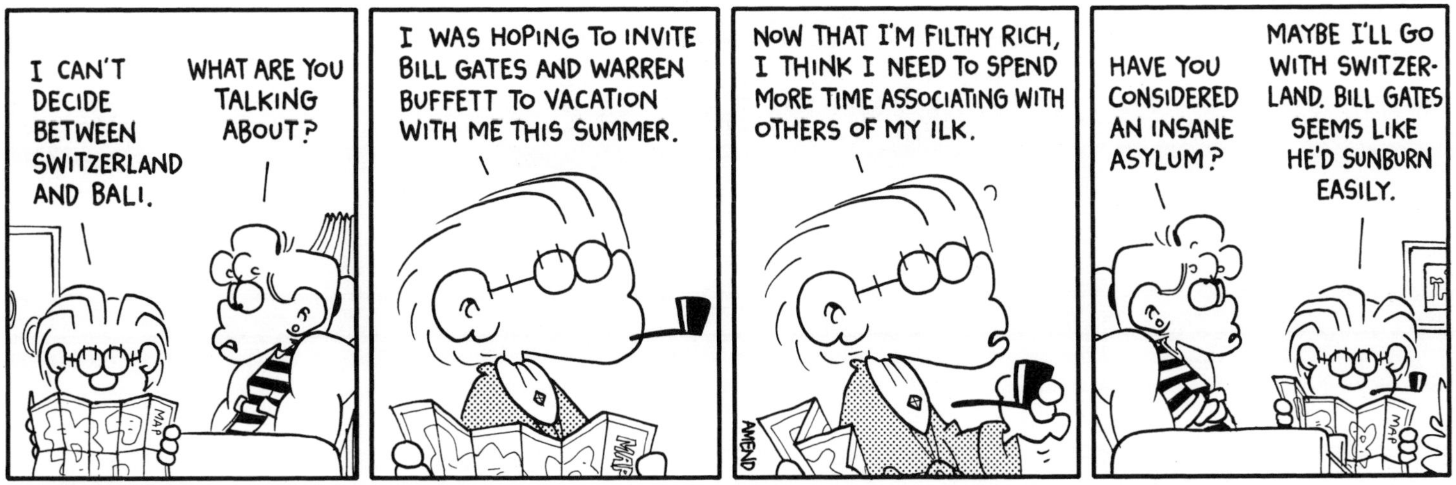
I CAN'T DECIDE BETWEEN SWITZERLAND AND BALI.
WHAT ARE YOU TALKING ABOUT?
MAP
I WAS HOPING TO INVITE BILL GATES AND WARREN BUFFETT TO VACATION WITH ME THIS SUMMER.
NOW THAT I'M FILTHY RICH, I THINK I NEED TO SPEND MORE TIME ASSOCIATING WITH OTHERS OF MY ILK.
HAVE YOU CONSIDERED AN INSANE ASYLUM?
MAYBE I'LL GO WITH SWITZER-LAND. BILL GATES SEEMS LIKE HE'D SUNBURN EASILY.

June 7, 1996

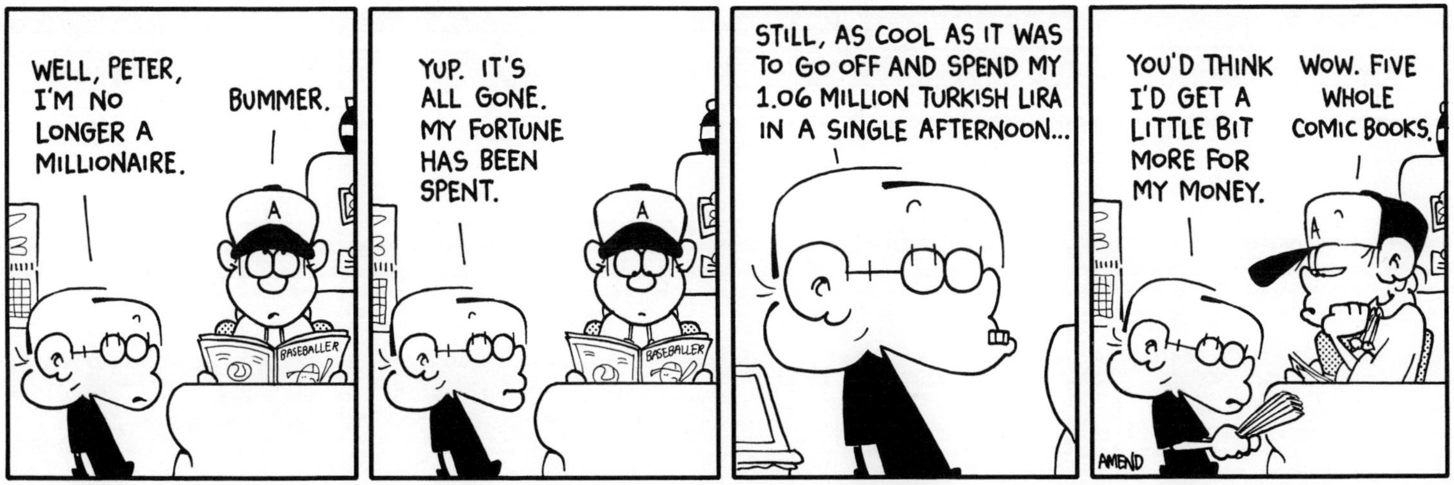
WELL, PETER, I'M NO LONGER A MILLIONAIRE.
BUMMER.
BASEBALLER
YUP. IT'S ALL GONE. MY FORTUNE HAS BEEN SPENT.
STILL, AS COOL AS IT WAS TO GO OFF AND SPEND MY 1.06 MILLION TURKISH LIRA IN A SINGLE AFTERNOON...
YOU'D THINK I'D GET A LITTLE BIT MORE FOR MY MONEY.
WOW. FIVE WHOLE COMIC BOOKS.

June 8, 1996

May 26, 1996

I just made these problems up, but it turns out the second one is crazy hard and this strip is actually cited in a math book.

June 2, 1996

212

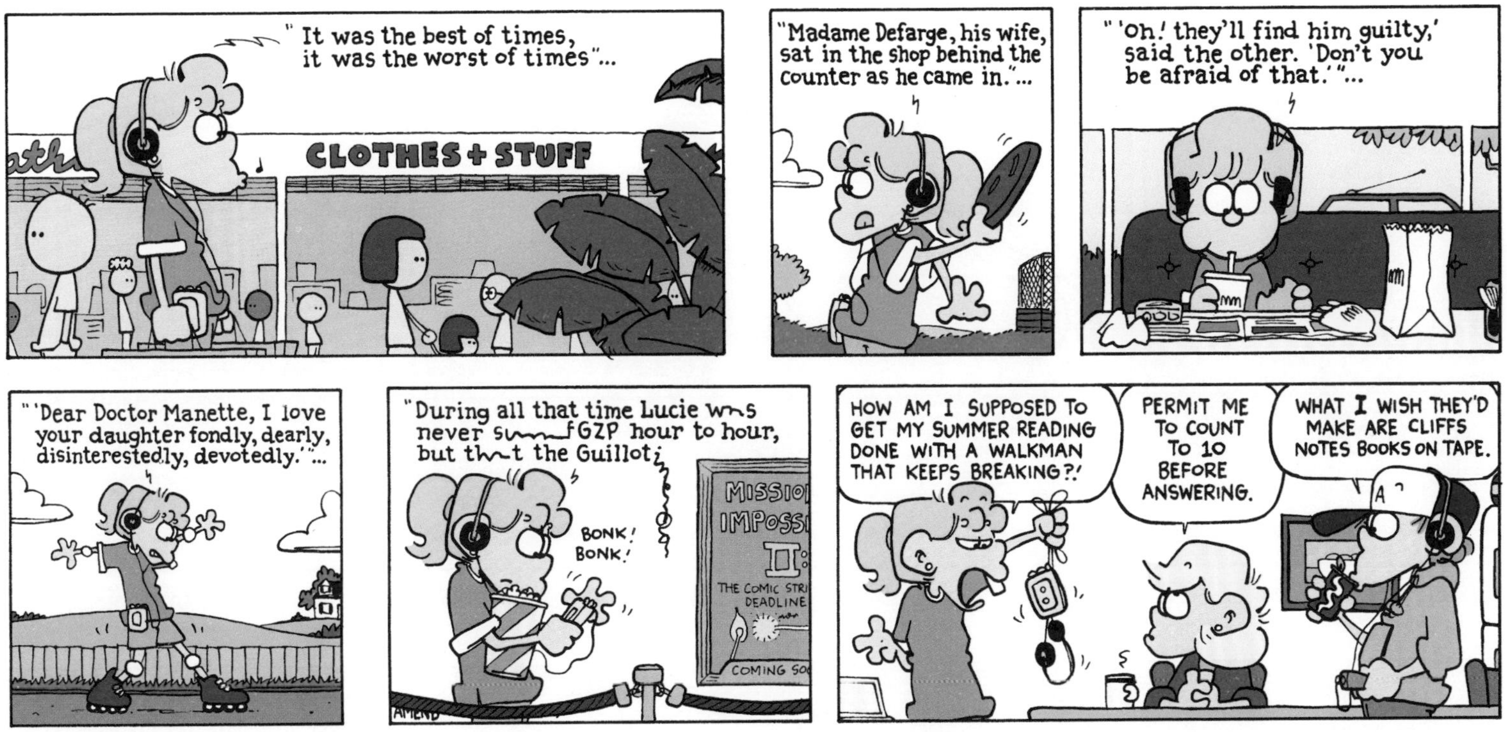

"It was the best of times, it was the worst of times"...
CLOTHES + STUFF
"Madame Defarge, his wife, sat in the shop behind the counter as he came in."...
"'Oh! they'll find him guilty,' said the other. 'Don't you be afraid of that.'"...
"'Dear Doctor Manette, I love your daughter fondly, dearly, disinterestedly, devotedly.'"...
"During all that time Lucie was never s fGZP hour to hour, but that the Guillot
BONK! BONK!
MISSION IMPOSSI
THE COMIC STRI DEADLINE
COMING SOO
AMEND
HOW AM I SUPPOSED TO GET MY SUMMER READING DONE WITH A WALKMAN THAT KEEPS BREAKING?!
PERMIT ME TO COUNT TO 10 BEFORE ANSWERING.
WHAT I WISH THEY'D MAKE ARE CLIFFS NOTES BOOKS ON TAPE.

June 16, 1996

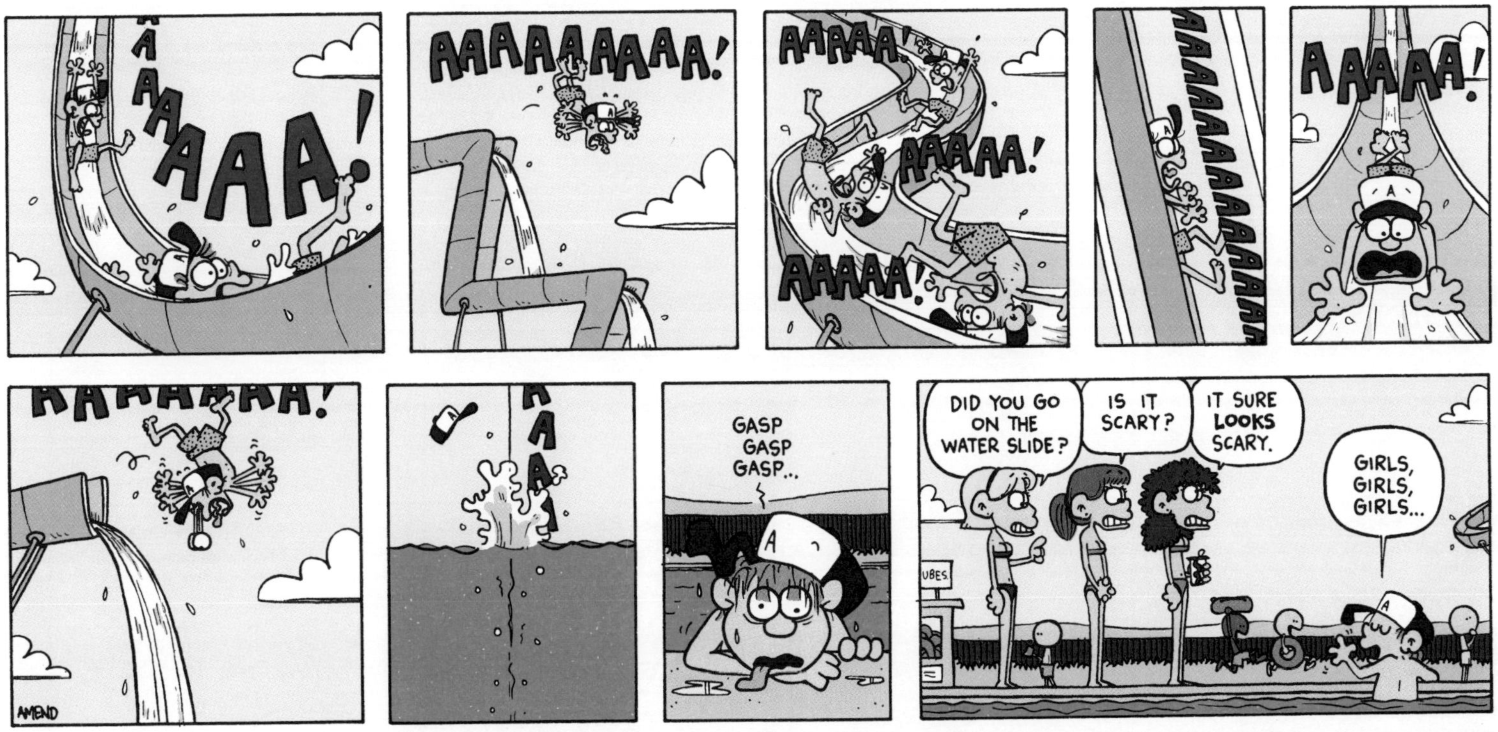

AAAAAA!
AAAAAAAAAA!
AAAAA!
AAAAA!
AAAAA!
AAAAAAAAAAAAAA
AAAAA!
AAAAAAA!
AAA
GASP GASP GASP...
DID YOU GO ON THE WATER SLIDE?
IS IT SCARY?
IT SURE LOOKS SCARY.
GIRLS, GIRLS, GIRLS...
AMEND

August 11, 1996

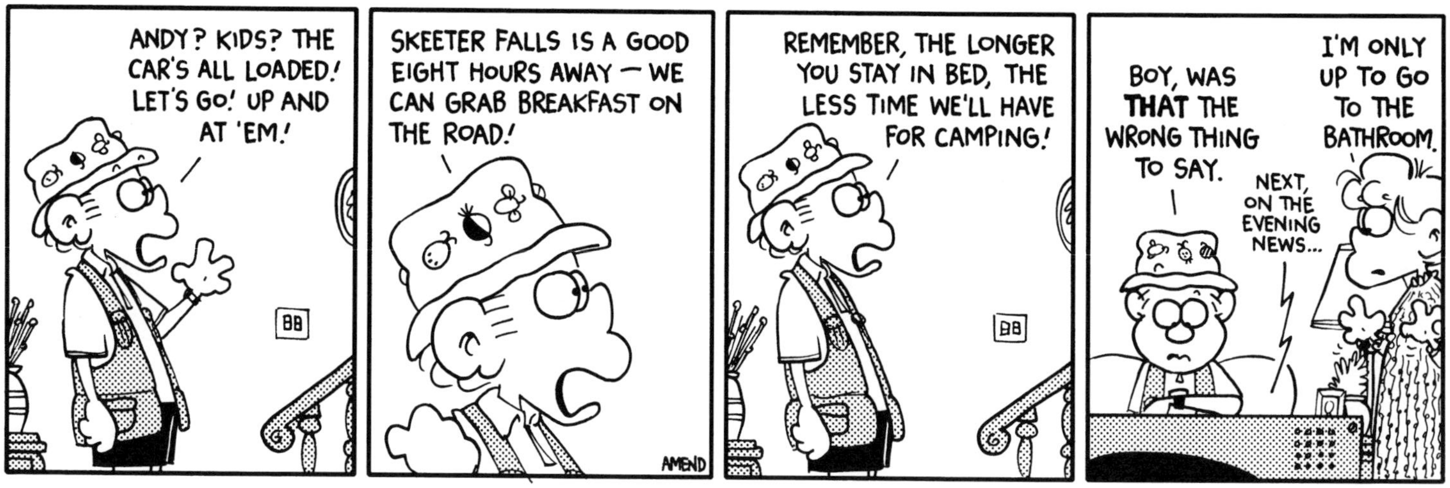
ANDY? KIDS? THE CAR'S ALL LOADED! LET'S GO! UP AND AT 'EM!
SKEETER FALLS IS A GOOD EIGHT HOURS AWAY — WE CAN GRAB BREAKFAST ON THE ROAD!
REMEMBER, THE LONGER YOU STAY IN BED, THE LESS TIME WE'LL HAVE FOR CAMPING!
BOY, WAS **THAT** THE WRONG THING TO SAY.
I'M ONLY UP TO GO TO THE BATHROOM.
NEXT, ON THE EVENING NEWS...
AMEND

August 12, 1996

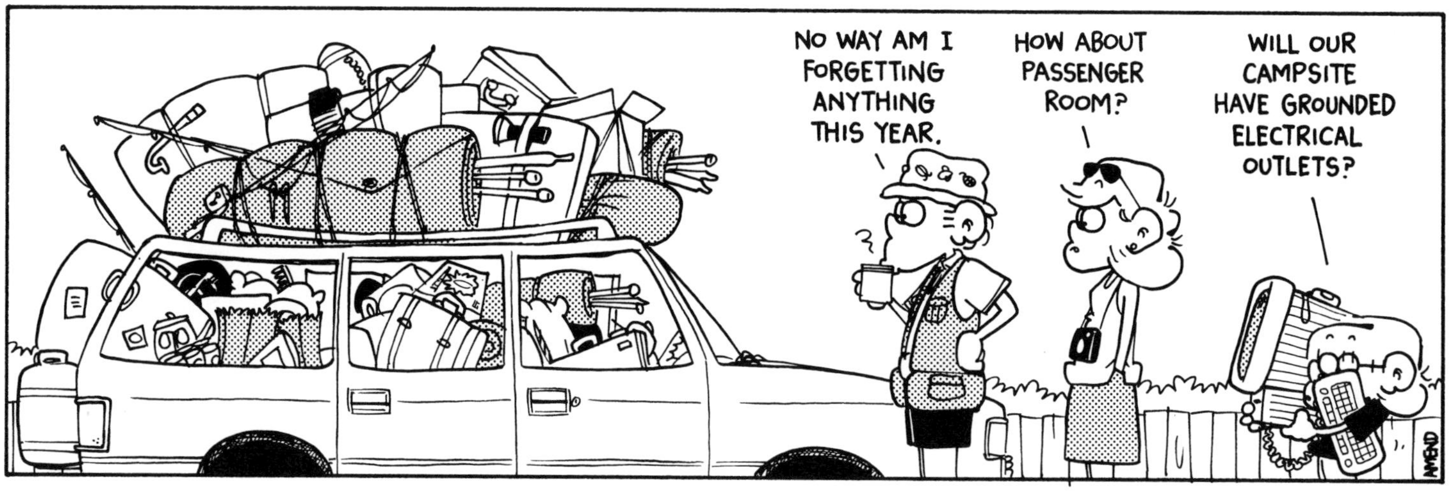
NO WAY AM I FORGETTING ANYTHING THIS YEAR.
HOW ABOUT PASSENGER ROOM?
WILL OUR CAMPSITE HAVE GROUNDED ELECTRICAL OUTLETS?
AMEND

August 13, 1996

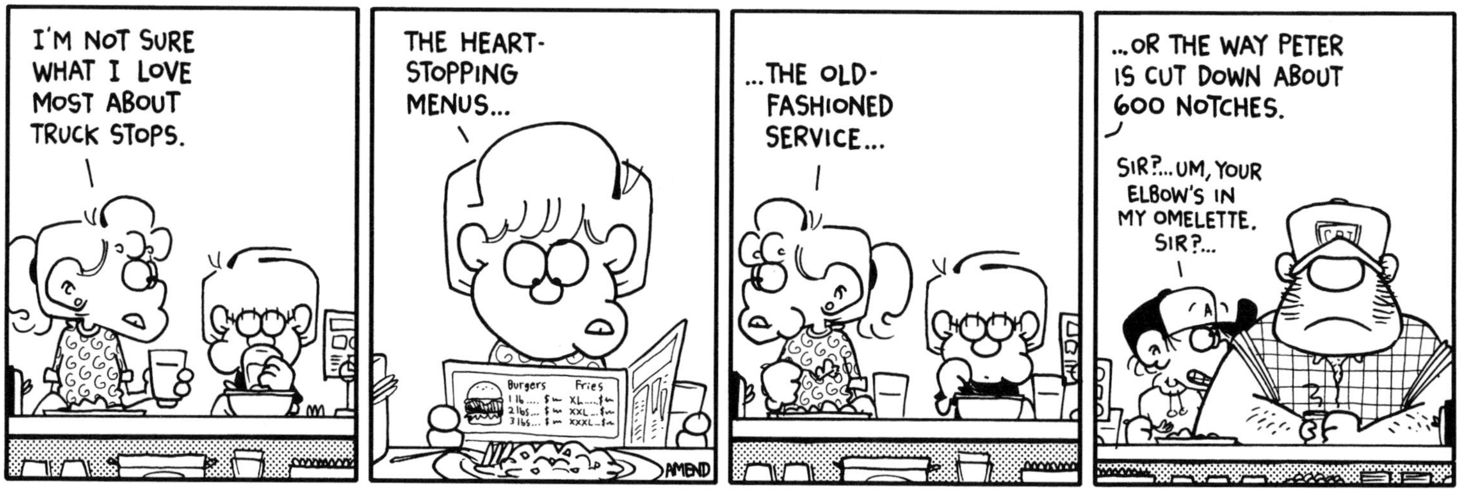
I'M NOT SURE WHAT I LOVE MOST ABOUT TRUCK STOPS.
THE HEART-STOPPING MENUS...
Burgers
Fries
...THE OLD-FASHIONED SERVICE...
...OR THE WAY PETER IS CUT DOWN ABOUT 600 NOTCHES.
SIR?...UM, YOUR ELBOW'S IN MY OMELETTE. SIR?...
AMEND

August 14, 1996

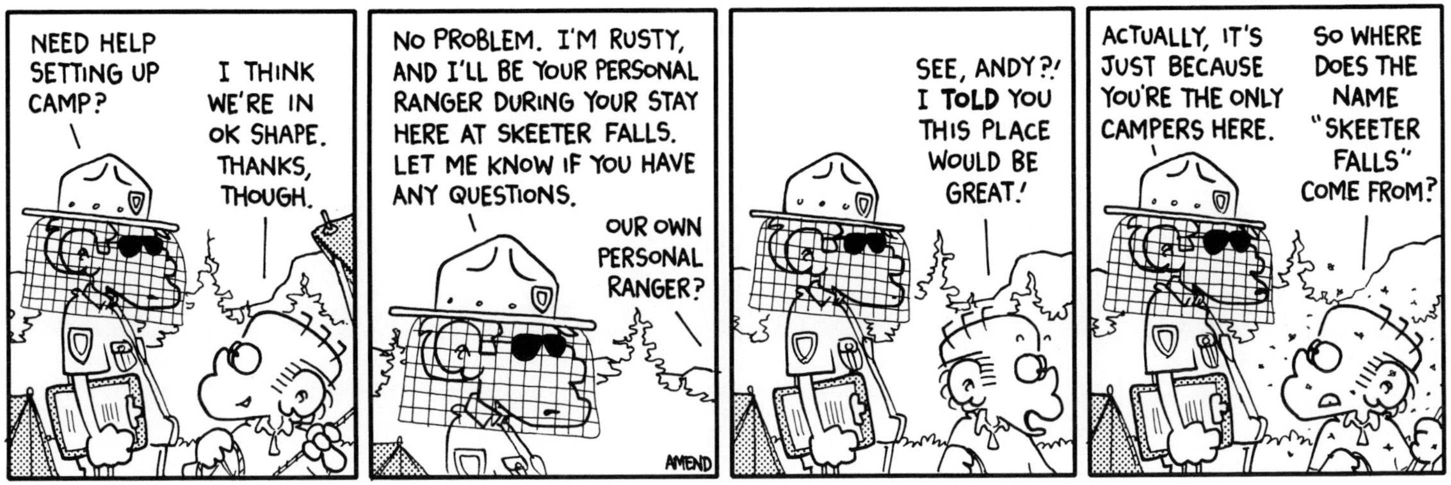
NEED HELP SETTING UP CAMP?
I THINK WE'RE IN OK SHAPE. THANKS, THOUGH.
NO PROBLEM. I'M RUSTY, AND I'LL BE YOUR PERSONAL RANGER DURING YOUR STAY HERE AT SKEETER FALLS. LET ME KNOW IF YOU HAVE ANY QUESTIONS.
OUR OWN PERSONAL RANGER?
AMEND
SEE, ANDY?! I TOLD YOU THIS PLACE WOULD BE GREAT!
ACTUALLY, IT'S JUST BECAUSE YOU'RE THE ONLY CAMPERS HERE.
SO WHERE DOES THE NAME "SKEETER FALLS" COME FROM?

August 15, 1996

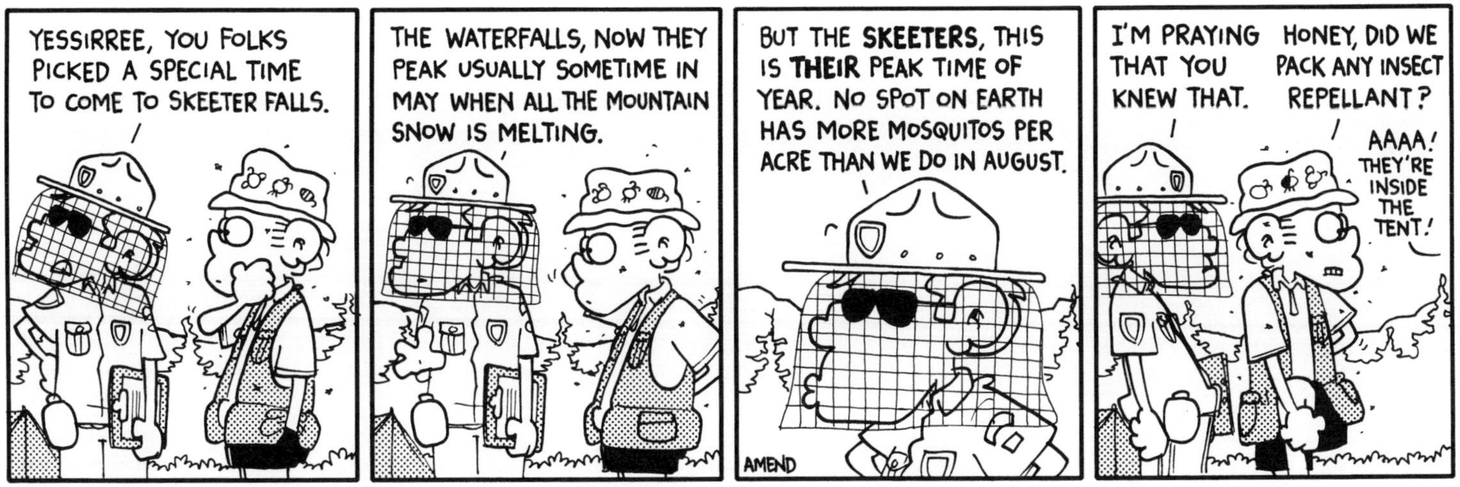
YESSIRREE, YOU FOLKS PICKED A SPECIAL TIME TO COME TO SKEETER FALLS.
THE WATERFALLS, NOW THEY PEAK USUALLY SOMETIME IN MAY WHEN ALL THE MOUNTAIN SNOW IS MELTING.
BUT THE SKEETERS, THIS IS THEIR PEAK TIME OF YEAR. NO SPOT ON EARTH HAS MORE MOSQUITOS PER ACRE THAN WE DO IN AUGUST.
AMEND
I'M PRAYING THAT YOU KNEW THAT.
HONEY, DID WE PACK ANY INSECT REPELLANT?
AAAA! THEY'RE INSIDE THE TENT!

August 16, 1996

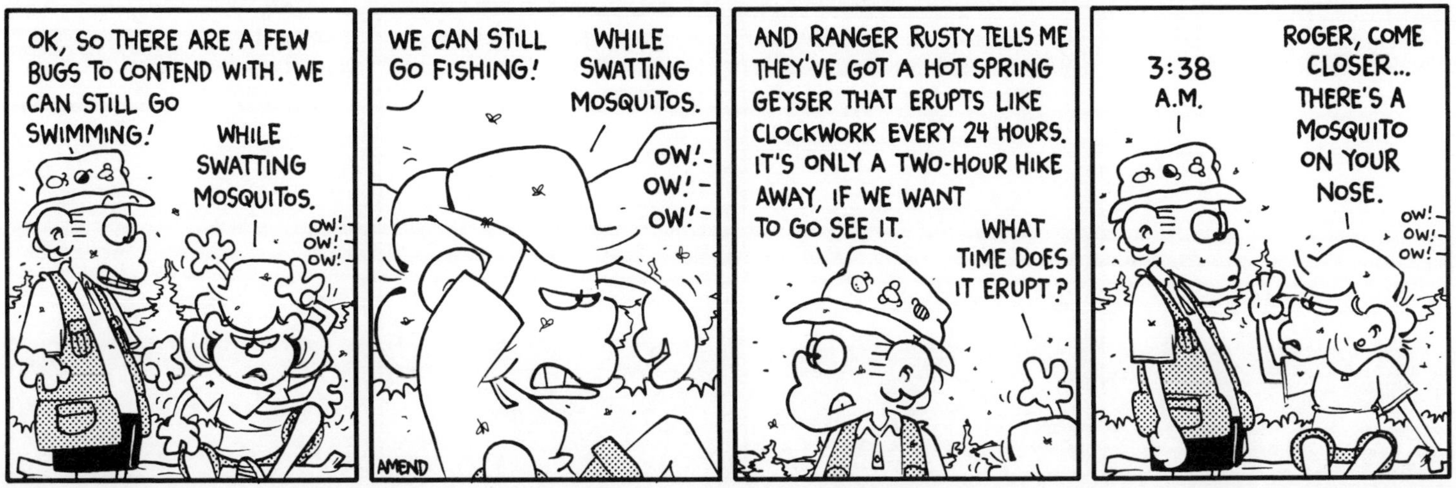
OK, SO THERE ARE A FEW BUGS TO CONTEND WITH. WE CAN STILL GO SWIMMING!
WHILE SWATTING MOSQUITOS.
OW! OW! OW!
WE CAN STILL GO FISHING!
WHILE SWATTING MOSQUITOS.
OW! OW! OW!
AMEND
AND RANGER RUSTY TELLS ME THEY'VE GOT A HOT SPRING GEYSER THAT ERUPTS LIKE CLOCKWORK EVERY 24 HOURS. IT'S ONLY A TWO-HOUR HIKE AWAY, IF WE WANT TO GO SEE IT.
WHAT TIME DOES IT ERUPT?
3:38 A.M.
ROGER, COME CLOSER... THERE'S A MOSQUITO ON YOUR NOSE.
OW! OW! OW!

August 17, 1996

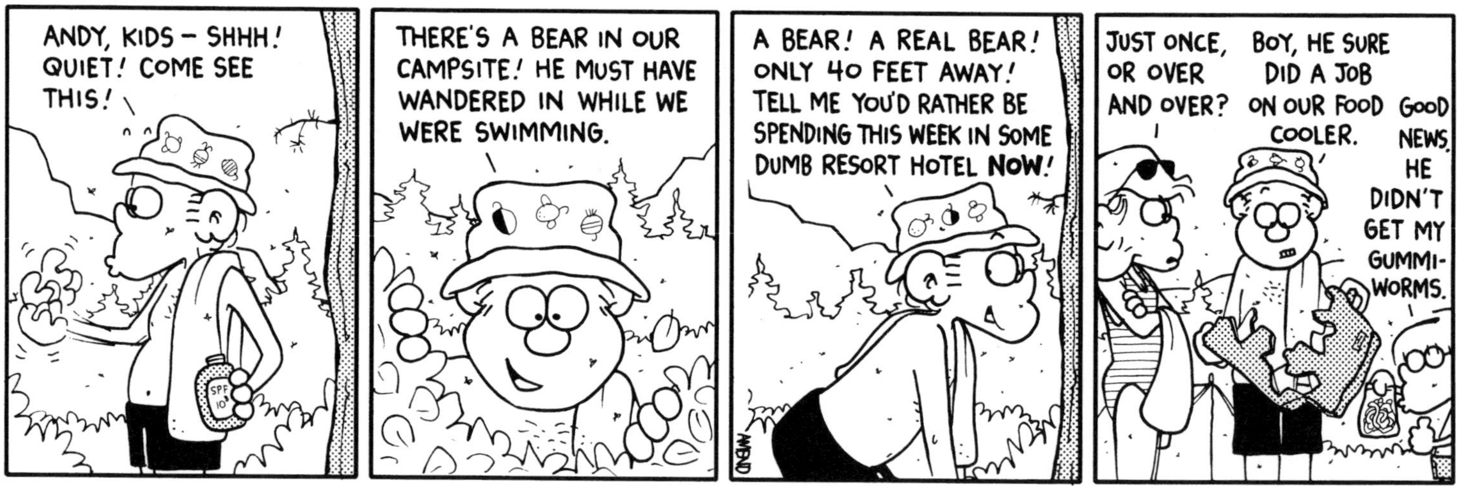
ANDY, KIDS – SHHH! QUIET! COME SEE THIS!
THERE'S A BEAR IN OUR CAMPSITE! HE MUST HAVE WANDERED IN WHILE WE WERE SWIMMING.
A BEAR! A REAL BEAR! ONLY 40 FEET AWAY! TELL ME YOU'D RATHER BE SPENDING THIS WEEK IN SOME DUMB RESORT HOTEL NOW!
JUST ONCE, OR OVER AND OVER?
BOY, HE SURE DID A JOB ON OUR FOOD COOLER.
GOOD NEWS, HE DIDN'T GET MY GUMMI-WORMS.
SPF 10
AMEND

August 19, 1996

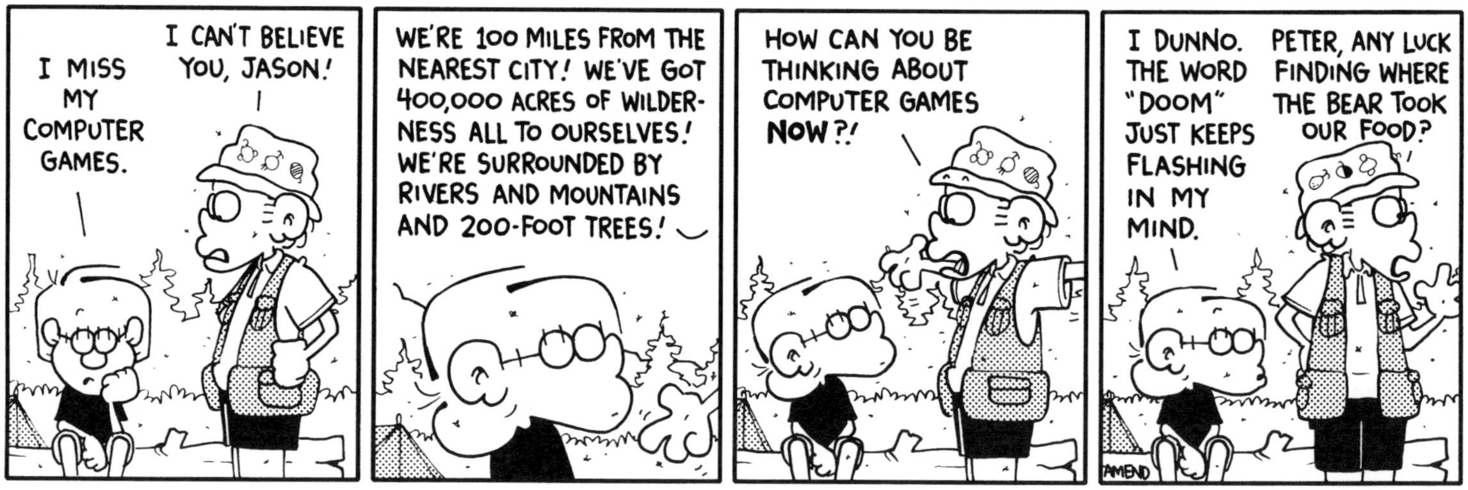
I MISS MY COMPUTER GAMES.
I CAN'T BELIEVE YOU, JASON!
WE'RE 100 MILES FROM THE NEAREST CITY! WE'VE GOT 400,000 ACRES OF WILDERNESS ALL TO OURSELVES! WE'RE SURROUNDED BY RIVERS AND MOUNTAINS AND 200-FOOT TREES!
HOW CAN YOU BE THINKING ABOUT COMPUTER GAMES NOW?!
I DUNNO. THE WORD "DOOM" JUST KEEPS FLASHING IN MY MIND.
PETER, ANY LUCK FINDING WHERE THE BEAR TOOK OUR FOOD?
AMEND

August 20, 1996

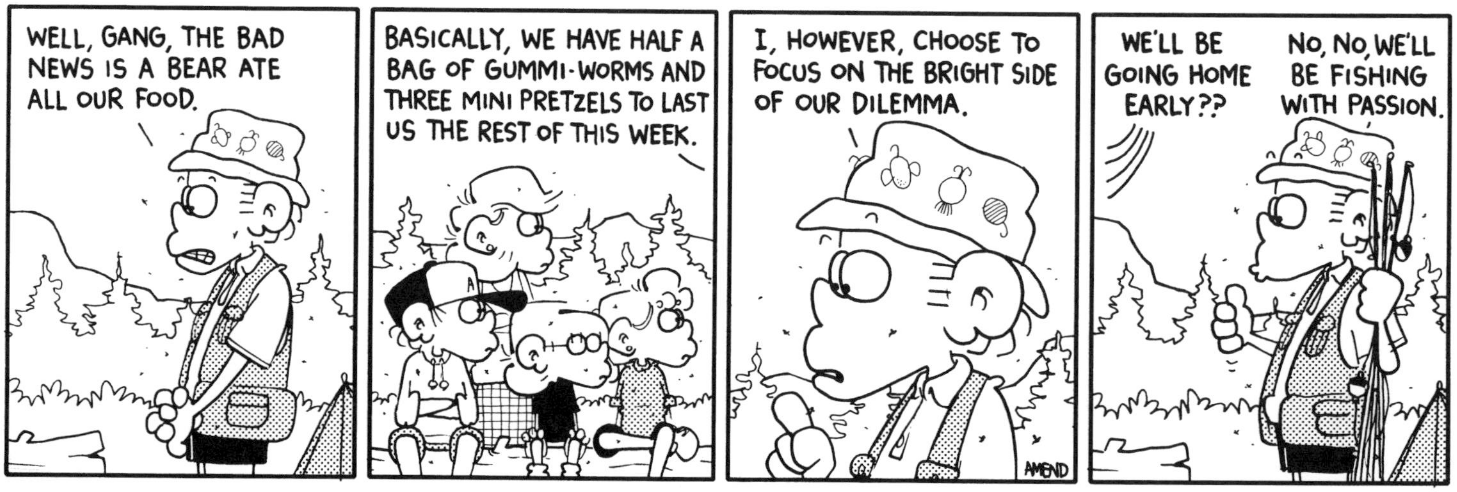
WELL, GANG, THE BAD NEWS IS A BEAR ATE ALL OUR FOOD.
BASICALLY, WE HAVE HALF A BAG OF GUMMI-WORMS AND THREE MINI PRETZELS TO LAST US THE REST OF THIS WEEK.
I, HOWEVER, CHOOSE TO FOCUS ON THE BRIGHT SIDE OF OUR DILEMMA.
WE'LL BE GOING HOME EARLY??
NO, NO, WE'LL BE FISHING WITH PASSION.
AMEND

August 21, 1996

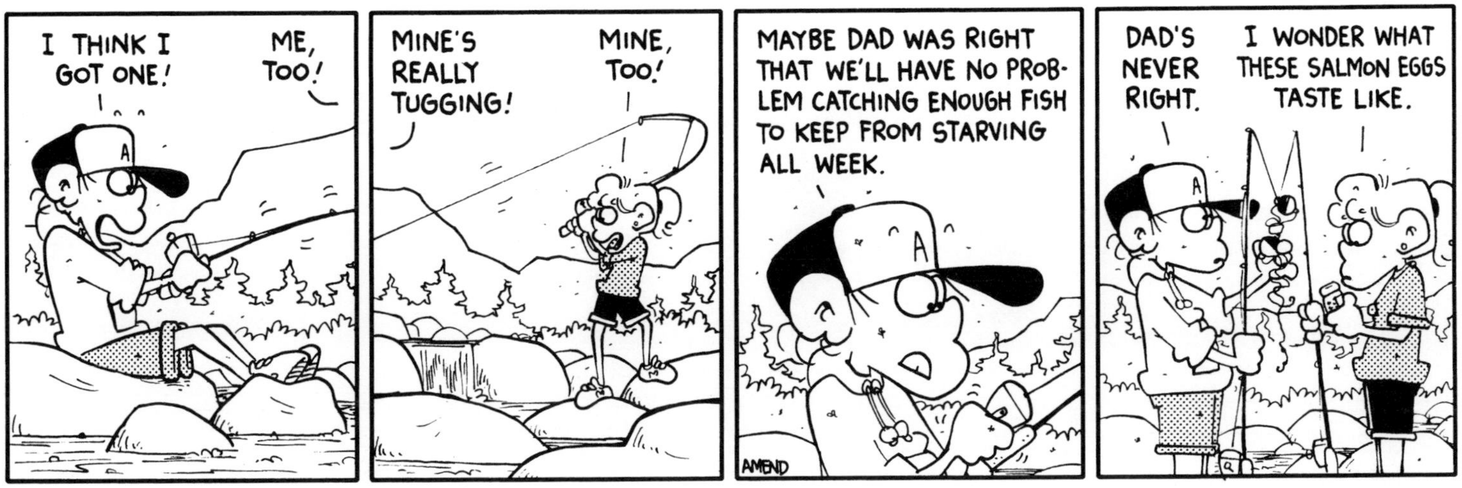

I THINK I GOT ONE!
ME, TOO!
MINE'S REALLY TUGGING!
MINE, TOO!
MAYBE DAD WAS RIGHT THAT WE'LL HAVE NO PROB-LEM CATCHING ENOUGH FISH TO KEEP FROM STARVING ALL WEEK.
AMEND
DAD'S NEVER RIGHT.
I WONDER WHAT THESE SALMON EGGS TASTE LIKE.

August 22, 1996

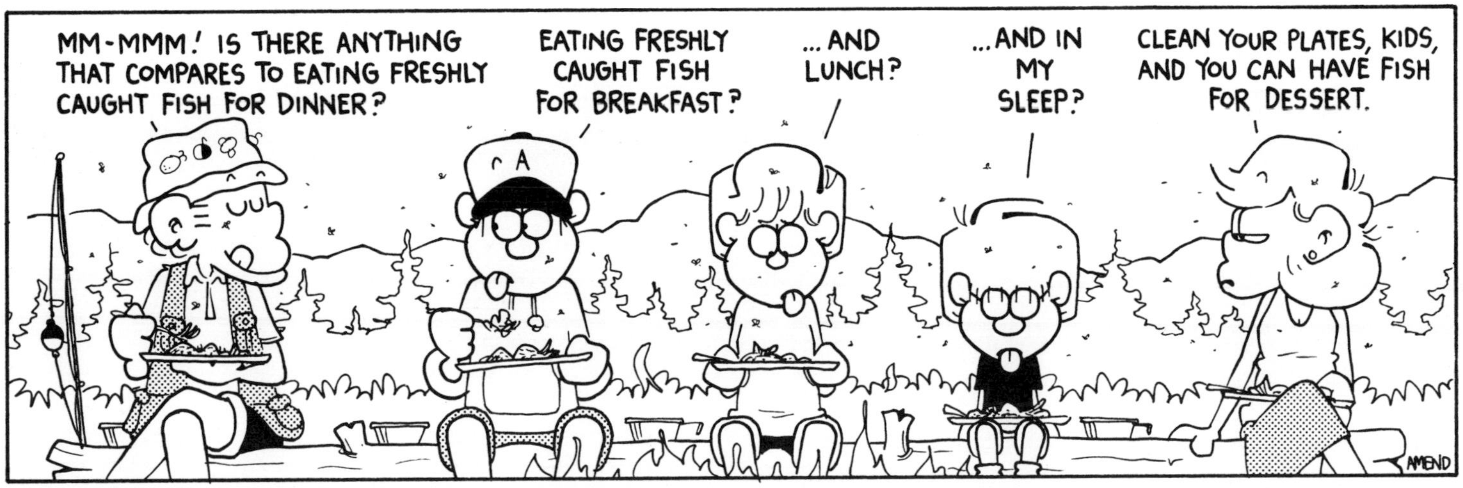

MM-MMM! IS THERE ANYTHING THAT COMPARES TO EATING FRESHLY CAUGHT FISH FOR DINNER?
EATING FRESHLY CAUGHT FISH FOR BREAKFAST?
...AND LUNCH?
...AND IN MY SLEEP?
CLEAN YOUR PLATES, KIDS, AND YOU CAN HAVE FISH FOR DESSERT.
AMEND

August 23, 1996

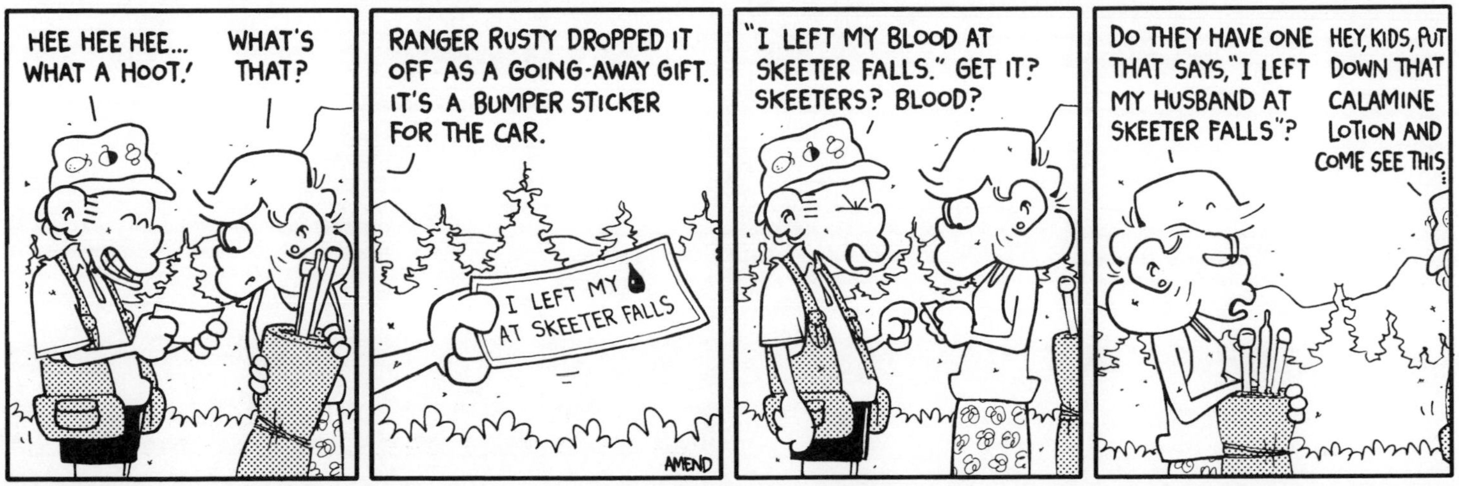

HEE HEE HEE... WHAT A HOOT!
WHAT'S THAT?
RANGER RUSTY DROPPED IT OFF AS A GOING-AWAY GIFT. IT'S A BUMPER STICKER FOR THE CAR.
I LEFT MY
AT SKEETER FALLS
AMEND
"I LEFT MY BLOOD AT SKEETER FALLS." GET IT? SKEETERS? BLOOD?
DO THEY HAVE ONE THAT SAYS, "I LEFT MY HUSBAND AT SKEETER FALLS"?
HEY, KIDS, PUT DOWN THAT CALAMINE LOTION AND COME SEE THIS.

August 24, 1996

This might be a good time to mention the availability of ad space on foxtrot.com.

August 25, 1996

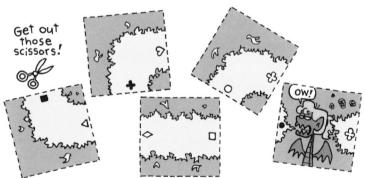
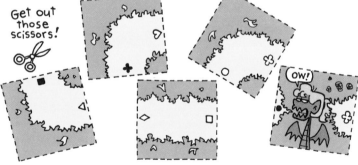
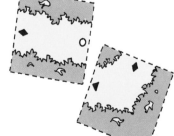

There's a company in Vermont that makes jigsaw puzzles where the pieces can go in more than one spot. I thought I'd give it a try myself.

October 13, 1996

June 21, 1996

February 22, 1997

I was reading a lot of Dr. Seuss to my kids during this era.

October 6, 1997

December 16, 1996

December 17, 1996

220

December 18, 1996

December 19, 1996

Apparently Paige doesn't proofread her dreams. It should be "Hermey."

December 20, 1996

December 21, 1996

I'm sure George Lucas didn't revamp the original trilogy just so I could have fun with the idea, but I'm grateful just the same.

January 27, 1997

January 28, 1997

January 29, 1997

WAIT A MINUTE — YOU'D HAVE JASON SKYWALKER TURN TO THE DARK SIDE OF THE FORCE?!

ABSOLUTELY. YOU BET.

I MEAN, THINK ABOUT IT. DARTH VADER WANTS SOMEONE TO HELP HIM RULE THE GALAXY. THE **GALAXY**! JASON CAN'T HELP IT IF HIS BROTHER LUKE'S A FOOL.

OBI-WAN HAS TAUGHT YOU WELL.

I WILL NOT FIGHT YOU, FATHER.

HE'S TALKING TO ME, YOU DOOFUS.

January 30, 1997

SO WHAT WOULD HAPPEN TO DARTH JASON AT THE END OF "RETURN OF THE JEDI"?

HE'D SNEAK OFF THE NEW DEATH STAR JUST BEFORE THE REBELS BLOW IT UP.

THE CURRENT ENDING IS JUST TOO DARN HAPPY. **MY** VERSION WOULD LEAVE MOVIEGOERS CHILLED WITH THE KNOWLEDGE THAT THIS NEW ARCH-VILLAIN IS LURKING SOMEWHERE OUT THERE, READY TO RESURFACE WHEN THE SEQUELS EVENTUALLY GET MADE.

SO HOW WOULD HE ESCAPE?

MY IDEA IS TO MAKE HIM A MASTER OF DISGUISE.

THEY **DID** IT, R2!

LUCKY SHOT. I MEAN, BLEEP BLOOP.

January 31, 1997

PETER! PETER! I GOT A LETTER FROM LUCASFILM!

OPEN IT UP! WHAT'S IT SAY?!

"DEAR MR. FOX:
    WE HAVE HAD A CHANCE TO REVIEW YOUR RECENT CORRESPONDENCE."

"UNFORTUNATELY, ALL WORK ON THE 'STAR WARS SPECIAL EDITION' TRILOGY WAS COMPLETED PRIOR TO RECEIPT OF YOUR LETTER AND WE THEREFORE HAVE NO CHOICE BUT TO PASS ON YOUR IDEAS."

OH, WELL.

THAT'S NOT AN "UN" — IT'S A LITTLE BLOB OF TONER.

AT LEAST THEY RETURNED MY DARTH JASON ACTION-FIGURE PROTOTYPE.

February 1, 1997

223

Ironically, I didn't launch my "own" FoxTrot website until twelve years later. Guess I'm not trendy.

March 10, 1997

March 11, 1997

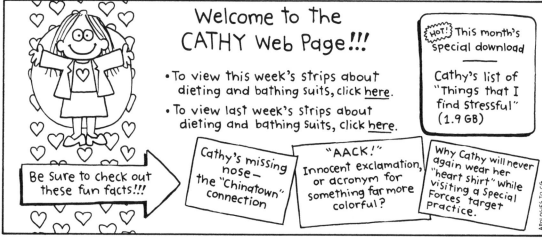

March 12, 1997

Panel 1 (March 13, 1997):

So, DO YOU THINK I SHOULD SEND MY WEB SITE IDEAS TO THE CARTOONISTS, OR TO THEIR SYNDICATES?

CAN WE INCLUDE THE TRASH CAN AS OPTION THREE?

Welcome to the DOONESBURY Web Page !!!

- To read today's strip, click <u>here</u>.
- To read the 22-page interview with German Finance Minister Theo Waigel from the November issue of The Economist, which helps put the punchline in some context, click <u>here</u>.

New! Download a listing of the entire cast of Doonesbury characters (not recommended for modems 28.8 kbps and slower)

AN IMPORTANT MESSAGE FROM UNCLE DUKE

Kids, I'm just <u>pretending</u> to take all those drugs.

A Special Sneak-Peek at One of Next Week's Strips!!!

What is it, Al? Sir, the Ethiopian ambassador wants to know if it's all right to eat you.

March 13, 1997

Panel 2 (March 14, 1997):

BUT THERE ALREADY **IS** A "DILBERT" WEB SITE, DOOFUS.

THAT DOESN'T MEAN THEY WON'T WANT FRESH IDEAS AT SOME POINT.

Welcome to the DILBERT ®™ⓘ etc. Web Page !!!

- For today's cartoon, complete with cubicle-placement suggestions, click <u>here</u>.
- To e-mail an idea to cartoonist Scott Adams, click <u>here</u>.
- For an explanation why you won't see a dime for your contribution, click <u>here</u>.

This page is sponsored by THE NATION OF JAPAN
Because we really like it when American workers read cartoons all day long.

For a list of Dilbert merchandise now licensed, click <u>here</u>.

For a list of Dilbert merchandise licensed since that last list was created, click <u>here</u>.

DOGBERT'S QUESTION OF THE WEEK
Will this be the year that Wally snaps?
Scott's answer on Monday

Army fatigues? This isn't "casual day"!

March 14, 1997

Panel 3 (March 15, 1997):

I HEAR YOU'VE GIVEN UP TRYING TO DESIGN WEB SITES FOR CARTOONISTS.

LET'S JUST SAY MY IDEAS WEREN'T GETTING THE RECEPTION I EXPECTED.

OH? WHO'D YOU HEAR FROM?

WELL, JIM DAVIS, WHO DOES "GARFIELD," SENT ME AN ENVELOPE FULL OF CONFETTI.

...WHICH I INITIALLY TOOK AS A SIGN THAT HE WANTED ME TO CELEBRATE OUR NEW PARTNERSHIP.

UNTIL YOU NOTICED IT WAS MADE FROM THE LETTER YOU SENT HIM.

THEN CHARLES SCHULZ SENT ME ASHES, WHICH I AT FIRST TOOK TO MEAN HE THOUGHT MY IDEAS WERE HOT...

March 15, 1997

225

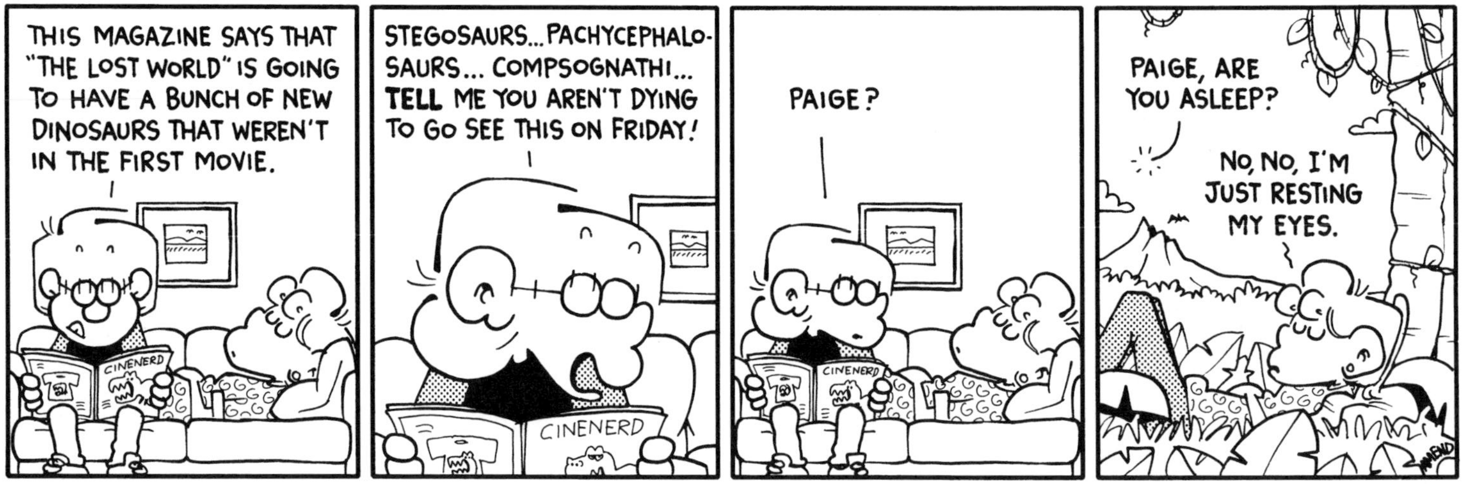
THIS MAGAZINE SAYS THAT "THE LOST WORLD" IS GOING TO HAVE A BUNCH OF NEW DINOSAURS THAT WEREN'T IN THE FIRST MOVIE.
CINENERD
STEGOSAURS... PACHYCEPHALOSAURS... COMPSOGNATHI... TELL ME YOU AREN'T DYING TO GO SEE THIS ON FRIDAY!
CINENERD
PAIGE?
CINENERD
PAIGE, ARE YOU ASLEEP?
NO, NO, I'M JUST RESTING MY EYES.
AMEND

May 19, 1997

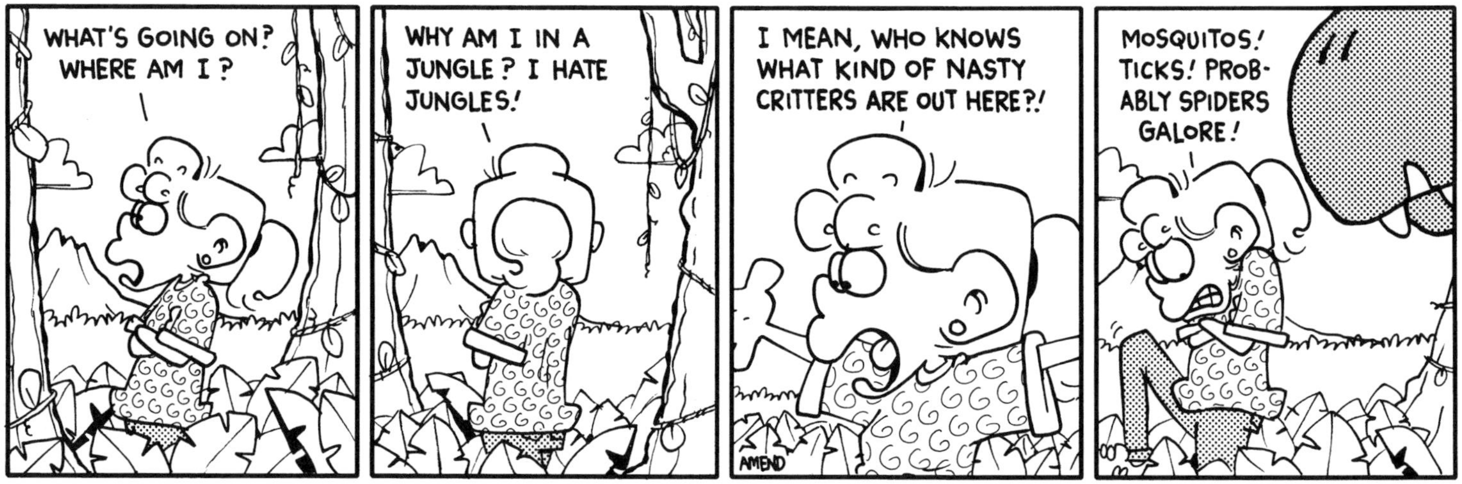
WHAT'S GOING ON? WHERE AM I?
WHY AM I IN A JUNGLE? I HATE JUNGLES!
I MEAN, WHO KNOWS WHAT KIND OF NASTY CRITTERS ARE OUT HERE?!
AMEND
MOSQUITOS! TICKS! PROBABLY SPIDERS GALORE!

May 20, 1997

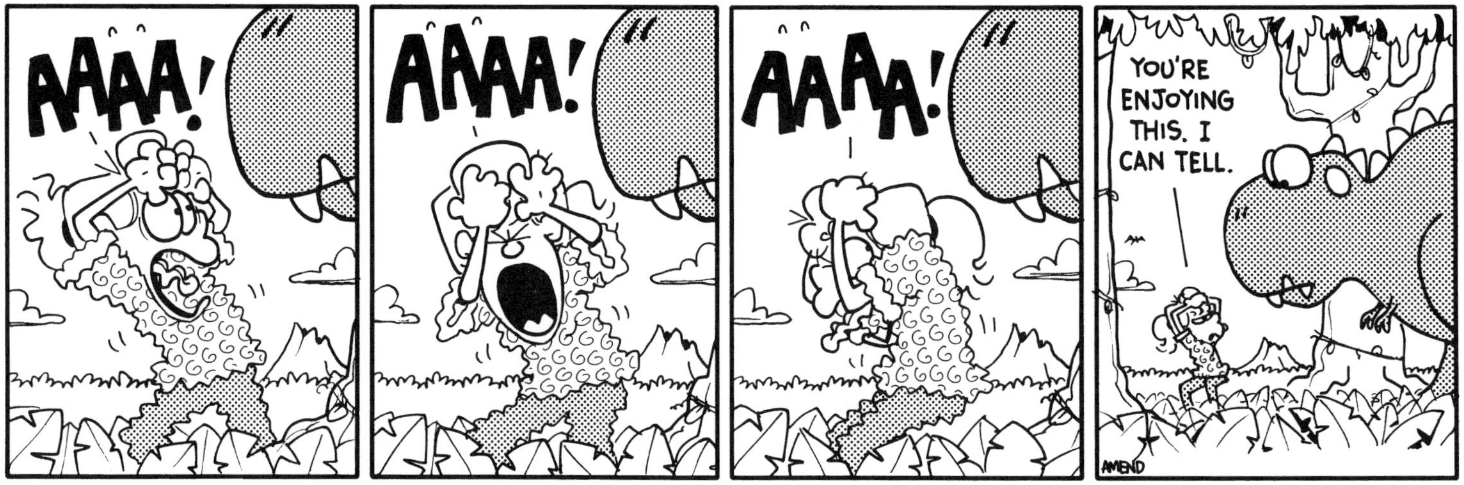
AAAA!
AAAA!
AAAA!
YOU'RE ENJOYING THIS. I CAN TELL.
AMEND

May 21, 1997

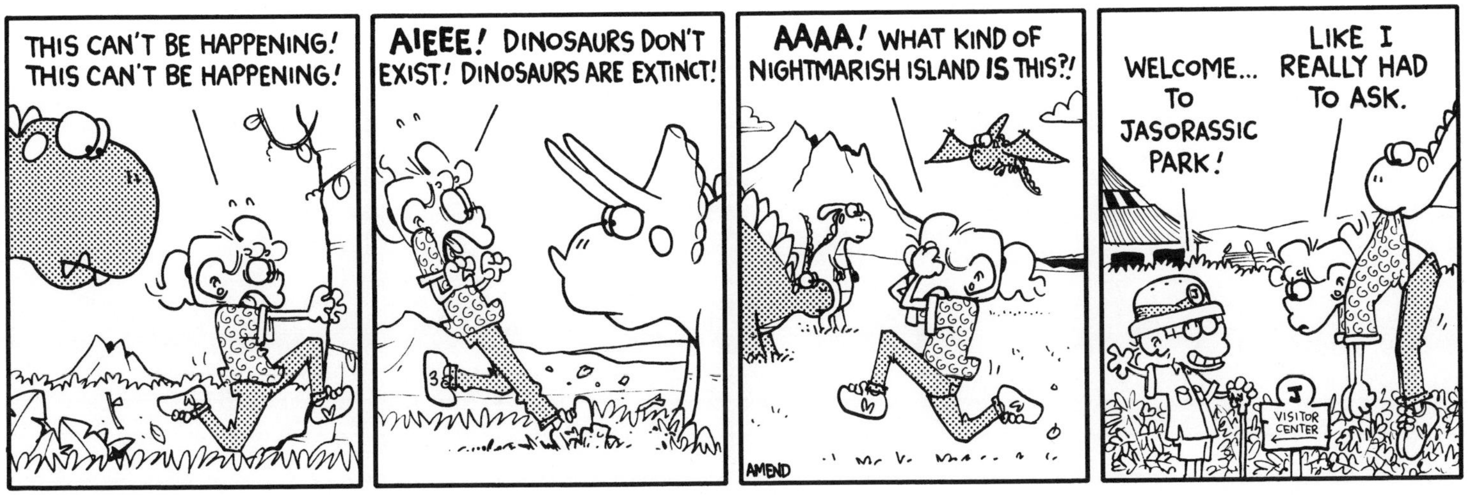
THIS CAN'T BE HAPPENING! THIS CAN'T BE HAPPENING!
AIEEE! DINOSAURS DON'T EXIST! DINOSAURS ARE EXTINCT!
AAAA! WHAT KIND OF NIGHTMARISH ISLAND IS THIS?!
AMEND
WELCOME... TO JASORASSIC PARK!
LIKE I REALLY HAD TO ASK.
VISITOR CENTER

May 22, 1997

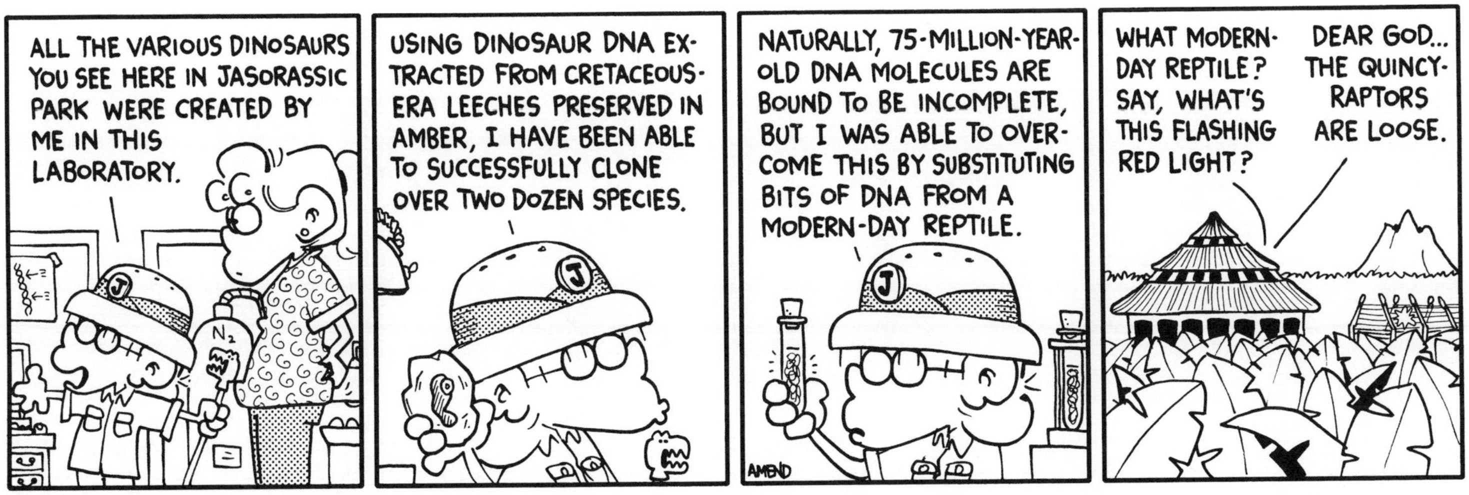
ALL THE VARIOUS DINOSAURS YOU SEE HERE IN JASORASSIC PARK WERE CREATED BY ME IN THIS LABORATORY.
USING DINOSAUR DNA EXTRACTED FROM CRETACEOUS-ERA LEECHES PRESERVED IN AMBER, I HAVE BEEN ABLE TO SUCCESSFULLY CLONE OVER TWO DOZEN SPECIES.
NATURALLY, 75-MILLION-YEAR-OLD DNA MOLECULES ARE BOUND TO BE INCOMPLETE, BUT I WAS ABLE TO OVERCOME THIS BY SUBSTITUTING BITS OF DNA FROM A MODERN-DAY REPTILE.
AMEND
WHAT MODERN-DAY REPTILE? SAY, WHAT'S THIS FLASHING RED LIGHT?
DEAR GOD... THE QUINCY-RAPTORS ARE LOOSE.

May 23, 1997

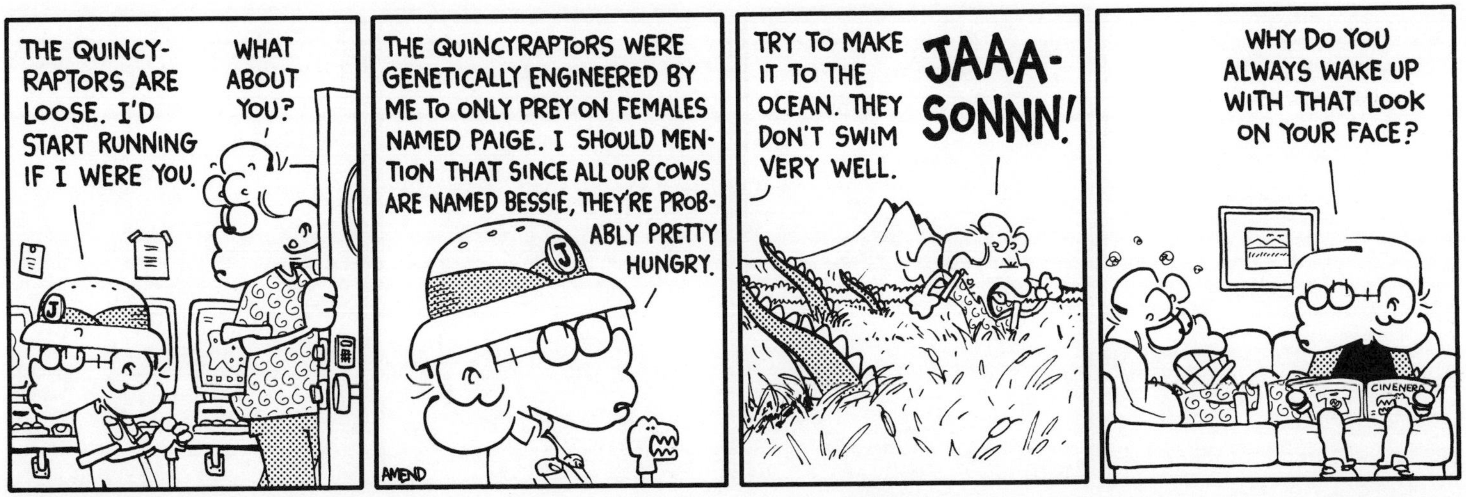
THE QUINCY-RAPTORS ARE LOOSE. I'D START RUNNING IF I WERE YOU.
WHAT ABOUT YOU?
THE QUINCYRAPTORS WERE GENETICALLY ENGINEERED BY ME TO ONLY PREY ON FEMALES NAMED PAIGE. I SHOULD MENTION THAT SINCE ALL OUR COWS ARE NAMED BESSIE, THEY'RE PROBABLY PRETTY HUNGRY.
AMEND
TRY TO MAKE IT TO THE OCEAN. THEY DON'T SWIM VERY WELL.
JAAA-SONNN!
WHY DO YOU ALWAYS WAKE UP WITH THAT LOOK ON YOUR FACE?
CINENERD

May 24, 1997

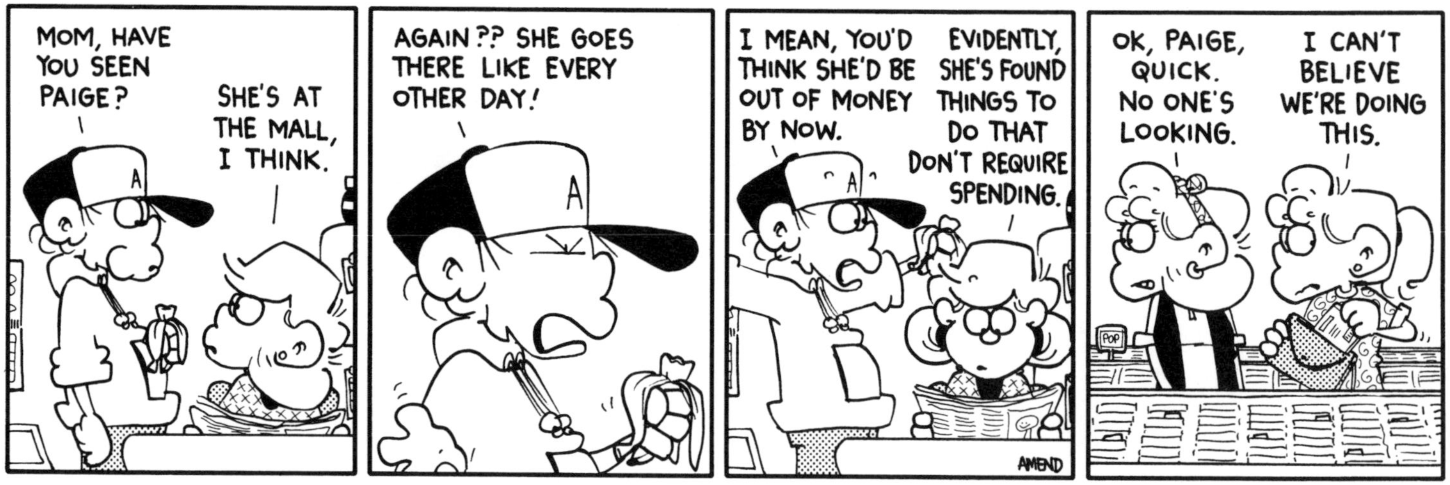
MOM, HAVE YOU SEEN PAIGE?
SHE'S AT THE MALL, I THINK.
AGAIN?? SHE GOES THERE LIKE EVERY OTHER DAY!
I MEAN, YOU'D THINK SHE'D BE OUT OF MONEY BY NOW.
EVIDENTLY, SHE'S FOUND THINGS TO DO THAT DON'T REQUIRE SPENDING.
OK, PAIGE, QUICK. NO ONE'S LOOKING.
I CAN'T BELIEVE WE'RE DOING THIS.

June 2, 1997

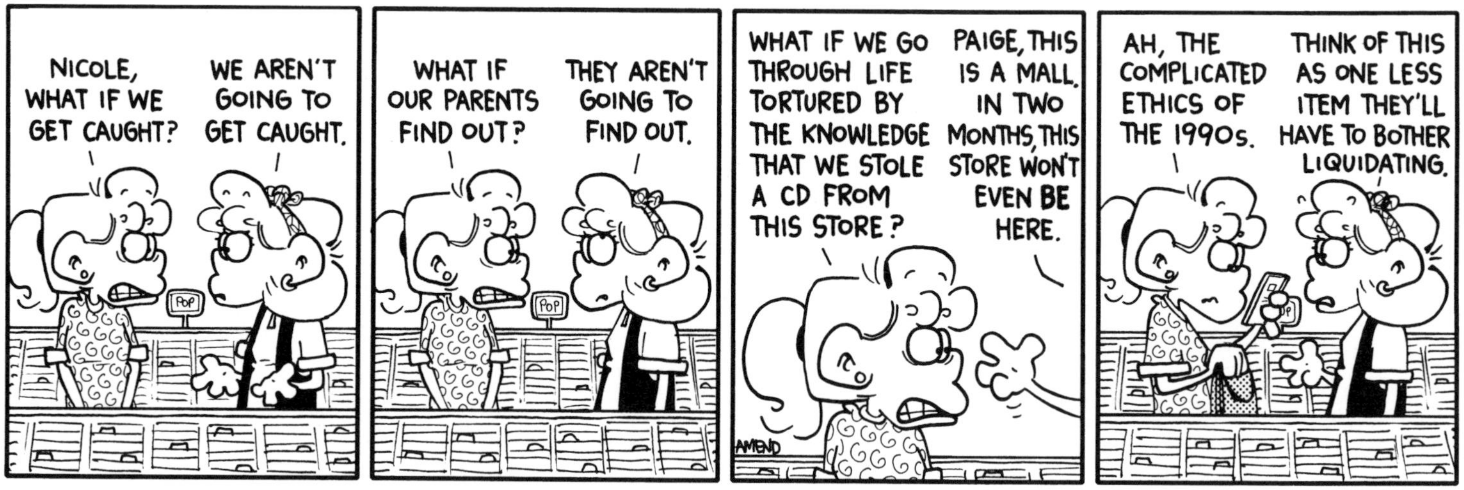
NICOLE, WHAT IF WE GET CAUGHT?
WE AREN'T GOING TO GET CAUGHT.
WHAT IF OUR PARENTS FIND OUT?
THEY AREN'T GOING TO FIND OUT.
WHAT IF WE GO THROUGH LIFE TORTURED BY THE KNOWLEDGE THAT WE STOLE A CD FROM THIS STORE?
PAIGE, THIS IS A MALL. IN TWO MONTHS, THIS STORE WON'T EVEN BE HERE.
AH, THE COMPLICATED ETHICS OF THE 1990s.
THINK OF THIS AS ONE LESS ITEM THEY'LL HAVE TO BOTHER LIQUIDATING.

June 3, 1997

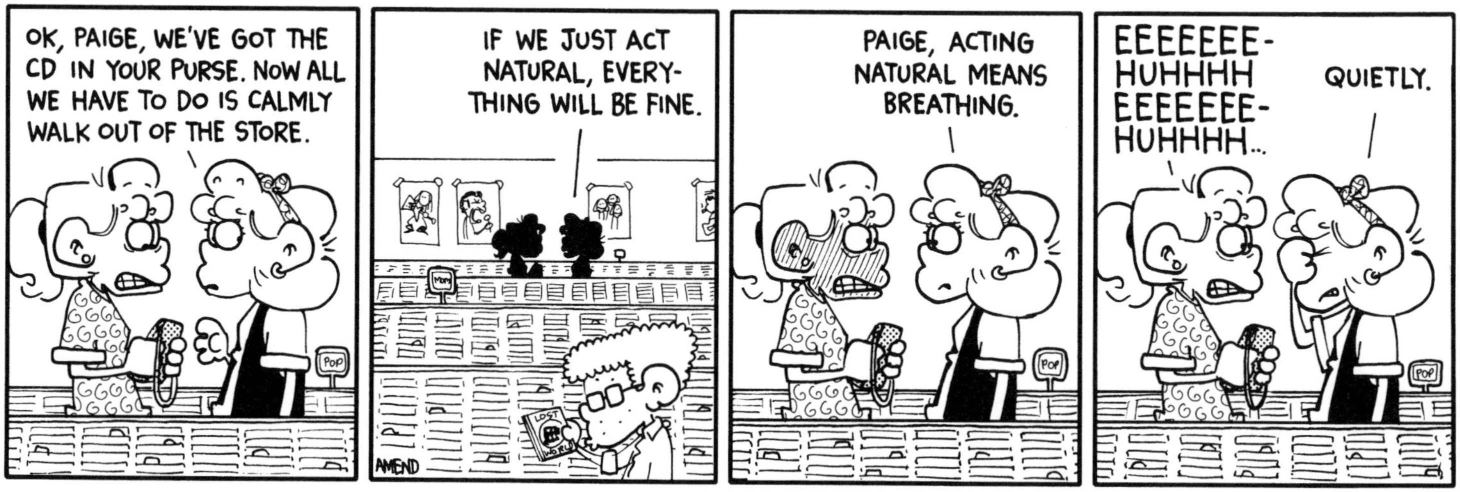
OK, PAIGE, WE'VE GOT THE CD IN YOUR PURSE. NOW ALL WE HAVE TO DO IS CALMLY WALK OUT OF THE STORE.
IF WE JUST ACT NATURAL, EVERYTHING WILL BE FINE.
PAIGE, ACTING NATURAL MEANS BREATHING.
EEEEEEE-HUHHHH EEEEEEE-HUHHHH...
QUIETLY.

June 4, 1997

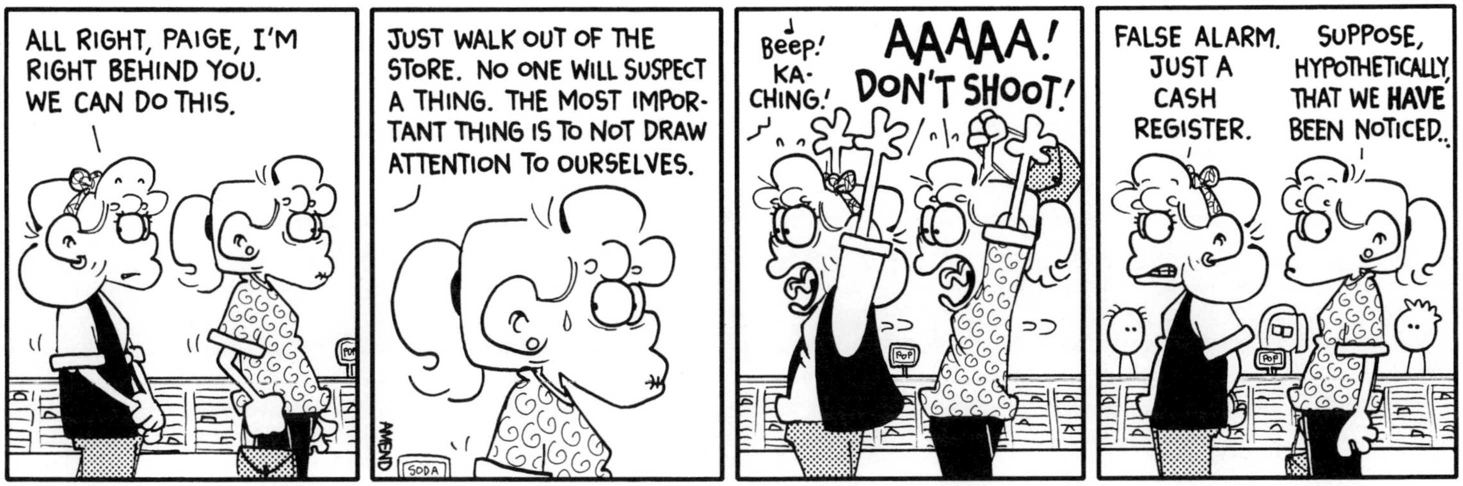
ALL RIGHT, PAIGE, I'M RIGHT BEHIND YOU. WE CAN DO THIS.
JUST WALK OUT OF THE STORE. NO ONE WILL SUSPECT A THING. THE MOST IMPORTANT THING IS TO NOT DRAW ATTENTION TO OURSELVES.
SODA
Beep! KA-CHING!
AAAAA! DON'T SHOOT!
POP
FALSE ALARM. JUST A CASH REGISTER.
SUPPOSE, HYPOTHETICALLY, THAT WE HAVE BEEN NOTICED..
AMEND

June 5, 1997

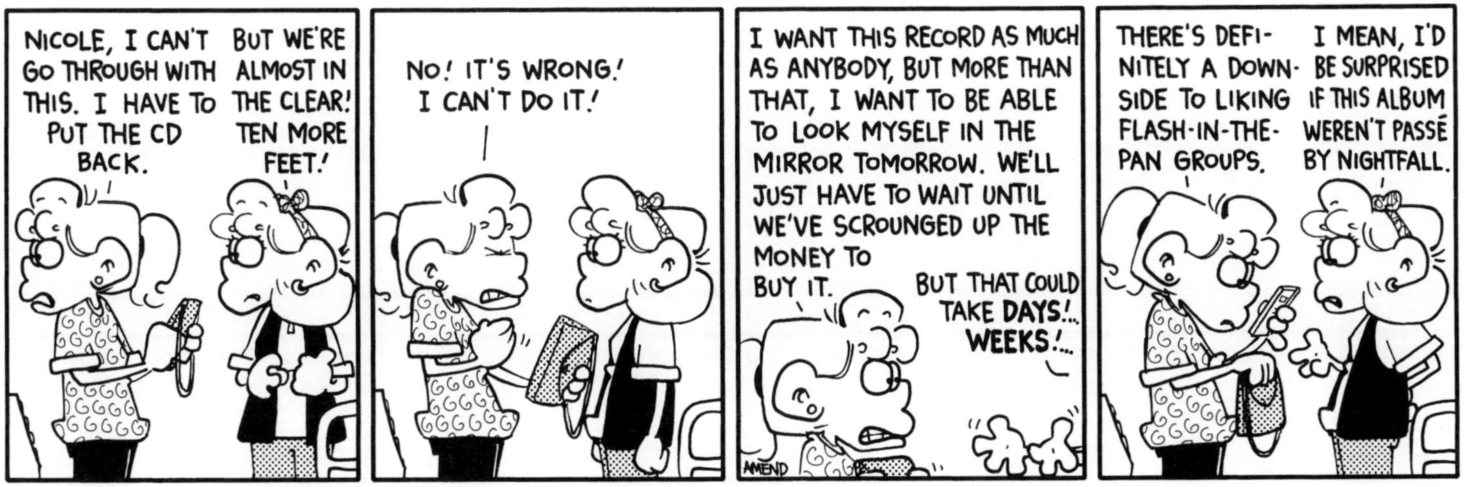
NICOLE, I CAN'T GO THROUGH WITH THIS. I HAVE TO PUT THE CD BACK.
BUT WE'RE ALMOST IN THE CLEAR! TEN MORE FEET!
NO! IT'S WRONG! I CAN'T DO IT!
I WANT THIS RECORD AS MUCH AS ANYBODY, BUT MORE THAN THAT, I WANT TO BE ABLE TO LOOK MYSELF IN THE MIRROR TOMORROW. WE'LL JUST HAVE TO WAIT UNTIL WE'VE SCROUNGED UP THE MONEY TO BUY IT.
BUT THAT COULD TAKE DAYS!... WEEKS!...
THERE'S DEFINITELY A DOWNSIDE TO LIKING FLASH-IN-THE-PAN GROUPS.
I MEAN, I'D BE SURPRISED IF THIS ALBUM WEREN'T PASSÉ BY NIGHTFALL.
AMEND

June 6, 1997

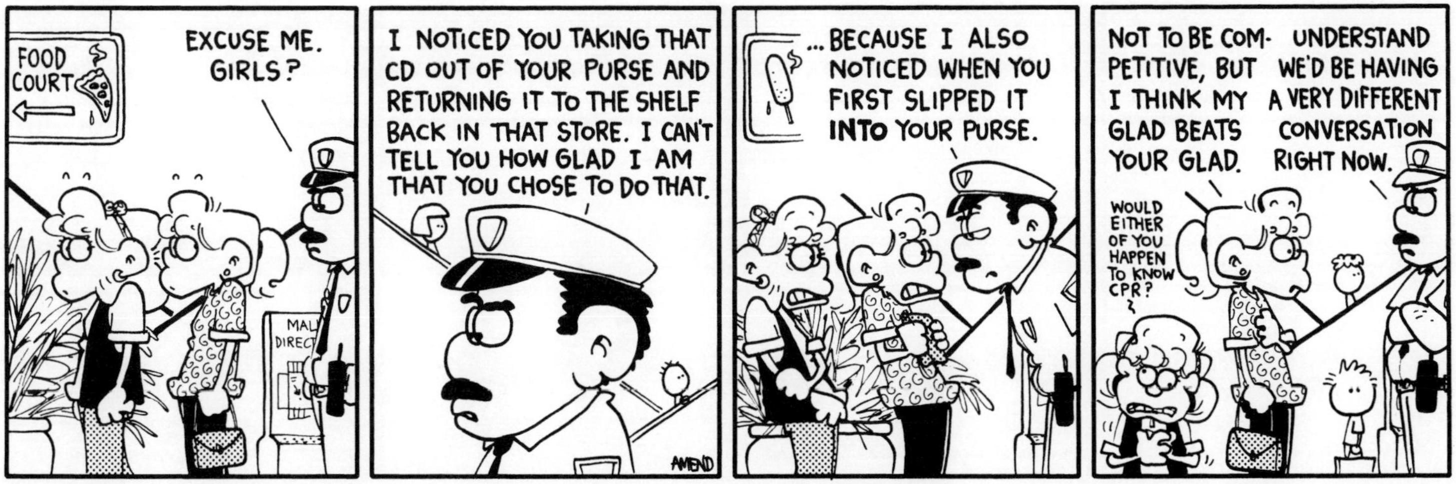
FOOD COURT
EXCUSE ME. GIRLS?
MALL DIRECT
I NOTICED YOU TAKING THAT CD OUT OF YOUR PURSE AND RETURNING IT TO THE SHELF BACK IN THAT STORE. I CAN'T TELL YOU HOW GLAD I AM THAT YOU CHOSE TO DO THAT.
AMEND
...BECAUSE I ALSO NOTICED WHEN YOU FIRST SLIPPED IT INTO YOUR PURSE.
NOT TO BE COMPETITIVE, BUT I THINK MY GLAD BEATS YOUR GLAD.
UNDERSTAND WE'D BE HAVING A VERY DIFFERENT CONVERSATION RIGHT NOW.
WOULD EITHER OF YOU HAPPEN TO KNOW CPR?

June 7, 1997

PAIGE! PAIGE! I GOT A JOB FOR THE SUMMER!

GET OUT! WHERE?!

AT THE PAVILIONPLEX-22 MOVIE THEATER! I FILLED OUT AN APPLICATION LAST WEEK AND THEY JUST CALLED TO SAY I CAN START TOMORROW!

COOL.

JUST THINK! ME... IN THE **FILM INDUSTRY!** I ALWAYS KNEW THAT IF I HELD OUT LONG ENOUGH, A DREAM JOB LIKE THIS WOULD SOMEDAY COME MY WAY!

ORDINARILY, I'D START YOU ON THE RESTROOM STALLS, BUT WE'VE GOT MAJOR SODA SPILLAGE IN THEATER 18.

WHY DID YOU ASK IF I OWNED KNEE PADS?

June 9, 1997

FOX, THEATERS 1 THROUGH 7 NEED CLEANING.

PETER, THEATERS 8 THROUGH 15 NEED CLEANING.

FOX, THEATERS 16 THROUGH 22 NEED CLEANING.

FINALLY, THEY'LL ALL BE DONE.

THEATERS 1 THROUGH 7 ARE READY FOR CLEANING AGAIN.

I'M BEGINNING TO SEE A REAL DOWNSIDE TO THIS JOB.

June 10, 1997

HOW'S PETER'S MOVIE THEATER JOB GOING?

JUST GREAT, FROM WHAT HE TELLS ME.

HE SAYS THEY MAY EVEN LET HIM WORK THE CONCESSION STAND TONIGHT.

HE SHOULD DO WELL AT THAT. WE FOXES ARE NATURAL SALESMEN.

REALLY? HE STRIKES ME AS BEING JUST A LITTLE TOO HONEST.

WOULD YOU LIKE OUR CHEESE-LIKE SAUCE ON YOUR NACHOS, OR SOME OILY FAKE BUTTER ON YOUR POPCORN, MA'AM?

PETER, MAY I SPEAK TO YOU FOR A SECOND?

June 11, 1997

230

June 12, 1997

Panel 1:
WHAT'S THIS?? I ORDERED A **LARGE** ROOT BEER.
UM, YOU ORDERED A SMALL.

Panel 2:
IT'S HOT... I'M THIRSTY... WHY WOULD I HAVE ORDERED A SMALL?! "LARGE," I DEFINITELY ORDERED A LARGE!
MA'AM, YOU MAY HAVE **MEANT** TO SAY "LARGE," BUT THE REALITY IS YOU SAID "SMALL."

Panel 3:
LOOK, YOU CLOD, HAVE YOU NEVER HEARD THE EXPRESSION, "THE CUSTOMER IS ALWAYS RIGHT"?!
BUT YOU'RE WRONG.

Panel 4:
I MUST SAY, FOX, YOU'RE THE FIRST EMPLOYEE I'VE HAD WHO **WANTED** TO GO BACK TO MOPPING BATHROOMS.
ACTUALLY, I SHOULD MOP THE CONCESSION AREA FIRST.

June 13, 1997

Panel 1:
HOW WAS WORK, SWEETIE?
UGGH. THIS JOB IS A LOT HARDER THAN I THOUGHT IT'D BE.

Panel 2:
I FIGURED BY WORKING IN A MOVIE THEATER, I'D GET TO BASICALLY HANG OUT AND WATCH MOVIES FOR FREE ALL SUMMER. ALL I'VE SEEN SO FAR ARE ABOUT THREE MINUTES OF "THE LOST WORLD" ON WEDNESDAY.

Panel 3:
AND THAT WAS ONLY BECAUSE I HAD TO RUSH IN AND BREAK UP TWO PSYCHOS HAVING A POPCORN FIGHT.

Panel 4:
SAY, DIDN'T JASON AND PAIGE GO SEE THAT MOVIE ON WEDNESDAY?
FORTUNATELY, IT WAS DARK, SO THEY MISTOOK ME FOR AN AUTHORITY FIGURE.

June 14, 1997

Panel 1:
HERE YOU GO, PETER. PAY DAY.
YOWZA!

Panel 2:
THIS IS SO EXCITING! I'VE NEVER EVER GOTTEN A PAY-CHECK BEFORE! MAYBE I SHOULD FRAME IT... OR HAVE IT BRONZED... OR BLOWN UP INTO A POSTER!

Panel 3:
WELL, WHATEVER YOU DECIDE, YOU'VE EARNED IT. KEEP UP THE GOOD WORK.

Panel 4:
UM, STANDING NEXT TO A THEATER CONCESSION STAND IS PROBABLY NOT THE BEST PLACE TO LOOK AT THAT.
THERE MUST BE SOME MISTAKE...THIS WON'T EVEN BUY TWO BOXES OF MILK DUDS.

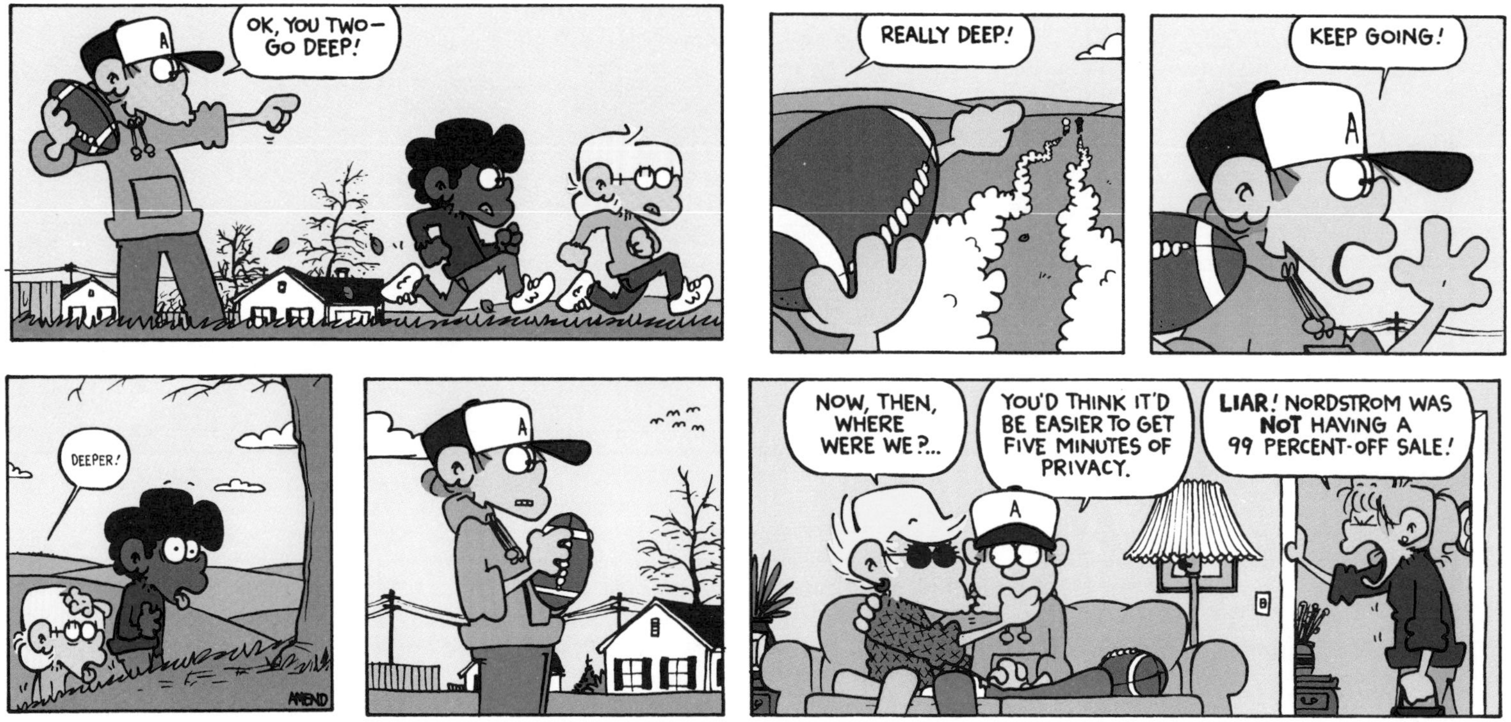
OK, YOU TWO—GO DEEP!
REALLY DEEP!
KEEP GOING!
DEEPER!
AMEND
NOW, THEN, WHERE WERE WE?...
YOU'D THINK IT'D BE EASIER TO GET FIVE MINUTES OF PRIVACY.
LIAR! NORDSTROM WAS NOT HAVING A 99 PERCENT-OFF SALE!

December 1, 1996

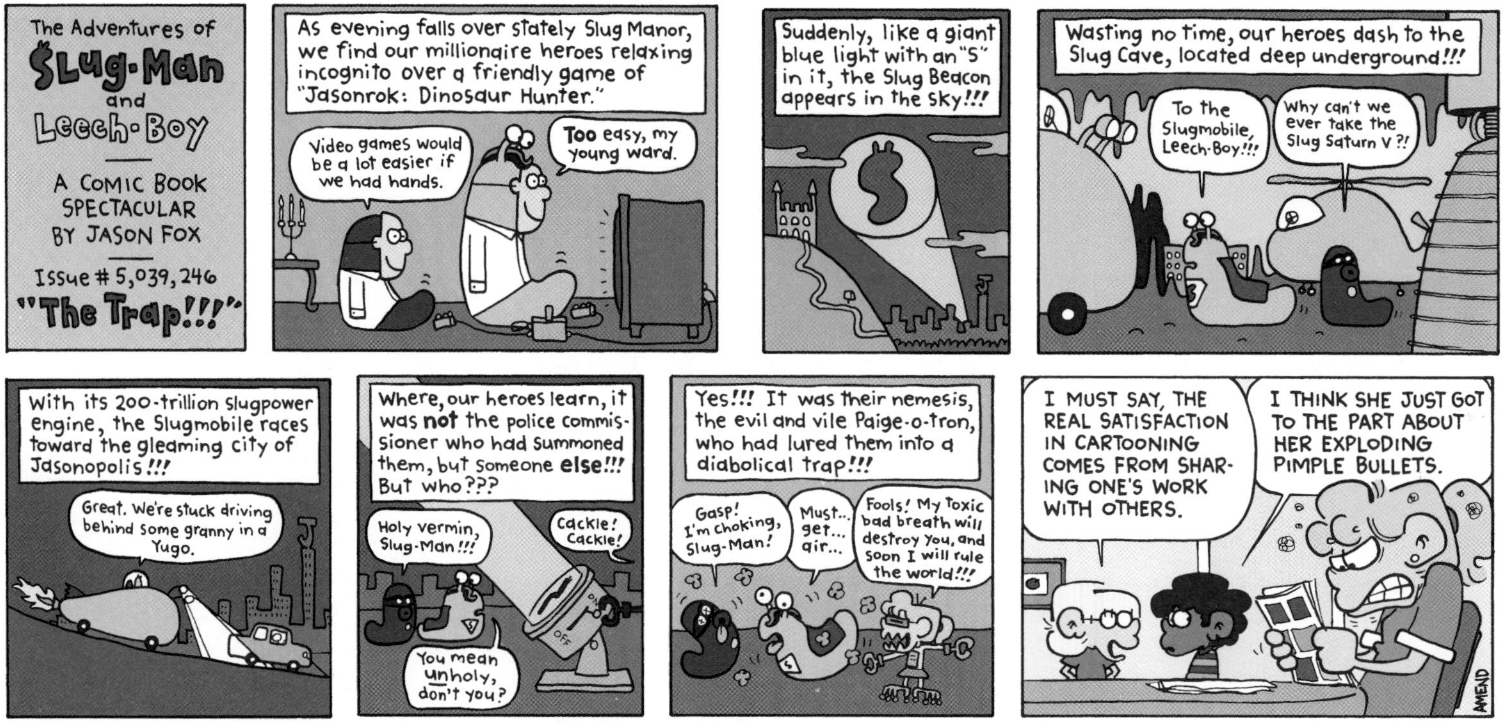
The Adventures of $lug-Man and Leech-Boy
A COMIC BOOK SPECTACULAR BY JASON FOX
Issue # 5,039,246
"The Trap!!!"
As evening falls over stately Slug Manor, we find our millionaire heroes relaxing incognito over a friendly game of "Jasonrok: Dinosaur Hunter."
Video games would be a lot easier if we had hands.
Too easy, my young ward.
Suddenly, like a giant blue light with an "S" in it, the Slug Beacon appears in the sky!!!
Wasting no time, our heroes dash to the Slug Cave, located deep underground!!!
To the Slugmobile, Leech-Boy!!!
Why can't we ever take the Slug Saturn V?!
With its 200-trillion slugpower engine, the Slugmobile races toward the gleaming city of Jasonopolis!!!
Great. We're stuck driving behind some granny in a Yugo.
Where, our heroes learn, it was not the police commissioner who had summoned them, but someone else!!! But who???
Holy vermin, Slug-Man!!!
Cackle! Cackle!
You mean unholy, don't you?
OFF
Yes!!! It was their nemesis, the evil and vile Paige-o-tron, who had lured them into a diabolical trap!!!
Gasp! I'm choking, Slug-Man!
Must... get... air...
Fools! My toxic bad breath will destroy you, and soon I will rule the world!!!
I MUST SAY, THE REAL SATISFACTION IN CARTOONING COMES FROM SHARING ONE'S WORK WITH OTHERS.
I THINK SHE JUST GOT TO THE PART ABOUT HER EXPLODING PIMPLE BULLETS.
AMEND

April 27, 1997

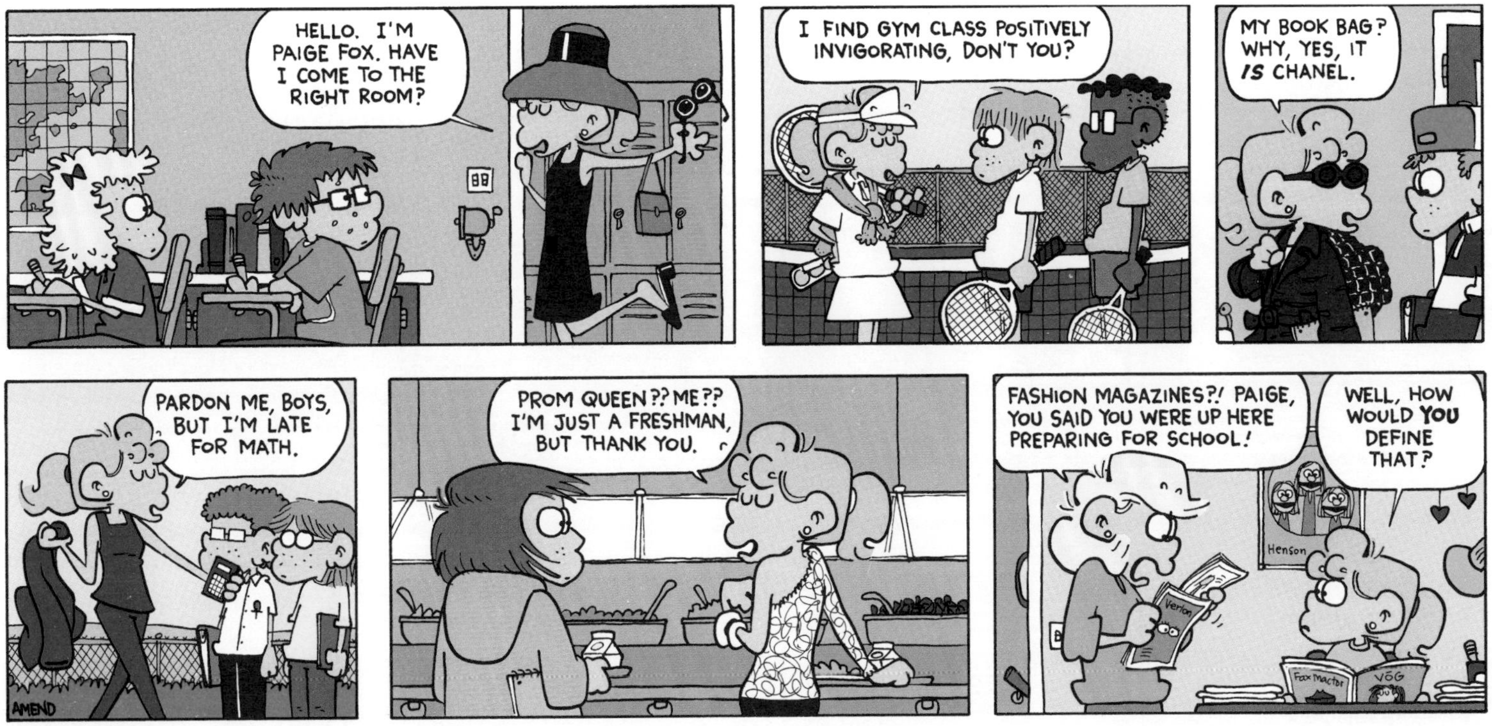
HELLO. I'M PAIGE FOX. HAVE I COME TO THE RIGHT ROOM?
I FIND GYM CLASS POSITIVELY INVIGORATING, DON'T YOU?
MY BOOK BAG? WHY, YES, IT *IS* CHANEL.
PARDON ME, BOYS, BUT I'M LATE FOR MATH.
PROM QUEEN?? ME?? I'M JUST A FRESHMAN, BUT THANK YOU.
FASHION MAGAZINES?! PAIGE, YOU SAID YOU WERE UP HERE PREPARING FOR SCHOOL!
WELL, HOW WOULD **YOU** DEFINE THAT?
Henson
VÖG
AMEND

August 31, 1997

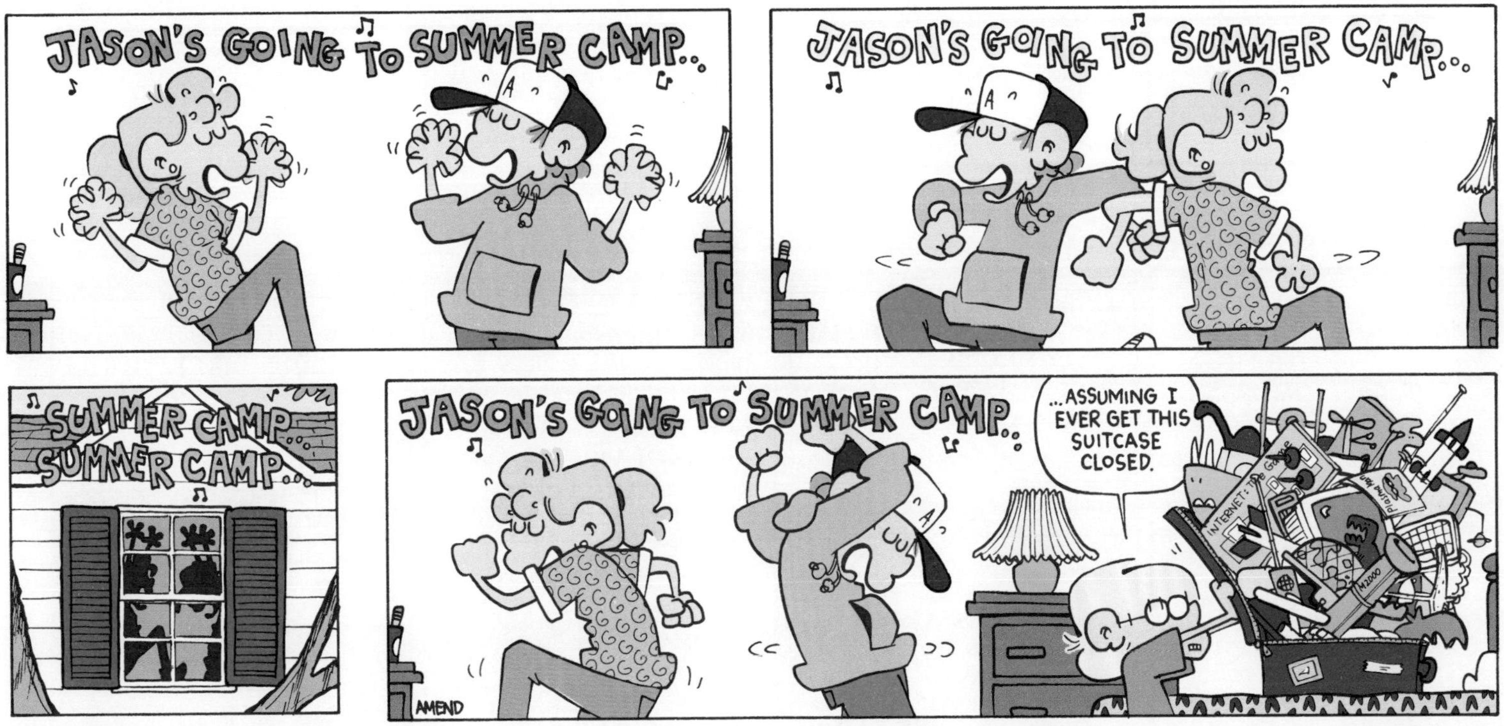
JASON'S GOING TO SUMMER CAMP...
JASON'S GOING TO SUMMER CAMP...
SUMMER CAMP... SUMMER CAMP...
JASON'S GOING TO SUMMER CAMP...
...ASSUMING I EVER GET THIS SUITCASE CLOSED.
AMEND

June 22, 1997

Doing a long story line over the summer seemed like a fun, creative challenge.

YOUR FATHER'S GETTING THE CAR. NOW, YOU'RE SURE YOU DIDN'T FORGET ANYTHING?

PRETTY SURE.

YOU'VE GOT YOUR TOOTHBRUSH?

YUP.

FLASHLIGHT?

YUP.

DAD GAVE YOU SOME SPENDING MONEY?

NOT ENOUGH, BUT YEAH.

LAKE BOHRMORE SCIENCE CAMP

WELL, THEN, I GUESS WE'LL SEE YOU IN AUGUST, SWEETIE.

WAIT. I DID FORGET SOMETHING.

WHAT'S THAT?

TO SAY I'LL MISS YOU, MOM.

June 23, 1997

THINK ABOUT IT, MARCUS! WE'RE GOING TO BE AT THIS SCIENCE CAMP TOGETHER ALL SUMMER!

YOU AND ME! THE TWO MUSKETEERS!

BOTH FOR ONE AND ONE FOR BOTH!

SURROUNDED BY COMPUTERS... LASERS... A PALEONTOLOGY LAB... LIFE JUST DOESN'T GET ANY BETTER THAN THIS!

HOLY COW!

JASON! MARCUS!

IT DOES, HOWEVER, GET WAY, WAY WORSE.

I DIDN'T KNOW SHE WAS COMING HERE...

June 24, 1997

JASON! MARCUS!

DEAR GOD.

IT'S EILEEN JACOBSON FROM SCHOOL!

I CAN'T BELIEVE YOU GUYS ARE ENROLLED AT CAMP BOHRMORE, TOO! THIS IS AWESOME!

WE JUST GOT HERE. HOW 'BOUT YOU?

I GOT IN A COUPLE HOURS AGO. OH, MAN, I DIDN'T THINK I WAS GOING TO KNOW ANYBODY HERE, BUT NOW IT TURNS OUT I CAN HANG OUT WITH YOU TWO ALL SUMMER! I'M SO PSYCHED!

YOU KNOW, JASON, I'VE NEVER FORGOTTEN THAT TIME WE WENT OUT FOR ICE CREAM TOGETHER.

EXCUSE ME WHILE I TRY TO FIND SOME HEMLOCK TO SWALLOW.

YOU TWO WENT OUT FOR ICE CREAM?? WHEN WAS THIS??

June 25, 1997

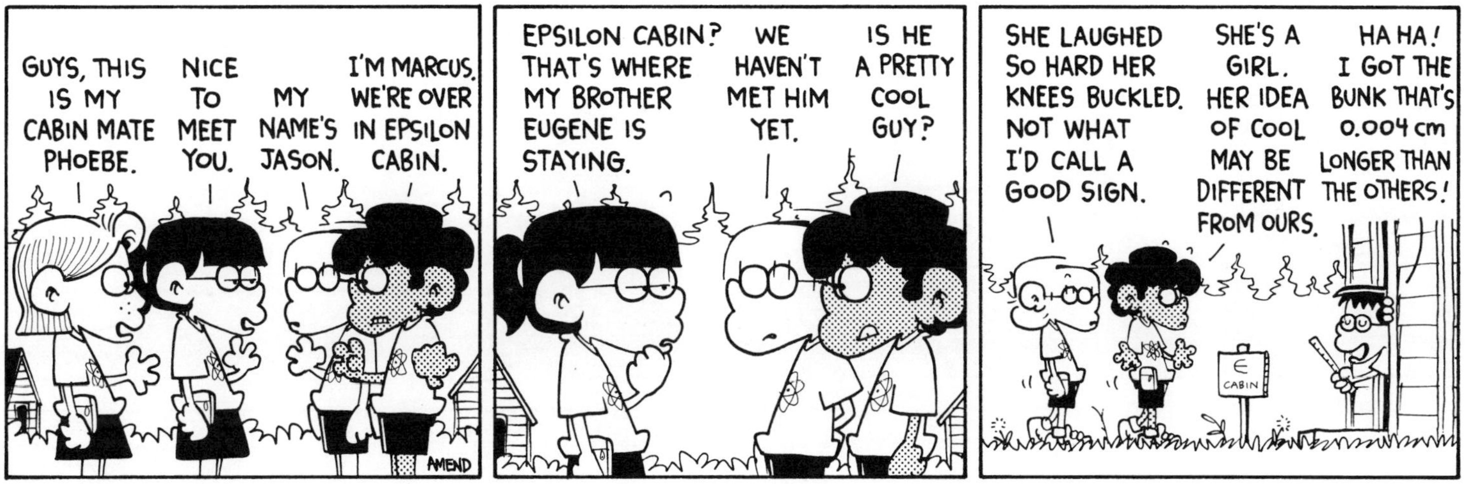
GUYS, THIS IS MY CABIN MATE PHOEBE.
NICE TO MEET YOU.
MY NAME'S JASON.
I'M MARCUS. WE'RE OVER IN EPSILON CABIN.
EPSILON CABIN? THAT'S WHERE MY BROTHER EUGENE IS STAYING.
WE HAVEN'T MET HIM YET.
IS HE A PRETTY COOL GUY?
SHE LAUGHED SO HARD HER KNEES BUCKLED. NOT WHAT I'D CALL A GOOD SIGN.
SHE'S A GIRL. HER IDEA OF COOL MAY BE DIFFERENT FROM OURS.
HA HA! I GOT THE BUNK THAT'S 0.004 cm LONGER THAN THE OTHERS!
CABIN
AMEND

June 26, 1997

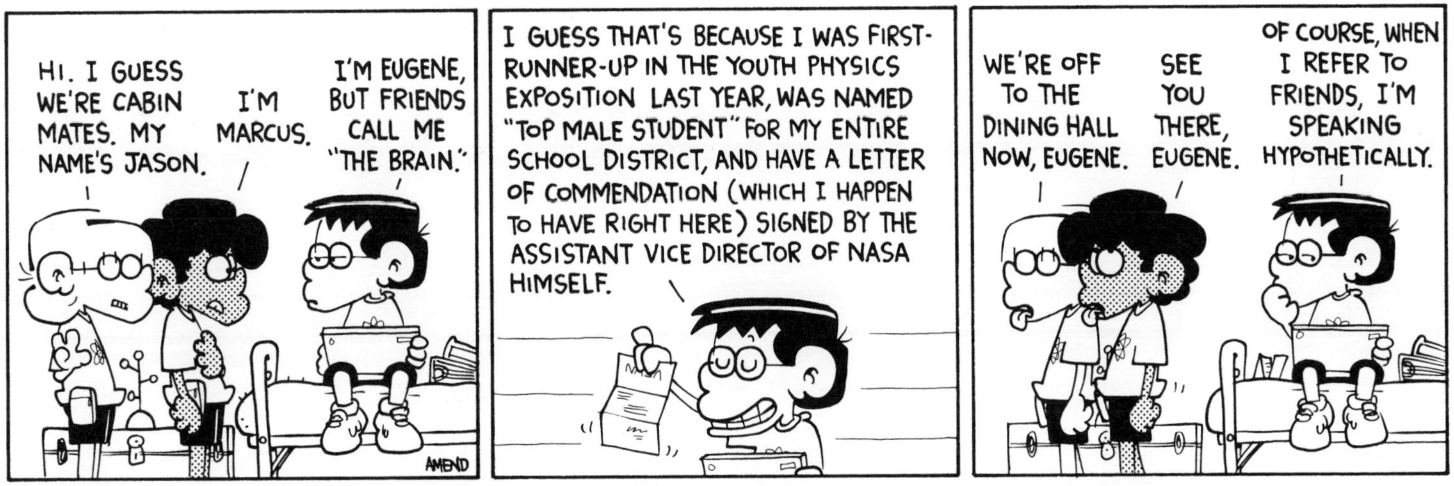
HI. I GUESS WE'RE CABIN MATES. MY NAME'S JASON.
I'M MARCUS.
I'M EUGENE, BUT FRIENDS CALL ME "THE BRAIN."
I GUESS THAT'S BECAUSE I WAS FIRST-RUNNER-UP IN THE YOUTH PHYSICS EXPOSITION LAST YEAR, WAS NAMED "TOP MALE STUDENT" FOR MY ENTIRE SCHOOL DISTRICT, AND HAVE A LETTER OF COMMENDATION (WHICH I HAPPEN TO HAVE RIGHT HERE) SIGNED BY THE ASSISTANT VICE DIRECTOR OF NASA HIMSELF.
WE'RE OFF TO THE DINING HALL NOW, EUGENE.
SEE YOU THERE, EUGENE.
OF COURSE, WHEN I REFER TO FRIENDS, I'M SPEAKING HYPOTHETICALLY.
AMEND

June 27, 1997

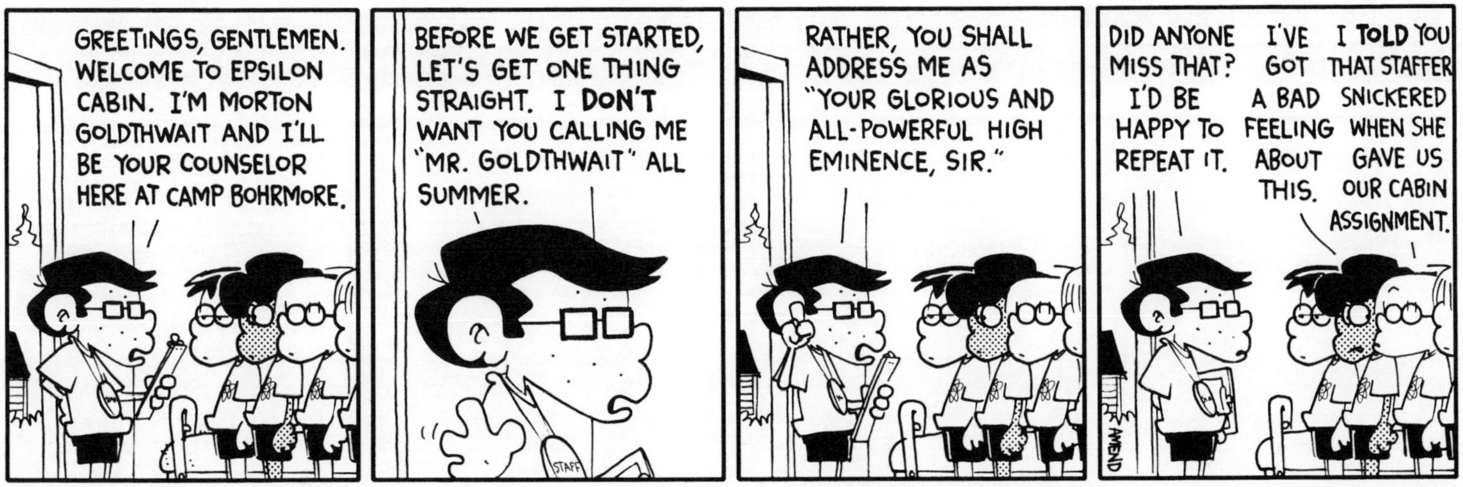
GREETINGS, GENTLEMEN. WELCOME TO EPSILON CABIN. I'M MORTON GOLDTHWAIT AND I'LL BE YOUR COUNSELOR HERE AT CAMP BOHRMORE.
BEFORE WE GET STARTED, LET'S GET ONE THING STRAIGHT. I DON'T WANT YOU CALLING ME "MR. GOLDTHWAIT" ALL SUMMER.
STAFF
RATHER, YOU SHALL ADDRESS ME AS "YOUR GLORIOUS AND ALL-POWERFUL HIGH EMINENCE, SIR."
DID ANYONE MISS THAT? I'D BE HAPPY TO REPEAT IT.
I'VE GOT A BAD FEELING ABOUT THIS.
I TOLD YOU THAT STAFFER SNICKERED WHEN SHE GAVE US OUR CABIN ASSIGNMENT.
AMEND

June 28, 1997

Because not every paper carried both the Sunday and the dailies, each had to make sense without the other.

June 29, 1997

July 6, 1997

Niels Bohr was a Nobel Prize–winning physicist, probably most famous for his model of atomic structure.

The little paper on the wall in panel two spells out GOOD JOB in ASCII.

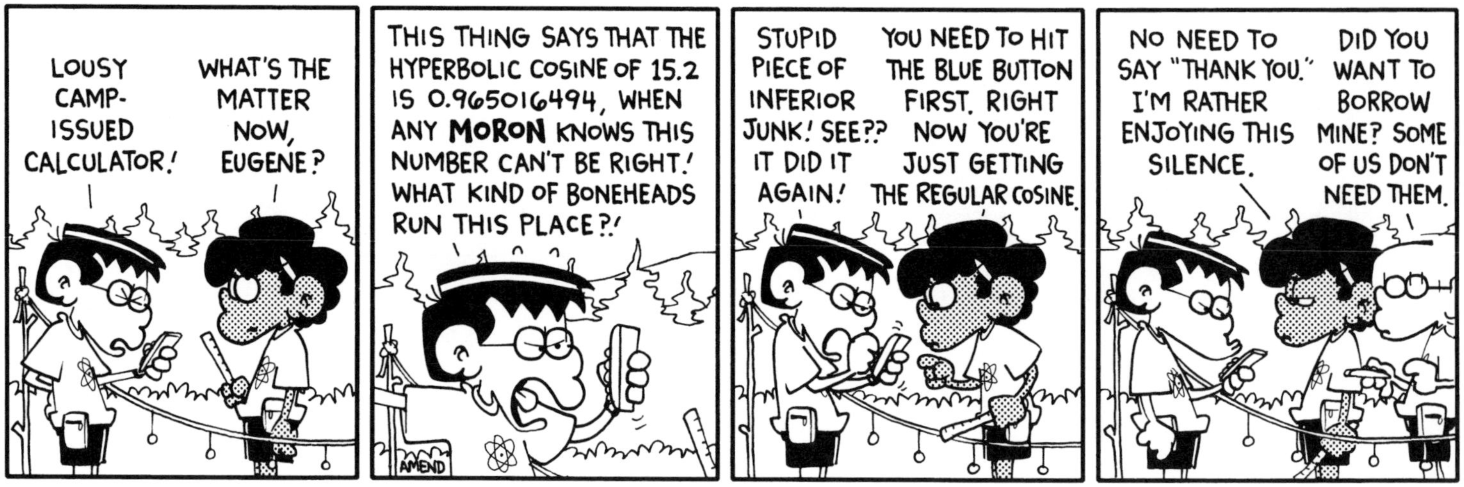
LOUSY CAMP-ISSUED CALCULATOR!
WHAT'S THE MATTER NOW, EUGENE?
THIS THING SAYS THAT THE HYPERBOLIC COSINE OF 15.2 IS 0.9650164494, WHEN ANY **MORON** KNOWS THIS NUMBER CAN'T BE RIGHT! WHAT KIND OF BONEHEADS RUN THIS PLACE?!
AMEND
STUPID PIECE OF INFERIOR JUNK! SEE?? IT DID IT AGAIN!
YOU NEED TO HIT THE BLUE BUTTON FIRST. RIGHT NOW YOU'RE JUST GETTING THE REGULAR COSINE.
NO NEED TO SAY "THANK YOU." I'M RATHER ENJOYING THIS SILENCE.
DID YOU WANT TO BORROW MINE? SOME OF US DON'T NEED THEM.

July 3, 1997

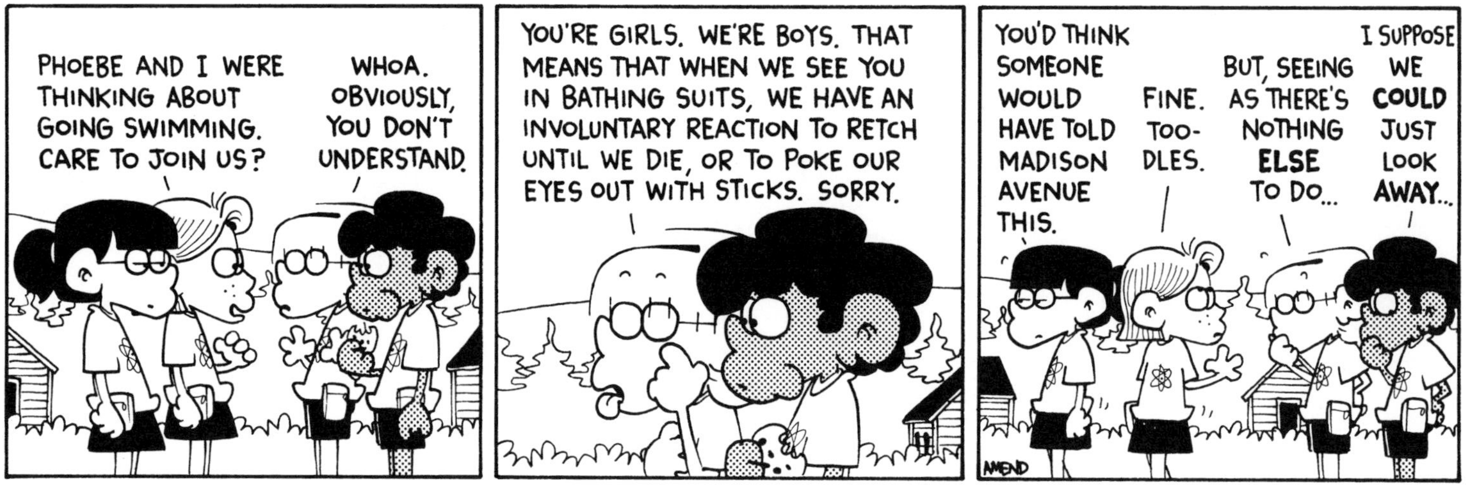
PHOEBE AND I WERE THINKING ABOUT GOING SWIMMING. CARE TO JOIN US?
WHOA. OBVIOUSLY, YOU DON'T UNDERSTAND.
YOU'RE GIRLS. WE'RE BOYS. THAT MEANS THAT WHEN WE SEE YOU IN BATHING SUITS, WE HAVE AN INVOLUNTARY REACTION TO RETCH UNTIL WE DIE, OR TO POKE OUR EYES OUT WITH STICKS. SORRY.
YOU'D THINK SOMEONE WOULD HAVE TOLD MADISON AVENUE THIS.
FINE. TOO-DLES.
BUT, SEEING AS THERE'S NOTHING **ELSE** TO DO...
I SUPPOSE WE **COULD** JUST LOOK **AWAY**...
AMEND

July 4, 1997

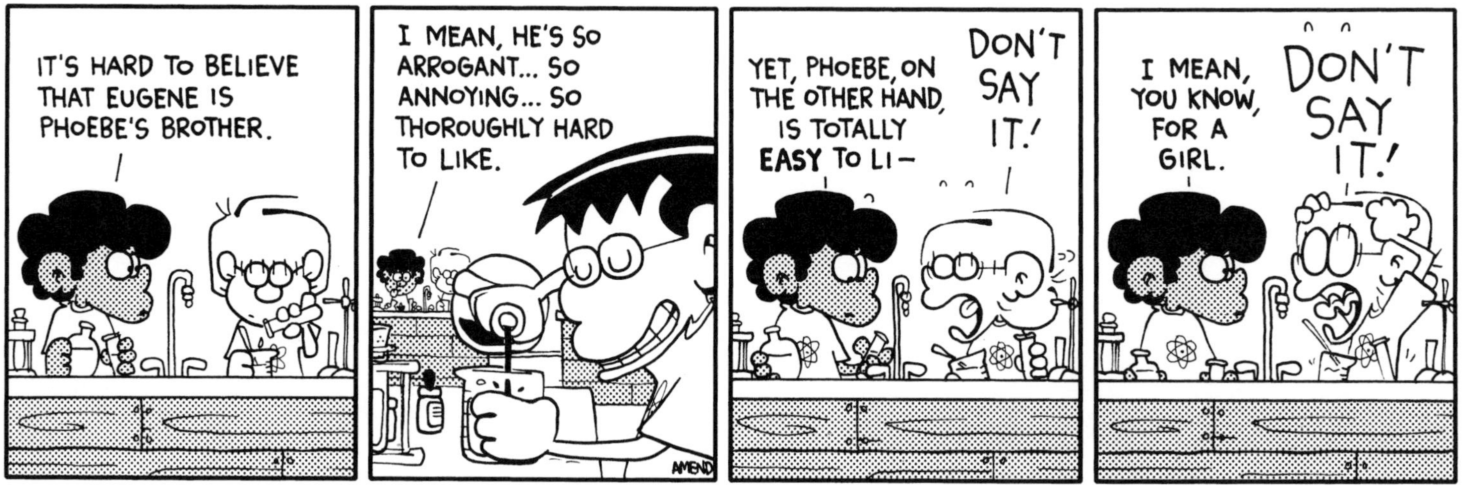
IT'S HARD TO BELIEVE THAT EUGENE IS PHOEBE'S BROTHER.
I MEAN, HE'S SO ARROGANT... SO ANNOYING... SO THOROUGHLY HARD TO LIKE.
AMEND
YET, PHOEBE, ON THE OTHER HAND, IS TOTALLY **EASY** TO LI–
DON'T SAY IT!
I MEAN, YOU KNOW, FOR A GIRL.
DON'T SAY IT!

July 5, 1997

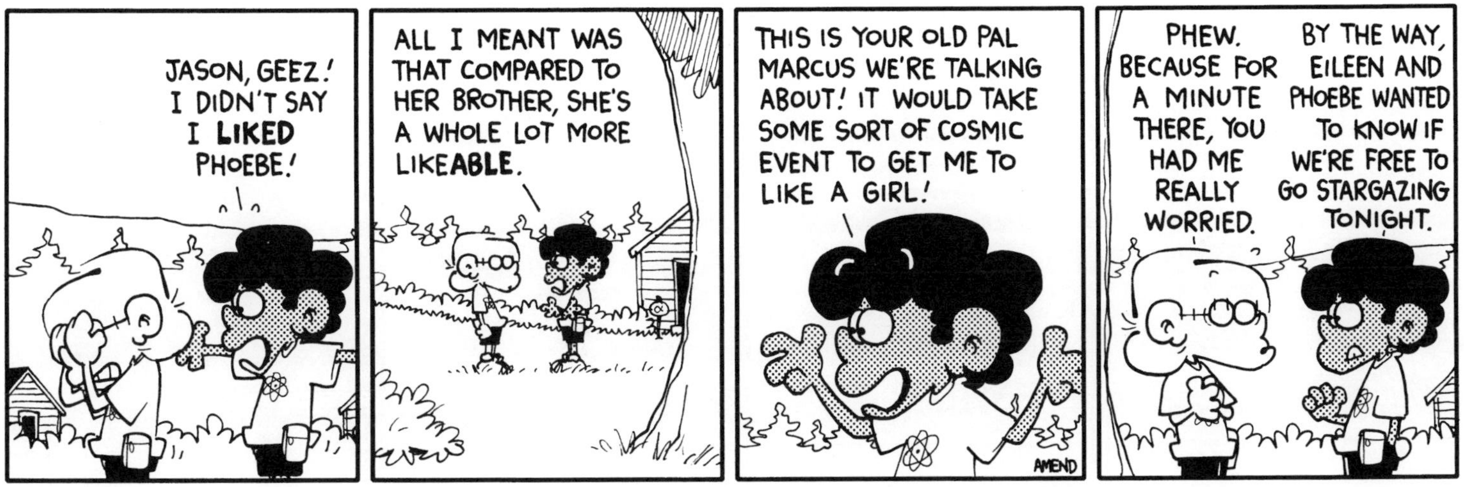
JASON, GEEZ! I DIDN'T SAY I **LIKED** PHOEBE!
ALL I MEANT WAS THAT COMPARED TO HER BROTHER, SHE'S A WHOLE LOT MORE LIKE**ABLE**.
THIS IS YOUR OLD PAL MARCUS WE'RE TALKING ABOUT! IT WOULD TAKE SOME SORT OF COSMIC EVENT TO GET ME TO LIKE A GIRL!
AMEND
PHEW. BECAUSE FOR A MINUTE THERE, YOU HAD ME REALLY WORRIED.
BY THE WAY, EILEEN AND PHOEBE WANTED TO KNOW IF WE'RE FREE TO GO STARGAZING TONIGHT.

July 7, 1997

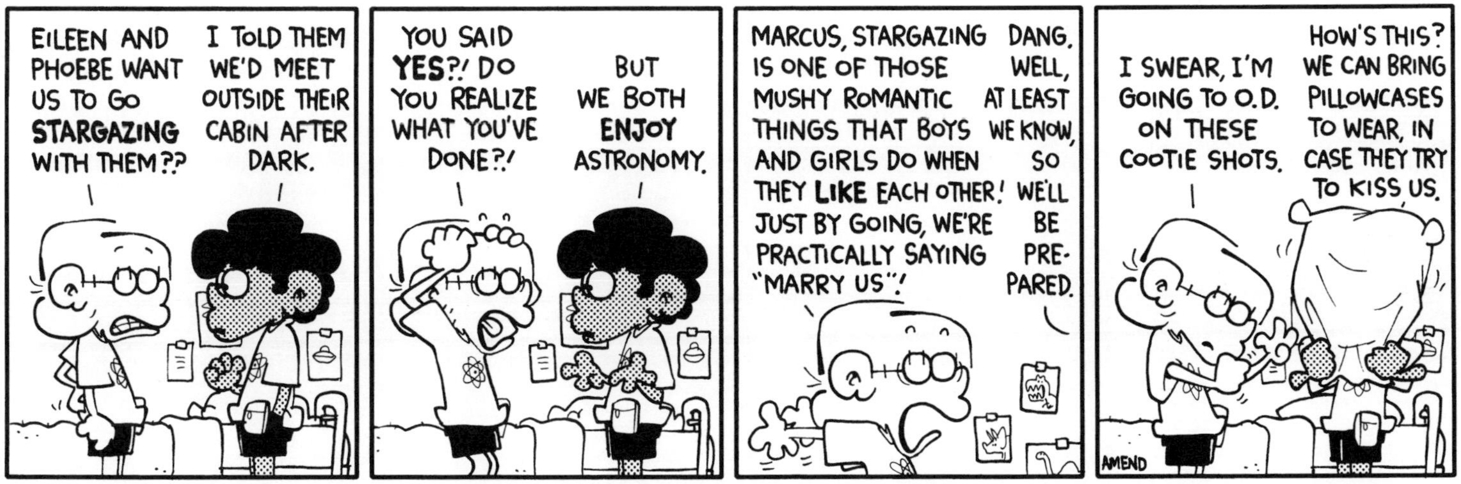
EILEEN AND PHOEBE WANT US TO GO **STARGAZING** WITH THEM??
I TOLD THEM WE'D MEET OUTSIDE THEIR CABIN AFTER DARK.
YOU SAID **YES**?! DO YOU REALIZE WHAT YOU'VE DONE?!
BUT WE BOTH **ENJOY** ASTRONOMY.
MARCUS, STARGAZING IS ONE OF THOSE MUSHY ROMANTIC THINGS THAT BOYS AND GIRLS DO WHEN THEY **LIKE** EACH OTHER! JUST BY GOING, WE'RE PRACTICALLY SAYING "MARRY US"!
DANG. WELL, AT LEAST WE KNOW, SO WE'LL BE PRE-PARED.
I SWEAR, I'M GOING TO O.D. ON THESE COOTIE SHOTS.
HOW'S THIS? WE CAN BRING PILLOWCASES TO WEAR, IN CASE THEY TRY TO KISS US.
AMEND

July 8, 1997

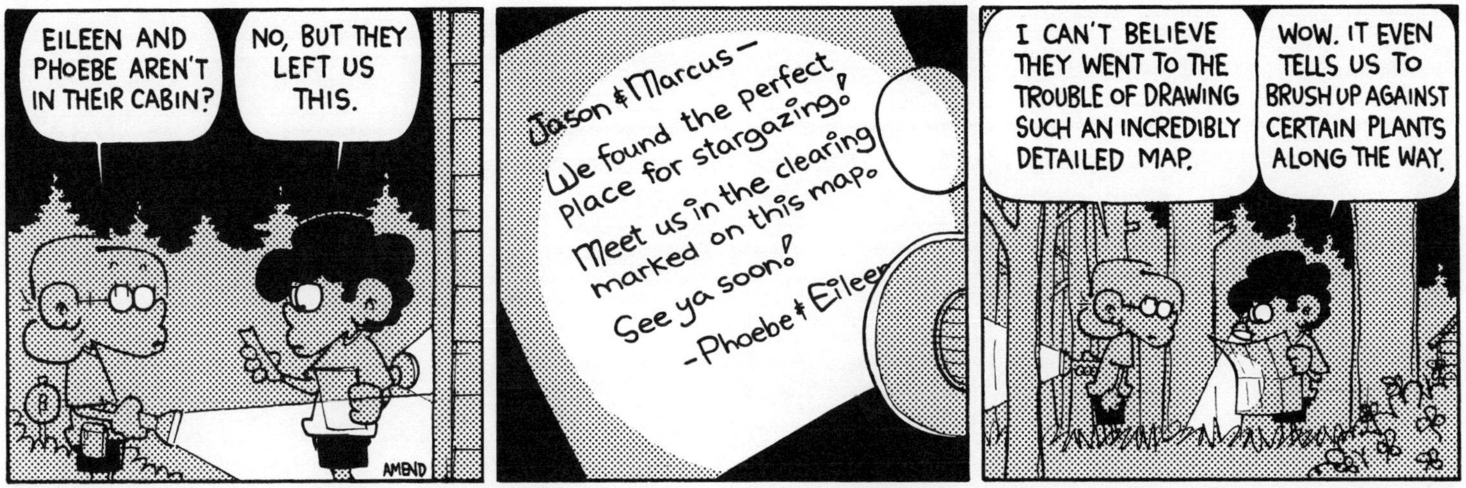
EILEEN AND PHOEBE AREN'T IN THEIR CABIN?
NO, BUT THEY LEFT US THIS.
AMEND
Jason & Marcus—
We found the perfect place for stargazing!
Meet us in the clearing marked on this map.
See ya soon!
-Phoebe & Eileen
I CAN'T BELIEVE THEY WENT TO THE TROUBLE OF DRAWING SUCH AN INCREDIBLY DETAILED MAP.
WOW. IT EVEN TELLS US TO BRUSH UP AGAINST CERTAIN PLANTS ALONG THE WAY.

July 9, 1997

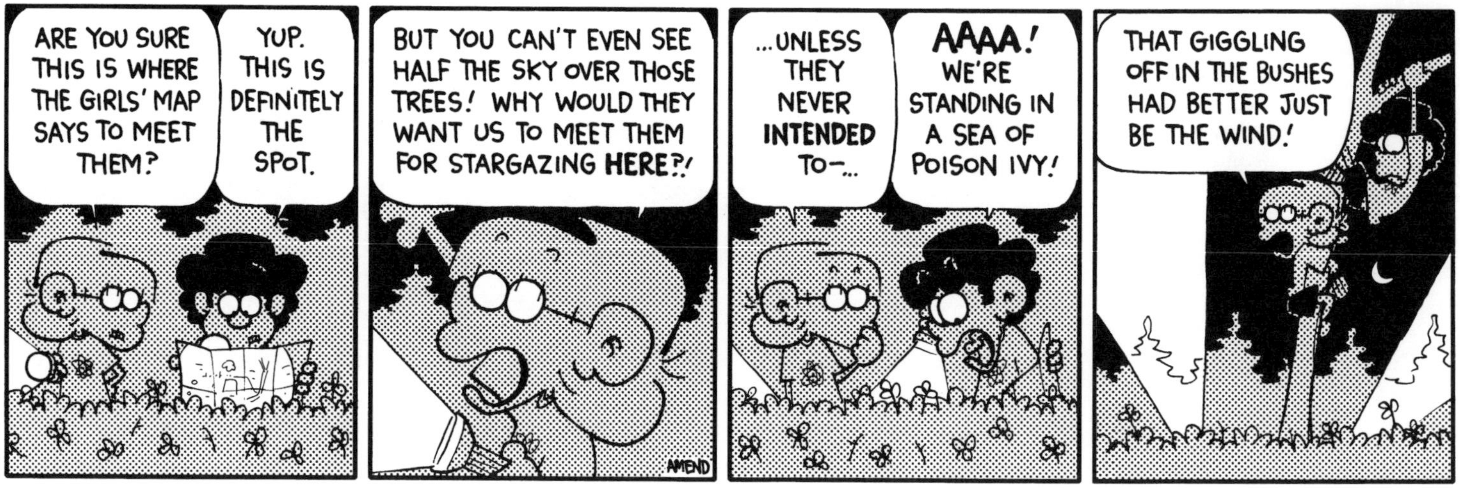
ARE YOU SURE THIS IS WHERE THE GIRLS' MAP SAYS TO MEET THEM?
YUP. THIS IS DEFINITELY THE SPOT.
BUT YOU CAN'T EVEN SEE HALF THE SKY OVER THOSE TREES! WHY WOULD THEY WANT US TO MEET THEM FOR STARGAZING **HERE**?!
...UNLESS THEY NEVER **INTENDED** TO—...
AAAA! WE'RE STANDING IN A SEA OF POISON IVY!
THAT GIGGLING OFF IN THE BUSHES HAD BETTER JUST BE THE WIND!
AMEND

July 10, 1997

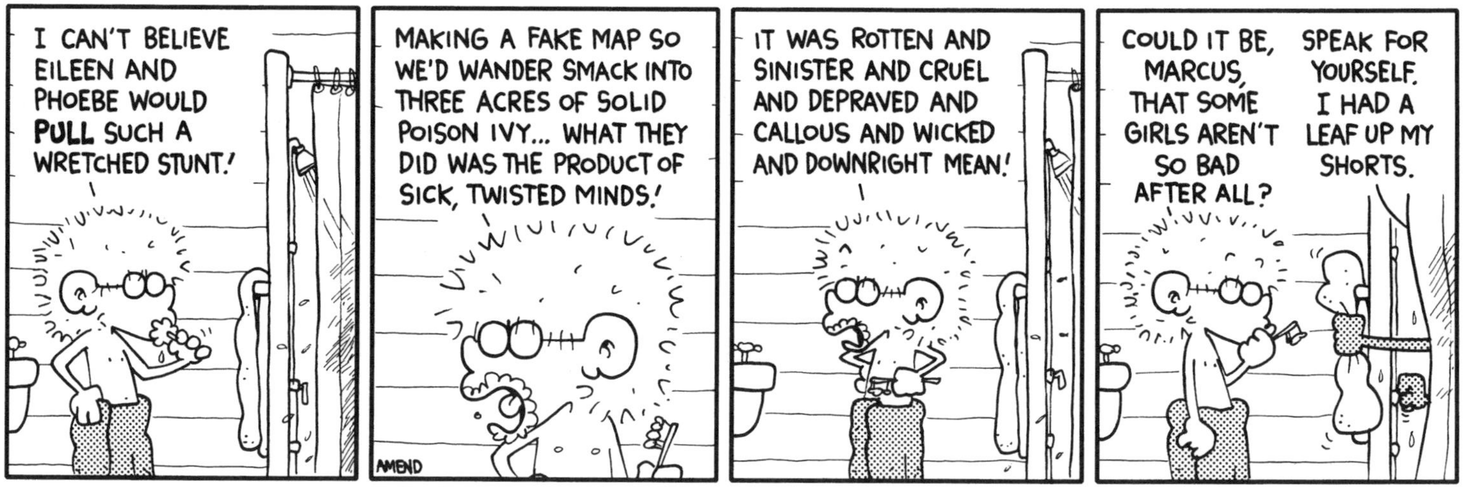
I CAN'T BELIEVE EILEEN AND PHOEBE WOULD **PULL** SUCH A WRETCHED STUNT!
MAKING A FAKE MAP SO WE'D WANDER SMACK INTO THREE ACRES OF SOLID POISON IVY... WHAT THEY DID WAS THE PRODUCT OF SICK, TWISTED MINDS!
AMEND
IT WAS ROTTEN AND SINISTER AND CRUEL AND DEPRAVED AND CALLOUS AND WICKED AND DOWNRIGHT MEAN!
COULD IT BE, MARCUS, THAT SOME GIRLS AREN'T SO BAD AFTER ALL?
SPEAK FOR YOURSELF. I HAD A LEAF UP MY SHORTS.

July 11, 1997

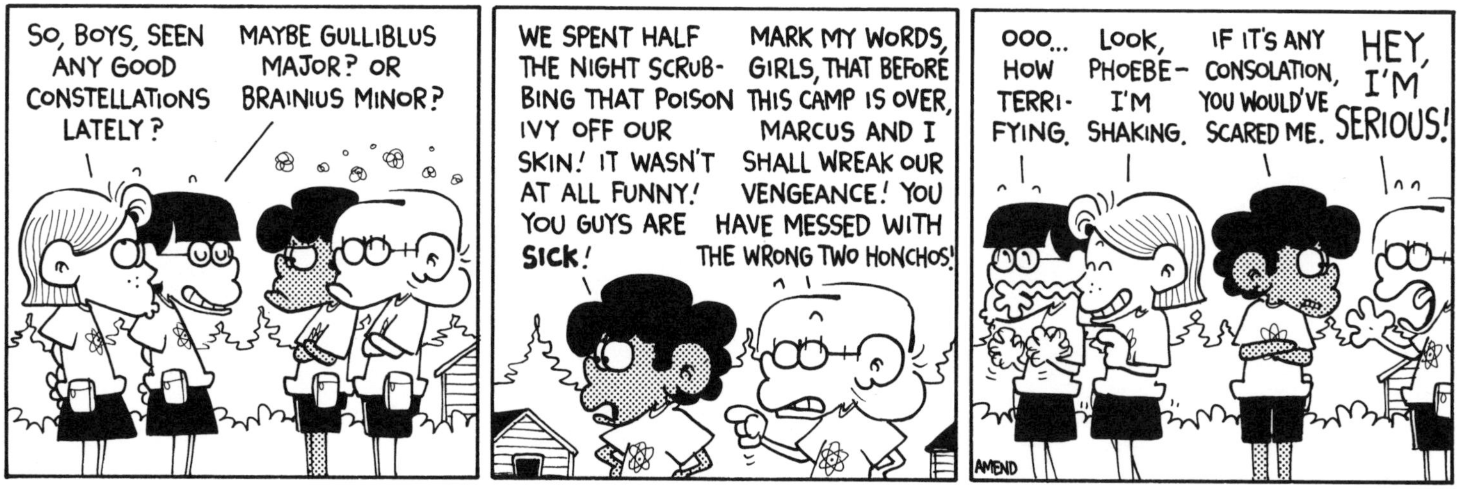
SO, BOYS, SEEN ANY GOOD CONSTELLATIONS LATELY?
MAYBE GULLIBLUS MAJOR? OR BRAINIUS MINOR?
WE SPENT HALF THE NIGHT SCRUBBING THAT POISON IVY OFF OUR SKIN! IT WASN'T AT ALL FUNNY! YOU GUYS ARE **SICK**!
MARK MY WORDS, GIRLS, THAT BEFORE THIS CAMP IS OVER, MARCUS AND I SHALL WREAK OUR VENGEANCE! YOU HAVE MESSED WITH THE WRONG TWO HONCHOS!
OOO... HOW TERRIFYING.
LOOK, PHOEBE— I'M SHAKING.
IF IT'S ANY CONSOLATION, YOU WOULD'VE SCARED ME.
HEY, I'M SERIOUS!
AMEND

July 12, 1997

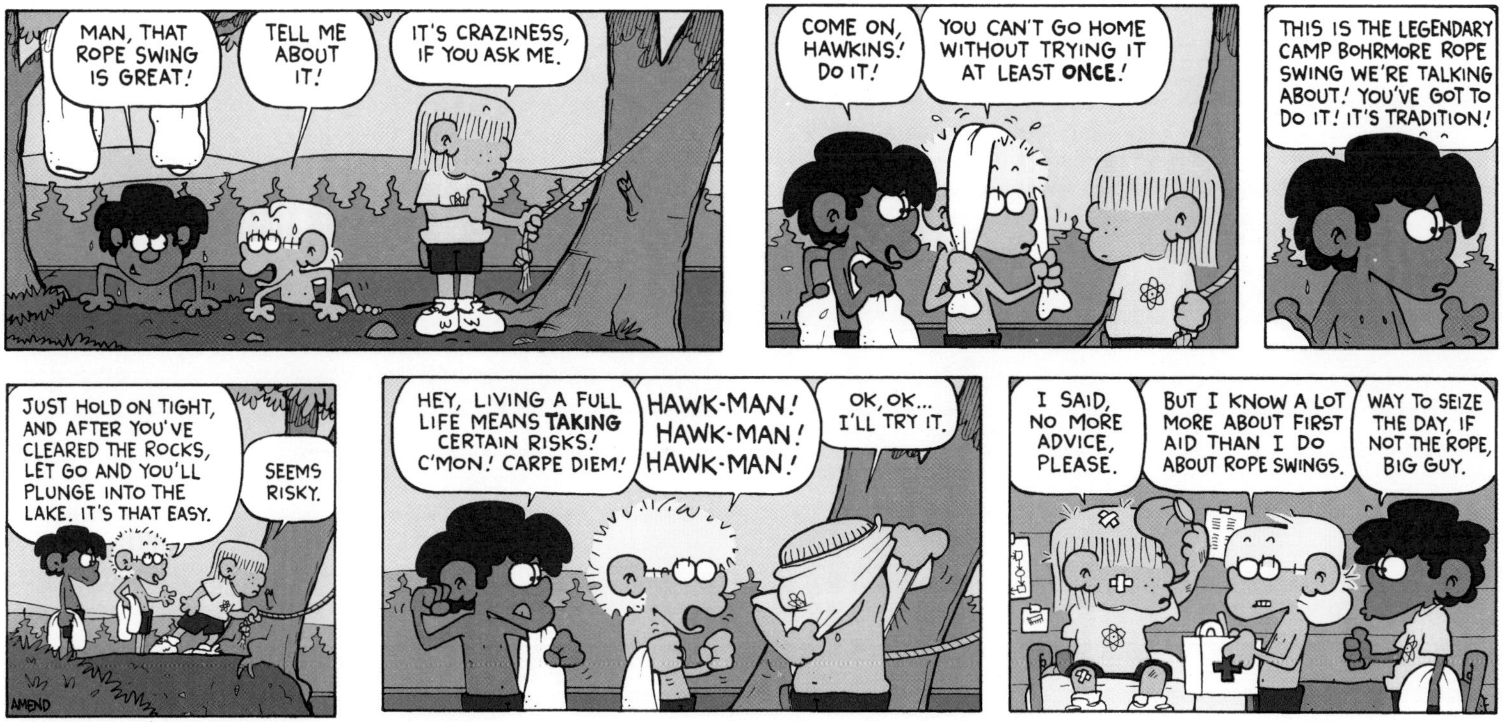
MAN, THAT ROPE SWING IS GREAT!
TELL ME ABOUT IT!
IT'S CRAZINESS, IF YOU ASK ME.
COME ON, HAWKINS! DO IT!
YOU CAN'T GO HOME WITHOUT TRYING IT AT LEAST **ONCE**!
THIS IS THE LEGENDARY CAMP BOHRMORE ROPE SWING WE'RE TALKING ABOUT! YOU'VE GOT TO DO IT! IT'S TRADITION!
JUST HOLD ON TIGHT, AND AFTER YOU'VE CLEARED THE ROCKS, LET GO AND YOU'LL PLUNGE INTO THE LAKE. IT'S THAT EASY.
SEEMS RISKY.
AMEND
HEY, LIVING A FULL LIFE MEANS **TAKING** CERTAIN RISKS! C'MON! CARPE DIEM!
HAWK-MAN! HAWK-MAN! HAWK-MAN!
OK, OK... I'LL TRY IT.
I SAID, NO MORE ADVICE, PLEASE.
BUT I KNOW A LOT MORE ABOUT FIRST AID THAN I DO ABOUT ROPE SWINGS.
WAY TO SEIZE THE DAY, IF NOT THE ROPE, BIG GUY.

July 20, 1997

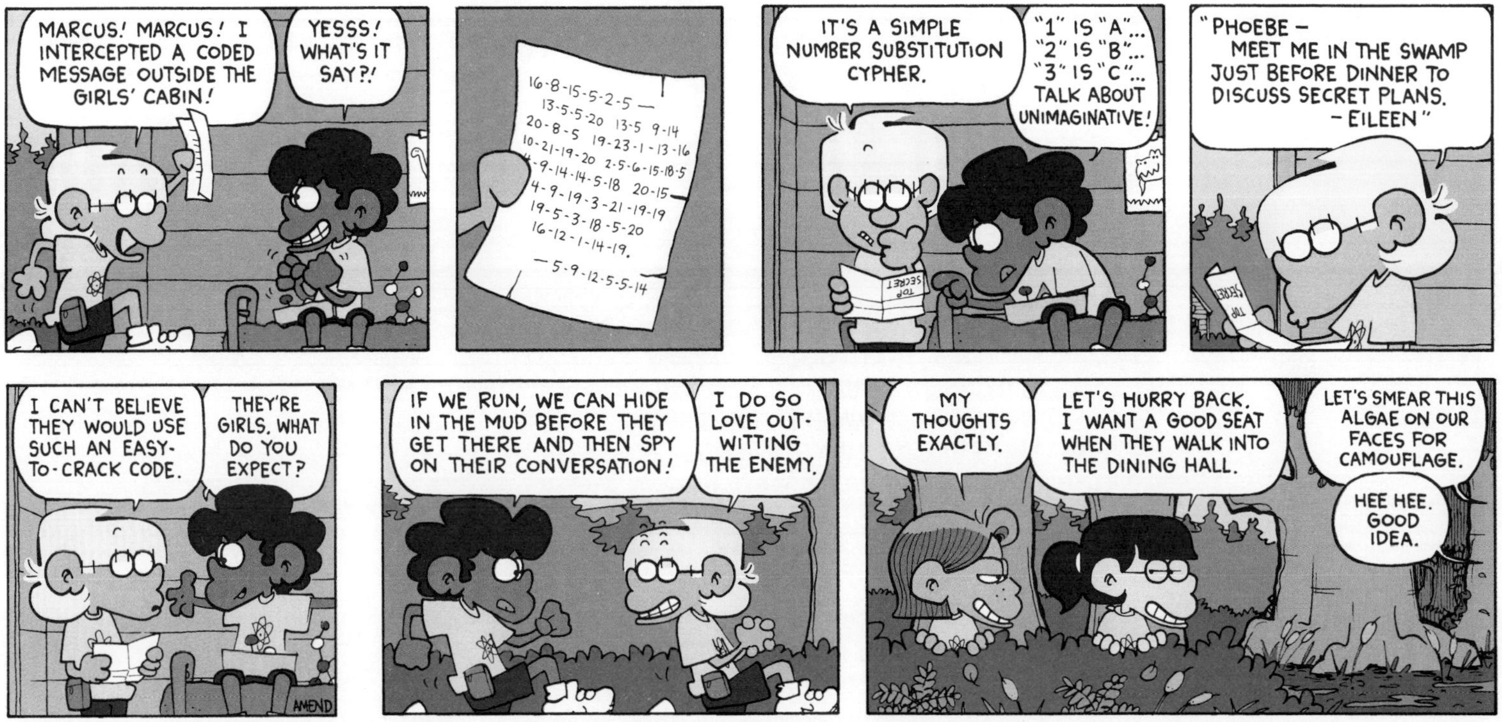
MARCUS! MARCUS! I INTERCEPTED A CODED MESSAGE OUTSIDE THE GIRLS' CABIN!
YESSS! WHAT'S IT SAY?!
16-8-15-5-2-5 — 13-5-5-20 13-5 9-14 20-8-5 19-23-1-13-16 10-21-19-20 2-5-6-15-18-5 4-9-14-14-5-18 20-15 4-9-19-3-21-19-19 19-5-3-18-5-20 16-12-1-14-19. —5-9-12-5-5-14
IT'S A SIMPLE NUMBER SUBSTITUTION CYPHER.
"1" IS "A"... "2" IS "B"... "3" IS "C"... TALK ABOUT UNIMAGINATIVE!
TOP SECRET
"PHOEBE — MEET ME IN THE SWAMP JUST BEFORE DINNER TO DISCUSS SECRET PLANS. - EILEEN"
I CAN'T BELIEVE THEY WOULD USE SUCH AN EASY-TO-CRACK CODE.
THEY'RE GIRLS. WHAT DO YOU EXPECT?
AMEND
IF WE RUN, WE CAN HIDE IN THE MUD BEFORE THEY GET THERE AND THEN SPY ON THEIR CONVERSATION!
I DO SO LOVE OUT-WITTING THE ENEMY.
MY THOUGHTS EXACTLY.
LET'S HURRY BACK. I WANT A GOOD SEAT WHEN THEY WALK INTO THE DINING HALL.
LET'S SMEAR THIS ALGAE ON OUR FACES FOR CAMOUFLAGE.
HEE HEE. GOOD IDEA.

July 13, 1997

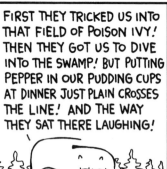

Panel 1: NOW THEY'VE DONE IT! NOW THEY'VE GONE TOO FAR! / PBBSPT! PBBSPT!

Panel 2: FIRST THEY TRICKED US INTO THAT FIELD OF POISON IVY! THEN THEY GOT US TO DIVE INTO THE SWAMP! BUT PUTTING PEPPER IN OUR PUDDING CUPS AT DINNER JUST PLAIN CROSSES THE LINE! AND THE WAY THEY SAT THERE LAUGHING!

Panel 3: I MEAN, WHO DO EILEEN AND PHOEBE THINK THEY **ARE**?!?

Panel 4: ...US?? / I'D SAY THEY'RE OUR EQUALS, EXCEPT WE'RE GETTING WHOOPED.

July 14, 1997

Panel 1: WHAT'S THAT? / THE RULES FOR THE BIG CAMP BOHRMORE SCIENCE CONTEST.

Panel 2: "WORKING IN TEAMS OF TWO, APPLY ONE OR MORE OF THE SCIENTIFIC PRINCIPLES YOU'VE LEARNED THIS SUMMER IN THE DESIGN AND EXECUTION OF AN EXPERIMENT OR DEMONSTRATION OF YOUR CHOOSING." COOL... THERE'S EVEN A BIG TROPHY!

Panel 3: MARCUS, YOU AND I ARE GOING TO WIN THIS PRIZE. / ASSUMING WE CAN SOMEHOW BEAT THAT STUPID EUGENE.

Panel 4: STUPID? MOI? DO I NEED TO SHOW YOU MY TRANSCRIPT AGAIN? / HEY, EUGENE— I HEAR THERE ARE SOME AMAZING PROTOZOANS AT THE BOTTOM OF THE LAKE. / HERE. YOU CAN BORROW MY MICROSCOPE.

July 15, 1997

Panel 1: HOW'S YOUR BIG SCIENCE PROJECT COMING ALONG? / FINE. / GO AWAY, EUGENE.

Panel 2: "FINE"? THAT'S TOO BAD, BECAUSE THE PROJECT HAWKINS AND I ARE DOING IS COMING ALONG **GLORIOUSLY**. IT'S GOING TO TAKE MUCH MORE THAN "FINE" TO BEAT **ME** IN THIS CONTEST.

Panel 3: EUGENE, YOU NIMROD! YOU LEFT THE CAP OFF THIS TEST TUBE OVERNIGHT, AND NOW OUR MOLARITY'S ALL MESSED UP!

Panel 4: STILL, WE'RE DOING BETTER THAN "FINE." / MARCUS, PASS ME THOSE ELECTRODES. / TRUST ME— GO AWAY, EUGENE.

July 16, 1997

July 17, 1997

July 18, 1997

July 19, 1997

Because I had to turn in each week of strips as soon as they were finished, I didn't know how this story would ultimately unfold as I wrote it. Rather stressful.

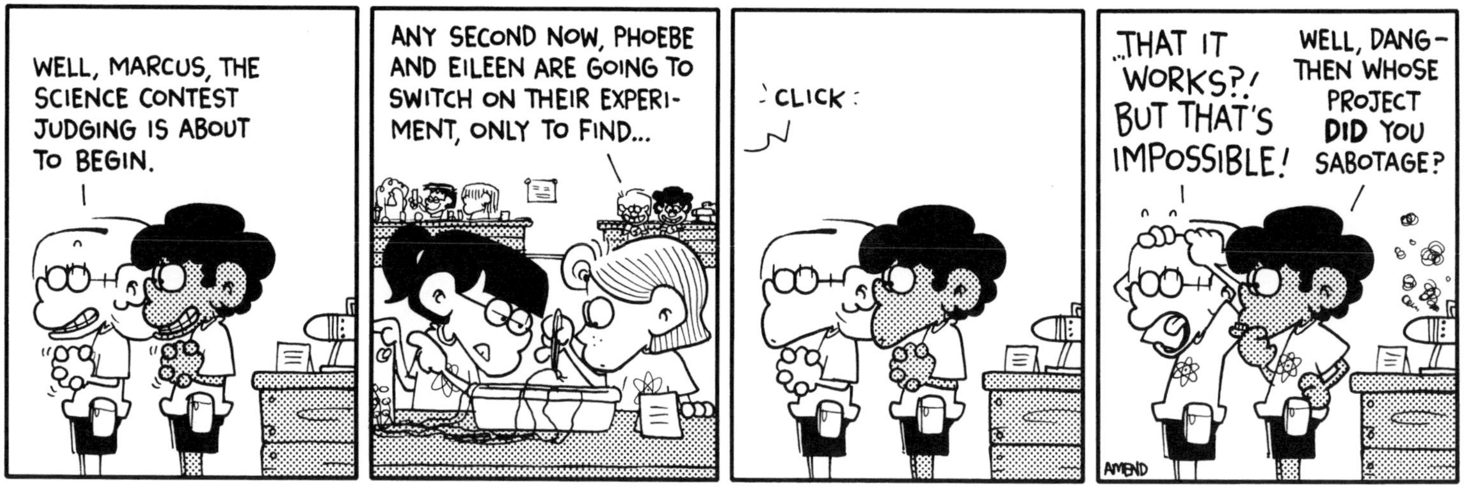
WELL, MARCUS, THE SCIENCE CONTEST JUDGING IS ABOUT TO BEGIN.
ANY SECOND NOW, PHOEBE AND EILEEN ARE GOING TO SWITCH ON THEIR EXPERIMENT, ONLY TO FIND...
CLICK
...THAT IT WORKS?! BUT THAT'S IMPOSSIBLE!
WELL, DANG— THEN WHOSE PROJECT DID YOU SABOTAGE?
AMEND

July 21, 1997

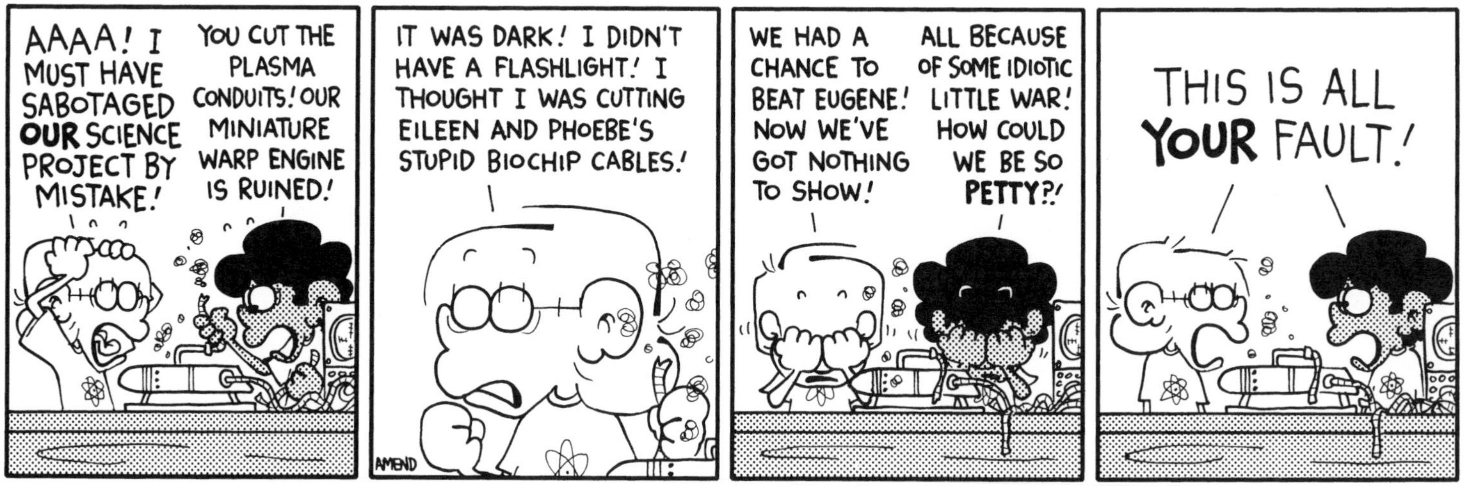
AAAA! I MUST HAVE SABOTAGED OUR SCIENCE PROJECT BY MISTAKE!
YOU CUT THE PLASMA CONDUITS! OUR MINIATURE WARP ENGINE IS RUINED!
IT WAS DARK! I DIDN'T HAVE A FLASHLIGHT! I THOUGHT I WAS CUTTING EILEEN AND PHOEBE'S STUPID BIOCHIP CABLES!
AMEND
WE HAD A CHANCE TO BEAT EUGENE! NOW WE'VE GOT NOTHING TO SHOW!
ALL BECAUSE OF SOME IDIOTIC LITTLE WAR! HOW COULD WE BE SO PETTY?!
THIS IS ALL YOUR FAULT!

July 22, 1997

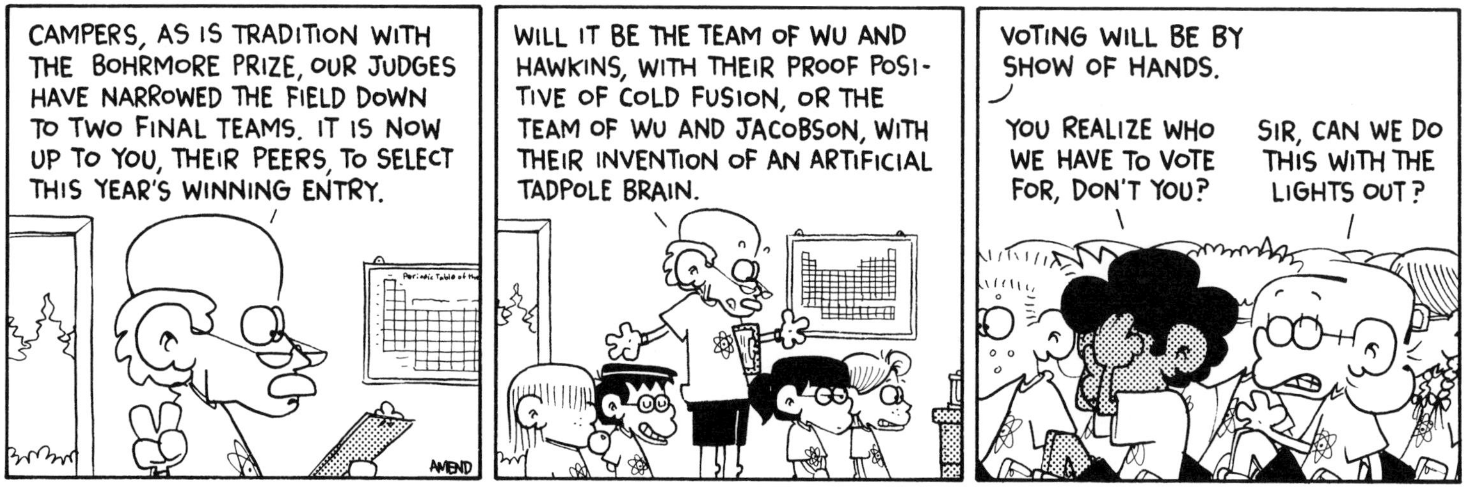
CAMPERS, AS IS TRADITION WITH THE BOHRMORE PRIZE, OUR JUDGES HAVE NARROWED THE FIELD DOWN TO TWO FINAL TEAMS. IT IS NOW UP TO YOU, THEIR PEERS, TO SELECT THIS YEAR'S WINNING ENTRY.
AMEND
WILL IT BE THE TEAM OF WU AND HAWKINS, WITH THEIR PROOF POSITIVE OF COLD FUSION, OR THE TEAM OF WU AND JACOBSON, WITH THEIR INVENTION OF AN ARTIFICIAL TADPOLE BRAIN.
VOTING WILL BE BY SHOW OF HANDS.
YOU REALIZE WHO WE HAVE TO VOTE FOR, DON'T YOU?
SIR, CAN WE DO THIS WITH THE LIGHTS OUT?

July 23, 1997

OK, THAT'S NINE VOTES FOR EUGENE AND MR. HAWKINS. NOW, HOW MANY OF YOU THINK THAT PHOEBE AND EILEEN HERE SHOULD WIN?

...5...6...7...8...

EIGHT VOTES... ANY MORE?... DID I GET EVERYONE?...

WELL, THEN, I GUESS WE HAVE OUR WIN— WAIT!

July 24, 1997

WHAT'S WRONG WITH US, MARCUS??

WE GO INTO THE SCIENCE CONTEST TRYING TO SABOTAGE THE GIRLS' EXPERIMENT, AND INSTEAD WE END UP CASTING THE DECIDING VOTES TO AWARD THEM FIRST PRIZE!

IT'S LIKE NO MATTER WHAT WE DO, PHOEBE AND EILEEN COME OUT ON TOP! THEY'RE JUST GIRLS! WHY CAN'T WE EVER BEAT THEM??

IF ONLY WE DIDN'T HAVE TO BEAT THEM.

THE PROBLEM WITH UNWRITTEN RULES IS THEY'RE SO HARD TO DOUBLE-CHECK.

July 25, 1997

WELL, GIRLS, IT'S YOUR LUCKY DAY.

BIG TIME.

AFTER SOME DISCUSSION, MARCUS AND I HAVE DECIDED TO TAKE THE HIGH ROAD AND FORGIVE YOU FOR YOUR MANY DIABOLICAL ACTIONS AGAINST US THIS SUMMER. WE WILL NO LONGER SEEK REVENGE.

THE POISON IVY INCIDENT? FORGIVEN. THE PUDDING CUP INCIDENT? FORGIVEN. THE SNAILS IN OUR BEDSHEETS? ALL FORGIVEN.

BASICALLY, WHAT YOU'RE SAYING IS WE KICKED YOUR FANNIES.

BIG TIME.

THOSE ARE YOUR WORDS, NOT OURS.

UM, IF YOU WOULDN'T MIND SIGNING THIS DECLARATION OF TRUCE...

July 26, 1997

245

July 28, 1997

July 29, 1997

I can't remember whether the lack of shading dots here is due to deadline constraints or concerns about legibility. Probably the former.

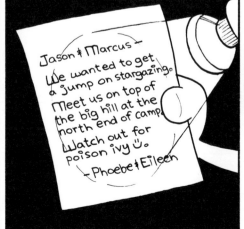

246

July 30, 1997

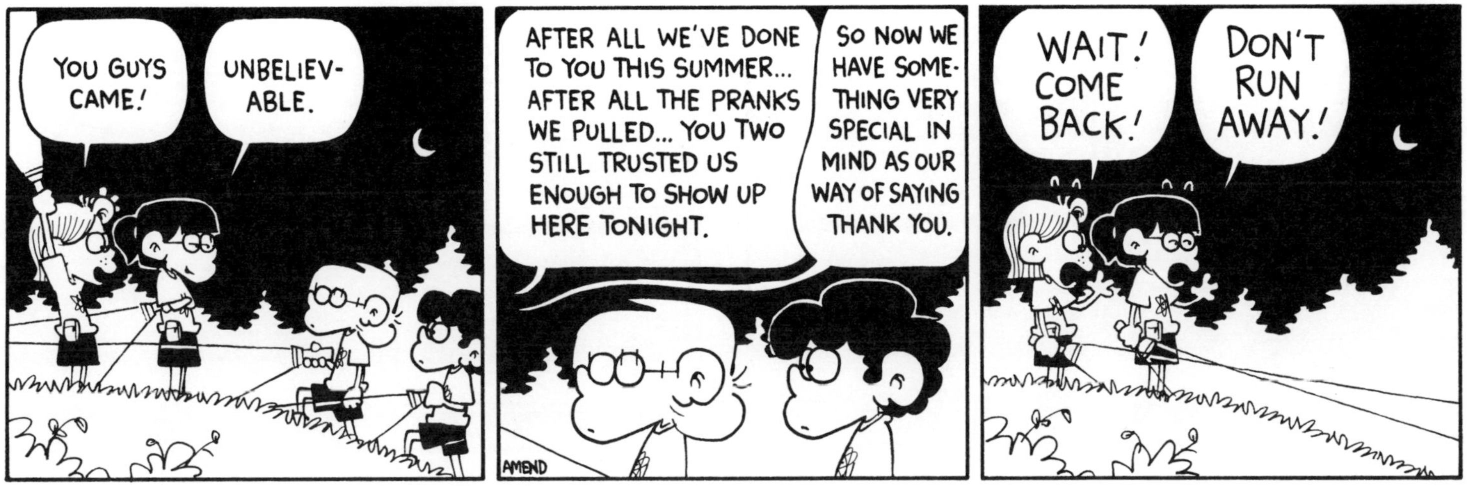
YOU GUYS CAME!
UNBELIEVABLE.
AFTER ALL WE'VE DONE TO YOU THIS SUMMER... AFTER ALL THE PRANKS WE PULLED... YOU TWO STILL TRUSTED US ENOUGH TO SHOW UP HERE TONIGHT.
SO NOW WE HAVE SOMETHING VERY SPECIAL IN MIND AS OUR WAY OF SAYING THANK YOU.
AMEND
WAIT! COME BACK!
DON'T RUN AWAY!
July 31, 1997

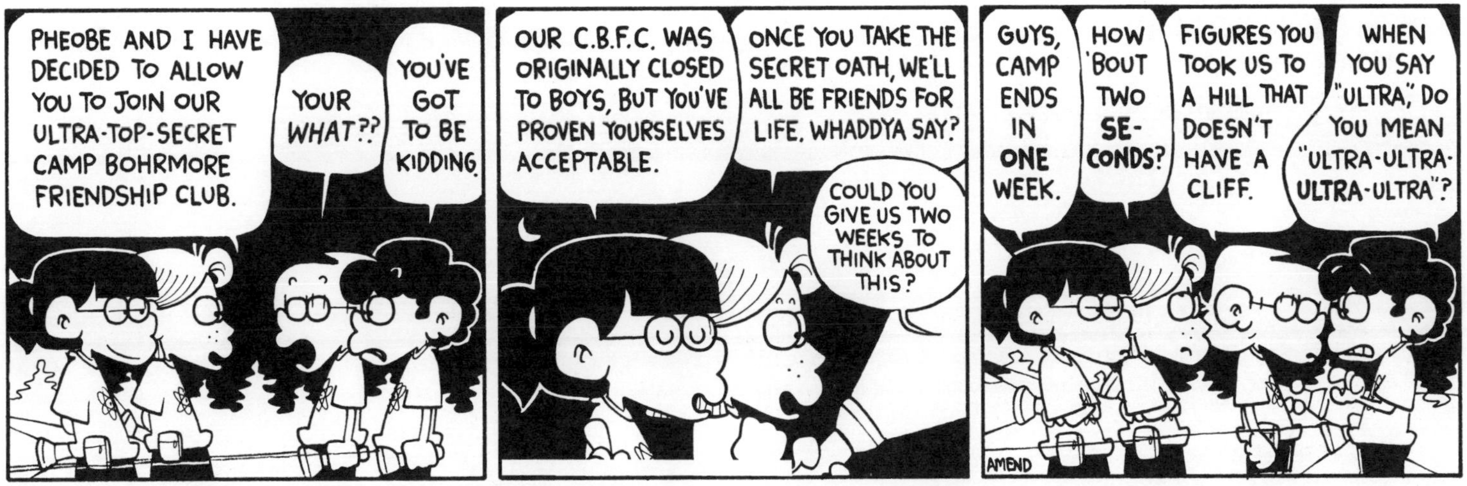
PHEOBE AND I HAVE DECIDED TO ALLOW YOU TO JOIN OUR ULTRA-TOP-SECRET CAMP BOHRMORE FRIENDSHIP CLUB.
YOUR WHAT??
YOU'VE GOT TO BE KIDDING.
OUR C.B.F.C. WAS ORIGINALLY CLOSED TO BOYS, BUT YOU'VE PROVEN YOURSELVES ACCEPTABLE.
ONCE YOU TAKE THE SECRET OATH, WE'LL ALL BE FRIENDS FOR LIFE. WHADDYA SAY?
COULD YOU GIVE US TWO WEEKS TO THINK ABOUT THIS?
GUYS, CAMP ENDS IN ONE WEEK.
HOW 'BOUT TWO SECONDS?
FIGURES YOU TOOK US TO A HILL THAT DOESN'T HAVE A CLIFF.
WHEN YOU SAY "ULTRA," DO YOU MEAN "ULTRA-ULTRA-ULTRA-ULTRA"?
AMEND
August 1, 1997

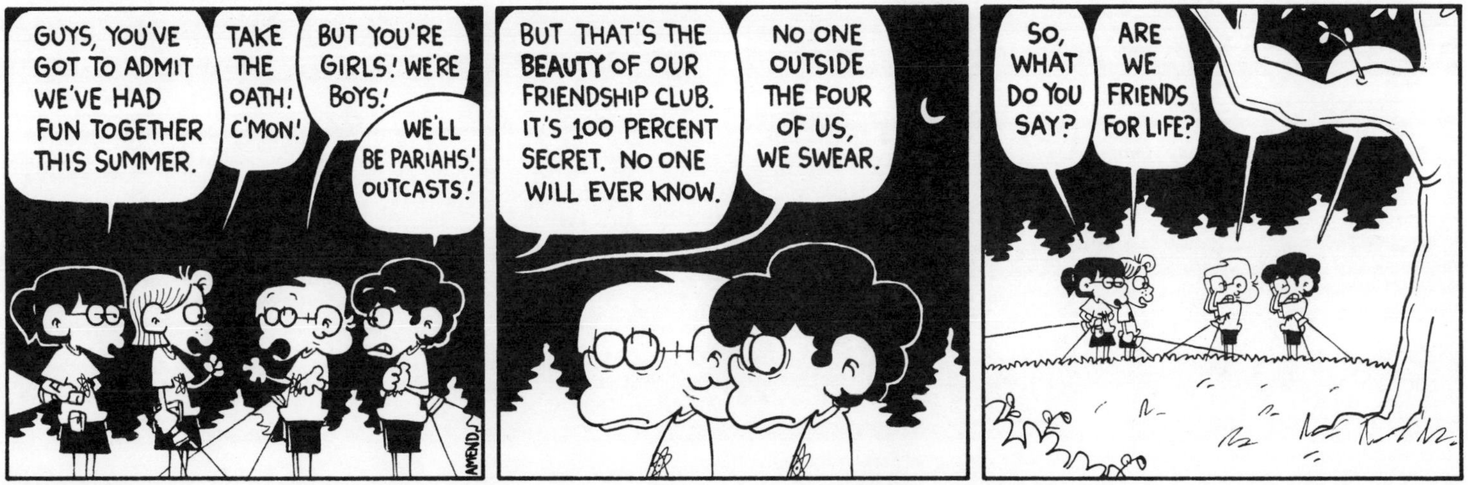
GUYS, YOU'VE GOT TO ADMIT WE'VE HAD FUN TOGETHER THIS SUMMER.
TAKE THE OATH! C'MON!
BUT YOU'RE GIRLS! WE'RE BOYS!
WE'LL BE PARIAHS! OUTCASTS!
AMEND
BUT THAT'S THE BEAUTY OF OUR FRIENDSHIP CLUB. IT'S 100 PERCENT SECRET. NO ONE WILL EVER KNOW.
NO ONE OUTSIDE THE FOUR OF US, WE SWEAR.
SO, WHAT DO YOU SAY?
ARE WE FRIENDS FOR LIFE?
August 2, 1997

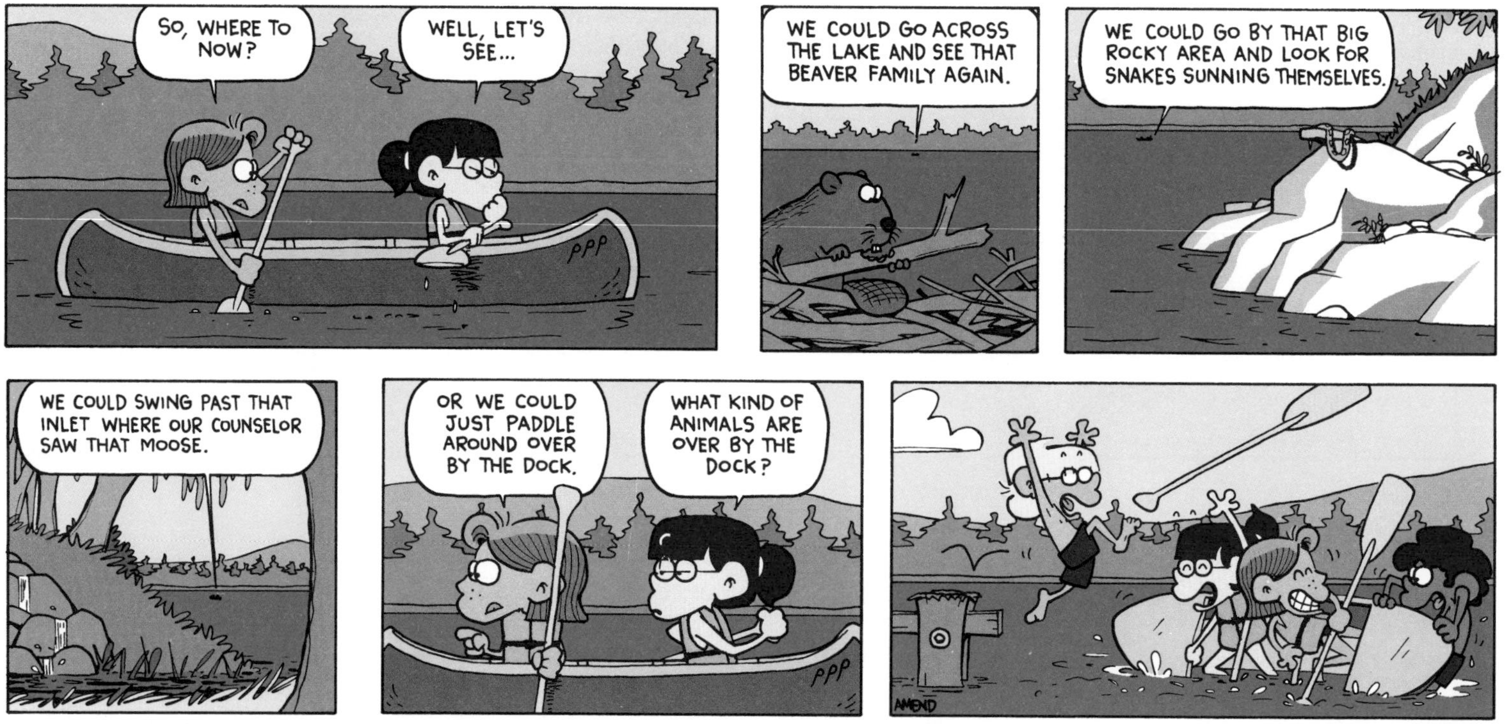
SO, WHERE TO NOW?
WELL, LET'S SEE...
WE COULD GO ACROSS THE LAKE AND SEE THAT BEAVER FAMILY AGAIN.
WE COULD GO BY THAT BIG ROCKY AREA AND LOOK FOR SNAKES SUNNING THEMSELVES.
WE COULD SWING PAST THAT INLET WHERE OUR COUNSELOR SAW THAT MOOSE.
OR WE COULD JUST PADDLE AROUND OVER BY THE DOCK.
WHAT KIND OF ANIMALS ARE OVER BY THE DOCK?
AMEND

July 27, 197

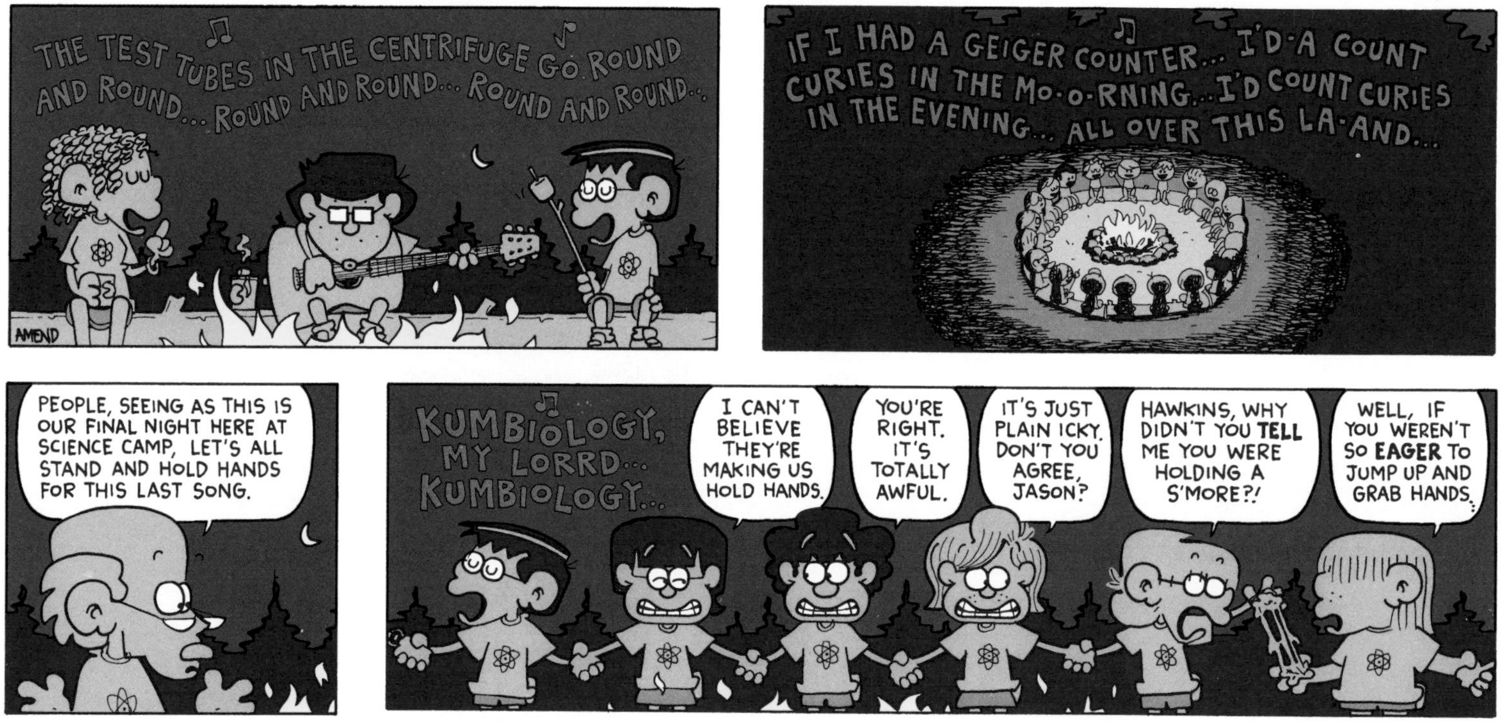
THE TEST TUBES IN THE CENTRIFUGE GO ROUND AND ROUND... ROUND AND ROUND... ROUND AND ROUND...
AMEND
IF I HAD A GEIGER COUNTER... I'D-A COUNT CURIES IN THE MO-O-RNING... I'D COUNT CURIES IN THE EVENING... ALL OVER THIS LA-AND...
PEOPLE, SEEING AS THIS IS OUR FINAL NIGHT HERE AT SCIENCE CAMP, LET'S ALL STAND AND HOLD HANDS FOR THIS LAST SONG.
KUMBIOLOGY, MY LORRD... KUMBIOLOGY...
I CAN'T BELIEVE THEY'RE MAKING US HOLD HANDS.
YOU'RE RIGHT. IT'S TOTALLY AWFUL.
IT'S JUST PLAIN ICKY. DON'T YOU AGREE, JASON?
HAWKINS, WHY DIDN'T YOU TELL ME YOU WERE HOLDING A S'MORE?!
WELL, IF YOU WEREN'T SO EAGER TO JUMP UP AND GRAB HANDS...

August 3, 1997

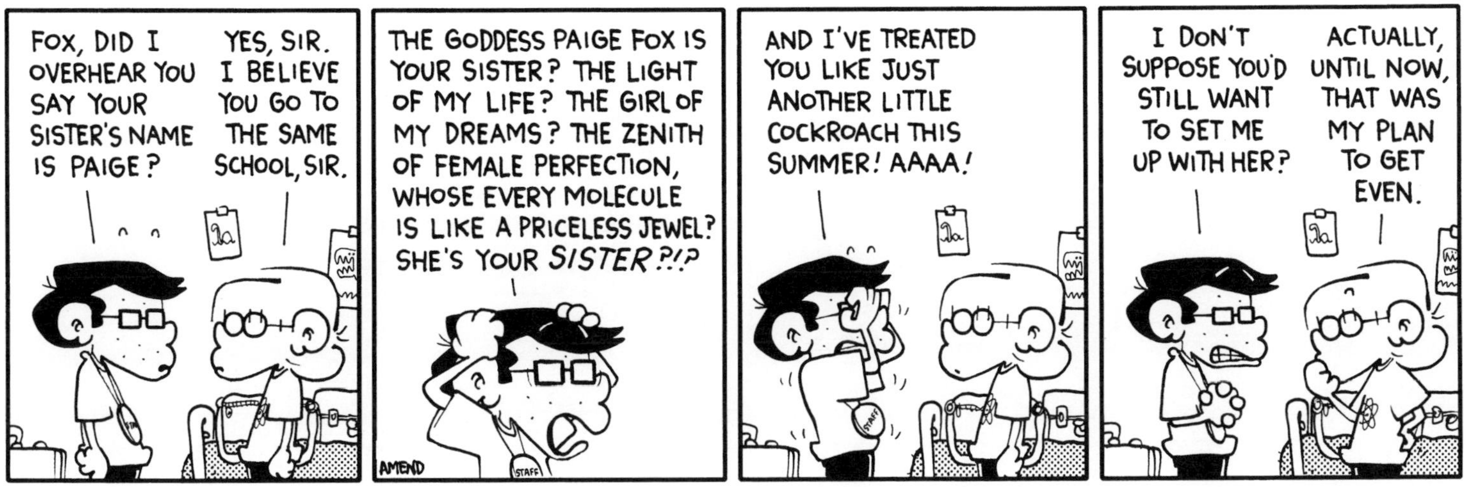
FOX, DID I OVERHEAR YOU SAY YOUR SISTER'S NAME IS PAIGE?
YES, SIR. I BELIEVE YOU GO TO THE SAME SCHOOL, SIR.
THE GODDESS PAIGE FOX IS YOUR SISTER? THE LIGHT OF MY LIFE? THE GIRL OF MY DREAMS? THE ZENITH OF FEMALE PERFECTION, WHOSE EVERY MOLECULE IS LIKE A PRICELESS JEWEL? SHE'S YOUR *SISTER*?!?
AMEND
STAFF
AND I'VE TREATED YOU LIKE JUST ANOTHER LITTLE COCKROACH THIS SUMMER! AAAA!
I DON'T SUPPOSE YOU'D STILL WANT TO SET ME UP WITH HER?
ACTUALLY, UNTIL NOW, THAT WAS MY PLAN TO GET EVEN.

August 4, 1997

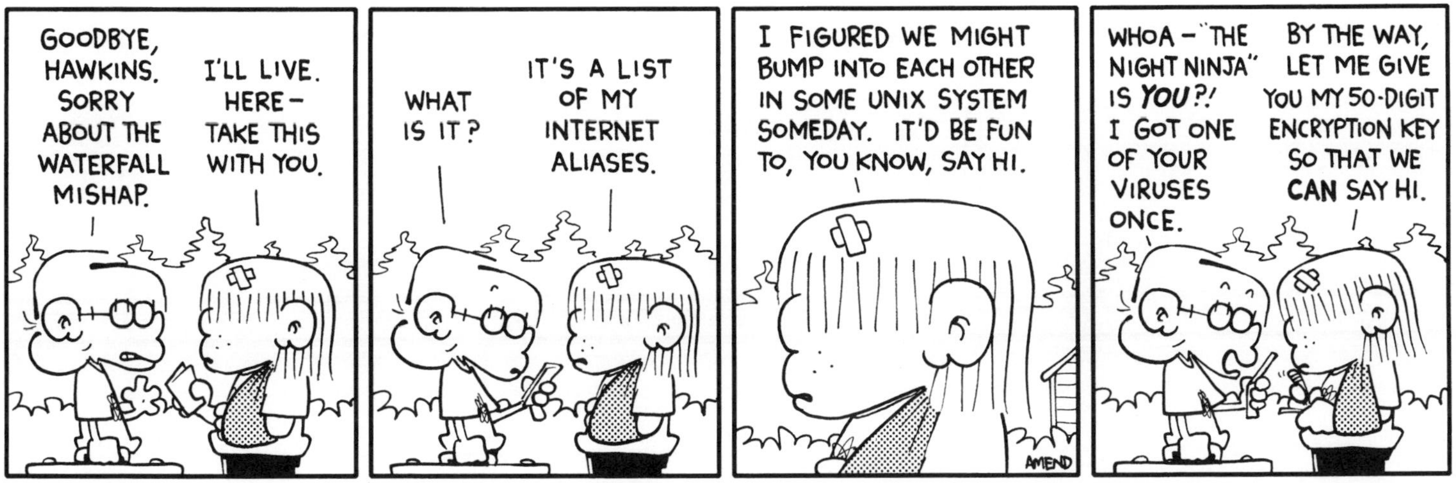
GOODBYE, HAWKINS. SORRY ABOUT THE WATERFALL MISHAP.
I'LL LIVE. HERE– TAKE THIS WITH YOU.
WHAT IS IT?
IT'S A LIST OF MY INTERNET ALIASES.
I FIGURED WE MIGHT BUMP INTO EACH OTHER IN SOME UNIX SYSTEM SOMEDAY. IT'D BE FUN TO, YOU KNOW, SAY HI.
AMEND
WHOA – "THE NIGHT NINJA" IS *YOU*?! I GOT ONE OF YOUR VIRUSES ONCE.
BY THE WAY, LET ME GIVE YOU MY 50-DIGIT ENCRYPTION KEY SO THAT WE **CAN** SAY HI.

August 5, 1997

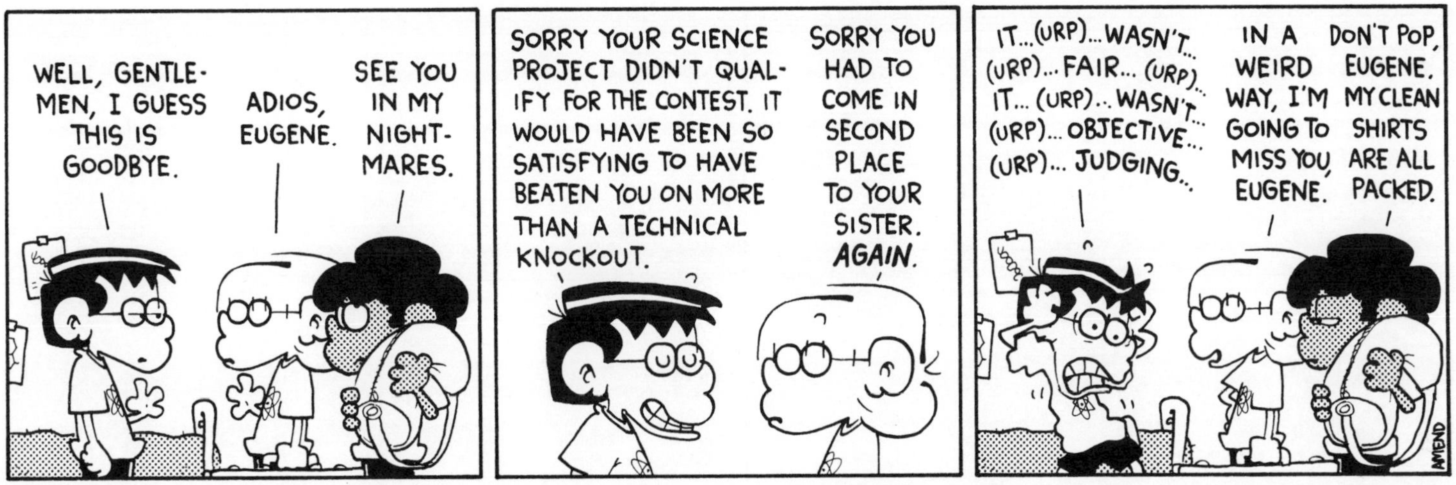
WELL, GENTLEMEN, I GUESS THIS IS GOODBYE.
ADIOS, EUGENE.
SEE YOU IN MY NIGHTMARES.
SORRY YOUR SCIENCE PROJECT DIDN'T QUALIFY FOR THE CONTEST. IT WOULD HAVE BEEN SO SATISFYING TO HAVE BEATEN YOU ON MORE THAN A TECHNICAL KNOCKOUT.
SORRY YOU HAD TO COME IN SECOND PLACE TO YOUR SISTER. ***AGAIN***.
IT... (URP)... WASN'T... (URP)... FAIR... (URP) IT... (URP)... WASN'T... (URP)... OBJECTIVE... (URP)... JUDGING...
IN A WEIRD WAY, I'M GOING TO MISS YOU, EUGENE.
DON'T POP, EUGENE. MY CLEAN SHIRTS ARE ALL PACKED.
AMEND

August 6, 1997

August 7, 1997

August 8, 1997

I was really pleased with the way this story worked out. I was also really glad it didn't kill me. It came close.

August 9, 1997

September 14, 1997

I wish I could think up jokes like this more often. They're fun to draw.

September 28, 1997

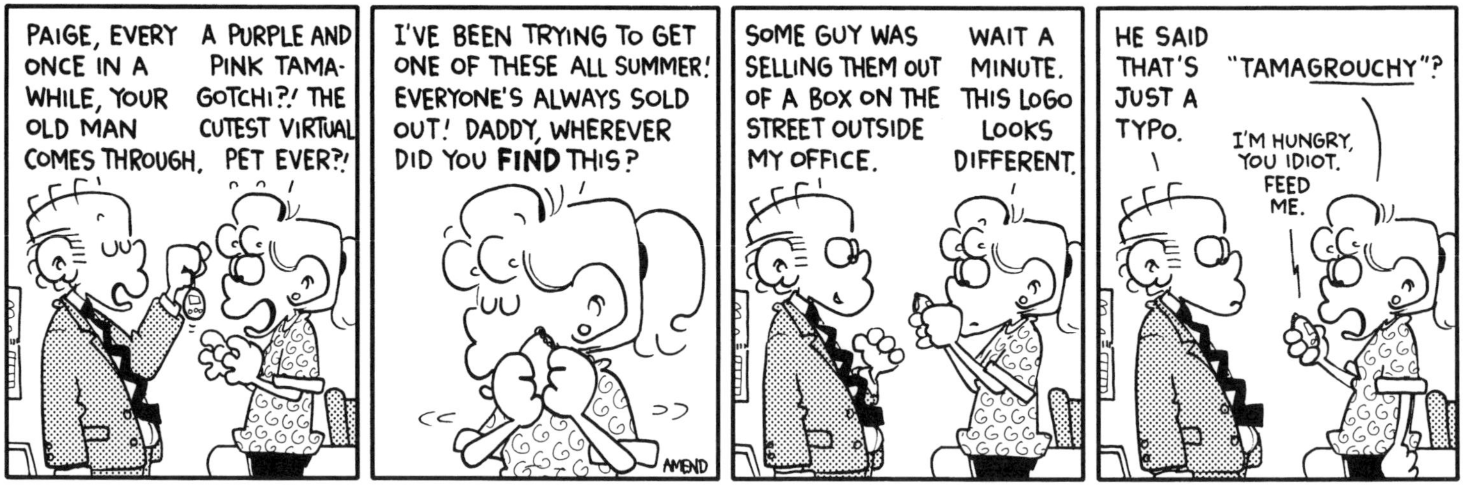
PAIGE, EVERY ONCE IN A WHILE, YOUR OLD MAN COMES THROUGH.
A PURPLE AND PINK TAMAGOTCHI?! THE CUTEST VIRTUAL PET EVER?!
I'VE BEEN TRYING TO GET ONE OF THESE ALL SUMMER! EVERYONE'S ALWAYS SOLD OUT! DADDY, WHEREVER DID YOU FIND THIS?
AMEND
SOME GUY WAS SELLING THEM OUT OF A BOX ON THE STREET OUTSIDE MY OFFICE.
WAIT A MINUTE. THIS LOGO LOOKS DIFFERENT.
HE SAID THAT'S JUST A TYPO.
"TAMAGROUCHY"?
I'M HUNGRY, YOU IDIOT. FEED ME.

August 18, 1997

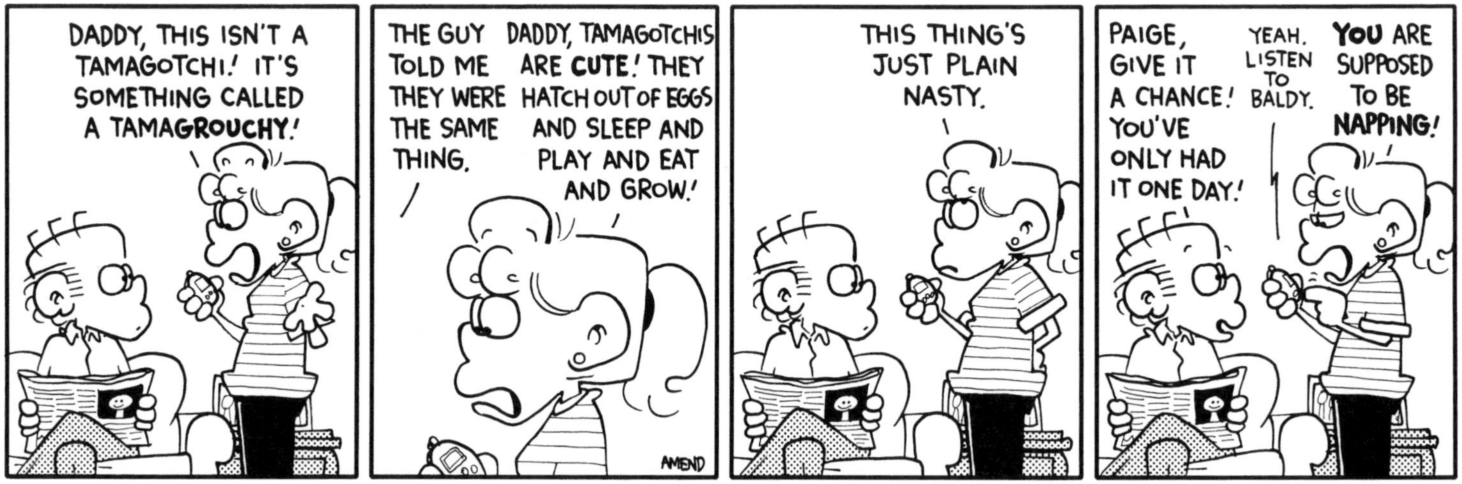
DADDY, THIS ISN'T A TAMAGOTCHI! IT'S SOMETHING CALLED A TAMAGROUCHY!
THE GUY TOLD ME THEY WERE THE SAME THING.
DADDY, TAMAGOTCHIS ARE CUTE! THEY HATCH OUT OF EGGS AND SLEEP AND PLAY AND EAT AND GROW!
AMEND
THIS THING'S JUST PLAIN NASTY.
PAIGE, GIVE IT A CHANCE! YOU'VE ONLY HAD IT ONE DAY!
YEAH. LISTEN TO BALDY.
YOU ARE SUPPOSED TO BE NAPPING!

August 19, 1997

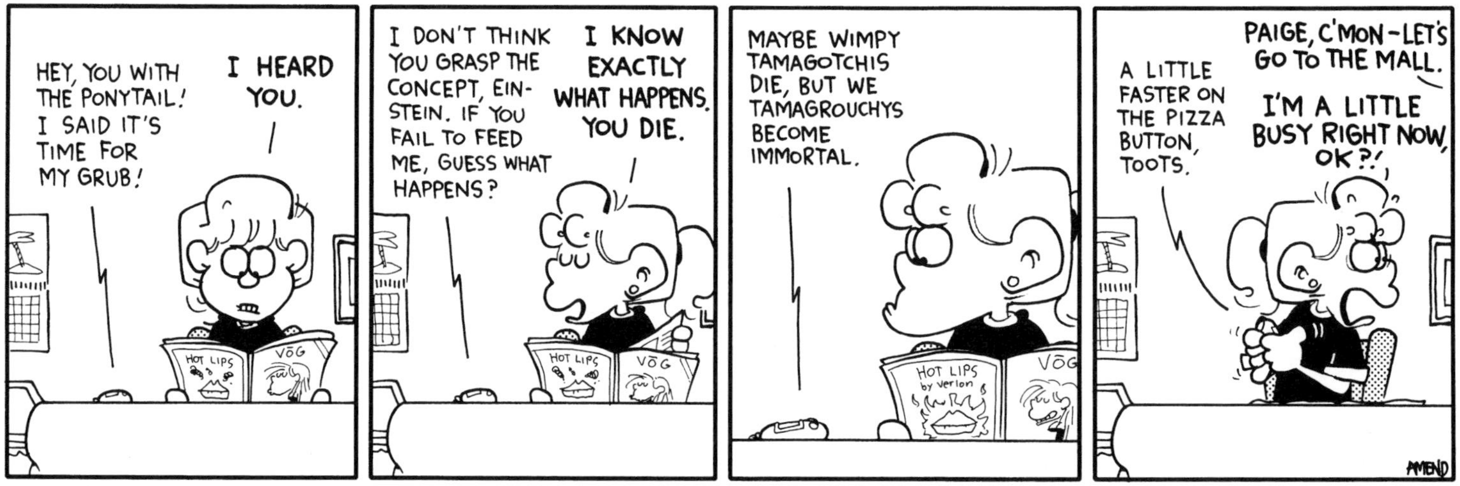
HEY, YOU WITH THE PONYTAIL! I SAID IT'S TIME FOR MY GRUB!
I HEARD YOU.
HOT LIPS
VŌG
I DON'T THINK YOU GRASP THE CONCEPT, EINSTEIN. IF YOU FAIL TO FEED ME, GUESS WHAT HAPPENS?
I KNOW EXACTLY WHAT HAPPENS. YOU DIE.
MAYBE WIMPY TAMAGOTCHIS DIE, BUT WE TAMAGROUCHYS BECOME IMMORTAL.
A LITTLE FASTER ON THE PIZZA BUTTON, TOOTS.
PAIGE, C'MON-LET'S GO TO THE MALL.
I'M A LITTLE BUSY RIGHT NOW, OK?!
AMEND

August 20, 1997

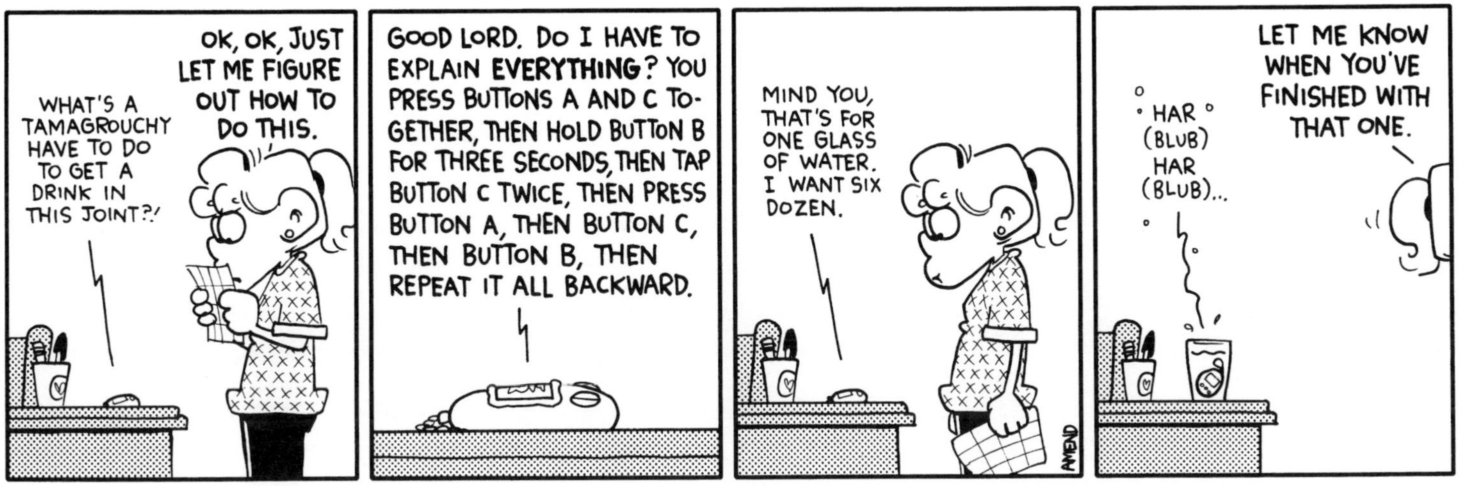

WHAT'S A TAMAGROUCHY HAVE TO DO TO GET A DRINK IN THIS JOINT?!
OK, OK, JUST LET ME FIGURE OUT HOW TO DO THIS.
GOOD LORD. DO I HAVE TO EXPLAIN **EVERYTHING**? YOU PRESS BUTTONS A AND C TOGETHER, THEN HOLD BUTTON B FOR THREE SECONDS, THEN TAP BUTTON C TWICE, THEN PRESS BUTTON A, THEN BUTTON C, THEN BUTTON B, THEN REPEAT IT ALL BACKWARD.
MIND YOU, THAT'S FOR ONE GLASS OF WATER. I WANT SIX DOZEN.
AMEND
HAR (BLUB) HAR (BLUB)...
LET ME KNOW WHEN YOU'VE FINISHED WITH THAT ONE.

August 21, 1997

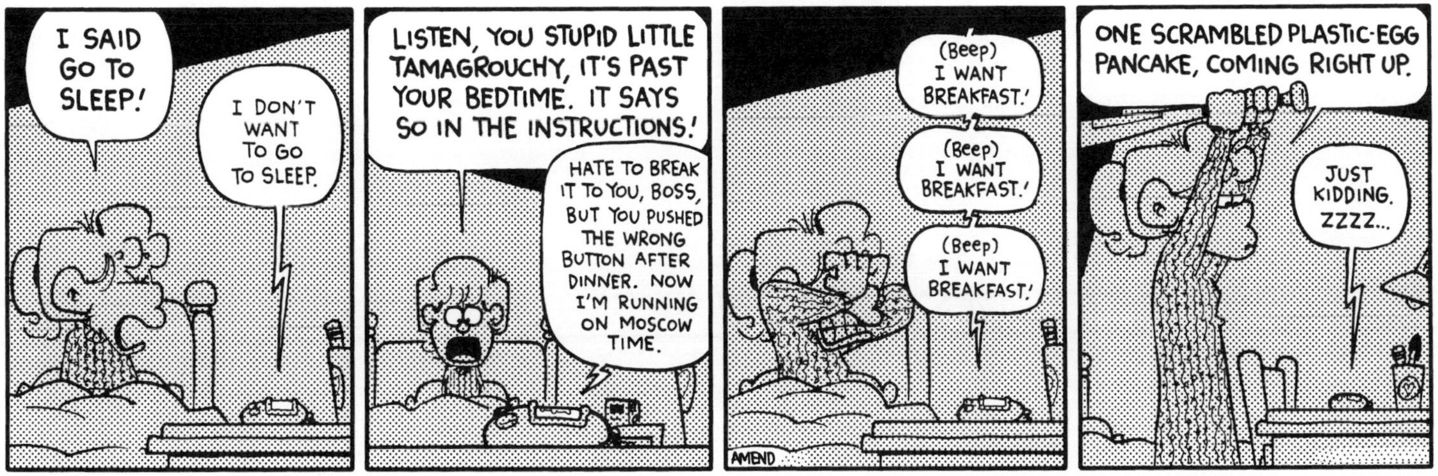

I SAID GO TO SLEEP!
I DON'T WANT TO GO TO SLEEP.
LISTEN, YOU STUPID LITTLE TAMAGROUCHY, IT'S PAST YOUR BEDTIME. IT SAYS SO IN THE INSTRUCTIONS!
HATE TO BREAK IT TO YOU, BOSS, BUT YOU PUSHED THE WRONG BUTTON AFTER DINNER. NOW I'M RUNNING ON MOSCOW TIME.
(Beep) I WANT BREAKFAST!
(Beep) I WANT BREAKFAST!
(Beep) I WANT BREAKFAST!
AMEND
ONE SCRAMBLED PLASTIC-EGG PANCAKE, COMING RIGHT UP.
JUST KIDDING. ZZZZ...

August 22 1997

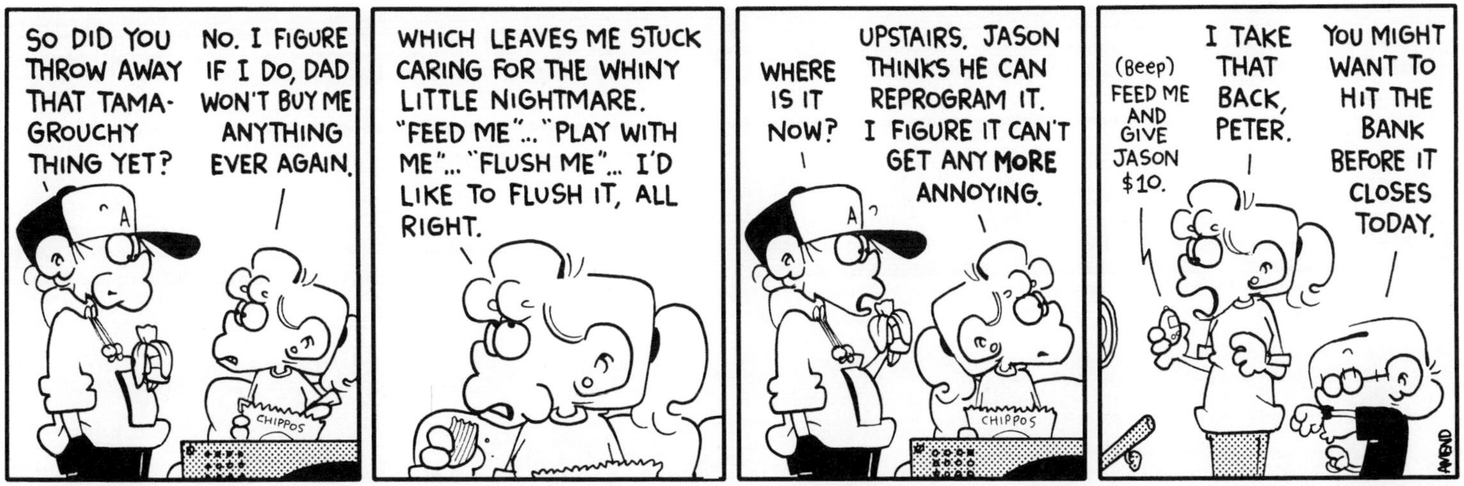

SO DID YOU THROW AWAY THAT TAMA-GROUCHY THING YET?
NO. I FIGURE IF I DO, DAD WON'T BUY ME ANYTHING EVER AGAIN.
CHIPPOS
WHICH LEAVES ME STUCK CARING FOR THE WHINY LITTLE NIGHTMARE. "FEED ME"... "PLAY WITH ME"... "FLUSH ME"... I'D LIKE TO FLUSH IT, ALL RIGHT.
WHERE IS IT NOW?
UPSTAIRS. JASON THINKS HE CAN REPROGRAM IT. I FIGURE IT CAN'T GET ANY **MORE** ANNOYING.
CHIPPOS
(Beep) FEED ME AND GIVE JASON $10.
I TAKE THAT BACK, PETER.
YOU MIGHT WANT TO HIT THE BANK BEFORE IT CLOSES TODAY.
AMEND

August 23, 1997

MOM! MOM! GUESS WHAT?!

WHAT?

MISS O'MALLEY SAID MARCUS AND I COULD BE THE A-V BOYS FOR OUR CLASS THIS FALL!

A-V BOYS?

AUDIO-VISUAL. WE'LL BE IN CHARGE OF SETTING UP THE EQUIPMENT FOR SHOWING FILMS AND STUFF IN CLASS. IT'LL BE A LOT OF WORK, BUT I THINK IT'LL BE FUN.

WELL, I'M SURE YOU'RE UP TO THE TASK.

WE'RE RUNNING THE SURROUND SOUND CABLES TOMORROW.

REMIND ME TO START SCREENING MY PHONE CALLS AGAIN.

September 8, 1997

I'M THINKING WE'RE GOING TO NEED FIVE OR SIX BIG SPEAKERS.

MARCUS, MARCUS, MARCUS.

MAYBE THAT'S FINE FOR **TRADITIONAL** SURROUND SOUND SETUPS, BUT I THOUGHT WE WERE TRYING TO RAISE THE BAR HERE. JMX-SOUND™ SHOULD BE SOMETHING TOTALLY NEW.

WHEN WE FIRST TURN ON THAT MOVIE PROJECTOR, I WANT OUR CLASSMATES TO **KNOW** IT.

I MEANT FIVE OR SIX SPEAKERS PER STUDENT.

OK, NOW WE'RE ON THE SAME PAGE.

September 9, 1997

MISS O'MALLEY SAYS THIS IS THE PROJECTOR YOU AND I WILL BE IN CHARGE OF RUNNING.

SHE SAID IT WAS PRETTY SIMPLE TO OPERATE.

JUST YOUR BASIC 16mm.

YUP, YUP.

NO FANCY LENSES... NO FANCY ELECTRONICS... NO FANCY AUDIO OUTPUT JACKS... NO GIZMOS THAT A NOVICE MIGHT FIND FRIGHTENINGLY COMPLEX.

NOT YET, ANYWAY.

SO, DO YOU WANT TO DRILL THROUGH THE BACK OR THE FRONT?

September 10, 1997

September 11, 1997

September 12, 1997

September 13, 1997

September 29, 1997

September 30, 1997

October 1, 1997

October 2, 1997

October 3, 1997

October 4, 1997

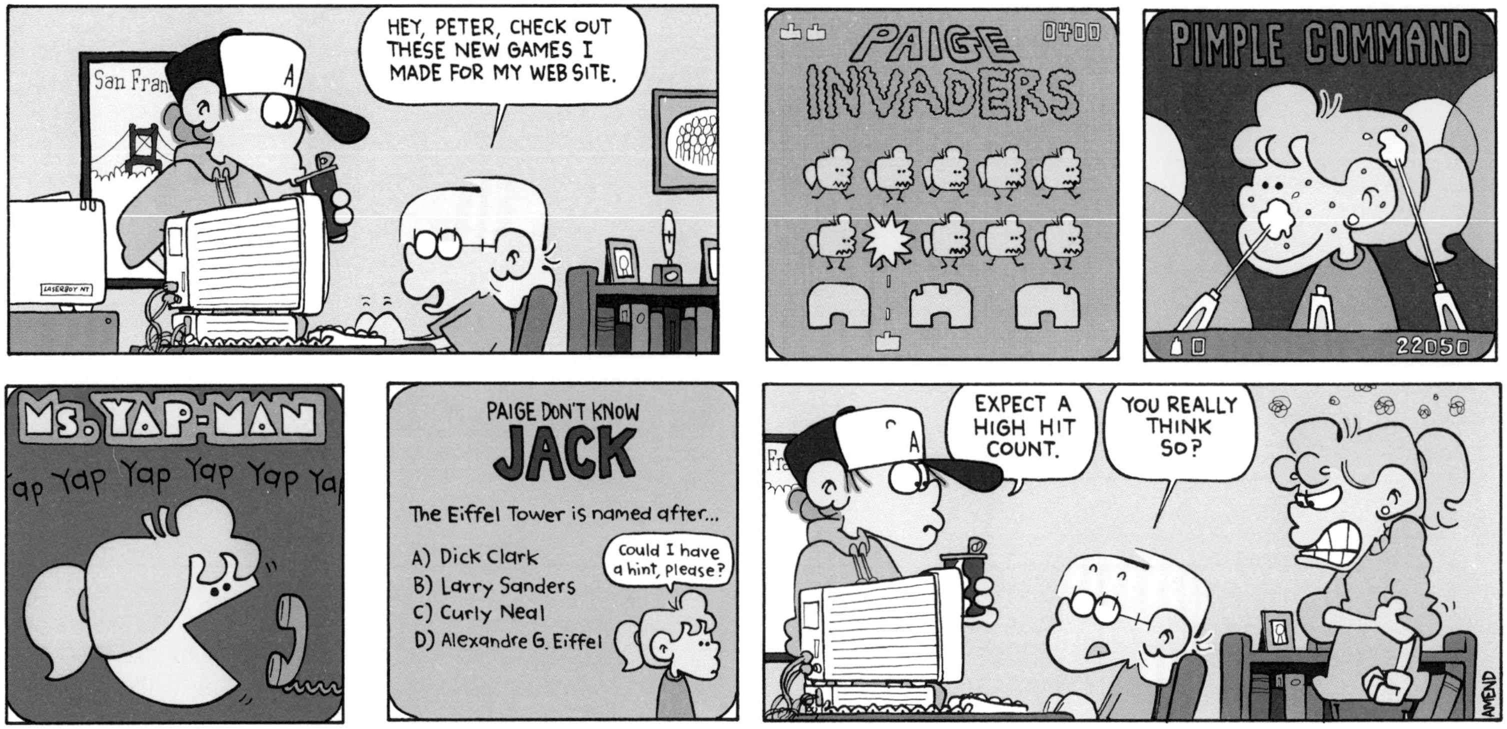
HEY, PETER, CHECK OUT THESE NEW GAMES I MADE FOR MY WEB SITE.
San Fran
0400
PAIGE INVADERS
PIMPLE COMMAND
22050
Ms. YAP-MAN
Yap Yap Yap Yap Yap Yap
PAIGE DON'T KNOW
JACK
The Eiffel Tower is named after...
A) Dick Clark
B) Larry Sanders
C) Curly Neal
D) Alexandre G. Eiffel
Could I have a hint, please?
EXPECT A HIGH HIT COUNT.
YOU REALLY THINK SO?
AMEND

October 12, 1997

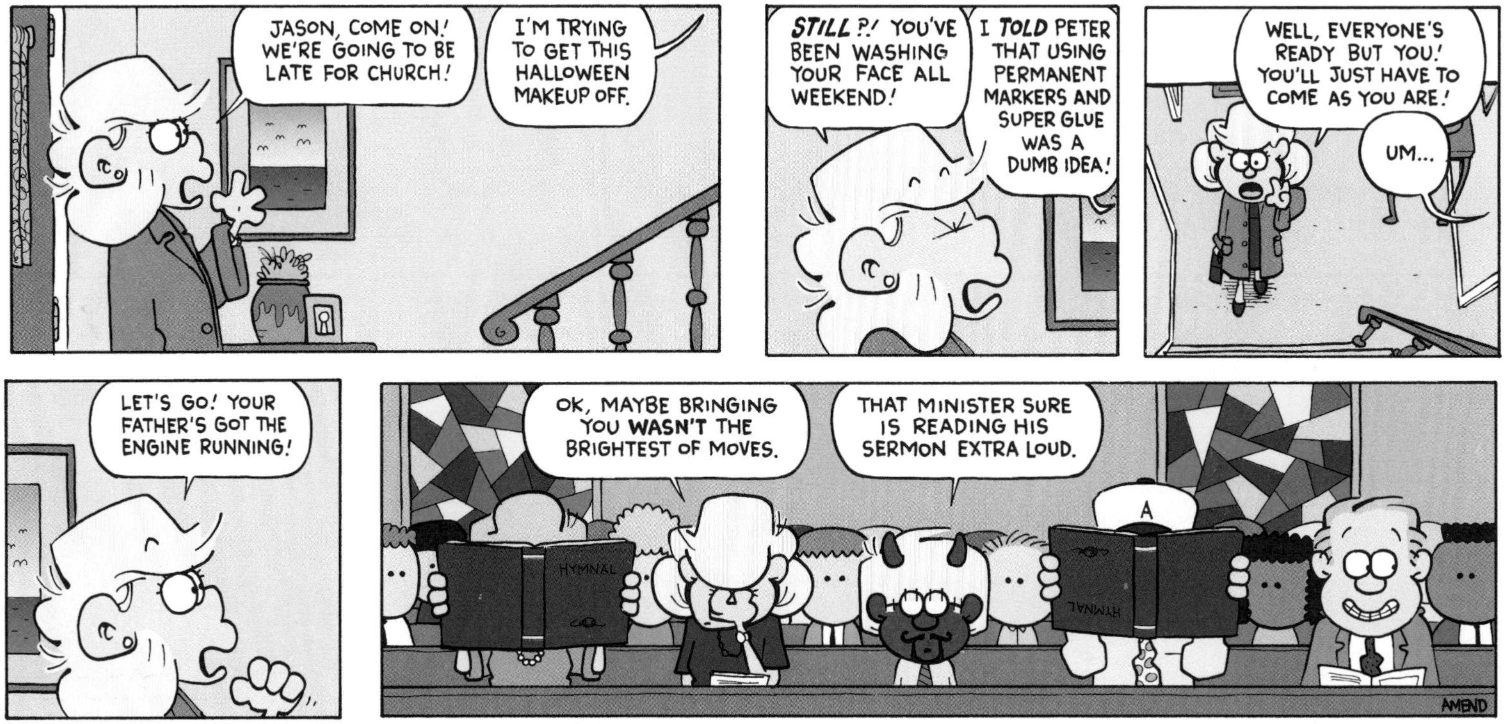
JASON, COME ON! WE'RE GOING TO BE LATE FOR CHURCH!
I'M TRYING TO GET THIS HALLOWEEN MAKEUP OFF.
STILL?! YOU'VE BEEN WASHING YOUR FACE ALL WEEKEND!
I TOLD PETER THAT USING PERMANENT MARKERS AND SUPER GLUE WAS A DUMB IDEA!
WELL, EVERYONE'S READY BUT YOU! YOU'LL JUST HAVE TO COME AS YOU ARE!
UM...
LET'S GO! YOUR FATHER'S GOT THE ENGINE RUNNING!
OK, MAYBE BRINGING YOU WASN'T THE BRIGHTEST OF MOVES.
THAT MINISTER SURE IS READING HIS SERMON EXTRA LOUD.
HYMNAL
HYMNAL
AMEND

November 2, 1997

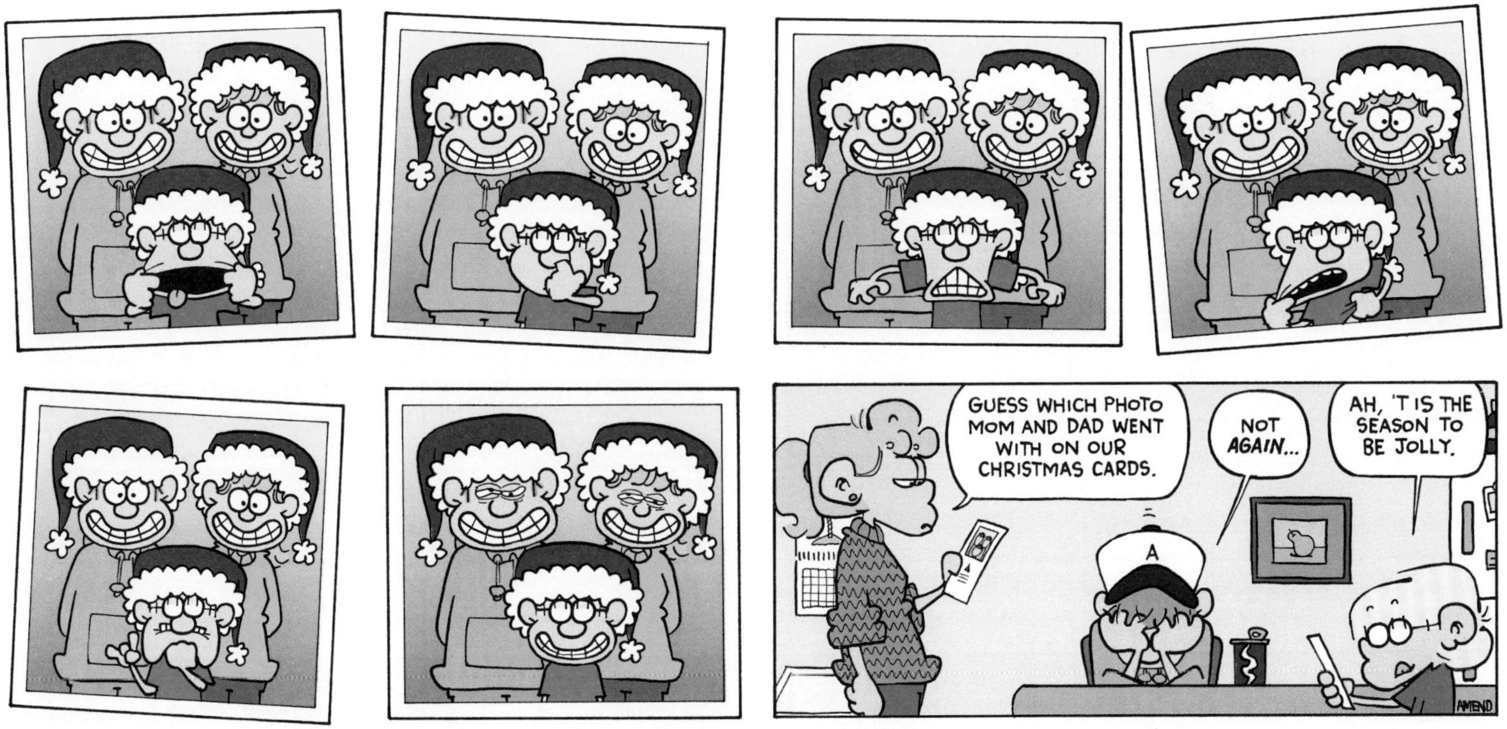
GUESS WHICH PHOTO MOM AND DAD WENT WITH ON OUR CHRISTMAS CARDS.
NOT AGAIN...
AH, 'T IS THE SEASON TO BE JOLLY.
AMEND

December 7, 1997

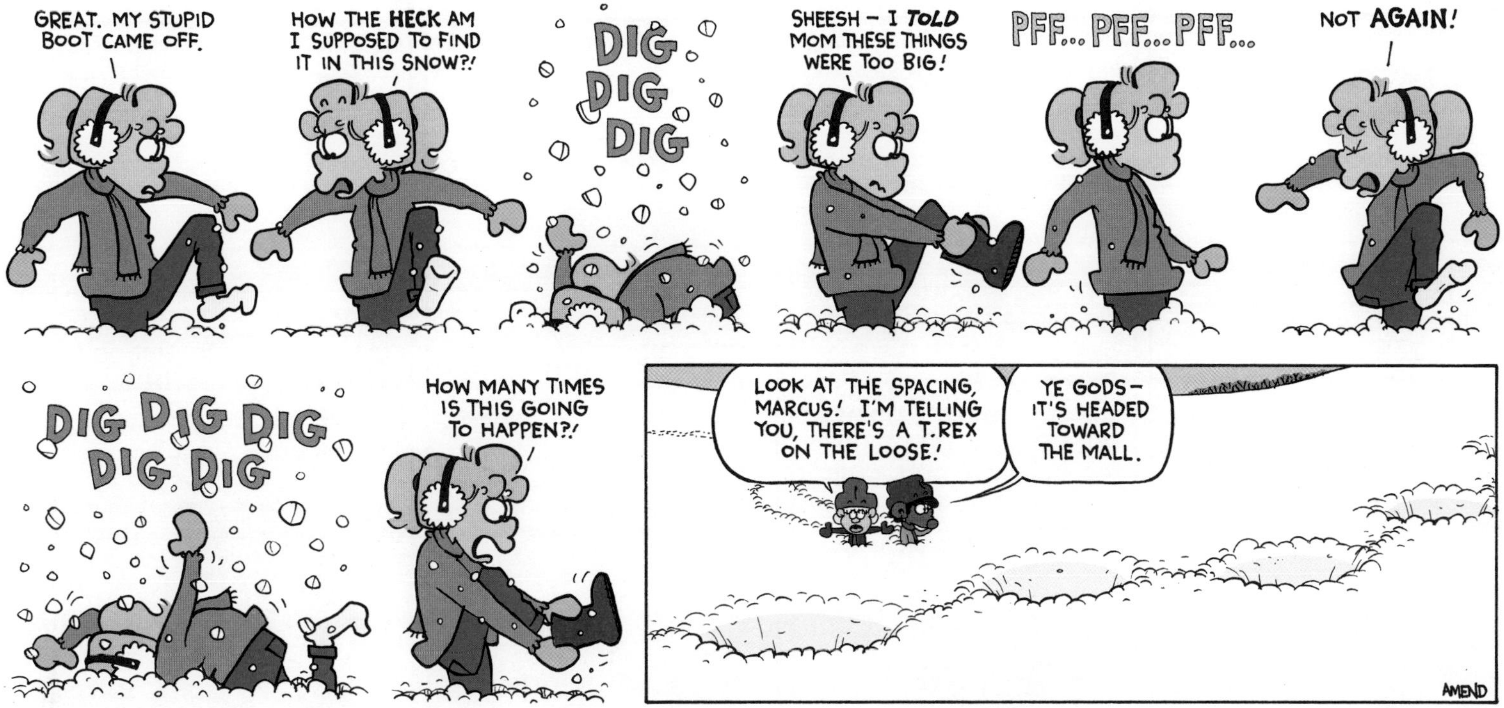
GREAT. MY STUPID BOOT CAME OFF.
HOW THE HECK AM I SUPPOSED TO FIND IT IN THIS SNOW?!
DIG DIG DIG
SHEESH – I TOLD MOM THESE THINGS WERE TOO BIG!
PFF... PFF... PFF...
NOT AGAIN!
DIG DIG DIG DIG DIG
HOW MANY TIMES IS THIS GOING TO HAPPEN?!
LOOK AT THE SPACING, MARCUS! I'M TELLING YOU, THERE'S A T. REX ON THE LOOSE!
YE GODS – IT'S HEADED TOWARD THE MALL.
AMEND

January 11, 1998

October 20, 1997

October 21, 1997

Blizzard actually let me be a beta tester for StarCraft, but my baby iMac could barely run it. I cried a lot.

October 22, 1997

  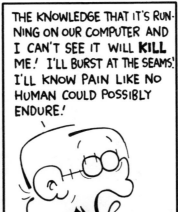 

October 23, 1997

October 24, 1997

October 25, 1997

261

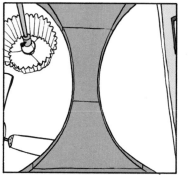

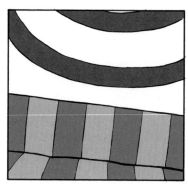

January 18, 1998

Paige's biology teacher is based on one of my college friends.

January 25, 1998

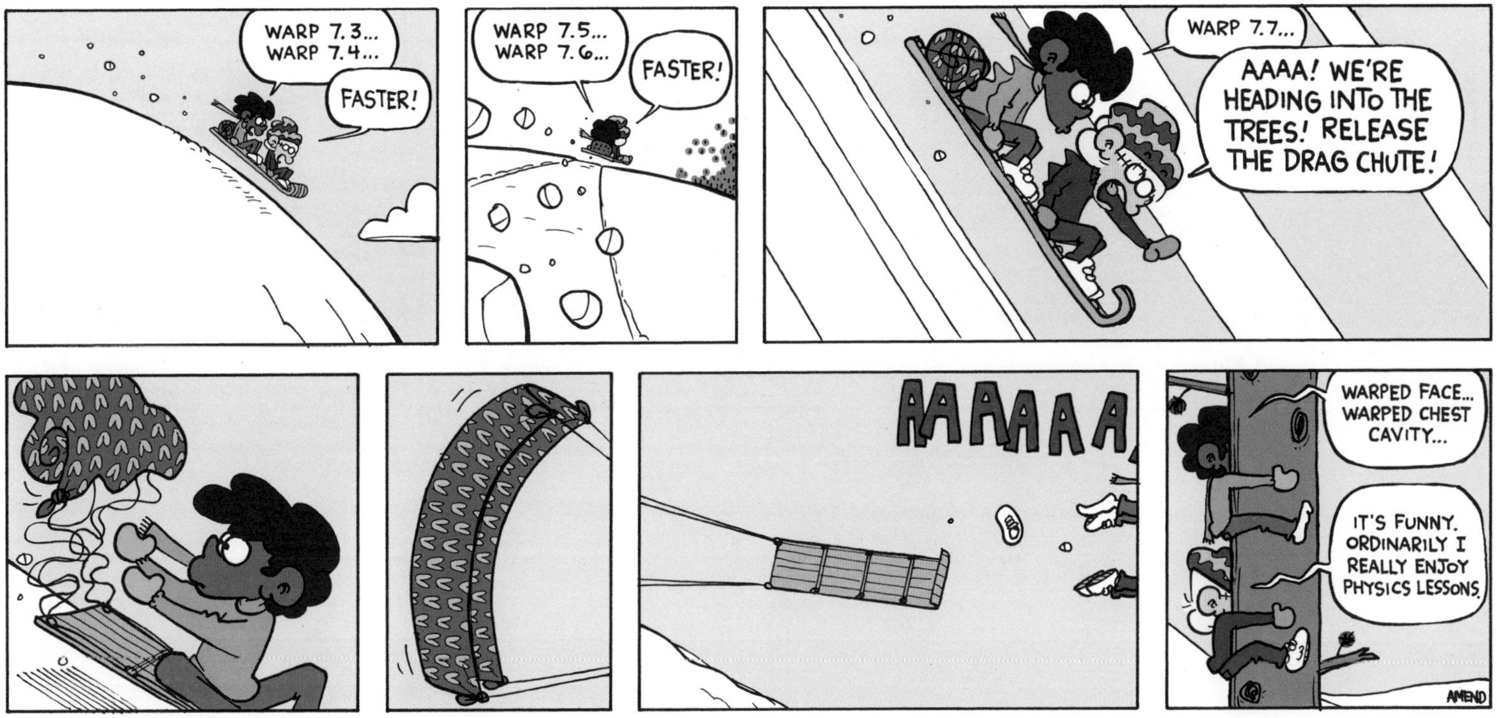
WARP 7.3...
WARP 7.4...
FASTER!
WARP 7.5...
WARP 7.6...
FASTER!
WARP 7.7...
AAAA! WE'RE HEADING INTO THE TREES! RELEASE THE DRAG CHUTE!
AAAAAA
WARPED FACE... WARPED CHEST CAVITY...
IT'S FUNNY. ORDINARILY I REALLY ENJOY PHYSICS LESSONS.
AMEND

February 1, 1998

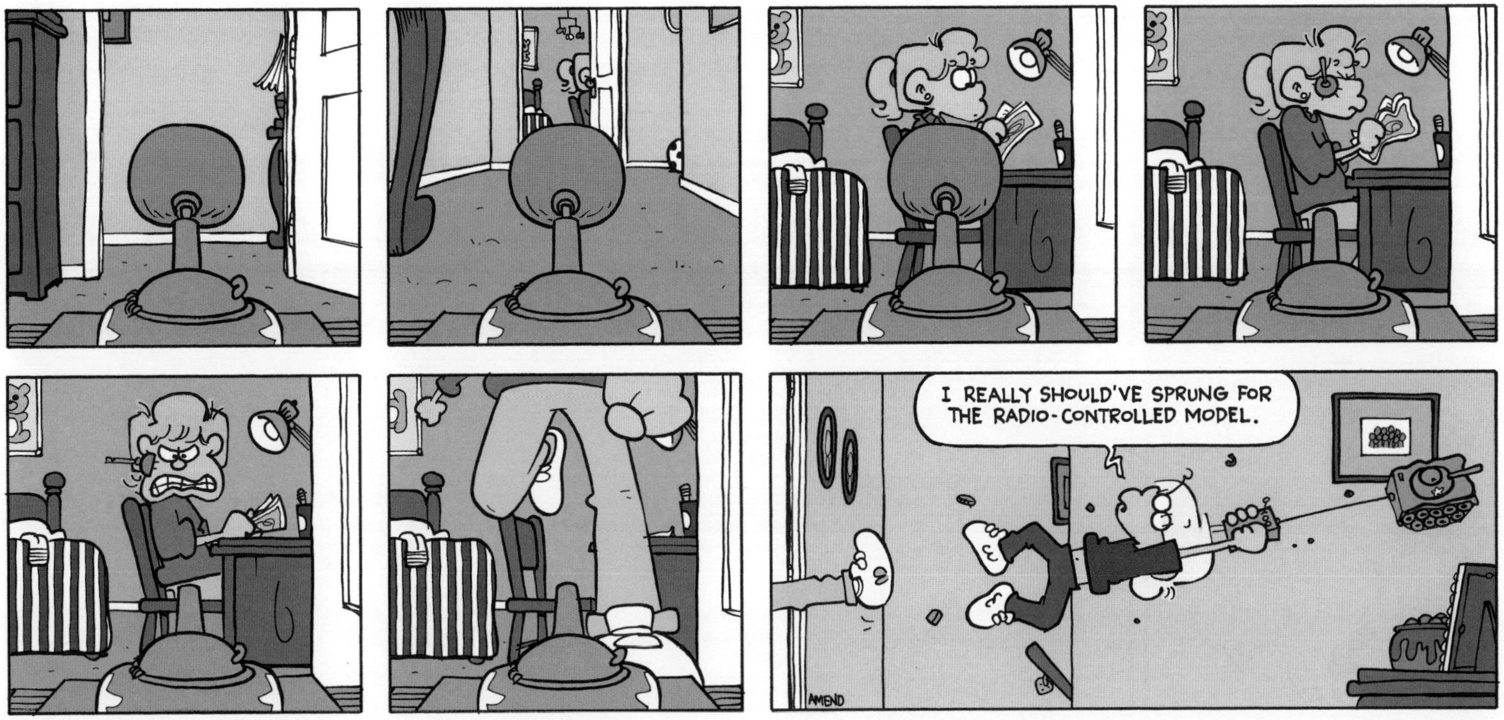
I REALLY SHOULD'VE SPRUNG FOR THE RADIO-CONTROLLED MODEL.
AMEND

March 15, 1998

Right after *Titanic* opened, Oprah had a show with James Cameron, and as I watched woman after woman stand up and gush, I thought, "Hmm . . . I could have fun with this."

WELL, SWEETIE, WE'VE FINALLY CAUGHT UP WITH THE REST OF THE WORLD AND HAVE NOW SEEN "TITANIC."

I'VE GOT TO SAY, FOR A THREE-HOUR FLICK, THAT WAS PRETTY GOOD.

"PRETTY GOOD"?! "PRETTY GOOD"?!

THE MOST MOVING, EXCITING, WONDERFUL, HEART-WRENCHING, TOUCHING, ROMANTIC, POWERFUL, EYE-OPENING, TRAGIC, PERFECT LOVE STORY I THINK I'VE EVER SEEN AND YOU THINK IT'S JUST "*PRETTY GOOD*"?!?!

UH-OH.

I'M NOT SURE I WANT TO GO HOME WITH YOU TONIGHT, ROGER.

February 2, 1998

HONK!

SNIFF!

HONK! HONK! HONK!

COLD? FLU?

AHH AHH AHHHH..

"TITANIC" SOUNDTRACK.

February 3, 1998

ANDY, YOU MIGHT WANT TO UPDATE THE MESSAGE ON YOUR ANSWERING MACHINE.

OH?

IT'S THE ONE YOU PUT ON THERE LAST MONDAY ABOUT NOT BEING IN BECAUSE YOU WERE CATCHING A MATINEE SCREENING OF "TITANIC."

WHAT'S WRONG WITH IT?

WELL, NOTHING... IF YOU'VE BEEN SEEING MATINEES OF "TITANIC" FOR 10 DAYS STRAIGHT.

DON'T TELL ME.

YOU KNOW, THIS MAN IN FRONT OF ME AT TODAY'S SCREENING CRIED JUST LIKE THAT.

February 4, 1998

YOU KNOW, MOM, ACCORDING TO MY CINEGEEK MAGAZINE, THEY USED A 44-FOOT MODEL FOR A LOT OF THOSE SHOTS OF THE TITANIC.

AND AT THE END? WHERE EVERYONE'S SUPPOSEDLY FREEZING IN THE OCEAN? THEY FILMED IT IN A HEATED INDOOR POOL AND ADDED ALL THE FOGGY BREATH WITH COMPUTERS.

IN FACT, FOR THIS ONE SCENE WITH JACK AND ROSE RUNNING AWAY FROM A WALL OF WATER...

JASON, ARE YOU **TRYING** TO SABOTAGE MY LOVE OF THE MOVIE?!

DAD, IF SHE'S FIGURED OUT YOUR PLAN, DO I STILL GET PAID?

WELL, I'M OFF TO THE 6:00 SCREENING. THE TV DINNERS ARE WHERE THEY WERE LAST NIGHT.

February 5, 1998

SWEETHEART, DON'T YOU THINK YOU MIGHT BE GETTING JUST A LITTLE CARRIED AWAY?

YOU'VE SEEN "TITANIC" **HOW** MANY TIMES NOW? TWENTY-FOUR?

WATCHING IT OVER AND OVER ISN'T GOING TO CHANGE THE ENDING... THE BOAT **SINKS!** IT'S SAD, BUT WHAT'S DONE IS DONE!

I KNOW, BUT AT LEAST WHILE I'M IN THE THEATER, IT'S LIKE EVERYONE'S STILL ALIVE FOR THOSE SIX HOURS.

UM, DON'T YOU MEAN THREE HOURS?

I CAN'T DRIVE ALL THE WAY TO THE CINEPLEX AND JUST SEE IT ONCE.

February 6, 1998

ROGER, I KNOW IT MUST SEEM WEIRD THAT I'VE GONE SO GOO-GOO OVER "TITANIC."

BUT SOMETHING ABOUT THAT FILM HAS RESONATED WITH ME LIKE NOTHING HAS IN WHO KNOWS HOW LONG.

IT'S MADE ME WANT TO LIVE! TO LOVE! TO MAKE EACH DAY COUNT! TO GET OUT AND **DO** THINGS!

LIKE WHAT?

I'M FLYING, JACK! ... I MEAN, ROGER.

ACTUALLY, I'D RATHER YOU **DIDN'T** USE MY REAL NAME RIGHT NOW.

February 7, 1998

CLASS, LAST YEAR I NOTICED A PROBLEM WITH THE WAY VALENTINE'S DAY CARDS WERE BEING EXCHANGED.

IT SEEMED SOME OF YOU WERE GETTING LOTS OF CARDS WHILE OTHERS WERE GETTING VERY FEW. I'VE DECIDED THAT AS FIFTH-GRADERS, YOU'RE TOO YOUNG TO HAVE TO DEAL WITH THAT SORT OF STRESS.

SO THIS YEAR, I WANT YOU TO BRING ENOUGH CARDS FOR ALL OF YOUR CLASSMATES. THAT'LL MAKE THINGS FAIR.

OF COURSE, THIS MAY INTRODUCE ANOTHER SORT OF STRESS... WE HAVE TO GIVE CARDS TO GIRLS?!? WE HAVE TO GIVE CARDS TO BOYS?!?

February 9, 1998

I'M SO PSYCHED WE HAVE TO GIVE VALENTINE'S CARDS TO EVERYONE IN THE CLASS. NOT ME.

THINK ABOUT IT, JASON — IF WE JUST GAVE THEM TO THE PEOPLE WE LIKED, IT'D BE AWFULLY EMBARASSING. HOW SO?

YOU KNOW, YOU AND I SINGLING EACH OTHER OUT IN SUCH AN OBVIOUS WAY.

AH, THE THINGS I'LL SAY TO SNAG A CHOCOLATE PUDDING CUP. JASON, STOP! THAT'S A FIRE EXIT!

February 10, 1998

MOM SAYS DINNER'S IN A HALF-HOUR. HEE HEE HEE...

WHAT'S SO FUNNY? I HAVE TO GIVE VALENTINE'S CARDS TO ALL THE GIRLS IN MY CLASS THIS YEAR, AND I JUST CAME UP WITH THE PERFECT IDEA.

I'LL GO TO THE GROCERY STORE, BUY A BLOB OF STEAK, CHOP IT UP, PUT A BIT IN EACH ENVELOPE AND WRITE, "FOR YOU, VALENTINE, A PIECE OF MY HEART."

YOU KNOW, FIVE YEARS FROM NOW WHEN YOU CAN'T BUY YOURSELF A DATE... NOW, FOR EILEEN JACOBSON, WHO LIKES ME, I'LL NEED TO FIND SOMETHING EVEN GROSSER.

February 11, 1998

February 12, 1998

February 13, 1998

February 14, 1998

267

February 16, 1998

February 17, 1998

February 18, 1998

February 19, 1998

February 20, 1998

February 21, 1998

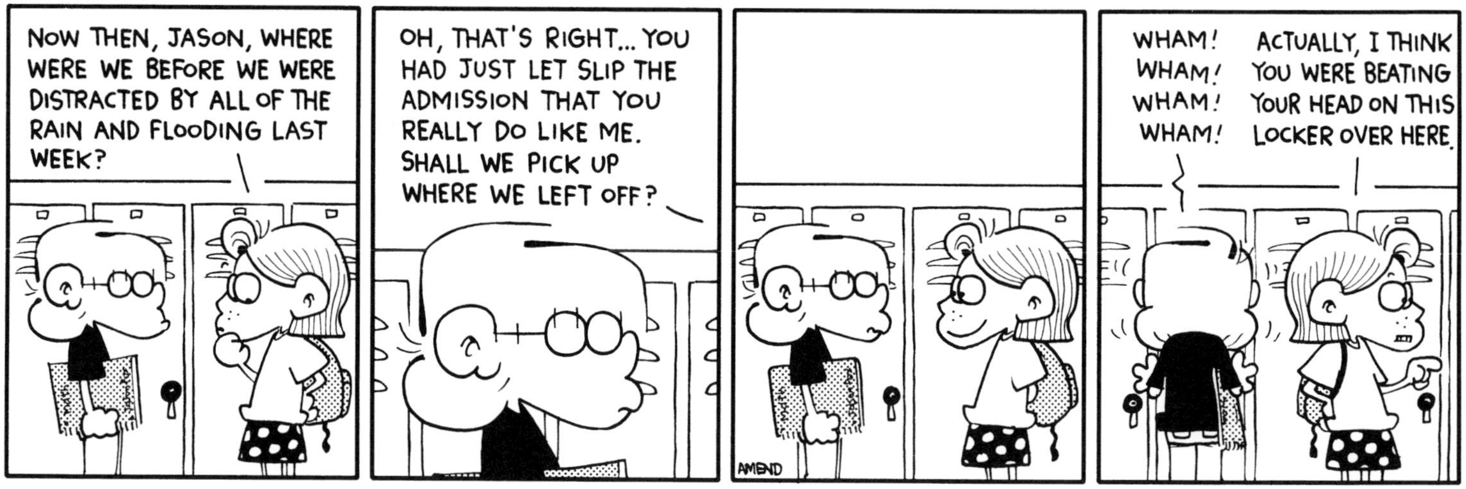
NOW THEN, JASON, WHERE WERE WE BEFORE WE WERE DISTRACTED BY ALL OF THE RAIN AND FLOODING LAST WEEK?
OH, THAT'S RIGHT... YOU HAD JUST LET SLIP THE ADMISSION THAT YOU REALLY DO LIKE ME. SHALL WE PICK UP WHERE WE LEFT OFF?
AMEND
WHAM! WHAM! WHAM! WHAM!
ACTUALLY, I THINK YOU WERE BEATING YOUR HEAD ON THIS LOCKER OVER HERE.

March 2, 1998

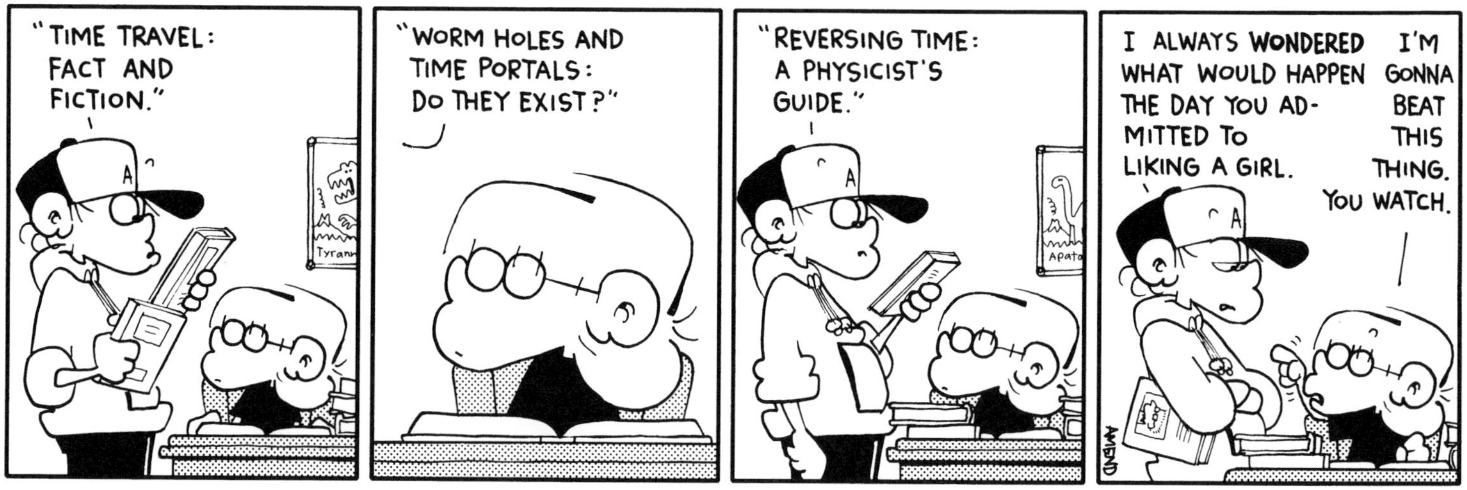
"TIME TRAVEL: FACT AND FICTION."
"WORM HOLES AND TIME PORTALS: DO THEY EXIST?"
"REVERSING TIME: A PHYSICIST'S GUIDE."
I ALWAYS WONDERED WHAT WOULD HAPPEN THE DAY YOU ADMITTED TO LIKING A GIRL.
I'M GONNA BEAT THIS THING. YOU WATCH.
AMEND

March 3, 1998

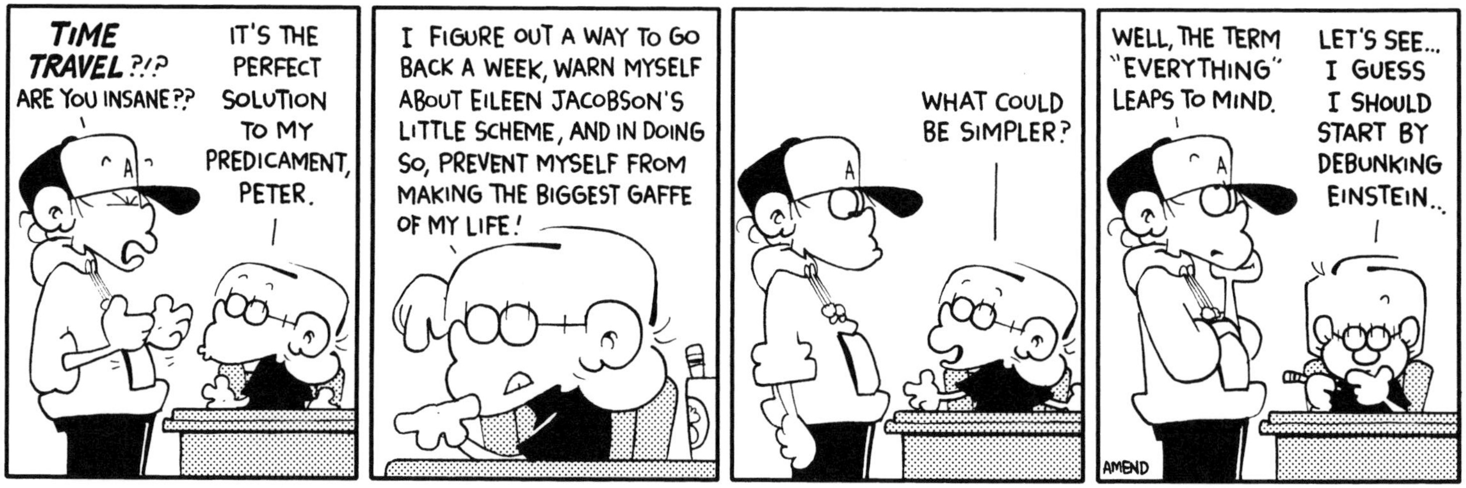
TIME TRAVEL?!? ARE YOU INSANE??
IT'S THE PERFECT SOLUTION TO MY PREDICAMENT, PETER.
I FIGURE OUT A WAY TO GO BACK A WEEK, WARN MYSELF ABOUT EILEEN JACOBSON'S LITTLE SCHEME, AND IN DOING SO, PREVENT MYSELF FROM MAKING THE BIGGEST GAFFE OF MY LIFE!
WHAT COULD BE SIMPLER?
WELL, THE TERM "EVERYTHING" LEAPS TO MIND.
LET'S SEE... I GUESS I SHOULD START BY DEBUNKING EINSTEIN...
AMEND

March 4, 1998

JASON, YOU HAVEN'T TOUCHED YOUR DINNER AT ALL!

SORRY, MOM. I'M ON A SUPER CRASH DIET.

WHAT?? YOU'RE NOTHING BUT SKIN AND BONES AS IT IS!

I KNOW, BUT IF I WANT TO TRAVEL BACK IN TIME, I NEED TO GET MY BODY'S REST MASS DOWN TO ABSOLUTE ZERO SO THAT I CAN EXCEED THE SPEED OF LIGHT.

IT'S A PAIN, BUT THAT STUFF I TOLD EILEEN JACOBSON LAST WEEK HAS GOT TO BE UNDONE.

SO THIS CRASH DIET HAS NOTHING TO DO WITH MY SERVING EGGPLANT LOAF TONIGHT?

TOTALLY A COINCIDENCE. BUT I APPRECIATE THE HELP.

March 5, 1998

PETER, I'M GOING TO NEED YOUR HELP.

WITH WHAT?

AS YOU KNOW, I'VE BEEN PURSUING TIME TRAVEL AS THE SOLUTION TO MY RECENT EILEEN JACOBSON PROBLEM.

WELL, IF MY THEORIES ON THE SUBJECT ARE CORRECT, I'M GOING TO NEED TO EXCEED THE SPEED OF LIGHT, WHICH IS ROUGHLY 670 MILLION MPH. MOST PHYSICISTS SAY IT'S IMPOSSIBLE, BUT I SAY IT CAN BE DONE.

WHERE DO I COME IN?

I'VE SEEN HOW YOU DRIVE ON THE FREEWAY.

YOU'RE TALKING NINE-DIGIT SPEEDS. I'VE ONLY FLIRTED WITH FOUR.

March 6, 1998

WELL, EILEEN, YOU'VE LUCKED OUT.

OH?

I SPENT THIS ENTIRE WEEK RESEARCHING TIME TRAVEL SO THAT I COULD GO BACK AND STOP MYSELF FROM EVER SAYING THAT I LIKED YOU, BUT I'VE CONCLUDED IT CAN'T BE DONE.

AND BELIEVE ME, I WORKED HARDER ON THIS THAN I'VE WORKED ON ANYTHING IN MY LIFE. DAY AND NIGHT, NIGHT AND DAY, SEARCHING, PRAYING, AGONIZING FOR THE SOLUTION THAT WOULD GET ME OUT OF THIS BIND. BUT, ALAS, A HAPPY ENDING WASN'T TO BE.

SO... LOOKS LIKE I'M YOUR BEAU.

AND... I'VE LUCKED OUT HOW EXACTLY?

March 7, 1998

271

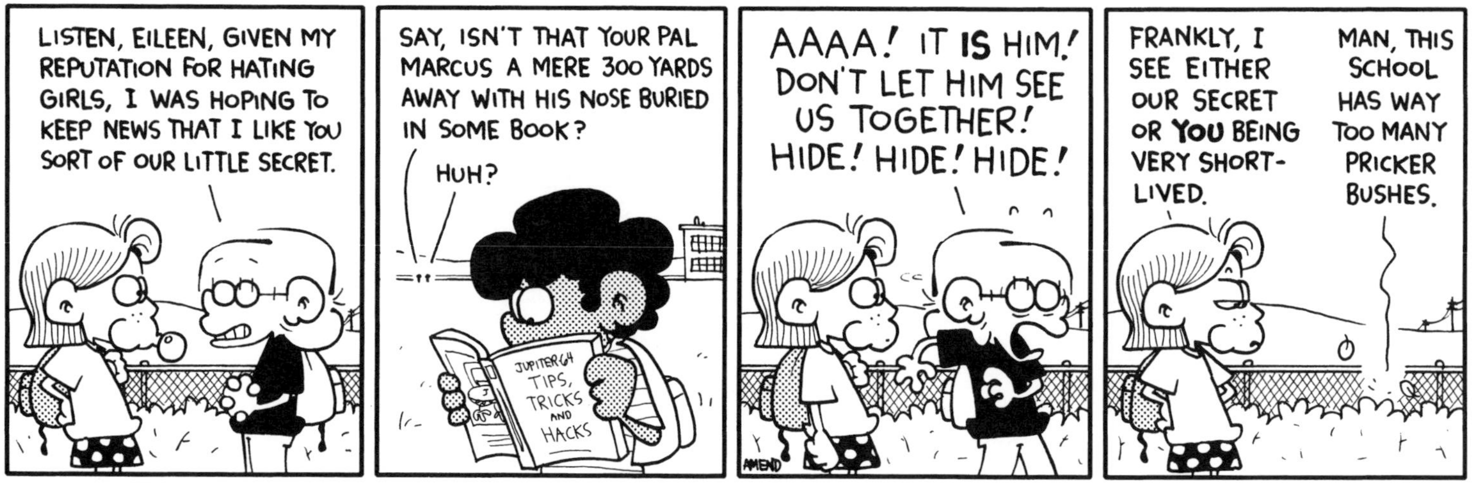
LISTEN, EILEEN, GIVEN MY REPUTATION FOR HATING GIRLS, I WAS HOPING TO KEEP NEWS THAT I LIKE YOU SORT OF OUR LITTLE SECRET.
SAY, ISN'T THAT YOUR PAL MARCUS A MERE 300 YARDS AWAY WITH HIS NOSE BURIED IN SOME BOOK?
HUH?
JUPITER 64 TIPS, TRICKS AND HACKS
AAAA! IT IS HIM! DON'T LET HIM SEE US TOGETHER! HIDE! HIDE! HIDE!
AMEND
FRANKLY, I SEE EITHER OUR SECRET OR YOU BEING VERY SHORT-LIVED.
MAN, THIS SCHOOL HAS WAY TOO MANY PRICKER BUSHES.

March 16, 1998

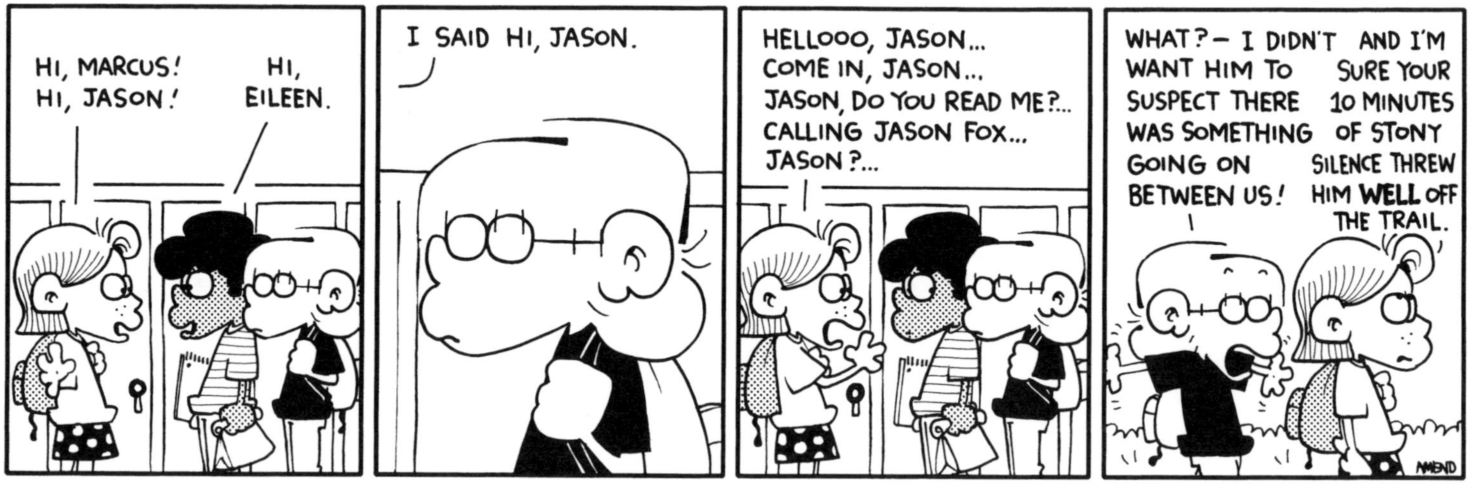
HI, MARCUS! HI, JASON!
HI, EILEEN.
I SAID HI, JASON.
HELLOOO, JASON... COME IN, JASON... JASON, DO YOU READ ME?... CALLING JASON FOX... JASON?...
WHAT?– I DIDN'T WANT HIM TO SUSPECT THERE WAS SOMETHING GOING ON BETWEEN US!
AND I'M SURE YOUR 10 MINUTES OF STONY SILENCE THREW HIM WELL OFF THE TRAIL.
AMEND

March 17, 1998

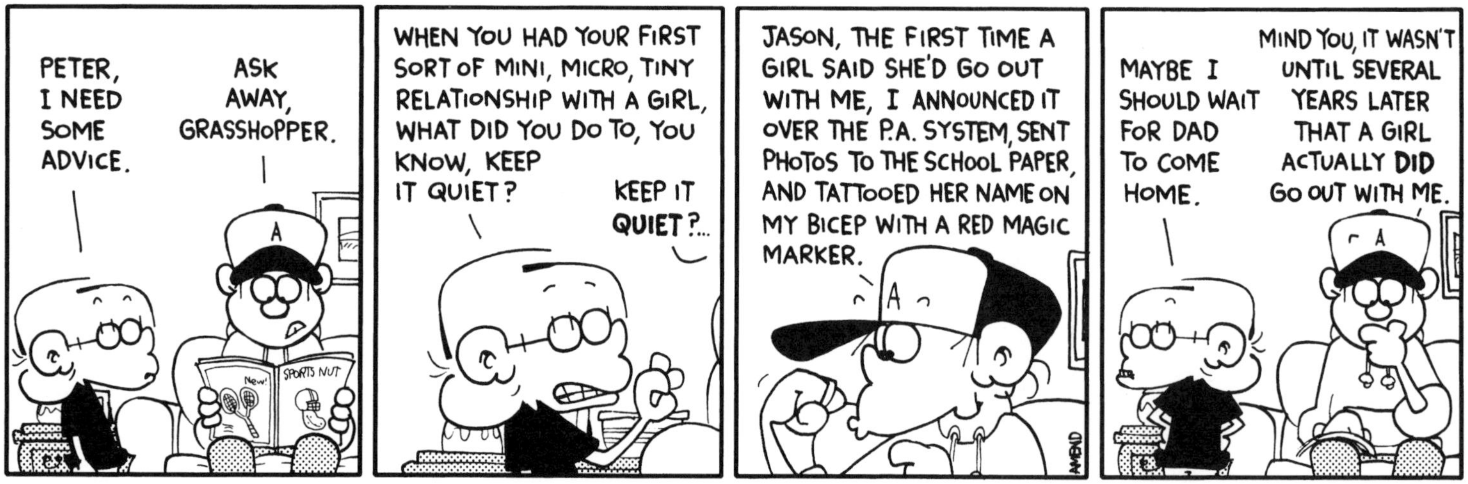
PETER, I NEED SOME ADVICE.
ASK AWAY, GRASSHOPPER.
SPORTS NUT
WHEN YOU HAD YOUR FIRST SORT OF MINI, MICRO, TINY RELATIONSHIP WITH A GIRL, WHAT DID YOU DO TO, YOU KNOW, KEEP IT QUIET?
KEEP IT QUIET?...
JASON, THE FIRST TIME A GIRL SAID SHE'D GO OUT WITH ME, I ANNOUNCED IT OVER THE P.A. SYSTEM, SENT PHOTOS TO THE SCHOOL PAPER, AND TATTOOED HER NAME ON MY BICEP WITH A RED MAGIC MARKER.
AMEND
MAYBE I SHOULD WAIT FOR DAD TO COME HOME.
MIND YOU, IT WASN'T UNTIL SEVERAL YEARS LATER THAT A GIRL ACTUALLY DID GO OUT WITH ME.

March 18, 1998

I CAN'T BELIEVE HOW IDIOTIC I'VE BEEN, EILEEN.

OH?

I'VE SPENT ALL WEEK SCARED TO DEATH SOMEONE'S GOING TO OVERHEAR US TALKING AND FIND OUT THAT I LIKE YOU. WELL, I WAS THINKING ABOUT THE MOVIE "TITANIC," WHEN (BOINK!) IT HIT ME...

THAT YOU SHOULD JUST IGNORE WHAT OTHER PEOPLE THINK AND FOLLOW YOUR OWN HEART?

NO, NO— WE SHOULD JUST SECRETLY COMMUNICATE BY SEMAPHORE.

MORE AND MORE I SEE THE WISDOM IN KEEPING OUR RELATIONSHIP HIDDEN.

March 19, 1998

JASON, I WISH YOU'D STOP ACTING SO WEIRD!

WHAT DO YOU MEAN?

WHAT DO I MEAN?! YOU WON'T BE SEEN WITH ME... YOU WON'T SAY HI TO ME IN FRONT OF YOUR FRIENDS... YOU WANT US TO COMMUNICATE IN SOME SECRET CODE...

IS YOUR LIKING ME REALLY SO EMBARRASSING TO YOU THAT IT'S WORTH CRIPPLING OUR FRIENDSHIP JUST TO KEEP IT SECRET??

I'M WAITING FOR AN ANSWER.

AND I'LL GIVE YOU ONE, JUST AS SOON AS THAT KID I MET ONCE TURNS HIS BACK COMPLETELY TOWARD US.

March 20, 1998

GIVE ANY THOUGHT TO WHAT WE TALKED ABOUT?

YOU WERE RIGHT, EILEEN.

IT'S OBVIOUS THE ROOT OF ALL OUR PROBLEMS IS MY OBSESSION WITH KEEPING THIS THING SECRET. THE ONLY SOLUTION IS TO JUST GRIT MY TEETH, TAKE THE PLUNGE, AND ADMIT TO THE WORLD THAT I LIKE YOU.

YOU'RE SURE?

YUP. IN EXACTLY 11 DAYS I PLAN TO SHOUT IT FROM THE ROOFTOPS: "I LIKE EILEEN!"

THAT WOULDN'T BE APRIL FOOL'S DAY, BY ANY CHANCE, WOULD IT?

DANG. I CAN'T BELIEVE YOU CAUGHT THAT.

March 21, 1998

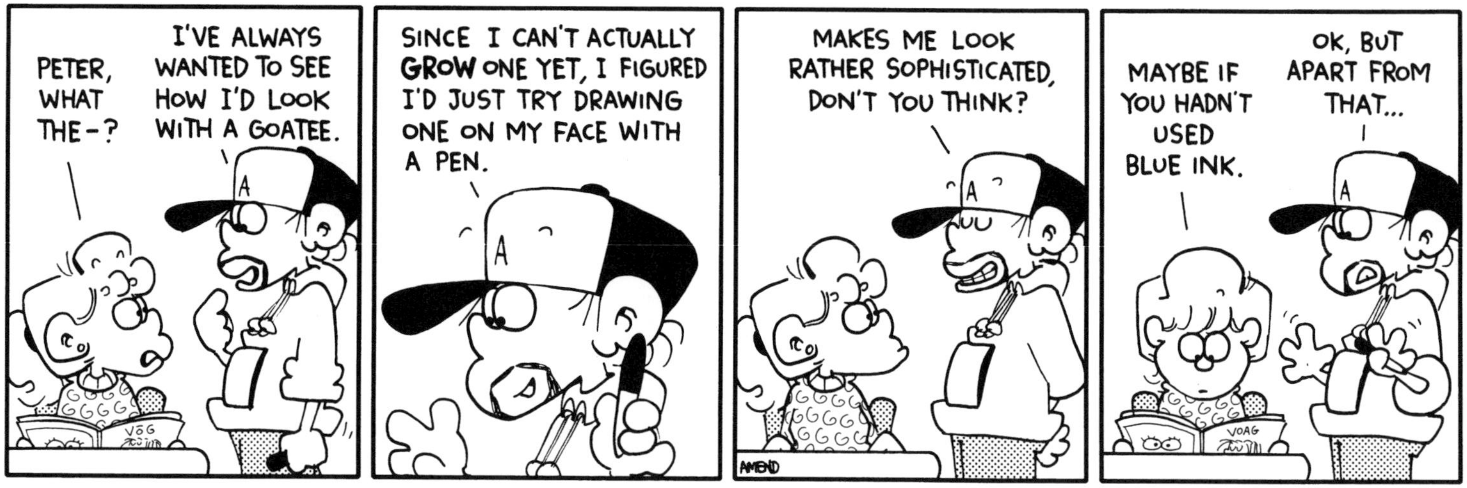
PETER, WHAT THE-?
I'VE ALWAYS WANTED TO SEE HOW I'D LOOK WITH A GOATEE.
SINCE I CAN'T ACTUALLY GROW ONE YET, I FIGURED I'D JUST TRY DRAWING ONE ON MY FACE WITH A PEN.
MAKES ME LOOK RATHER SOPHISTICATED, DON'T YOU THINK?
MAYBE IF YOU HADN'T USED BLUE INK.
OK, BUT APART FROM THAT...

March 23, 1998

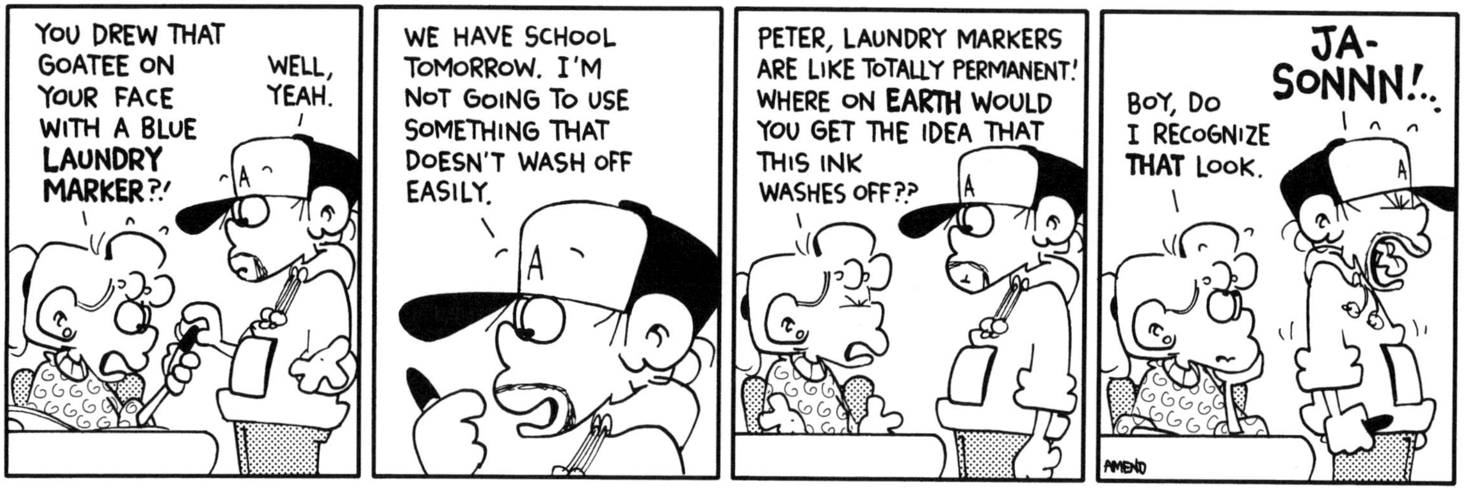
YOU DREW THAT GOATEE ON YOUR FACE WITH A BLUE LAUNDRY MARKER?!
WELL, YEAH.
WE HAVE SCHOOL TOMORROW. I'M NOT GOING TO USE SOMETHING THAT DOESN'T WASH OFF EASILY.
PETER, LAUNDRY MARKERS ARE LIKE TOTALLY PERMANENT! WHERE ON EARTH WOULD YOU GET THE IDEA THAT THIS INK WASHES OFF??
BOY, DO I RECOGNIZE THAT LOOK.
JA-SONNN!..

March 24, 1998

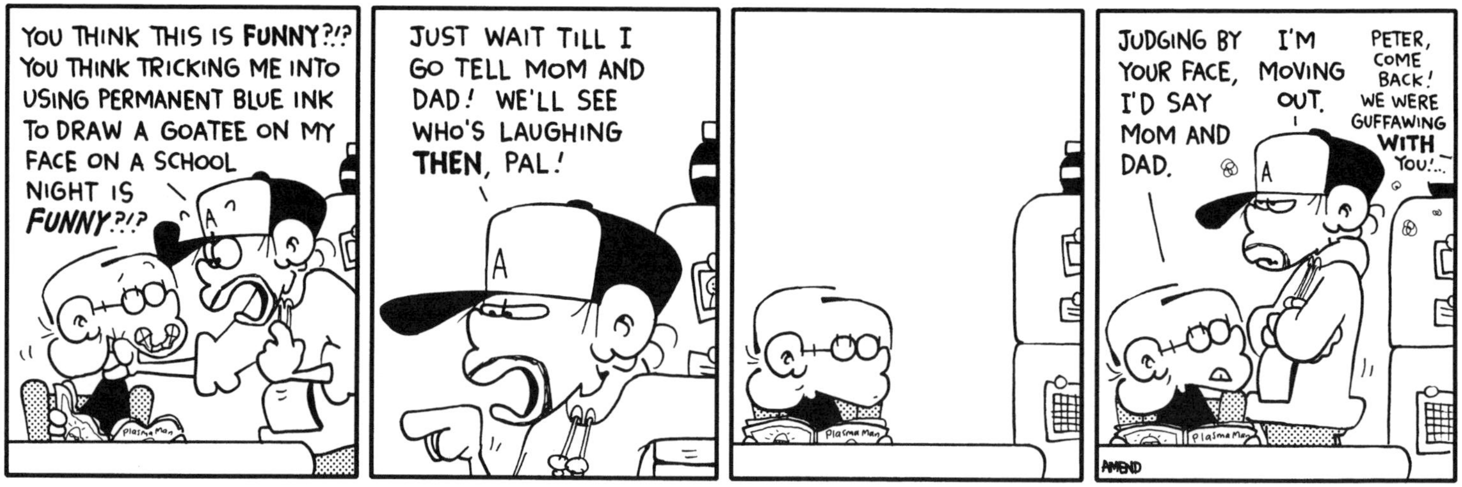
YOU THINK THIS IS FUNNY?!? YOU THINK TRICKING ME INTO USING PERMANENT BLUE INK TO DRAW A GOATEE ON MY FACE ON A SCHOOL NIGHT IS FUNNY?!?
JUST WAIT TILL I GO TELL MOM AND DAD! WE'LL SEE WHO'S LAUGHING THEN, PAL!
JUDGING BY YOUR FACE, I'D SAY MOM AND DAD.
I'M MOVING OUT.
PETER, COME BACK! WE WERE GUFFAWING WITH YOU!..

March 25, 1998

PETER, CALM DOWN. I'LL THINK OF SOMETHING.

CALM DOWN?! SCHOOL IS IN 12 HOURS AND I'VE GOT A BLUE GOATEE ON MY FACE!

YOU'RE TALKING TO A CHEMISTRY WIZ, REMEMBER? I'LL JUST PUT A FEW CHOICE SOLVENTS ONTO THIS RAG AND THAT INDELIBLE INK WILL SMEAR RIGHT OFF!

ORRR... MAYBE JUST SMEAR.

AAAA! MY WHOLE FACE IS BLUE!

March 26, 1998

I BORROWED SOME OF MOM'S MAKEUP. I'LL HAVE THAT BLUE INK HIDDEN IN NO TIME.

WAIT A SECOND! I DON'T WANT **YOU** DOING THIS!

THE ONLY MAKEUP JOBS YOU KNOW HOW TO DO ARE MONSTER FACES FOR HALLO-WEEN. WHERE'S PAIGE?... SHE KNOWS HOW TO PUT THIS STUFF ON PROPERLY.

NO COMMENTS. JUST DO IT.

NOW, THEN, DRACULA OR FRANKENSTEIN?

March 27, 1998

HEH HEH... DARE I ASK HOW SCHOOL WENT?

LET'S JUST SAY YOU LUCKED-OUT BIG TIME.

WITH THIS STUPID BLUE INK ALL OVER MY FACE, THE GIRLS DECIDED I LOOKED LIKE LEONARDO DICAPRIO TOWARD THE END OF "TITANIC," WHILE THE GUYS THOUGHT I RESEMBLED SOME ALIEN BEING FROM "STAR TREK."

FORTUNATELY, BETWEEN THE TEASING ON ONE HAND, AND THE GOOGLY-EYED FAWNING ON THE OTHER, IT ALL KIND OF AVERAGED OUT OK.

ODD... I WAS UNDER THE IMPRESSION THAT GIRLS **LIKED** LEONARDO.

IT'S FUNNY, YOU AND I SHARE SO MANY GENES, AND YET...

March 28, 1998

JASON, LOOK, I'M REALLY HAPPY THAT YOU LIKE ME, DON'T GET ME WRONG.

BUT THE EXTENT TO WHICH YOU'VE BEEN GOING TO HIDE THIS NEWS FROM YOUR FRIENDS IS REALLY STARTING TO BOTHER ME.

LIKING SOMEONE SHOULD MEAN A WILLINGNESS TO SAY, "TO HECK WITH EMBARRASSMENT"! SERIOUSLY, DON'T YOU AGREE?!

IN SPIRIT. DRAT—I THINK WE'VE BEEN SPOTTED.

I MEAN, LORD KNOWS *I'VE* SAID TO HECK WITH EMBARRASSMENT.

March 30, 1998

PHEW. FALSE ALARM.

JASON, WILL YOU COOL IT WITH THE DISGUISES?!

EILEEN, YOU DON'T UNDERSTAND THE FIFTH-GRADE MALE ETHOS. IF THE GUYS FIND OUT THAT I LIKE YOU—A *GIRL*—I'M KAPUT! FINISHED! RUINED!

THEY'LL MAKE FUN OF ME! TEASE ME! TAUNT ME TILL I DIE!

HOW DO YOU KNOW?

WELL, I'D DO IT TO **THEM.**

YOU DID SAY FIFTH GRADE, AND NOT, OH, FIRST OR SECOND, CORRECT?

March 31, 1998

LOOK, JASON, I DON'T WANT YOU TO BE TEASED BY YOUR FRIENDS, I REALLY DON'T.

BUT I DON'T WANT TO BE TREATED THE WAY YOU'VE BEEN TREATING ME RECENTLY, EITHER.

SO THE WAY I SEE IT, YOU'VE GOT A DECISION TO MAKE: WHICH DO YOU LIKE **MORE**—ME, OR YOUR PRECIOUS "GIRL HATER" REPUTATION? YOU CAN'T HAVE BOTH, SO WHAT'S IT GOING TO BE?

UM... I'LL TELL YOU TOMORROW.

YOU SAID THAT YESTERDAY.

ER... AND IT'S NOT TOMORROW YET, IS IT?

April 1, 1998

276

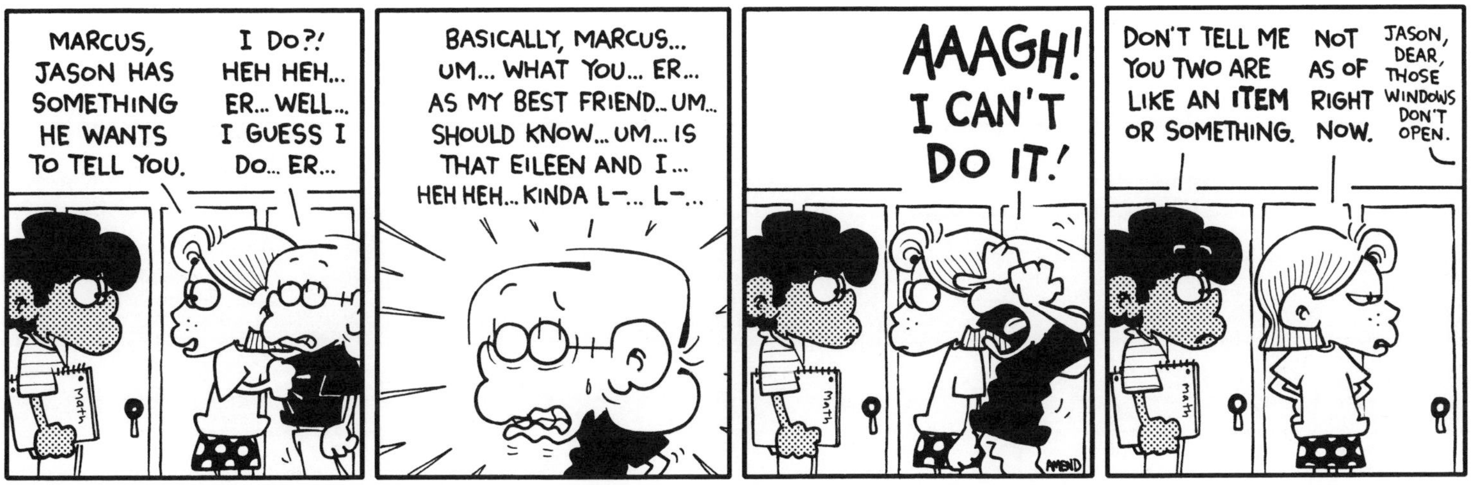
MARCUS, JASON HAS SOMETHING HE WANTS TO TELL YOU.
I DO?! HEH HEH... ER... WELL... I GUESS I DO... ER...
BASICALLY, MARCUS... UM... WHAT YOU... ER... AS MY BEST FRIEND... UM... SHOULD KNOW... UM... IS THAT EILEEN AND I... HEH HEH... KINDA L-... L-...
AAAGH! I CAN'T DO IT!
DON'T TELL ME YOU TWO ARE LIKE AN ITEM OR SOMETHING.
NOT AS OF RIGHT NOW.
JASON, DEAR, THOSE WINDOWS DON'T OPEN.
AMEND

April 2, 1998

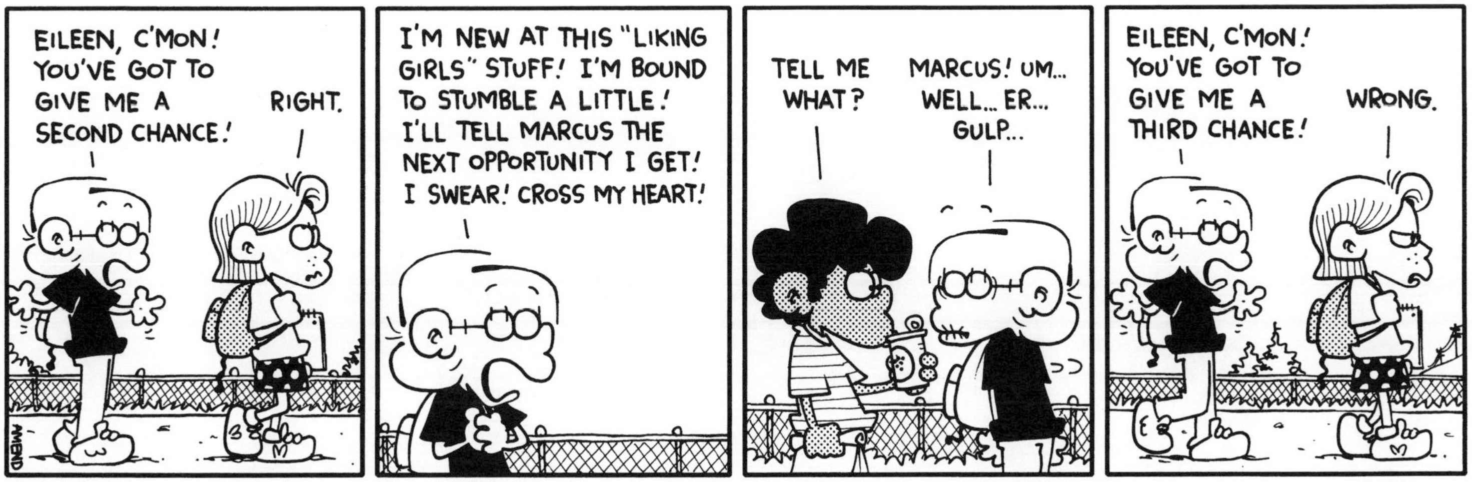
EILEEN, C'MON! YOU'VE GOT TO GIVE ME A SECOND CHANCE!
RIGHT.
AMEND
I'M NEW AT THIS "LIKING GIRLS" STUFF! I'M BOUND TO STUMBLE A LITTLE! I'LL TELL MARCUS THE NEXT OPPORTUNITY I GET! I SWEAR! CROSS MY HEART!
TELL ME WHAT?
MARCUS! UM... WELL... ER... GULP...
EILEEN, C'MON! YOU'VE GOT TO GIVE ME A THIRD CHANCE!
WRONG.

April 3, 1998

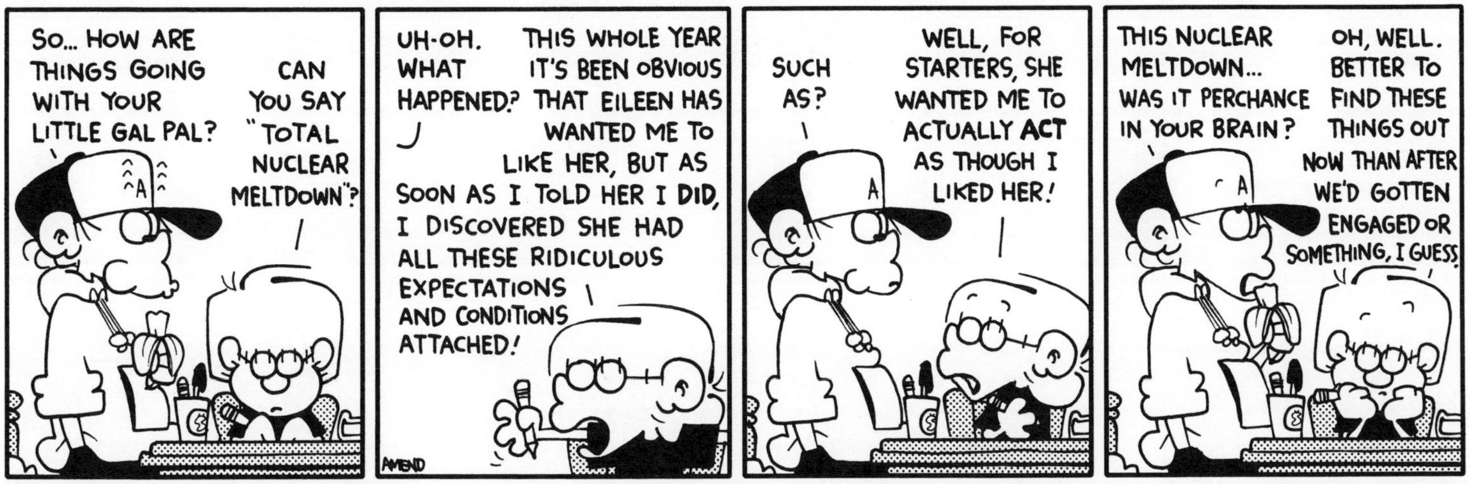
SO... HOW ARE THINGS GOING WITH YOUR LITTLE GAL PAL?
CAN YOU SAY "TOTAL NUCLEAR MELTDOWN"?
UH-OH. WHAT HAPPENED?
THIS WHOLE YEAR IT'S BEEN OBVIOUS THAT EILEEN HAS WANTED ME TO LIKE HER, BUT AS SOON AS I TOLD HER I DID, I DISCOVERED SHE HAD ALL THESE RIDICULOUS EXPECTATIONS AND CONDITIONS ATTACHED!
AMEND
SUCH AS?
WELL, FOR STARTERS, SHE WANTED ME TO ACTUALLY ACT AS THOUGH I LIKED HER!
THIS NUCLEAR MELTDOWN... WAS IT PERCHANCE IN YOUR BRAIN?
OH, WELL. BETTER TO FIND THESE THINGS OUT NOW THAN AFTER WE'D GOTTEN ENGAGED OR SOMETHING, I GUESS.

April 4, 1998

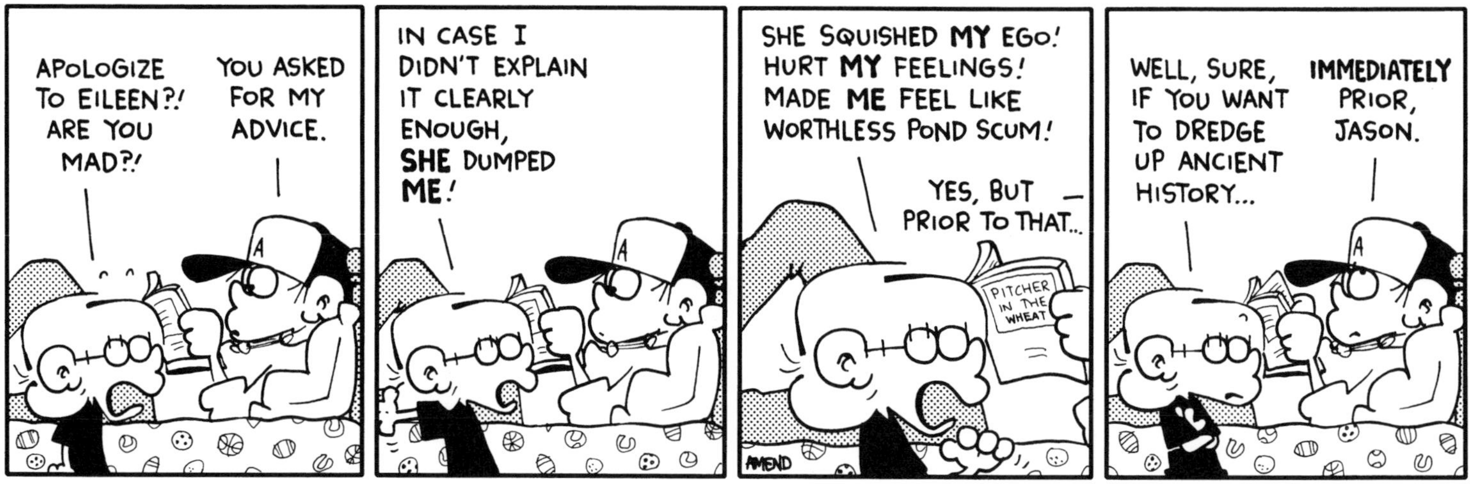
APOLOGIZE TO EILEEN?! ARE YOU MAD?!
YOU ASKED FOR MY ADVICE.
IN CASE I DIDN'T EXPLAIN IT CLEARLY ENOUGH, SHE DUMPED ME!
SHE SQUISHED MY EGO! HURT MY FEELINGS! MADE ME FEEL LIKE WORTHLESS POND SCUM!
YES, BUT PRIOR TO THAT...
PITCHER IN THE WHEAT
WELL, SURE, IF YOU WANT TO DREDGE UP ANCIENT HISTORY...
IMMEDIATELY PRIOR, JASON.
AMEND
April 6, 1998

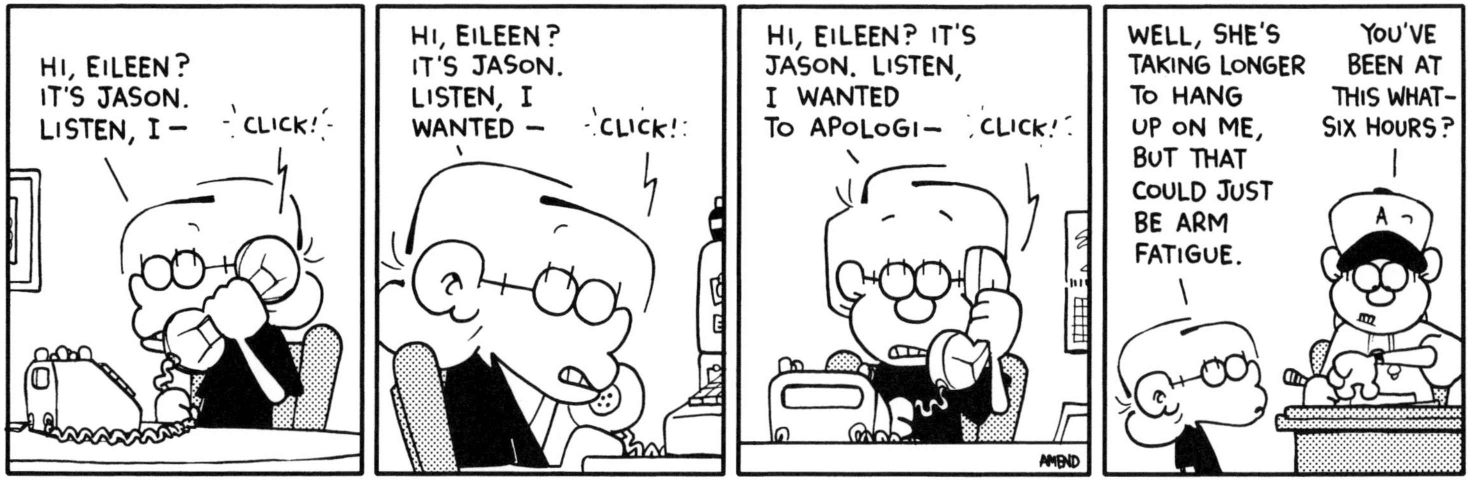
HI, EILEEN? IT'S JASON. LISTEN, I –
CLICK!
HI, EILEEN? IT'S JASON. LISTEN, I WANTED –
CLICK!
HI, EILEEN? IT'S JASON. LISTEN, I WANTED TO APOLOGI–
CLICK!
AMEND
WELL, SHE'S TAKING LONGER TO HANG UP ON ME, BUT THAT COULD JUST BE ARM FATIGUE.
YOU'VE BEEN AT THIS WHAT–SIX HOURS?
April 7, 1998

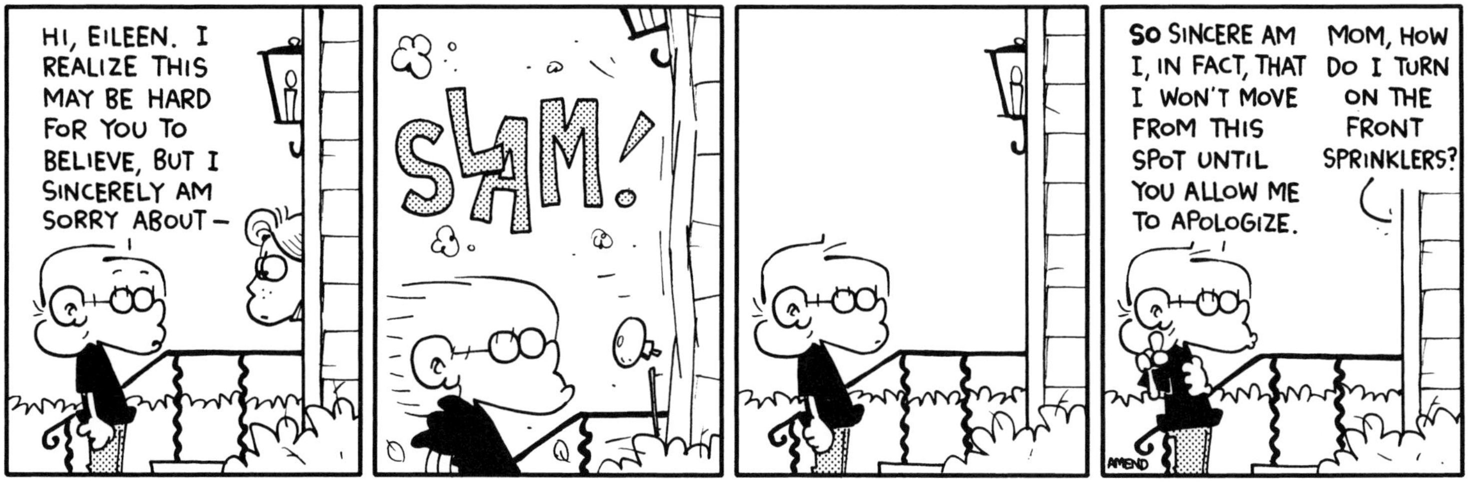
HI, EILEEN. I REALIZE THIS MAY BE HARD FOR YOU TO BELIEVE, BUT I SINCERELY AM SORRY ABOUT –
SLAM!
SO SINCERE AM I, IN FACT, THAT I WON'T MOVE FROM THIS SPOT UNTIL YOU ALLOW ME TO APOLOGIZE.
MOM, HOW DO I TURN ON THE FRONT SPRINKLERS?
AMEND
April 8, 1998

April 9, 1998

April 10, 1998

April 11, 1998

It was fun to advance the Jason-Eileen relationship for a while, but in the end I needed most of it back in the bottle.

As a former bench warmer, I like having a character who's even worse at baseball than I was.

April 5, 1998

April 12, 1998

THE BEST OF
FoxTrot

Volume Two

by Bill Amend

Andrews McMeel
Publishing, LLC

Kansas City • Sydney • London

FoxTrot is distributed internationally by Universal Uclick.

 For information, write Andrews McMeel Publishing, LLC, an Andrews McMeel Universal company, 1130 Walnut Street, Kansas City, Missouri 64106.

10 11 12 13 14 SDB 10 9 8 7 6 5 4 3 2 1

ISBN: 978-0-7407-7733-2
Library of Congress Control Number: 2009929504

www.andrewsmcmeel.com
www.foxtrot.com

May 10, 1998

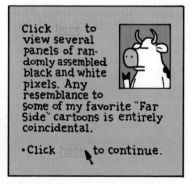

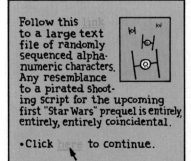

I still don't see how numbers can be copyrighted.

May 17, 1998

April 20, 1998

I'm pretty sure these strips were written after my three-year-old daughter started loudly rhyming "uck" words while we were in the middle of a store.

April 21, 1998

April 22, 1998

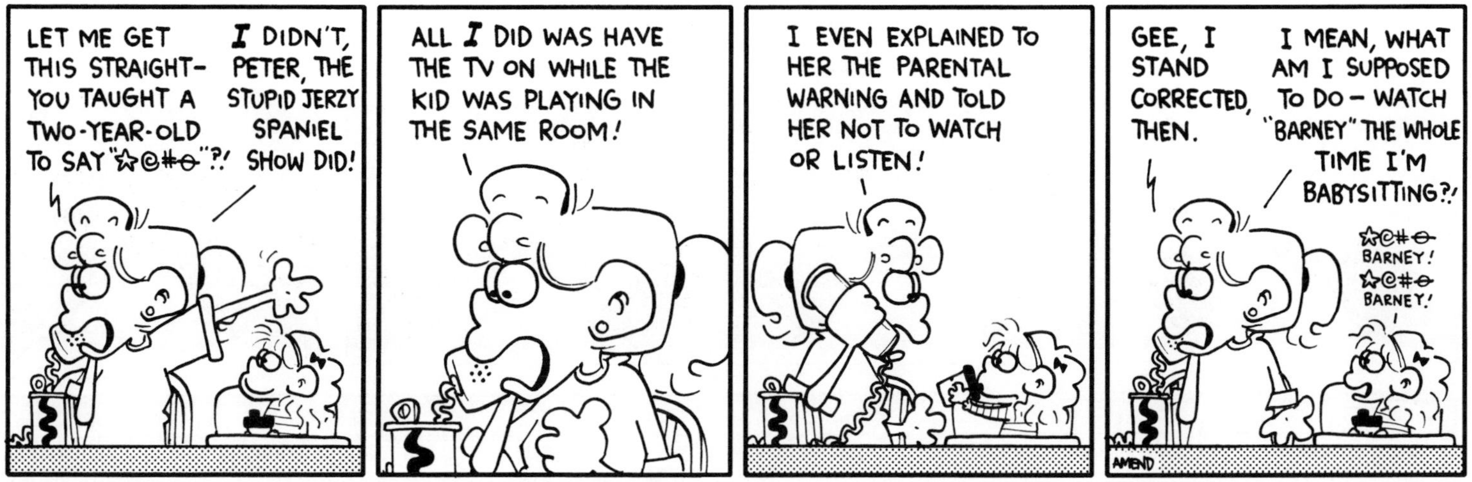
LET ME GET THIS STRAIGHT– YOU TAUGHT A TWO-YEAR-OLD TO SAY "☆@#⊖"?!
I DIDN'T, PETER, THE STUPID JERZY SPANIEL SHOW DID!
ALL I DID WAS HAVE THE TV ON WHILE THE KID WAS PLAYING IN THE SAME ROOM!
I EVEN EXPLAINED TO HER THE PARENTAL WARNING AND TOLD HER NOT TO WATCH OR LISTEN!
GEE, I STAND CORRECTED, THEN.
I MEAN, WHAT AM I SUPPOSED TO DO – WATCH "BARNEY" THE WHOLE TIME I'M BABYSITTING?!
☆@#⊖ BARNEY! ☆@#⊖ BARNEY!
AMEND

April 23, 1998

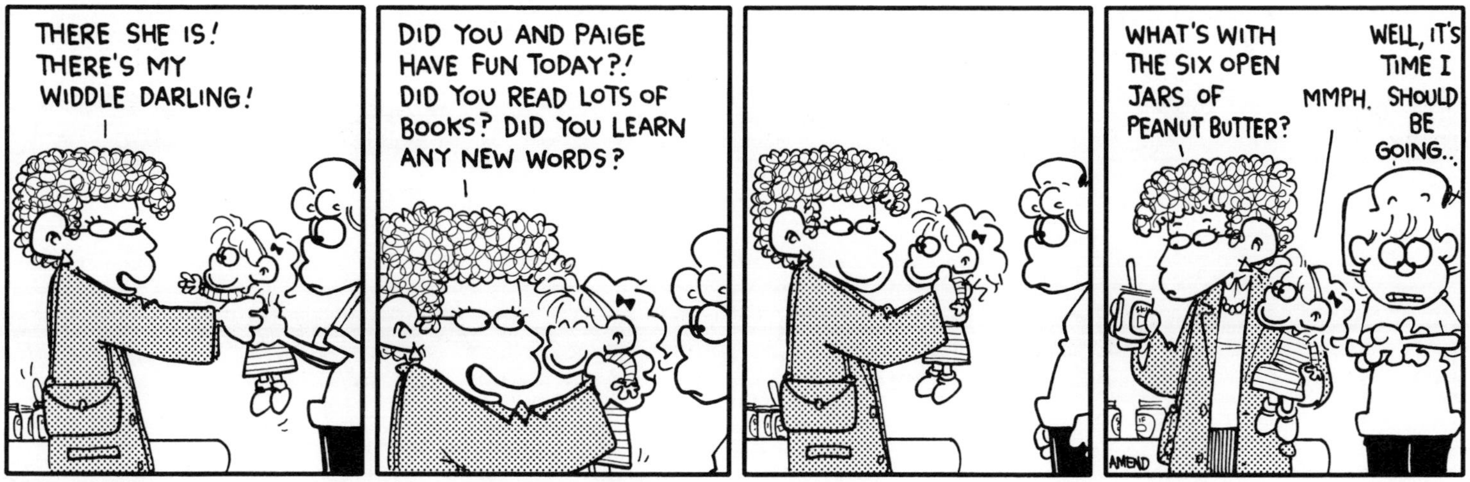
THERE SHE IS! THERE'S MY WIDDLE DARLING!
DID YOU AND PAIGE HAVE FUN TODAY?! DID YOU READ LOTS OF BOOKS? DID YOU LEARN ANY NEW WORDS?
WHAT'S WITH THE SIX OPEN JARS OF PEANUT BUTTER?
MMPH.
WELL, IT'S TIME I SHOULD BE GOING...
AMEND

April 24, 1998

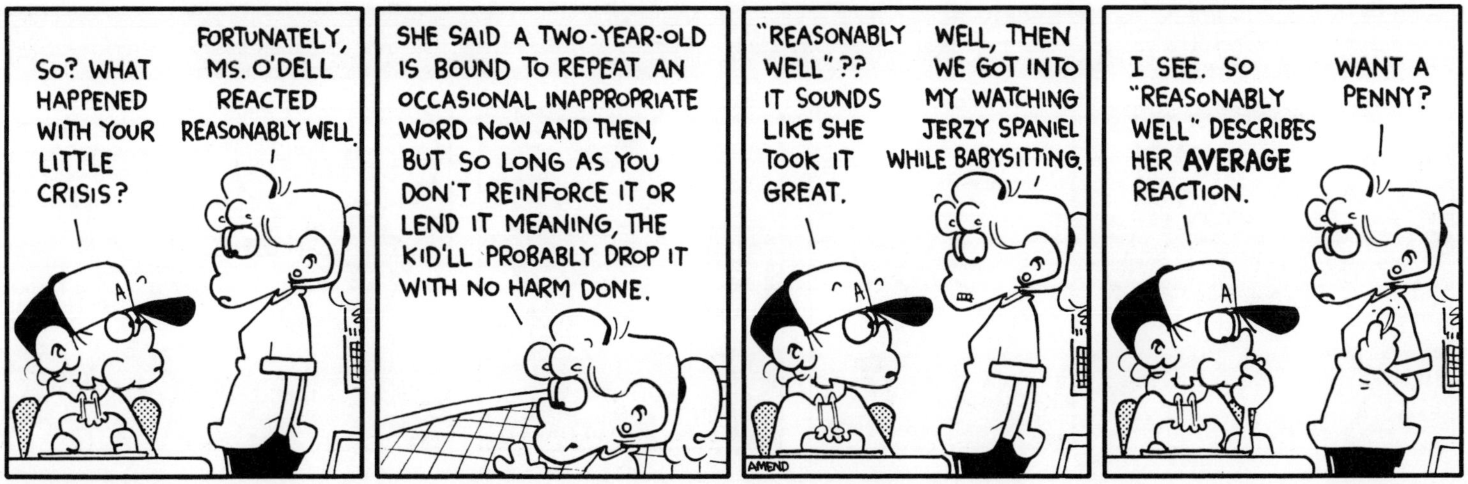
SO? WHAT HAPPENED WITH YOUR LITTLE CRISIS?
FORTUNATELY, MS. O'DELL REACTED REASONABLY WELL.
SHE SAID A TWO-YEAR-OLD IS BOUND TO REPEAT AN OCCASIONAL INAPPROPRIATE WORD NOW AND THEN, BUT SO LONG AS YOU DON'T REINFORCE IT OR LEND IT MEANING, THE KID'LL PROBABLY DROP IT WITH NO HARM DONE.
"REASONABLY WELL"?? IT SOUNDS LIKE SHE TOOK IT GREAT.
WELL, THEN WE GOT INTO MY WATCHING JERZY SPANIEL WHILE BABYSITTING.
I SEE. SO "REASONABLY WELL" DESCRIBES HER AVERAGE REACTION.
WANT A PENNY?
AMEND

April 25, 1998

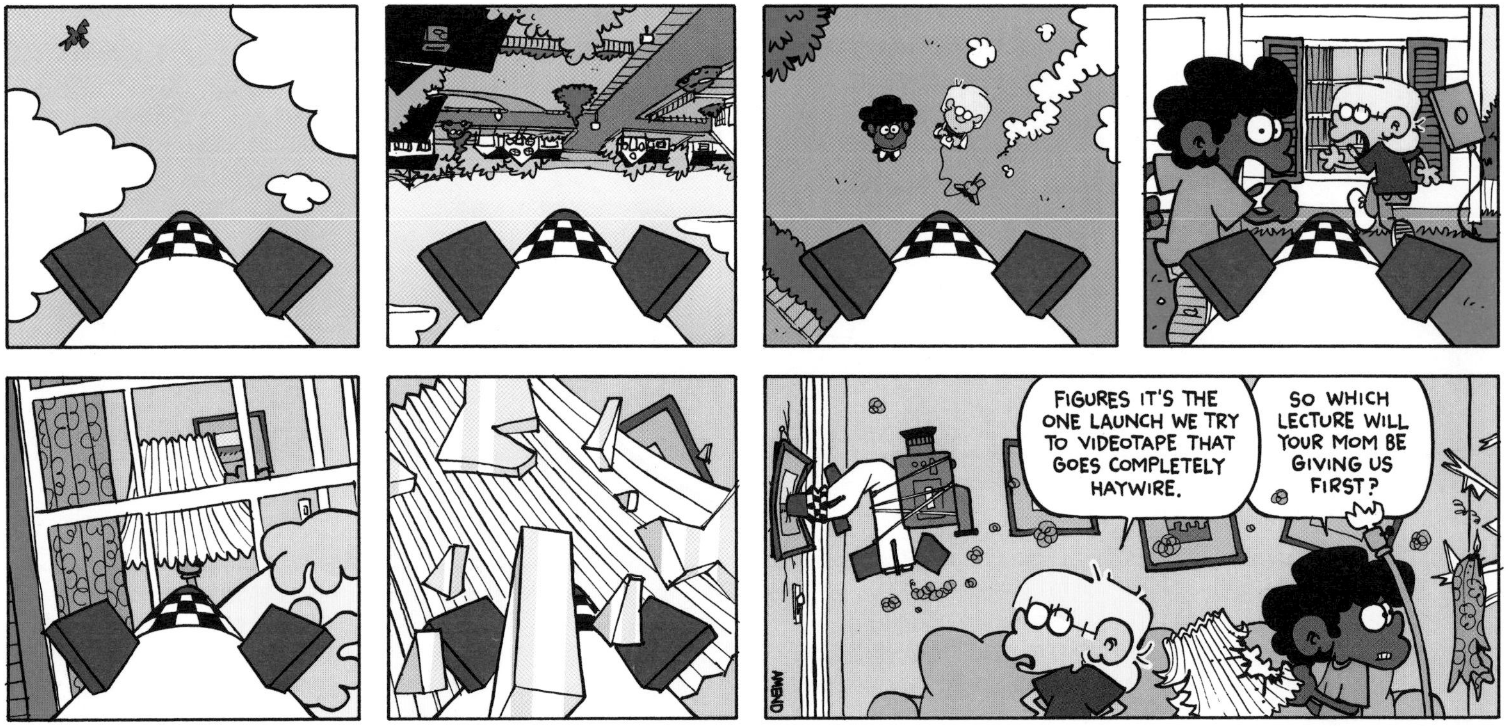
FIGURES IT'S THE ONE LAUNCH WE TRY TO VIDEOTAPE THAT GOES COMPLETELY HAYWIRE.
SO WHICH LECTURE WILL YOUR MOM BE GIVING US FIRST?
AMEND

May 31, 1998

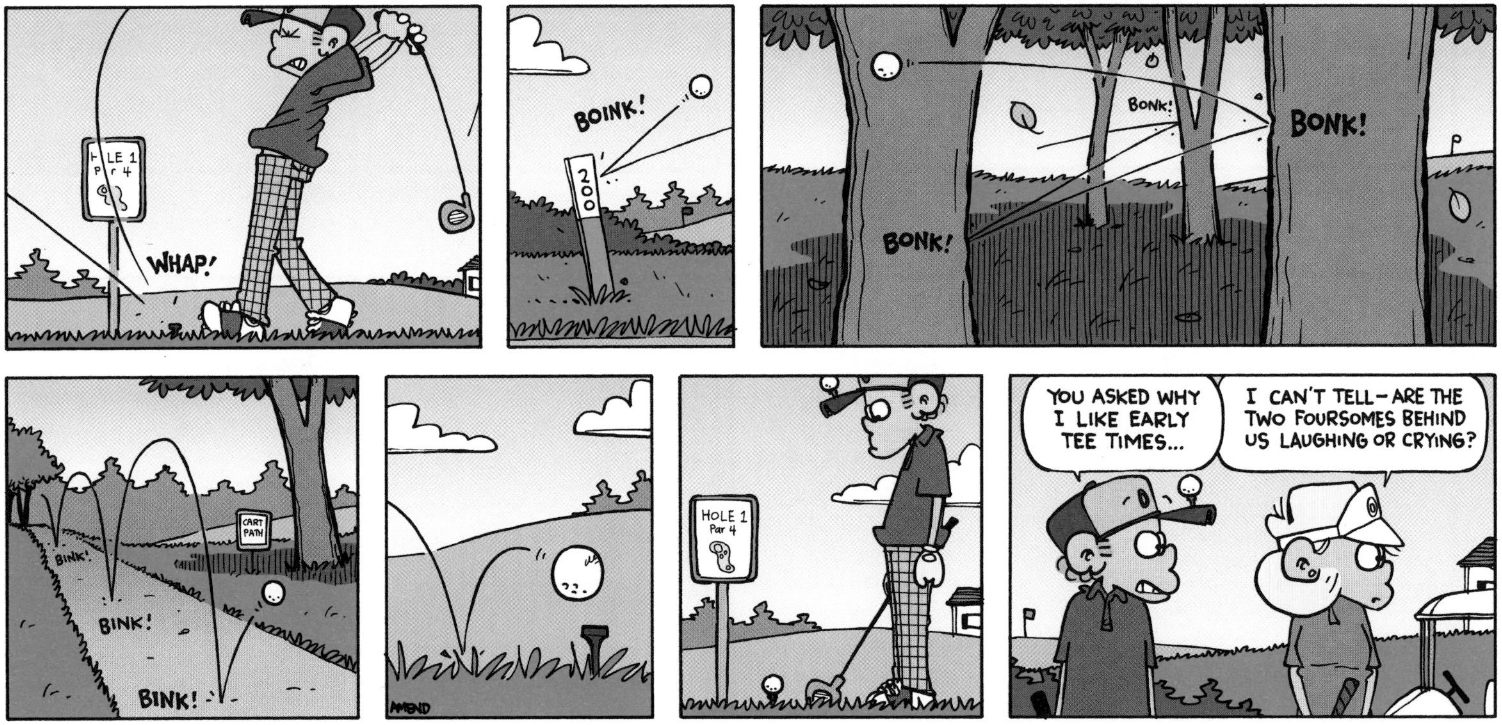
HOLE 1
Par 4
WHAP!
BOINK!
200
BONK!
BONK!
BONK!
CART PATH
BINK!
BINK!
BINK!
AMEND
HOLE 1
Par 4
YOU ASKED WHY I LIKE EARLY TEE TIMES...
I CAN'T TELL—ARE THE TWO FOURSOMES BEHIND US LAUGHING OR CRYING?

June 14, 1998

See? There are applications for math in all kinds of places.

May 21, 1998

July 6, 1998

July 9, 1998

My spoof of the Beanie Babies craze. As with the *Titanic* strips, it's fun to let Andy Fox go nutso once in a while.

June 1, 1998

June 2, 1998

June 3, 1998

8

ANDY, WHAT *IS* ALL THIS?? — MY NEW HOBBY. I'M COLLECTING BITTY BABIES.

AREN'T THEY ADORABLE?! AREN'T THEY TO DIE FOR?! AND BEFORE YOU START WHINING ABOUT THE COST, KEEP IN MIND THEIR INVESTMENT POTENTIAL.

TAKE THAT "CUDSIE THE COW" YOU'RE HOLDING. ACCORDING TO THIS ONE WEB SITE, HE'S GONE UP TWO CENTS IN VALUE SINCE I BOUGHT HIM THIS MORNING.

TWO CENTS?? WHO *CARES*?? — WELL, GIVEN HOW MANY "CUDSIES" I PURCHASED...

June 4, 1998

THIS ARTICLE IN THE JUNE "BITTY BABIER" SAYS IF YOU STACK WINE BOXES SIDEWAYS, YOU CAN STORE YOUR BITTY BABIES IN A LUXURIOUS HI-RISE OF CUBBY HOLES.

WE HAVE A COUPLE WINE BOXES IN THE BASEMENT, DON'T WE? — DEAR, I DON'T WANT TO SOUND JUDGMENTAL, BUT AREN'T YOU A LITTLE OLD FOR ALL THIS?

ROGER, SOME OF THESE BITTIES SELL FOR THOUSANDS OF DOLLARS. IT'S GOTTEN TO WHERE **ONLY** A GROWN-UP CAN AFFORD THIS HOBBY. — MOM, WHY'S THERE A "FOR SALE" SIGN IN YOUR CAR WINDOW?

... OR, AT LEAST, **ALMOST** AFFORD THIS HOBBY. — OK, MAYBE I **DO** WANT TO SOUND A LITTLE JUDGMENTAL AT THIS POINT.

June 5, 1998

WHAT HAPPENED TO ALL YOUR BITTY BABIES? — I SOLD THEM TO A DEALER HERE IN TOWN.

WHY?? I THOUGHT YOU WERE LIKE TOTALLY GOO-GOO OVER THEM! — I WAS. THAT'S WHY I HAD TO LET THEM GO.

THEY DESERVED A BETTER LIFE THAN WHAT I COULD OFFER: DAYS AND NIGHTS LOCKED UP IN A DARK, IMPENETRABLE, PRISON-LIKE STEAMER TRUNK. THEY NEED TO BE OUT... ON BEDS, BOOKCASES, SHELVES... BRINGING JOY TO ALL WHO SEE THEM!

COULDN'T YOU DO THAT HERE? — I TRIED IT FOR 15 MINUTES. — QUINCY PUKED UP ANOTHER TAG. WERE YOU MISSING A "SLOPS THE PIG"?

June 6, 1998

9

June 15, 1998

Kids often write me asking if I'll ever show Jason without his glasses. I guess this strip wasn't what they wanted.

June 16, 1998

10

June 17, 1998

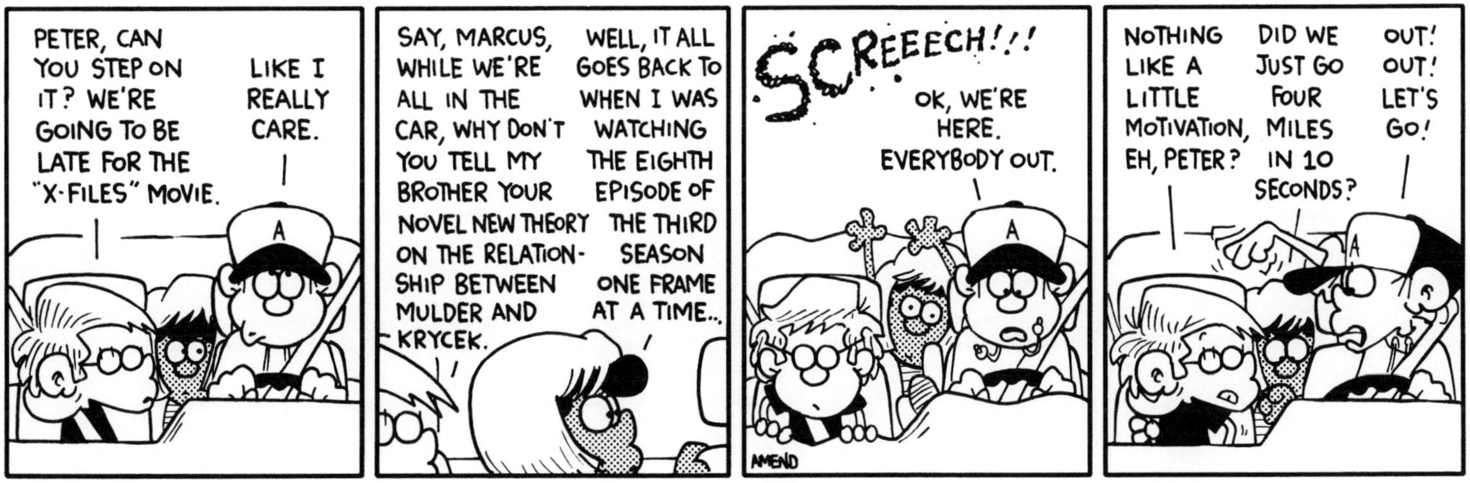
PETER, CAN YOU STEP ON IT? WE'RE GOING TO BE LATE FOR THE "X-FILES" MOVIE.
LIKE I REALLY CARE.
SAY, MARCUS, WHILE WE'RE ALL IN THE CAR, WHY DON'T YOU TELL MY BROTHER YOUR NOVEL NEW THEORY ON THE RELATIONSHIP BETWEEN MULDER AND KRYCEK.
WELL, IT ALL GOES BACK TO WHEN I WAS WATCHING THE EIGHTH EPISODE OF THE THIRD SEASON ONE FRAME AT A TIME...
SCREEECH!!!
OK, WE'RE HERE. EVERYBODY OUT.
AMEND
NOTHING LIKE A LITTLE MOTIVATION, EH, PETER?
DID WE JUST GO FOUR MILES IN 10 SECONDS?
OUT! OUT! LET'S GO!

June 18, 1998

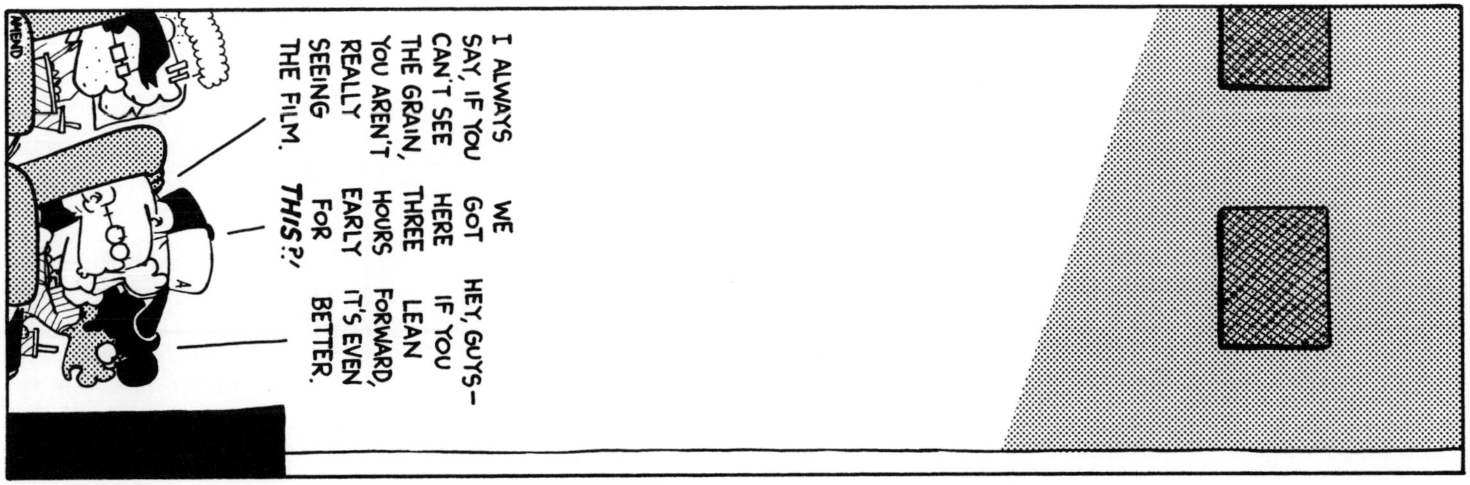
AMEND
I ALWAYS SAY, IF YOU CAN'T SEE THE GRAIN, YOU AREN'T REALLY SEEING THE FILM.
WE GOT HERE THREE HOURS EARLY FOR THIS?!
HEY, GUYS– IF YOU LEAN FORWARD, IT'S EVEN BETTER.

June 19, 1998

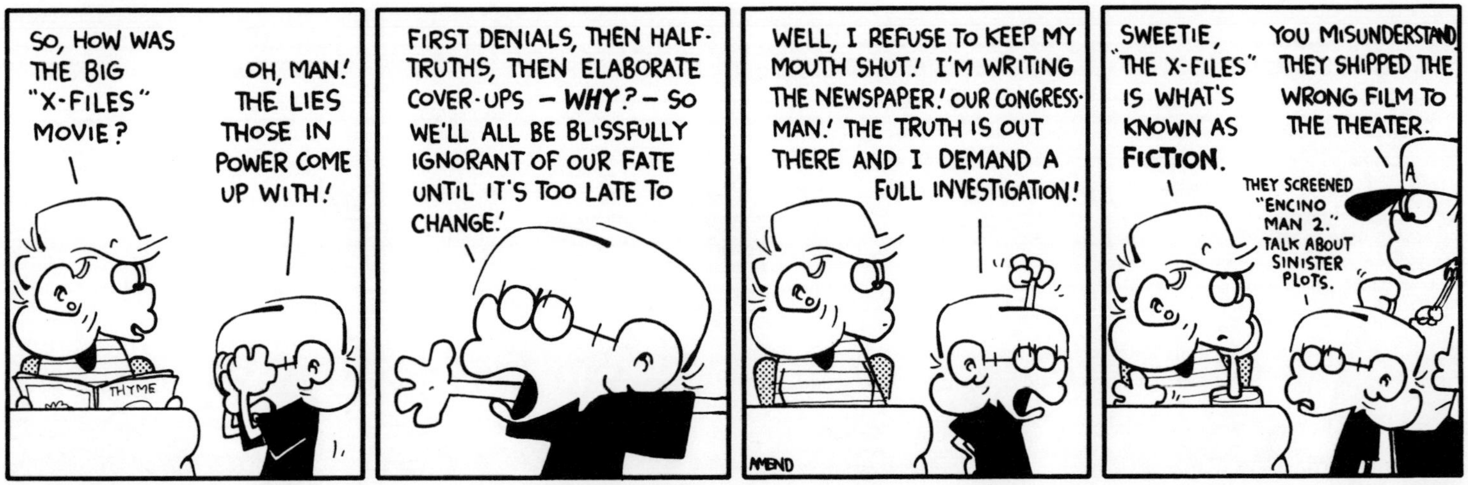
SO, HOW WAS THE BIG "X-FILES" MOVIE?
OH, MAN! THE LIES THOSE IN POWER COME UP WITH!
THYME
FIRST DENIALS, THEN HALF-TRUTHS, THEN ELABORATE COVER-UPS – WHY? – SO WE'LL ALL BE BLISSFULLY IGNORANT OF OUR FATE UNTIL IT'S TOO LATE TO CHANGE!
WELL, I REFUSE TO KEEP MY MOUTH SHUT! I'M WRITING THE NEWSPAPER! OUR CONGRESSMAN! THE TRUTH IS OUT THERE AND I DEMAND A FULL INVESTIGATION!
AMEND
SWEETIE, "THE X-FILES" IS WHAT'S KNOWN AS FICTION.
YOU MISUNDERSTAND. THEY SHIPPED THE WRONG FILM TO THE THEATER.
THEY SCREENED "ENCINO MAN 2." TALK ABOUT SINISTER PLOTS.

June 20, 1998

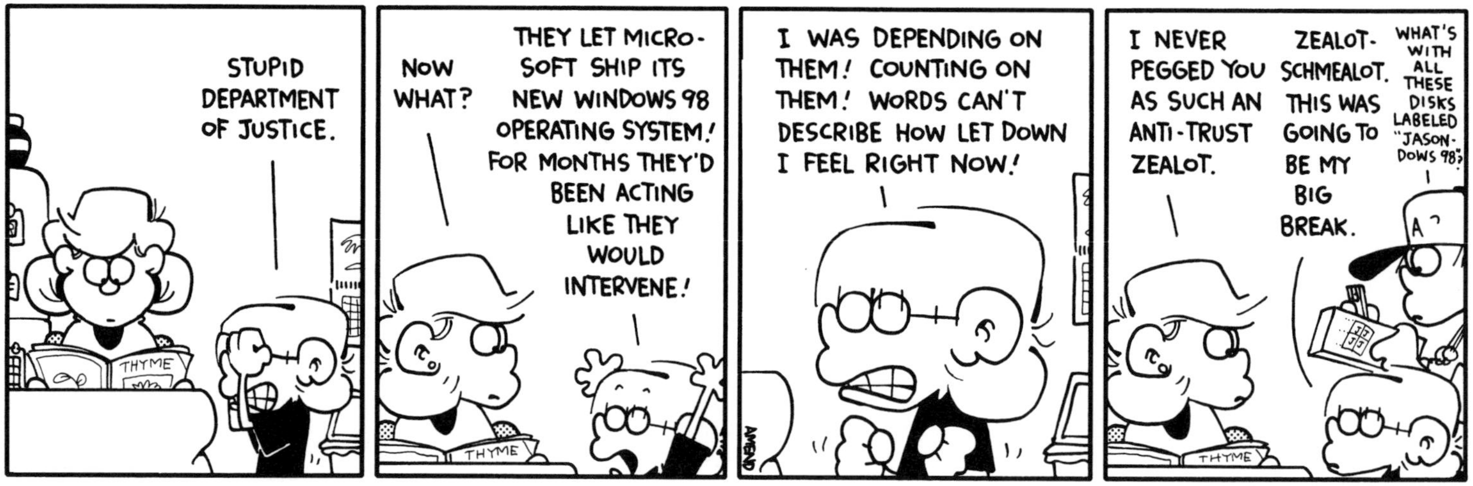
STUPID DEPARTMENT OF JUSTICE.
NOW WHAT?
THEY LET MICRO-SOFT SHIP ITS NEW WINDOWS 98 OPERATING SYSTEM! FOR MONTHS THEY'D BEEN ACTING LIKE THEY WOULD INTERVENE!
I WAS DEPENDING ON THEM! COUNTING ON THEM! WORDS CAN'T DESCRIBE HOW LET DOWN I FEEL RIGHT NOW!
I NEVER PEGGED YOU AS SUCH AN ANTI-TRUST ZEALOT.
ZEALOT-SCHMEALOT. THIS WAS GOING TO BE MY BIG BREAK.
WHAT'S WITH ALL THESE DISKS LABELED "JASON-DOWS 98"?
THYME
AMEND

June 29, 1998

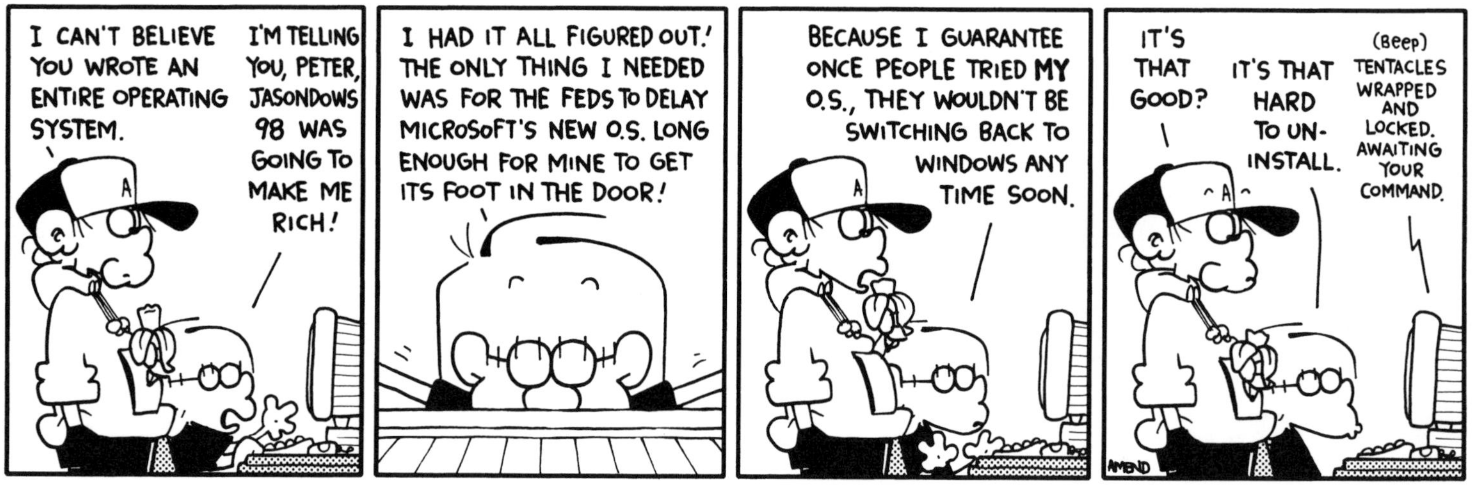
I CAN'T BELIEVE YOU WROTE AN ENTIRE OPERATING SYSTEM.
I'M TELLING YOU, PETER, JASONDOWS 98 WAS GOING TO MAKE ME RICH!
I HAD IT ALL FIGURED OUT! THE ONLY THING I NEEDED WAS FOR THE FEDS TO DELAY MICROSOFT'S NEW O.S. LONG ENOUGH FOR MINE TO GET ITS FOOT IN THE DOOR!
BECAUSE I GUARANTEE ONCE PEOPLE TRIED MY O.S., THEY WOULDN'T BE SWITCHING BACK TO WINDOWS ANY TIME SOON.
IT'S THAT GOOD?
IT'S THAT HARD TO UN-INSTALL.
(Beep) TENTACLES WRAPPED AND LOCKED. AWAITING YOUR COMMAND.
AMEND

June 30, 1998

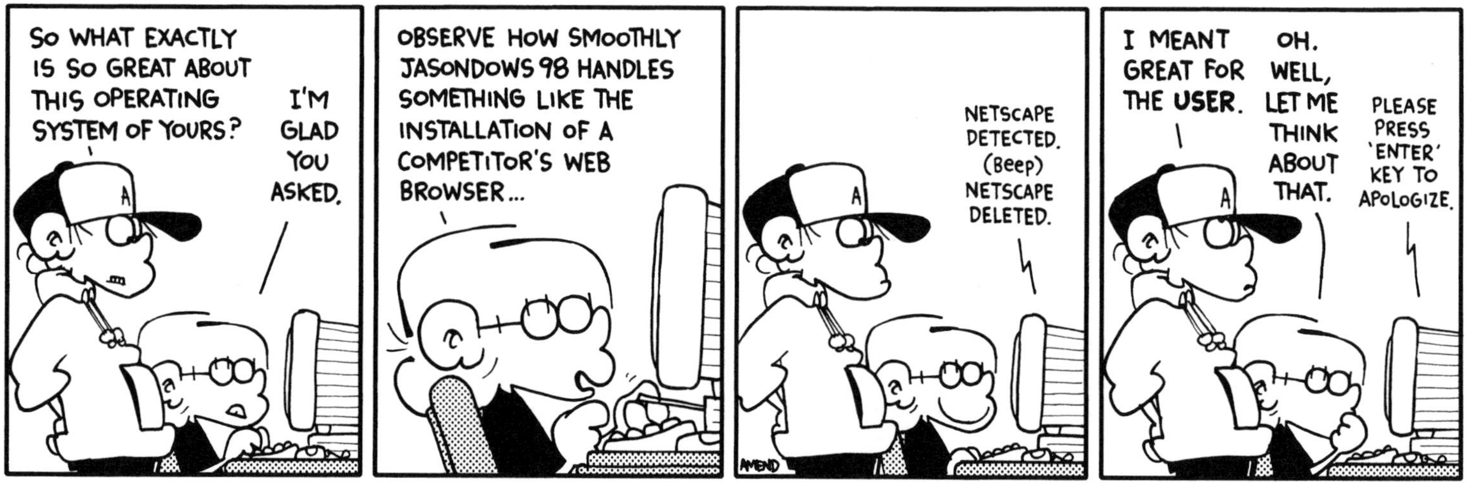
SO WHAT EXACTLY IS SO GREAT ABOUT THIS OPERATING SYSTEM OF YOURS?
I'M GLAD YOU ASKED.
OBSERVE HOW SMOOTHLY JASONDOWS 98 HANDLES SOMETHING LIKE THE INSTALLATION OF A COMPETITOR'S WEB BROWSER...
NETSCAPE DETECTED. (Beep) NETSCAPE DELETED.
I MEANT GREAT FOR THE USER.
OH. WELL, LET ME THINK ABOUT THAT.
PLEASE PRESS 'ENTER' KEY TO APOLOGIZE.
AMEND

July 1, 1998

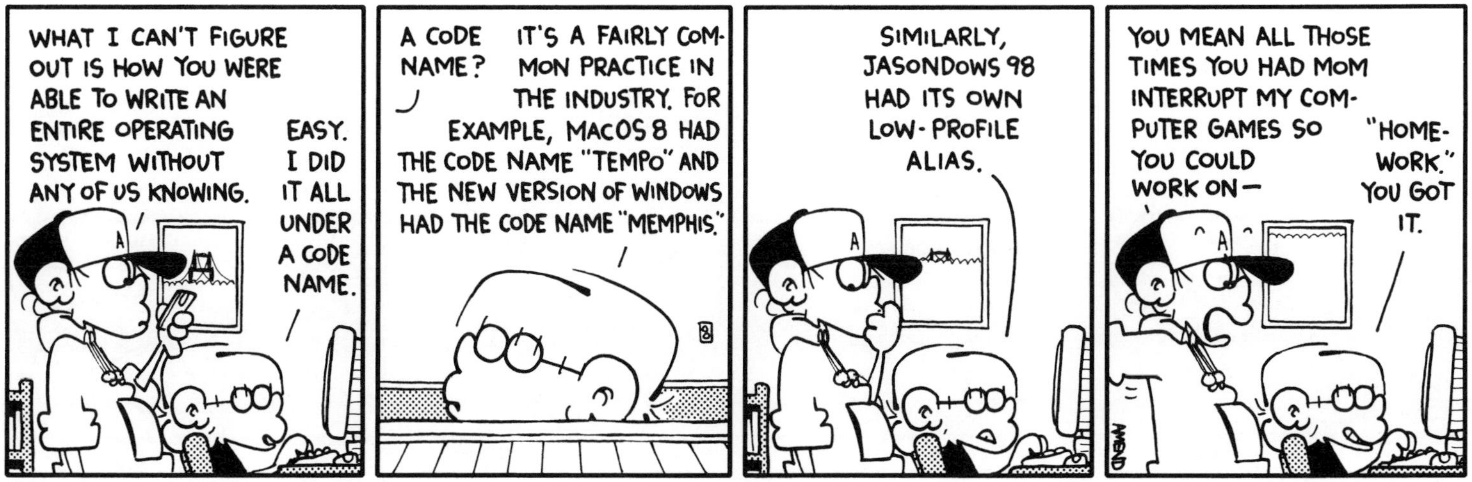
WHAT I CAN'T FIGURE OUT IS HOW YOU WERE ABLE TO WRITE AN ENTIRE OPERATING SYSTEM WITHOUT ANY OF US KNOWING.
EASY. I DID IT ALL UNDER A CODE NAME.
A CODE NAME?
IT'S A FAIRLY COMMON PRACTICE IN THE INDUSTRY. FOR EXAMPLE, MACOS 8 HAD THE CODE NAME "TEMPO" AND THE NEW VERSION OF WINDOWS HAD THE CODE NAME "MEMPHIS."
SIMILARLY, JASONDOWS 98 HAD ITS OWN LOW-PROFILE ALIAS.
YOU MEAN ALL THOSE TIMES YOU HAD MOM INTERRUPT MY COMPUTER GAMES SO YOU COULD WORK ON—
"HOMEWORK." YOU GOT IT.

July 2, 1998

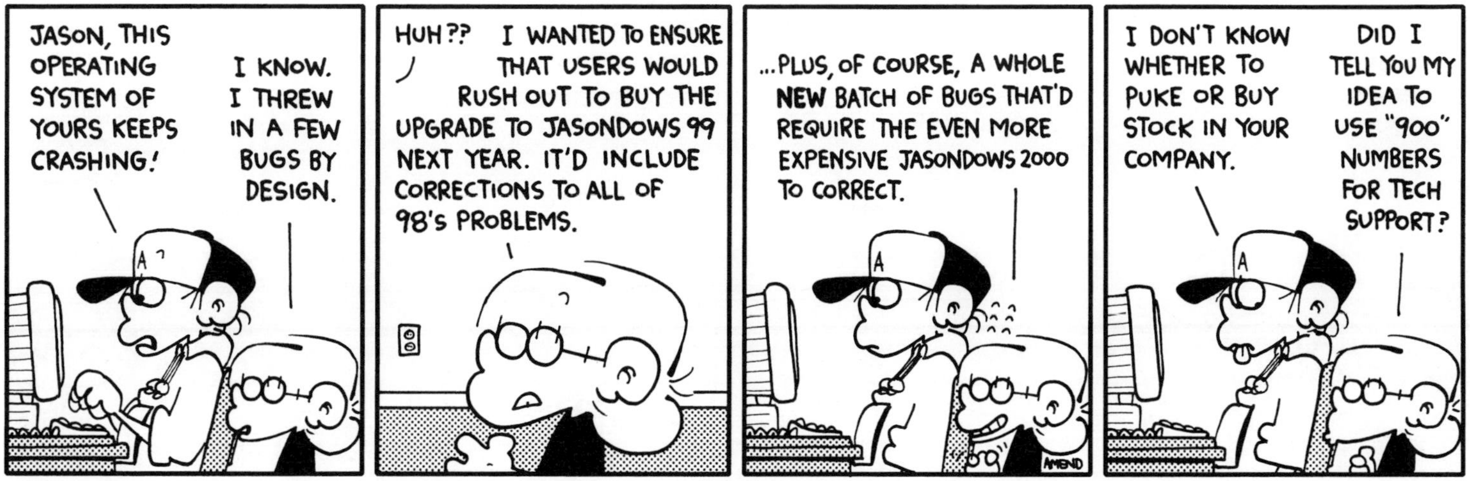
JASON, THIS OPERATING SYSTEM OF YOURS KEEPS CRASHING!
I KNOW. I THREW IN A FEW BUGS BY DESIGN.
HUH??
I WANTED TO ENSURE THAT USERS WOULD RUSH OUT TO BUY THE UPGRADE TO JASONDOWS 99 NEXT YEAR. IT'D INCLUDE CORRECTIONS TO ALL OF 98'S PROBLEMS.
...PLUS, OF COURSE, A WHOLE NEW BATCH OF BUGS THAT'D REQUIRE THE EVEN MORE EXPENSIVE JASONDOWS 2000 TO CORRECT.
I DON'T KNOW WHETHER TO PUKE OR BUY STOCK IN YOUR COMPANY.
DID I TELL YOU MY IDEA TO USE "900" NUMBERS FOR TECH SUPPORT?

July 3, 1998

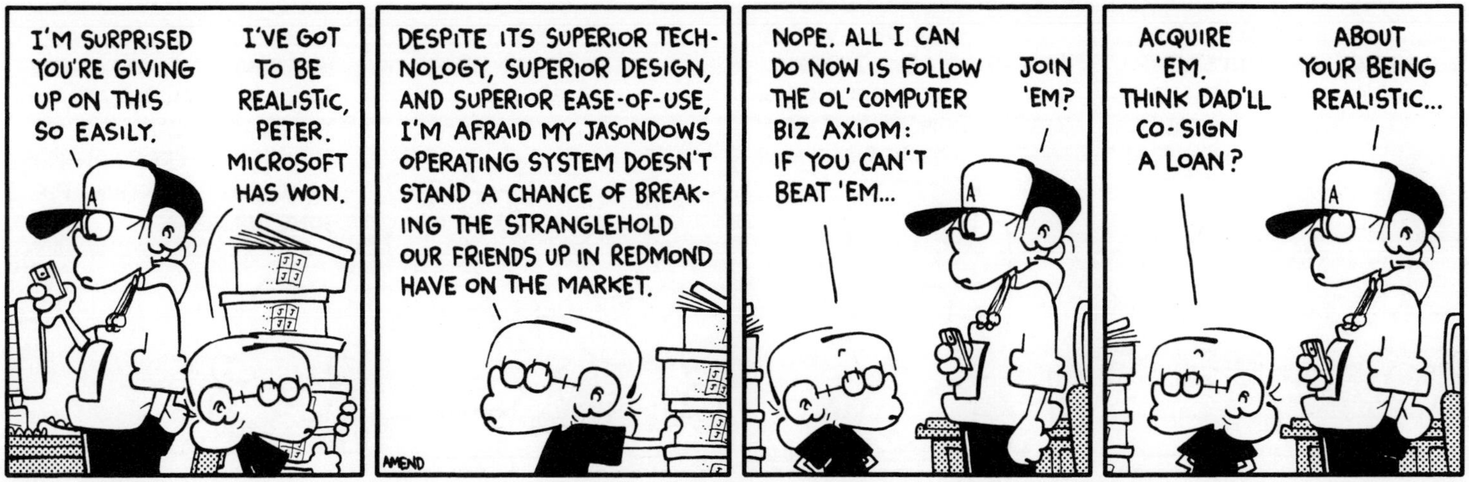
I'M SURPRISED YOU'RE GIVING UP ON THIS SO EASILY.
I'VE GOT TO BE REALISTIC, PETER. MICROSOFT HAS WON.
DESPITE ITS SUPERIOR TECHNOLOGY, SUPERIOR DESIGN, AND SUPERIOR EASE-OF-USE, I'M AFRAID MY JASONDOWS OPERATING SYSTEM DOESN'T STAND A CHANCE OF BREAKING THE STRANGLEHOLD OUR FRIENDS UP IN REDMOND HAVE ON THE MARKET.
NOPE. ALL I CAN DO NOW IS FOLLOW THE OL' COMPUTER BIZ AXIOM: IF YOU CAN'T BEAT 'EM...
JOIN 'EM?
ACQUIRE 'EM. THINK DAD'LL CO-SIGN A LOAN?
ABOUT YOUR BEING REALISTIC...

July 4, 1998

I thought about starting a vegetable garden but then decided it'd be easier to let my characters do it.

Panel 1: ROGER, LOOK! THE FIRST ZUCCHINI FROM MY GARDEN! / I DIDN'T KNOW YOU PLANTED ZUCCHINI.

Panel 2: I WASN'T GOING TO, BUT SOMEONE TOLD ME THEY WERE EASY TO GROW, AND SINCE I'M NEW AT THIS, I FIGURED EASY IS GOOD. AND JUST THINK— WE'LL HAVE 23 MORE OF THESE SOON.

Panel 3: HOW CAN YOU BE SO SURE OF THE NUMBER? / THAT'S HOW MANY I PLANTED, SILLY.

Panel 4: UM, I'M PRETTY SURE YOU GET MORE THAN ONE ZUCCHINI PER PLANT. / HOW MANY MORE? / HEY, MOM— WHAT'S WITH THESE 4 MILLION GREEN THINGS?

July 27, 1998

Panel 1: PAIGE, WHAT'S THE PLURAL OF "ZUCCHINI"?

Panel 2: IS IT "ZUCCHINI" OR "ZUCCHINIS"? / HMM. I'M NOT SURE. WHY?

Panel 3: WELL, GIVEN WHAT I'VE SEEN OF MOM'S GARDEN, IT'S SOMETHING THAT MIGHT BE USEFUL TO KNOW.

Panel 4: ... ALONG WITH SCIENTIFIC NOTATION. / THAT'S ONE DAY'S HARVEST?? / ONE HOUR'S.

July 28, 1998

Panel 1: WHAT'S THIS? / ZUCCHINI SALAD, ZUCCHINI STIR-FRY, AND A LITTLE SOMETHING I'M CALLING "ZUCCHINI SURPRISE."

Panel 2: THIS IS A JOKE, RIGHT? / PAIGE, I'VE GOT SIX ZILLION ZUCCHINIS GROWING IN OUR BACK YARD RIGHT NOW.

Panel 3: WE HAVE TO EAT THEM, OR THEY'LL GO BAD.

Panel 4: I KNOW, BUT WHY COULDN'T YOU HAVE PLANTED **TACOS** OR SOMETHING? / TELL YOU WHAT— IF YOU CLEAN YOUR PLATE, YOU CAN HAVE ICE CREAM ON YOUR ZUCCHINI PIE.

July 29, 1998

MOM, I'LL BE AT DENISE'S HOUSE.

OH, PETER, WAIT! AS LONG AS YOU'RE GOING OVER THERE, WHY DON'T YOU BRING HER AND HER PARENTS ONE OR TWO ZUCCHINIS FROM OUR GARDEN?

HERE YOU GO. BETTER TAKE THE STATION WAGON.

MOM, THAT ISN'T "ONE OR TWO."

OK, SO I ROUNDED UP A LITTLE.

MOM, PLEASE. THESE ARE PEOPLE I WANT TO LIKE ME.

IN THAT CASE, MIGHT I SUGGEST INCLUDING ONE OF THESE PRIZE BIG BERTHAS?

July 30, 1998

MOM! PLEASE! THIS IS THE EIGHTH NIGHT IN A ROW YOU'VE SERVED ZUCCHINI FOR DINNER!

I'M SORRY, JASON, BUT I DON'T KNOW WHAT ELSE TO DO.

EVERY TIME I GO OUT TO THE GARDEN, THERE ARE ANOTHER TWO DOZEN ZUCCHINIS TO PICK. I HAD NO IDEA THESE THINGS GREW SO FAST.

THEY'RE LIKE SOME SORT OF MUTANT, SPACE-ALIEN CROP.

I WISH YOU'D TOLD ME THAT SOONER. ...SECONDS?

SPEAKING OF THINGS MUTANT...

July 31, 1998

HEY, PAIGE, CHECK OUT THESE BICEPS.

I'M LIKE THE BEEFIEST I'VE EVER BEEN IN MY LIFE. ARMS... LEGS... CHEST... I'M OFF TO THE SWIMMING POOL TO SHOW OFF.

AND I OWE IT ALL TO MOM'S HOME-GROWN ZUCCHINIS.

I THOUGHT THEY HAD LIKE ZERO CALORIES.

LET ME CLARIFY: CARRYING MOM'S HOME-GROWN ZUCCHINIS.

AH.

WELL, I THINK THE HARVEST, AT LAST, IS SHOWING SIGNS OF WANING.

August 1, 1998

I like Jason's last line here.

August 9, 1998

16

October 9, 1998

October 19, 1998

I think water molecules are supposed to look more like Mickey Mouse heads. My apologies for Jason's error.

October 21, 1998

I remember being worried that no one would get this joke.

August 10, 1998

Figuring out how to draw Lara Croft as a FoxTrot character was a fun challenge.

August 11, 1998

18

August 12, 1998

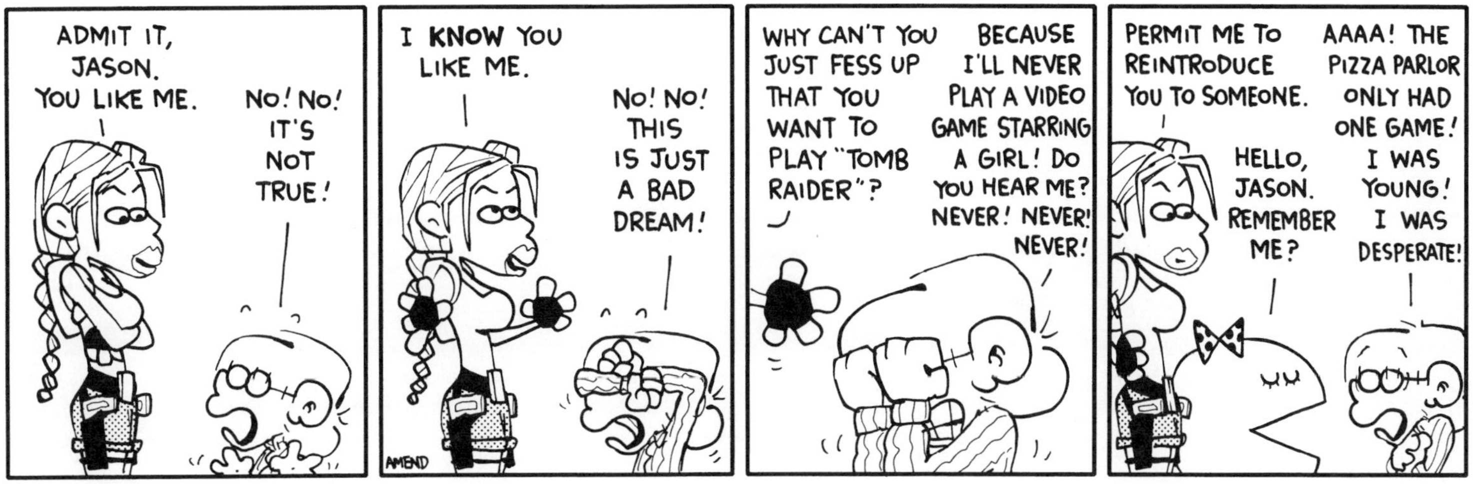
ADMIT IT, JASON. YOU LIKE ME.
NO! NO! IT'S NOT TRUE!
I KNOW YOU LIKE ME.
NO! NO! THIS IS JUST A BAD DREAM!
AMEND
WHY CAN'T YOU JUST FESS UP THAT YOU WANT TO PLAY "TOMB RAIDER"?
BECAUSE I'LL NEVER PLAY A VIDEO GAME STARRING A GIRL! DO YOU HEAR ME? NEVER! NEVER! NEVER!
PERMIT ME TO REINTRODUCE YOU TO SOMEONE.
HELLO, JASON. REMEMBER ME?
AAAA! THE PIZZA PARLOR ONLY HAD ONE GAME! I WAS YOUNG! I WAS DESPERATE!

August 13, 1998

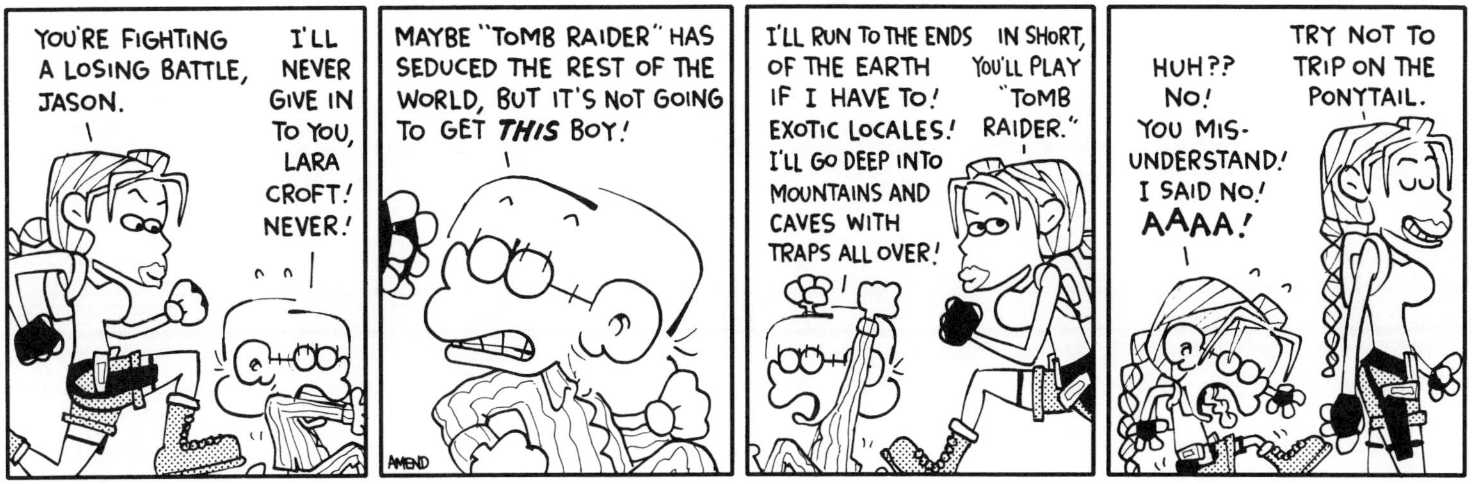
YOU'RE FIGHTING A LOSING BATTLE, JASON.
I'LL NEVER GIVE IN TO YOU, LARA CROFT! NEVER!
MAYBE "TOMB RAIDER" HAS SEDUCED THE REST OF THE WORLD, BUT IT'S NOT GOING TO GET THIS BOY!
AMEND
I'LL RUN TO THE ENDS OF THE EARTH IF I HAVE TO! EXOTIC LOCALES! I'LL GO DEEP INTO MOUNTAINS AND CAVES WITH TRAPS ALL OVER!
IN SHORT, YOU'LL PLAY "TOMB RAIDER."
HUH?? NO! YOU MISUNDERSTAND! I SAID NO! AAAA!
TRY NOT TO TRIP ON THE PONYTAIL.

August 14, 1998

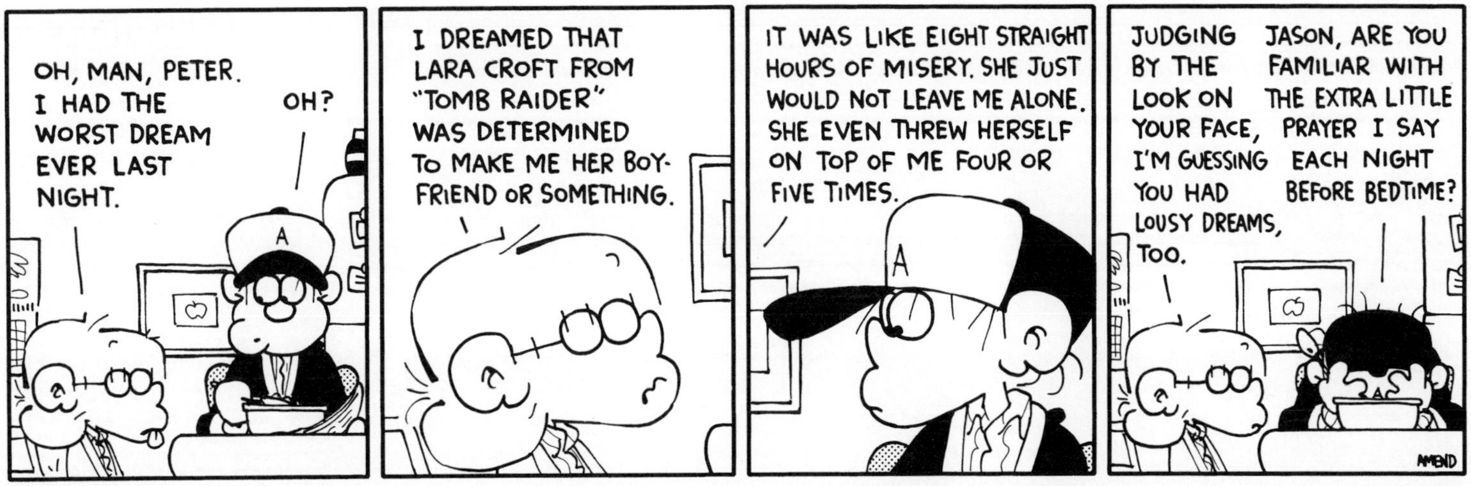
OH, MAN, PETER. I HAD THE WORST DREAM EVER LAST NIGHT.
OH?
I DREAMED THAT LARA CROFT FROM "TOMB RAIDER" WAS DETERMINED TO MAKE ME HER BOYFRIEND OR SOMETHING.
IT WAS LIKE EIGHT STRAIGHT HOURS OF MISERY. SHE JUST WOULD NOT LEAVE ME ALONE. SHE EVEN THREW HERSELF ON TOP OF ME FOUR OR FIVE TIMES.
JUDGING BY THE LOOK ON YOUR FACE, I'M GUESSING YOU HAD LOUSY DREAMS, TOO.
JASON, ARE YOU FAMILIAR WITH THE EXTRA LITTLE PRAYER I SAY EACH NIGHT BEFORE BEDTIME?
AMEND

August 15, 1998

August 31, 1998

September 1, 1998

September 2, 1998

September 3, 1998

September 4, 1998

September 5, 1998

21

WOW. YOU KNOW, THIS "DILBERT" PHENOMENON IS AMAZING TO ME.

FIVE YEARS AGO I HADN'T EVEN HEARD OF THE COMIC STRIP, AND NOW IT'S EVERY- WHERE I LOOK. BOOKS... CALENDARS... OFFICE SUPPLY ADS... HIS OWN ICE CREAM FLAVOR... NOW I READ ABOUT AN UPCOMING TV SERIES...

WHATEVER SCOTT ADAMS' SECRET FORMULA IS, IT SURE HAS BEEN SUCCESSFUL.

I'M A LITTLE SURPRISED OTHER CARTOONISTS HAVEN'T TRIED TO COPY IT.

HONEY, PLEASE. THESE ARE ARTISTS. THEY HAVE INTEGRITY.

SO, LIKE MY NEW HAIR- CUT?

September 28, 1998

APPARENTLY "DILBERT's" BIG LEAP FROM OBSCURITY TO PROMINENCE BEGAN SOON AFTER SCOTT ADAMS STARTED INCLUDING HIS INTERNET ADDRESS BETWEEN THE PANELS OF HIS STRIP, BEFORE SUCH THINGS WERE COMMON.

NOW THAT EVERYONE IS DOING IT, I WONDER WHAT A CARTOONIST COULD DO TO DISTINGUISH HIMSELF FROM THE PACK.

WWW. foxtrot .com

... WITHOUT LOOKING TOO DESPERATE.

I'M SURE IT'S ALL PART OF THE CREATIVE CHALLENGE.

September 29, 1998

I SUSPECT ANOTHER THING THAT'S REALLY HELPED "DILBERT" SUCCEED COMMER- CIALLY IS ITS THREE- PANEL FORMAT.

HOW IS THAT AN ADVAN- TAGE?

SO MANY OF THE OTHER STRIPS I SEE ARE FOUR PANELS. THAT MEANS SCOTT ADAMS GETS AN INSTANT 33-PERCENT PRODUCTIVITY JUMP ON HIS COMPETITORS. THIS IS PROBABLY HOW HE HAS THE TIME FOR ALL THOSE LUCRATIVE SIDE PROJECTS.

I'LL BET ANY FOUR-PANEL CARTOONISTS REALIZING THIS MUST BE BEATING THEIR HEADS ON THEIR DESKS RIGHT ABOUT NOW.

NNOOTT NNOOTT LLIITTEERRAALLLLYY,, OOFF CCOOUURRSSEE.:

22

September 30, 1998

ANOTHER CLEVER THING SCOTT ADAMS DID EARLY ON WAS TO ESTABLISH AN ELECTRONIC NEWSLETTER FOR FANS.

MOM, I'M OFF TO THE BOOKSTORE.

I IMAGINE THIS GIVES HIM QUITE A LEG UP ON THE COMPETITION, SINCE I'D WAGER CARTOONISTS DON'T HAVE MUCH P.R. MACHINERY AT THEIR DISPOSAL.

I HEAR THERE'S THIS GREAT NEW BOOK THAT'S JUST COME OUT.

THINK ABOUT IT — THE POWER TO INFORM AN ARMY OF FANS THE INSTANT YOU HAVE A NEW PRODUCT FOR SALE.

IT'S ONLY $12.95, TOO! A BARGAIN!

THE ONLY THING THAT COULD TOP THAT WOULD BE TO PLUG THAT STUFF IN THE STRIP ITSELF.

OH, COME ON — NO ONE COULD BE THAT SHAMELESS.

DID I MENTION THE ISBN NUMBER?

0-8362-

October 1, 1998

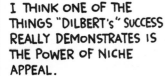

I THINK ONE OF THE THINGS "DILBERT'S" SUCCESS REALLY DEMONSTRATES IS THE POWER OF NICHE APPEAL.

ORIGINALLY, THE STRIP WAS ABOUT ALL SORTS OF TOPICS. BUT ONCE SCOTT ADAMS REALIZED HE WAS STRIKING A CHORD WITH THE WORLD'S CUBICLE DWELLERS, HE FOCUSED ALMOST EXCLUSIVELY ON WORKPLACE HUMOR, AND SINCE THEN HE'S BECOME FILTHY RICH.

I GUESS THE LESSON FOR OTHER CARTOONISTS IS, IF YOU WANT TO MAKE IT BIG, FIND AN UNDERSERVED TARGET AUDIENCE AND GO AFTER IT.

RIGHT, KIDS?

MOM! JASON CALLED ME "HAGGIS FACE"!

NO, NO — I CALLED YOU "LASSIE."

October 2, 1998

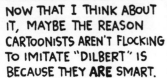

NOW THAT I THINK ABOUT IT, MAYBE THE REASON CARTOONISTS AREN'T FLOCKING TO IMITATE "DILBERT" IS BECAUSE THEY ARE SMART.

MAYBE THEY RECOGNIZE THAT "DILBERT" IS SUCCESSFUL BECAUSE IT IS "DILBERT" — IT ISN'T TRYING TO FOLLOW SOMEONE ELSE'S FORMULA.

MAYBE THE KEY TO A GOOD COMIC STRIP IS TO FIND AND INCORPORATE IDEAS THAT OTHERS AREN'T CURRENTLY USING.

MOM! DAD! CHECK OUT THIS COOL STUFFED TIGER I FOUND!

PERHAPS I SHOULD INCLUDE THE RECENT PAST IN THERE AS WELL.

I DON'T KNOW. THERE'S SOMETHING TO BE SAID FOR NOSTALGIA.

October 3, 1998

23

I had to rewind this scene on our VCR about a zillion times to get Jabba's dialogue right.

November 1, 1998

November 8, 1998

24

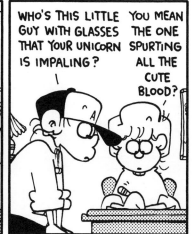

January 27, 1999

February 17, 1999

March 10, 1999

John Book was Harrison Ford's character in *Witness*.

November 9, 1998

November 10, 1998

November 11, 1998

November 12, 1998

November 13, 1998

November 14, 1998

November 23, 1998

November 24, 1998

November 25, 1998

November 26, 1998

November 27, 1998

November 28, 1998

This Scrooge story line was ridiculously fun to write and draw.

December 7, 1998

December 8, 1998

30

December 9, 1998

December 10, 1998

December 11, 1998

December 12, 1998

December 14, 1998

December 15, 1998

December 16, 1998

December 17, 1998

December 18, 1998

December 19, 1998

33

January 11, 1999

Even at the time, the dot-com bubble seemed insane.

January 12, 1999

34

January 13, 1999

January 14, 1999

January 15, 1999

January 16, 1999

February 1, 1999

February 2, 1999

36

February 3, 1999

PAIGE, I DON'T THINK YOU UNDERSTAND! I'VE SPENT HUNDREDS OF HOURS TRYING TO DEFEAT THE RED ORB GUARDIAN IN THIS VIDEO GAME!

YOU HAVE TO TELL ME HOW YOU GOT PAST HIM! YOU **HAVE** TO!

DID YOU USE THE FLAMING SWORD? THE SCREAMING SWORD? THE SWORD OF DEATH? THE SWORD OF PAIN? THE AX OF VENGEANCE? THE MACE OF MIGHT? THE RAZOR ARROWS? THE EXPLODING ARROWS? WHAT? WHAT? WHAT?

IF YOU **MUST** KNOW, I SIMPLY WALKED RIGHT BY HIM.

WELL, OF COURSE YOU DID ONCE HE WAS DEAD. WAIT! I KNOW! IT WAS THE SWORD OF FURY! AM I RIGHT?!

I DON'T THINK **YOU** UNDERSTAND, JASON...

February 4, 1999

SO THE SECRET TO GETTING PAST THE RED ORB GUARDIAN IS TO **NOT** ATTACK HIM??

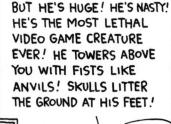

BUT HE'S HUGE! HE'S NASTY! HE'S THE MOST LETHAL VIDEO GAME CREATURE EVER! HE TOWERS ABOVE YOU WITH FISTS LIKE ANVILS! SKULLS LITTER THE GROUND AT HIS FEET!

AND YOU'RE NOT SUPPOSED TO EVEN **TRY** TO TAKE THIS GUY ON IN A FIGHT??

WOW. TALK ABOUT COUNTER-INTUITIVE.

REFRESH MY MEMORY. YOU SPEND **HOW** MANY NANOSECONDS IN THE REAL WORLD EACH DAY?

February 5, 1999

WHY SO GLUM?

I SPENT AN ENTIRE MONTH TRYING TO KILL THIS ONE VIDEO GAME FOE, AND IT TURNS OUT ALL I HAD TO DO WAS WALK PAST HIM!

WHO **KNEW** YOU WEREN'T SUPPOSED TO CLUB HIM OR KICK HIM OR LOB FIRE-BALLS AT HIS HEAD, JUST BECAUSE HE'S HUGE AND FIERCE AND CAN SQUASH YOU AT WILL!

YOU'VE HEARD THE SAYING, "DISCRETION IS THE BETTER PART OF VALOR"? THINK OF THIS AS A VALUABLE LIFE LESSON.

A "LIFE LESSON"? WHO THE HECK WANTS LIFE LESSONS IN THEIR VIDEO GAMES, MOTHER!

SHEESH. NEXT THING YOU KNOW, THEY'LL TRY STICKING THEM IN THE FUNNIES.

OH, SHOOT— I LEFT THE RAW CHICKEN OUT ALL NIGHT. WELL, I'M SURE IT'S FINE...

February 6, 1999

37

February 22, 1999

February 23, 1999

February 24, 1999

February 25, 1999

February 26, 1999

February 27, 1999

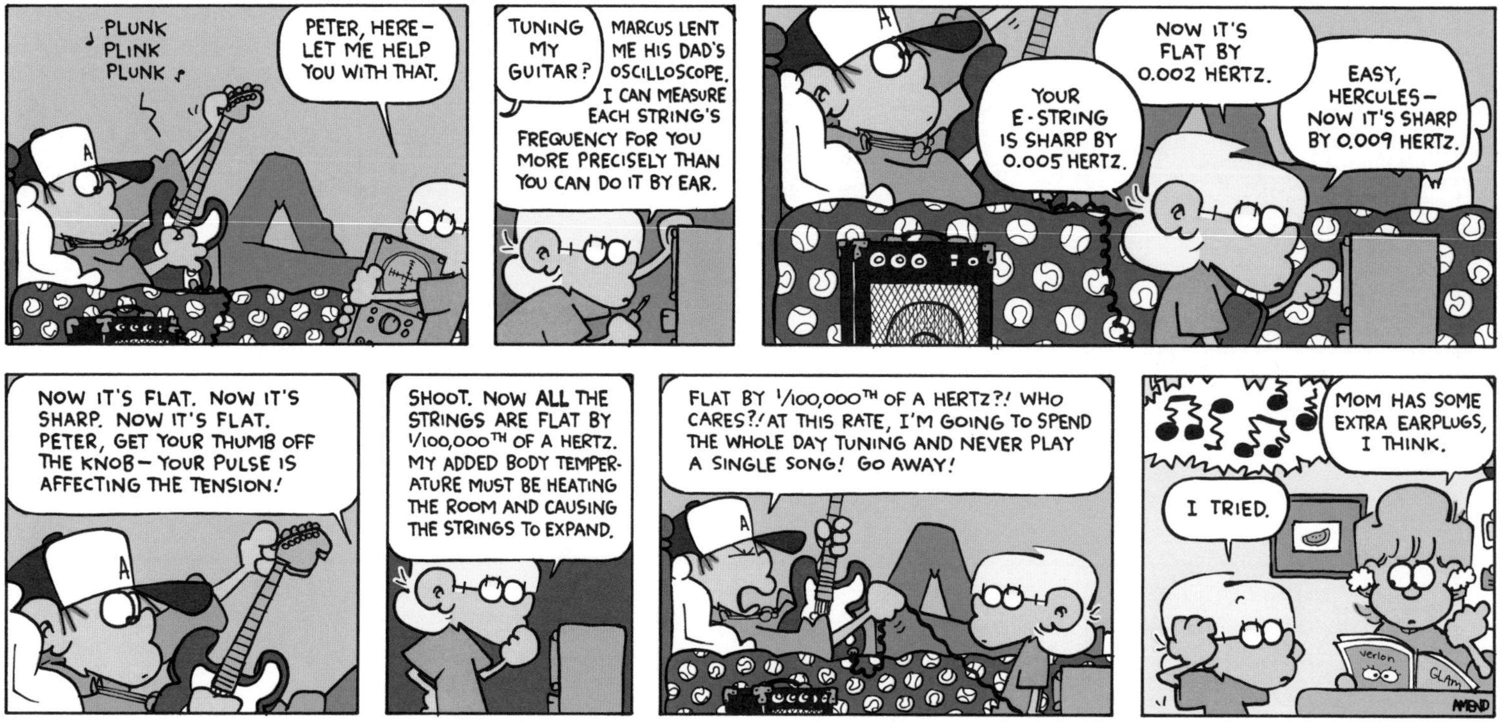
PLUNK
PLUNK
PLUNK
PETER, HERE– LET ME HELP YOU WITH THAT.
TUNING MY GUITAR?
MARCUS LENT ME HIS DAD'S OSCILLOSCOPE. I CAN MEASURE EACH STRING'S FREQUENCY FOR YOU MORE PRECISELY THAN YOU CAN DO IT BY EAR.
YOUR E-STRING IS SHARP BY 0.005 HERTZ.
NOW IT'S FLAT BY 0.002 HERTZ.
EASY, HERCULES– NOW IT'S SHARP BY 0.009 HERTZ.
NOW IT'S FLAT. NOW IT'S SHARP. NOW IT'S FLAT. PETER, GET YOUR THUMB OFF THE KNOB– YOUR PULSE IS AFFECTING THE TENSION!
SHOOT. NOW ALL THE STRINGS ARE FLAT BY 1/100,000TH OF A HERTZ. MY ADDED BODY TEMPERATURE MUST BE HEATING THE ROOM AND CAUSING THE STRINGS TO EXPAND.
FLAT BY 1/100,000TH OF A HERTZ?! WHO CARES?! AT THIS RATE, I'M GOING TO SPEND THE WHOLE DAY TUNING AND NEVER PLAY A SINGLE SONG! GO AWAY!
MOM HAS SOME EXTRA EARPLUGS, I THINK.
I TRIED.
AMEND

March 21, 1999

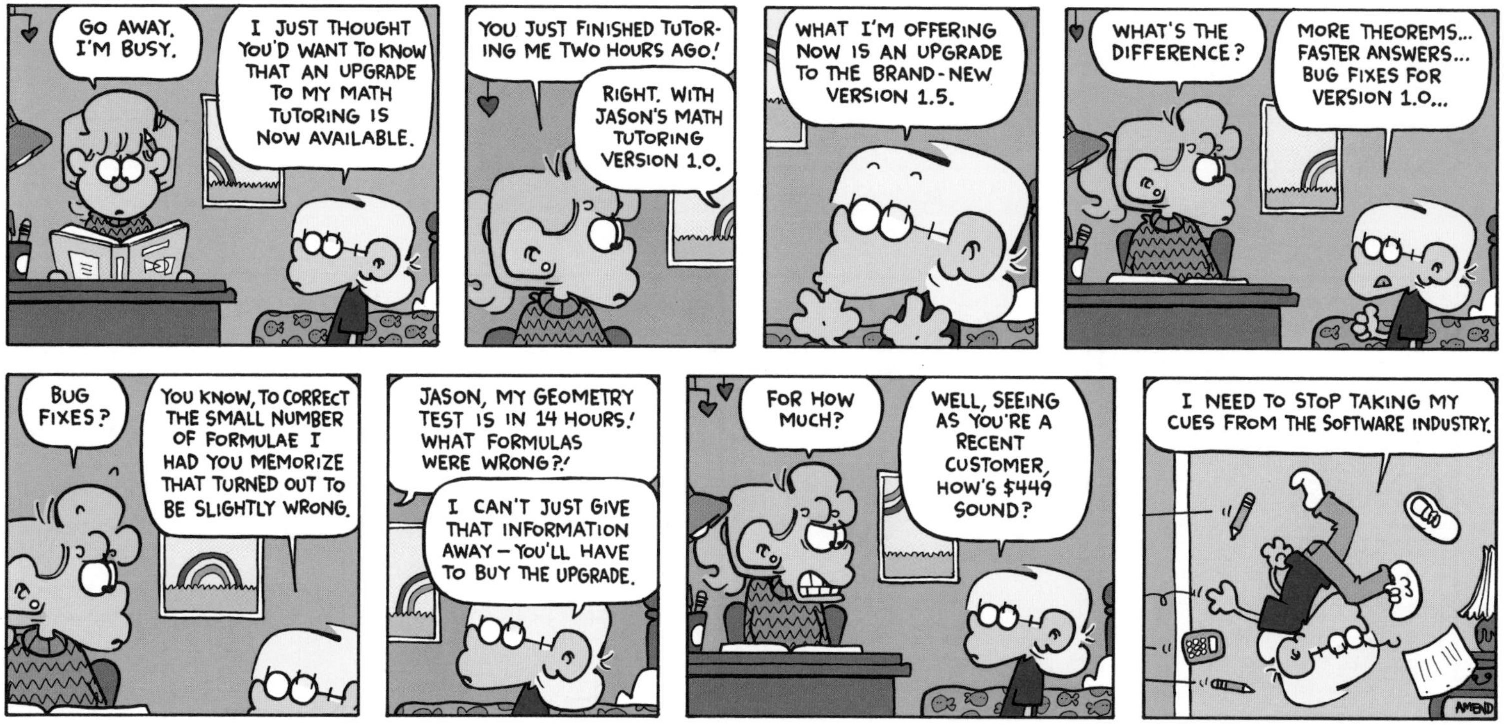
GO AWAY. I'M BUSY.
I JUST THOUGHT YOU'D WANT TO KNOW THAT AN UPGRADE TO MY MATH TUTORING IS NOW AVAILABLE.
YOU JUST FINISHED TUTORING ME TWO HOURS AGO!
RIGHT. WITH JASON'S MATH TUTORING VERSION 1.0.
WHAT I'M OFFERING NOW IS AN UPGRADE TO THE BRAND-NEW VERSION 1.5.
WHAT'S THE DIFFERENCE?
MORE THEOREMS... FASTER ANSWERS... BUG FIXES FOR VERSION 1.0...
BUG FIXES?
YOU KNOW, TO CORRECT THE SMALL NUMBER OF FORMULAE I HAD YOU MEMORIZE THAT TURNED OUT TO BE SLIGHTLY WRONG.
JASON, MY GEOMETRY TEST IS IN 14 HOURS! WHAT FORMULAS WERE WRONG?!
I CAN'T JUST GIVE THAT INFORMATION AWAY– YOU'LL HAVE TO BUY THE UPGRADE.
FOR HOW MUCH?
WELL, SEEING AS YOU'RE A RECENT CUSTOMER, HOW'S $449 SOUND?
I NEED TO STOP TAKING MY CUES FROM THE SOFTWARE INDUSTRY.
AMEND

April 4, 1999

April 11, 1999

Welcome to the Jason Fox STAR WARS EPISODE I Rumors Web Page!!!

Greetings, fellow "Star Wars" fans! With less than four weeks to go before the big event, new details about the movie are leaking out faster than a Tatooine pod race!

Spoilers ahead! Beware!

First, confirmation of last week's report here that John Williams' score departs rather drastically from his earlier SW works. "He's sort of big on kazoos now," states one well-placed insider. Another source would only characterize the new sound as "highly experimental."

Speaking of music, we erred in our earlier report that "Titanic's" own Celine Dion would sing the ballad "A Long Time Ago" over the end credits. Sources now tell us the song will run during the opening title crawl and will take full advantage of THX surround sound.

Bad news for special effects fans. Apparently stung by criticism from his mailman that the trailers looked "too digital," George Lucas has ordered all computer-generated images removed from the film. CGI character Jar Jar Binks will reportedly be renamed "Jar Jar Binks, Master of Invisibility."

Finally, rumors continue to swirl of a last-minute voice recasting. A number of spies report that fitness guru Richard Simmons has been hired to rerecord all of lead villain Darth Maul's dialogue. "We think audiences will be surprised at how well he growls," says one Skywalker Ranch informant.

Ironic that my idea of a horrible rumor was "no Jar-Jar Binks."

April 25, 1999

41

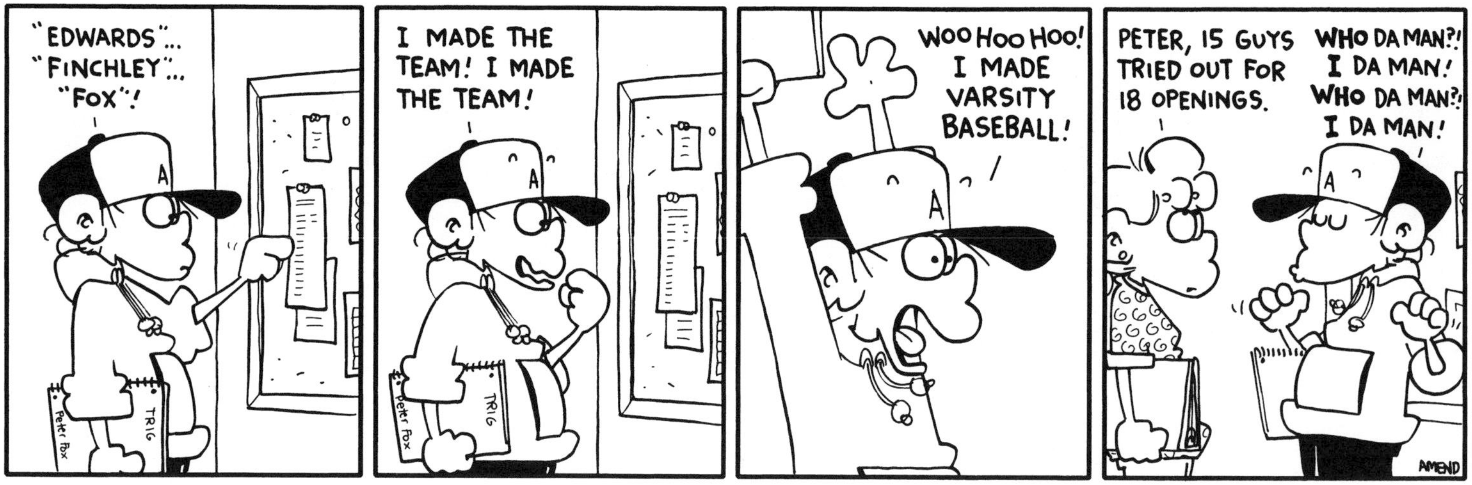
"EDWARDS"... "FINCHLEY"... "FOX"!
Peter Fox
TRIG
I MADE THE TEAM! I MADE THE TEAM!
WOO HOO HOO! I MADE VARSITY BASEBALL!
PETER, 15 GUYS TRIED OUT FOR 18 OPENINGS.
WHO DA MAN?! I DA MAN! WHO DA MAN?! I DA MAN!
AMEND

April 12, 1999

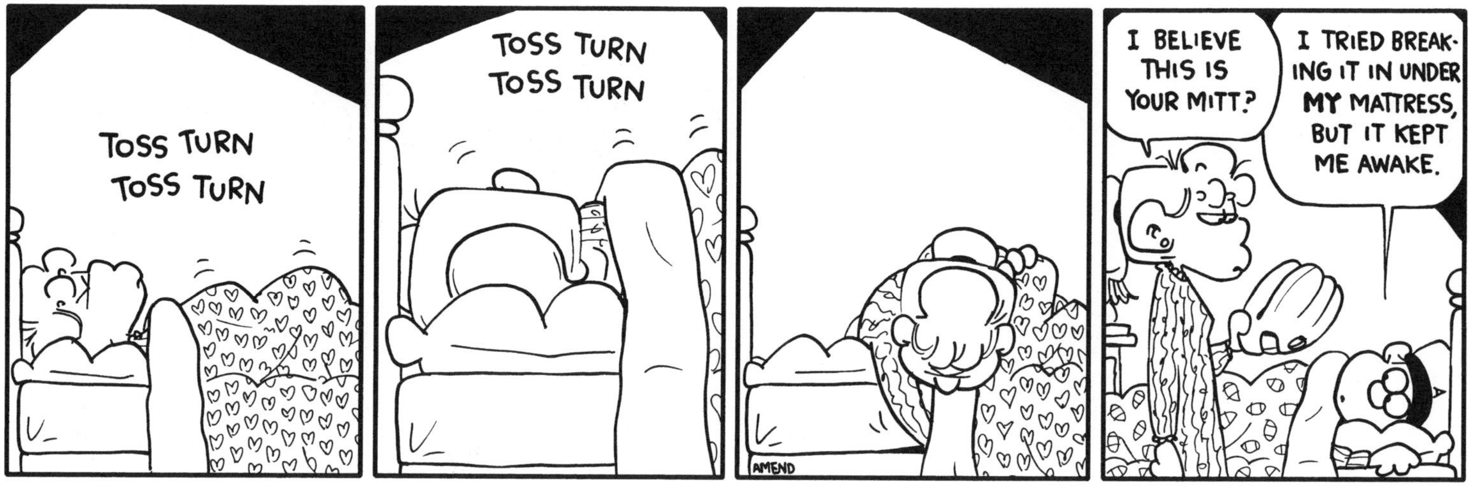
TOSS TURN TOSS TURN
TOSS TURN TOSS TURN
AMEND
I BELIEVE THIS IS YOUR MITT?
I TRIED BREAKING IT IN UNDER MY MATTRESS, BUT IT KEPT ME AWAKE.

April 13, 1999

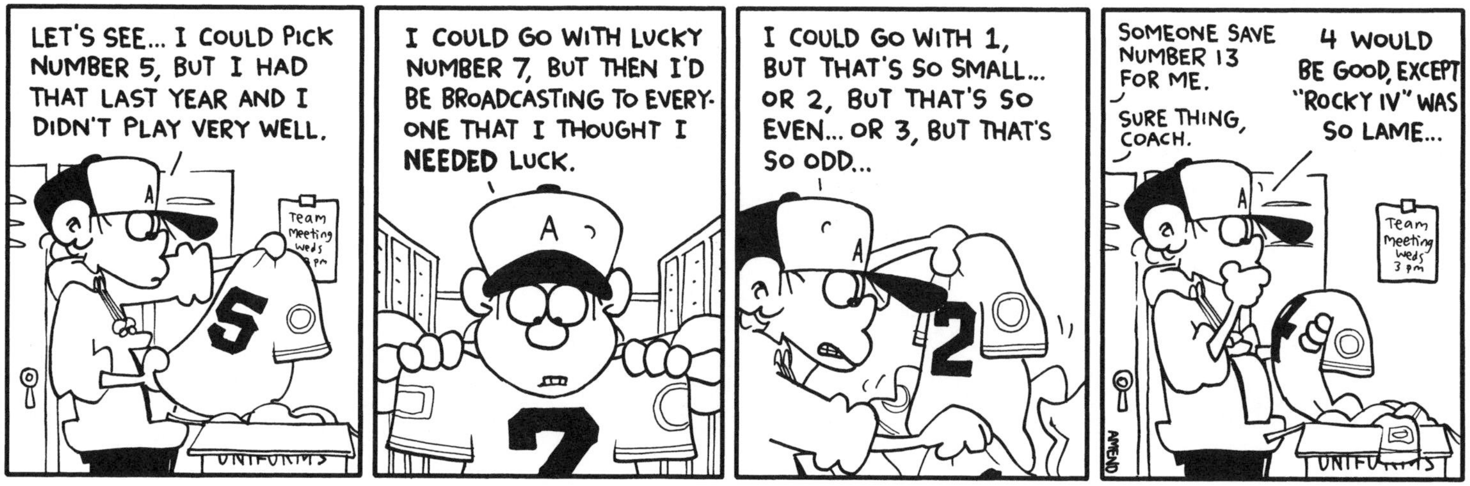
LET'S SEE... I COULD PICK NUMBER 5, BUT I HAD THAT LAST YEAR AND I DIDN'T PLAY VERY WELL.
Team Meeting Weds 3 pm
I COULD GO WITH LUCKY NUMBER 7, BUT THEN I'D BE BROADCASTING TO EVERYONE THAT I THOUGHT I NEEDED LUCK.
I COULD GO WITH 1, BUT THAT'S SO SMALL... OR 2, BUT THAT'S SO EVEN... OR 3, BUT THAT'S SO ODD...
SOMEONE SAVE NUMBER 13 FOR ME.
SURE THING, COACH.
4 WOULD BE GOOD, EXCEPT "ROCKY IV" WAS SO LAME...
Team Meeting Weds 3 pm
AMEND

April 14, 1999

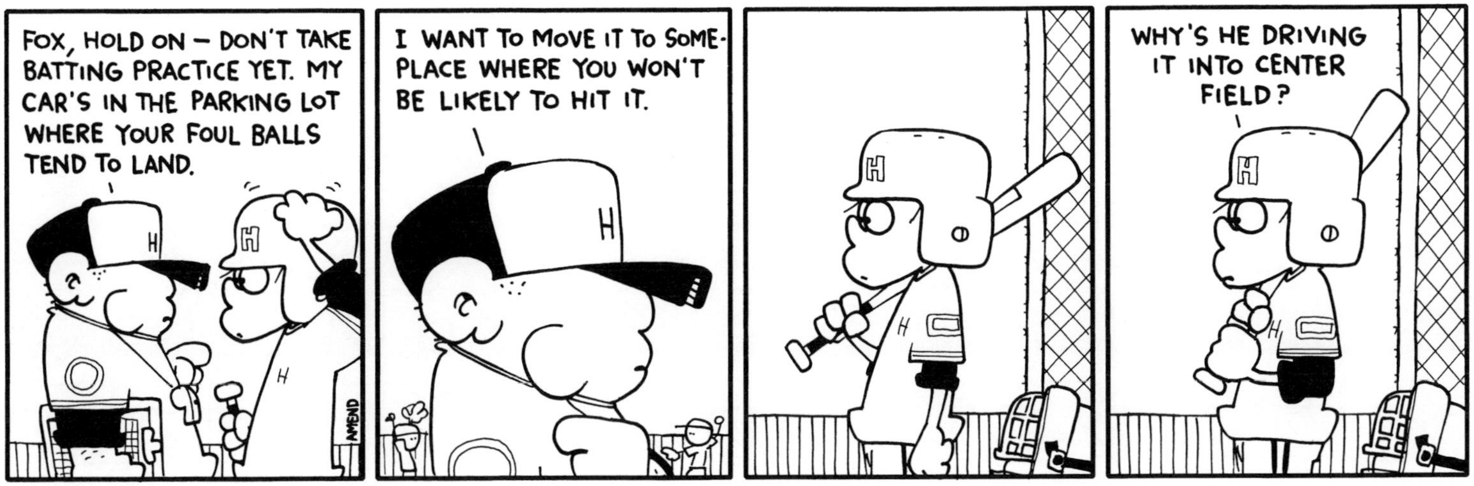
FOX, HOLD ON – DON'T TAKE BATTING PRACTICE YET. MY CAR'S IN THE PARKING LOT WHERE YOUR FOUL BALLS TEND TO LAND.
I WANT TO MOVE IT TO SOME-PLACE WHERE YOU WON'T BE LIKELY TO HIT IT.
WHY'S HE DRIVING IT INTO CENTER FIELD?

April 15, 1999

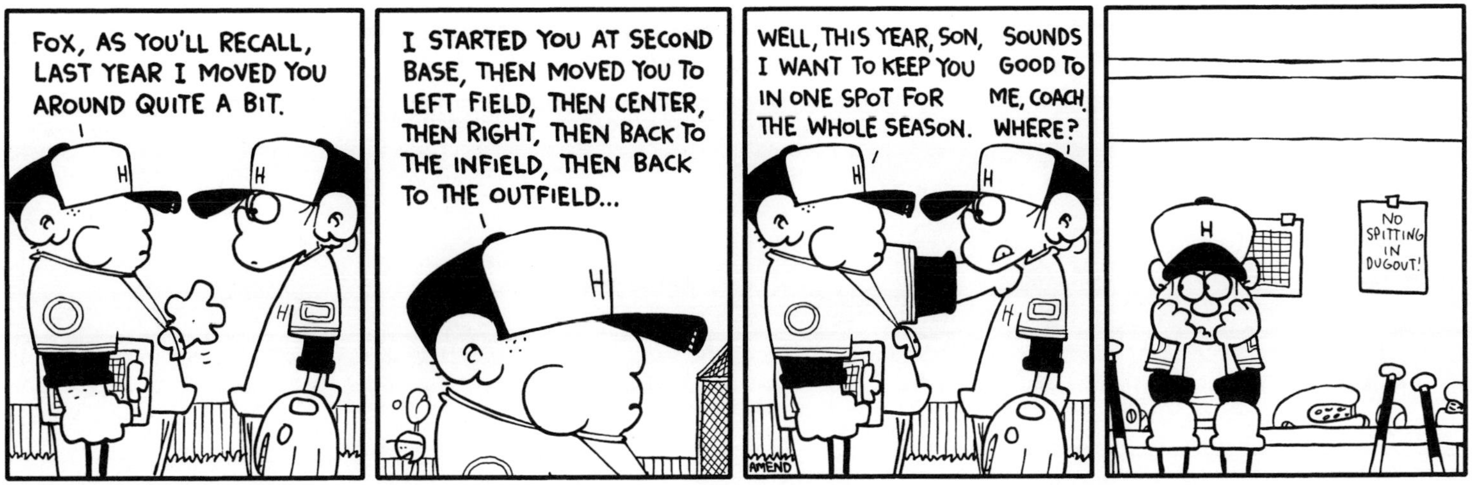
FOX, AS YOU'LL RECALL, LAST YEAR I MOVED YOU AROUND QUITE A BIT.
I STARTED YOU AT SECOND BASE, THEN MOVED YOU TO LEFT FIELD, THEN CENTER, THEN RIGHT, THEN BACK TO THE INFIELD, THEN BACK TO THE OUTFIELD...
WELL, THIS YEAR, SON, I WANT TO KEEP YOU IN ONE SPOT FOR THE WHOLE SEASON.
SOUNDS GOOD TO ME, COACH. WHERE?
NO SPITTING IN DUGOUT!

April 16, 1999

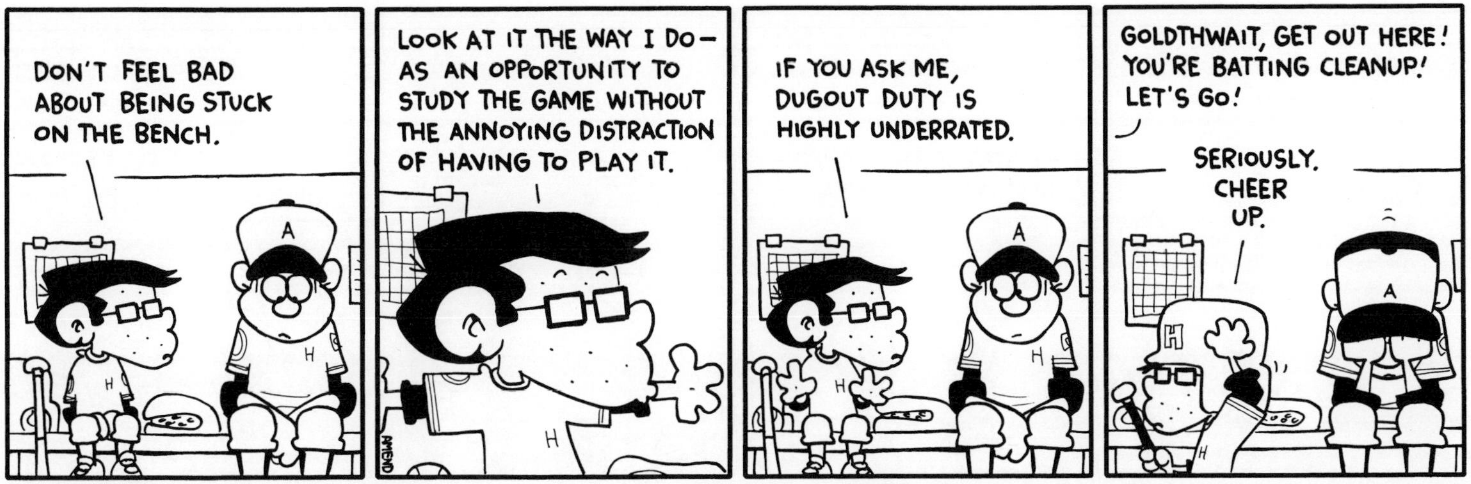
DON'T FEEL BAD ABOUT BEING STUCK ON THE BENCH.
LOOK AT IT THE WAY I DO – AS AN OPPORTUNITY TO STUDY THE GAME WITHOUT THE ANNOYING DISTRACTION OF HAVING TO PLAY IT.
IF YOU ASK ME, DUGOUT DUTY IS HIGHLY UNDERRATED.
GOLDTHWAIT, GET OUT HERE! YOU'RE BATTING CLEANUP! LET'S GO!
SERIOUSLY. CHEER UP.

April 17, 1999

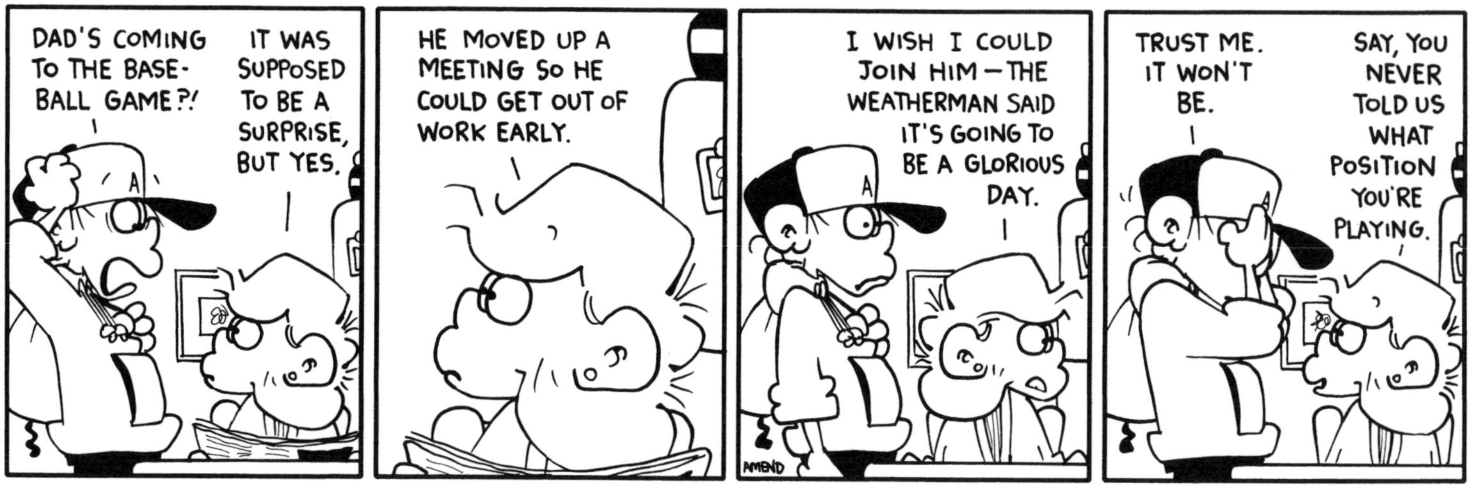
DAD'S COMING TO THE BASE-BALL GAME?!
IT WAS SUPPOSED TO BE A SURPRISE, BUT YES.
HE MOVED UP A MEETING SO HE COULD GET OUT OF WORK EARLY.
I WISH I COULD JOIN HIM—THE WEATHERMAN SAID IT'S GOING TO BE A GLORIOUS DAY.
TRUST ME. IT WON'T BE.
SAY, YOU NEVER TOLD US WHAT POSITION YOU'RE PLAYING.
AMEND

April 19, 1999

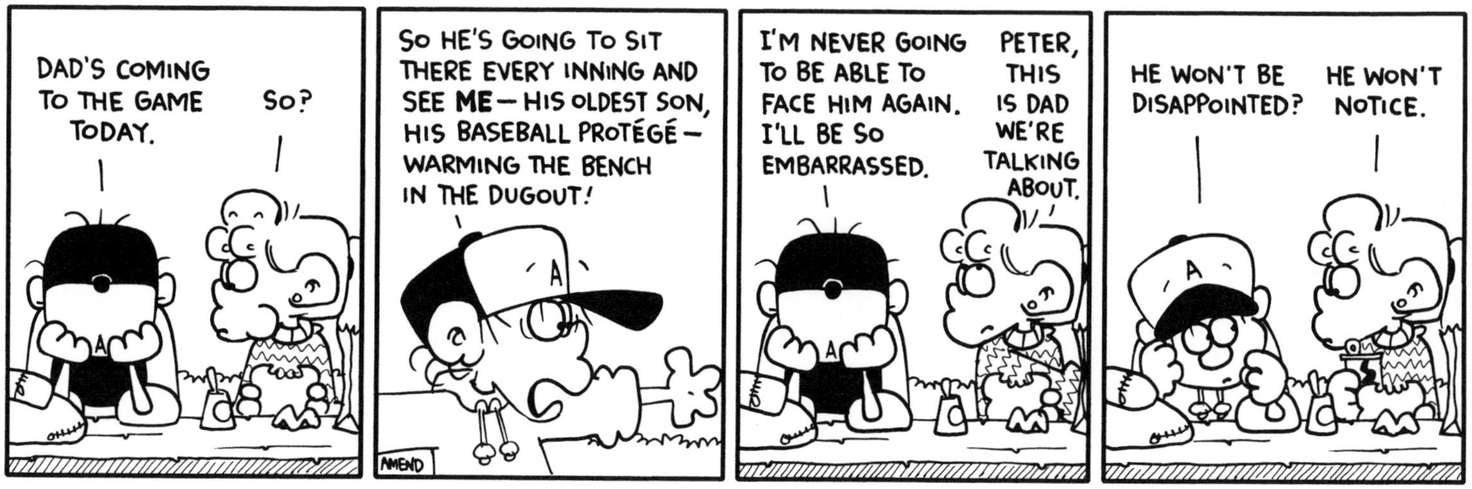
DAD'S COMING TO THE GAME TODAY.
SO?
SO HE'S GOING TO SIT THERE EVERY INNING AND SEE **ME**—HIS OLDEST SON, HIS BASEBALL PROTÉGÉ—WARMING THE BENCH IN THE DUGOUT!
I'M NEVER GOING TO BE ABLE TO FACE HIM AGAIN. I'LL BE SO EMBARRASSED.
PETER, THIS IS DAD WE'RE TALKING ABOUT.
HE WON'T BE DISAPPOINTED?
HE WON'T NOTICE.
AMEND

April 20, 1999

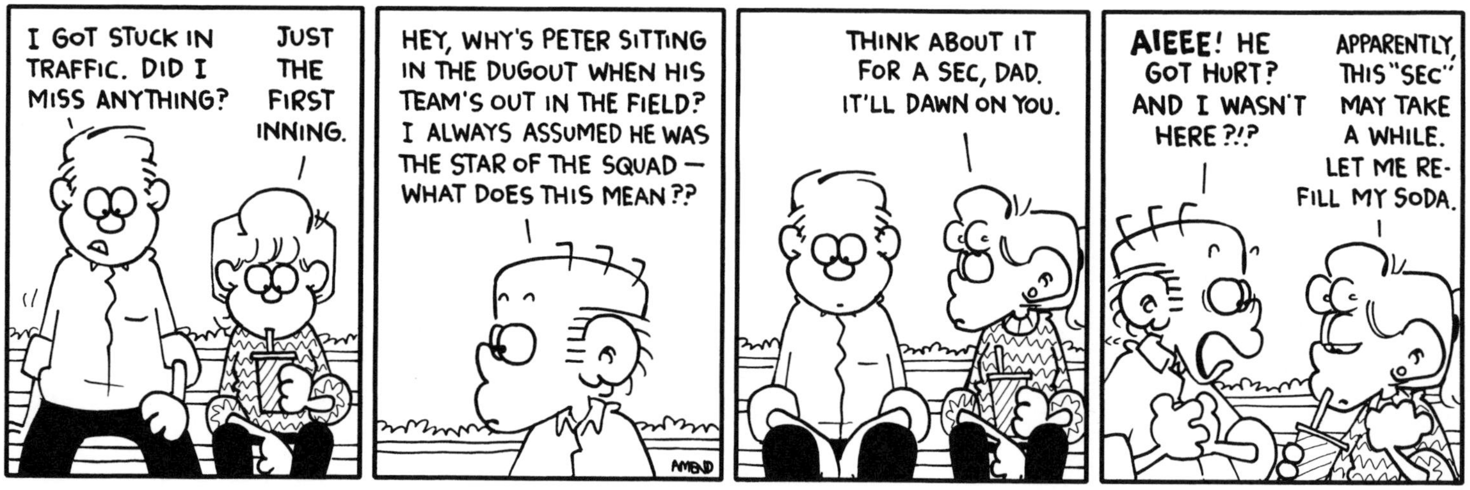
I GOT STUCK IN TRAFFIC. DID I MISS ANYTHING?
JUST THE FIRST INNING.
HEY, WHY'S PETER SITTING IN THE DUGOUT WHEN HIS TEAM'S OUT IN THE FIELD? I ALWAYS ASSUMED HE WAS THE STAR OF THE SQUAD—WHAT DOES THIS MEAN??
THINK ABOUT IT FOR A SEC, DAD. IT'LL DAWN ON YOU.
AIEEE! HE GOT HURT? AND I WASN'T HERE?!?
APPARENTLY, THIS "SEC" MAY TAKE A WHILE. LET ME RE-FILL MY SODA.
AMEND

April 21, 1999

IT'S THE LAST INNING AND PETER HASN'T PLAYED AT ALL.

HE'S JUST SAT THERE ON THE BENCH. THE COACH DOESN'T EVEN LOOK LIKE HE WOULD **CONSIDER** PUTTING PETER IN THE GAME.

DOES THIS MEAN WHAT I THINK IT MEANS?

'FRAID SO, DAD.

MY SON'S IN THE STARTING PITCHER ROTATION!

I WISH YOU WOULDN'T MAKE ME CHOKE WHILE I'M EATING A HOT DOG.

April 22, 1999

PETER FOX! YOU DA MAN!

DADDY, I DON'T KNOW HOW TO TELL YOU THIS GENTLY.

PETER ISN'T GOING TO PLAY IN TODAY'S GAME, OR ANY OTHER GAME, MOST LIKELY. HE'S THE LOW GUY ON THE TOTEM POLE... FOURTH STRING, IF THAT... VARSITY BASEBALL'S DESIGNATED BENCH-WARMER.

YOU JUST **ASSUMED** HE WAS A STAR. THE TRUTH IS HE'S NOT.

PETER FOX! YOU DA MAN!

DADDY, DON'T BE SO CLUELESS. YOU ACT LIKE NOTHING'S CHANGED.

April 23, 1999

I CAN'T BELIEVE DAD CHEERED ME ON LIKE THAT TODAY.

I MEAN, EVEN AFTER HE SAW I WAS JUST A BENCH-WARMER, A FOURTH-STRINGER, A **NOBODY**, HE KEPT RIGHT ON YELLING, "RAH, RAH, PETER! RAH, RAH, PETER!"

I THOUGHT FOR SURE HE'D THINK I WAS A FAILURE. I THOUGHT FOR SURE HE'D BE DISAPPOINTED.

SOMETIMES OUR DAD'S PRETTY COOL.

FOR A GUY WHO SAYS "RAH."

April 24, 1999

I thought it was good to see this side of Roger.

45

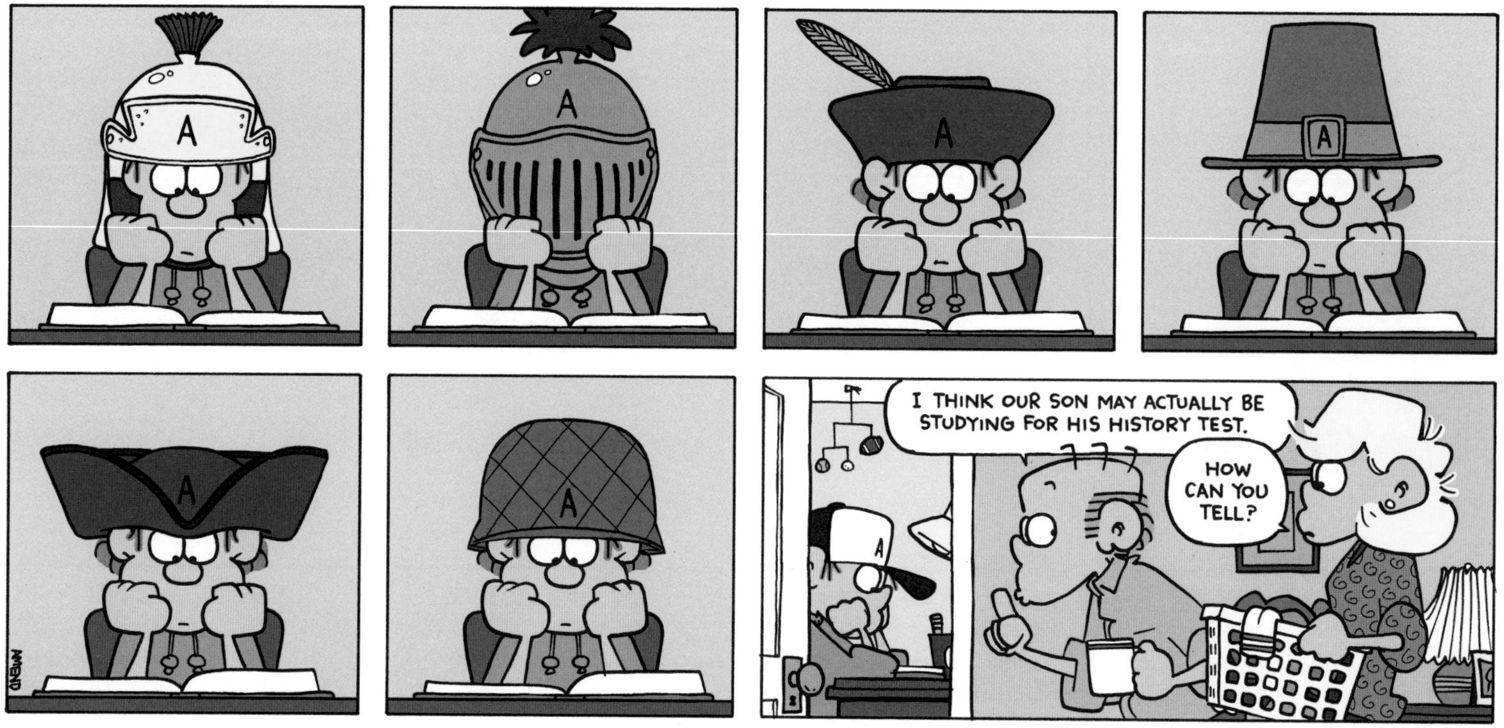
I THINK OUR SON MAY ACTUALLY BE STUDYING FOR HIS HISTORY TEST.
HOW CAN YOU TELL?
AMEND

May 9, 1999

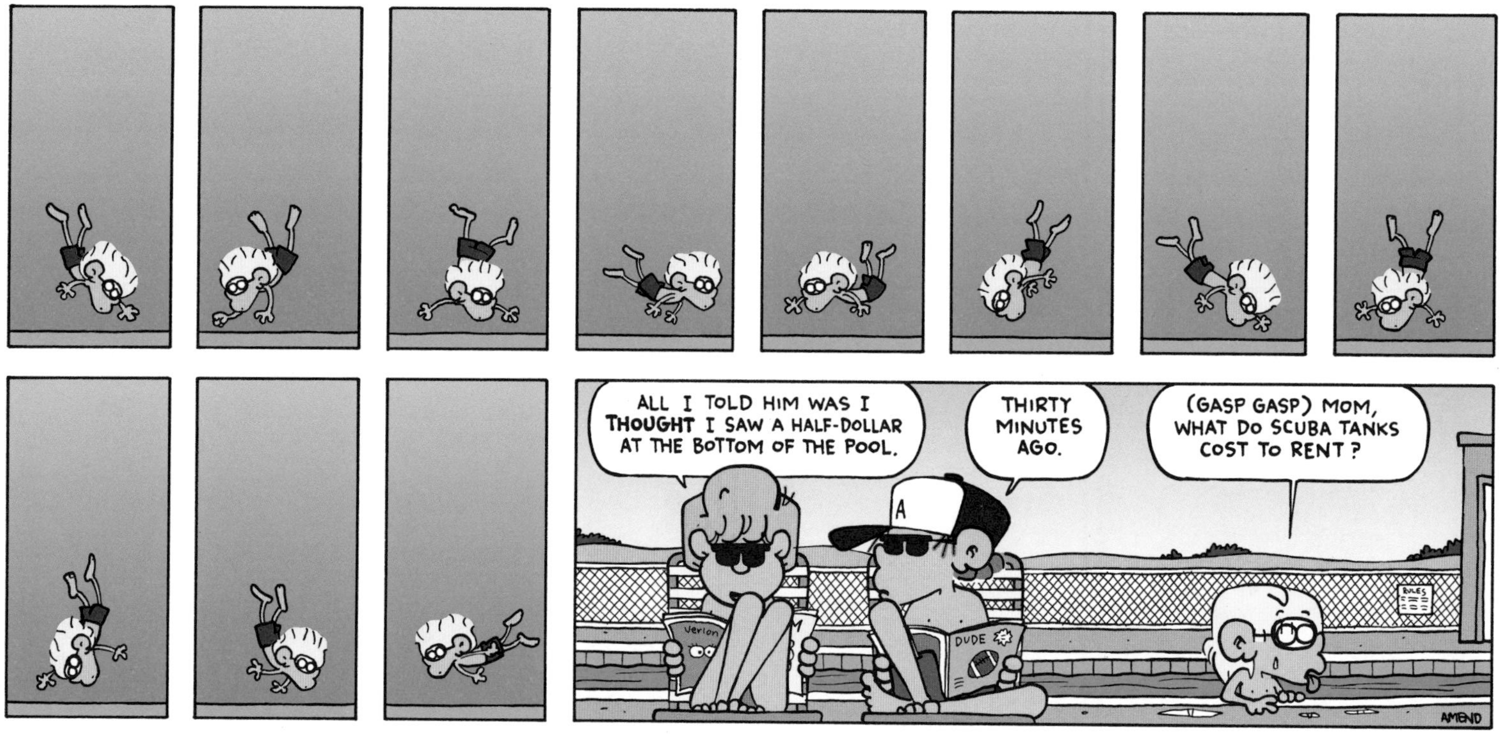
ALL I TOLD HIM WAS I **THOUGHT** I SAW A HALF-DOLLAR AT THE BOTTOM OF THE POOL.
THIRTY MINUTES AGO.
(GASP GASP) MOM, WHAT DO SCUBA TANKS COST TO RENT?
DUDE
AMEND

July 4, 1999

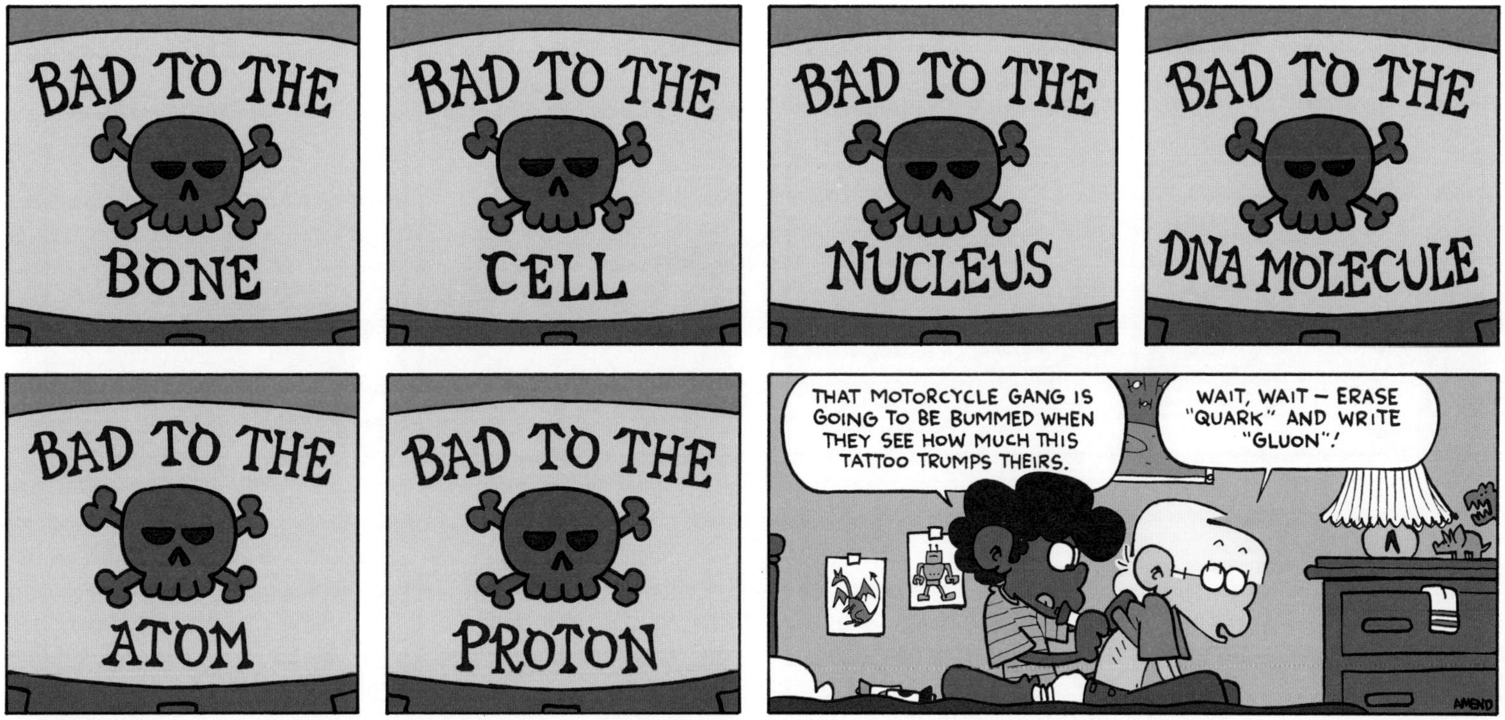
BAD TO THE BONE
BAD TO THE CELL
BAD TO THE NUCLEUS
BAD TO THE DNA MOLECULE
BAD TO THE ATOM
BAD TO THE PROTON
THAT MOTORCYCLE GANG IS GOING TO BE BUMMED WHEN THEY SEE HOW MUCH THIS TATTOO TRUMPS THEIRS.
WAIT, WAIT – ERASE "QUARK" AND WRITE "GLUON"!
AMEND
July 11, 1999

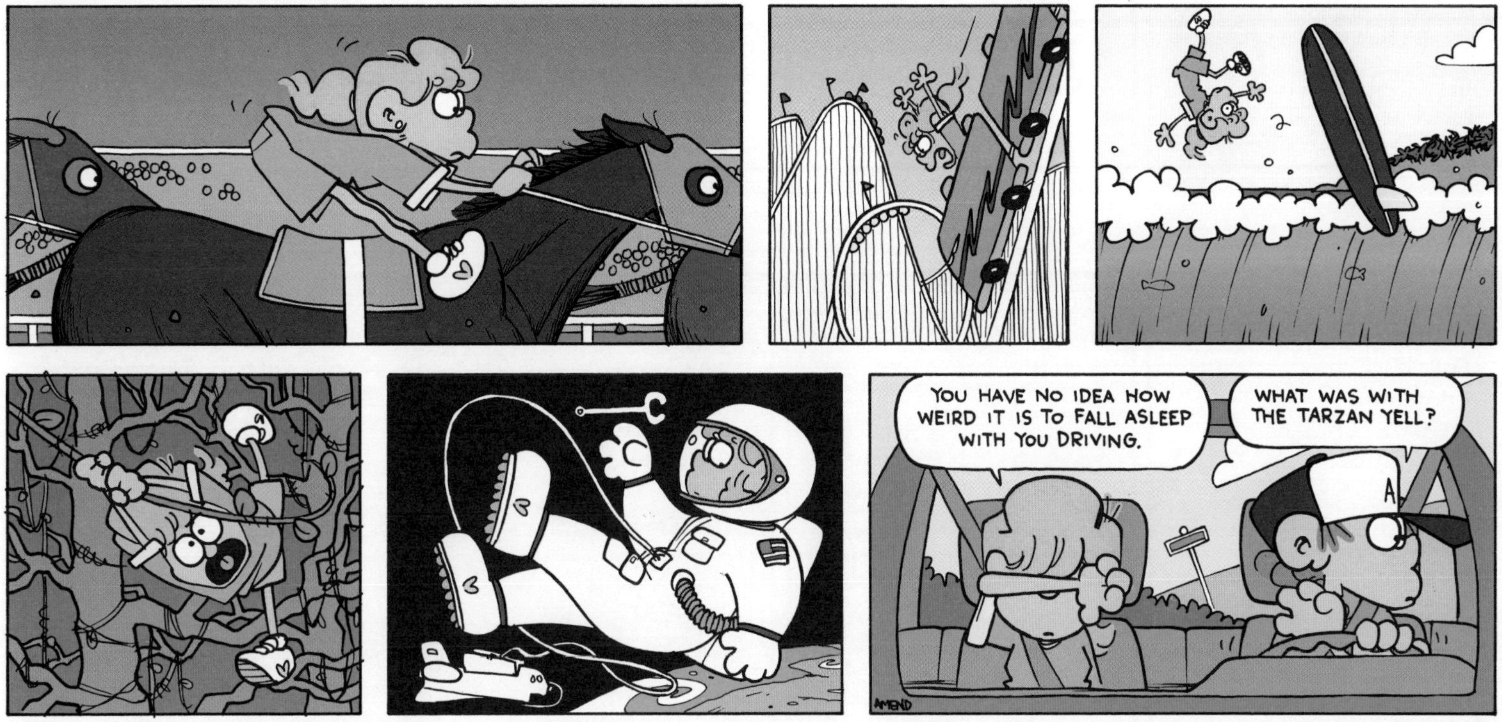
YOU HAVE NO IDEA HOW WEIRD IT IS TO FALL ASLEEP WITH YOU DRIVING.
WHAT WAS WITH THE TARZAN YELL?
AMEND
August 1, 1999

DAD SAYS YOU'RE GOING BACK TO WORK AT THE MOVIE THEATER.

YEAH. I'M NOT REALLY LOOKING FORWARD TO IT, THOUGH.

WHY? I THOUGHT YOU LIKED WORKING THERE.

THAT WAS LAST SUMMER. THINGS HAVE CHANGED SINCE THEN.

WHAT'S DIFFERENT? THE MANAGEMENT? THE PAY? THE HOURS?

"STAR WARS" WASN'T PLAYING THEN.

AH.

...ON ALL 22 SCREENS.

I SENSE MUCH FEAR IN YOU.

June 7, 1999

NOW, PETER, THE THING TO KEEP IN MIND WITH THESE "STAR WARS" FANS IS THEY'RE JUST ORDINARY PEOPLE, MOSTLY.

SURE, THEY LIKE TO DRESS UP IN COSTUMES. AND WAVE PLASTIC LIGHTSABERS. AND GIVE STANDING OVATIONS TO THE LUCASFILM LOGO. AND SLEEP ON SIDEWALKS FOR TICKETS.

BUT OTHER THAN THAT, THEY REALLY ARE JUST LIKE YOU AND ME.

AT LAST WE WILL REVEAL OURSELVES TO THE RESTROOM.

...ONLY INSANE.

MR. MAUL, SIR? YOU DROPPED YOUR STRAW.

June 8, 1999

HI. I'D LIKE SIX TICKETS FOR "THE PHANTOM MENACE" ON YOUR BIGGEST SCREEN.

FOR WHICH SHOW TIME?

WHAT DO YOU MEAN, WHICH SHOW TIME?

THERE ARE SIX SHOW TIMES— 11:30, 2:00, 4:30, 7:00, 9:30 AND MIDNIGHT.

RIGHT. I WANT ONE TICKET FOR EACH SCREENING.

OH.

YOU MUST BE NEW. I DIDN'T SEE YOU HERE YESTERDAY.

YOU MAY NOT SEE ME HERE TOMORROW, EITHER.

June 9, 1999

48

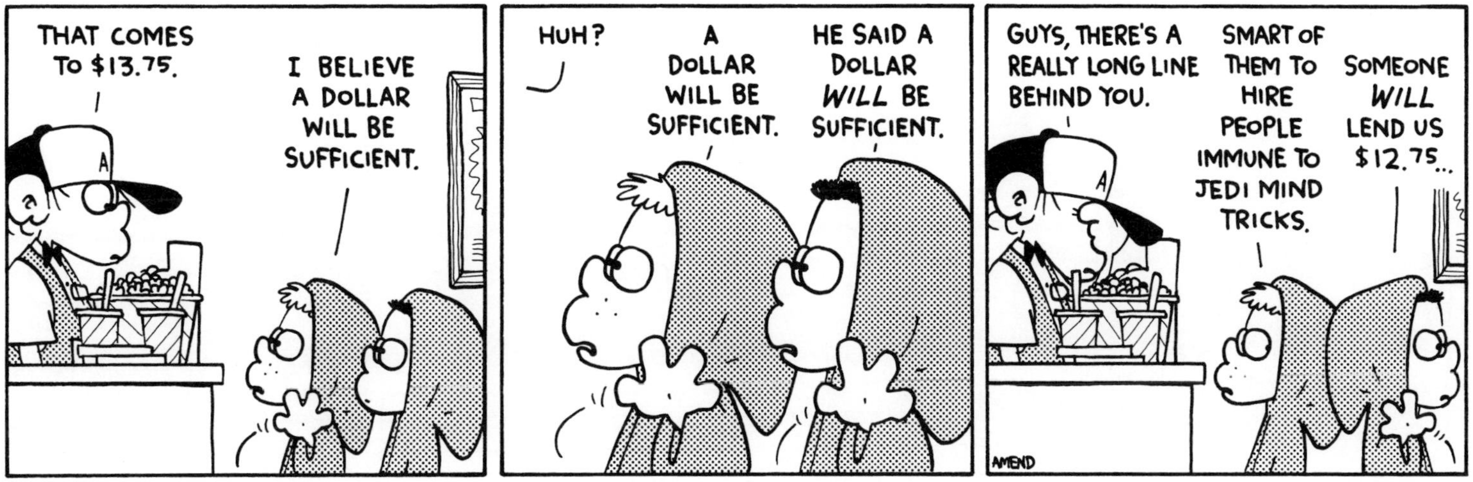
THAT COMES TO $13.75.
I BELIEVE A DOLLAR WILL BE SUFFICIENT.
HUH?
A DOLLAR WILL BE SUFFICIENT.
HE SAID A DOLLAR *WILL* BE SUFFICIENT.
GUYS, THERE'S A REALLY LONG LINE BEHIND YOU.
SMART OF THEM TO HIRE PEOPLE IMMUNE TO JEDI MIND TRICKS.
SOMEONE *WILL* LEND US $12.75...
AMEND

June 10, 1999

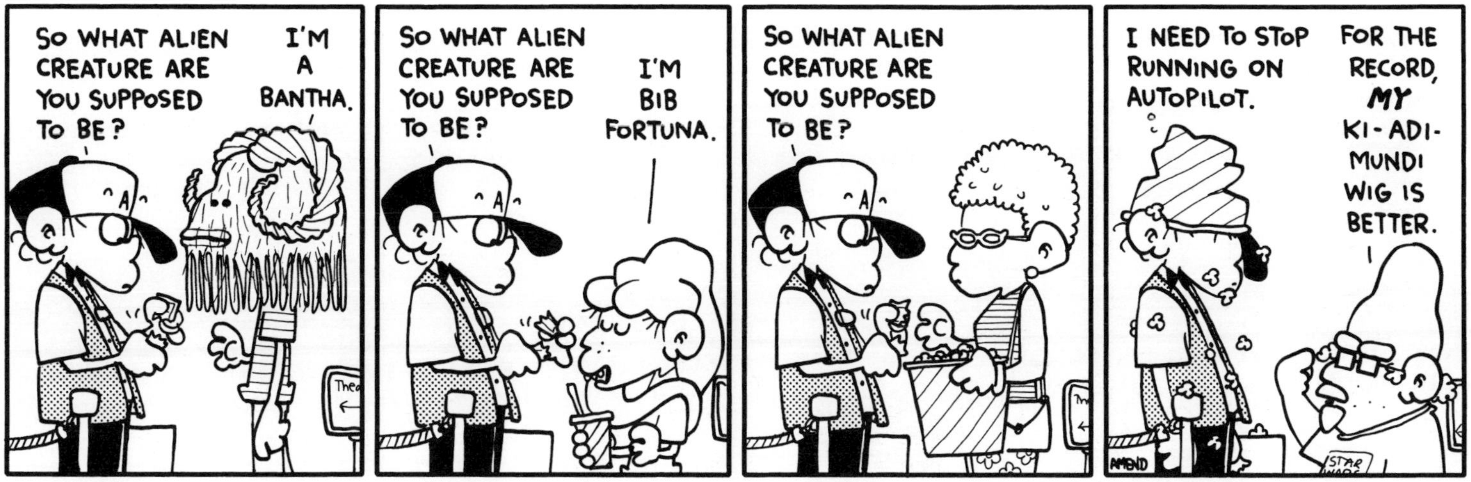
SO WHAT ALIEN CREATURE ARE YOU SUPPOSED TO BE?
I'M A BANTHA.
SO WHAT ALIEN CREATURE ARE YOU SUPPOSED TO BE?
I'M BIB FORTUNA.
SO WHAT ALIEN CREATURE ARE YOU SUPPOSED TO BE?
I NEED TO STOP RUNNING ON AUTOPILOT.
FOR THE RECORD, *MY* KI-ADI-MUNDI WIG IS BETTER.
AMEND

June 11, 1999

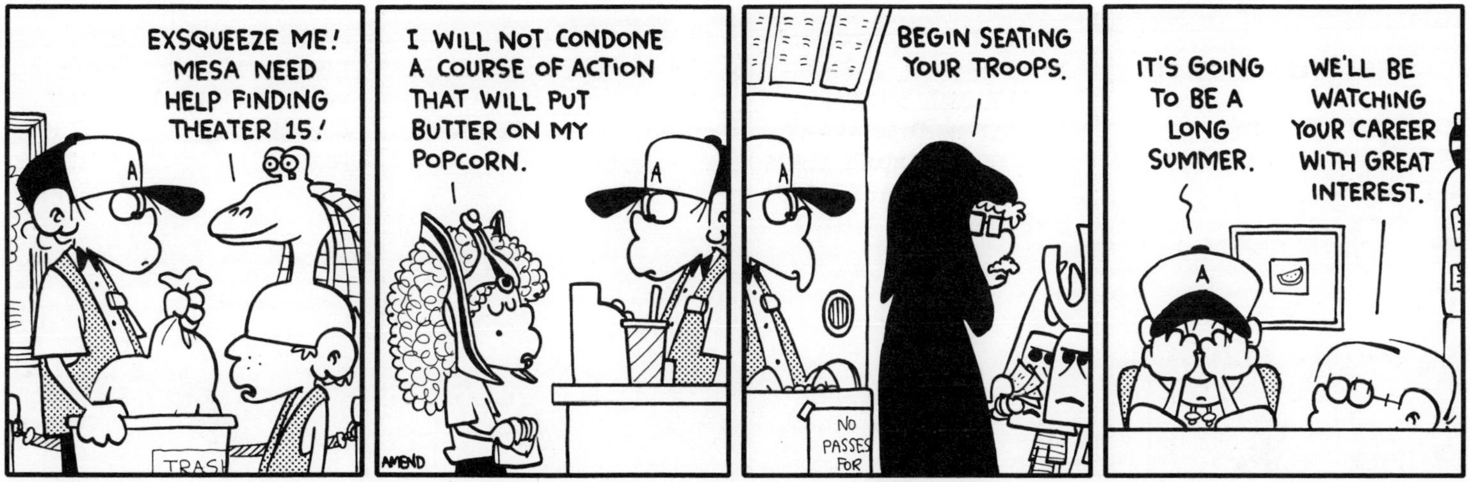
EXSQUEEZE ME! MESA NEED HELP FINDING THEATER 15!
I WILL NOT CONDONE A COURSE OF ACTION THAT WILL PUT BUTTER ON MY POPCORN.
AMEND
BEGIN SEATING YOUR TROOPS.
NO PASSES FOR
IT'S GOING TO BE A LONG SUMMER.
WE'LL BE WATCHING YOUR CAREER WITH GREAT INTEREST.

June 12, 1999

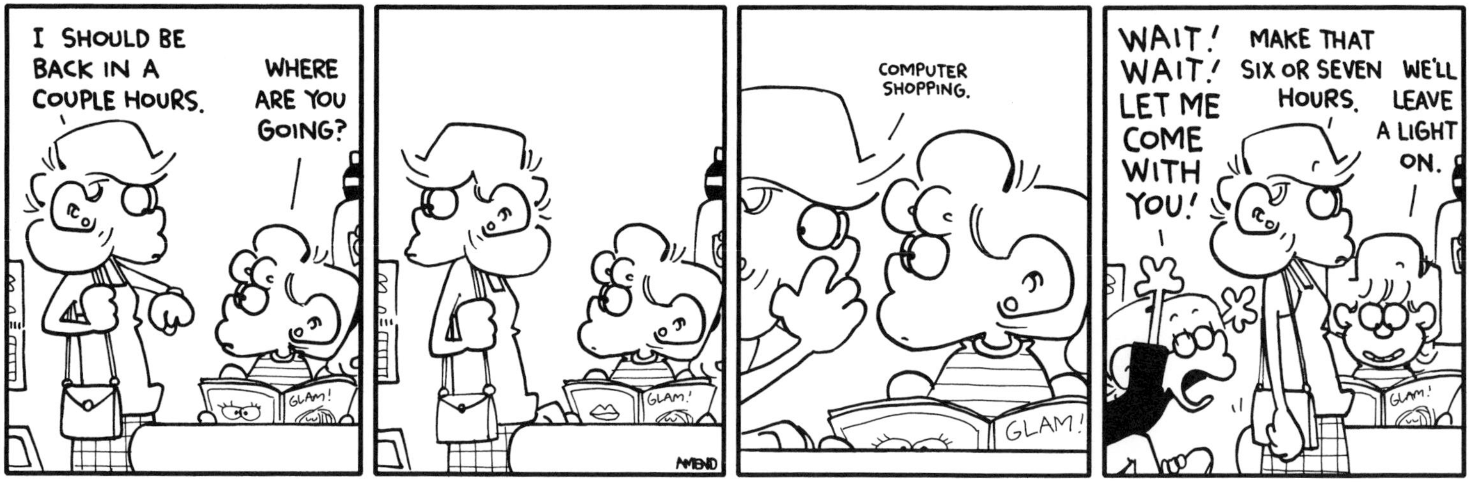
I SHOULD BE BACK IN A COUPLE HOURS.
WHERE ARE YOU GOING?
COMPUTER SHOPPING.
WAIT! WAIT! LET ME COME WITH YOU!
MAKE THAT SIX OR SEVEN HOURS.
WE'LL LEAVE A LIGHT ON.

August 9, 1999

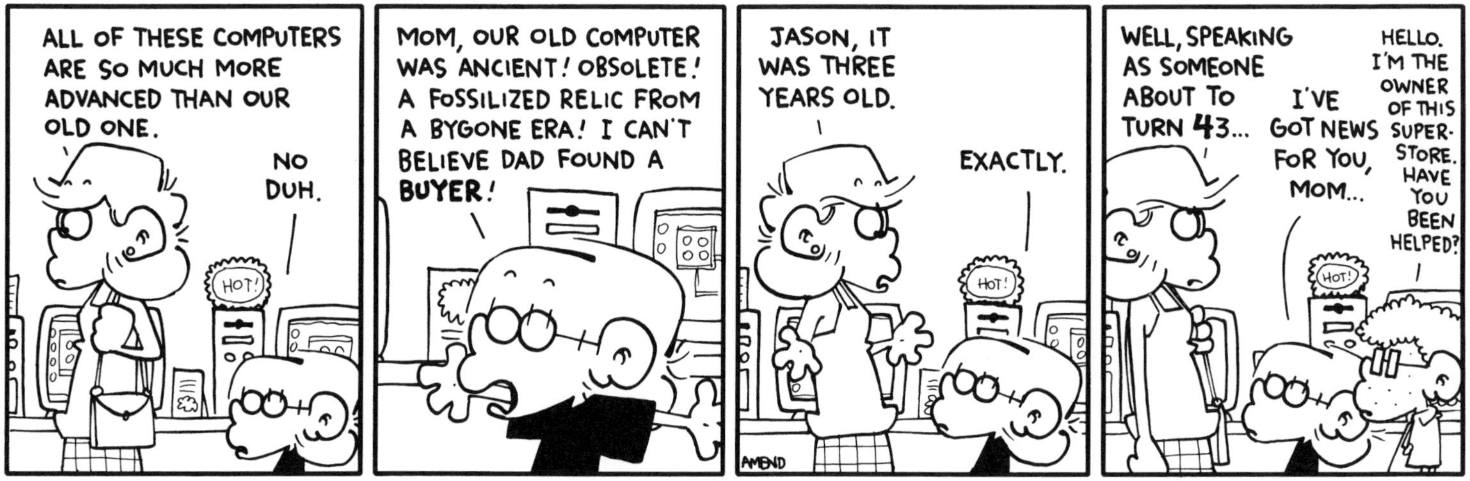
ALL OF THESE COMPUTERS ARE SO MUCH MORE ADVANCED THAN OUR OLD ONE.
NO DUH.
MOM, OUR OLD COMPUTER WAS ANCIENT! OBSOLETE! A FOSSILIZED RELIC FROM A BYGONE ERA! I CAN'T BELIEVE DAD FOUND A BUYER!
JASON, IT WAS THREE YEARS OLD.
EXACTLY.
WELL, SPEAKING AS SOMEONE ABOUT TO TURN 43...
I'VE GOT NEWS FOR YOU, MOM...
HELLO. I'M THE OWNER OF THIS SUPER-STORE. HAVE YOU BEEN HELPED?

August 10, 1999

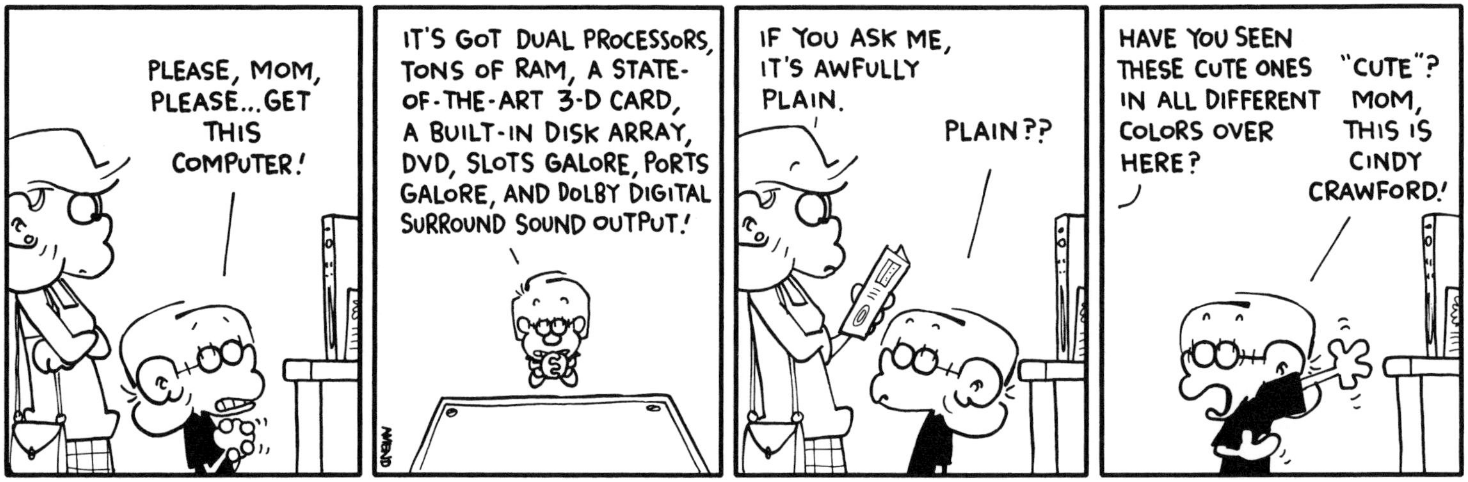
PLEASE, MOM, PLEASE...GET THIS COMPUTER!
IT'S GOT DUAL PROCESSORS, TONS OF RAM, A STATE-OF-THE-ART 3-D CARD, A BUILT-IN DISK ARRAY, DVD, SLOTS GALORE, PORTS GALORE, AND DOLBY DIGITAL SURROUND SOUND OUTPUT!
IF YOU ASK ME, IT'S AWFULLY PLAIN.
PLAIN??
HAVE YOU SEEN THESE CUTE ONES IN ALL DIFFERENT COLORS OVER HERE?
"CUTE"? MOM, THIS IS CINDY CRAWFORD!

August 11, 1999

I remember struggling to come up with a good name for an iMac spoof. I had a eureka moment with "iFruit."

August 12, 1999

August 13, 1999

August 14, 1999

51

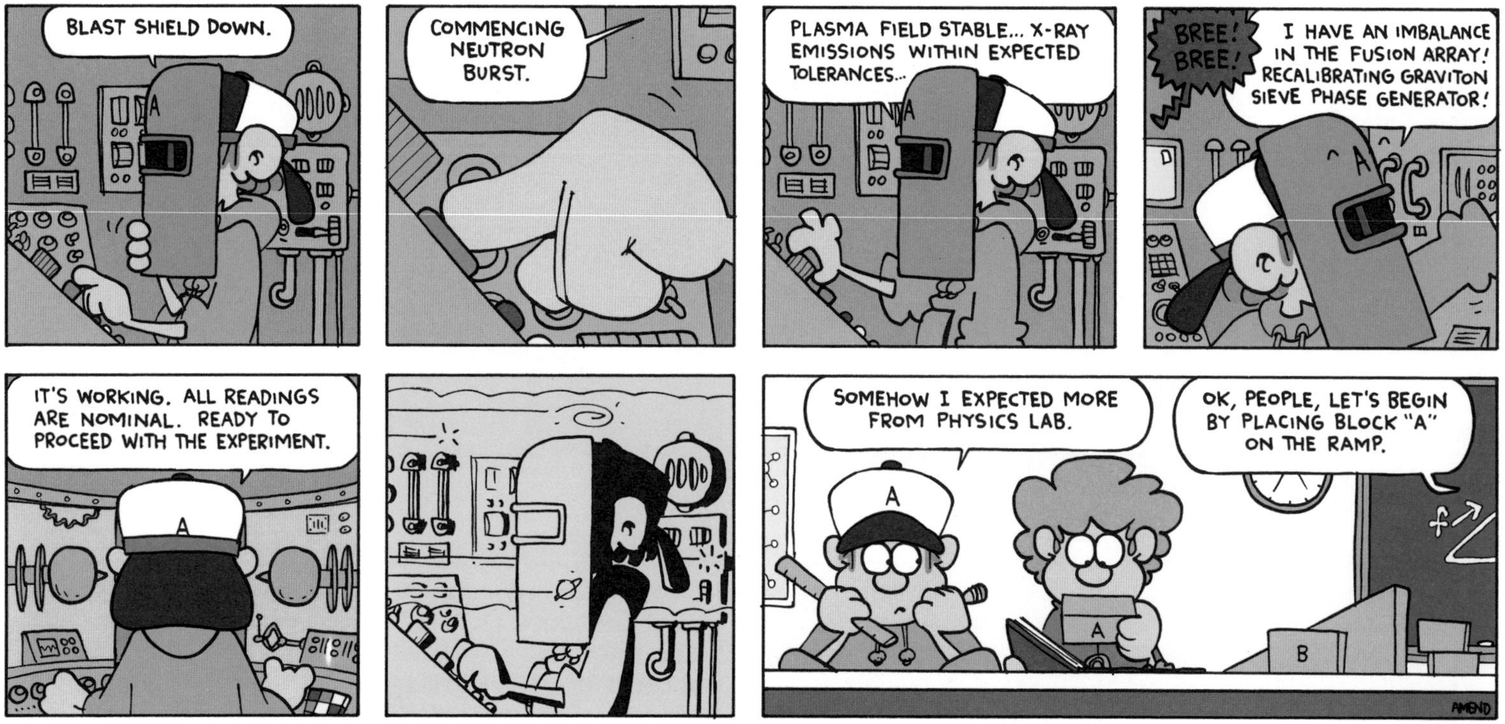
BLAST SHIELD DOWN.
COMMENCING NEUTRON BURST.
PLASMA FIELD STABLE... X-RAY EMISSIONS WITHIN EXPECTED TOLERANCES...
BREE! BREE!
I HAVE AN IMBALANCE IN THE FUSION ARRAY! RECALIBRATING GRAVITON SIEVE PHASE GENERATOR!
IT'S WORKING. ALL READINGS ARE NOMINAL. READY TO PROCEED WITH THE EXPERIMENT.
SOMEHOW I EXPECTED MORE FROM PHYSICS LAB.
OK, PEOPLE, LET'S BEGIN BY PLACING BLOCK "A" ON THE RAMP.
AMEND

September 12, 1999

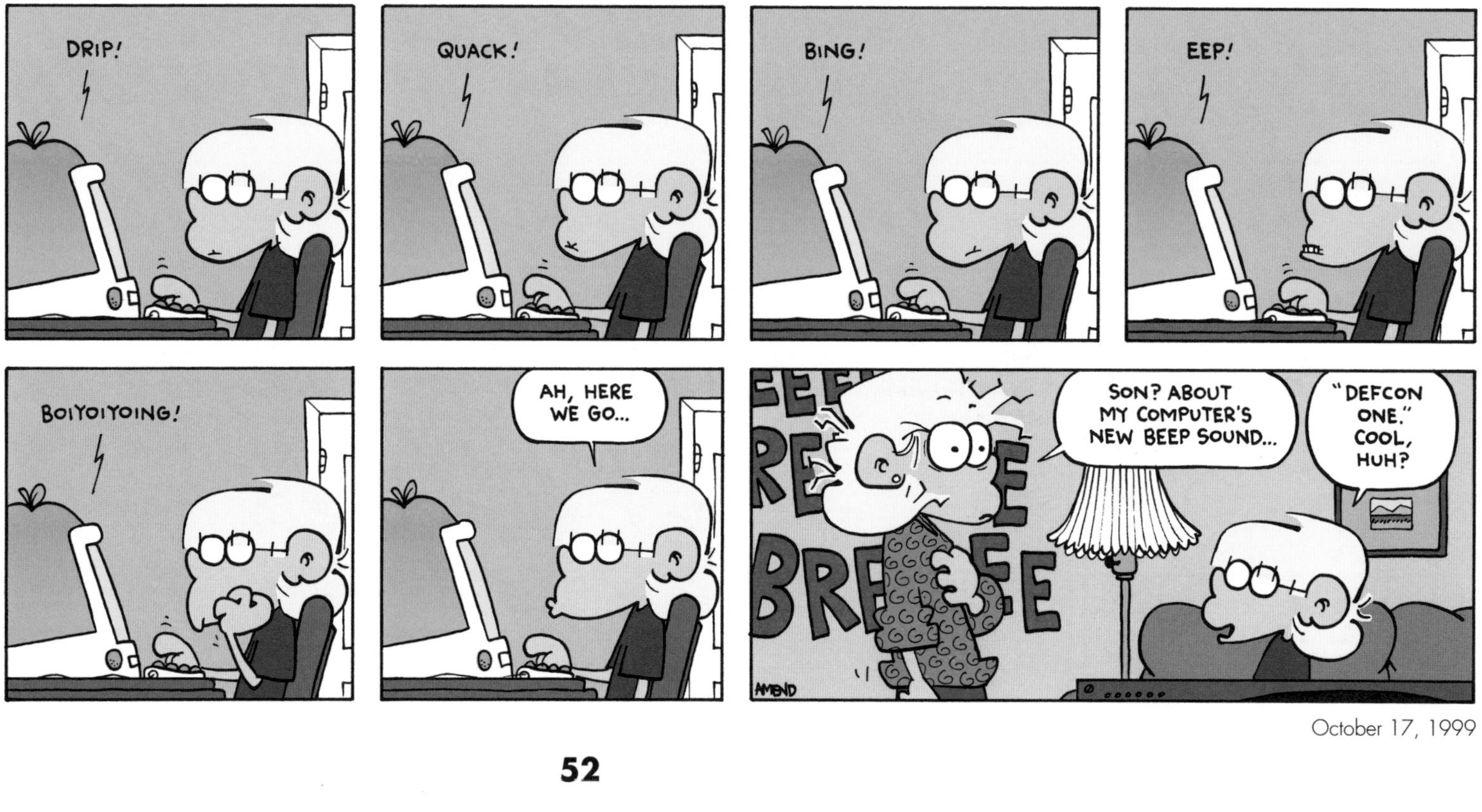
DRIP!
QUACK!
BING!
EEP!
BOIYOIYOING!
AH, HERE WE GO...
SON? ABOUT MY COMPUTER'S NEW BEEP SOUND...
"DEFCON ONE." COOL, HUH?
AMEND

October 17, 1999

September 15, 1999

September 17, 1999

September 21, 1999

THINK YOU HAVE ENOUGH BOOKS IN THERE?

BOOKS?

MOM, I'M ON MY WAY TO **SCHOOL**.

CORRECTION: THINK YOU HAVE ENOUGH POKÉMON CARDS IN THERE?

TRUTHFULLY?

October 11, 1999

HAVE YOU SEEN ALL THESE TRADING CARDS OUR SON IS AMASSING?

IT'S THE POKÉMON GAME. ALL THE KIDS AT HIS SCHOOL ARE PLAYING IT.

APPARENTLY, JASON'S GOT EVERY CARD EXCEPT ONE, AND HE'S BEEN BUYING PACKS LIKE CRAZY TRYING TO GET IT.

HE'S BORROWED HIS NEXT 37 ALLOWANCES. IT'S LIKE A SICKNESS.

SO HE DOESN'T HAVE **ONE CARD!** WHAT'S THE BIG DEAL?!

DID I MENTION I HAVE THE CHARIZARD CARD AND YOU DON'T?

ONLY 814 TIMES TODAY, EILEEN.

October 12, 1999

LET'S SEE... I SHOULD PROBABLY PUT THIS GLASS OF WATER IN THE SOUTH-EAST.

WHAT ARE YOU DOING?

FENG-SHUIING MY ROOM. IT'S THE ANCIENT CHINESE ART OF ARRANGING ONE'S ENVIRONMENT TO MAXIMIZE POSITIVE ENERGY. I WANT TO UP MY ODDS OF SUCCESS WHEN I OPEN THIS NEW PACK OF POKÉMON CARDS.

I'LL ADMIT CHANGING THE GRAIN OF MY CARPET TO FACE THE RIGHT WAY WAS A PAIN, BUT IF IT'LL GET ME A HOLO-FOIL CHARIZARD CARD, THE THREE DAYS IT TOOK WILL BE WORTH IT.

YOU'VE GOT YOUR USUAL "I THINK I'M GOING TO PUKE" FACE ON, I SEE.

SHOULD I DO IT IN THE SOUTHEAST AS WELL?

October 13, 1999

October 14, 1999

October 15, 1999

October 16, 1999

October 18, 1999

October 19, 1999

October 20, 1999

October 21, 1999

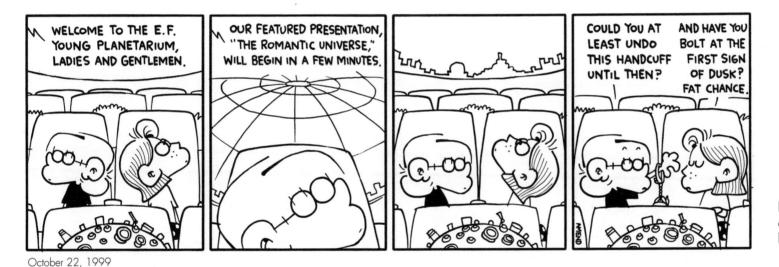

October 22, 1999

I named the planetarium after one of my physics buddies.

October 23, 1999

October 26, 1999

October 28, 1999

October 29, 1999

October 30, 1999

November 3, 1999

December 2, 1999

59

I'd pay good money for one of those hats.

October 31, 1999

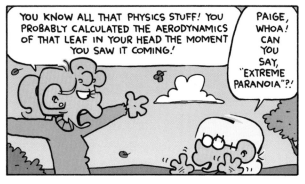

November 7, 1999

November 11, 1999

November 13, 1999

December 10, 1999

November 15, 1999

November 16, 1999

November 17, 1999

62

WHAT ARE YOU DOING?

PLANNING OUT OUR THANKSGIVING DINNER.

WITH MY MOTHER COMING, EVERYTHING HAS TO BE ABSOLUTELY PERFECT AND TASTEFUL, BECAUSE THAT'S HOW **SHE'D** DO IT. I HAVE TO MEASURE UP TO HER.

SHE CARES ABOUT THAT?

I CARE ABOUT THAT.

FUNNY YOU SHOULD STRESS THE NEED FOR GOOD TASTE.

TURKEY IN A CURRY-YOGURT-RICE-PASTE CRUST. TRY AND TOP **THAT**.

November 18, 1999

KIDS, I REALLY NEED YOU TO HELP CLEAN UP THE HOUSE THIS WEEK.

WHY?

BECAUSE YOUR GRAND-MOTHER'S COMING AND IT'S IMPORTANT THAT IT'S SPOTLESS WHEN SHE GETS HERE.

WHY?

WELL, BECAUSE OTHERWISE SHE'LL TAKE IT UPON HERSELF TO CLEAN THE WHOLE HOUSE FOR US, AND WE DON'T WANT THAT.

SPEAK FOR YOUR-SELF.

I SAID, WE DON'T WANT THAT!

LOOK, JUST BECAUSE **YOU** HAVE "ISSUES"...

I'VE LET MY ROOM GET EXTRA MESSY ON PURPOSE.

November 19, 1999

OK, I THINK I'VE GOT EVERYTHING I NEED FOR THANKSGIVING.

TURKEY... STUFFING... CRAN-BERRIES... POTATOES... BABY ONIONS... GREEN BEANS... SWEET POTATOES... PIE FILLING... NOTHING TO DO NOW BUT WAIT FOR MY MOTHER TO ARRIVE.

ANTACIDS! ANTACIDS! I KNEW I FORGOT SOMETHING!

November 20, 1999

November 22, 1999

November 23, 1999

Drawing this one was easier than usual.

64

November 24, 1999

I'VE RUINED THANKSGIVING DINNER.

WHAT HAP-PENED?

I TRIED TOO HARD. I TRIED TO COOK TOO MANY THINGS WITH ALL SORTS OF FANCY RECIPES AND ENDED UP BURNING IT ALL. ALL BECAUSE I WANTED TO PROVE I'M EQUAL TO MY MOTHER.

NOW WHAT'S SHE GOING TO THINK OF ME?!

THAT YOU'RE A CHIP OFF THE OL' BLOCK?

HUH? WHAT DO YOU MEAN?

SPEAKING OF CHIPS, PETER WANTS TO KNOW IF HE CAN HAVE DORITOS FOR DINNER.

November 25, 1999

ANDREA, I WENT THROUGH THIS SAME THING WITH MY MOTHER.

I ALWAYS FELT A NEED TO PROVE I COULD DO THINGS AS WELL AS SHE, AND USUALLY ALL THAT WOULD HAPPEN IS I WOULD MAKE A ROYAL MESS OF IT ALL. SOMETHING ABOUT TRYING TOO HARD.

HOW COULD YOU GOOF SOMETHING UP? YOU'RE PERFECT!

BUT DON'T YOU SEE? YOU ONLY THINK THAT BECAUSE YOU'RE MY DAUGHTER.

NO, I'M QUOTING THAT NEW YORK TIMES STORY ABOUT YOU.

OK, BUT IT'S ALSO A DAUGHTER'S PERSPECTIVE.

WAY TO NOT BOTCH ANY DINNER, MOM. I KNOW.

November 26, 1999

WELL, I FOR ONE WOULD LIKE TO RAISE A GLASS IN THANKSGIVING.

FOR FAMILY.

FOR UNDERSTANDING.

FOR FIRE EXTINGUISHERS.

FOR PIZZA DELIVERY.

THINK SANTA'D PAY MONEY FOR THESE BIG CHUNKS OF COAL?

November 27, 1999

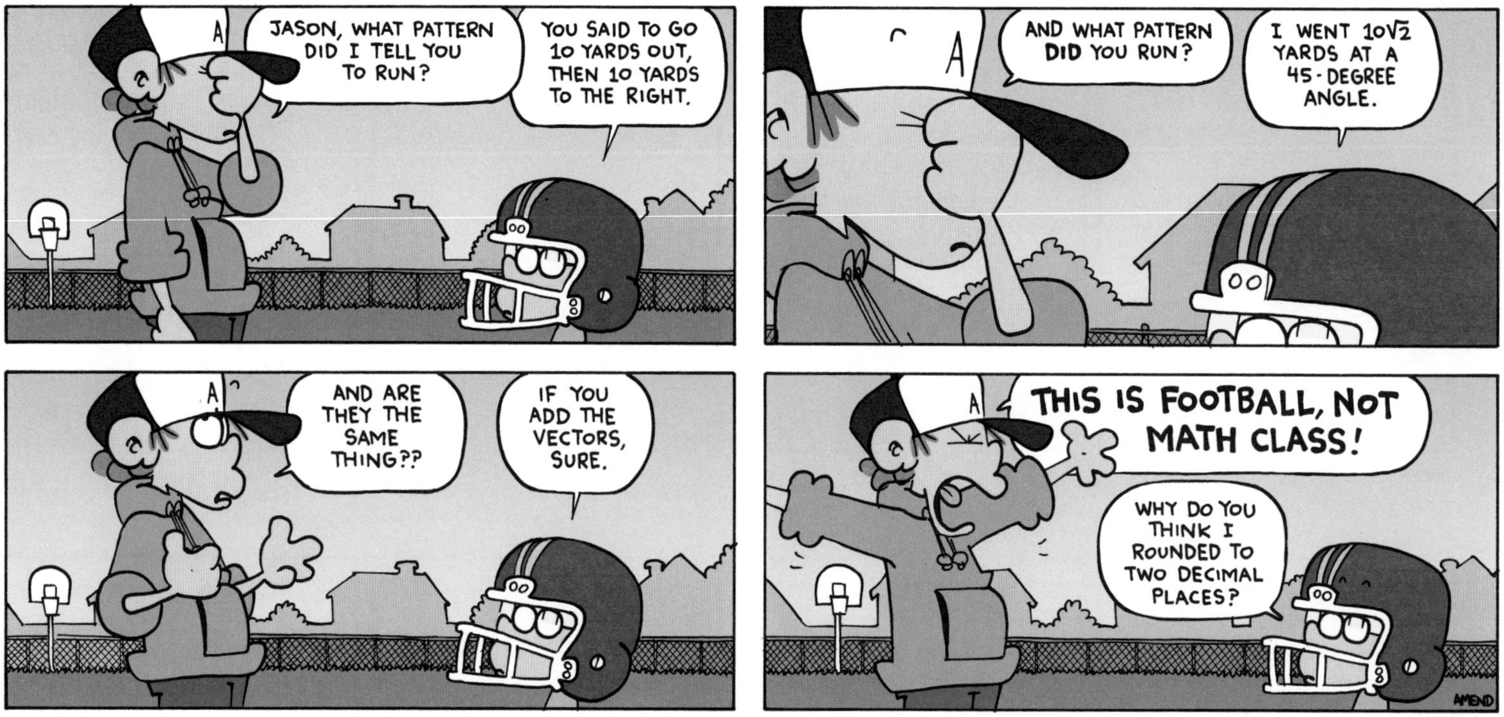
JASON, WHAT PATTERN DID I TELL YOU TO RUN?
YOU SAID TO GO 10 YARDS OUT, THEN 10 YARDS TO THE RIGHT.
AND WHAT PATTERN DID YOU RUN?
I WENT $10\sqrt{2}$ YARDS AT A 45-DEGREE ANGLE.
AND ARE THEY THE SAME THING??
IF YOU ADD THE VECTORS, SURE.
THIS IS FOOTBALL, NOT MATH CLASS!
WHY DO YOU THINK I ROUNDED TO TWO DECIMAL PLACES?
AMEND

November 14, 1999

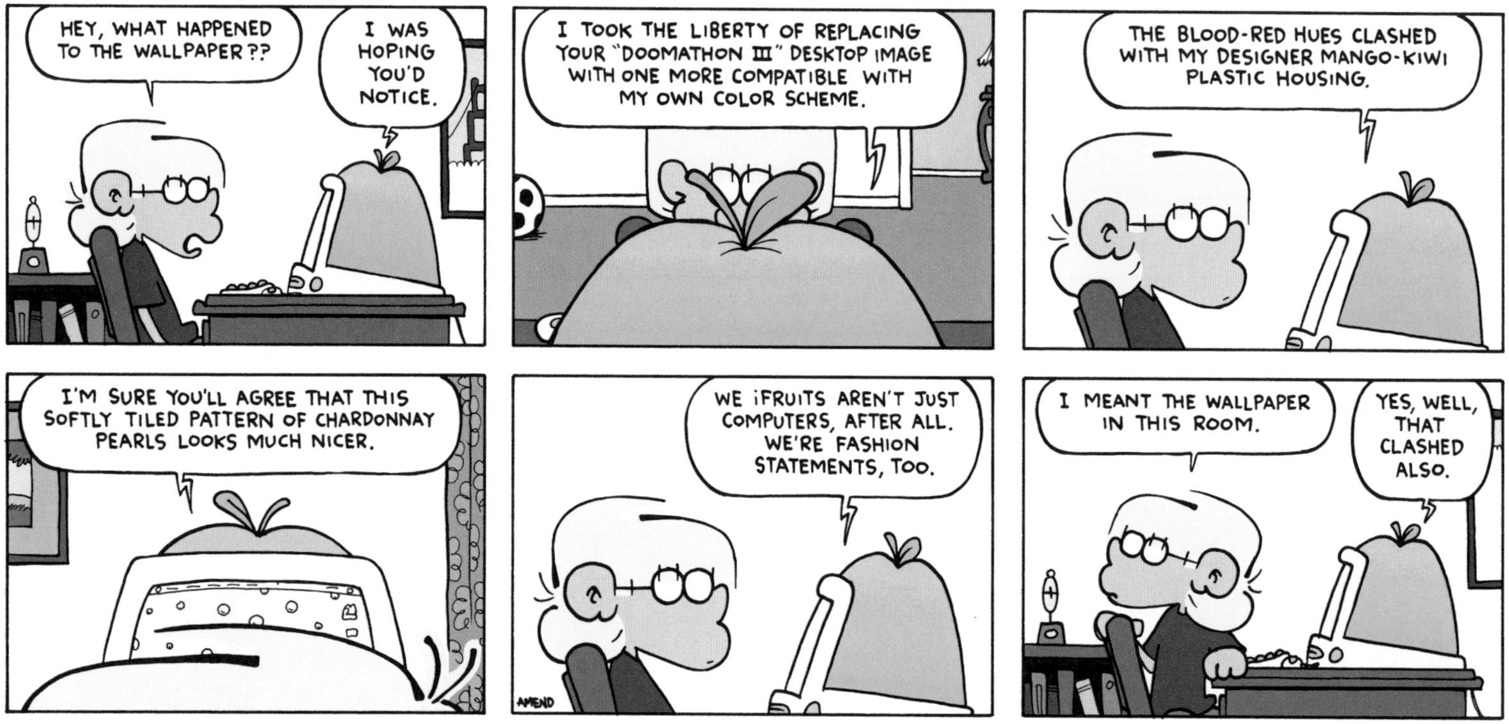
HEY, WHAT HAPPENED TO THE WALLPAPER??
I WAS HOPING YOU'D NOTICE.
I TOOK THE LIBERTY OF REPLACING YOUR "DOOMATHON III" DESKTOP IMAGE WITH ONE MORE COMPATIBLE WITH MY OWN COLOR SCHEME.
THE BLOOD-RED HUES CLASHED WITH MY DESIGNER MANGO-KIWI PLASTIC HOUSING.
I'M SURE YOU'LL AGREE THAT THIS SOFTLY TILED PATTERN OF CHARDONNAY PEARLS LOOKS MUCH NICER.
WE iFRUITS AREN'T JUST COMPUTERS, AFTER ALL. WE'RE FASHION STATEMENTS, TOO.
I MEANT THE WALLPAPER IN THIS ROOM.
YES, WELL, THAT CLASHED ALSO.
AMEND

January, 30, 2000

December 4, 1999

December 6, 1999

A few readers didn't get this one. Jason's loading up for a big burp.

December 7, 1999

I had so much fun with the Scrooge strips, I tried spoofing another Christmas classic the following year.

WHAT ARE YOU DOING?

WRITING A TV SCRIPT.

IT OCCURS TO ME THAT MOST OF THE HOLIDAY SPECIALS WE WATCH EVERY YEAR ARE OVER 30 YEARS OLD. I THOUGHT IT MIGHT BE A GOOD TIME TO SUBMIT A NEW IDEA TO THE NETWORKS.

SO YOU'VE COME UP WITH ONE?

WELL, I HAD A LITTLE HELP FROM MOM.

"THE MRS. GRINCH WHO WAS TOO CHEAP FOR CHRISTMAS."

JASON, YOUR WISH LIST WAS 800 PAGES!

THINK I DREW HER FACE GROUCHY ENOUGH?

December 13, 1999

Trying to draw like Dr. Seuss and Chuck Jones was the hardest part.

Every kid down in Kidville liked Christmas a lot.

But Mrs. Grinch, who looked down on Kidville, did NOT.

Mrs. Grinch HATED Christmas! The gifts and the presents!

She wanted those kids to live like poor PEASANTS!

A $5,000 computer?!? Are you mad?!?

Cheap-skate.

December 14, 1999

How she hated the spending!

No, you can't have a new stereo!

How she hated it all!

No, you can't have a leather coat!

Mrs. Grinch hated ANYTHING that came from a mall!

No, you can't have 500 cases of Pokémon cards!

Could it be that her wallet was two sizes too small?

Hey! Get out of there!

Maybe if you cleaned out all of these old "Titanic" ticket stubs...

December 15, 1999

68

How did the woman get so tight-fisted?

This gift list is too long!

Her concept of Christmas so thoroughly twisted?

How can you kids be so materialistic?!

In Kidville it's thought, in Kidville they say...

Buy me this! Buy me that!

...that Mrs. Grinch must have just been born this way.

I don't want a toy. I want world peace.

Freak.

visit Santa

December 16, 1999

Thought mean Mrs. Grinch, from her Mrs. Grinch lair...

...(where she looked down on Kidville with an icy Grinch stare):

"Soon will be Christmas, and we know what THAT means..."

"Ham! Turkey! Roast Beast! NOTHING made of soybeans!"

It's appall-ing!

December 17, 1999

Then Mrs. Grinch got an idea.

An AWFUL idea!

Mrs. Grinch got a HORRIBLE, AWFUL idea!

But did she listen to us? Noooo.

It's a good idea. Be quiet.

December 18, 1999

"I know JUST what to do!" Mrs. Grinch laughed to herself...

...as she grabbed her Grinch keychain from off of her shelf.

And while Kidville was sleeping, Mrs. Grinch did speed...

...to buy cheap WHOLE-SOME presents! What a wretched Grinch deed!

Give me all your flash cards!

December 20, 1999

She replaced the kids' toys with tofu and tomes!

Video games scrapped for old books of old poems!

EMILY DICKINSON

BLOOD ARENA 3

Mrs. Grinch took the Jet Skis! The rockets! The cars!

In their stead she left packets of granola fruit bars!

I'm so good to them!

December 21, 1999

Just at that moment a little kid boy, saw Mrs. Grinch swap practical clothes for his toy.

Um...

Jason Fox

"Why, Santy Claus, why?" asked the sweet little tyke. "Why are you trading these socks for my bike?"

"My dear little lad," the mean Mrs. Grinch lied, "these socks are much better than some bike you can ride."

"These socks are unbleached! This wool is undyed! The yarn in these socks was organically farmed with pride!"

Oh joy.

December 22, 1999

70

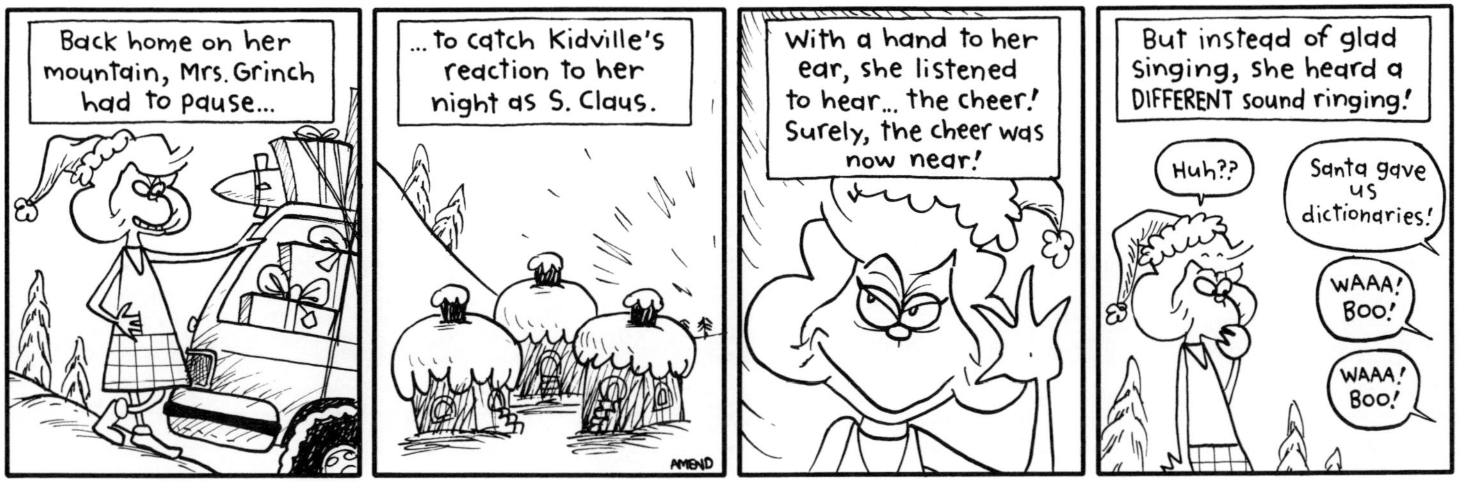
Back home on her mountain, Mrs. Grinch had to pause...
... to catch Kidville's reaction to her night as S. Claus.
With a hand to her ear, she listened to hear... the cheer! Surely, the cheer was now near!
But instead of glad singing, she heard a DIFFERENT sound ringing!
Huh??
Santa gave us dictionaries!
WAAA! Boo!
WAAA! Boo!
AMEND
December 23, 1999

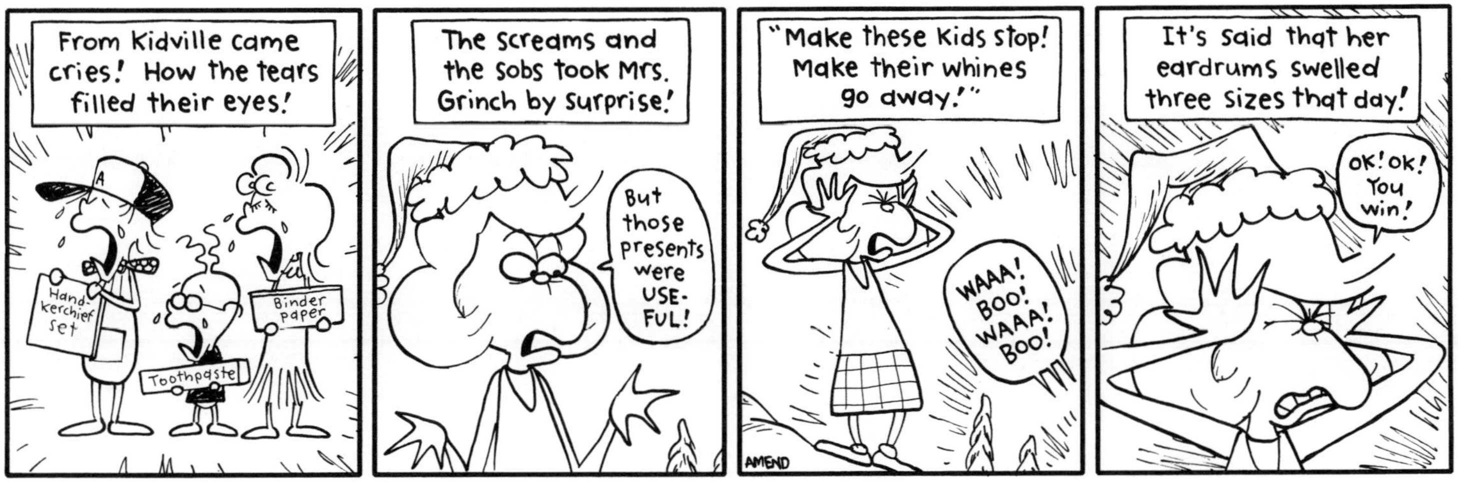
From Kidville came cries! How the tears filled their eyes!
Hand-kerchief set
Toothpaste
Binder paper
The screams and the sobs took Mrs. Grinch by surprise!
But those presents were USE-FUL!
"Make these kids stop! Make their whines go away!"
WAAA! BOO! WAAA! BOO!
AMEND
It's said that her eardrums swelled three sizes that day!
OK! OK! You win!
December 24, 1999

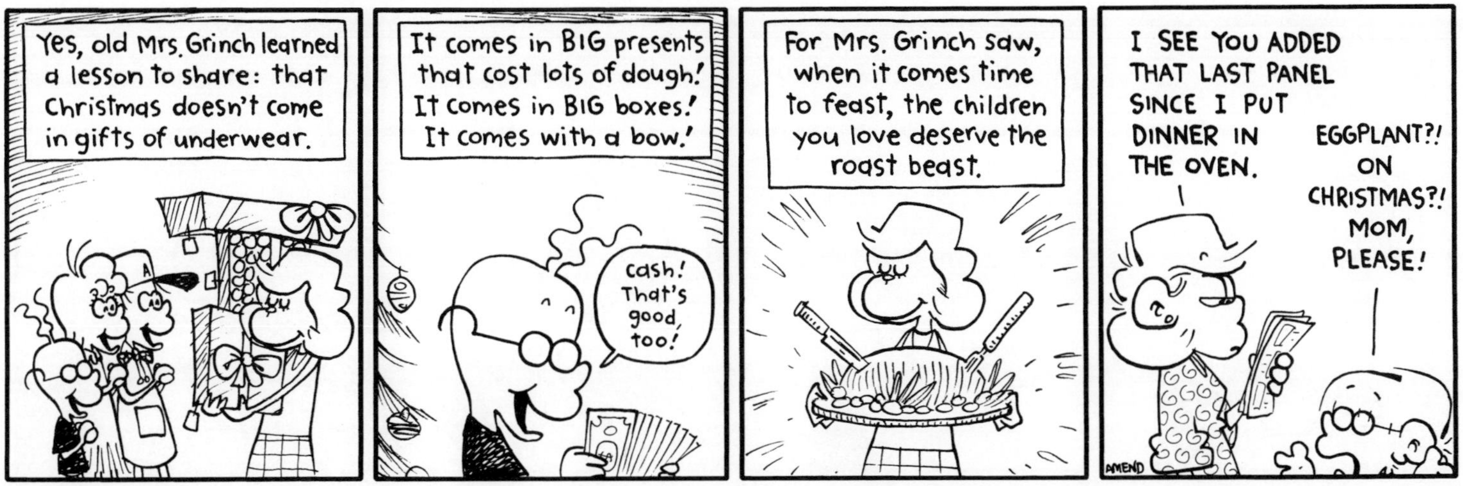
Yes, old Mrs. Grinch learned a lesson to share: that Christmas doesn't come in gifts of underwear.
It comes in BIG presents that cost lots of dough! It comes in BIG boxes! It comes with a bow!
Cash! That's good, too!
For Mrs. Grinch saw, when it comes time to feast, the children you love deserve the roast beast.
I SEE YOU ADDED THAT LAST PANEL SINCE I PUT DINNER IN THE OVEN.
EGGPLANT?! ON CHRISTMAS?! MOM, PLEASE!
AMEND
December 25, 1999

December 30, 1999

This circa 1900 FoxTrot style is kinda intriguing. I should fiddle with time more someday.

December 31, 1999

72

January 27, 2000

February 13, 2000

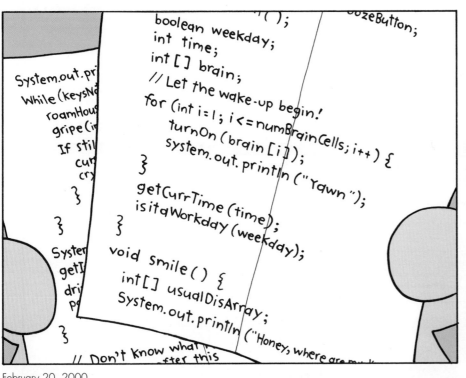

February 20, 2000

One of the creators of the Java language complimented me on this strip. That felt nice, especially since I don't know Java and had to fake it.

January 3, 2000

January 4, 2000

January 19, 2000

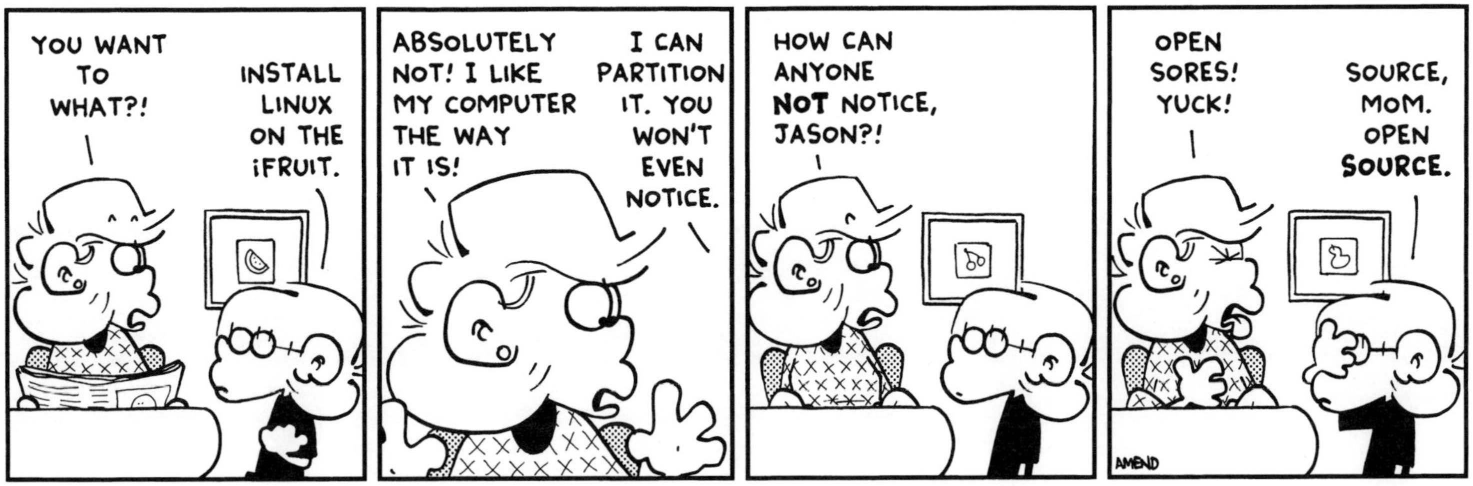
YOU WANT TO WHAT?!
INSTALL LINUX ON THE iFRUIT.
ABSOLUTELY NOT! I LIKE MY COMPUTER THE WAY IT IS!
I CAN PARTITION IT. YOU WON'T EVEN NOTICE.
HOW CAN ANYONE **NOT** NOTICE, JASON?!
OPEN SORES! YUCK!
SOURCE, MOM. OPEN **SOURCE**.
AMEND

February 7, 2000

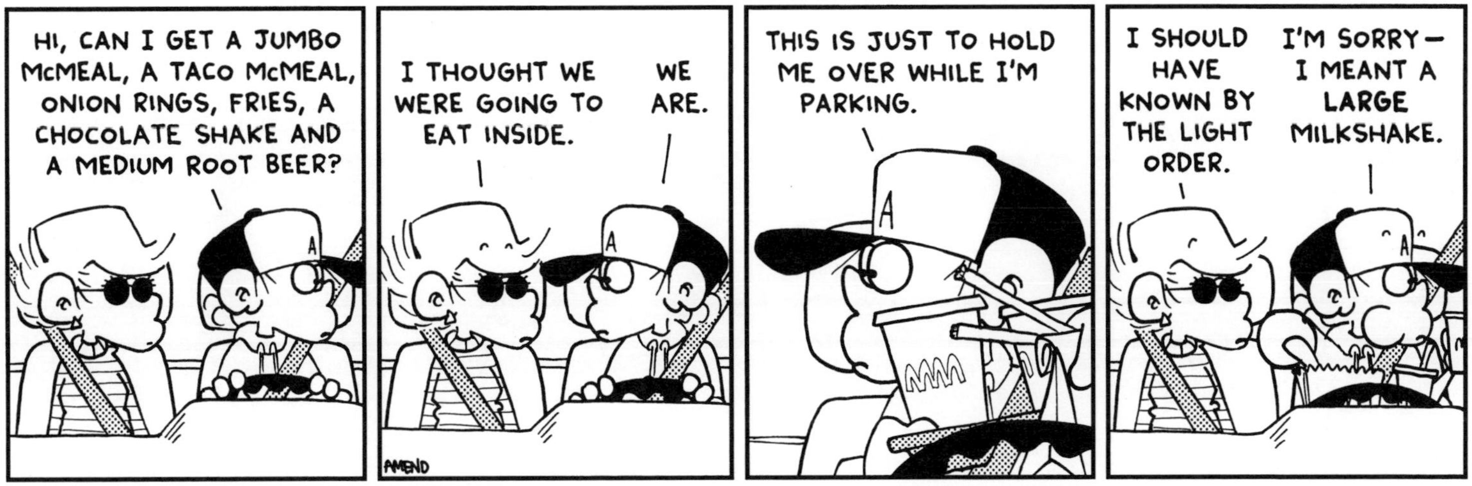
HI, CAN I GET A JUMBO McMEAL, A TACO McMEAL, ONION RINGS, FRIES, A CHOCOLATE SHAKE AND A MEDIUM ROOT BEER?
I THOUGHT WE WERE GOING TO EAT INSIDE.
WE ARE.
AMEND
THIS IS JUST TO HOLD ME OVER WHILE I'M PARKING.
I SHOULD HAVE KNOWN BY THE LIGHT ORDER.
I'M SORRY— I MEANT A **LARGE** MILKSHAKE.

March 8, 2000

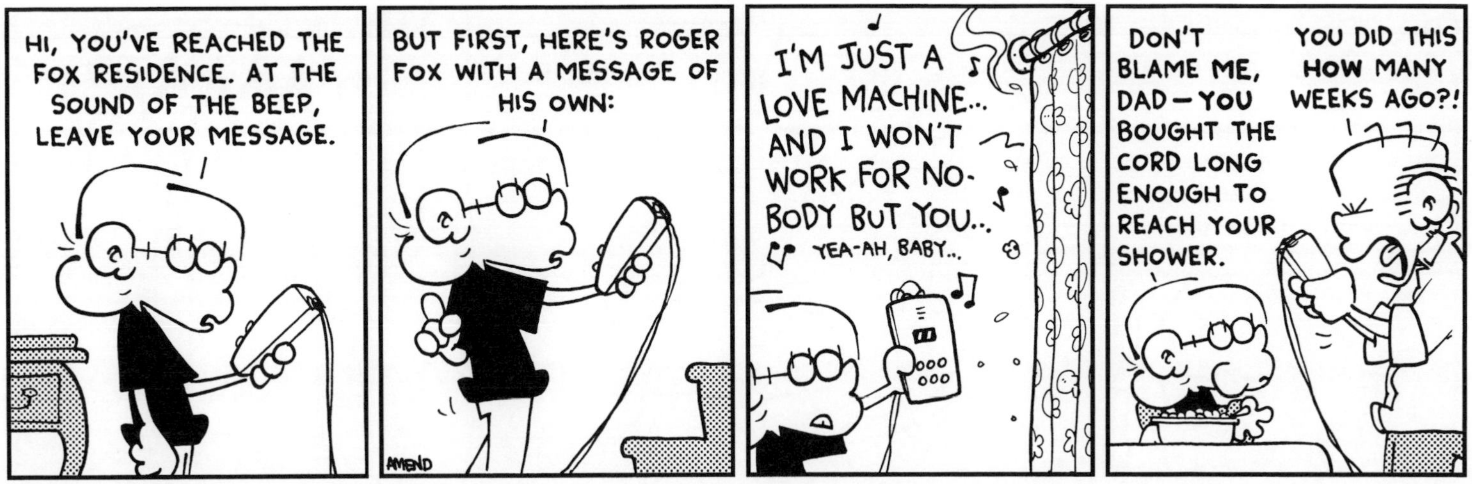
HI, YOU'VE REACHED THE FOX RESIDENCE. AT THE SOUND OF THE BEEP, LEAVE YOUR MESSAGE.
BUT FIRST, HERE'S ROGER FOX WITH A MESSAGE OF HIS OWN:
AMEND
I'M JUST A LOVE MACHINE... AND I WON'T WORK FOR NO-BODY BUT YOU...
YEA-AH, BABY...
DON'T BLAME ME, DAD—**YOU** BOUGHT THE CORD LONG ENOUGH TO REACH YOUR SHOWER.
YOU DID THIS **HOW MANY** WEEKS AGO?!

March 21, 2000

February 14, 2000

February 15, 2000

A rare FoxTrot cliffhanger.

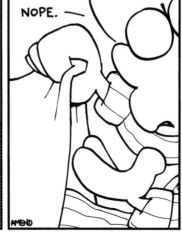

76

February 16, 2000

February 17, 2000

February 18, 2000

February 19, 2000

February 21, 2000

February 22, 2000

February 23, 2000

February 24, 2000

February 25, 2000

February 26, 2000

79

I have nothing against the Backstreet Boys. It's all Jason. Really.

March 25, 2000

At least one prominent newspaper wouldn't run this one.

March 27, 2000

80

April 7, 2000

I HAD THE MOST WONDERFUL DREAM LAST NIGHT.

ME TOO.

April 2, 2000

WHATCHA DOING?

STUDYING FOR EXAMS.

WHAT?? DID I JUST HEAR JASON FOX USE THE "S" WORD??

WHAT'S HAPPENED TO MY LITTLE GENIUS BROTHER?! COULD IT BE THAT THE KING OF NERDS IS NOT SO KINGLY AFTER ALL?! THAT HE HAS TO LOWER HIMSELF AND STUDY LIKE THE REST OF US FOR A CHANGE?!

AS WE MORTALS LIKE TO SAY: HA HA HA!

"ADVANCED READINGS IN GAUGE FIELD THEORY."

I'M STUDYING FOR GRAD SCHOOL FINALS. I DON'T WANT TO HAVE TO CRAM WHEN I'M THERE.

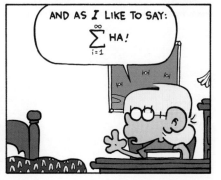

AND AS I LIKE TO SAY:
$$\sum_{i=1}^{\infty} \text{HA}!$$

I think I spent more time trying to come up with a good nerdy book title than I did writing and drawing the strip.

May 21, 2000

81

JASON! STOP! LET SOMEONE ELSE CLEAR THE TABLE!

YET ONE MORE CHORE MOM'LL NEVER ASK ME TO DO AGAIN.

OBVIOUSLY, YOU ONLY LOOK LIKE YOU DON'T KNOW WHAT YOU'RE DOING.

April 10, 2000

I CAN'T REMEMBER THE LAST TIME WE PLAYED CHESS TOGETHER, PAIGE.

I'LL LET YOU CHOOSE— RED OR BLACK?

WELL, LET'S SEE...

THIS RED CLASHES WITH MY SWEATER, SO I'LL TAKE BLACK.

SUDDENLY THE MEMORIES RUSH BACK.

ICK. DO THESE BOARDS ALL HAVE TO COME IN PLAID?

April 11, 2000

LET'S SEE... SHOULD I GET THE HIGH-FAT MILK, OR THE LOW-FAT?...

THE HIGH-FAT.

SHOULD I GET THE EXTRA-THICK BACON, OR THE REGULAR?...

THE EXTRA-THICK.

SHOULD I GET THE LOW-CAL FROZEN PIZZA, OR THE FOUR-CHEESE, ALL-MEAT, HUNGRY-DUDE EDITION?...

DAD, YOU HAVE TO ASK??

YOU'RE A LOT MORE FUN TO SHOP WITH THAN YOUR MOTHER.

YOU'RE ONLY BUYING THREE?

May 3, 2000

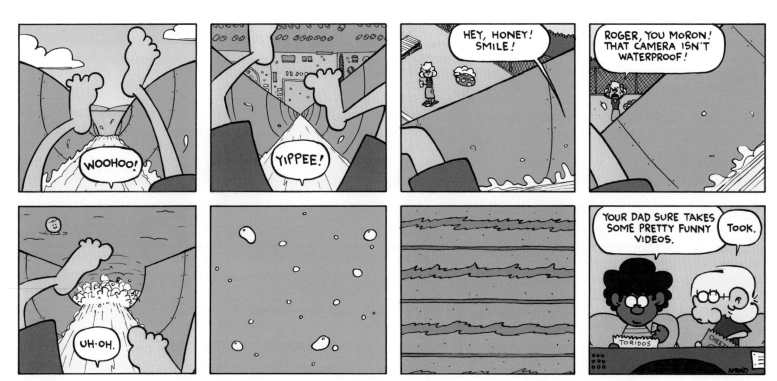

July 9, 2000

July 30, 2000

The equations are all related to the physics of what Jason is doing in each panel.

I did these back when Peter Jackson was still a relative unknown, so I didn't have a lot of photos to work from. I think I did an okay caricature, considering.

JASON TELLS ME THERE'S A BIG "LORD OF THE RINGS" MOVIE TRILOGY IN THE WORKS.

WOW. HE MUST BE ECSTATIC.

ACTUALLY, HE'S PRETTY DEPRESSED.

THAT THEY WON'T BE AS GOOD AS THE BOOKS?

THAT HE AND MARCUS MISSED THE CASTING CALL.

GOOD LORD. CAN YOU IMAGINE?

WILL THE TWO HOBBITS PLEASE CLIMB OUT OF THE BALROG COSTUME?!

April 17, 2000

I NEED FRODO AND SAMWISE ON THE SET, PLEASE.

FRODO AND SAM? I NEED YOU ON THE SET, PLEASE.

NOW!

YOU KNOW, YOU MIGHT HAVE TOLD US THAT ROOT BEER STAINS MITHRIL.

April 18, 2000

I liked that these strips gave me an excuse to skim through the books looking for ideas.

ACTION! I HAD A FUNNY DREAM AN HOUR OR TWO BEFORE WE STOPPED, MR. FRODO. OR MAYBE IT WASN'T A DREAM. FUNNY IT WAS ANYWAY.

WELL, WHAT WAS IT? I HAVEN'T SEEN OR THOUGHT OF ANYTHING TO MAKE ME SMILE SINCE WE LEFT LOTHLORIEN.

CUT! WHAT ARE YOU TWO DOING?! THOSE LINES AREN'T IN THE SCRIPT!

THEY'RE IN THE BOOK.

WE HAVE IT MEMORIZED.

SOMEBODY GET ME CASTING ON THE PHONE.

COULDN'T YOU THANK THEM LATER?

THIS ROPE SHOULD BE MADE OF ELVEN HITHLAIN, BY THE WAY.

April 19, 2000

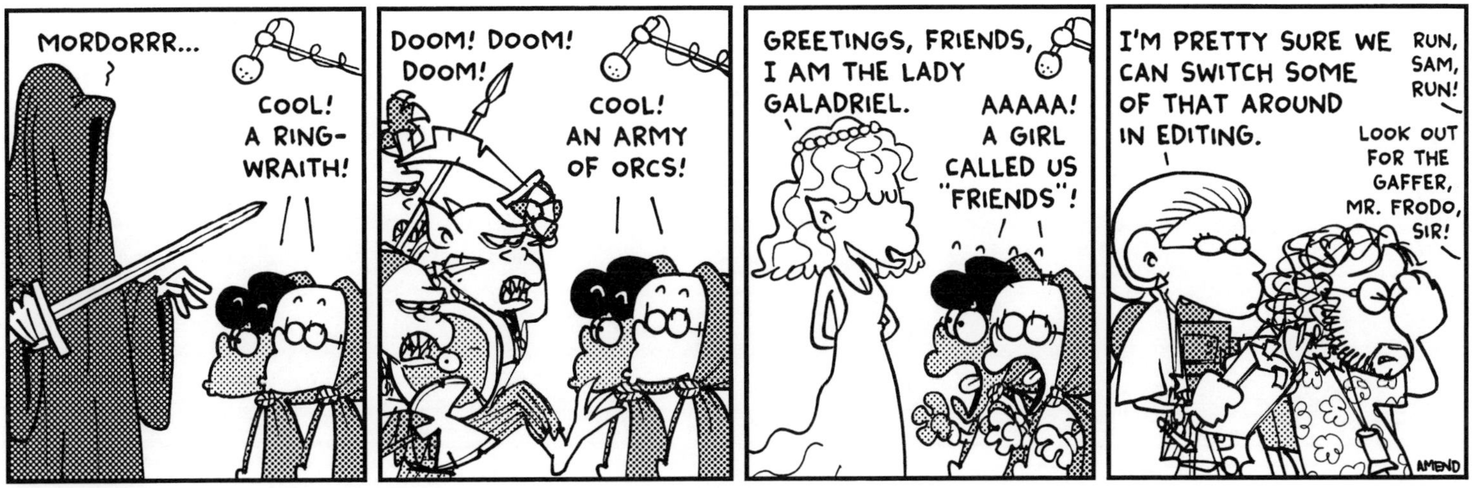
MORDORRR...
COOL! A RING-WRAITH!
DOOM! DOOM! DOOM!
COOL! AN ARMY OF ORCS!
GREETINGS, FRIENDS, I AM THE LADY GALADRIEL.
AAAAA! A GIRL CALLED US "FRIENDS"!
I'M PRETTY SURE WE CAN SWITCH SOME OF THAT AROUND IN EDITING.
RUN, SAM, RUN!
LOOK OUT FOR THE GAFFER, MR. FRODO, SIR!
AMEND

April 20, 2000

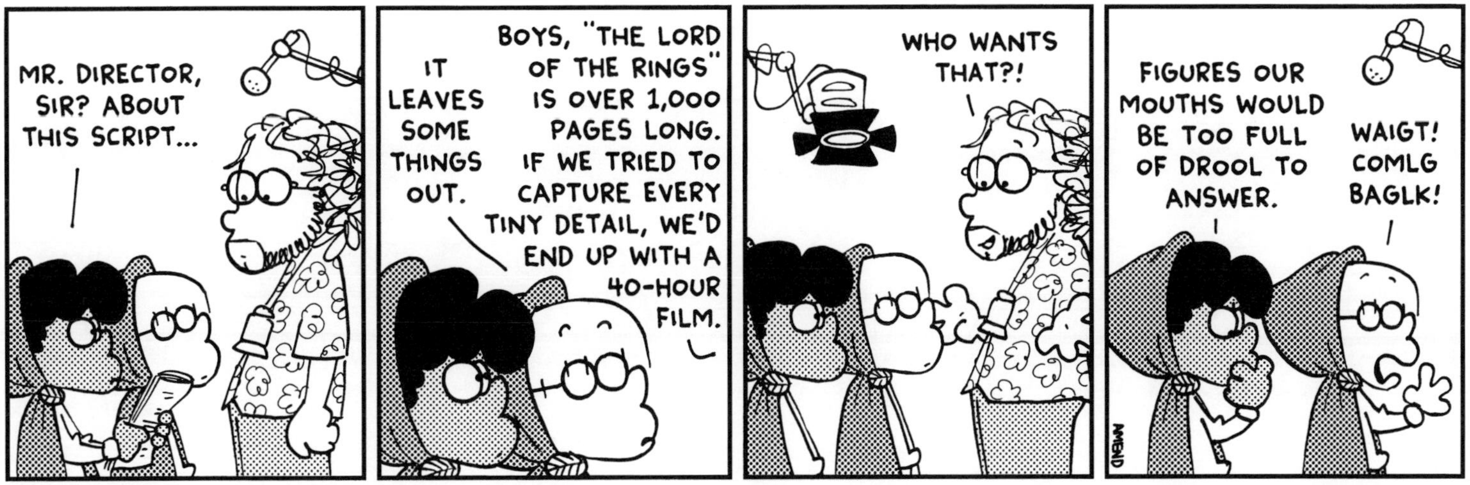
MR. DIRECTOR, SIR? ABOUT THIS SCRIPT...
IT LEAVES SOME THINGS OUT.
BOYS, "THE LORD OF THE RINGS" IS OVER 1,000 PAGES LONG. IF WE TRIED TO CAPTURE EVERY TINY DETAIL, WE'D END UP WITH A 40-HOUR FILM.
WHO WANTS THAT?!
AMEND
FIGURES OUR MOUTHS WOULD BE TOO FULL OF DROOL TO ANSWER.
WAIGT! COMLG BAGLK!

April 21, 2000

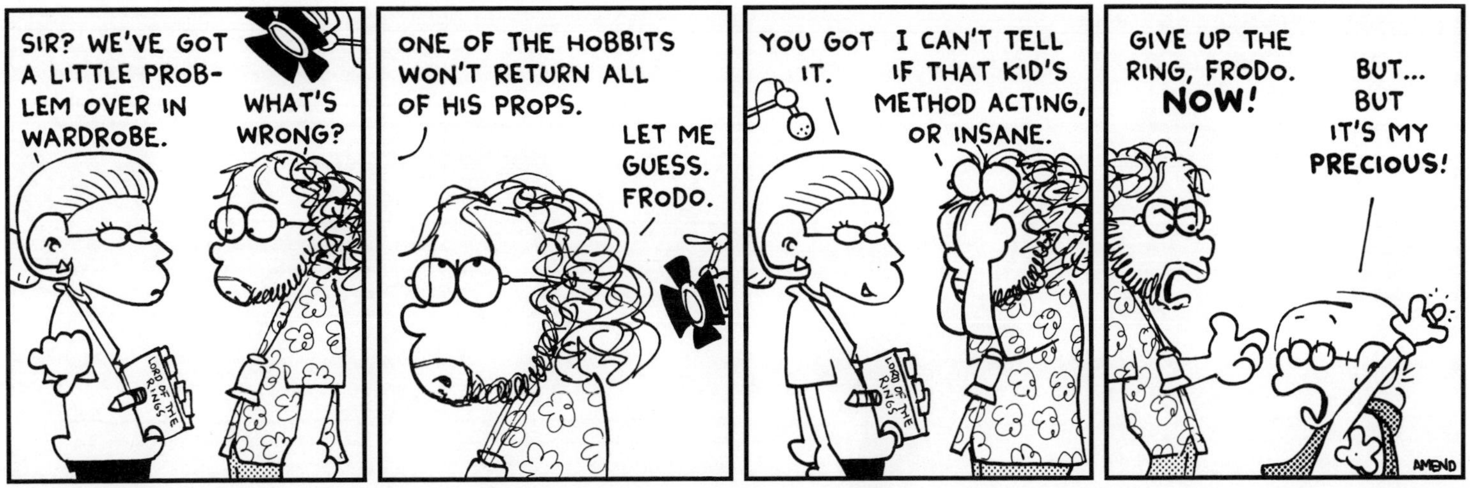
SIR? WE'VE GOT A LITTLE PROB-LEM OVER IN WARDROBE.
WHAT'S WRONG?
LORD OF THE RINGS
ONE OF THE HOBBITS WON'T RETURN ALL OF HIS PROPS.
LET ME GUESS. FRODO.
YOU GOT IT.
I CAN'T TELL IF THAT KID'S METHOD ACTING, OR INSANE.
LORD OF THE RINGS
GIVE UP THE RING, FRODO. **NOW!**
BUT... BUT IT'S MY **PRECIOUS!**
AMEND

April 22, 2000

THERE WE GO.

YOU CUT SUCH A SMALL SLICE OF PIZZA, PETER. ARE YOU FEELING OK?   SURE.

WHY DO YOU ASK?   NEVER MIND.

May 10, 2000

GOOD LORD. ALL BUT SEVEN COMIC STRIPS TODAY HAVE JOKES ABOUT GOLF.

WHAT ARE THESE CAR-TOONISTS THINKING?! WHAT KIND OF GROUP MIND-ROT IS AT WORK HERE?!

ROGER, TAKE A LOOK AT THIS— IS IT APPALLING OR WHAT?!

NO KIDDING! SEVEN STRIPS DON'T EVEN MENTION GOLF!   I GIVE UP.   I LOVED MARY WORTH'S LINE ABOUT SAND TRAPS.

May 18, 2000

I LIKE TO BALANCE LIKE THIS AND IMAGINE THERE'S A POOL OF LAVA BELOW.

OR A PIT OF SNAKES AND DEADLY ALLIGATORS.

OR A...   HI GUYS!

OK, NOW I'M REALLY SCARED TO FALL.   DOES LAVA BURN OFF COOTIES?

May 19, 2000

86

May 25, 2000

May 27, 2000

Several months after Sparky Schulz passed away, there was an effort to get cartoonists to do tribute strips to run on the same day. This was mine.

June 1, 2000

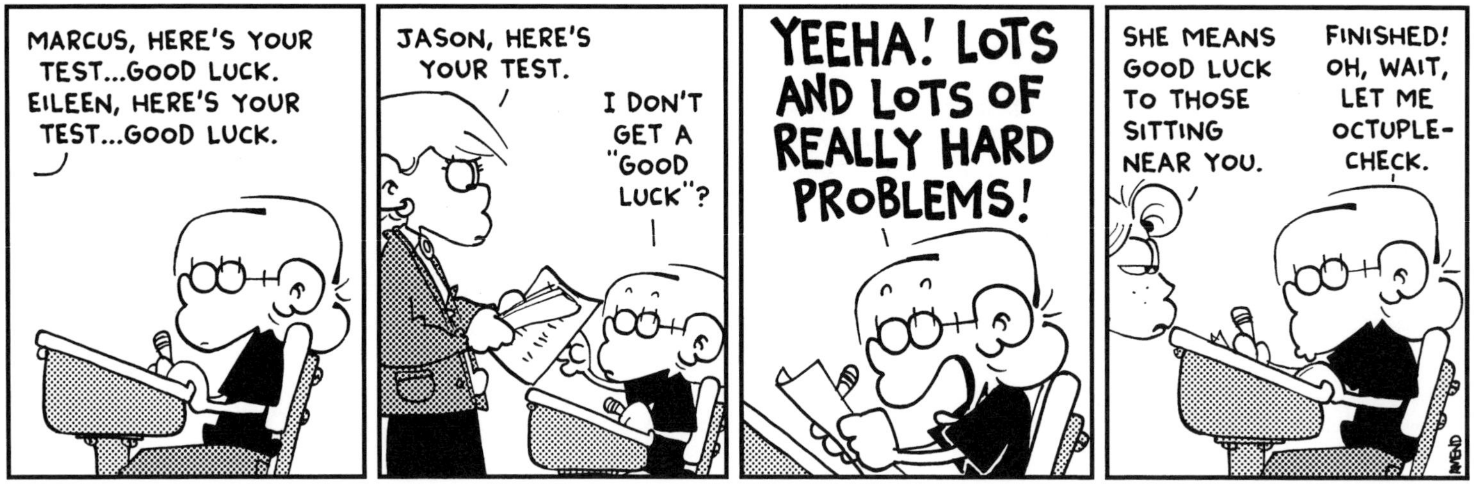
MARCUS, HERE'S YOUR TEST...GOOD LUCK. EILEEN, HERE'S YOUR TEST...GOOD LUCK.
JASON, HERE'S YOUR TEST.
I DON'T GET A "GOOD LUCK"?
YEEHA! LOTS AND LOTS OF REALLY HARD PROBLEMS!
SHE MEANS GOOD LUCK TO THOSE SITTING NEAR YOU.
FINISHED! OH, WAIT, LET ME OCTUPLE-CHECK.
AMEND
June 2, 2000

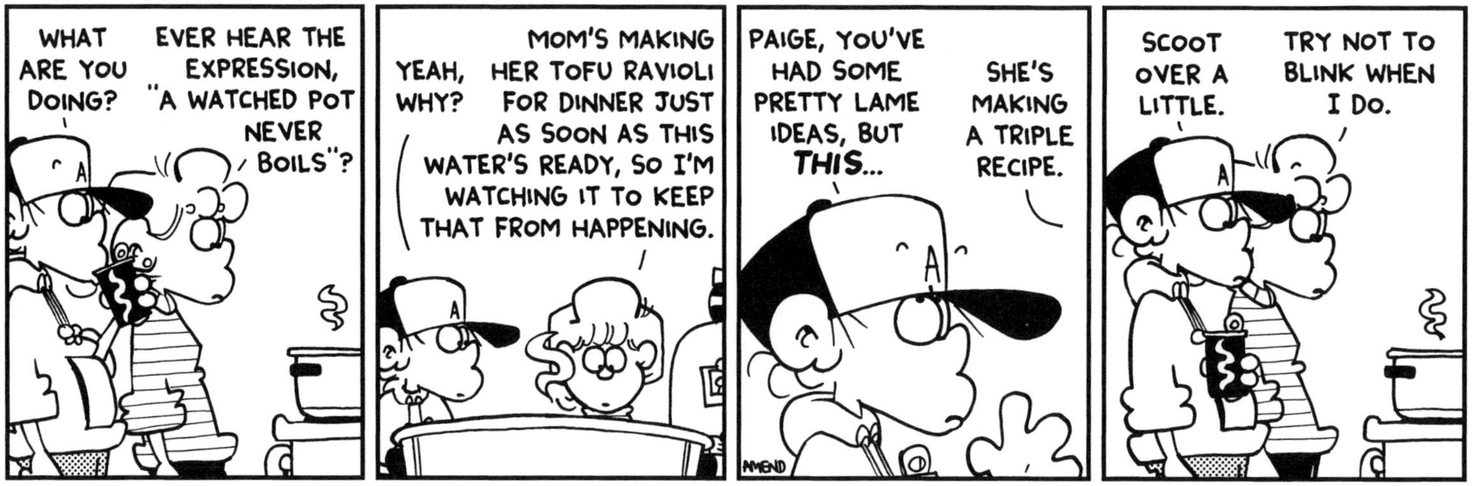
WHAT ARE YOU DOING?
EVER HEAR THE EXPRESSION, "A WATCHED POT NEVER BOILS"?
YEAH, WHY?
MOM'S MAKING HER TOFU RAVIOLI FOR DINNER JUST AS SOON AS THIS WATER'S READY, SO I'M WATCHING IT TO KEEP THAT FROM HAPPENING.
PAIGE, YOU'VE HAD SOME PRETTY LAME IDEAS, BUT THIS...
SHE'S MAKING A TRIPLE RECIPE.
SCOOT OVER A LITTLE.
TRY NOT TO BLINK WHEN I DO.
AMEND
August 29, 2000

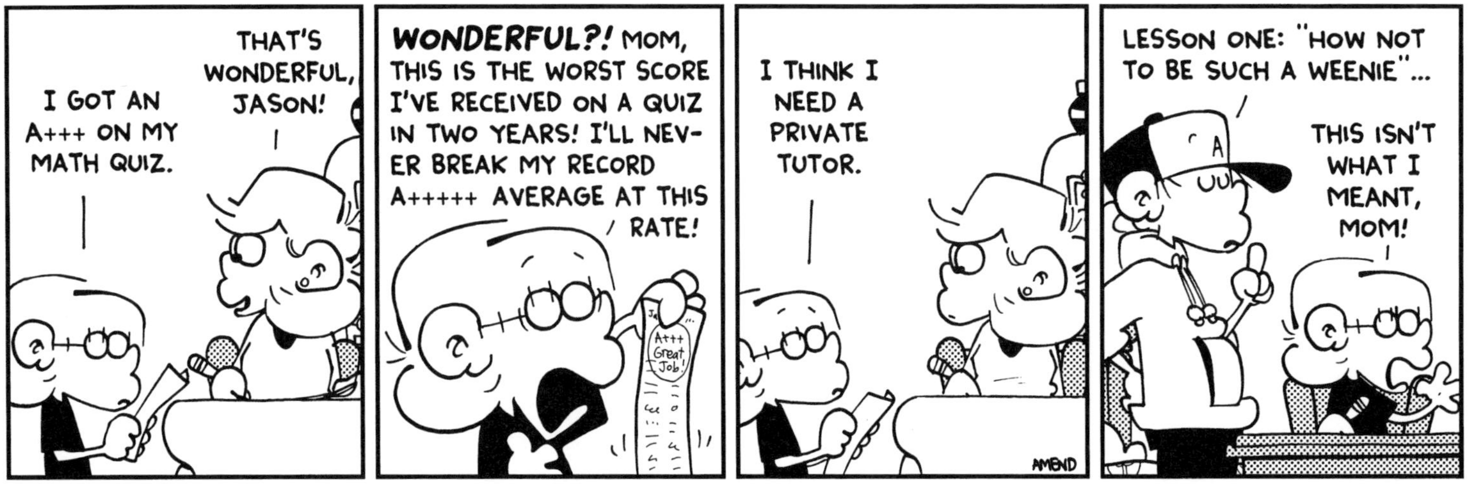
I GOT AN A+++ ON MY MATH QUIZ.
THAT'S WONDERFUL, JASON!
WONDERFUL?! MOM, THIS IS THE WORST SCORE I'VE RECEIVED ON A QUIZ IN TWO YEARS! I'LL NEVER BREAK MY RECORD A+++++ AVERAGE AT THIS RATE!
A+++ Great Job!
I THINK I NEED A PRIVATE TUTOR.
AMEND
LESSON ONE: "HOW NOT TO BE SUCH A WEENIE"...
THIS ISN'T WHAT I MEANT, MOM!
September 18, 2000

August 6, 2000

October 22, 2000

I like how this strip works as both a joke and a little puzzle.

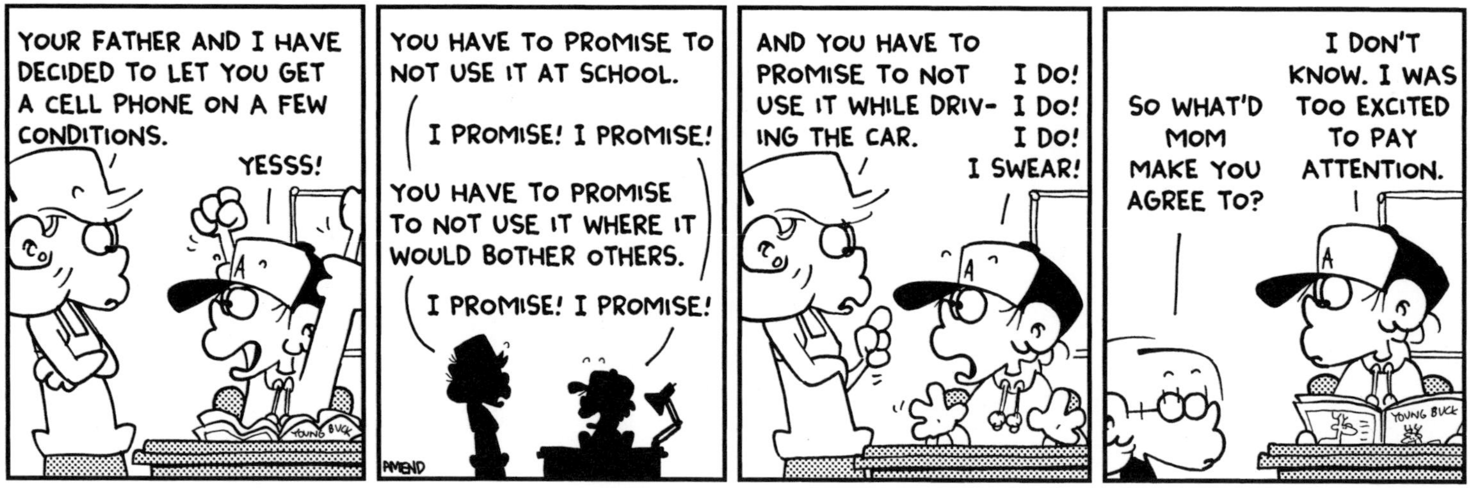
YOUR FATHER AND I HAVE DECIDED TO LET YOU GET A CELL PHONE ON A FEW CONDITIONS.
YESSS!
YOU HAVE TO PROMISE TO NOT USE IT AT SCHOOL.
I PROMISE! I PROMISE!
YOU HAVE TO PROMISE TO NOT USE IT WHERE IT WOULD BOTHER OTHERS.
I PROMISE! I PROMISE!
AMEND
AND YOU HAVE TO PROMISE TO NOT USE IT WHILE DRIVING THE CAR.
I DO! I DO! I DO! I SWEAR!
SO WHAT'D MOM MAKE YOU AGREE TO?
I DON'T KNOW. I WAS TOO EXCITED TO PAY ATTENTION.
YOUNG BUCK

August 9, 2000

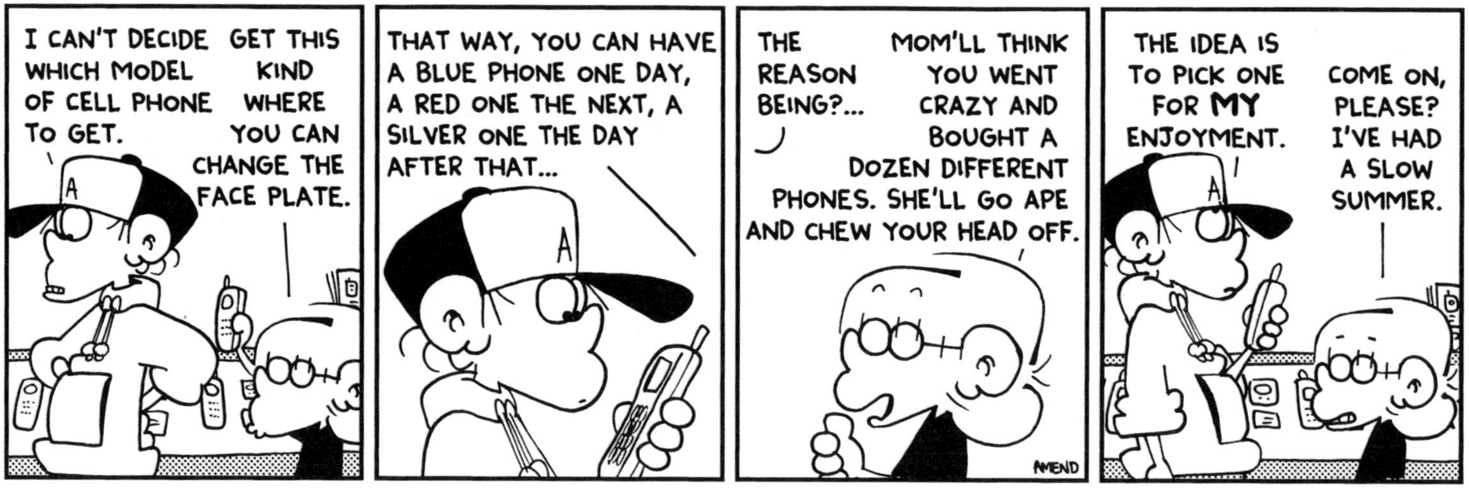
I CAN'T DECIDE WHICH MODEL OF CELL PHONE TO GET.
GET THIS KIND WHERE YOU CAN CHANGE THE FACE PLATE.
THAT WAY, YOU CAN HAVE A BLUE PHONE ONE DAY, A RED ONE THE NEXT, A SILVER ONE THE DAY AFTER THAT...
THE REASON BEING?...
MOM'LL THINK YOU WENT CRAZY AND BOUGHT A DOZEN DIFFERENT PHONES. SHE'LL GO APE AND CHEW YOUR HEAD OFF.
AMEND
THE IDEA IS TO PICK ONE FOR MY ENJOYMENT.
COME ON, PLEASE? I'VE HAD A SLOW SUMMER.

August 10, 2000

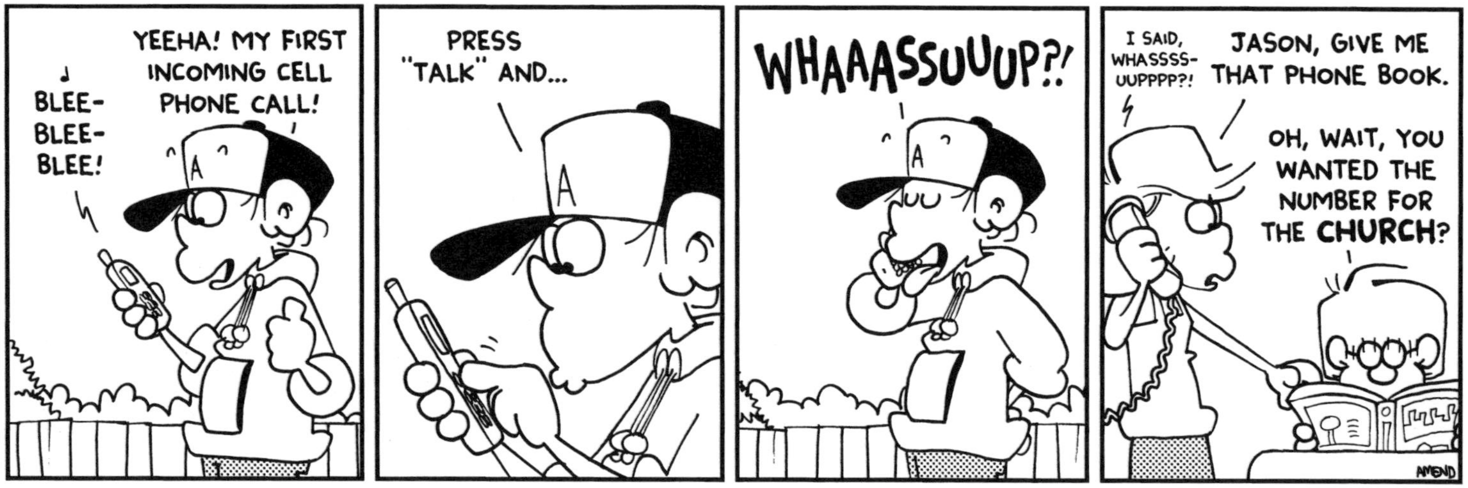
BLEE-BLEE-BLEE!
YEEHA! MY FIRST INCOMING CELL PHONE CALL!
PRESS "TALK" AND...
WHAAASSUUUP?!
I SAID, WHASSSS-UUPPPP?!
JASON, GIVE ME THAT PHONE BOOK.
OH, WAIT, YOU WANTED THE NUMBER FOR THE CHURCH?
AMEND

August 12, 2000

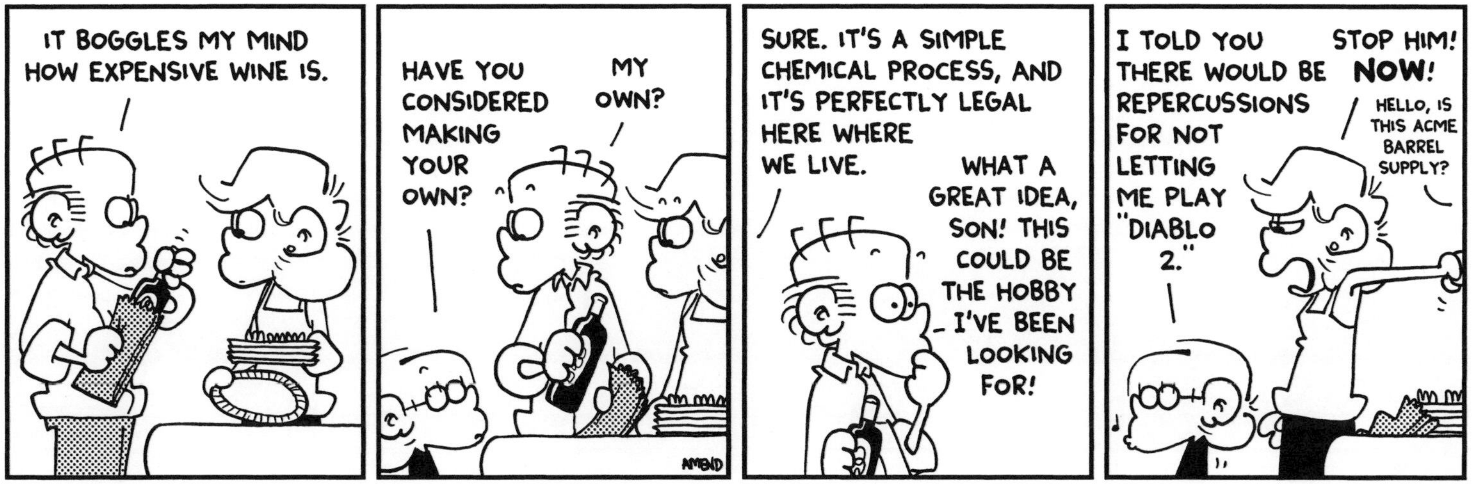
IT BOGGLES MY MIND HOW EXPENSIVE WINE IS.
HAVE YOU CONSIDERED MAKING YOUR OWN?
MY OWN?
SURE. IT'S A SIMPLE CHEMICAL PROCESS, AND IT'S PERFECTLY LEGAL HERE WHERE WE LIVE.
WHAT A GREAT IDEA, SON! THIS COULD BE THE HOBBY I'VE BEEN LOOKING FOR!
I TOLD YOU THERE WOULD BE REPERCUSSIONS FOR NOT LETTING ME PLAY "DIABLO 2."
STOP HIM! NOW!
HELLO, IS THIS ACME BARREL SUPPLY?

August 14, 2000

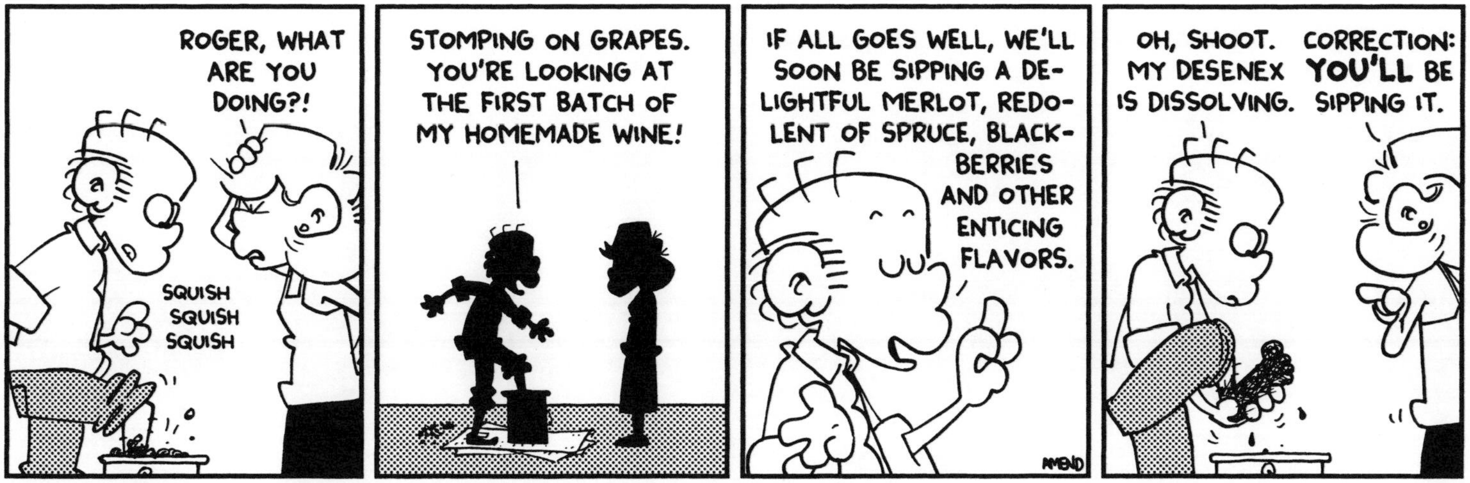
ROGER, WHAT ARE YOU DOING?!
SQUISH SQUISH SQUISH
STOMPING ON GRAPES. YOU'RE LOOKING AT THE FIRST BATCH OF MY HOMEMADE WINE!
IF ALL GOES WELL, WE'LL SOON BE SIPPING A DELIGHTFUL MERLOT, REDOLENT OF SPRUCE, BLACKBERRIES AND OTHER ENTICING FLAVORS.
OH, SHOOT. MY DESENEX IS DISSOLVING.
CORRECTION: YOU'LL BE SIPPING IT.

August 15, 2000

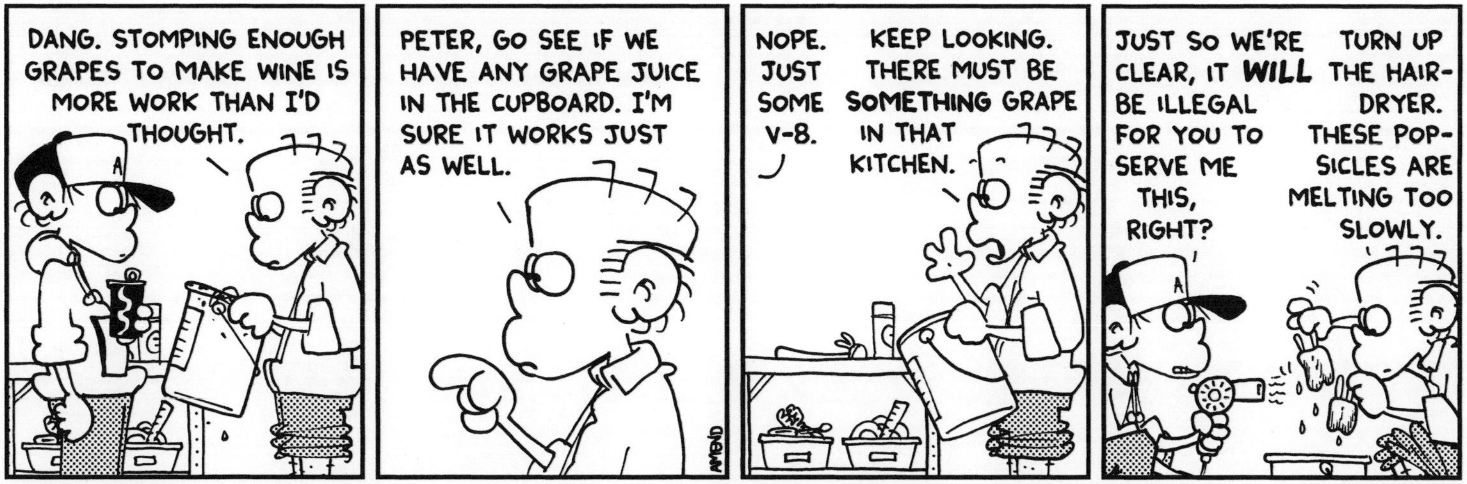
DANG. STOMPING ENOUGH GRAPES TO MAKE WINE IS MORE WORK THAN I'D THOUGHT.
PETER, GO SEE IF WE HAVE ANY GRAPE JUICE IN THE CUPBOARD. I'M SURE IT WORKS JUST AS WELL.
NOPE. JUST SOME V-8.
KEEP LOOKING. THERE MUST BE SOMETHING GRAPE IN THAT KITCHEN.
JUST SO WE'RE CLEAR, IT WILL BE ILLEGAL FOR YOU TO SERVE ME THIS, RIGHT?
TURN UP THE HAIRDRYER. THESE POPSICLES ARE MELTING TOO SLOWLY.

August 16, 2000

DARE I ASK HOW YOUR HOMEMADE WINE IS COMING ALONG?

PRETTY WELL. I JUST FINISHED BOTTLING IT.

WHO MADE THE LABELS?

JASON. AREN'T THEY GREAT?

I GUESS IN HONOR OF MY LITTLE ROGUE WINERY, HE GAVE THEM THIS WONDERFUL PIRATE MOTIF.

I SUPPOSE THAT'S ONE WAY TO INTERPRET THE BIG SKULL AND CROSSBONES.

REMIND ME TO SAY SOMETHING LIKE "AARGH!" WHEN I DRINK IT.

August 17, 2000

READY TO TRY MY CLOS DU ROGER HOMEMADE WINE?

DO I HAVE TO?

FIRST, I'LL UNCORK THE BOTTLE AND LET IT BREATHE FOR A WHILE.

IT WOULD BE NICE IF WE COULD BREATHE, TOO.

YOU HAVE TO ADMIT, IT'S A FULL-BODIED AND COMPLEX STENCH.

August 18, 2000

ANDY, AT LEAST GIVE MY HOMEMADE WINE A LITTLE CREDIT.

SURE, IT WAS A TAD FOAMY. SURE, IT HAD THAT AWFUL SMELL. SURE, IT HAD THOSE STRANGE BLOBS.

Cartoonist wins lottery again

BUT SURELY EVEN YOU WOULD AGREE...

OUR GARBAGE DISPOSAL IS NOW DRAINING BETTER THAN EVER.

OK, TRUE.

August 19, 2000

92

MOM! YOU PUT MY CLEAN SHIRTS AWAY WRONG!

YOU **KNOW** I LIKE THEM PILED IN ORDER! YOU PUT MY "DEEP SPACE NINE" SHIRT AFTER MY "VOYAGER" SHIRT, WHEN ANY FOOL COULD TELL YOU "DS9" COMES FIRST!

AND WHAT'S THIS "PHANTOM MENACE" SHIRT DOING IN HERE?! IT SHOULD BE IN MY LUCASFILM DRAWER! NEXT TIME YOU DO THE LAUNDRY, PUT MY CLOTHES WHERE THEY BELONG!

I SORTA SHOULDA SEEN THAT COMING.

August 21, 2000

Bee Bee Boop Beep Bee Bee Boop

Beep Bee Bee Boop Beep Bee Bee Boop Beep Bee Bee Boop Beep Bee Bee Boop Beep

Beee Beee Beeeeeee

CHECK IT OUT — I'M PLAYING LED ZEPPELIN!   THIS WOULD EXPLAIN OUR LAST PHONE BILL.

もしもし?

August 22, 2000

I'm pretty sure the little voice on the phone is saying "hello" in some far-off language, but I can't remember which.

CHECK OUT THESE PANTS I BOUGHT!

AREN'T THEY HIP?! AREN'T THEY COOL?! AREN'T THEY TOTALLY STYLIN'?!

HEY, I'VE GOT AN OLD PAIR JUST LIKE THESE! I SHOULD DIG THEM UP SO WE CAN GO AROUND LIKE TWINS!

WELCOME TO THE DARK SIDE OF RETRO.   WANT SOME PANTS?

October 17, 2000

September 11, 2000

September 12, 2000

September 13, 2000

September 14, 2000

September 15, 2000

September 16, 2000

October 30, 2000

November 6, 2000

96

November 21, 2000

November 12, 2000

November 26, 2000

"The Ghost of Tom Turkey" is a play on the Springsteen song "The Ghost of Tom Joad."

November 16, 2000

November 18, 2000

November 25, 2000

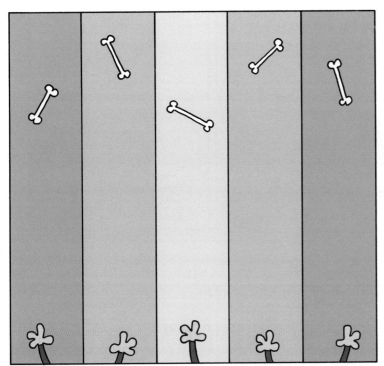

December 31, 2000

January 28, 2001

When I was a senior in high school I got to visit ILM and see the real AT-ATs. That doesn't have anything to do with this strip . . . I'm just bragging.

The Nutcracker didn't have as much to spoof as the Scrooge and Grinch stories, but I still had a great time with it.

PETER, YOU'RE THE COFFEE EXPERT — THINK FIVE SCOOPS OF INSTANT WILL BE ENOUGH?

FOR WHAT?

MOM'S TAKING ME TO "THE NUTCRACKER," AND I DON'T WANT TO FALL ASLEEP.

AFRAID THE BALLET WILL BE BORING?

AFRAID OF THE DREAMS I'LL HAVE.

HERR DROSSEL-ROGER, YOU SHOULDN'T HAVE.

DON'T HOLD IT SO CLOSE TO YOUR FACE.

December 18, 2000

WHY, HERR DROSSELROGER, WHAT AN INTERESTING GIFT.

IT'S A NOSE-CRACKER.

A WHAT?

A NOSECRACKER. IT CRACKS NOSES.

WHAT AM I SUPPOSED TO DO WITH A NOSECRACKER?

OW!

I'D SUGGEST GIVING IT AWAY. THAT'S WHAT *I* DID.

December 19, 2000

EEK! A MOUSE KING!

MUAA-HA-HA!

SAVE ME, NOSECRACKER! SAVE ME!

LEAD YOUR TOY ARMY AND VANQUISH THE FOUL VERMIN!

HE'S THE VERMIN!

MOUSE HORDE! TO THE TOY CHEST! LET NO FURBY ESCAPE OUR WRATH!

December 20, 2000

December 21, 2000

December 22, 2000

December 23, 2000

December 25, 2000

December 26, 2000

December 27, 2000

December 28, 2000

December 29, 2000

December 30, 2000

Jeff Thompson is an actual college friend. Why waste a good insult on a fictitious name, right?

January 16, 2001

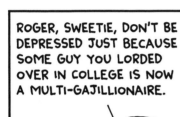

January 17, 2001

January 18, 2001

MOM SAYS YOU'RE WRITING A NOVEL.

YUP.

AND APPLYING TO THE PEACE CORPS. AND STARTING A BAND. AND RUNNING FOR OFFICE. AND TRYING OUT FOR A ROLE IN "G.I. JANE 2."

YUP YUP YUP YUP.

AND LOSING YOUR MARBLES BIG-TIME.

SHE TOLD YOU THAT?!

ACTUALLY, THAT I DIAGNOSED MYSELF.

SAY, MAYBE YOU CAN HELP ME WITH THESE MED-SCHOOL ESSAYS.

January 20, 2001

STILL STUCK?

IT'S SO FRUSTRATING.

I JUST KNOW THERE'S A GREAT NOVEL INSIDE OF ME TRYING TO GET OUT. I JUST KNOW IT!

QUINCY WENT THROUGH THAT ONCE.

YOUR IGUANA?

AFTER HE ATE PAIGE'S "CATCHER IN THE RYE." YEESH.

UM, IN CASE YOU MISSED THE "DO NOT DISTURB" SIGN...

January 24, 2001

COURIER. HMM. THAT DOESN'T FEEL RIGHT.

HELVETICA. NO. TOO PLAIN.

TIMES ROMAN. EEK. WAY TOO FORMAL.

WHAT'S THE PROBLEM?

I WANT TO USE A FONT THAT FITS MY WRITING STYLE.

If I may offer a suggestion...

January 25, 2001

HOW'S YOUR NOVEL COMING ALONG?

SO-SO. I WASN'T SURE WHAT TO WRITE FOR CHAPTER ONE, SO I SKIPPED TO CHAPTER TWO.

THEN I WASN'T SURE WHAT TO WRITE FOR CHAPTER TWO, SO I MOVED ON TO CHAPTER THREE.

SO YOU WROTE THAT?

NO, BUT I DID FINALLY MANAGE TO GET SOMETHING DOWN ON PAPER AFTER CHAPTER 57.

"THE END." I GUESS THAT'S A START.

DOES IT FEEL, YOU KNOW, SATISFYING?

January 27, 2001

WHAT'S THIS?

MY NOVEL. WANT TO READ IT?

YOU WROTE YOUR NOVEL IN A WEEKEND?! I THOUGHT YOU HAD WRITER'S BLOCK!

I DID, FOR A WHILE.

BUT AS SOON AS I SETTLED ON THE MAIN CHARACTER, IT WAS AS IF A SPIGOT JUST OPENED UP!

But won't the mission be dangerous, Agent Fox?

"Danger" is my middle name. That and "Handsome." And "Brilliant." And "Very Suave." Shall I go on?

In triplicate.

January 29, 2001

A shadowy sliver of a human shadow lowers himself spider-like down a wall.

Silently, he slips quietly into a room brimming with priceless objects of art and beauty.

Some more beautiful than others.

You're three seconds late, Agent Fox.

Trust me. I'm worth the wait.

YOUR CHARACTER HAS A FLING WITH A REDHEAD?!

I THOUGHT YOU MIGHT BE JEALOUS, SO I PUT TWO BLONDES IN THE NEXT CHAPTER.

January 30, 2001

January 31, 2001

Writing Roger's dialogue here was frighteningly easy. This causes me much concern.

February 1, 2001

February 2, 2001

Panel 1: SO WHAT'D YOU THINK OF MY SPY NOVEL? / ROGER, SWEETIE, YOU KNOW I LOVE YOU.

Panel 2: YOU KNOW I THINK THE WORLD OF YOU.

Panel 3: YOU KNOW I THINK YOU'RE PERFECTLY BRIGHT AND TALENTED IN ALL SORTS OF WAYS.

Panel 4: I SENSE A POSITIVE REVIEW COMING ON. / MAKE THAT *MODERATELY* BRIGHT.

February 3, 2001

Panel 1: A History of American Farming

Panel 2: By Peter Fox

Panel 3: ...who had a very rough time getting out of bed this morning and didn't eat breakfast and who pinched his left thumb in his gym locker and left his favorite pencil in the library and whose day got even worse when...

Panel 4: I'M ASSUMING THERE IS SUCH A THING AS A SYMPATHY GRADE. / YOUR TITLE PAGE IS LONGER THAN YOUR ESSAY.

February 26, 2001

Panel 1: I SEE THAT ANOTHER DOT-COM IS ABOUT TO GO BELLY-UP. / OH? WHAT'S THE TIP-OFF?

Panel 2: A BAD BUSINESS PLAN? LOUSY MANAGEMENT? PIE-IN-THE-SKY FORECASTS?

Panel 3: YOUR FATHER JUST BOUGHT THEIR STOCK. / IS THIS WHY YOU GAVE ME ALL THOSE SCHOLARSHIP APPLICATIONS?

March 6, 2001

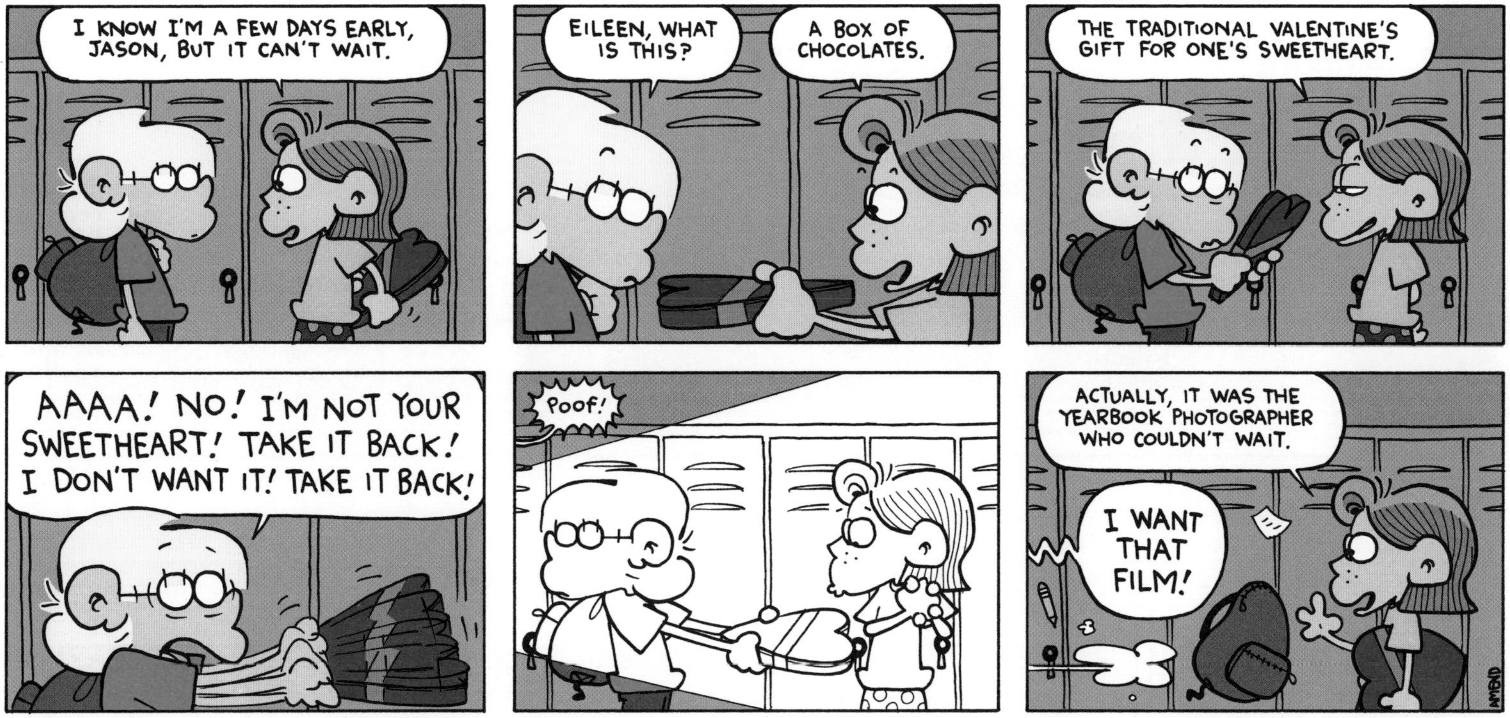
I KNOW I'M A FEW DAYS EARLY, JASON, BUT IT CAN'T WAIT.
EILEEN, WHAT IS THIS?
A BOX OF CHOCOLATES.
THE TRADITIONAL VALENTINE'S GIFT FOR ONE'S SWEETHEART.
AAAA! NO! I'M NOT YOUR SWEETHEART! TAKE IT BACK! I DON'T WANT IT! TAKE IT BACK!
Poof!
ACTUALLY, IT WAS THE YEARBOOK PHOTOGRAPHER WHO COULDN'T WAIT.
I WANT THAT FILM!
AMEND

February 11, 2001

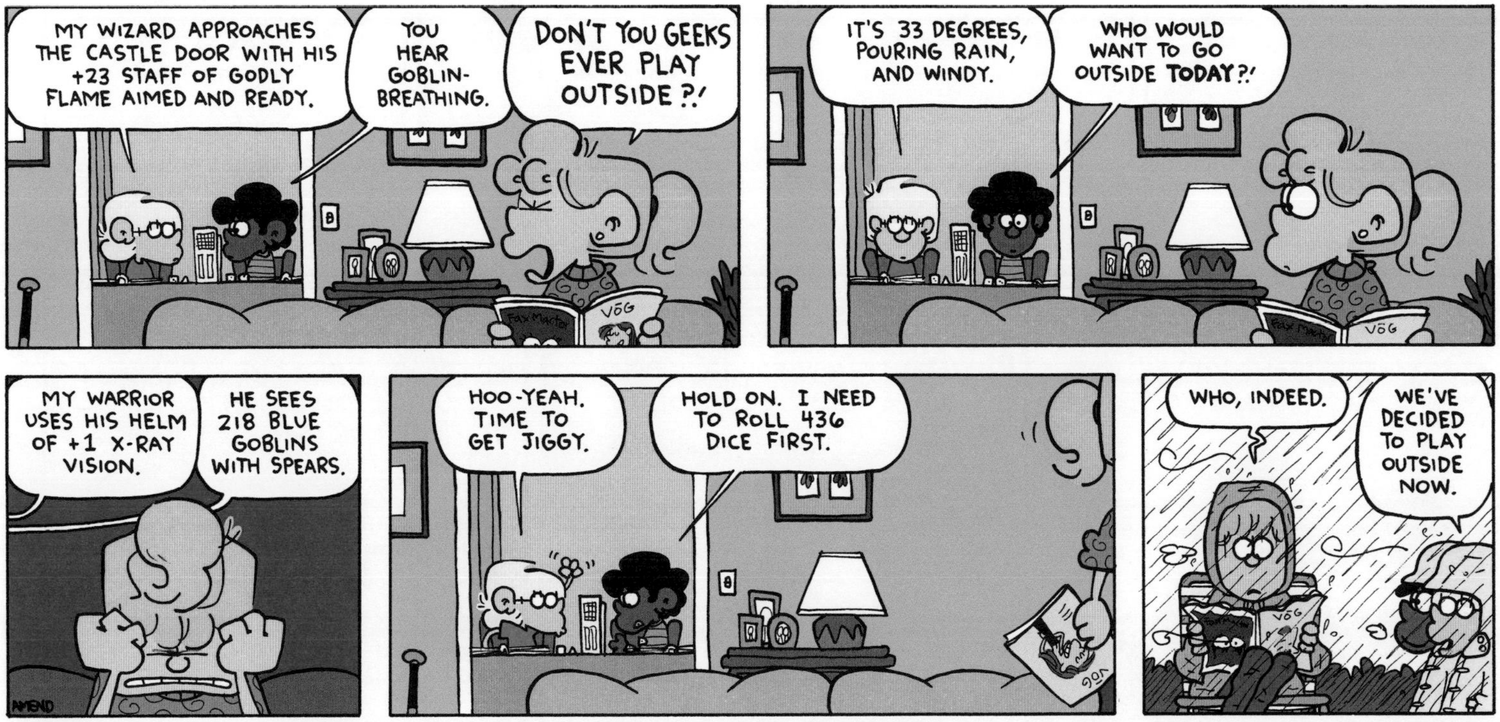
MY WIZARD APPROACHES THE CASTLE DOOR WITH HIS +23 STAFF OF GODLY FLAME AIMED AND READY.
YOU HEAR GOBLIN-BREATHING.
DON'T YOU GEEKS EVER PLAY OUTSIDE ?!
IT'S 33 DEGREES, POURING RAIN, AND WINDY.
WHO WOULD WANT TO GO OUTSIDE **TODAY** ?!
MY WARRIOR USES HIS HELM OF +1 X-RAY VISION.
HE SEES 218 BLUE GOBLINS WITH SPEARS.
AMEND
HOO-YEAH. TIME TO GET JIGGY.
HOLD ON. I NEED TO ROLL 436 DICE FIRST.
WHO, INDEED.
WE'VE DECIDED TO PLAY OUTSIDE NOW.

March 4, 2001

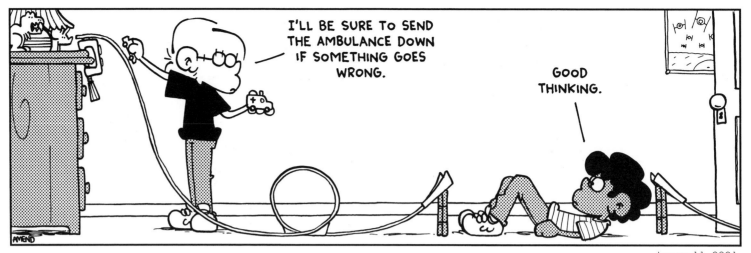

January 11, 2001

February 9, 2001

I screwed up and forgot to reverse Jason's hair in the reflections. Forgive me.

April 16, 2001

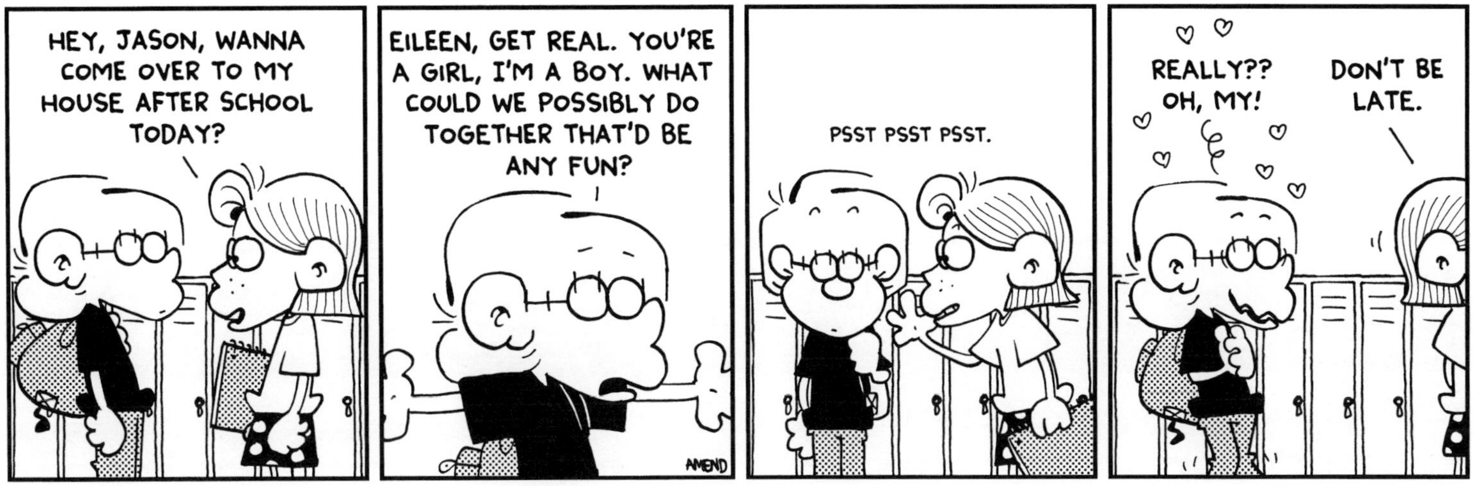
HEY, JASON, WANNA COME OVER TO MY HOUSE AFTER SCHOOL TODAY?
EILEEN, GET REAL. YOU'RE A GIRL, I'M A BOY. WHAT COULD WE POSSIBLY DO TOGETHER THAT'D BE ANY FUN?
AMEND
PSST PSST PSST.
REALLY?? OH, MY!
DON'T BE LATE.

March 19, 2001

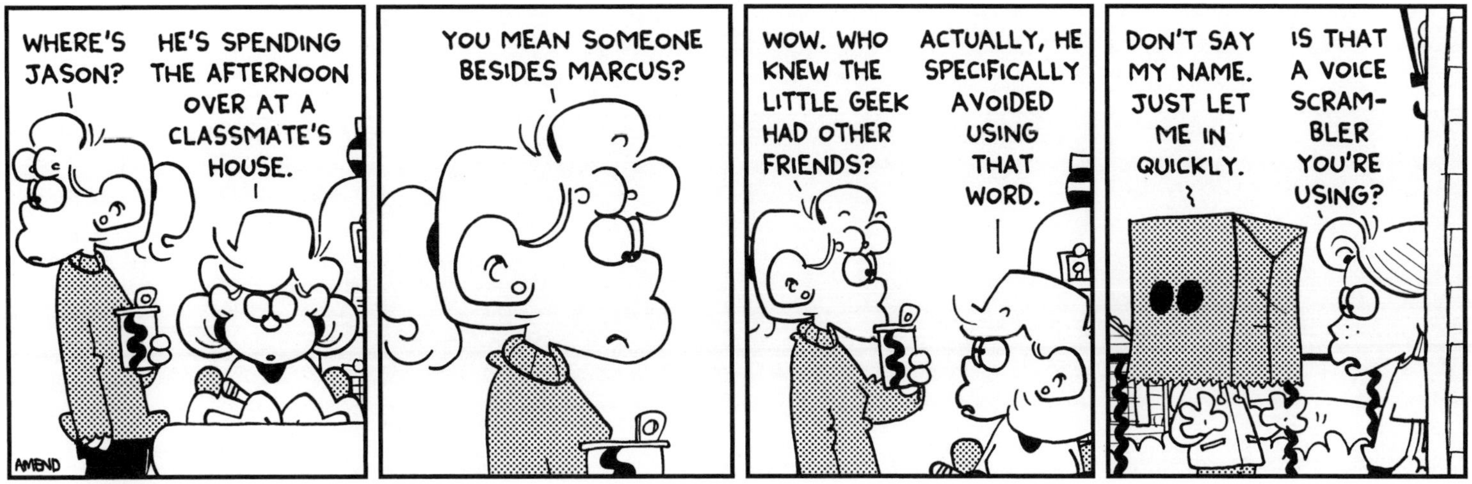
WHERE'S JASON?
HE'S SPENDING THE AFTERNOON OVER AT A CLASSMATE'S HOUSE.
AMEND
YOU MEAN SOMEONE BESIDES MARCUS?
WOW. WHO KNEW THE LITTLE GEEK HAD OTHER FRIENDS?
ACTUALLY, HE SPECIFICALLY AVOIDED USING THAT WORD.
DON'T SAY MY NAME. JUST LET ME IN QUICKLY.
IS THAT A VOICE SCRAM-BLER YOU'RE USING?

March 20, 2001

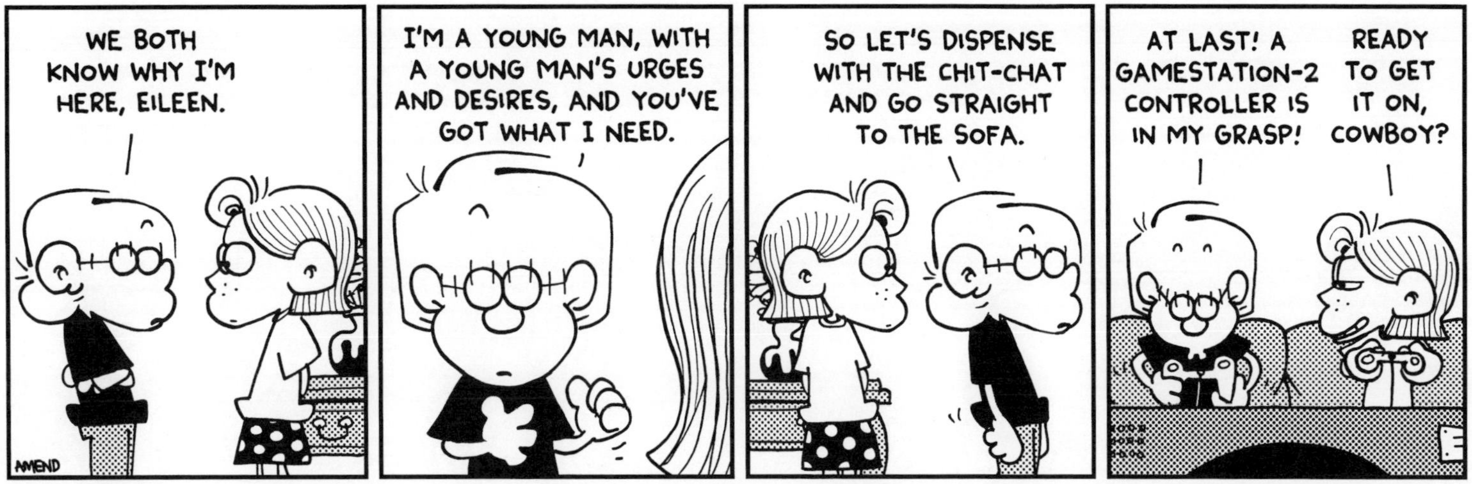
WE BOTH KNOW WHY I'M HERE, EILEEN.
AMEND
I'M A YOUNG MAN, WITH A YOUNG MAN'S URGES AND DESIRES, AND YOU'VE GOT WHAT I NEED.
SO LET'S DISPENSE WITH THE CHIT-CHAT AND GO STRAIGHT TO THE SOFA.
AT LAST! A GAMESTATION-2 CONTROLLER IS IN MY GRASP!
READY TO GET IT ON, COWBOY?

March 21, 2001

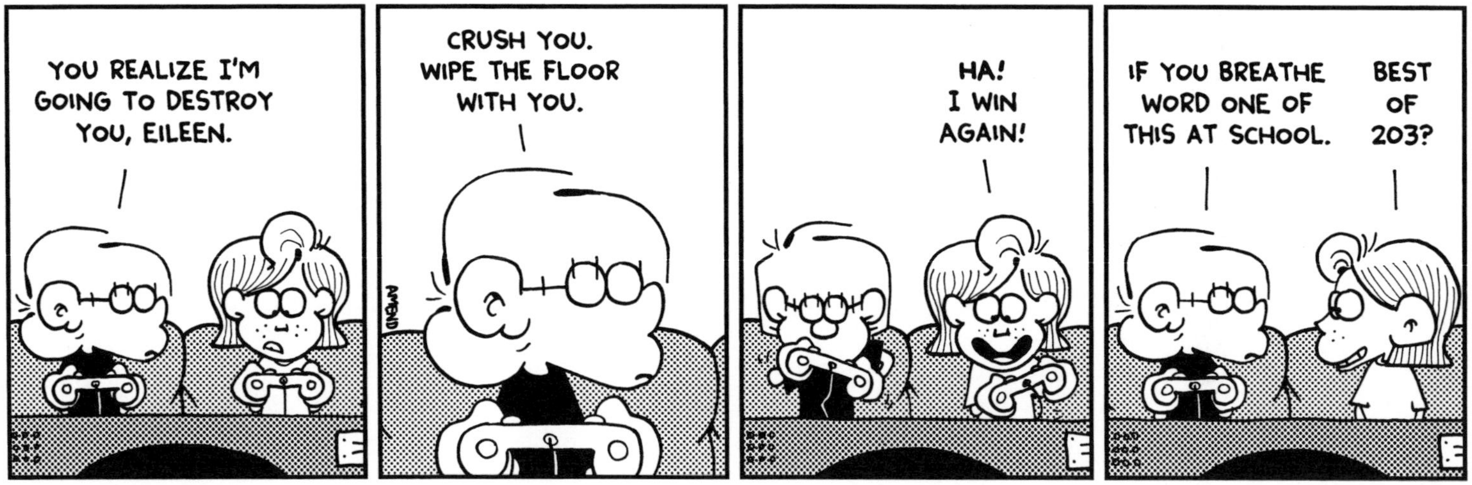
YOU REALIZE I'M GOING TO DESTROY YOU, EILEEN.
CRUSH YOU. WIPE THE FLOOR WITH YOU.
HA! I WIN AGAIN!
IF YOU BREATHE WORD ONE OF THIS AT SCHOOL.
BEST OF 203?

March 22, 2001

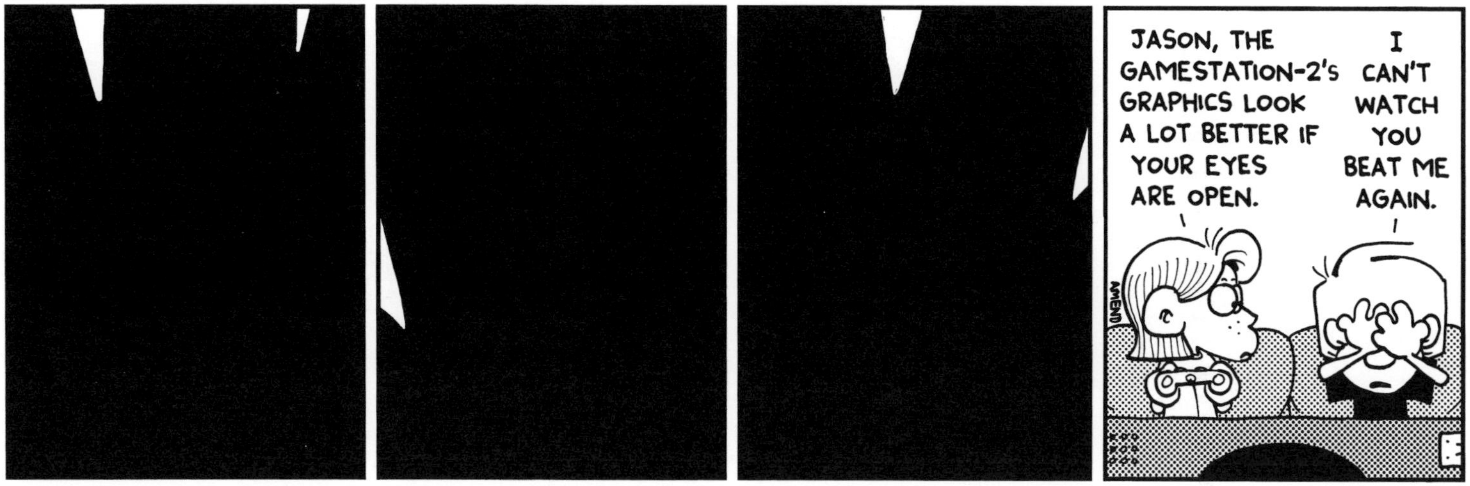
JASON, THE GAMESTATION-2's GRAPHICS LOOK A LOT BETTER IF YOUR EYES ARE OPEN.
I CAN'T WATCH YOU BEAT ME AGAIN.

March 23, 2001

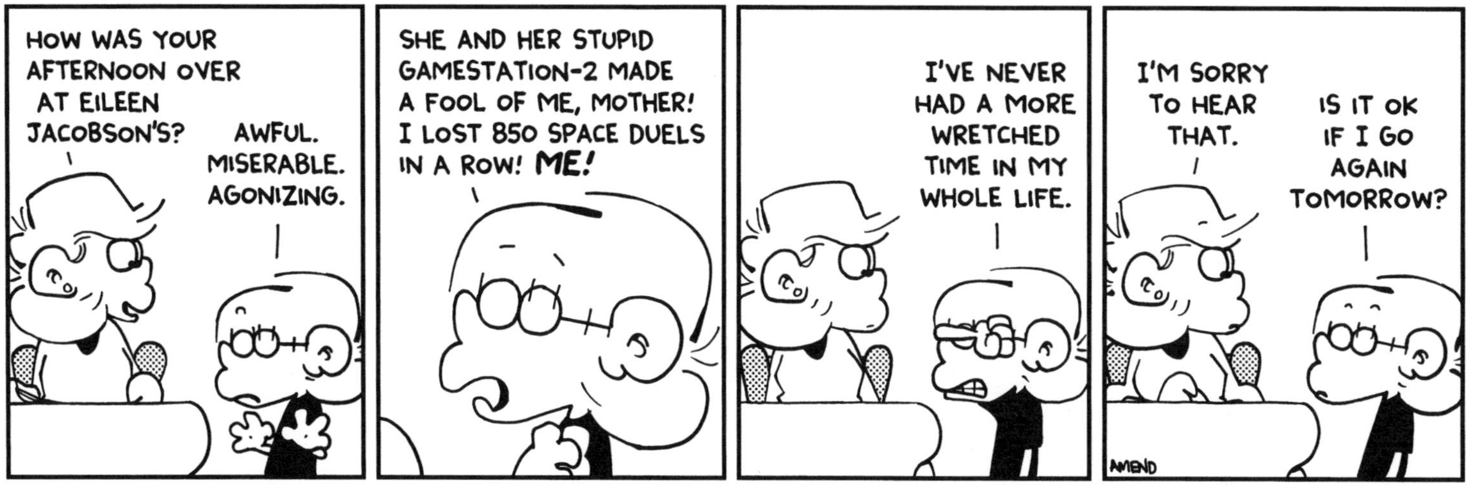
HOW WAS YOUR AFTERNOON OVER AT EILEEN JACOBSON'S?
AWFUL. MISERABLE. AGONIZING.
SHE AND HER STUPID GAMESTATION-2 MADE A FOOL OF ME, MOTHER! I LOST 850 SPACE DUELS IN A ROW! ME!
I'VE NEVER HAD A MORE WRETCHED TIME IN MY WHOLE LIFE.
I'M SORRY TO HEAR THAT.
IS IT OK IF I GO AGAIN TOMORROW?

March 24, 2001

This phrase was all the rage on the Web for a while.

March 12, 2001

March 13, 2001

March 27, 2001

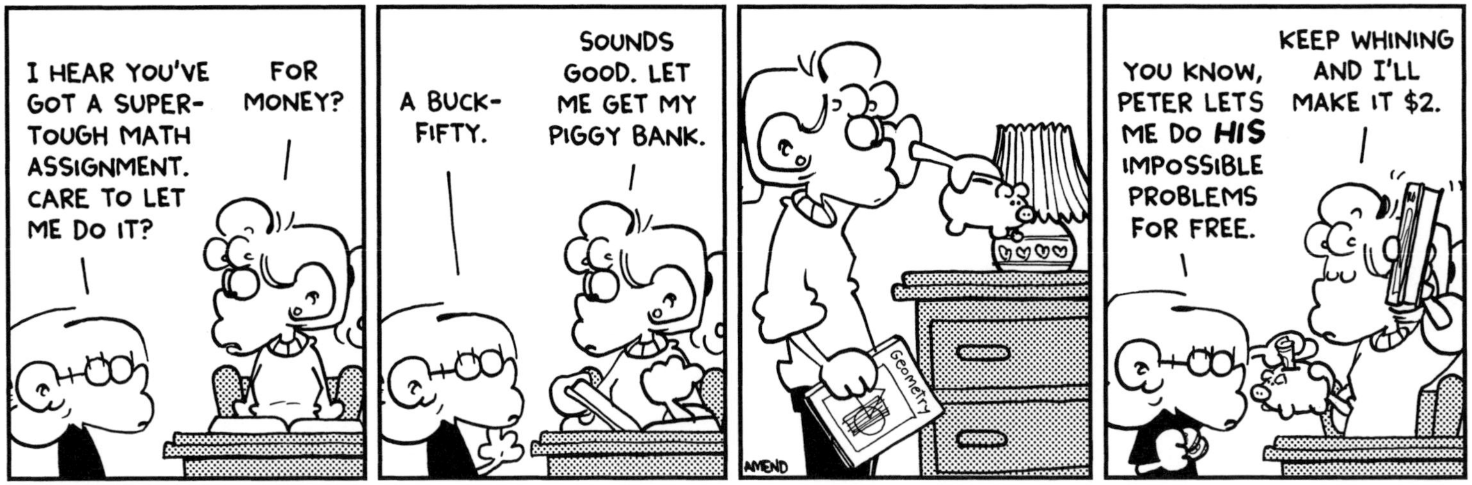
I HEAR YOU'VE GOT A SUPER-TOUGH MATH ASSIGNMENT. CARE TO LET ME DO IT?
FOR MONEY?
A BUCK-FIFTY.
SOUNDS GOOD. LET ME GET MY PIGGY BANK.
Geometry
YOU KNOW, PETER LETS ME DO **HIS** IMPOSSIBLE PROBLEMS FOR FREE.
KEEP WHINING AND I'LL MAKE IT $2.
AMEND

April 26, 2001

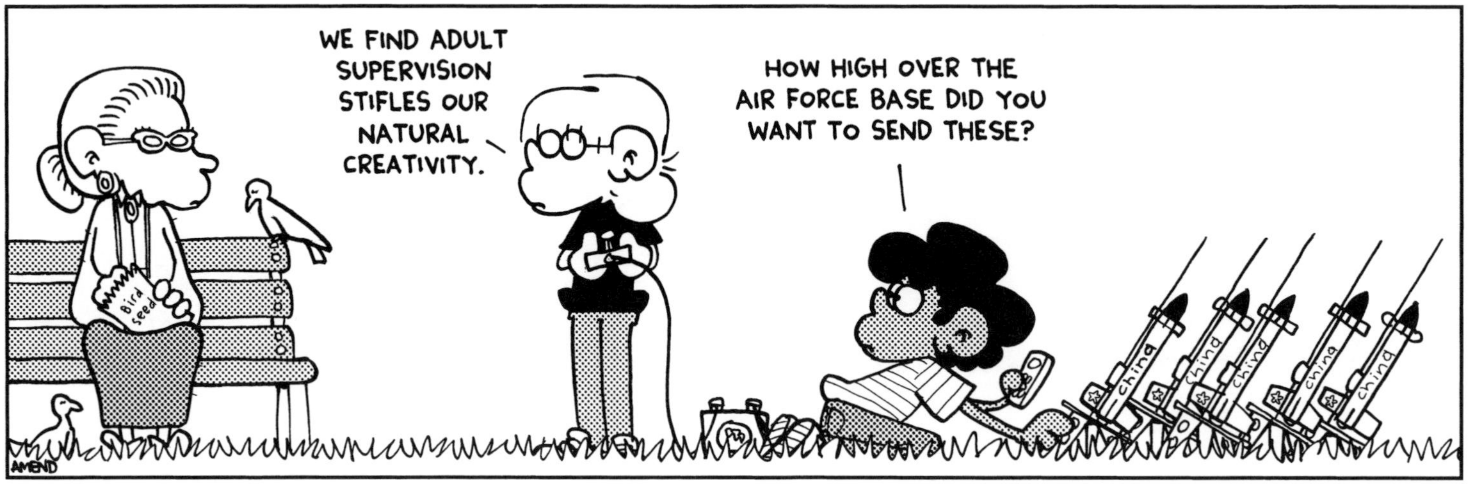
Bird seed
WE FIND ADULT SUPERVISION STIFLES OUR NATURAL CREATIVITY.
HOW HIGH OVER THE AIR FORCE BASE DID YOU WANT TO SEND THESE?
china
china
china
china
china
AMEND

April 27, 2001

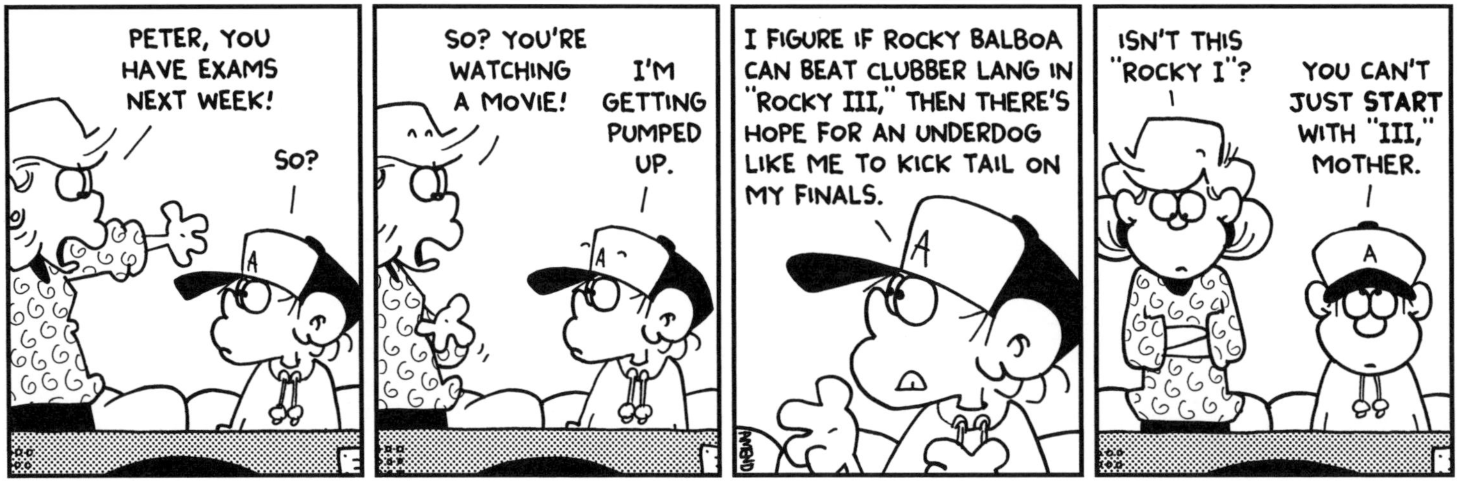
PETER, YOU HAVE EXAMS NEXT WEEK!
SO?
SO? YOU'RE WATCHING A MOVIE!
I'M GETTING PUMPED UP.
I FIGURE IF ROCKY BALBOA CAN BEAT CLUBBER LANG IN "ROCKY III," THEN THERE'S HOPE FOR AN UNDERDOG LIKE ME TO KICK TAIL ON MY FINALS.
ISN'T THIS "ROCKY I"?
YOU CAN'T JUST **START** WITH "III," MOTHER.
AMEND

May 15, 2001

April 1, 2001

June 24, 2001

Paige, Jason, and Marcus are all too young to be watching *Pulp Fiction*, but I liked the joke enough to ignore that fact.

COULD YOU TELL US WHERE THE LINE IS FOR "THE FELLOW-SHIP OF THE RING'S" FIRST SCREENING?

WHAT??

JASON, THAT MOVIE DOESN'T COME OUT FOR SIX MONTHS! THERE **IS** NO LINE!

WOO-HOO!

WE'RE FIRST!

I'LL GO GET OUR SLEEPING BAGS.

THIS POPCORN HAS UN-LIMITED REFILLS, RIGHT?

SIR, ABOUT MY HOURLY PAY...

June 19, 2001

In high school I made a movie called *Trek Wars*. Apparently, there's a sequel playing in Peter's theater.

YOU LOOK REALLY FAMILIAR.

YOU PROBABLY SAW MY "60 MINUTES" INTERVIEW.

AFTER MY DOT-COM WENT PUBLIC, I WAS NAMED BILLIONAIRE OF THE YEAR BY MOST OF THE BUSINESS PRESS. FORBES PUT ME ON THEIR COVER SIX TIMES.

WOW.

YUP.

OK, SO GO GRAB A UNIFORM AND I'LL SHOW YOU WHERE TO MOP.

YOU GOT IT, BOSS.

June 21, 2001

HOW WAS THE POOL?

THE WATER WAS COLD. :-P

BUT THE LIFEGUARDS WERE HOT. ;-)

AND THE SNACK BAR HAD THOSE CREAMCICLES I LIKE. :-)

I THINK YOUR SISTER MAY BE SPENDING TOO MUCH TIME IN CHAT ROOMS.

GOSH, REALLY?? <:-o

June 28, 2001

116

August 6, 2001

One of the challenges with vacation story lines is making them awful in new and interesting ways.

August 7, 2001

August 8, 2001

117

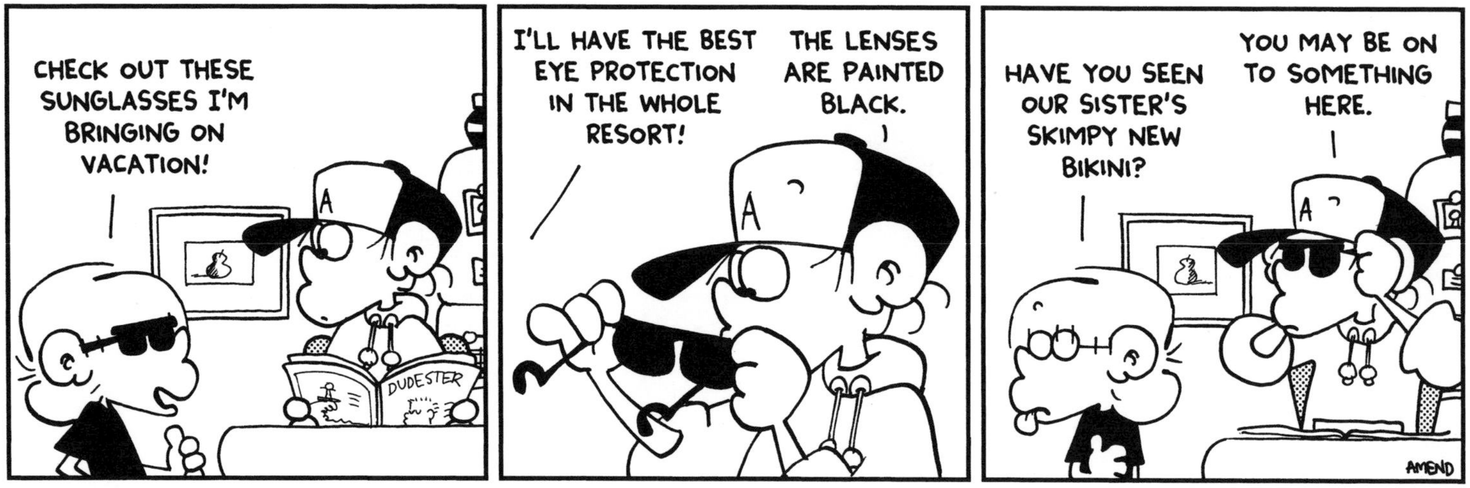
CHECK OUT THESE SUNGLASSES I'M BRINGING ON VACATION!
DUDESTER
I'LL HAVE THE BEST EYE PROTECTION IN THE WHOLE RESORT!
THE LENSES ARE PAINTED BLACK.
HAVE YOU SEEN OUR SISTER'S SKIMPY NEW BIKINI?
YOU MAY BE ON TO SOMETHING HERE.
AMEND

August 9, 2001

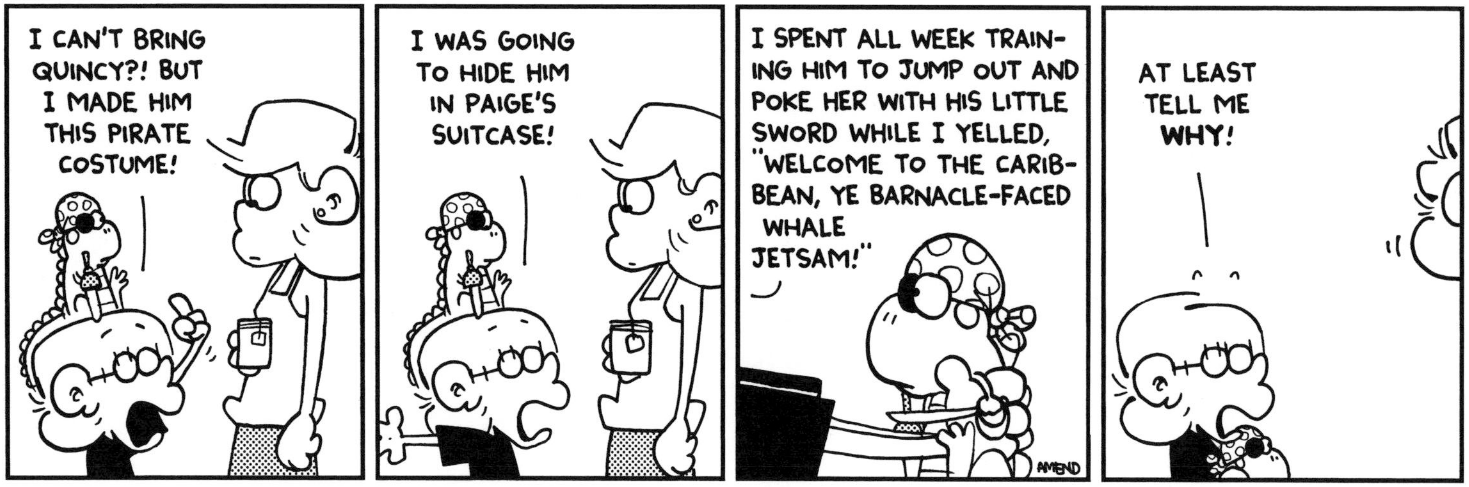
I CAN'T BRING QUINCY?! BUT I MADE HIM THIS PIRATE COSTUME!
I WAS GOING TO HIDE HIM IN PAIGE'S SUITCASE!
I SPENT ALL WEEK TRAINING HIM TO JUMP OUT AND POKE HER WITH HIS LITTLE SWORD WHILE I YELLED, "WELCOME TO THE CARIBBEAN, YE BARNACLE-FACED WHALE JETSAM!"
AMEND
AT LEAST TELL ME **WHY**!

August 10, 2001

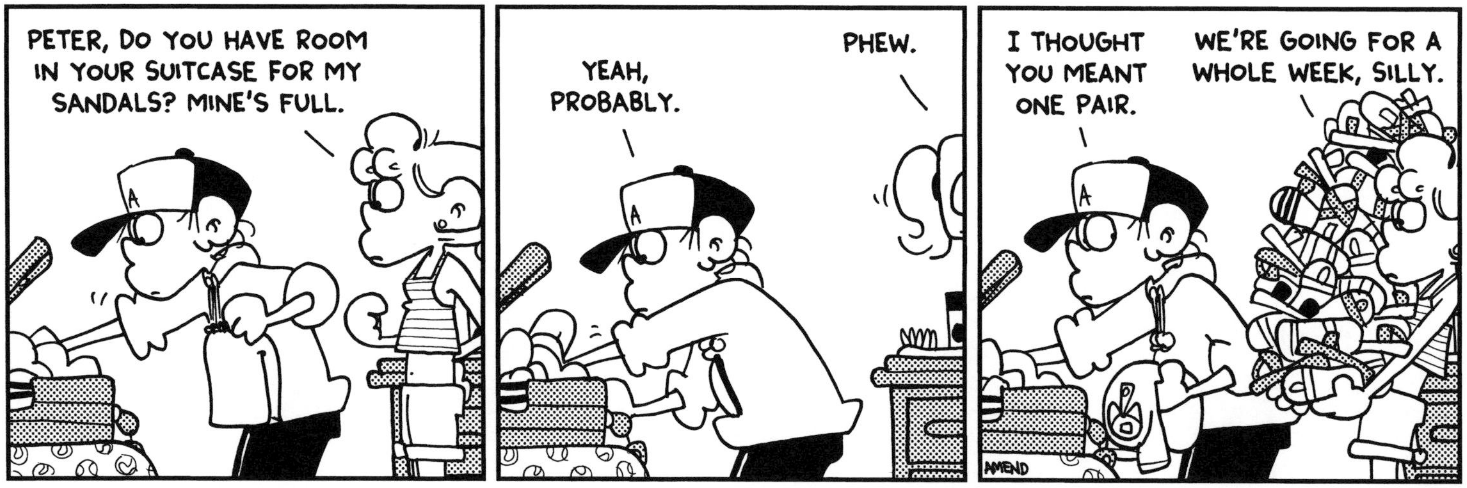
PETER, DO YOU HAVE ROOM IN YOUR SUITCASE FOR MY SANDALS? MINE'S FULL.
YEAH, PROBABLY.
PHEW.
I THOUGHT YOU MEANT ONE PAIR.
WE'RE GOING FOR A WHOLE WEEK, SILLY.
AMEND

August 11, 2001

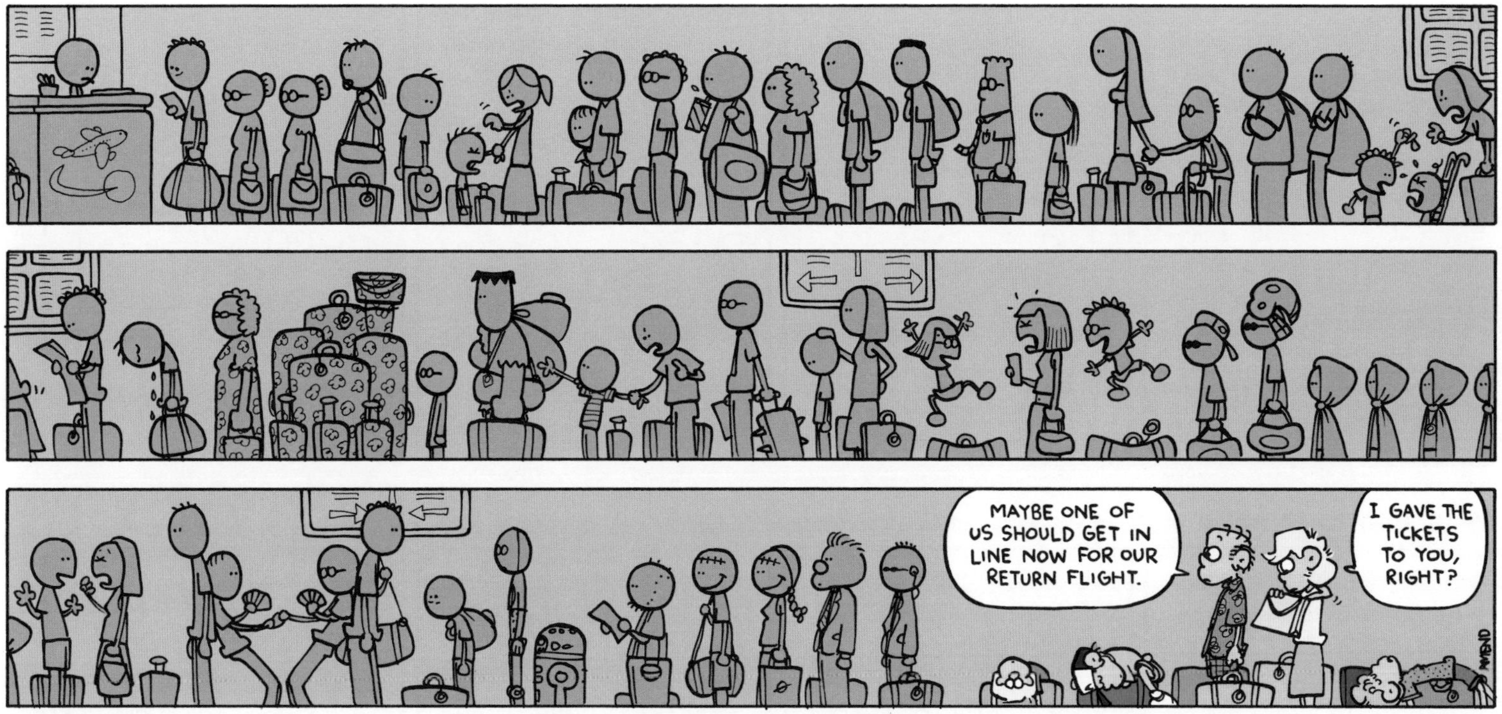
MAYBE ONE OF US SHOULD GET IN LINE NOW FOR OUR RETURN FLIGHT.
I GAVE THE TICKETS TO YOU, RIGHT?
AMEND

August 12, 2001

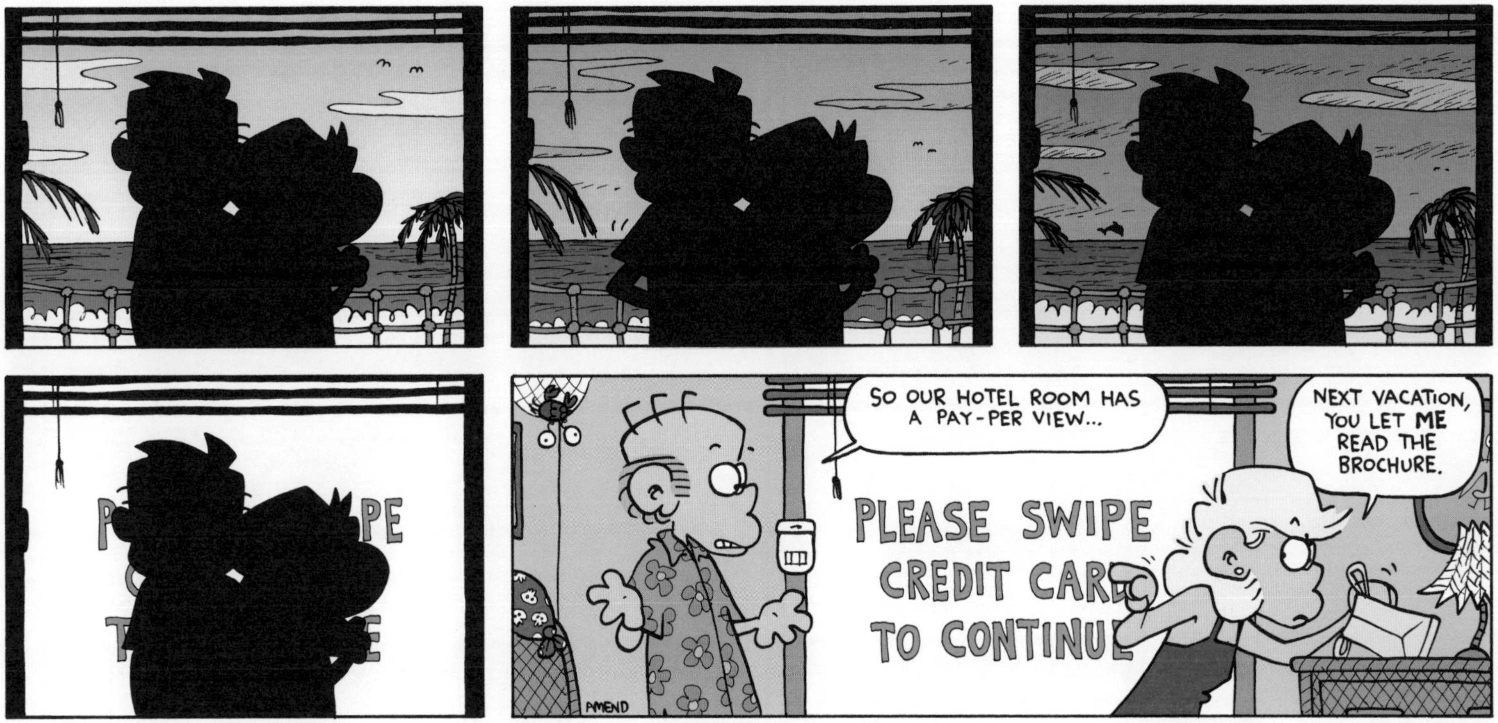
SO OUR HOTEL ROOM HAS A PAY-PER VIEW...
PLEASE SWIPE
CREDIT CAR
TO CONTINU
NEXT VACATION, YOU LET **ME** READ THE BROCHURE.
AMEND

August 19,2001

HEY, MON. WELCAM TO DE ISLES OF FUN-FUN CARIBBEANNY RESORT.

HI. DO YOU HAVE A RESERVATION FOR FOX?

FOX... FOX... YA, MON. YOU BE WID US ALL WEEK, MON.

WHOA, MON! YOU GOT TREE KIDS AND TWO ADULTS IN DE LIMBO SUITE?!

I DIDN'T REQUEST THE LIMBO SUITE.

"HOW LOW CAN YOU GO?"

I MEANT PRICE, NOT CEILING HEIGHT!

LOOK AT THIS CUTE LITTLE DOOR, MOM!

August 13, 2001

I HATE THIS PLACE.

ANDY, C'MON! WE'VE BEEN HERE FOR 30 MINUTES!

YOU HAVEN'T EVEN SEEN THE SIGHTS, AND ALREADY YOU'RE PASSING JUDGMENT! I THOUGHT YOU WANTED TO GO TO THE CARIBBEAN!

WE'RE AT A FAKE ISLAND RESORT SURROUNDED BY A BIG, FAKE OCEAN, ROGER! THERE'S NOTHING CARIBBEAN ABOUT THIS PLACE!

THE MUZAK ON THE ELEVATOR WAS CALYPSO...

DON'T MAKE ME HATE YOU, TOO, ROGER.

August 14, 2001

HEY, DAD! CHECK OUT ALL THE ACTIVITIES THIS PLACE HAS!

SNORKLING... BODY BOARDING... STEEL DRUM LESSONS... VOODOO DOLL PUPPETRY...

WHOA! THEY'VE GOT A FAKE HURRICANE SCHEDULED FOR TOMORROW NIGHT!

DID YOU HEAR THAT, HON?!

I WONDERED WHY ALL THE WALLS WERE FASTENED WITH VELCRO.

YOUR EYE TWITCHES LIKE THAT WHEN YOU'RE HAPPY, RIGHT?

120

August 15, 2001

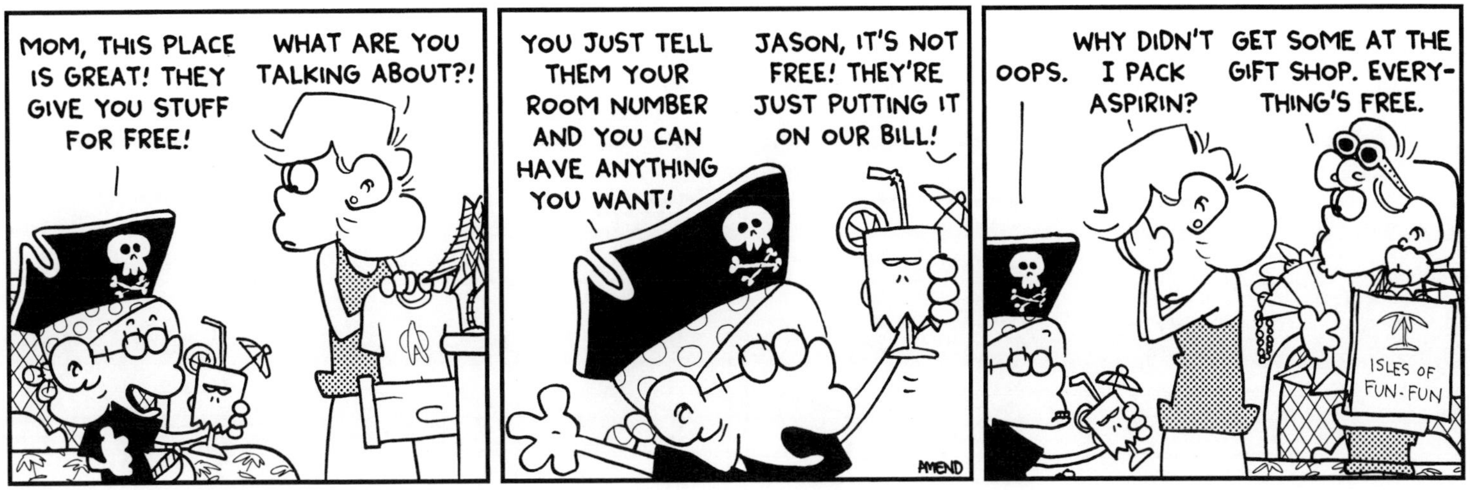
MOM, THIS PLACE IS GREAT! THEY GIVE YOU STUFF FOR FREE!
WHAT ARE YOU TALKING ABOUT?!
YOU JUST TELL THEM YOUR ROOM NUMBER AND YOU CAN HAVE ANYTHING YOU WANT!
JASON, IT'S NOT FREE! THEY'RE JUST PUTTING IT ON OUR BILL!
AMEND
OOPS.
WHY DIDN'T I PACK ASPIRIN?
GET SOME AT THE GIFT SHOP. EVERY-THING'S FREE.
ISLES OF FUN-FUN

August 16, 2001

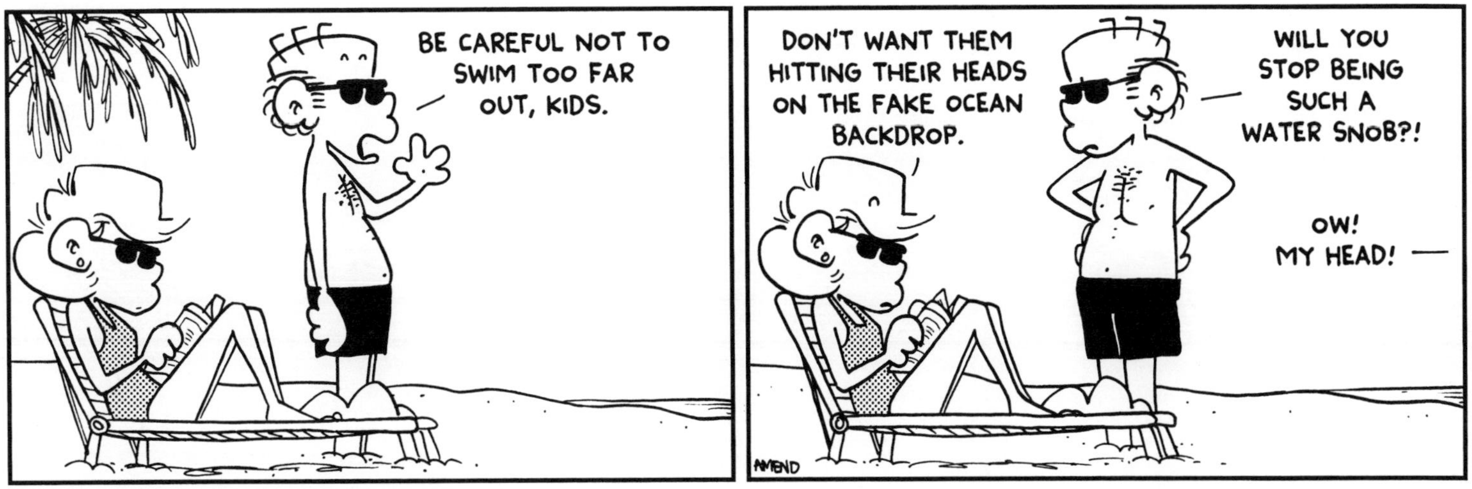
BE CAREFUL NOT TO SWIM TOO FAR OUT, KIDS.
DON'T WANT THEM HITTING THEIR HEADS ON THE FAKE OCEAN BACKDROP.
WILL YOU STOP BEING SUCH A WATER SNOB?!
OW! MY HEAD!
AMEND

August 17, 2001

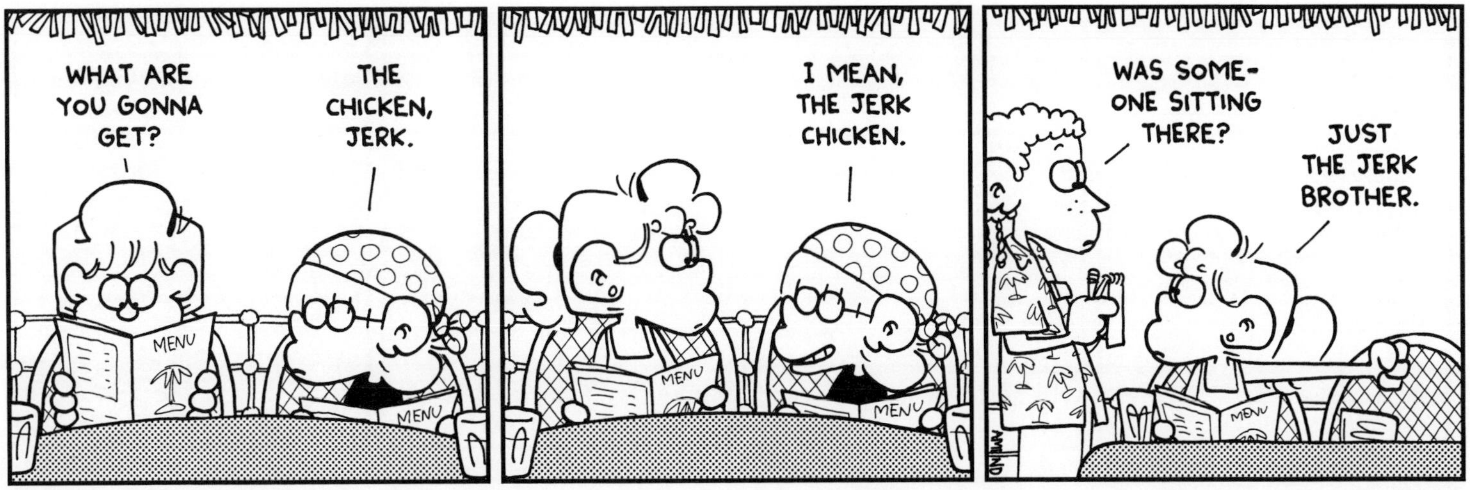
WHAT ARE YOU GONNA GET?
THE CHICKEN, JERK.
MENU
I MEAN, THE JERK CHICKEN.
WAS SOME-ONE SITTING THERE?
JUST THE JERK BROTHER.

August 18, 2001

THEY'RE HAVING STEEL DRUM MUSIC DOWN AT THE BEACH.

IS IT REAL, OR FAKE LIKE EVERY-THING ELSE HERE?

WILL YOU STOP BEATING UP ON THIS PLACE?! YOU WON'T HAVE A MOMENT OF FUN ON THIS TRIP IF ALL YOU DO IS LOOK FOR THINGS TO CRITICIZE!

SEE?! IT'S A REAL GUY PLAYING THE SYNTHESIZER!

WHOOPS. SORRY. I DIDN'T MEAN TO HIT BAGPIPES JUST THEN.

August 20, 2001

I like that Jason spells "skills" with a "z" even when speaking.

HEY, PETER! WATCH ME STAND UP ON THIS BOOGIE BOARD!

WOOHOO! DO I HAVE MAD SKILLZ OR WHAT?!

MAYBE IF YOU DID IT IN THE WATER.

WOULDN'T IT TIP OVER THEN?

August 21, 2001

CAN I BRING YOU A SODA?

NO, THANKS.

CAN I BRING YOU A SODA?

NO, THANKS.

YOOHOO... WAITER...

YES?

COULD YOU BRING ME A SODA, PLEASE?

August 22, 2001

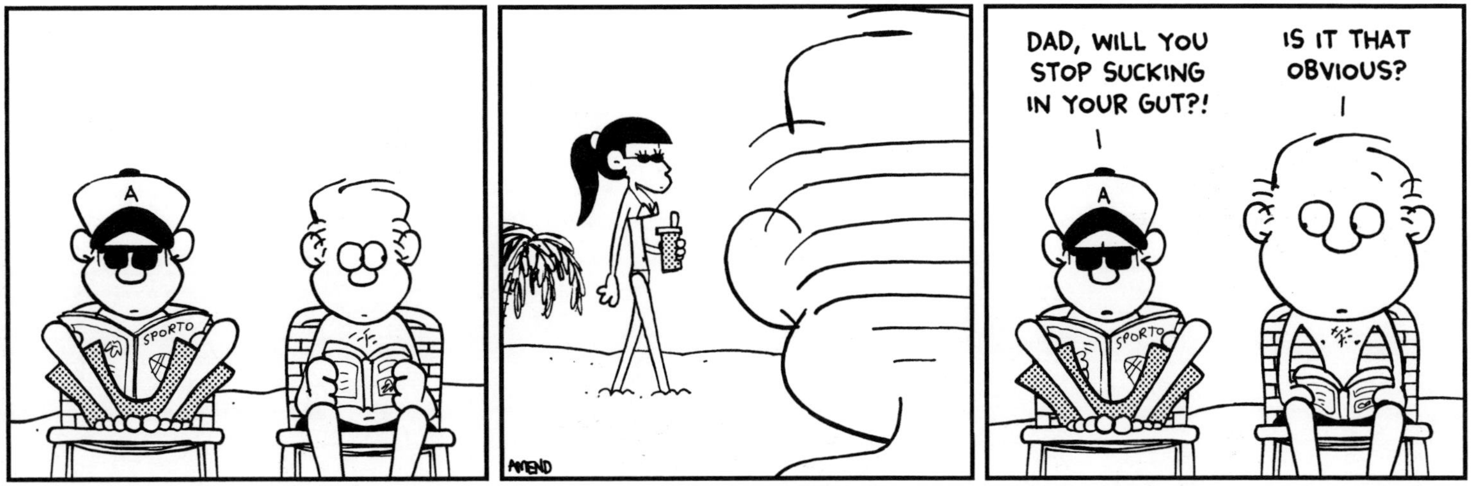
DAD, WILL YOU STOP SUCKING IN YOUR GUT?!
IS IT THAT OBVIOUS?
SPORTO
AMEND
August 23, 2001

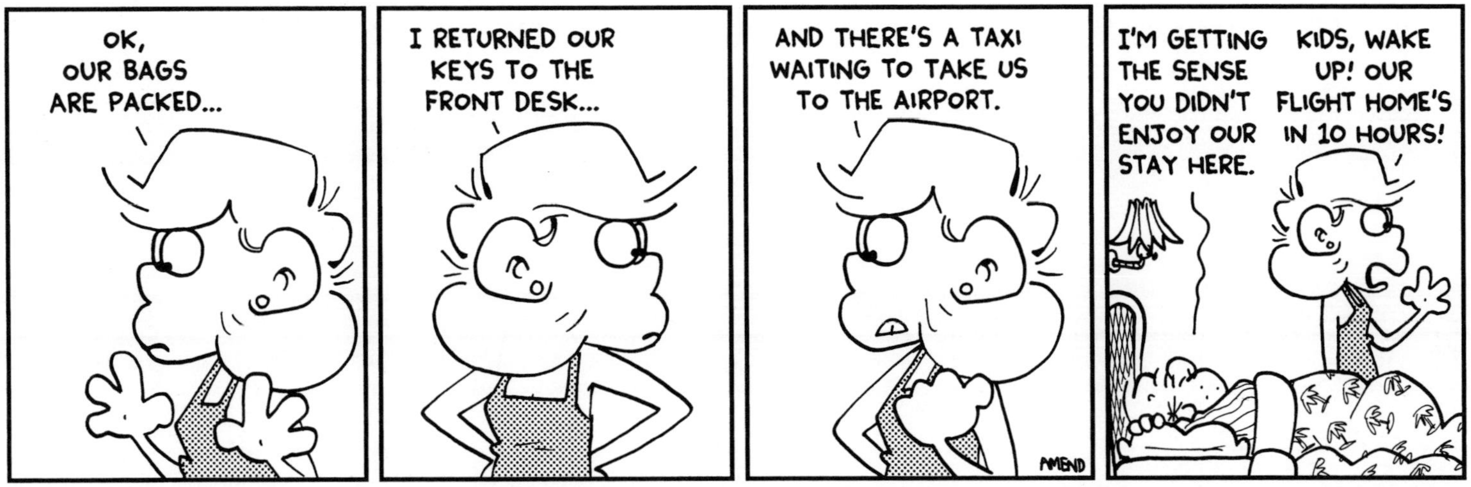
OK, OUR BAGS ARE PACKED...
I RETURNED OUR KEYS TO THE FRONT DESK...
AND THERE'S A TAXI WAITING TO TAKE US TO THE AIRPORT.
I'M GETTING THE SENSE YOU DIDN'T ENJOY OUR STAY HERE.
KIDS, WAKE UP! OUR FLIGHT HOME'S IN 10 HOURS!
AMEND
August 24, 2001

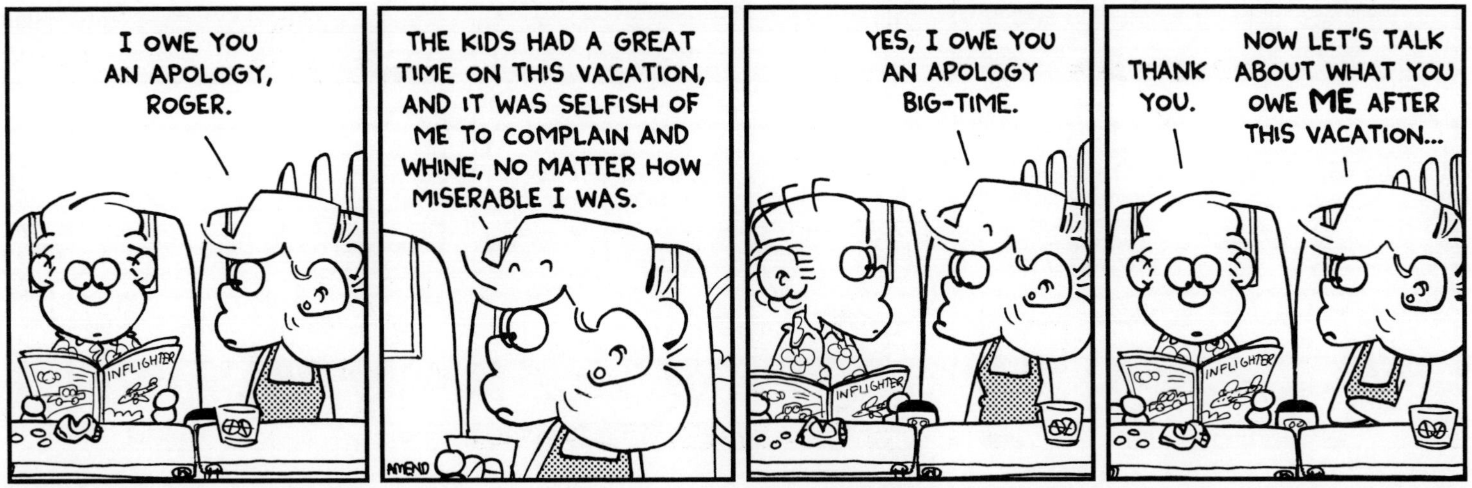
I OWE YOU AN APOLOGY, ROGER.
THE KIDS HAD A GREAT TIME ON THIS VACATION, AND IT WAS SELFISH OF ME TO COMPLAIN AND WHINE, NO MATTER HOW MISERABLE I WAS.
YES, I OWE YOU AN APOLOGY BIG-TIME.
THANK YOU.
NOW LET'S TALK ABOUT WHAT YOU OWE ME AFTER THIS VACATION...
INFLIGHTER
AMEND
August 25, 2001

Santa Claus (A) enters through chimney (B) and spots Christmas cookies (C) pulling string causing watering can (D) to fill bucket (E) striking match (F) lighting fuse (G) to rocket (H) which flies into wind chimes (I) that sound like a phone ringing, causing a groggy Dad (J) to lift receiver (K) pulling string and kicking boot (L) waking iguana (M) who sees ponytail (N) to attack and runs on treadmill (O) which cranks generator (P) powering angelic halo light (Q) above sleeping Jason (R) encouraging Santa (A) to give him lots and lots of presents(S).

December 23, 2001

May 12, 2002

124

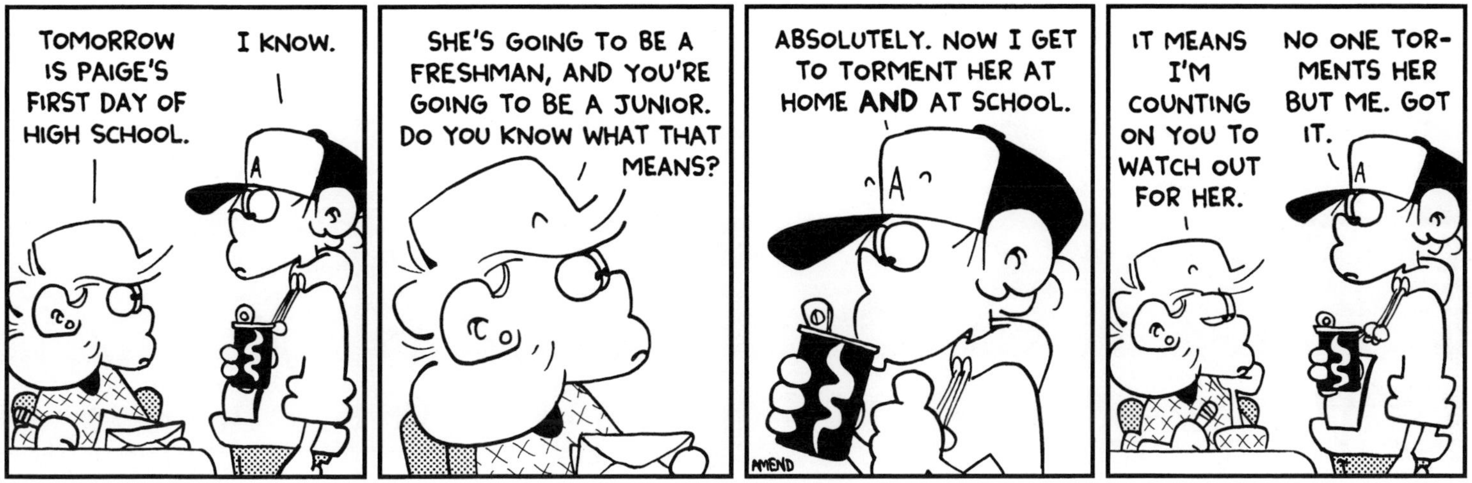
TOMORROW IS PAIGE'S FIRST DAY OF HIGH SCHOOL.
I KNOW.
SHE'S GOING TO BE A FRESHMAN, AND YOU'RE GOING TO BE A JUNIOR. DO YOU KNOW WHAT THAT MEANS?
ABSOLUTELY. NOW I GET TO TORMENT HER AT HOME AND AT SCHOOL.
IT MEANS I'M COUNTING ON YOU TO WATCH OUT FOR HER.
NO ONE TORMENTS HER BUT ME. GOT IT.
AMEND

September 3, 2001

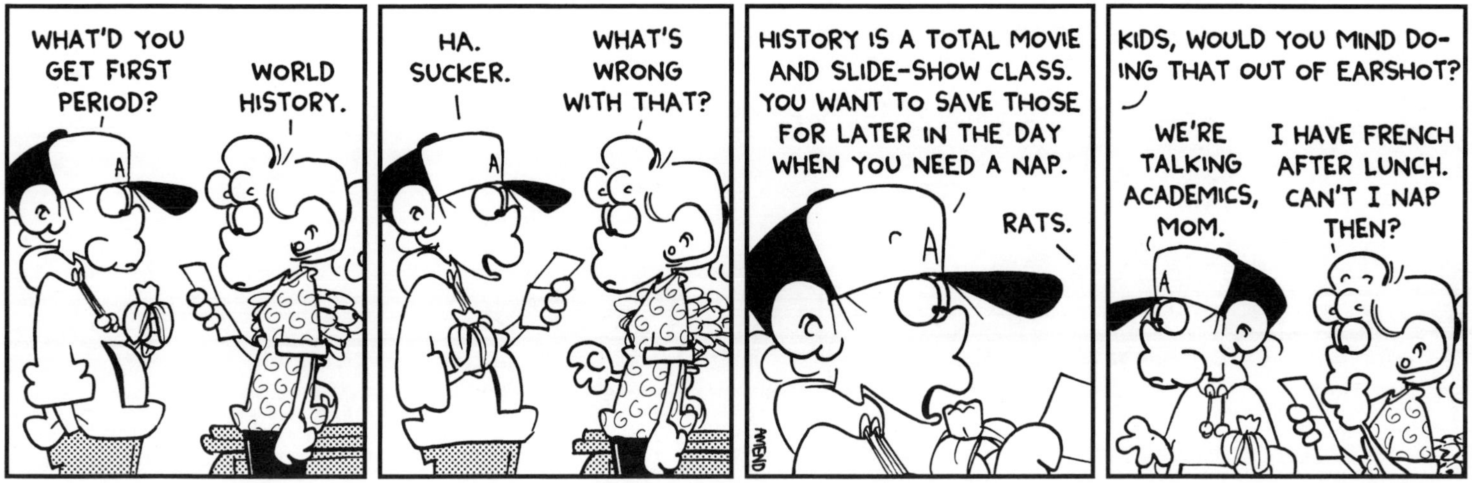
WHAT'D YOU GET FIRST PERIOD?
WORLD HISTORY.
HA. SUCKER.
WHAT'S WRONG WITH THAT?
HISTORY IS A TOTAL MOVIE AND SLIDE-SHOW CLASS. YOU WANT TO SAVE THOSE FOR LATER IN THE DAY WHEN YOU NEED A NAP.
RATS.
AMEND
KIDS, WOULD YOU MIND DOING THAT OUT OF EARSHOT?
WE'RE TALKING ACADEMICS, MOM.
I HAVE FRENCH AFTER LUNCH. CAN'T I NAP THEN?

September 4, 2001

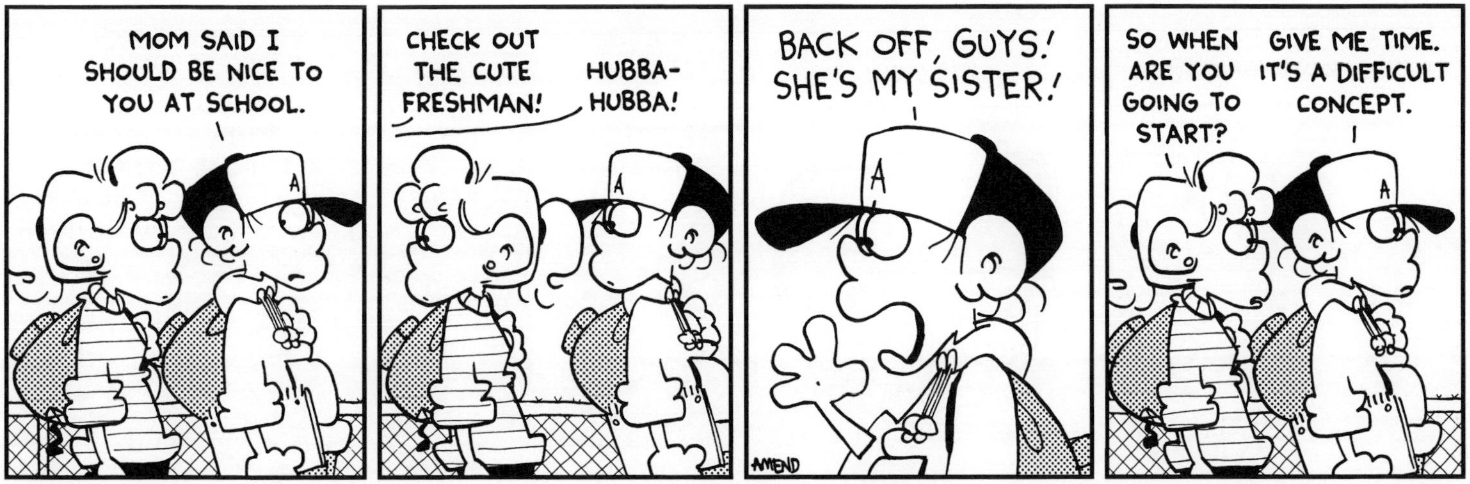
MOM SAID I SHOULD BE NICE TO YOU AT SCHOOL.
CHECK OUT THE CUTE FRESHMAN!
HUBBA-HUBBA!
BACK OFF, GUYS! SHE'S MY SISTER!
AMEND
SO WHEN ARE YOU GOING TO START?
GIVE ME TIME. IT'S A DIFFICULT CONCEPT.

September 5, 2001

PAIGE, WHAT ARE YOU DOING?

WRITING MY LOCKER COMBINATION ON MY HAND.

A TYPICAL NEWBIE FRESHMAN MISTAKE. AS SOON AS YOU PICK UP A BAR OF SOAP, YOU'RE DEAD. YOU NEED TO WRITE IT ON SOMETHING THAT NEVER GETS WASHED.

CAN I WRITE IT ON YOUR SWEATSHIRT, THEN?

HA HA.

THAT'S WHERE ALL OF MY IMPORTANT INFO GOES.

SO THAT'S NOT THE CHEM LAB I SMELL?

September 6, 2001

YOU GOT A CAFETERIA LUNCH??

YEAH, SO?

PAIGE, YOU ARE SUCH THE CLUELESS FRESHMAN. TRUST ME, THERE'S NOTHING MORE INEDIBLE THAN THE FOOD THIS SCHOOL SERVES.

EXCEPT MAYBE THE PEANUT BUTTER AND TOFU SANDWICHES MOM PACKED US TODAY.

I THOUGHT THOSE WERE MARSHMALLOWS.

OK, BUT YOU'RE STILL A FRESHMAN.

FRESH-CHICK.

September 7, 2001

I CAN'T BELIEVE HOW MUCH HOMEWORK THEY GIVE OUT IN HIGH SCHOOL!

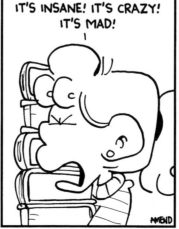

IT'S INSANE! IT'S CRAZY! IT'S MAD!

YOUR BROTHER PETER ALWAYS CLAIMS HE HAS NO HOMEWORK. INTERESTING.

PETER, GET IN HERE!

I THINK I'LL LIKE BEING A FRESHMAN.

CAN I HAVE MY BOOKS BACK NOW?

September 8, 2001

WASN'T THERE A TIME WHEN WE **ENJOYED** WATCHING TELEVISION?

Writing a humor strip the week of 9/11 wasn't easy.

September 24, 2001

DAD'S DONATING BLOOD??

YUP.

I THOUGHT HE WAS SCARED TO. YOU SAID HE WAS THE WORLD'S BIGGEST BABY AROUND NEEDLES.

SOMETIMES WE HAVE TO GROW UP, KIDDO.

WHOA. DID I JUST STUMBLE INTO "FOR BETTER OR FOR WORSE"?

YOU CAN STAY 10, SWEETIE. I DON'T MIND.

September 25, 2001

DID YOU REALLY DONATE BLOOD?

I DID.

DIDN'T IT HURT?

A LITTLE.

AND YOU DID IT ANYWAY?

I FIGURED DOING NOTHING WOULD HURT A LOT MORE.

September 26, 2001

127

September 27, 2001

September 28, 2001

September 29, 2001

October 18, 2001

October 25, 2001

October 26, 2001

129

October 30, 2001

October 31, 2001

November 24, 2001

December 22, 2001

December 26, 2001

January 1, 2002

SINCE WHEN DO YOU WEAR GLASSES, EILEEN?

IT'S A COSTUME, CAN'T YOU TELL?

I'M DRESSING UP THIS WEEK IN ANTICIPATION OF THE MOVIE EVERY BOOK FAN HAS BEEN WAITING LIKE CRAZY TO SEE!

"THE LORD OF THE RINGS" DOESN'T OPEN UNTIL **NEXT** MONTH, DOOFUS.

BESIDES, WHAT TOLKIEN CHARACTER SPORTS THAT HARRY POTTER EYEWEAR?

WHY DO I BOTHER WITH THESE MUGGLES?

November 12, 2001

YOU'RE WEARING A COSTUME ALL WEEK BECAUSE OF THE "HARRY POTTER" MOVIE?!

EILEEN, YOU ARE SUCH A LOSER! CAN'T YOU SEE HOW FOOLISH YOU LOOK?!

HEY, EVERYONE, CHECK OUT EILEEN! SHE'S ALL DRESSED UP LIKE HARRY POTTER!

WOW, SHE'S PULLING A JASON.

OK, **NOW** I FEEL LIKE A LOSER.

NO, NO! **I'M** DRESSING UP FOR "LORD OF THE RINGS"!

November 13, 2001

HEE HEE. EILEEN HAS CROSSED WANDS WITH THE WRONG "LORD OF THE RINGS" FAN.

LET HER WEAR HER STUPID HARRY POTTER GLASSES ALL WEEK... I'LL BE WEARING THIS BABY EVERY DAY FOR A MONTH!

I CAN'T WAIT TO HEAR HER SCREAM.

NICE DUMBLEDORE HAT.

IT'S A GANDALF HAT!

November 14, 2001

November 15, 2001

November 16, 2001

November 17, 2001

January 4, 2002

January 19, 2002

Basically, CHMOD 700 * restricts access to just the owner.

February 25, 2002

February 11, 2002

February 12, 2002

February 13, 2002

February 14, 2002

February 15, 2002

February 16, 2002

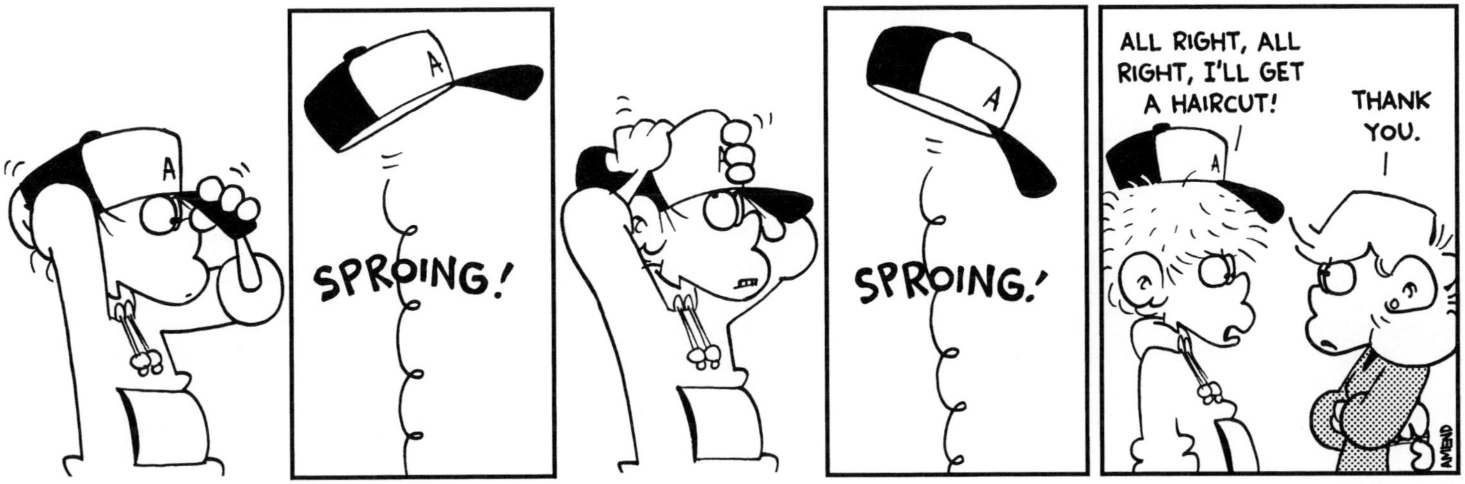
SPROING!
SPROING!
ALL RIGHT, ALL RIGHT, I'LL GET A HAIRCUT!
THANK YOU.
AMEND

February 18, 2002

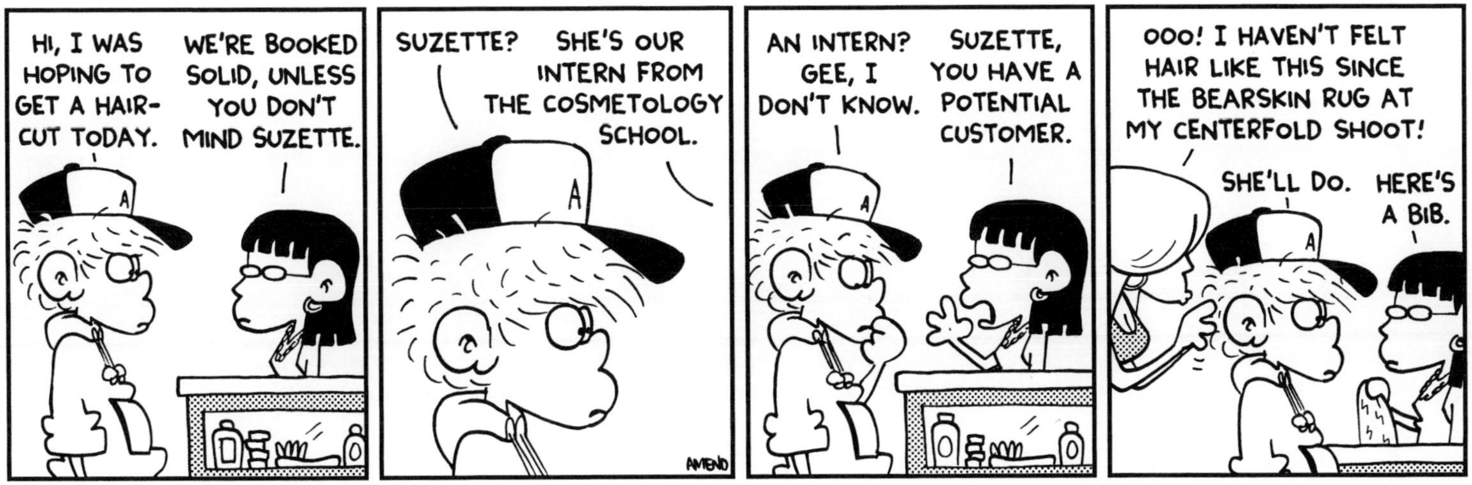
HI, I WAS HOPING TO GET A HAIR-CUT TODAY.
WE'RE BOOKED SOLID, UNLESS YOU DON'T MIND SUZETTE.
SUZETTE?
SHE'S OUR INTERN FROM THE COSMETOLOGY SCHOOL.
AMEND
AN INTERN? GEE, I DON'T KNOW.
SUZETTE, YOU HAVE A POTENTIAL CUSTOMER.
OOO! I HAVEN'T FELT HAIR LIKE THIS SINCE THE BEARSKIN RUG AT MY CENTERFOLD SHOOT!
SHE'LL DO.
HERE'S A BIB.

February 19, 2002

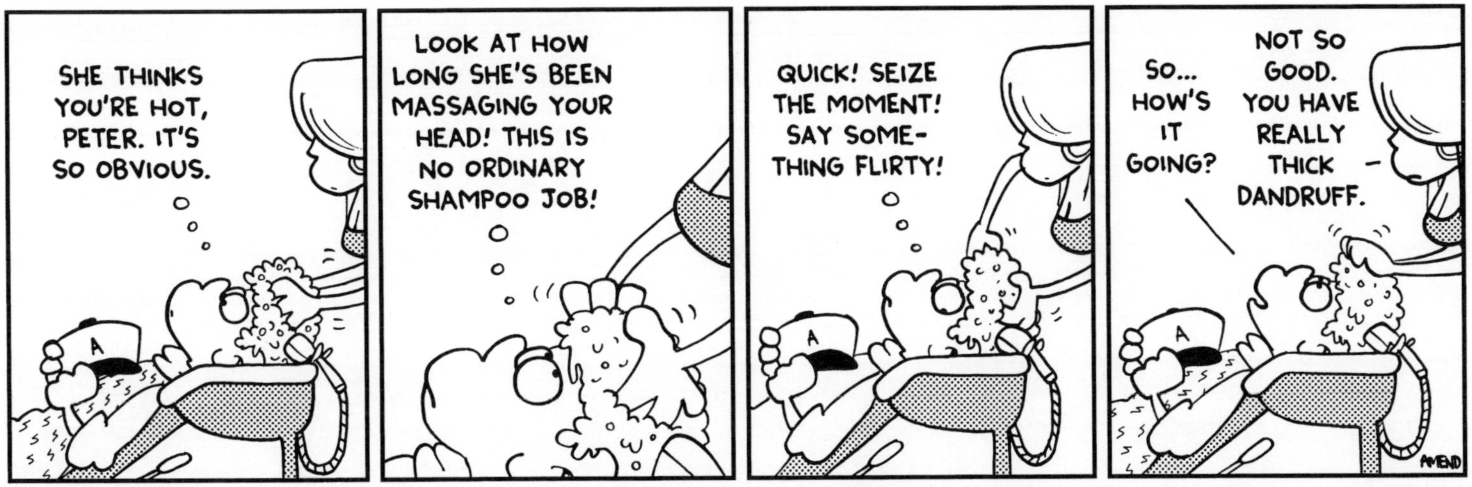
SHE THINKS YOU'RE HOT, PETER. IT'S SO OBVIOUS.
LOOK AT HOW LONG SHE'S BEEN MASSAGING YOUR HEAD! THIS IS NO ORDINARY SHAMPOO JOB!
QUICK! SEIZE THE MOMENT! SAY SOME-THING FLIRTY!
SO... HOW'S IT GOING?
NOT SO GOOD. YOU HAVE REALLY THICK DANDRUFF.
AMEND

February 20, 2002

THE MODELING PAID WELL ENOUGH, BUT IT WAS JUST SO MUCH WORK!

SNIP! SNIP! SNIP!

PUTTING **ON** SWIMSUITS! TAKING **OFF** SWIMSUITS! PUTTING **ON** LINGERIE! TAKING **OFF** LINGERIE!

THANK GOODNESS FOR THE OCCASIONAL NUDE JOBS.

SNIP! SNIP!

I'M SORRY—I JUST CUT YOUR EAR.

I DIDN'T NOTICE.

February 21, 2002

OOPSY-DOOPSY.

WHOOPSY-DAISY.

OH, FUDGY-WUDGY!

IT'S SO CUTE THE WAY YOU SAY THINGS.

DO WE HAVE A GLUEY GUNNY?

February 22, 2002

HOW'D YOUR HAIRCUT GO?

HOW'D IT GO? PICTURE THIS...

I SPENT 45 MINUTES IN A CHAIR WITH A FORMER LINGERIE MODEL RUNNING HER FINGERS ALL OVER MY HEAD AND NECK.

AND THEY ONLY CHARGED HALF-PRICE BECAUSE SHE'S STILL IN BEAUTICIAN'S SCHOOL.

I GUESS THE HALF-PRICE PART SOUNDS OK.

BEST... HAIRCUT... EVER.

February 23, 2002

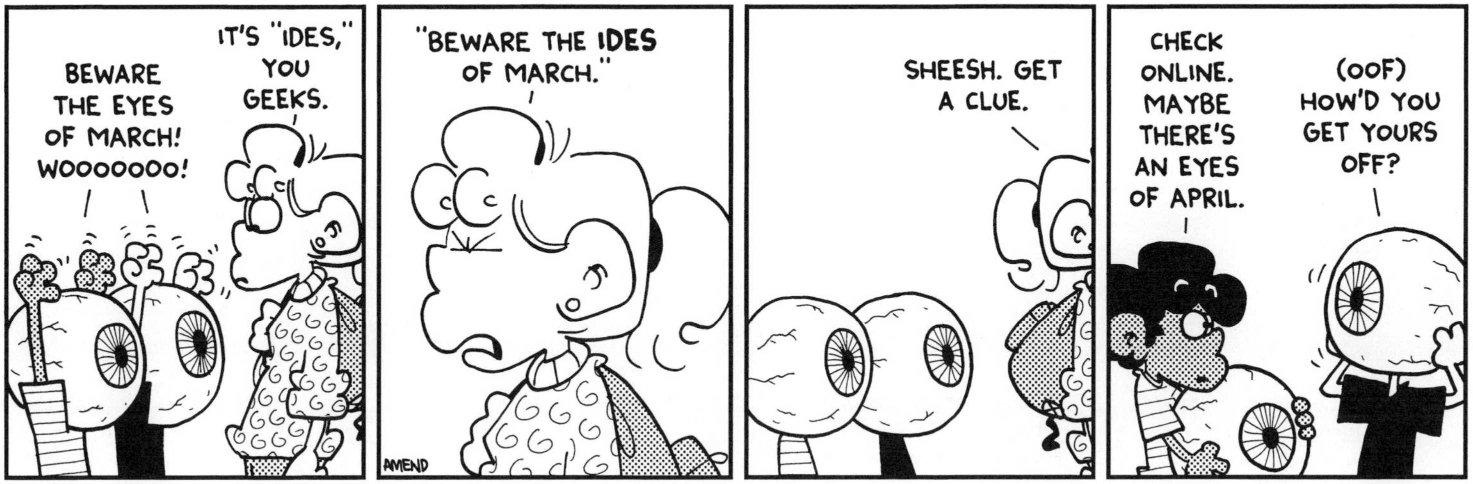
BEWARE THE EYES OF MARCH! WOOOOOOO!
IT'S "IDES," YOU GEEKS.
"BEWARE THE IDES OF MARCH."
AMEND
SHEESH. GET A CLUE.
CHECK ONLINE. MAYBE THERE'S AN EYES OF APRIL.
(OOF) HOW'D YOU GET YOURS OFF?

March 15, 2002

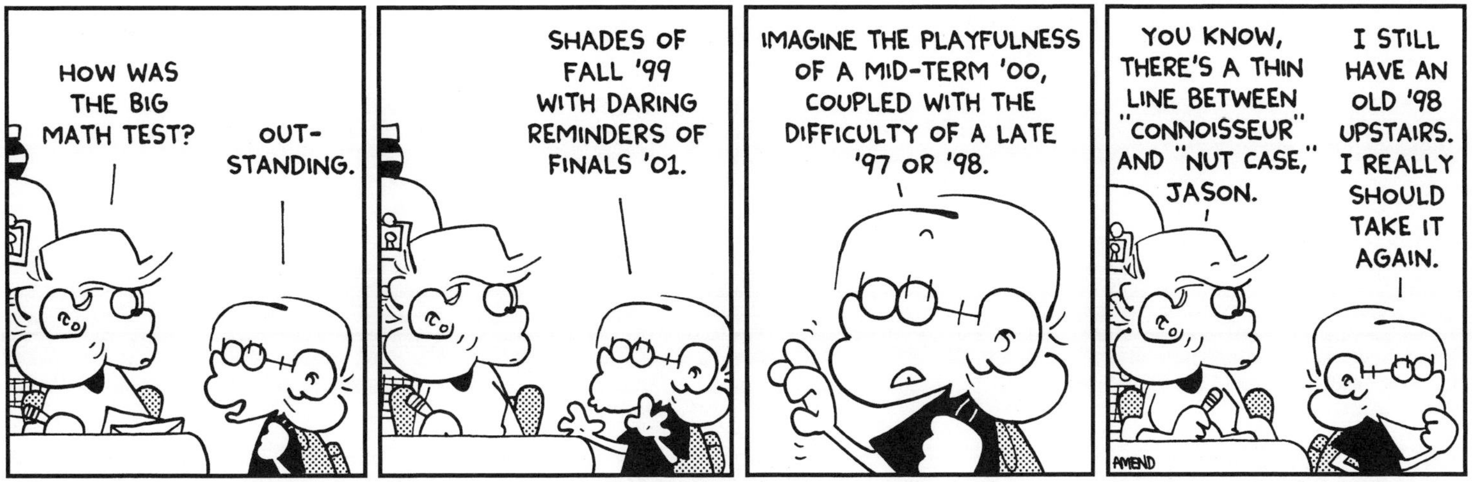
HOW WAS THE BIG MATH TEST?
OUT-STANDING.
SHADES OF FALL '99 WITH DARING REMINDERS OF FINALS '01.
IMAGINE THE PLAYFULNESS OF A MID-TERM '00, COUPLED WITH THE DIFFICULTY OF A LATE '97 OR '98.
YOU KNOW, THERE'S A THIN LINE BETWEEN "CONNOISSEUR" AND "NUT CASE," JASON.
I STILL HAVE AN OLD '98 UPSTAIRS. I REALLY SHOULD TAKE IT AGAIN.
AMEND

March 27, 2002

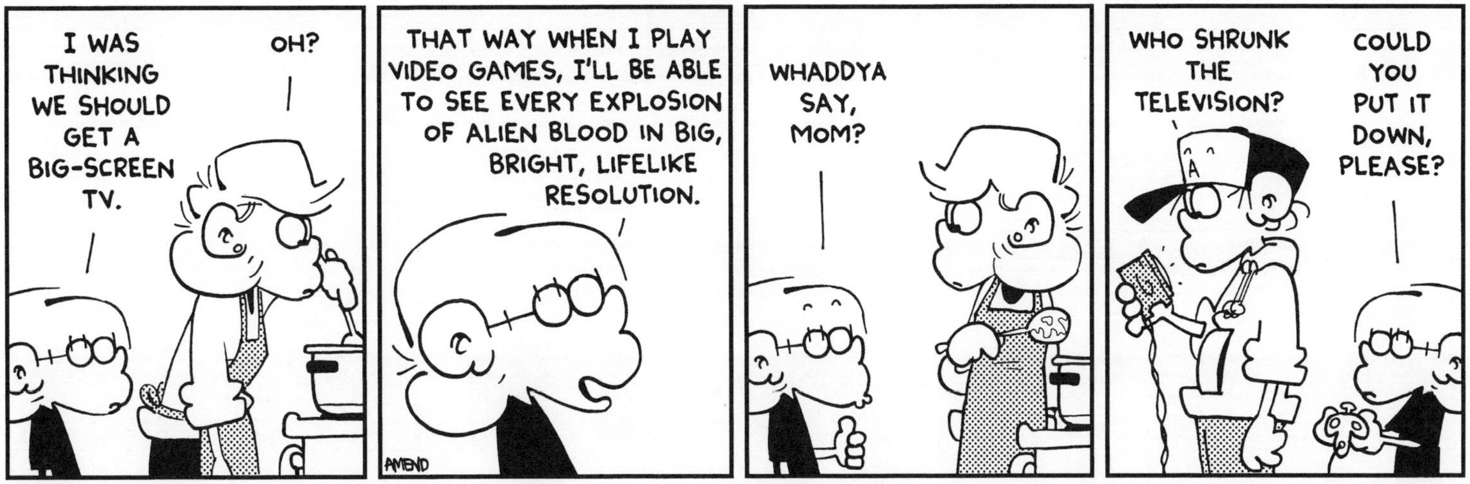
I WAS THINKING WE SHOULD GET A BIG-SCREEN TV.
OH?
THAT WAY WHEN I PLAY VIDEO GAMES, I'LL BE ABLE TO SEE EVERY EXPLOSION OF ALIEN BLOOD IN BIG, BRIGHT, LIFELIKE RESOLUTION.
AMEND
WHADDYA SAY, MOM?
WHO SHRUNK THE TELEVISION?
COULD YOU PUT IT DOWN, PLEASE?

April 13, 2002

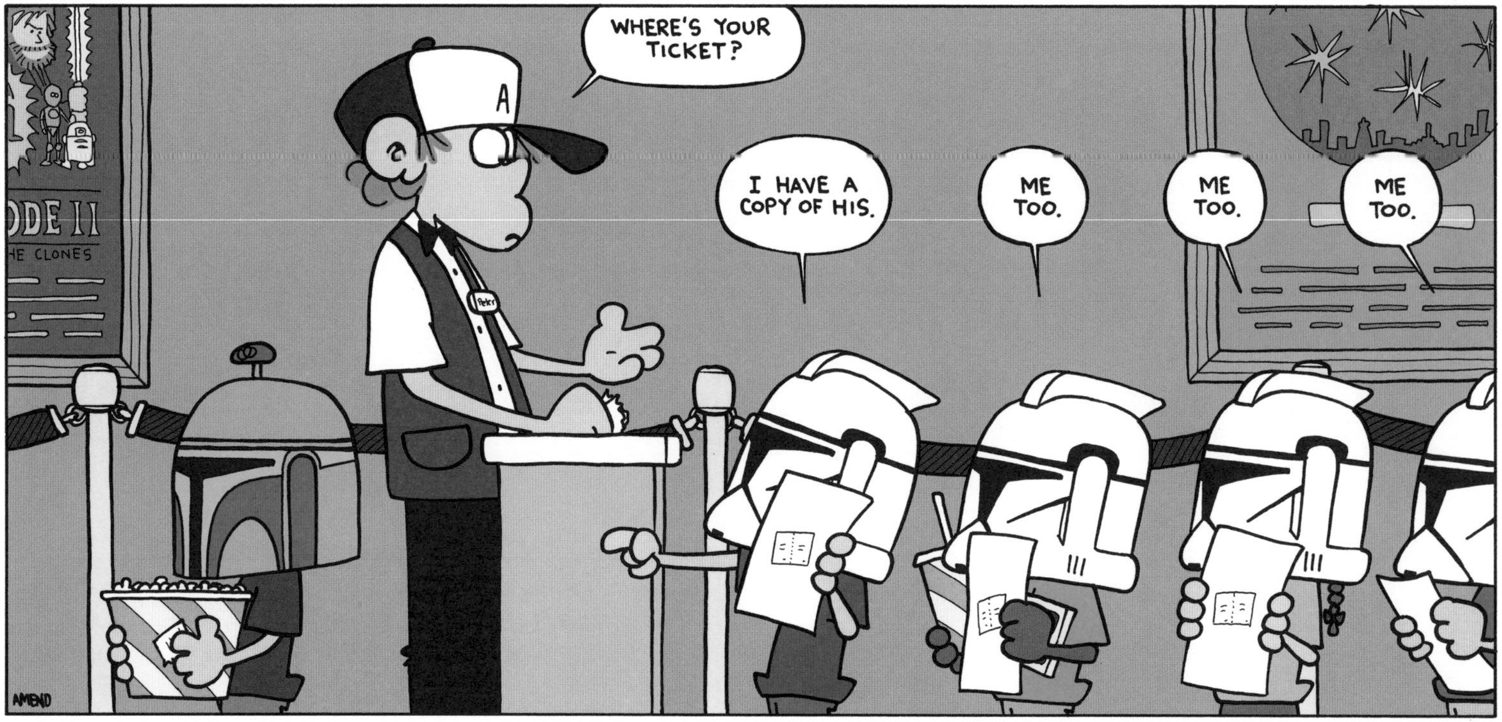
WHERE'S YOUR TICKET?
I HAVE A COPY OF HIS.
ME TOO.
ME TOO.
ME TOO.

May 19, 2002

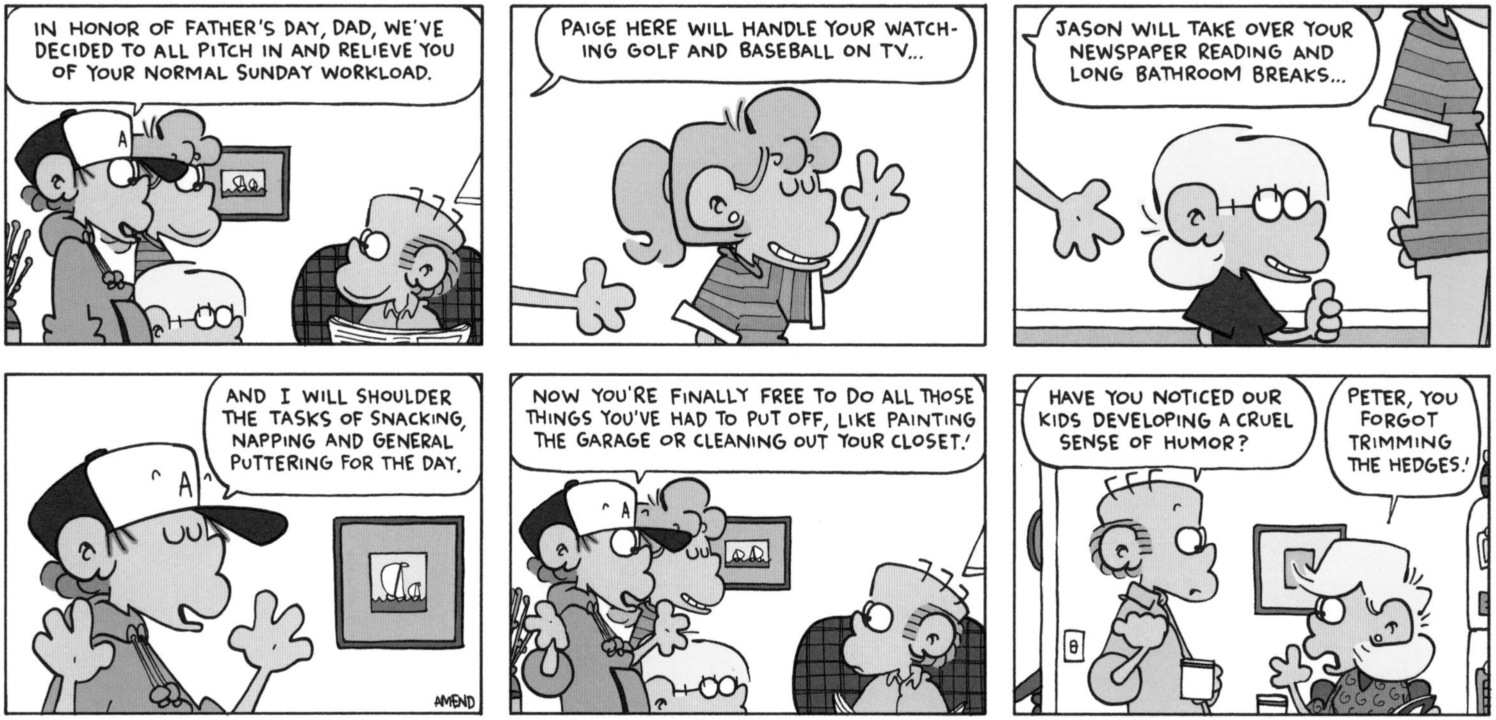
IN HONOR OF FATHER'S DAY, DAD, WE'VE DECIDED TO ALL PITCH IN AND RELIEVE YOU OF YOUR NORMAL SUNDAY WORKLOAD.
PAIGE HERE WILL HANDLE YOUR WATCHING GOLF AND BASEBALL ON TV...
JASON WILL TAKE OVER YOUR NEWSPAPER READING AND LONG BATHROOM BREAKS...
AND I WILL SHOULDER THE TASKS OF SNACKING, NAPPING AND GENERAL PUTTERING FOR THE DAY.
NOW YOU'RE FINALLY FREE TO DO ALL THOSE THINGS YOU'VE HAD TO PUT OFF, LIKE PAINTING THE GARAGE OR CLEANING OUT YOUR CLOSET!
HAVE YOU NOTICED OUR KIDS DEVELOPING A CRUEL SENSE OF HUMOR?
PETER, YOU FORGOT TRIMMING THE HEDGES!

June 16, 2002

June 30, 2002

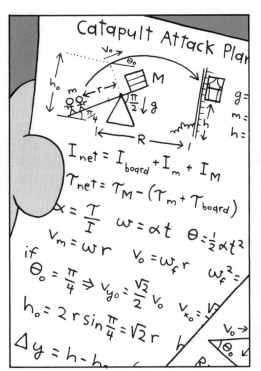

July 28, 2002

I was only a B student in college, so there's a chance my physics here isn't 100 percent correct.

141

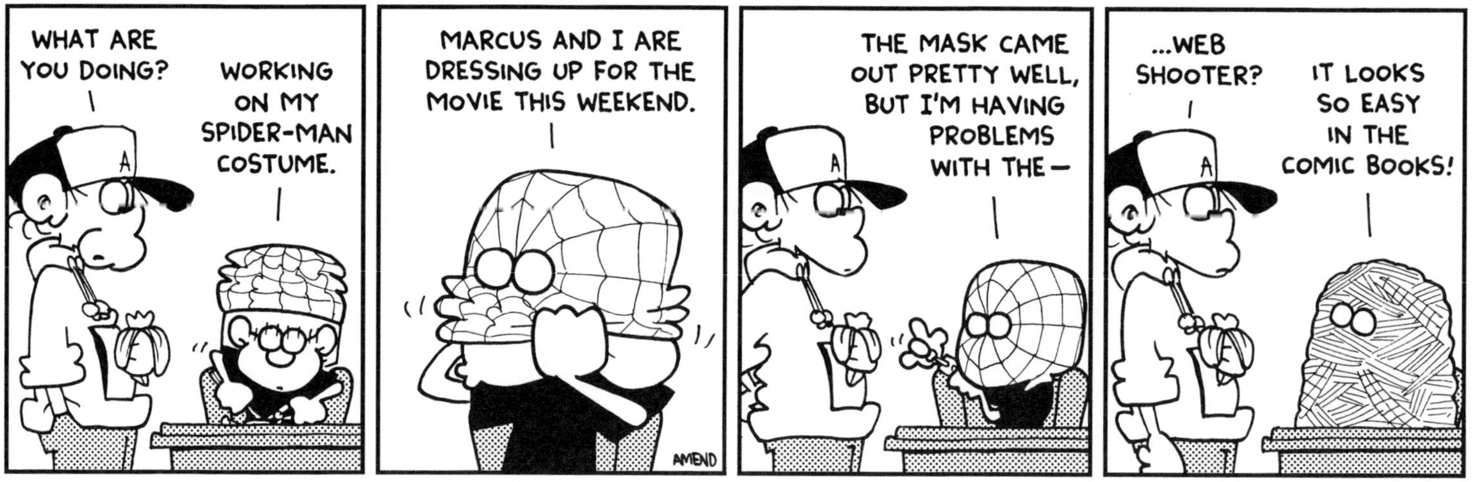
WHAT ARE YOU DOING?
WORKING ON MY SPIDER-MAN COSTUME.
MARCUS AND I ARE DRESSING UP FOR THE MOVIE THIS WEEKEND.
THE MASK CAME OUT PRETTY WELL, BUT I'M HAVING PROBLEMS WITH THE—
...WEB SHOOTER?
IT LOOKS SO EASY IN THE COMIC BOOKS!
AMEND

April 29, 2002

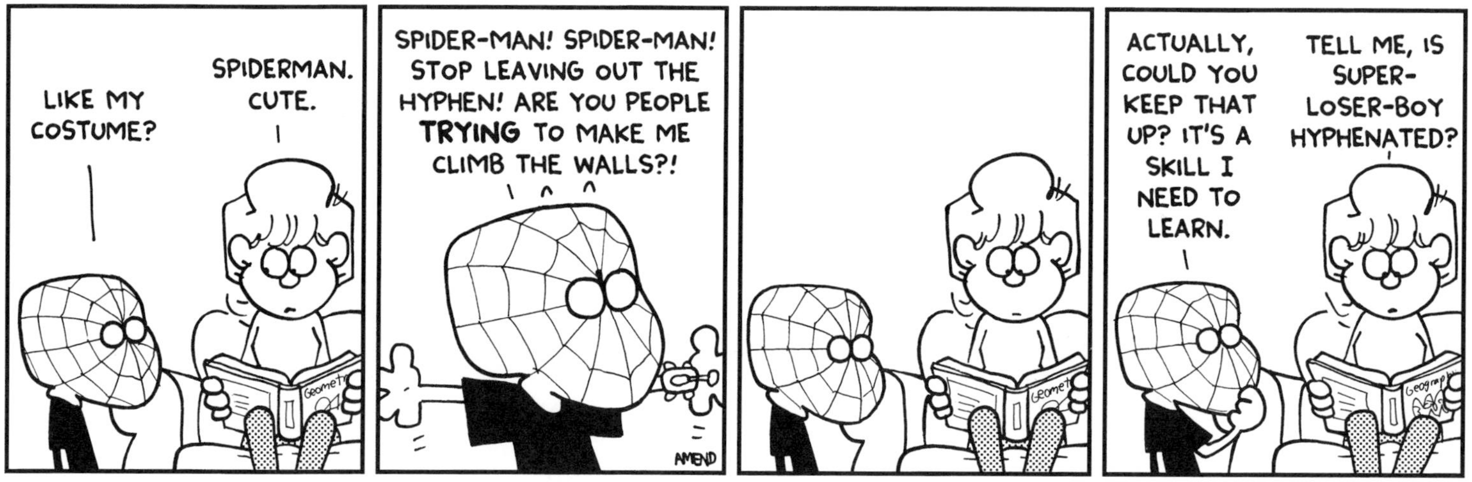
LIKE MY COSTUME?
SPIDERMAN. CUTE.
SPIDER-MAN! SPIDER-MAN! STOP LEAVING OUT THE HYPHEN! ARE YOU PEOPLE TRYING TO MAKE ME CLIMB THE WALLS?!
AMEND
ACTUALLY, COULD YOU KEEP THAT UP? IT'S A SKILL I NEED TO LEARN.
TELL ME, IS SUPER-LOSER-BOY HYPHENATED?

April 30, 2002

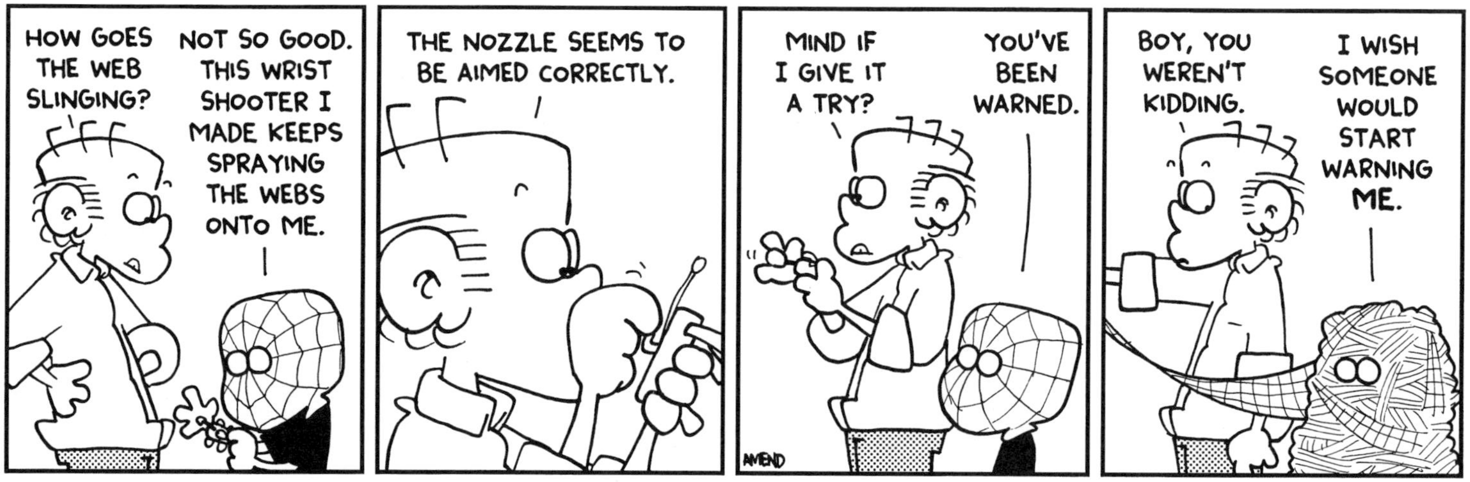
HOW GOES THE WEB SLINGING?
NOT SO GOOD. THIS WRIST SHOOTER I MADE KEEPS SPRAYING THE WEBS ONTO ME.
THE NOZZLE SEEMS TO BE AIMED CORRECTLY.
MIND IF I GIVE IT A TRY?
YOU'VE BEEN WARNED.
AMEND
BOY, YOU WEREN'T KIDDING.
I WISH SOMEONE WOULD START WARNING ME.

May 1, 2002

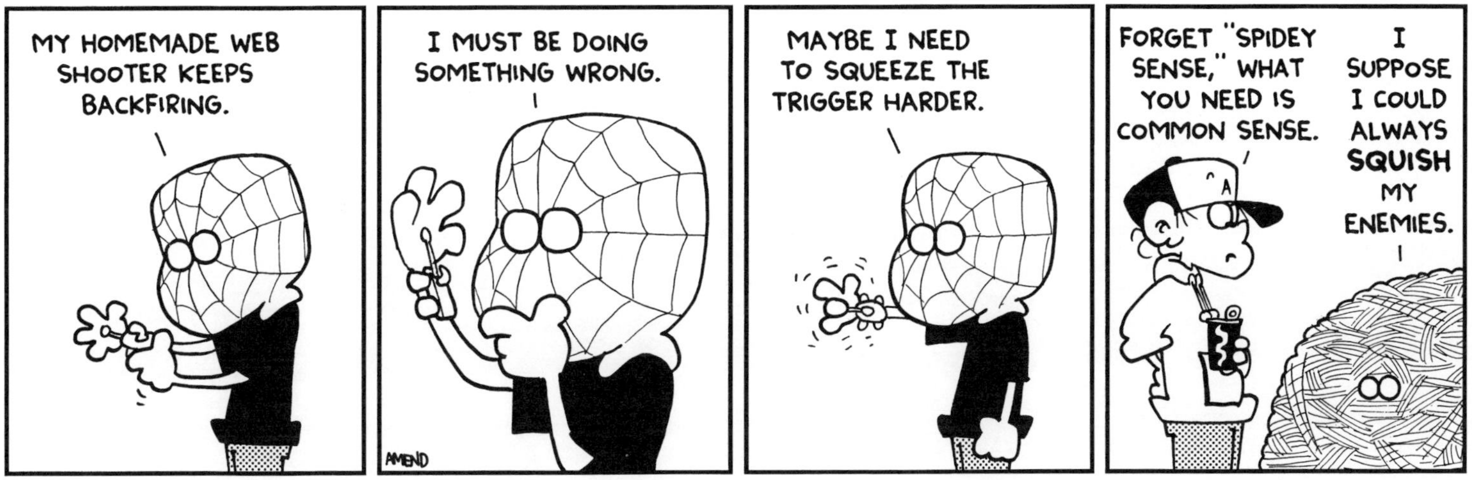
MY HOMEMADE WEB SHOOTER KEEPS BACKFIRING.
I MUST BE DOING SOMETHING WRONG.
MAYBE I NEED TO SQUEEZE THE TRIGGER HARDER.
FORGET "SPIDEY SENSE," WHAT YOU NEED IS COMMON SENSE.
I SUPPOSE I COULD ALWAYS **SQUISH** MY ENEMIES.

May 2, 2002

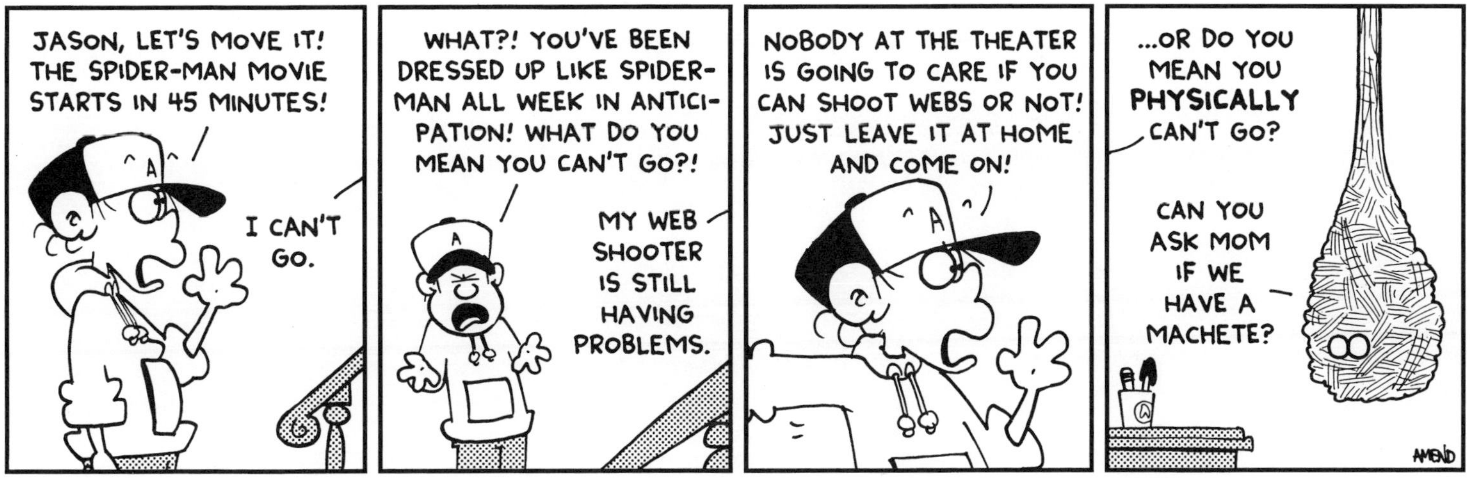
JASON, LET'S MOVE IT! THE SPIDER-MAN MOVIE STARTS IN 45 MINUTES!
I CAN'T GO.
WHAT?! YOU'VE BEEN DRESSED UP LIKE SPIDER-MAN ALL WEEK IN ANTICI-PATION! WHAT DO YOU MEAN YOU CAN'T GO?!
MY WEB SHOOTER IS STILL HAVING PROBLEMS.
NOBODY AT THE THEATER IS GOING TO CARE IF YOU CAN SHOOT WEBS OR NOT! JUST LEAVE IT AT HOME AND COME ON!
...OR DO YOU MEAN YOU **PHYSICALLY** CAN'T GO?
CAN YOU ASK MOM IF WE HAVE A MACHETE?

May 3, 2002

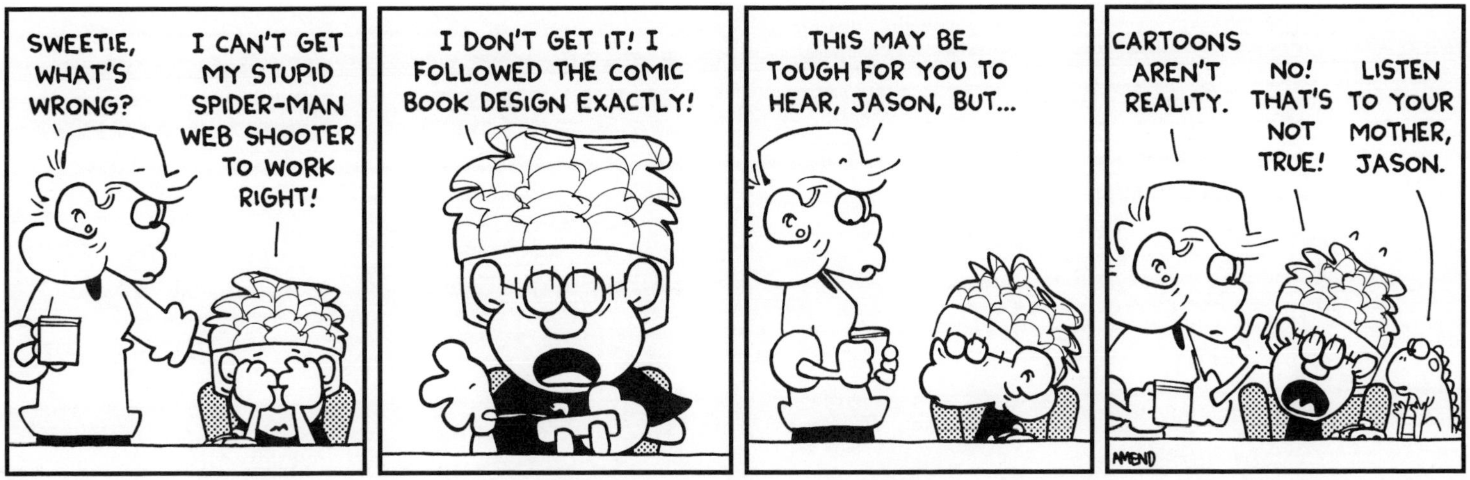
SWEETIE, WHAT'S WRONG?
I CAN'T GET MY STUPID SPIDER-MAN WEB SHOOTER TO WORK RIGHT!
I DON'T GET IT! I FOLLOWED THE COMIC BOOK DESIGN EXACTLY!
THIS MAY BE TOUGH FOR YOU TO HEAR, JASON, BUT...
CARTOONS AREN'T REALITY.
NO! THAT'S NOT TRUE!
LISTEN TO YOUR MOTHER, JASON.

May 4, 2002

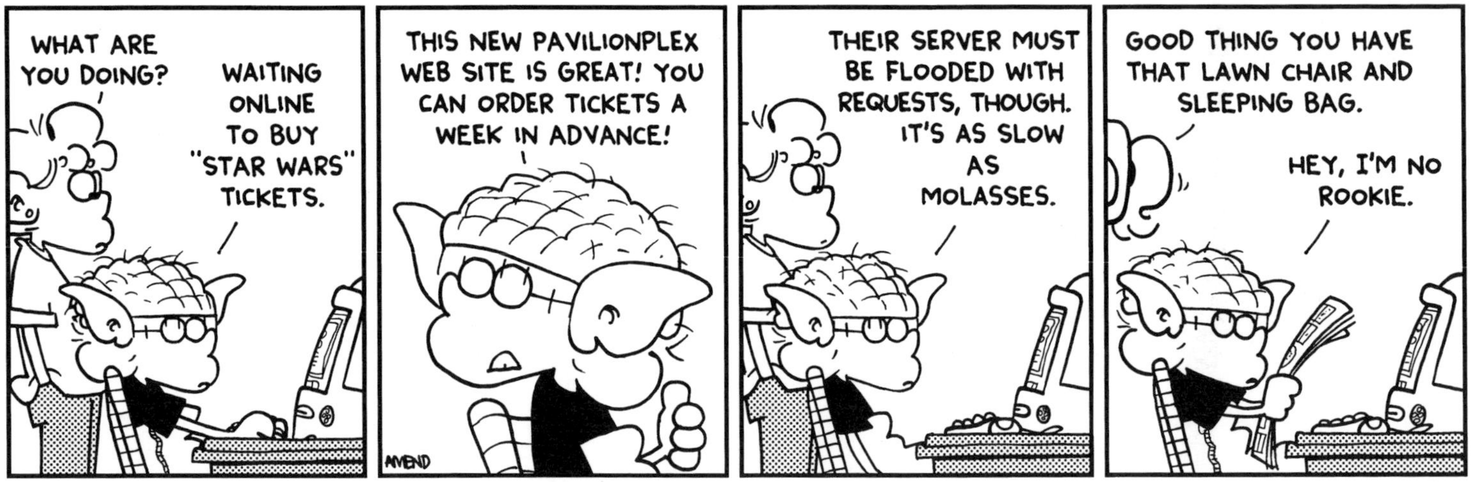
WHAT ARE YOU DOING?
WAITING ONLINE TO BUY "STAR WARS" TICKETS.
THIS NEW PAVILIONPLEX WEB SITE IS GREAT! YOU CAN ORDER TICKETS A WEEK IN ADVANCE!
AMEND
THEIR SERVER MUST BE FLOODED WITH REQUESTS, THOUGH. IT'S AS SLOW AS MOLASSES.
GOOD THING YOU HAVE THAT LAWN CHAIR AND SLEEPING BAG.
HEY, I'M NO ROOKIE.

May 13, 2002

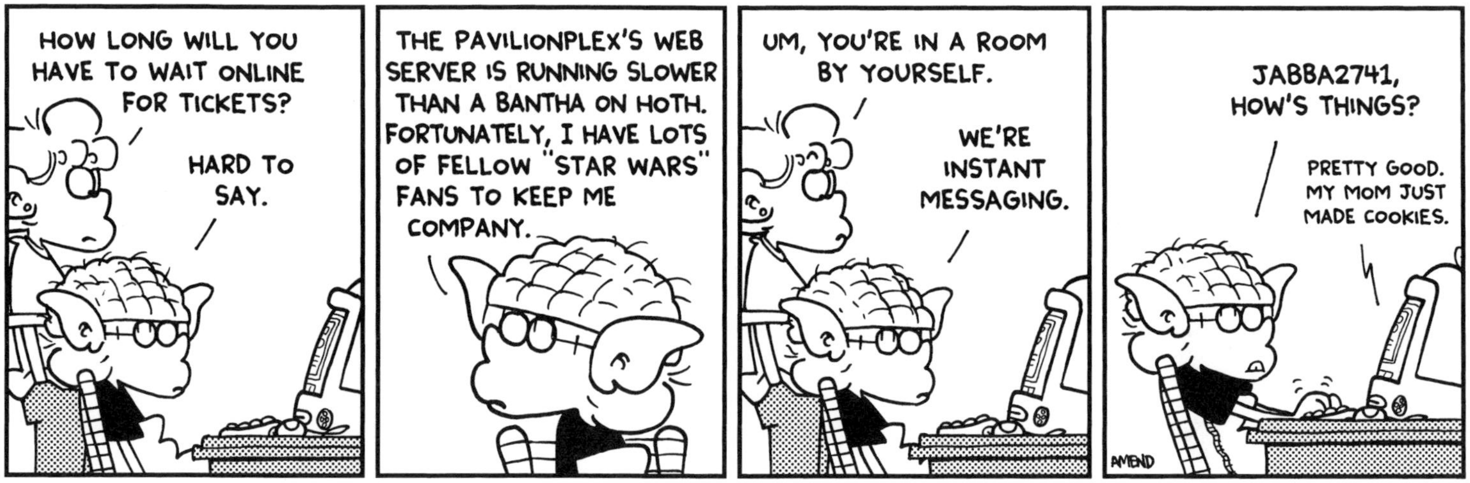
HOW LONG WILL YOU HAVE TO WAIT ONLINE FOR TICKETS?
HARD TO SAY.
THE PAVILIONPLEX'S WEB SERVER IS RUNNING SLOWER THAN A BANTHA ON HOTH. FORTUNATELY, I HAVE LOTS OF FELLOW "STAR WARS" FANS TO KEEP ME COMPANY.
UM, YOU'RE IN A ROOM BY YOURSELF.
WE'RE INSTANT MESSAGING.
JABBA2741, HOW'S THINGS?
PRETTY GOOD. MY MOM JUST MADE COOKIES.
AMEND

May 14, 2002

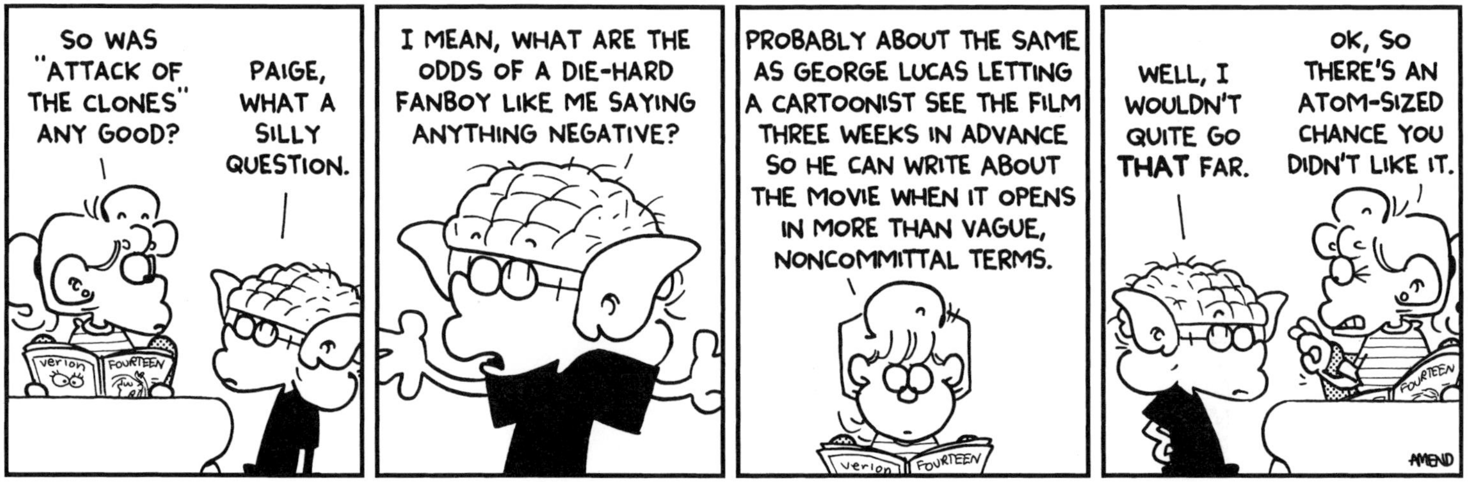
SO WAS "ATTACK OF THE CLONES" ANY GOOD?
PAIGE, WHAT A SILLY QUESTION.
verion
FOURTEEN
I MEAN, WHAT ARE THE ODDS OF A DIE-HARD FANBOY LIKE ME SAYING ANYTHING NEGATIVE?
PROBABLY ABOUT THE SAME AS GEORGE LUCAS LETTING A CARTOONIST SEE THE FILM THREE WEEKS IN ADVANCE SO HE CAN WRITE ABOUT THE MOVIE WHEN IT OPENS IN MORE THAN VAGUE, NONCOMMITTAL TERMS.
verion
FOURTEEN
WELL, I WOULDN'T QUITE GO THAT FAR.
OK, SO THERE'S AN ATOM-SIZED CHANCE YOU DIDN'T LIKE IT.
FOURTEEN
AMEND

May 18, 2002

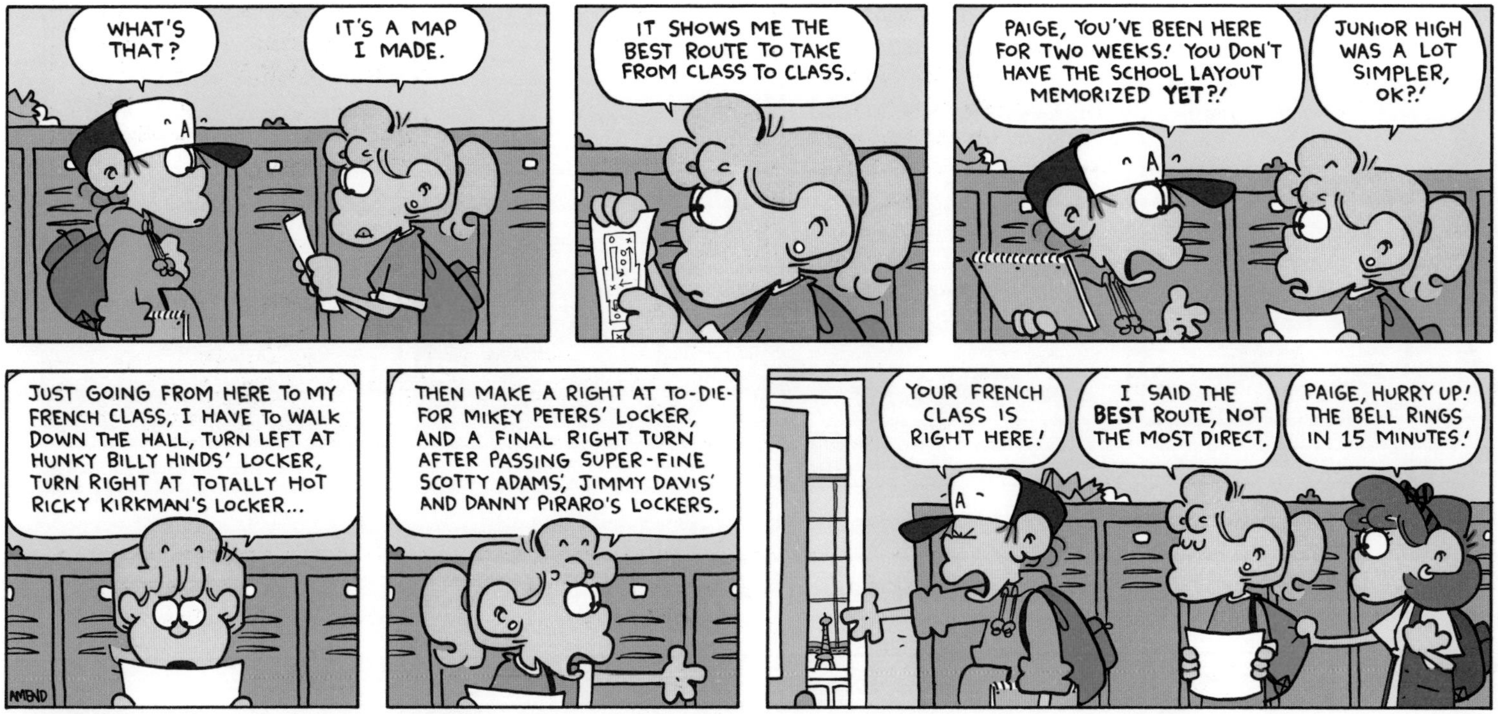
WHAT'S THAT?
IT'S A MAP I MADE.
IT SHOWS ME THE BEST ROUTE TO TAKE FROM CLASS TO CLASS.
PAIGE, YOU'VE BEEN HERE FOR TWO WEEKS! YOU DON'T HAVE THE SCHOOL LAYOUT MEMORIZED YET?!
JUNIOR HIGH WAS A LOT SIMPLER, OK?!
JUST GOING FROM HERE TO MY FRENCH CLASS, I HAVE TO WALK DOWN THE HALL, TURN LEFT AT HUNKY BILLY HINDS' LOCKER, TURN RIGHT AT TOTALLY HOT RICKY KIRKMAN'S LOCKER...
THEN MAKE A RIGHT AT TO-DIE-FOR MIKEY PETERS' LOCKER, AND A FINAL RIGHT TURN AFTER PASSING SUPER-FINE SCOTTY ADAMS', JIMMY DAVIS' AND DANNY PIRARO'S LOCKERS.
YOUR FRENCH CLASS IS RIGHT HERE!
I SAID THE BEST ROUTE, NOT THE MOST DIRECT.
PAIGE, HURRY UP! THE BELL RINGS IN 15 MINUTES!

September 15, 2002

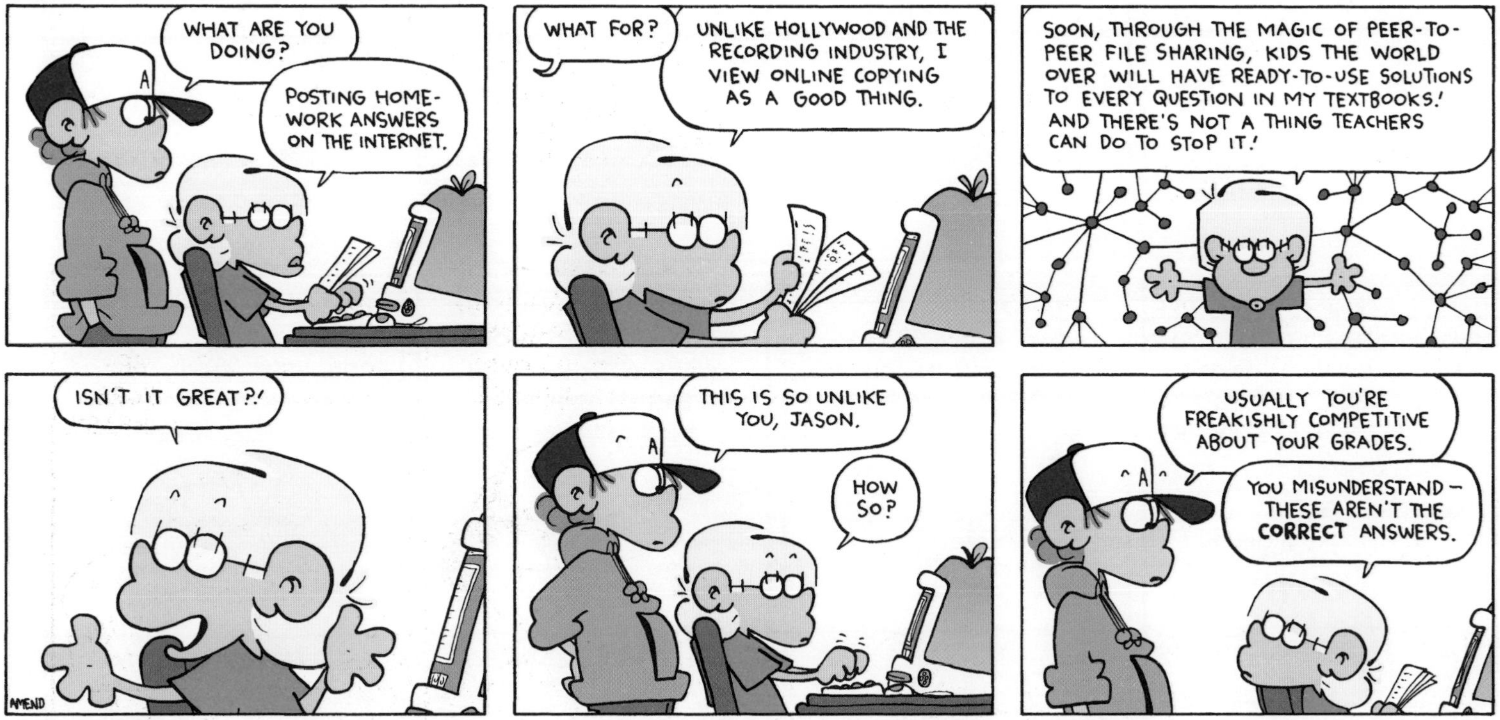
WHAT ARE YOU DOING?
POSTING HOME-WORK ANSWERS ON THE INTERNET.
WHAT FOR?
UNLIKE HOLLYWOOD AND THE RECORDING INDUSTRY, I VIEW ONLINE COPYING AS A GOOD THING.
SOON, THROUGH THE MAGIC OF PEER-TO-PEER FILE SHARING, KIDS THE WORLD OVER WILL HAVE READY-TO-USE SOLUTIONS TO EVERY QUESTION IN MY TEXTBOOKS! AND THERE'S NOT A THING TEACHERS CAN DO TO STOP IT!
ISN'T IT GREAT?!
THIS IS SO UNLIKE YOU, JASON.
HOW SO?
USUALLY YOU'RE FREAKISHLY COMPETITIVE ABOUT YOUR GRADES.
YOU MISUNDERSTAND— THESE AREN'T THE CORRECT ANSWERS.

September 29, 2002

Panel 1 (July 8, 2002):
YOU'RE READING A MARTHA STEWART MAGAZINE?
YOU BET I AM.

Panel 2:
IF HER STOCK-TRADING MESS DOESN'T GO AWAY, THE WORLD MAY SOON BE LOOKING FOR A NEW DOYENNE OF DOMESTICITY TO PUMP FULL OF CASH.

Panel 3:
WHAT DO YOU CARE?

Panel 4:
AND WHAT'S WITH THIS BLOND WIG?
DO YOU KNOW IF WE HAVE ANY DOILY SCISSORS?

July 8, 2002

Getting Jason to look like Martha Stewart was a huge pain. Not sure I pulled it off as well as I wanted.

Panel 5 (July 9, 2002):
JASON, YOU'RE A LUNATIC.
AM I?

Panel 6:
IF MARTHA STEWART ENDS UP GOING TO THE SLAMMER, *SOMEONE* HAS TO TAKE OVER HER ZILLION-DOLLAR EMPIRE.

Panel 7:
WHO BETTER THAN HER LONG-LOST, YOUNGER TWIN SISTER, JARTHA?

Panel 8:
STILL THINK I'M A LUNATIC?
NO. NO, THAT'S TOO KIND.

July 9, 2002

Panel 9 (July 10, 2002):
DARE I ASK WHY YOUR BROTHER IS WEARING A WIG?
HE HOPES TO BE THE NEXT MARTHA STEWART.

Panel 10:
MARTHA STEWART?! WHAT INTEREST DOES JASON HAVE IN COOKING AND ENTERTAINING?!

Panel 11:
I THINK HIS PLAN IS TO MELD HER SUPER-WOMAN WAYS WITH HIS OWN AREAS OF EXPERTISE.

Panel 12:
YOU WROTE THIS WEB BROWSER FROM SCRATCH?! WHEN?!
BE-FORE BREAKFAST.

146

July 10, 2002

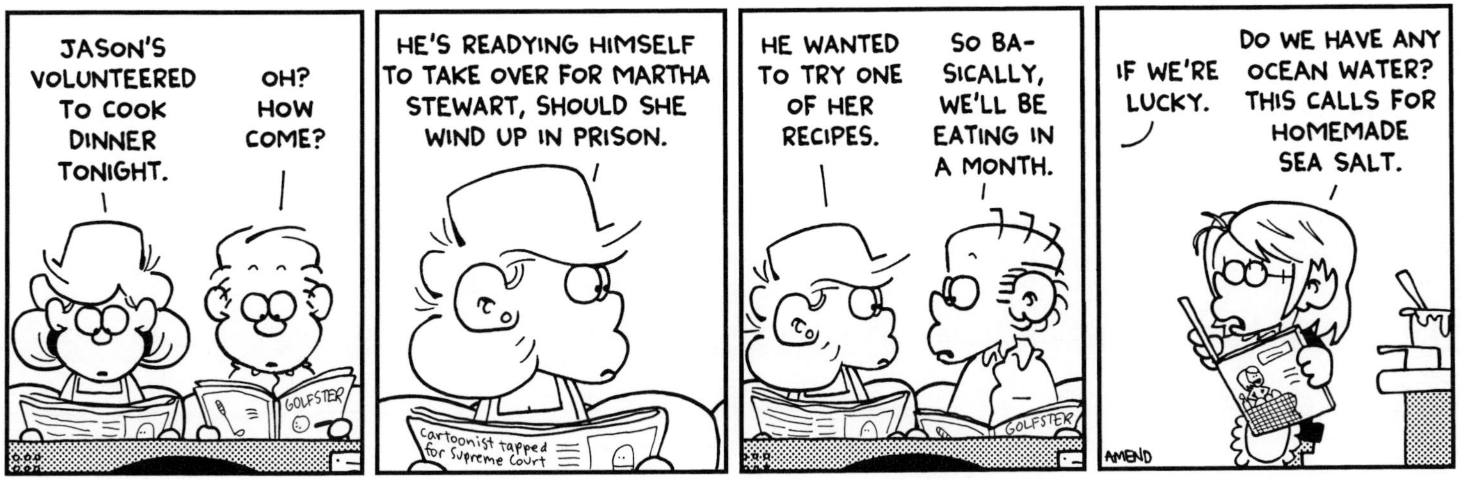
JASON'S VOLUNTEERED TO COOK DINNER TONIGHT.
OH? HOW COME?
GOLFSTER
HE'S READYING HIMSELF TO TAKE OVER FOR MARTHA STEWART, SHOULD SHE WIND UP IN PRISON.
Cartoonist tapped for Supreme Court
HE WANTED TO TRY ONE OF HER RECIPES.
SO BASICALLY, WE'LL BE EATING IN A MONTH.
GOLFSTER
IF WE'RE LUCKY.
DO WE HAVE ANY OCEAN WATER? THIS CALLS FOR HOMEMADE SEA SALT.
AMEND

July 11, 2002

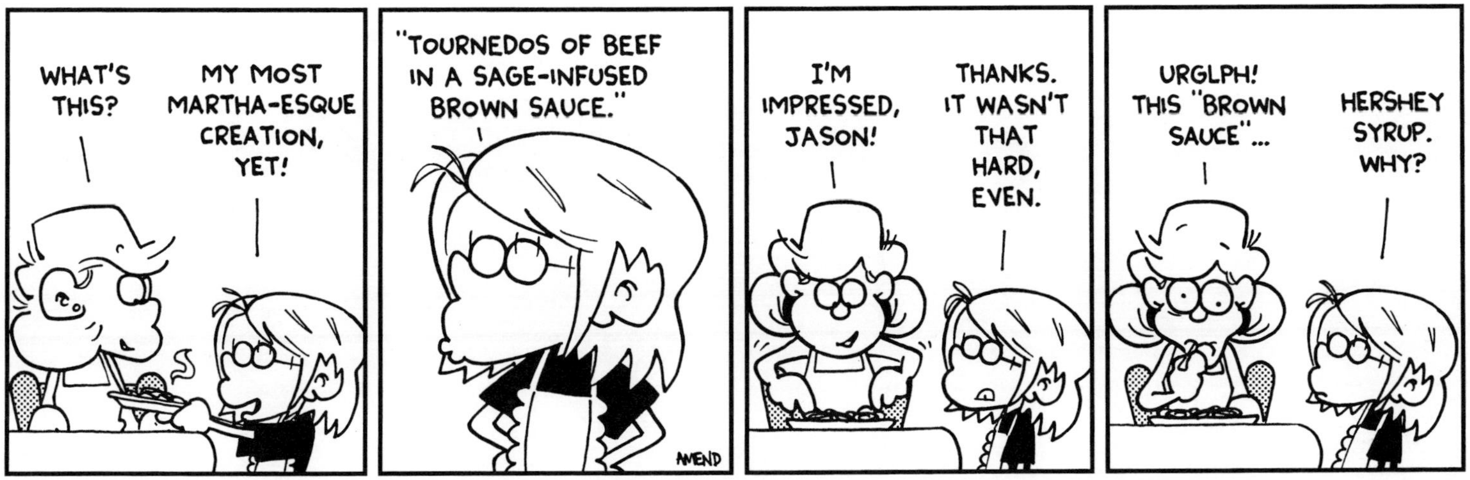
WHAT'S THIS?
MY MOST MARTHA-ESQUE CREATION, YET!
"TOURNEDOS OF BEEF IN A SAGE-INFUSED BROWN SAUCE."
AMEND
I'M IMPRESSED, JASON!
THANKS. IT WASN'T THAT HARD, EVEN.
URGLPH! THIS "BROWN SAUCE"...
HERSHEY SYRUP. WHY?

July 12, 2002

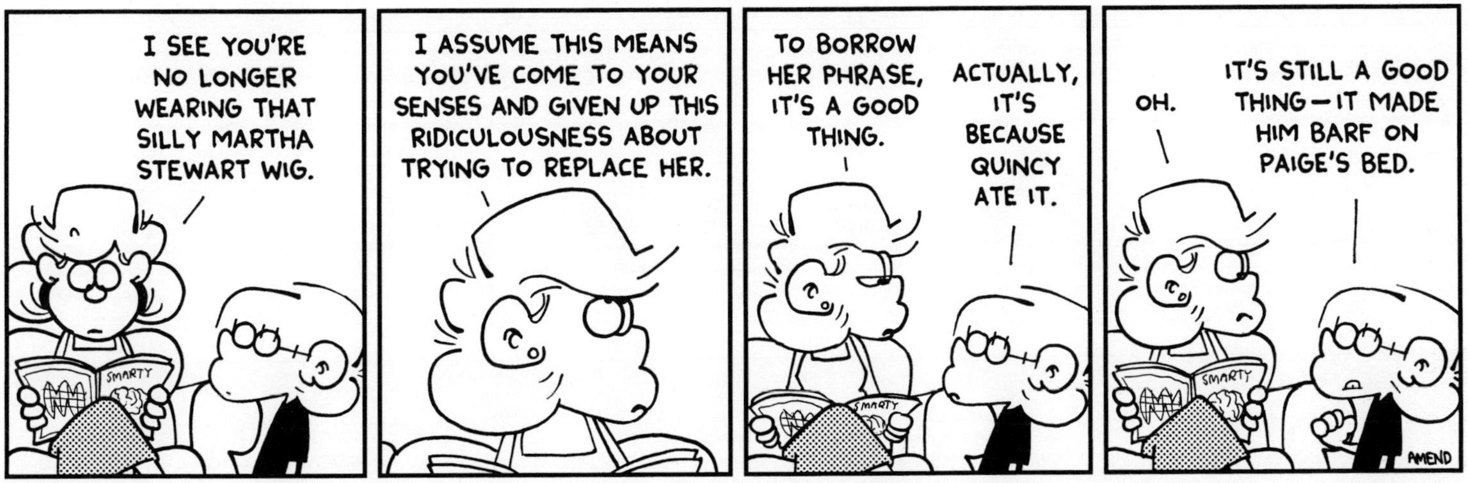
I SEE YOU'RE NO LONGER WEARING THAT SILLY MARTHA STEWART WIG.
SMARTY
I ASSUME THIS MEANS YOU'VE COME TO YOUR SENSES AND GIVEN UP THIS RIDICULOUSNESS ABOUT TRYING TO REPLACE HER.
TO BORROW HER PHRASE, IT'S A GOOD THING.
ACTUALLY, IT'S BECAUSE QUINCY ATE IT.
SMARTY
OH.
IT'S STILL A GOOD THING—IT MADE HIM BARF ON PAIGE'S BED.
SMARTY
AMEND

July 13, 2002

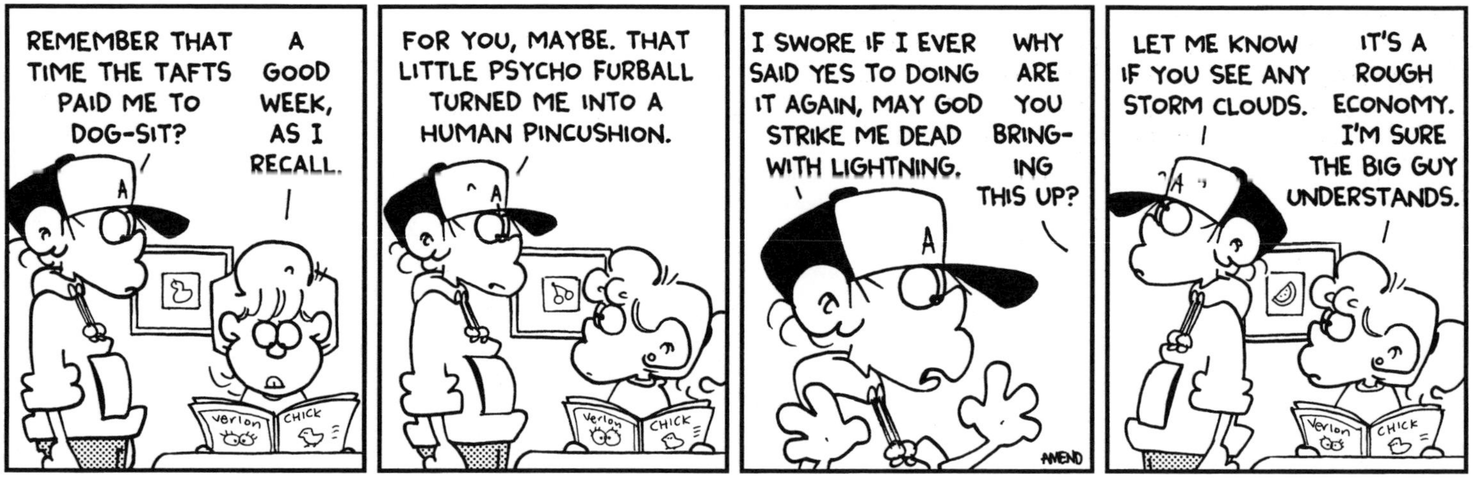
REMEMBER THAT TIME THE TAFTS PAID ME TO DOG-SIT?
A GOOD WEEK, AS I RECALL.
FOR YOU, MAYBE. THAT LITTLE PSYCHO FURBALL TURNED ME INTO A HUMAN PINCUSHION.
I SWORE IF I EVER SAID YES TO DOING IT AGAIN, MAY GOD STRIKE ME DEAD WITH LIGHTNING.
WHY ARE YOU BRING-ING THIS UP?
LET ME KNOW IF YOU SEE ANY STORM CLOUDS.
IT'S A ROUGH ECONOMY. I'M SURE THE BIG GUY UNDERSTANDS.

July 29, 2002

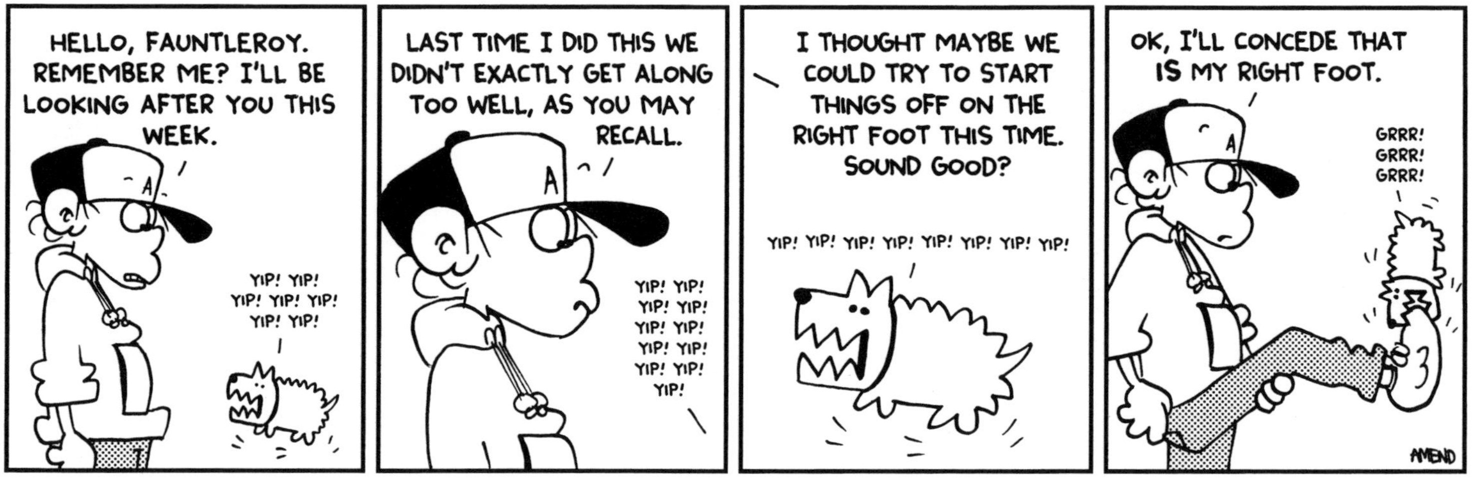
HELLO, FAUNTLEROY. REMEMBER ME? I'LL BE LOOKING AFTER YOU THIS WEEK.
YIP! YIP! YIP! YIP! YIP! YIP! YIP!
LAST TIME I DID THIS WE DIDN'T EXACTLY GET ALONG TOO WELL, AS YOU MAY RECALL.
YIP! YIP! YIP! YIP! YIP! YIP! YIP! YIP! YIP! YIP! YIP!
I THOUGHT MAYBE WE COULD TRY TO START THINGS OFF ON THE RIGHT FOOT THIS TIME. SOUND GOOD?
YIP! YIP! YIP! YIP! YIP! YIP! YIP! YIP!
OK, I'LL CONCEDE THAT IS MY RIGHT FOOT.
GRRR! GRRR! GRRR!

July 30, 2002

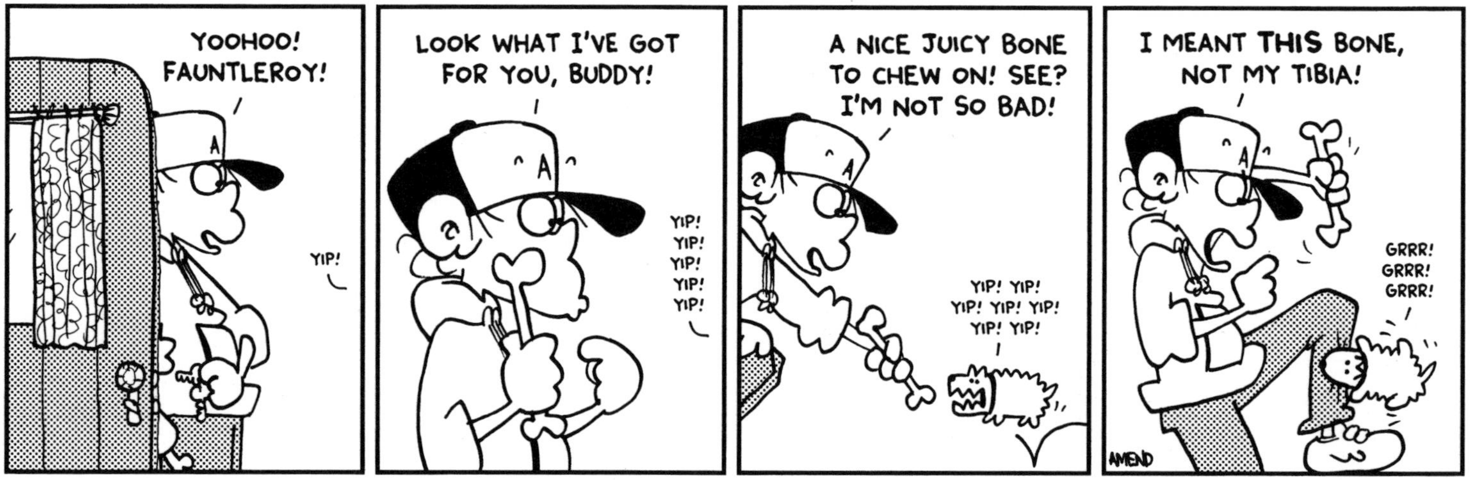
YOOHOO! FAUNTLEROY!
YIP!
LOOK WHAT I'VE GOT FOR YOU, BUDDY!
YIP! YIP! YIP! YIP! YIP!
A NICE JUICY BONE TO CHEW ON! SEE? I'M NOT SO BAD!
YIP! YIP! YIP! YIP! YIP! YIP! YIP!
I MEANT THIS BONE, NOT MY TIBIA!
GRRR! GRRR! GRRR!

July 31, 2002

August 1, 2002

August 2, 2002

This strip made me laugh while I was drawing it.

August 3, 2002

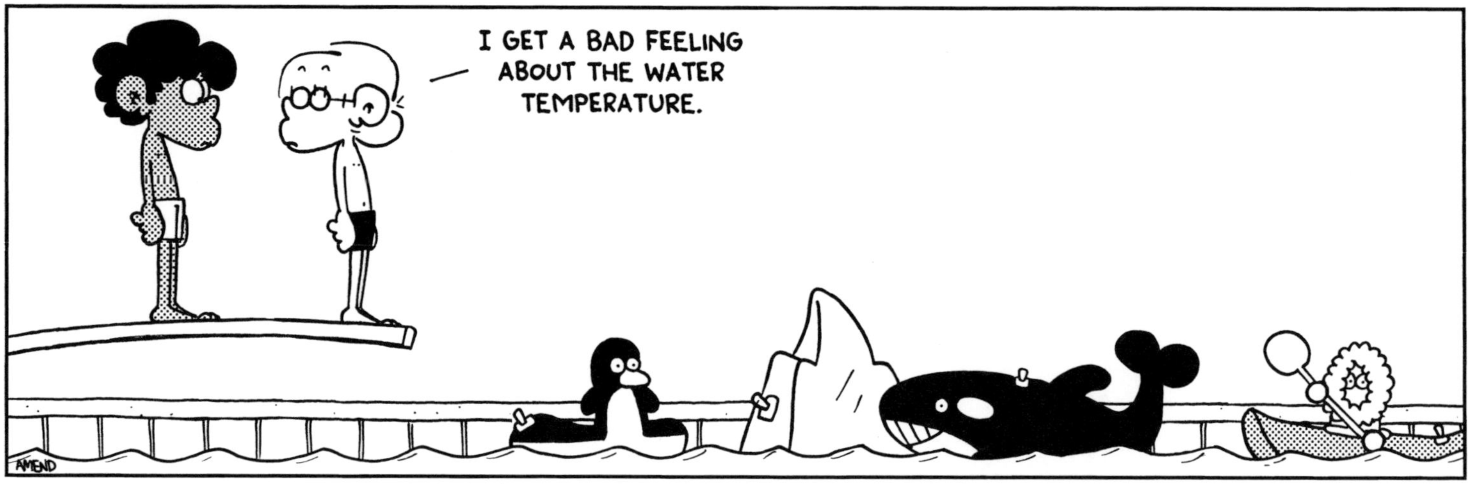
I GET A BAD FEELING ABOUT THE WATER TEMPERATURE.
AMEND

July 15, 2002

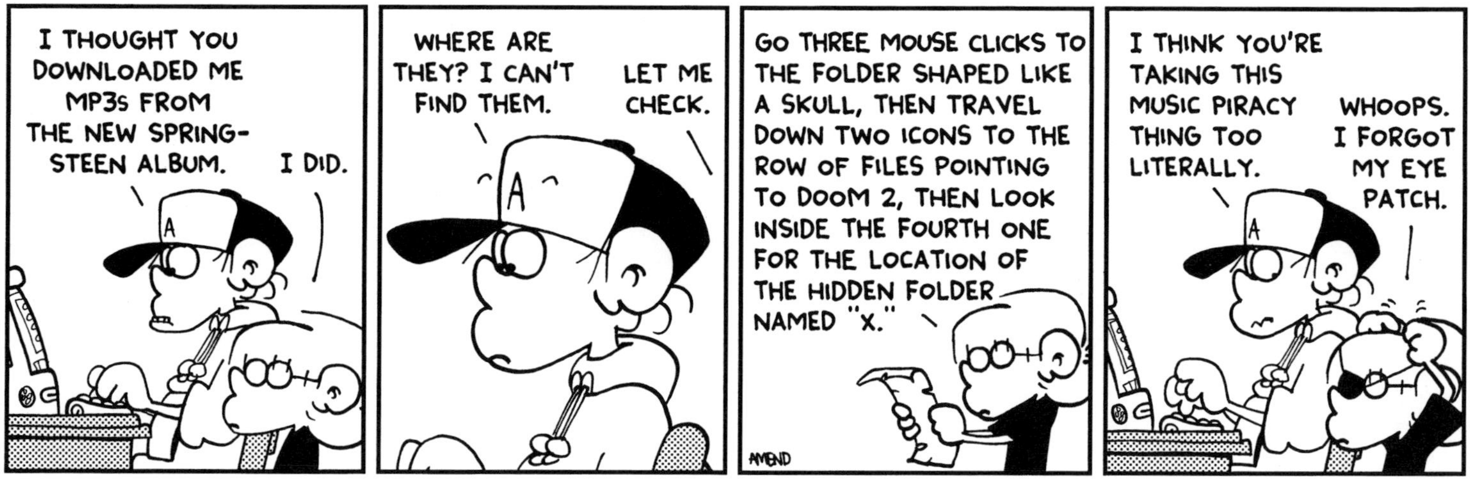
I THOUGHT YOU DOWNLOADED ME MP3s FROM THE NEW SPRING-STEEN ALBUM.
I DID.
WHERE ARE THEY? I CAN'T FIND THEM.
LET ME CHECK.
GO THREE MOUSE CLICKS TO THE FOLDER SHAPED LIKE A SKULL, THEN TRAVEL DOWN TWO ICONS TO THE ROW OF FILES POINTING TO DOOM 2, THEN LOOK INSIDE THE FOURTH ONE FOR THE LOCATION OF THE HIDDEN FOLDER NAMED "X."
AMEND
I THINK YOU'RE TAKING THIS MUSIC PIRACY THING TOO LITERALLY.
WHOOPS. I FORGOT MY EYE PATCH.

July 26, 2002

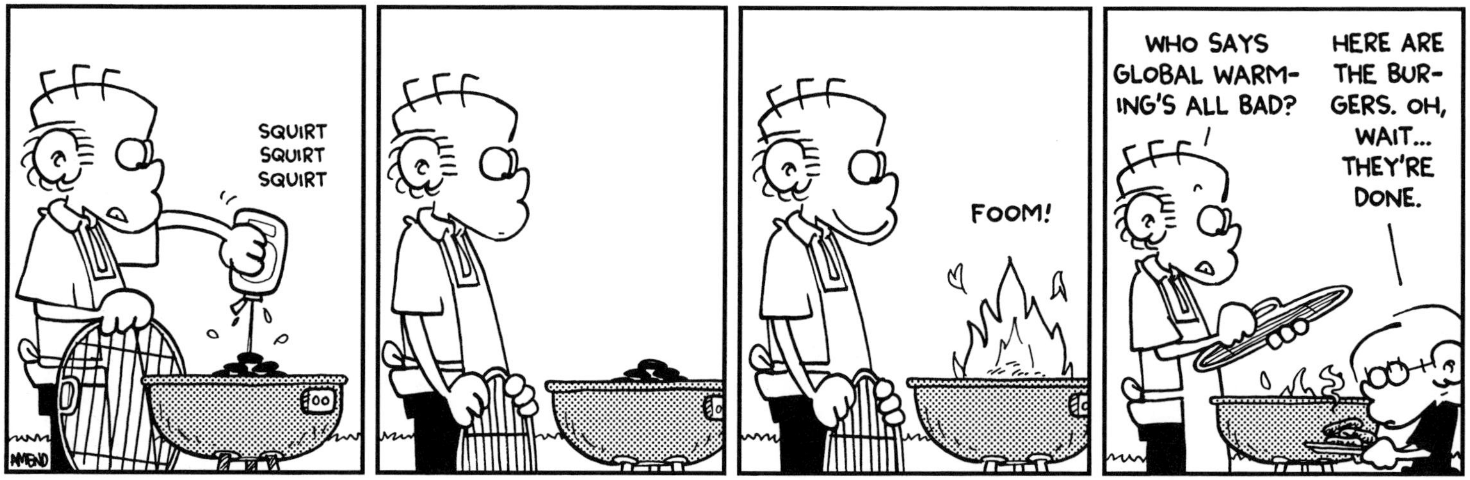
SQUIRT
SQUIRT
SQUIRT
AMEND
FOOM!
WHO SAYS GLOBAL WARM-ING'S ALL BAD?
HERE ARE THE BUR-GERS. OH, WAIT... THEY'RE DONE.

July 27, 2002

THEY SHOULD HAVE CAST **YOU** IN "THE MATRIX."

YOU SHOULD SEE ME WHEN IT'S CHOCOLATE.

July 24, 2002

WILL YOU SIGN MY PETITION?

WHAT'S IT FOR?

THE SCI-FI CHANNEL IS CANCELLING "FARSCAPE"! THIS IS TO DEMAND THEY RECONSIDER THIS OUTRAGEOUS AND UNBELIEVABLE ACT!

WHAT'S "FARSCAPE"?

I KNEW I SHOULD'VE DONE THIS ONLINE.

THERE'S A "SCI-FI CHANNEL"?

October 8, 2002

I got a lot of nice e-mail from *Farscape* fans after this strip ran.

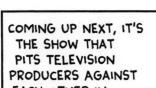

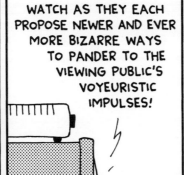

COMING UP NEXT, IT'S THE SHOW THAT PITS TELEVISION PRODUCERS AGAINST EACH OTHER IN FURIOUS COMPETITION!

WATCH AS THEY EACH PROPOSE NEWER AND EVER MORE BIZARRE WAYS TO PANDER TO THE VIEWING PUBLIC'S VOYEURISTIC IMPULSES!

AT STAKE ARE MILLIONS! WHO WILL WALK AWAY WITH IT?! WHOSE SHOW WILL LAND A NETWORK DEAL?!

FIND OUT, ON "REALITY SERIES: THE REALITY SERIES."

YOU JUST KNEW IT WOULD COME TO THIS.

January 30, 2003

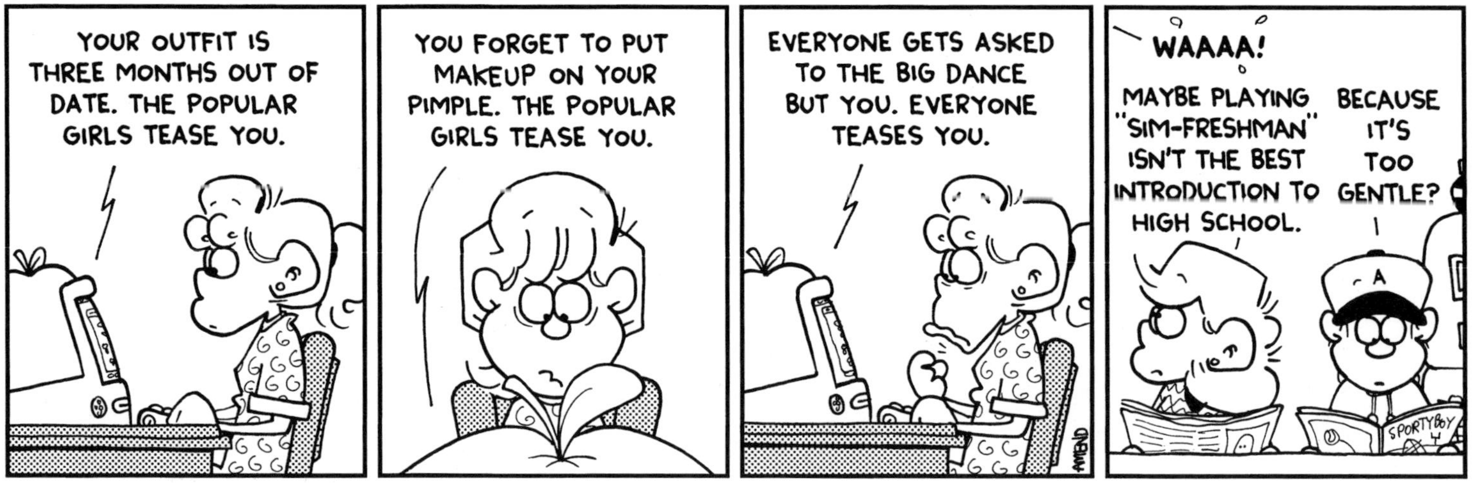
YOUR OUTFIT IS THREE MONTHS OUT OF DATE. THE POPULAR GIRLS TEASE YOU.
YOU FORGET TO PUT MAKEUP ON YOUR PIMPLE. THE POPULAR GIRLS TEASE YOU.
EVERYONE GETS ASKED TO THE BIG DANCE BUT YOU. EVERYONE TEASES YOU.
WAAAA!
MAYBE PLAYING "SIM-FRESHMAN" ISN'T THE BEST INTRODUCTION TO HIGH SCHOOL.
BECAUSE IT'S TOO GENTLE?

August 26, 2002

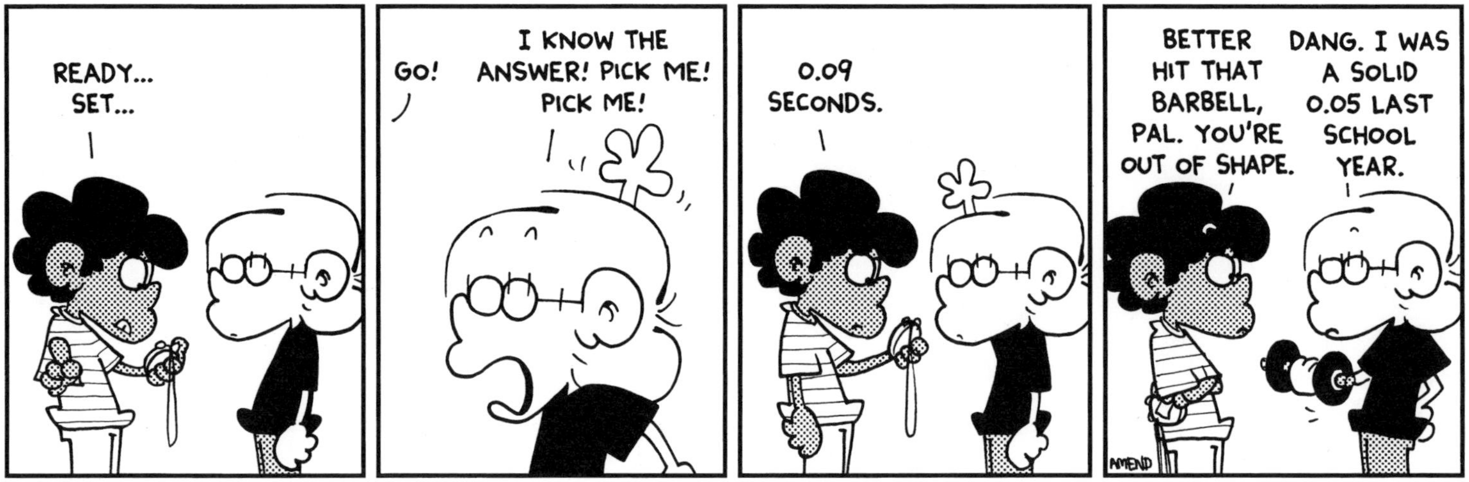
READY... SET...
GO!
I KNOW THE ANSWER! PICK ME! PICK ME!
0.09 SECONDS.
BETTER HIT THAT BARBELL, PAL. YOU'RE OUT OF SHAPE.
DANG. I WAS A SOLID 0.05 LAST SCHOOL YEAR.

August 27, 2002

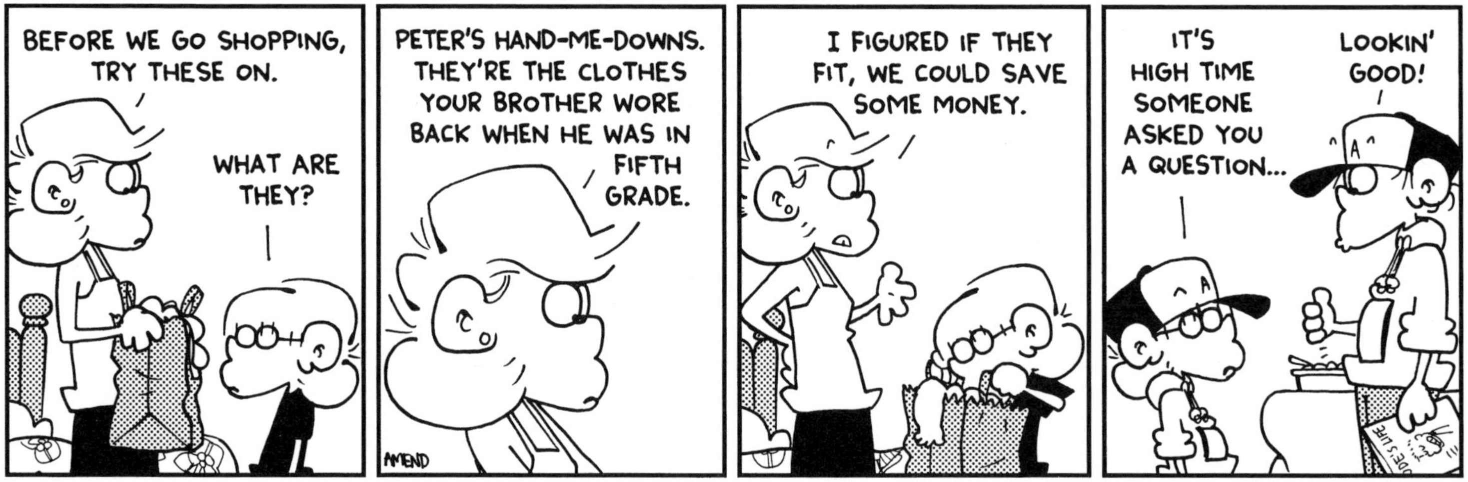
BEFORE WE GO SHOPPING, TRY THESE ON.
WHAT ARE THEY?
PETER'S HAND-ME-DOWNS. THEY'RE THE CLOTHES YOUR BROTHER WORE BACK WHEN HE WAS IN FIFTH GRADE.
I FIGURED IF THEY FIT, WE COULD SAVE SOME MONEY.
IT'S HIGH TIME SOMEONE ASKED YOU A QUESTION...
LOOKIN' GOOD!

August 29, 2002

I hadn't read *The Odyssey* in like twenty years, so I had to cross my fingers I didn't botch these too badly.

October 14, 2002

October 15, 2002

October 16, 2002

153

October 17, 2002

October 18, 2002

October 19, 2002

October 21, 2002

October 22, 2002

October 23, 2002

October 24, 2002

October 25, 2002

October 26, 2002

October 28, 2002

October 30, 2002

October 31, 2002

157

I met Bill Gates once, and he was much, much nicer to me than he should have been.

KEEP THE THERMOMETER UNDER YOUR TONGUE, PETER.

MGLRP.

103 DEGREES. I THOUGHT YOU FELT A LITTLE WARM.

I'M SICK?! I CAN'T BE SICK! NOT FOR THANKSGIVING!

IT'S THE ONE TIME OF THE YEAR WHEN I NEED ALL MY STRENGTH!

IT'S A MEAL. WHAT DO YOU NEED STRENGTH FOR?

PERHAPS YOU HAVEN'T NOTICED THE SIZE OF MY FORKFULS.

November 25, 2002

DOING OK?

BRRR. I'M FREEZING.

POOR PETER. THE MEDICINE SHOULD HELP SOON.

FEVERS OFTEN MAKE US FEEL CHILLY.

SO DO THERMOSTATS SET AT 60 DEGREES, MOTHER.

NONSENSE, PAIGE. IT'S HIS FEVER.

BRRR...

November 26, 2002

HOW'S OUR SICK BOY DOING?

SO-SO.

HE SLEPT UNTIL NOON, THEN SPENT THE REST OF THE DAY FORCING DOWN FLUIDS AND BABBLING INCOHERENTLY.

YOU KNOW, THAT SOUNDS FRIGHTENINGLY SIMILAR TO MY SOPHOMORE YEAR IN COLLEGE.

WHY? WERE YOU SICK A LOT?

November 27, 2002

158

November 28, 2002

November 29, 2002

November 30, 2002

December 5, 2002

December 12, 2002

160

December 19, 2002

December 26, 2002

December 31, 2002

January 2, 2003

January 13, 2003

January 14, 2003

January 15, 2003

SO HOW MANY LEVELS DOES "NICE CITY" HAVE?

WHO KNOWS.

RIGHT NOW I'M DOING THE "GOOD SON" SET OF MISSIONS. TALK ABOUT VIDEO GAME NIGHTMARES.

FIRST THERE WAS THE "MAKE YOUR BED" MISSION, THEN THE "DO YOUR HOMEWORK" MISSION, THEN THE "SET THE TABLE" MISSION...IT'S LIKE A VIRTUAL PARADE OF CHORES!

WHY DON'T YOU JUST QUIT?

IT BEATS THE REAL PARADE.

PETER, IS YOUR BED MADE?

January 16, 2003

I FOUND SOME CHEAT CODES FOR "NICE CITY" ON THE WEB.

WOOHOO! LET ME HAVE THEM!

PRESS A-B-UP-LEFT-A FOR UNLIMITED MONEY TO GIVE TO CHARITY... B-A-B-DOWN-UP TO MAKE THE DAYS EVEN SUNNIER...

DOWN-DOWN-RIGHT-A-A FOR SUPER-GOOD HUGS... AND B-UP-A-RIGHT-B TO ACCESS THE SECRET GLEE-CLUB MISSIONS.

AND I THOUGHT "RESIDENT EVIL" WAS SCARY.

HOW DO I UNDO THAT "SUNNIER" ONE?

January 17, 2003

THIS "NICE CITY" GAME IS AWFUL! I CAN'T TAKE IT ANYMORE!

WELL, LET'S SEE WHAT ELSE MAGG HAS APPROVED.

THAT MOTHERS AGAINST GORY GAMES LIST IS INCREDIBLY LAME, MOTHER! "PACIFIST-MAN"?? "MS. PACIFIST-MAN"?? "RESIDENT GOOD"?? "ETERNAL LIGHTNESS"??

ARE YOU **TRYING** TO MAKE ME QUIT PLAYING VIDEO GAMES ALTOGETHER?!

NEVER ASK QUESTIONS LIKE THAT.

DID YOU SEE THE SMILE ON HER FACE?!

January 18, 2003

January 21, 2003

I was a huge Disney geek as a kid, so drawing Jason as Steamboat Willie was a treat.

January 27, 2003

164

April 10, 2003

February 7, 2003

February 8, 2003

April 11, 2003

I was proud of this one. The dialogue is a haiku.

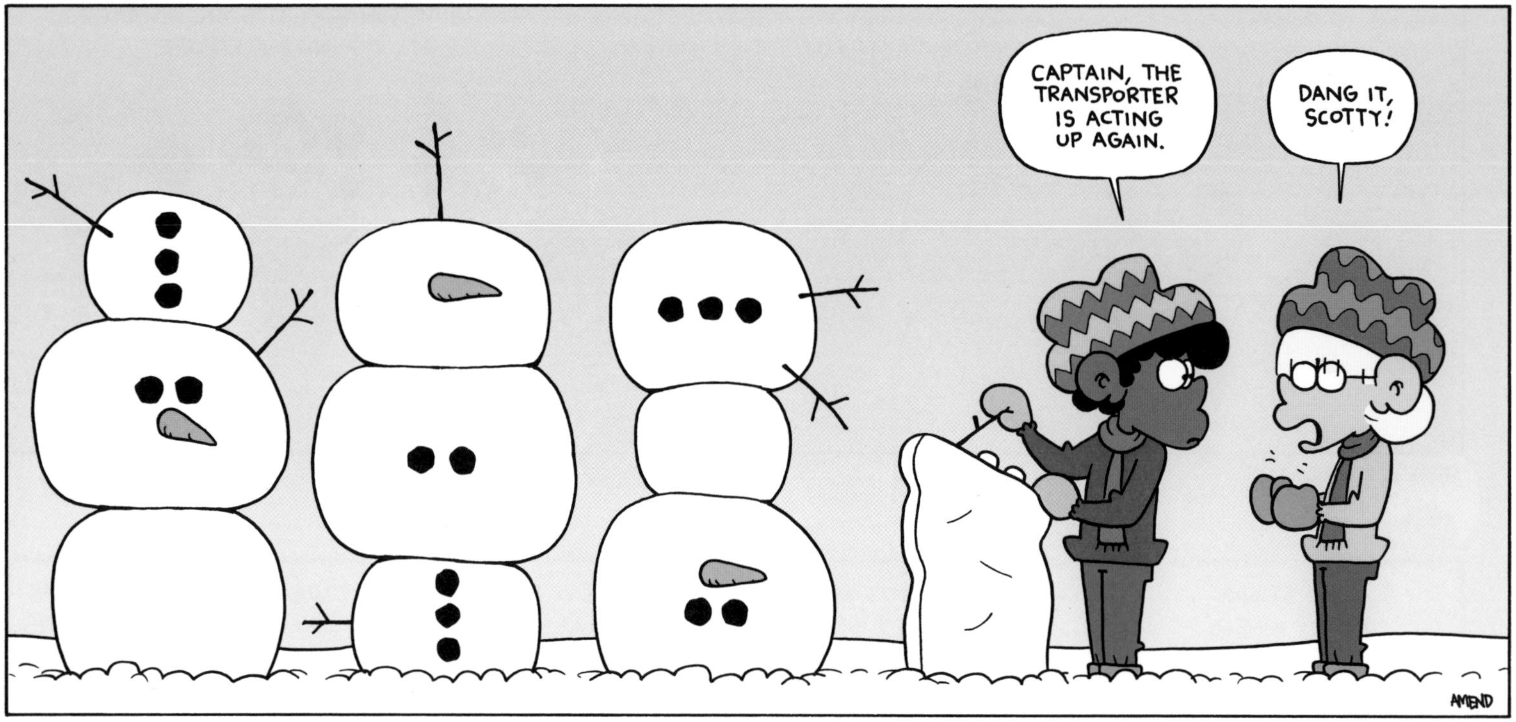
CAPTAIN, THE TRANSPORTER IS ACTING UP AGAIN.
DANG IT, SCOTTY!
AMEND

January 12, 2003

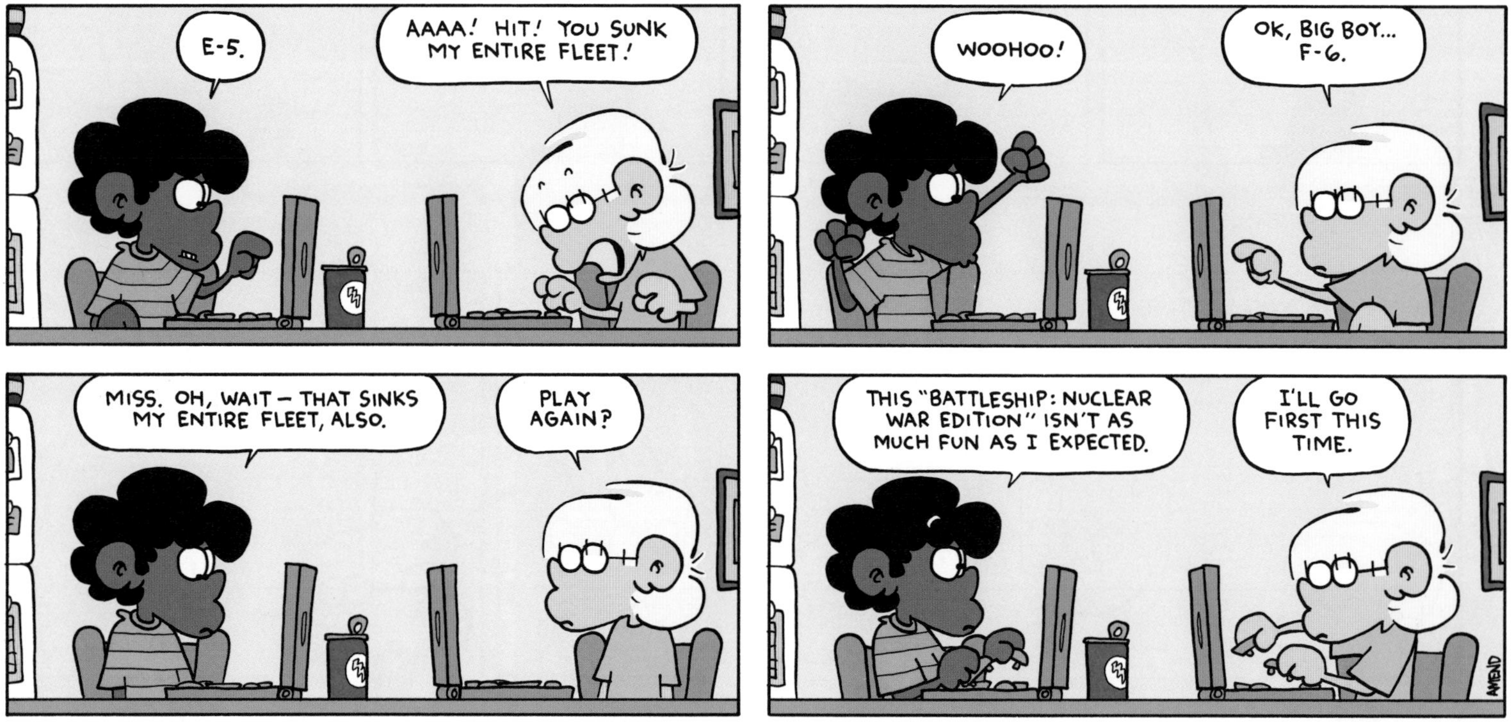
E-5.
AAAA! HIT! YOU SUNK MY ENTIRE FLEET!
WOOHOO!
OK, BIG BOY... F-6.
MISS. OH, WAIT — THAT SINKS MY ENTIRE FLEET, ALSO.
PLAY AGAIN?
THIS "BATTLESHIP: NUCLEAR WAR EDITION" ISN'T AS MUCH FUN AS I EXPECTED.
I'LL GO FIRST THIS TIME.
AMEND

February 2, 2003

February 17, 2003

February 18, 2003

February 19, 2003

I CAN'T WAIT TO SHOW THIS TO NICOLE! SHE'S GOING TO FLIP!

BUT DO I DARE RISK TAKING SOMETHING AS PRICELESS AS AN AUTOGRAPHED BACK-SYNC BOYS PHOTO TO SCHOOL?! IT COULD GET LOST! DAMAGED! **STOLEN!**

WHAT TO DO? THINK, PAIGE, THINK!

HELLO, IS THIS BRINKS ARMORED VEHICLES?

THINK AGAIN, PAIGE, THINK AGAIN.

February 20, 2003

PAIGE, YOU'RE GOING TO BE LATE FOR SCHOOL!

I DON'T KNOW WHAT TO DO WITH MY BACK-SYNC BOYS PHOTO!

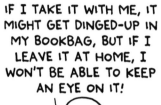

IF I TAKE IT WITH ME, IT MIGHT GET DINGED-UP IN MY BOOKBAG, BUT IF I LEAVE IT AT HOME, I WON'T BE ABLE TO KEEP AN EYE ON IT!

PAIGE, LEAVE IT HERE. I'M HOME. NOTHING WILL HAPPEN TO IT.

YOU PROMISE?

I PROMISE.

February 21, 2003

I SWEAR, MR. VIVONA IS A LOONY.

PAIGE, DO YOU REMEMBER THE CONVERSATION WE HAD RIGHT BEFORE YOU LEFT FOR SCHOOL?

THE ONE WHERE YOU PROMISED TO LOOK AFTER MY SIGNED BACKSYNC BOYS PHOTO WHILE I WAS AWAY?

WHAT ABOUT IT?

NOTHING, REALLY. I WAS JUST HOPING YOU'D FORGOTTEN.

DID SOMETHING HAPPEN TO MY PHOTO?!?

MAYBE I SHOULD BACK UP A LITTLE BEFORE ANSWERING...

168

February 22, 2003

JASON'S IGUANA CHEWED UP MY AUTOGRAPHED BACKSYNC BOYS PHOTO?!

MOTHER, YOU SAID YOU'D LOOK AFTER IT! YOU SAID NOTHING BAD WOULD HAPPEN!

YOU **PROMISED!**

JUST FOR THE RECORD, MY SHOELACES **WERE** CROSSED...

CURSE THESE LEGAL LOOP-HOLES.

February 24, 2003

SWEETIE, I'M REALLY SORRY.

YOU WERE HOME! YOU SAID YOU'D LOOK AFTER IT!

PAIGE, NOBODY CAN KEEP THEIR EYES ON A PICTURE OF THE BACKSYNC BOYS EVERY MINUTE OF THE DAY!

I CAN!

FINE. NOBODY MY AGE.

YOU **NEVER** WOULD HAVE LET QUINCY CHEW UP A DAVID CASSIDY PHOTO!

February 25, 2003

ARE YOU STILL MAD AT ME?

PAIGE?

I TOLD YOU HER EYES CAN SHOOT DAGGERS.

I'M JUST GLAD HER AIM STINKS.

February 26, 2003

169

I THINK YOU'RE BEING A LITTLE HARD ON MOM.

A LITTLE HARD?!

PETER, BECAUSE OF HER, MY AUTOGRAPHED PHOTO OF THE BACKSYNC BOYS WAS SHREDDED INTO CONFETTI!

WHAT DO YOU EXPECT ME TO DO— THANK HER?!

NO, NO, JASON AND I CAN DO THAT WELL ENOUGH.

BY THE WAY, IF I SEE EITHER OF YOU DOING THAT "HAPPY DANCE" AGAIN...

February 27, 2003

YOU LIED TO ME, MOTHER!
YOU LIED TO ME, MOTHER!
YOU LIED TO ME, MOTHER!
YOU LIED TO ME, MOTHER!

YOU LIED TO ME, MOTHER!
YOU LIED TO ME, MOTHER!
YOU LIED TO ME, MOTHER!
YOU LIED TO ME, MOTHER!

YOU LIED TO ME, MOTHER!
YOU LIED TO ME, MOTHER!
YOU LIED TO ME, MOTHER!
YOU LIED TO ME, MOTHER!

MOM'S NOT HOME, PAIGE.

I KNOW, I JUST DON'T WANT TO LOSE MY TRAIN OF THOUGHT.

February 28, 2003

YOU CAN'T SAY THIS IS ALL MOM'S FAULT, PAIGE.

SHE'S NOT THE ONE WHO LEFT HER BACKSYNC BOYS PHOTO OUT IN PLAIN SIGHT WHERE QUINCY COULD FIND IT.

NOW THAT I THINK ABOUT IT, SHE'S ALSO NOT THE ONE WHO SPENT MOST OF LAST SUMMER TEACHING HIS IGUANA TO CHEW UP MY THINGS.

ALL MOM'S FAULT. DEFINITELY.

EXACTLY. WHY MAKE THINGS COMPLICATED?

March 1, 2003

170

GO AWAY.

PAIGE, IS THERE ANYTHING I CAN DO? IS THERE ANY WAY TO MAKE IT UP TO YOU?

MY AUTOGRAPHED PHOTO OF THE BACKSYNC BOYS IS CONFETTI BECAUSE OF YOU, MOTHER! IT WAS MY MOST PRECIOUS AND PRICELESS POSSESSION!

THERE'S NOTHING THAT COULD EVEN **BEGIN** TO MAKE UP FOR IT! NOTHING!

ALTHOUGH THERE IS THIS ONE CUTE BRACELET AT NORDSTROM...

I'LL GO WARM UP THE CAR.

March 3, 2003

WHAT'S FOR DINNER?

STUFFED BEETLOAF.

MAYBE I SHOULD REPHRASE THAT...

WHAT'S FOR DINNER, MOTHER-WHO-LET-MY-BACKSYNC-BOYS-PHOTO-GET-RUINED?

MMM. SHRIMP COCKTAIL.

WHY'S MINE LOOK LIKE BEETLOAF?

March 4, 2003

ANDY, I WORRY THAT PAIGE IS STARTING TO TAKE ADVANTAGE OF YOUR GUILT OVER THIS BACKSYNC BOYS THING.

WHATEVER WOULD GIVE YOU THAT IMPRESSION?

MOTHER-WHO-RUINED-MY-LIFE? MY PILLOW ISN'T FLUFFED ENOUGH.

COMING!

CALL IT A HUNCH.

SINCE I'M UP, CAN I BAKE YOU SOME MORE COOKIES?

YOU'LL HAVE TO BRUSH MY TEETH AGAIN...

March 5, 2003

I'M TELLING YOU, NICOLE, I AM LIVING THE GOOD LIFE RIGHT NOW.

THIS WHOLE DESTROYED BACKSYNC BOYS PHOTO THING HAS GIVEN ME TOTAL LEVERAGE WITH MOM! SHE CLEANS MY ROOM... SHE LETS ME WATCH TV ALL I WANT... SHE BAKES ME COOKIES AT BEDTIME...

AND THE BEST PART IS, I DON'T SEE ANY END IN SIGHT!

PAIGE, LOOK WHAT JUST CAME IN THE MAIL!

BRING IT CLOSER. MY EYES AREN'T THAT GOOD.

March 6, 2003

YOU GOT 20 ENVELOPES, EACH WITH AN AUTOGRAPHED BACKSYNC BOYS PHOTO!

REMEMBER HOW YOU SAID YOU WROTE THEM A BUNCH OF LETTERS?! THEY MUST'VE NOT KEPT TRACK AND SENT YOU A PHOTO FOR EACH ONE!

PAIGE, ISN'T THIS GREAT?! ISN'T THIS WONDERFUL?! NOW YOU DON'T HAVE TO BE MISERABLE AND I DON'T HAVE TO KEEP TRYING TO CHEER YOU UP EVERY HALF-HOUR!

ARE YOU LISTENING? I SAID YOU DON'T HAVE TO BE MISERABLE.

WAAAA!

March 7, 2003

WILL YOU FORGIVE ME, MOTHER?

WHAT FOR?

FOR THE WAY I TREATED YOU AFTER QUINCY CHEWED UP MY PHOTO. I SAW YOU FELT GUILTY AND INSTEAD OF FORGIVING YOU, I MADE YOU JUMP THROUGH ALL SORTS OF HOOPS.

NOW I FEEL GUILTY.

AND YOU WANT ME TO FORGIVE YOU??

I SUPPOSE NOW YOU'LL WANT TO TEACH ME A LESSON.

EXACTLY. YOU'RE FORGIVEN.

172

March 8, 2003

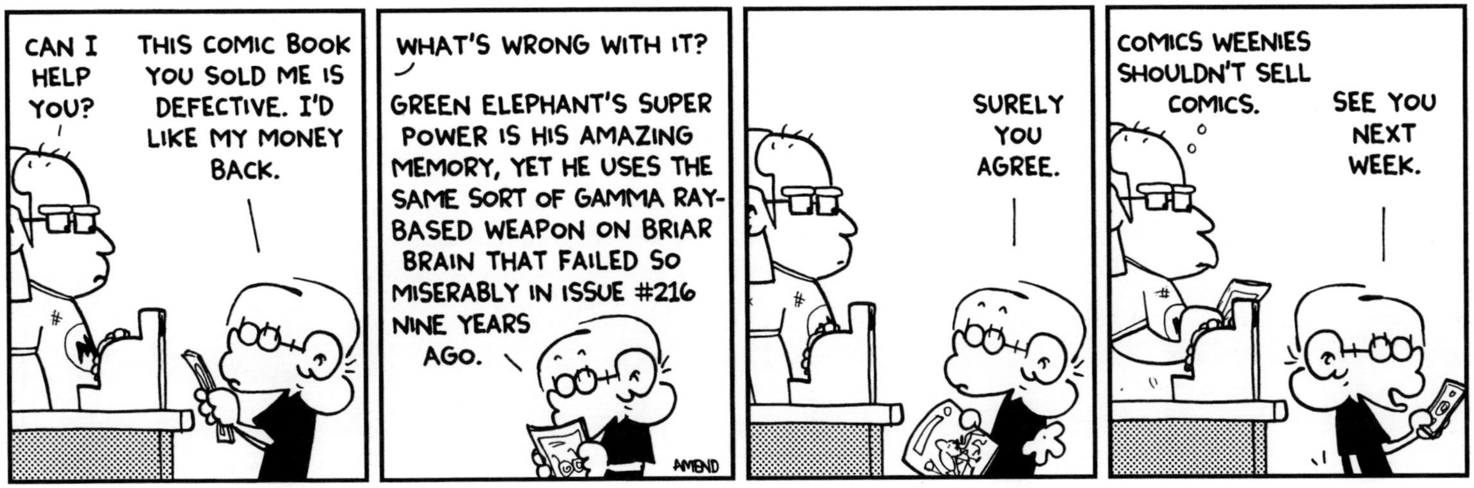
CAN I HELP YOU?
THIS COMIC BOOK YOU SOLD ME IS DEFECTIVE. I'D LIKE MY MONEY BACK.
WHAT'S WRONG WITH IT?
GREEN ELEPHANT'S SUPER POWER IS HIS AMAZING MEMORY, YET HE USES THE SAME SORT OF GAMMA RAY-BASED WEAPON ON BRIAR BRAIN THAT FAILED SO MISERABLY IN ISSUE #216 NINE YEARS AGO.
SURELY YOU AGREE.
COMICS WEENIES SHOULDN'T SELL COMICS.
SEE YOU NEXT WEEK.
April 12, 2003

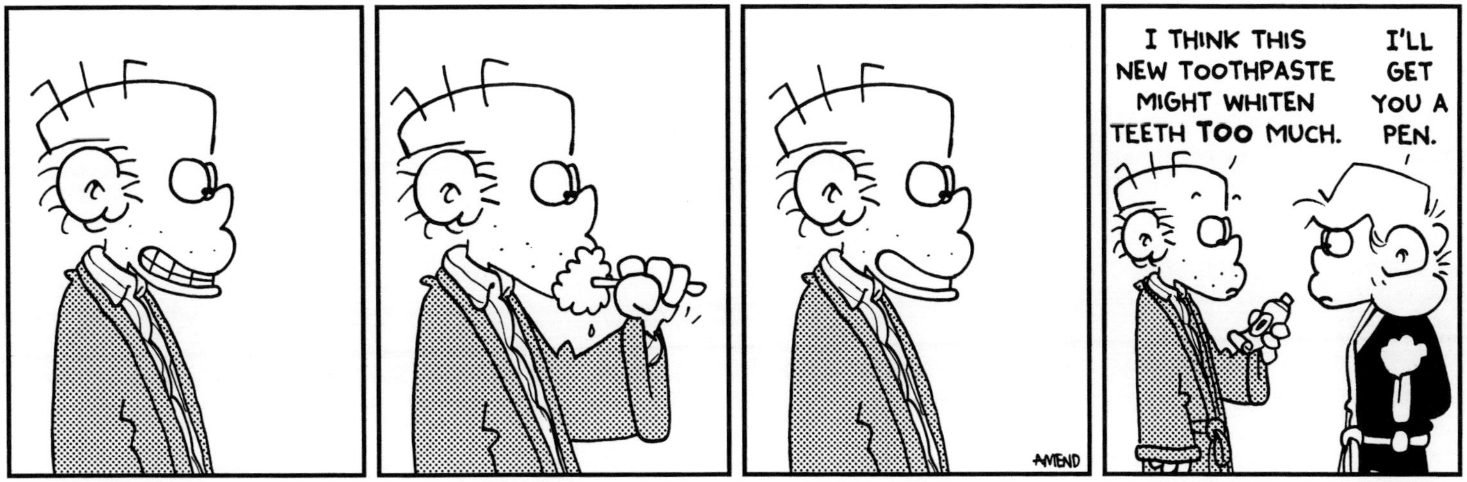
I THINK THIS NEW TOOTHPASTE MIGHT WHITEN TEETH **TOO** MUCH.
I'LL GET YOU A PEN.
April 21, 2003

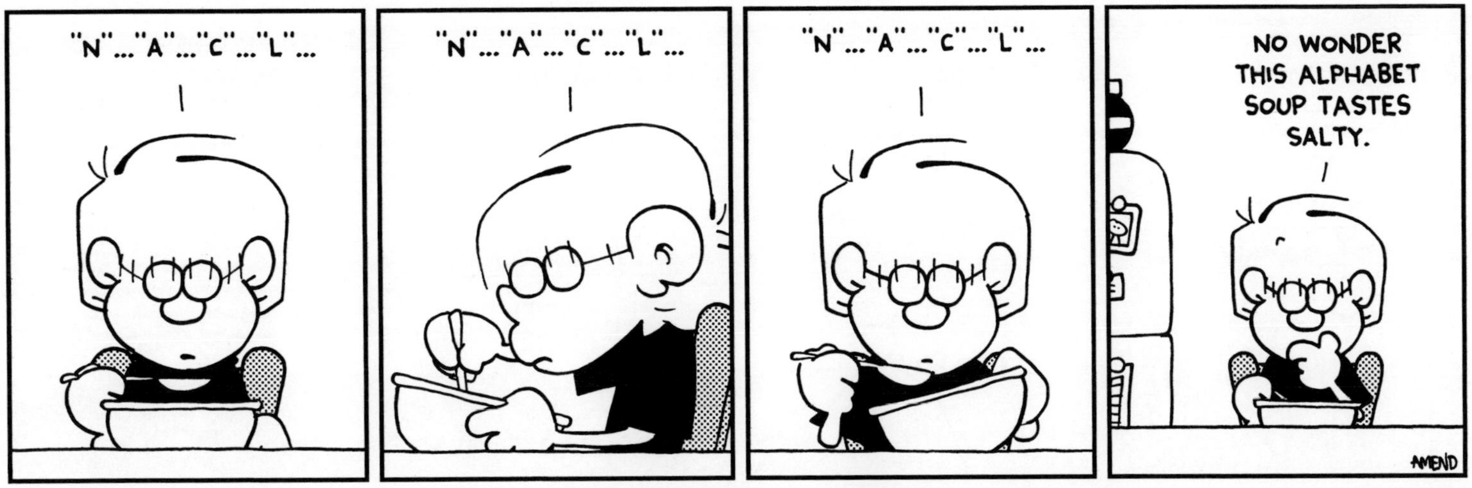
"N"..."A"..."C"..."L"...
"N"..."A"..."C"..."L"...
"N"..."A"..."C"..."L"...
NO WONDER THIS ALPHABET SOUP TASTES SALTY.
May 1, 2003

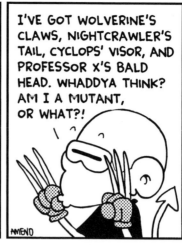

May 2, 2003

May 7, 2003

At least, there were zero
when I wrote this.

May 15, 2003

May 26, 2003

May 27, 2003

Randall Blair has done a lot of the design work for my Web site over the years. I don't pay much, but I can make you famous.

July 22, 2003

July 13, 2003

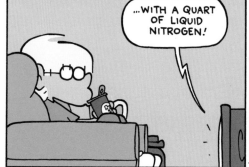

This was an actual recipe in *Popular Science* magazine, as I recall.

July 27, 2003

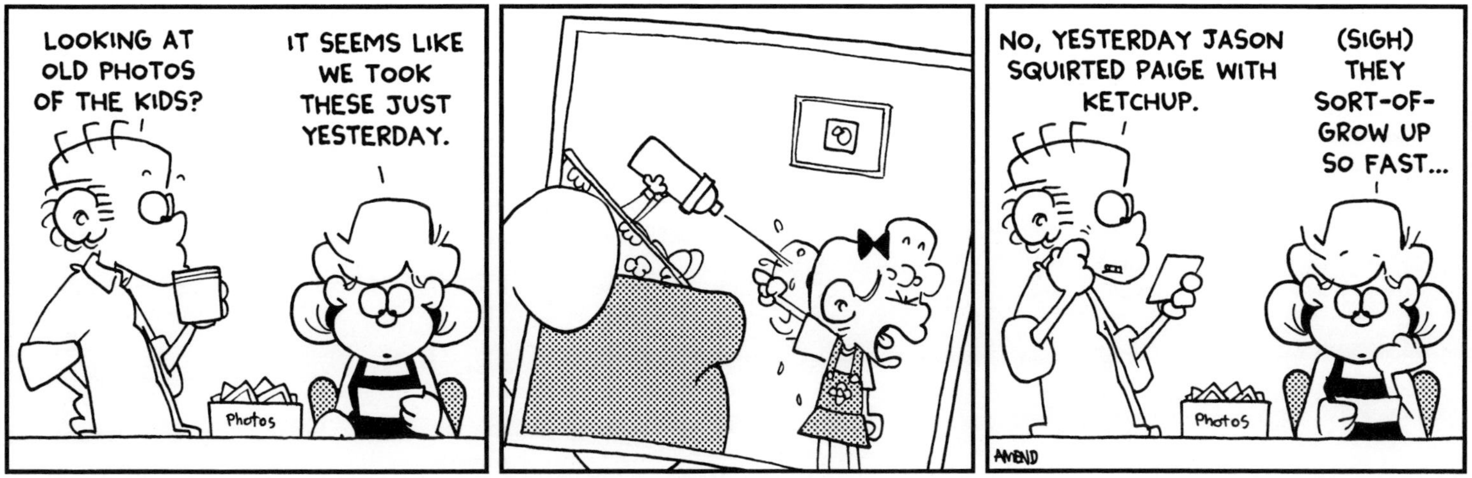
LOOKING AT OLD PHOTOS OF THE KIDS?
IT SEEMS LIKE WE TOOK THESE JUST YESTERDAY.
Photos
NO, YESTERDAY JASON SQUIRTED PAIGE WITH KETCHUP.
(SIGH) THEY SORT-OF-GROW UP SO FAST...
Photos
AMEND

June 23, 2003

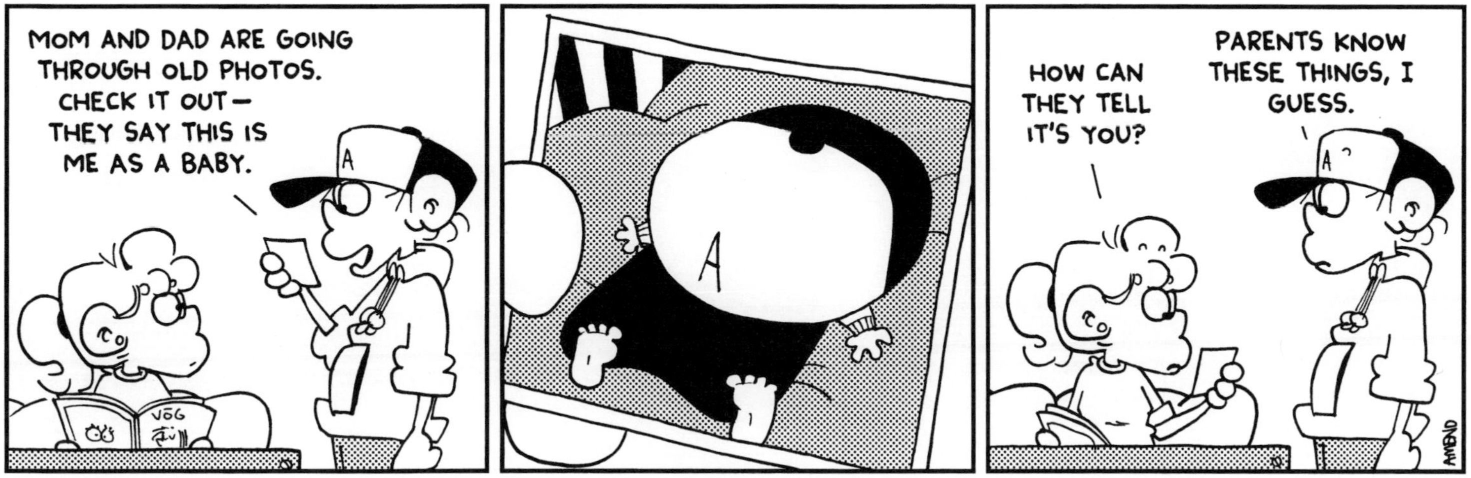
MOM AND DAD ARE GOING THROUGH OLD PHOTOS. CHECK IT OUT— THEY SAY THIS IS ME AS A BABY.
HOW CAN THEY TELL IT'S YOU?
PARENTS KNOW THESE THINGS, I GUESS.
AMEND

June 24, 2003

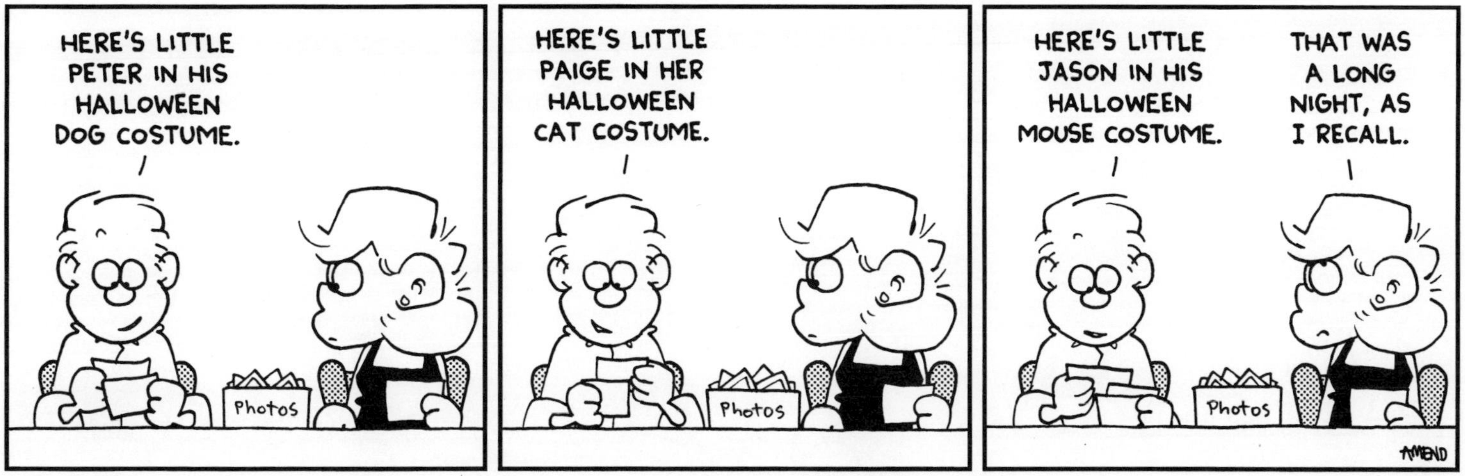
HERE'S LITTLE PETER IN HIS HALLOWEEN DOG COSTUME.
Photos
HERE'S LITTLE PAIGE IN HER HALLOWEEN CAT COSTUME.
Photos
HERE'S LITTLE JASON IN HIS HALLOWEEN MOUSE COSTUME.
THAT WAS A LONG NIGHT, AS I RECALL.
Photos
AMEND

June 25, 2003

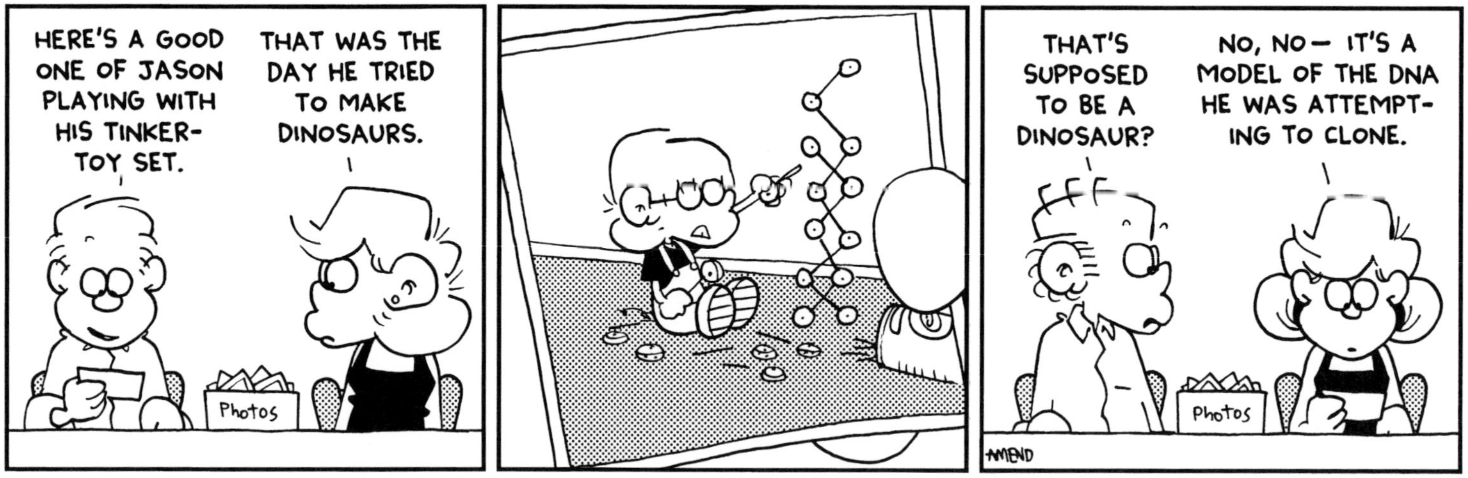
HERE'S A GOOD ONE OF JASON PLAYING WITH HIS TINKER-TOY SET.
THAT WAS THE DAY HE TRIED TO MAKE DINOSAURS.
Photos
THAT'S SUPPOSED TO BE A DINOSAUR?
NO, NO— IT'S A MODEL OF THE DNA HE WAS ATTEMPT-ING TO CLONE.
Photos
AMEND

June 26, 2003

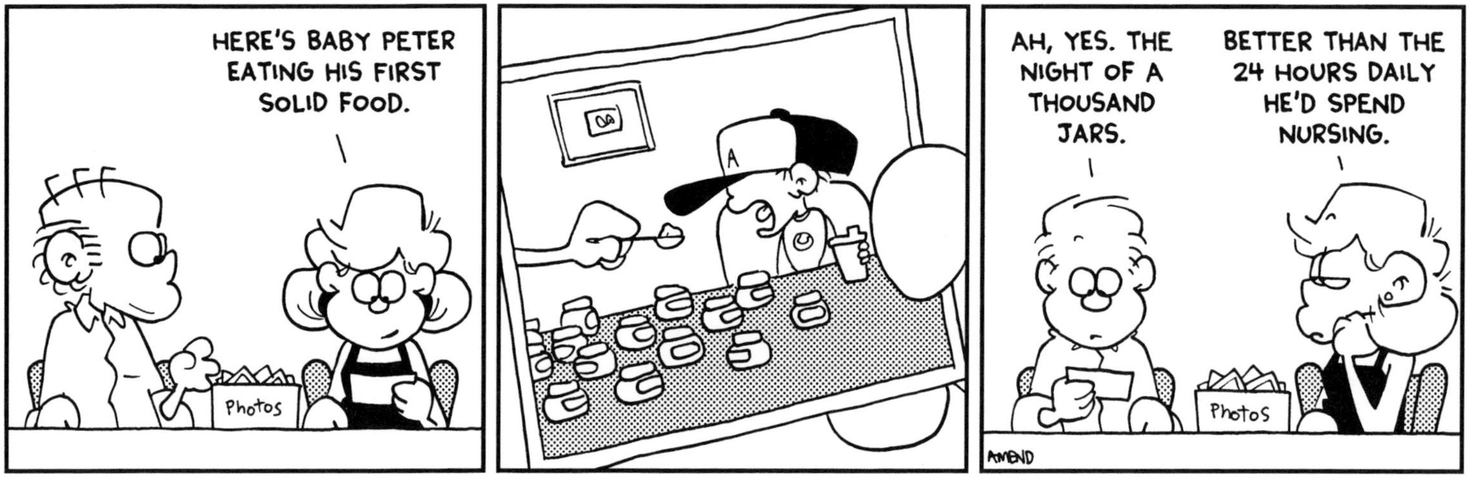
HERE'S BABY PETER EATING HIS FIRST SOLID FOOD.
Photos
AH, YES. THE NIGHT OF A THOUSAND JARS.
BETTER THAN THE 24 HOURS DAILY HE'D SPEND NURSING.
Photos
AMEND

June 27, 2003

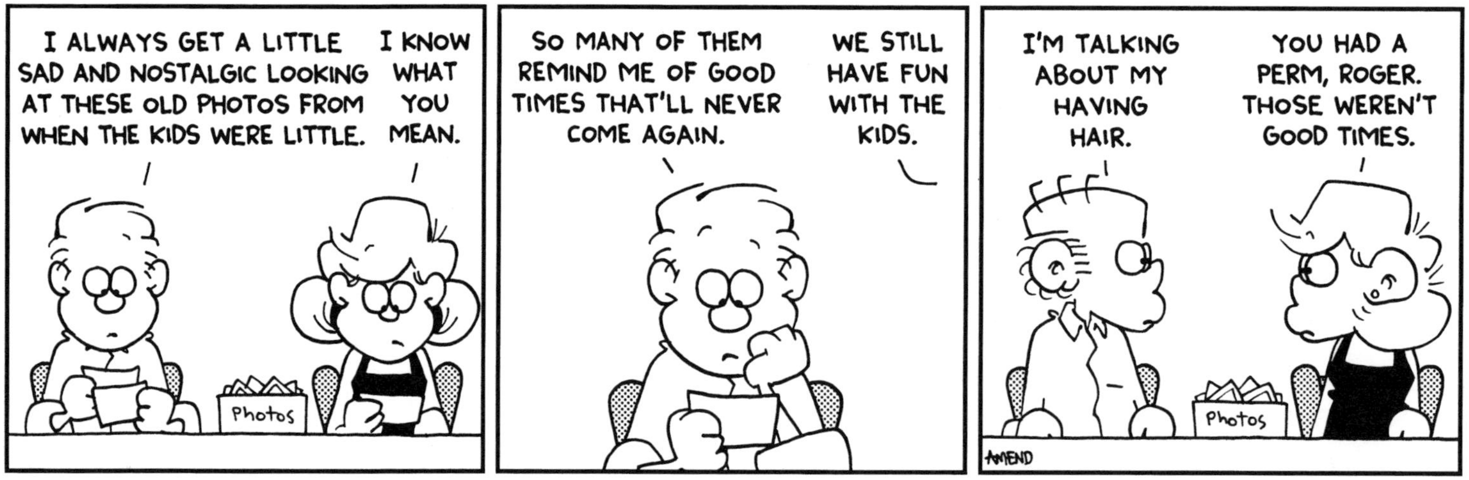
I ALWAYS GET A LITTLE SAD AND NOSTALGIC LOOKING AT THESE OLD PHOTOS FROM WHEN THE KIDS WERE LITTLE.
I KNOW WHAT YOU MEAN.
Photos
SO MANY OF THEM REMIND ME OF GOOD TIMES THAT'LL NEVER COME AGAIN.
WE STILL HAVE FUN WITH THE KIDS.
I'M TALKING ABOUT MY HAVING HAIR.
YOU HAD A PERM, ROGER. THOSE WEREN'T GOOD TIMES.
Photos
AMEND

June 28, 2003

WHAT ARE YOU DOING?

LEARNING HOW TO DO COMPUTER ANIMATION.

THE FILM "FINDING NEMO" HAS ME TOTALLY INSPIRED. I WANT TO MAKE MOVIES JUST LIKE IT.

WHEN DID YOU SEE IT?

I HAVEN'T YET.

YOU ARE SO READY FOR HOLLYWOOD.

$300 MILLION BOX OFFICE, BABY!

August 4, 2003

JASON, ABSOLUTELY NOT!

NO WAY, NO HOW! EVEN FOR YOU THIS IS A WEIRD REQUEST!

BUT I NEED ONE TO MAKE MY COMPUTER-ANIMATED MOVIE!

WHAT'S A SURFER FARM HAVE TO DO WITH ANIMATION?!

SERVER FARM! SERVER FARM!

August 5, 2003

I HEAR YOU'RE MAKING AN ANIMATED MOVIE.

YUP.

IT'S THE TENDER STORY OF A LEECH'S SEARCH FOR HIS MISSING SON. I'M CALLING IT "FINDING HEMO."

YOU CAN'T DO THAT! IT'S A TOTAL RIPOFF OF PIXAR!

SO?

SO THAT'S DREAMWORKS' TURF.

GOOD POINT. I'D HATE TO MAKE THEM MAD.

August 6, 2003

I got a less-than-happy e-mail from someone at Dreamworks after this ran.

179

The word "sucks" is a big no-no with a lot of newspapers, so it's fun to make it central to the joke so it can't be easily edited out.

YOU'RE MAKING A MOVIE ABOUT **LEECHES**?!

"FINDING HEMO." AND YOU KNOW WHAT'S THE BEST PART?

IF A CRITIC SAYS IT SUCKS, PEOPLE WILL JUST ASSUME THEY ARE TALKING ABOUT MY ACCURATE PORTRAYAL OF THE LEAD CHARACTERS.

AM I BRILLIANT, OR WHAT?

I'LL GO WITH "WHAT."

I'VE ALSO GOT A SKUNK CAMEO, IN CASE THEY ALSO SAY IT STINKS.

August 7, 2003

RENDERING ANIMATION... PLEASE WAIT...

RENDERING ANIMATION... PLEASE WAIT...

RENDERING ANIMATION... PLEASE WAIT...

I SEE WHERE THEY GOT THE IDEA FOR "A BUG'S LIFE."

FRAME ONE COMPLETED.

August 8, 2003

HOW GOES THE ANIMATION BUSINESS?

NOT SO GOOD. I'M THINKING OF THROWING IN THE TOWEL.

I HAD NO IDEA PRODUCING A FAMILY-CLASSIC SUMMER BLOCKBUSTER TOOK SO MUCH WORK! STORYBOARDS! VOICES! RENDERING EVERY SINGLE FRAME! IF THIS IS WHAT IT TAKES TO MAKE $300 MILLION THESE DAYS, FORGET IT!

JASON, YOU'VE BEEN AT IT FOR A DAY.

A DAY AND A HALF. DON'T REMIND ME.

AH, GENERATION DOT-COM.

WHY, I REMEMBER WHEN A KID LIKE ME COULD MAKE A BILLION IN HIS SLEEP!

180

August 9, 2003

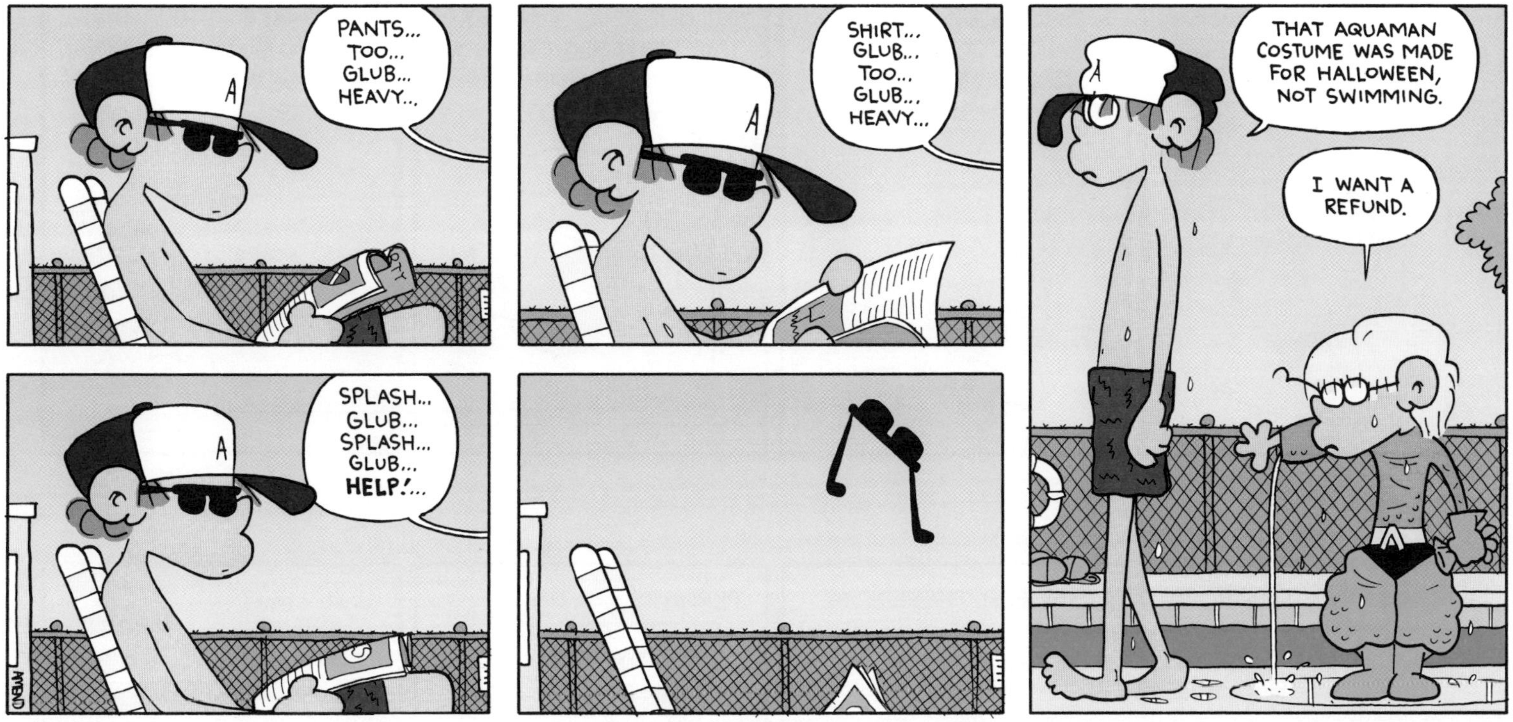
PANTS... TOO... GLUB... HEAVY...
SHIRT... GLUB... TOO... GLUB... HEAVY...
SPLASH... GLUB... SPLASH... GLUB... **HELP!**...
THAT AQUAMAN COSTUME WAS MADE FOR HALLOWEEN, NOT SWIMMING.
I WANT A REFUND.
AMEND

August 10, 2003

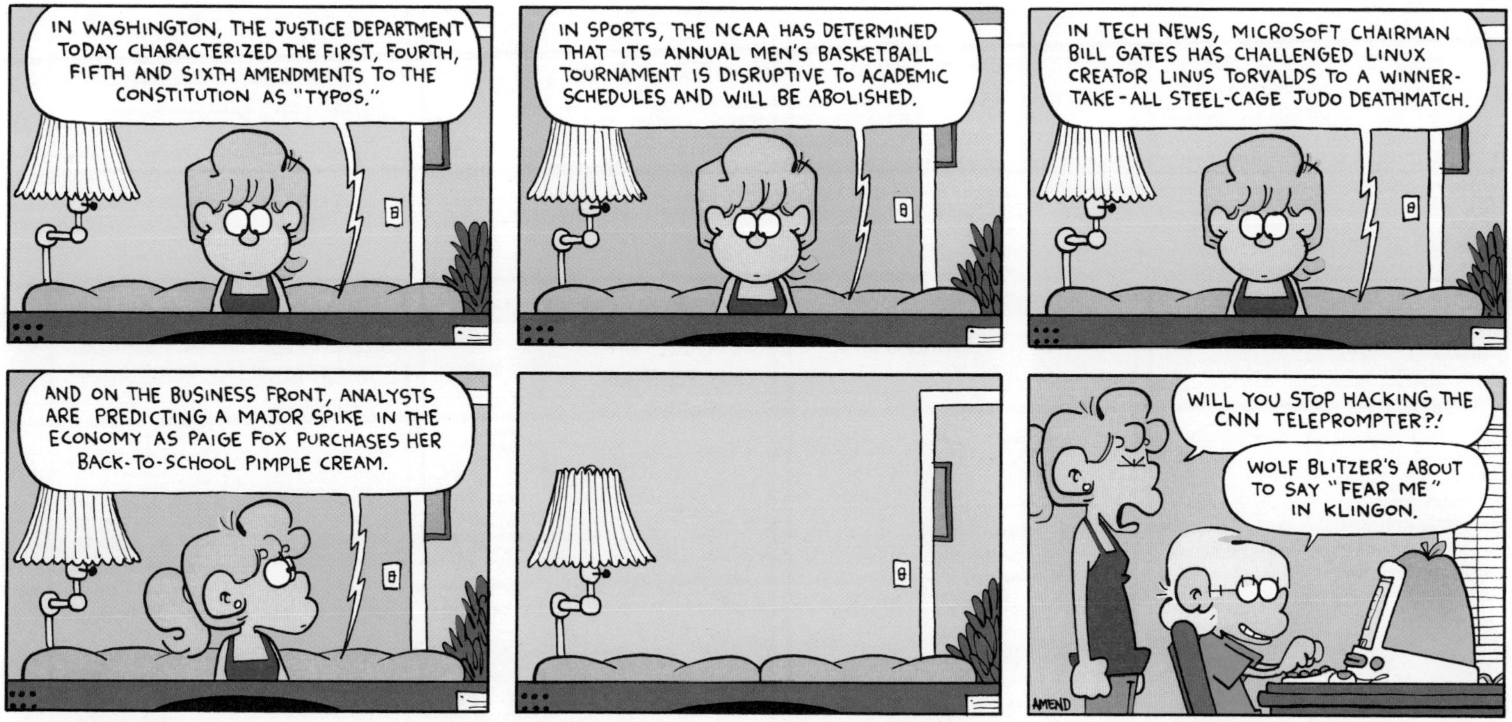
IN WASHINGTON, THE JUSTICE DEPARTMENT TODAY CHARACTERIZED THE FIRST, FOURTH, FIFTH AND SIXTH AMENDMENTS TO THE CONSTITUTION AS "TYPOS."
IN SPORTS, THE NCAA HAS DETERMINED THAT ITS ANNUAL MEN'S BASKETBALL TOURNAMENT IS DISRUPTIVE TO ACADEMIC SCHEDULES AND WILL BE ABOLISHED.
IN TECH NEWS, MICROSOFT CHAIRMAN BILL GATES HAS CHALLENGED LINUX CREATOR LINUS TORVALDS TO A WINNER-TAKE-ALL STEEL-CAGE JUDO DEATHMATCH.
AND ON THE BUSINESS FRONT, ANALYSTS ARE PREDICTING A MAJOR SPIKE IN THE ECONOMY AS PAIGE FOX PURCHASES HER BACK-TO-SCHOOL PIMPLE CREAM.
WILL YOU STOP HACKING THE CNN TELEPROMPTER?!
WOLF BLITZER'S ABOUT TO SAY "FEAR ME" IN KLINGON.
AMEND

August 24, 2003

ROGER, YOU KNOW THAT OLD LEISURE SUIT OF YOURS?

THAT HIDEOUS THING WITH THE FLARED PANTS AND WIDE LAPELS?

THE ONE THAT FOR YEARS I'VE BEEN BEGGING YOU TO BURN, AND YOU WOULDN'T?

REMEMBER THAT WHEN YOU GET HOME.

HEY, BABE. WHAT'S YOUR SIGN?

September 22, 2003

I AM DON IGUAN, THE LADIES' LIZARD.

JASON, PUT QUINCY BACK IN HIS CAGE.

I HAVE SLITHERED THE WORLD OVER IN SEARCH OF BEAUTY SUCH AS YOURS!

PERHAPS YOU'D LIKE TO COME BACK TO MY LAIR THIS EVENING.

I'LL LIGHT SOME CANDLES... PUT ON SOME BEETLE MUSIC...

I'M MARRIED. GO HIT ON YOUR SISTER.

September 23, 2003

I AM DON IGUAN, BABE MAGNET.

CHICK CATCHER.

DEVOTEE OF THE FEMALE FORM.

COULD YOU DIRECT ME TO A FEMALE FORM?

HOW 'BOUT A FEMALE FOREARM?

September 24, 2003

September 25, 2003

September 26, 2003

September 27, 2003

183

November 11, 2003

July 28, 2003

September 9, 2003

September 10, 2003

September 19, 2003

October 3, 2003

WHAT'S THIS? **AN INVITATION.**

I'M HAVING A PARTY AT MY HOUSE ON HALLOWEEN AND I WAS HOPING YOU COULD MAKE IT.

WAIT! WAIT! SCREAM LIKE THAT IN MY DICTAPHONE! I NEED SOUND EFFECTS!

October 20, 2003

MORTON GOLDTHWAIT WANTS ME TO COME TO HIS PARTY! **POOR PAIGE!**

HE'S THE BIGGEST DWEEB IN SCHOOL! IT'LL BE THE HALLOWEEN PARTY FROM HELL! **ACTUALLY, A HALLOWEEN PARTY FROM HELL MIGHT BE PRETTY COOL.**

GOOD POINT.

IT'LL BE THE HALLOWEEN PARTY FROM PURGATORY! **OR EVEN HEAVEN!**

October 21, 2003

I DON'T WANT TO GO TO MORTON GOLDTHWAIT'S HALLOWEEN PARTY!

HE'S A DWEEB! A DRIP! A MUTANT! A FREAK!

HE IS THE BIGGEST LITTLE NERD LOSER TWIT THIS SCHOOL HAS EVER SEEN!

THEN DON'T GO. **I DON'T WANT TO BE RUDE.**

October 22, 2003

UNBELIEVABLE.

YOU'RE REALLY GOING TO MORTON GOLDTHWAIT'S HALLOWEEN PARTY?

HE'S THE BIGGEST GEEK IN TOWN.'

DON'T RUB IT IN.

THAT'S WHAT I WAS GOING TO SAY.

October 23, 2003

NICOLE ACTUALLY AGREED TO GO TO GOLDTHWAIT'S PARTY WITH YOU?

OF COURSE.

SHE'S MY BEST FRIEND.

THAT'S WHAT BEST FRIENDS DO.

WHY'S YOUR PIGGY BANK SMASHED?

SHE'S ALSO MY EXPENSIVE FRIEND.

October 24, 2003

WHERE'S PAIGE?

GETTING HER COSTUME READY FOR MORTON GOLDTHWAIT'S PARTY.

I THOUGHT THAT WASN'T UNTIL NEXT WEEK.

SHE'S CONCERNED ABOUT HER IMAGE.

SHE WANTS TO PUT HER BEST FACE FORWARD?

MORE LIKE NO FACE FORWARD.

WHAT HAPPENS IF THEY PLAY STRIP "MAGIC: THE GATHERING"?

GOOD POINT. GOT SOME GLUE?

NOT PAIGE FOX

October 25, 2003

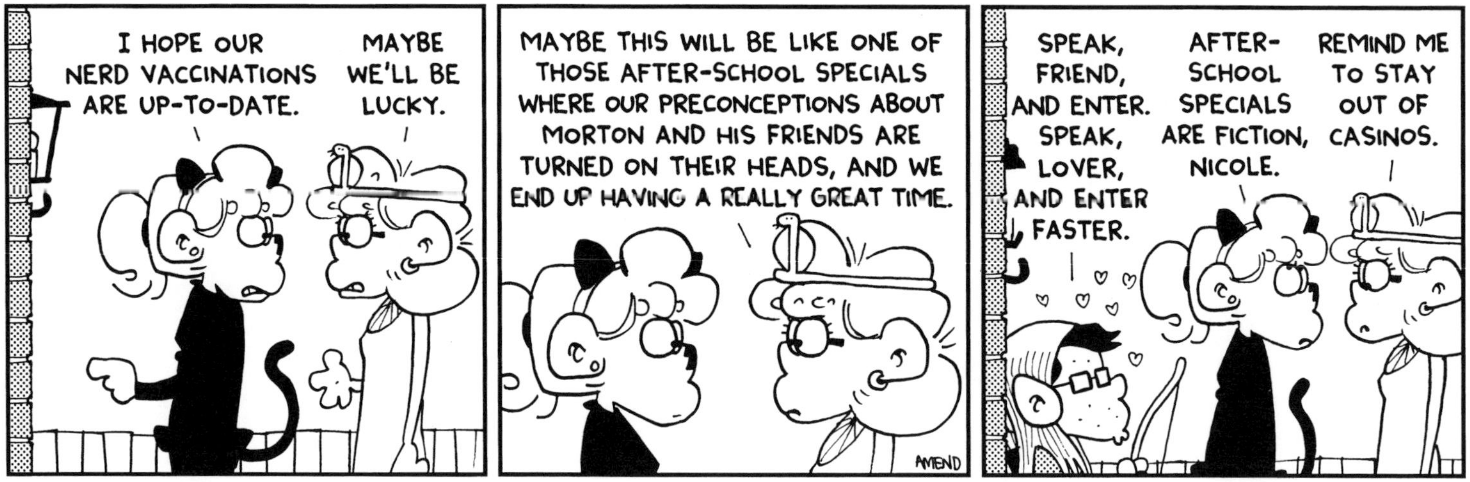
I HOPE OUR NERD VACCINATIONS ARE UP-TO-DATE.
MAYBE WE'LL BE LUCKY.
MAYBE THIS WILL BE LIKE ONE OF THOSE AFTER-SCHOOL SPECIALS WHERE OUR PRECONCEPTIONS ABOUT MORTON AND HIS FRIENDS ARE TURNED ON THEIR HEADS, AND WE END UP HAVING A REALLY GREAT TIME.
AMEND
SPEAK, FRIEND, AND ENTER. SPEAK, LOVER, AND ENTER FASTER.
AFTER-SCHOOL SPECIALS ARE FICTION, NICOLE.
REMIND ME TO STAY OUT OF CASINOS.

October 27, 2003

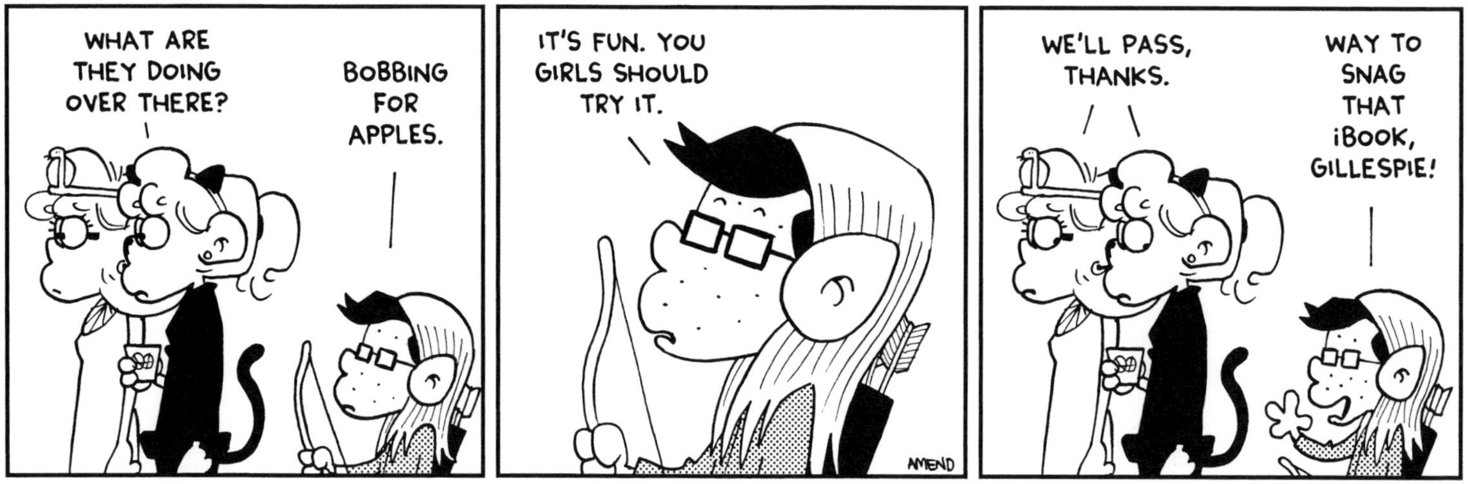
WHAT ARE THEY DOING OVER THERE?
BOBBING FOR APPLES.
IT'S FUN. YOU GIRLS SHOULD TRY IT.
AMEND
WE'LL PASS, THANKS.
WAY TO SNAG THAT iBOOK, GILLESPIE!

October 28, 2003

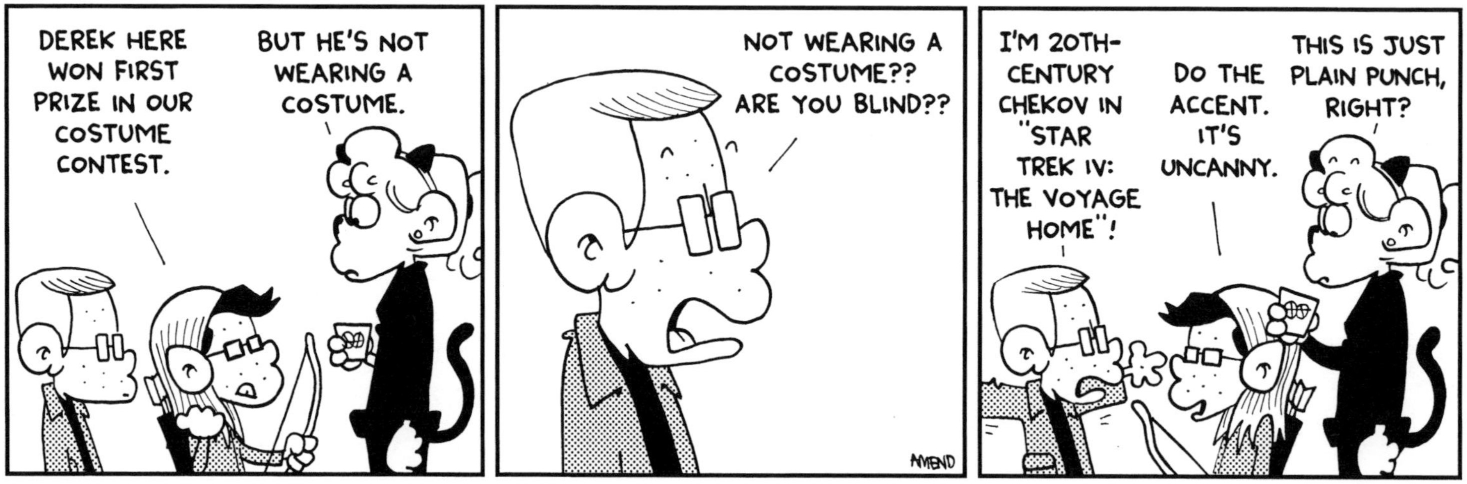
DEREK HERE WON FIRST PRIZE IN OUR COSTUME CONTEST.
BUT HE'S NOT WEARING A COSTUME.
NOT WEARING A COSTUME?? ARE YOU BLIND??
AMEND
I'M 20TH-CENTURY CHEKOV IN "STAR TREK IV: THE VOYAGE HOME"!
DO THE ACCENT. IT'S UNCANNY.
THIS IS JUST PLAIN PUNCH, RIGHT?

October 29, 2003

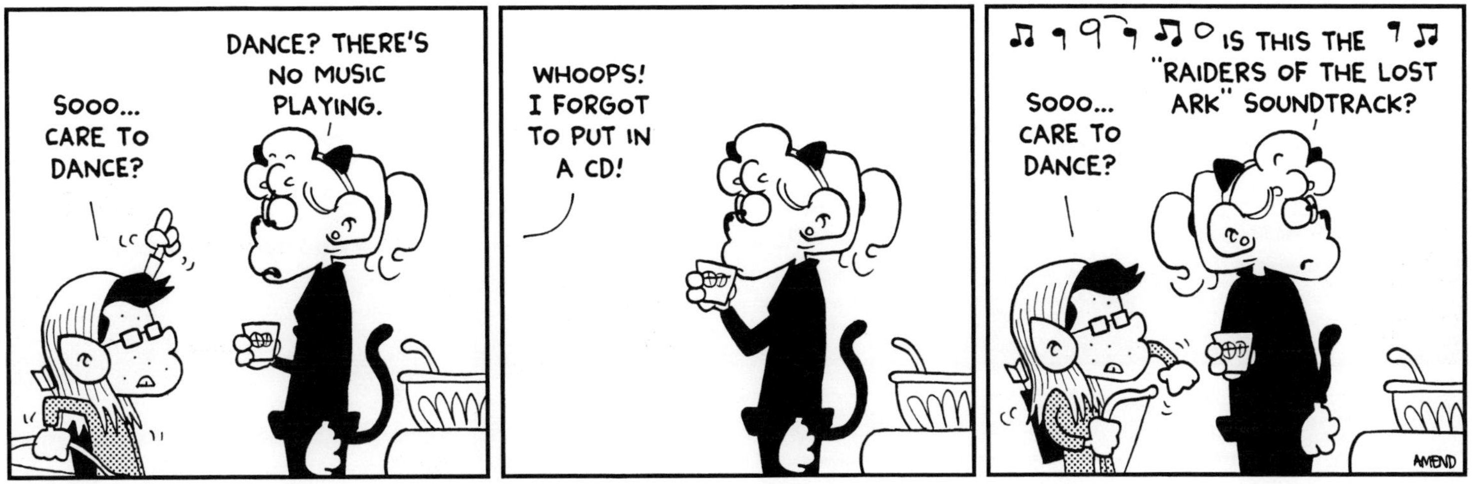
SOOO... CARE TO DANCE?
DANCE? THERE'S NO MUSIC PLAYING.
WHOOPS! I FORGOT TO PUT IN A CD!
SOOO... CARE TO DANCE?
IS THIS THE "RAIDERS OF THE LOST ARK" SOUNDTRACK?
AMEND

October 30, 2003

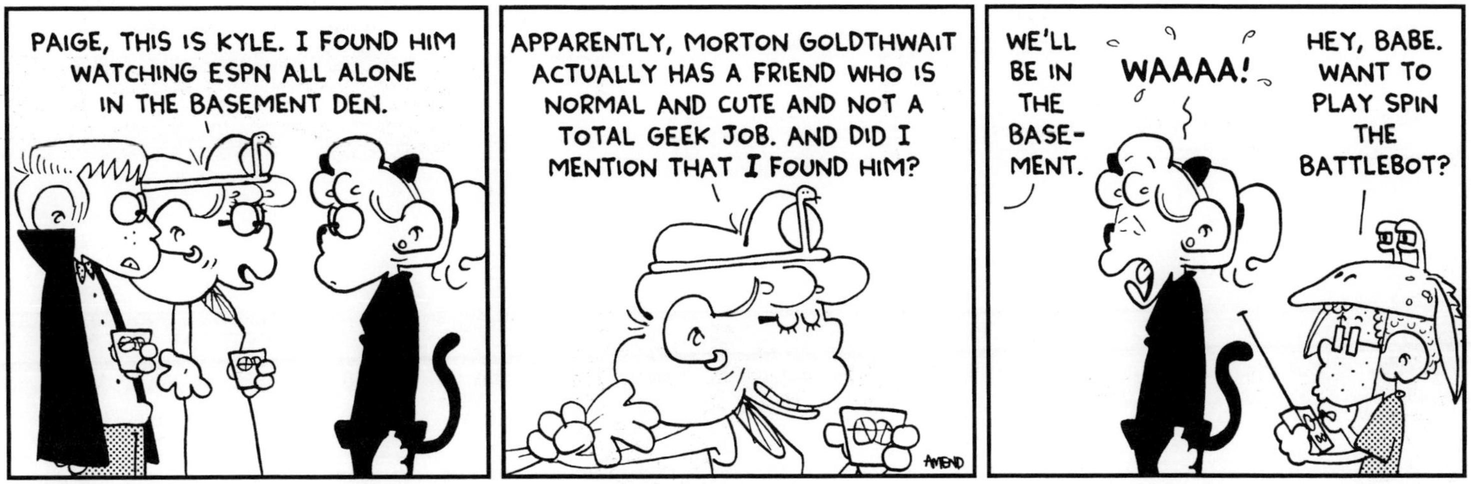
PAIGE, THIS IS KYLE. I FOUND HIM WATCHING ESPN ALL ALONE IN THE BASEMENT DEN.
APPARENTLY, MORTON GOLDTHWAIT ACTUALLY HAS A FRIEND WHO IS NORMAL AND CUTE AND NOT A TOTAL GEEK JOB. AND DID I MENTION THAT I FOUND HIM?
AMEND
WE'LL BE IN THE BASEMENT.
WAAAA!
HEY, BABE. WANT TO PLAY SPIN THE BATTLEBOT?

October 31, 2003

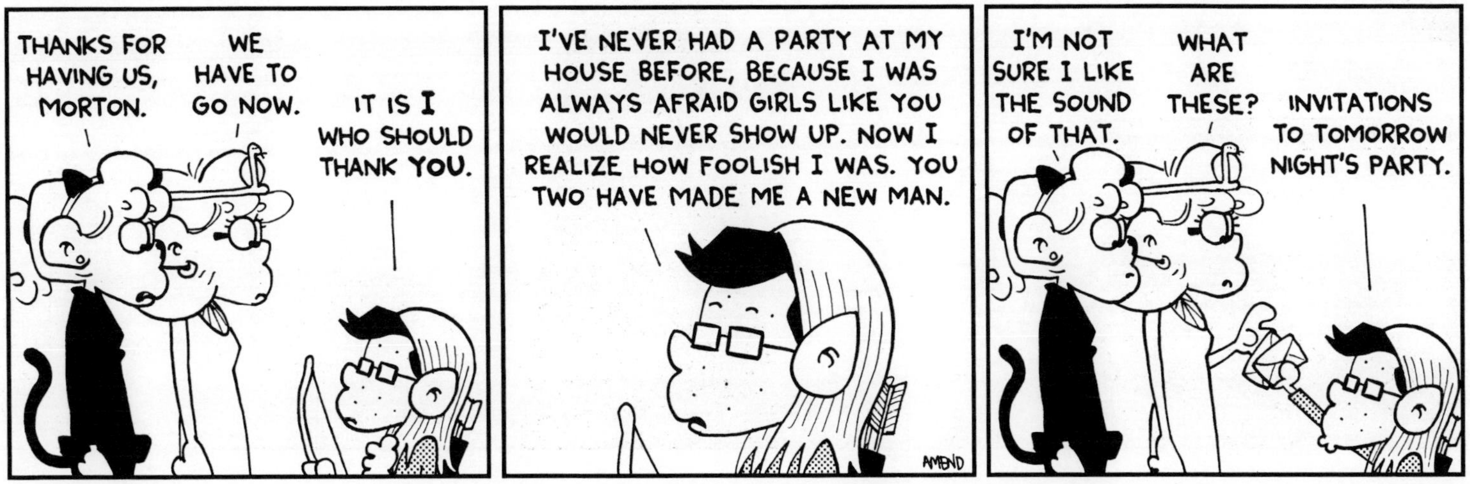
THANKS FOR HAVING US, MORTON.
WE HAVE TO GO NOW.
IT IS I WHO SHOULD THANK YOU.
I'VE NEVER HAD A PARTY AT MY HOUSE BEFORE, BECAUSE I WAS ALWAYS AFRAID GIRLS LIKE YOU WOULD NEVER SHOW UP. NOW I REALIZE HOW FOOLISH I WAS. YOU TWO HAVE MADE ME A NEW MAN.
AMEND
I'M NOT SURE I LIKE THE SOUND OF THAT.
WHAT ARE THESE?
INVITATIONS TO TOMORROW NIGHT'S PARTY.

November 1, 2003

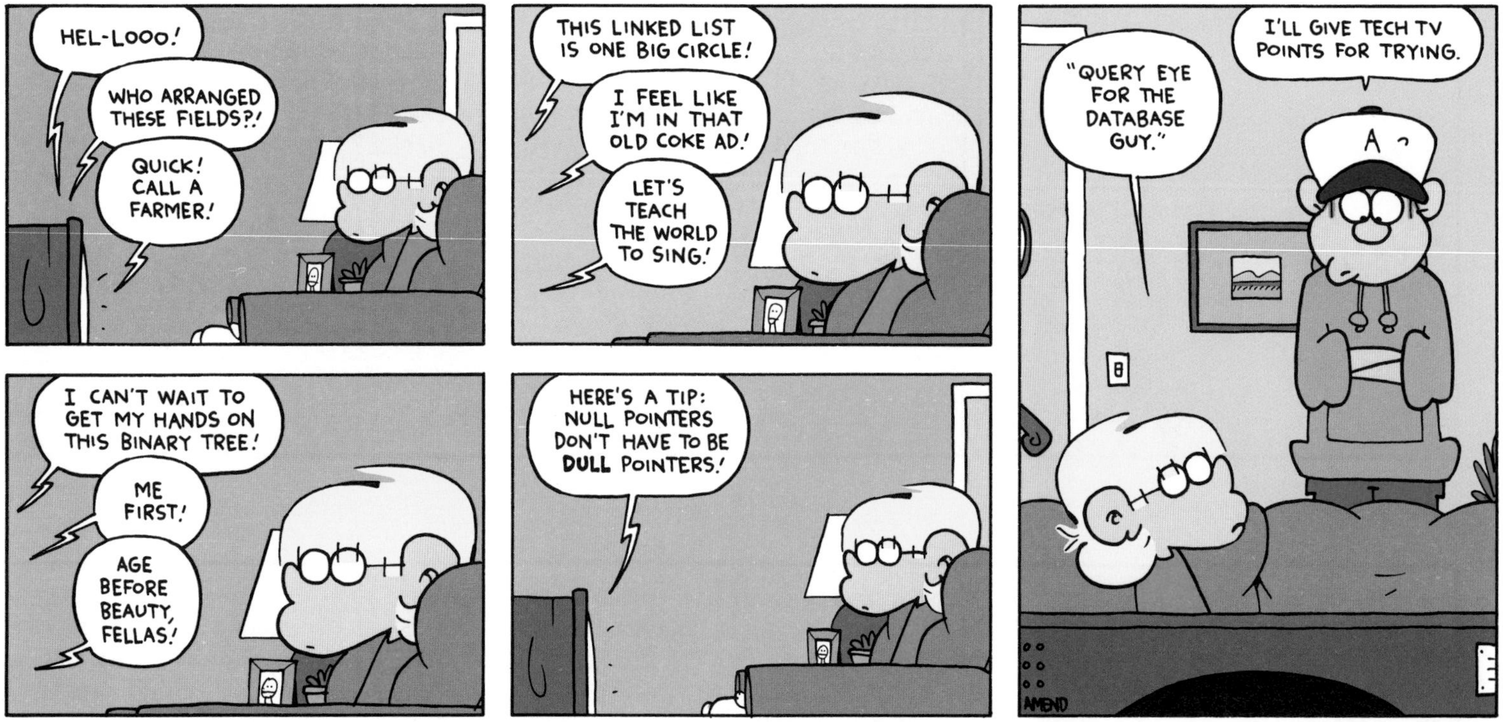
HEL-LOOO!
WHO ARRANGED THESE FIELDS?!
QUICK! CALL A FARMER!
THIS LINKED LIST IS ONE BIG CIRCLE!
I FEEL LIKE I'M IN THAT OLD COKE AD!
LET'S TEACH THE WORLD TO SING!
I CAN'T WAIT TO GET MY HANDS ON THIS BINARY TREE!
ME FIRST!
AGE BEFORE BEAUTY, FELLAS!
HERE'S A TIP: NULL POINTERS DON'T HAVE TO BE DULL POINTERS!
"QUERY EYE FOR THE DATABASE GUY."
I'LL GIVE TECH TV POINTS FOR TRYING.
AMEND

September 14, 2003

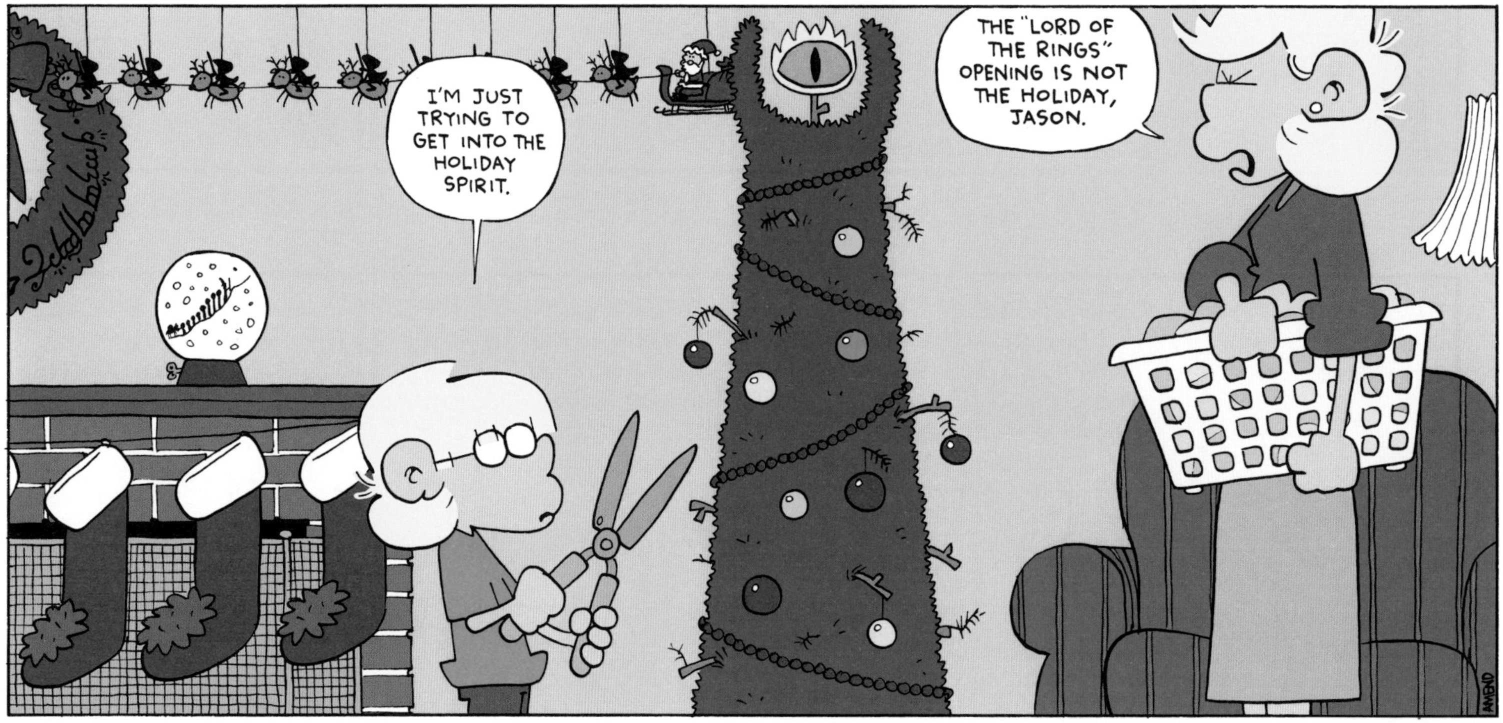
I'M JUST TRYING TO GET INTO THE HOLIDAY SPIRIT.
THE "LORD OF THE RINGS" OPENING IS NOT THE HOLIDAY, JASON.
AMEND

December 14, 2003

My wife had a huge Legolas crush. I feel Jason's pain in these strips.

December 15, 2003

December 16, 2003

December 17, 2003

December 18, 2003

December 19, 2003

December 20, 2003

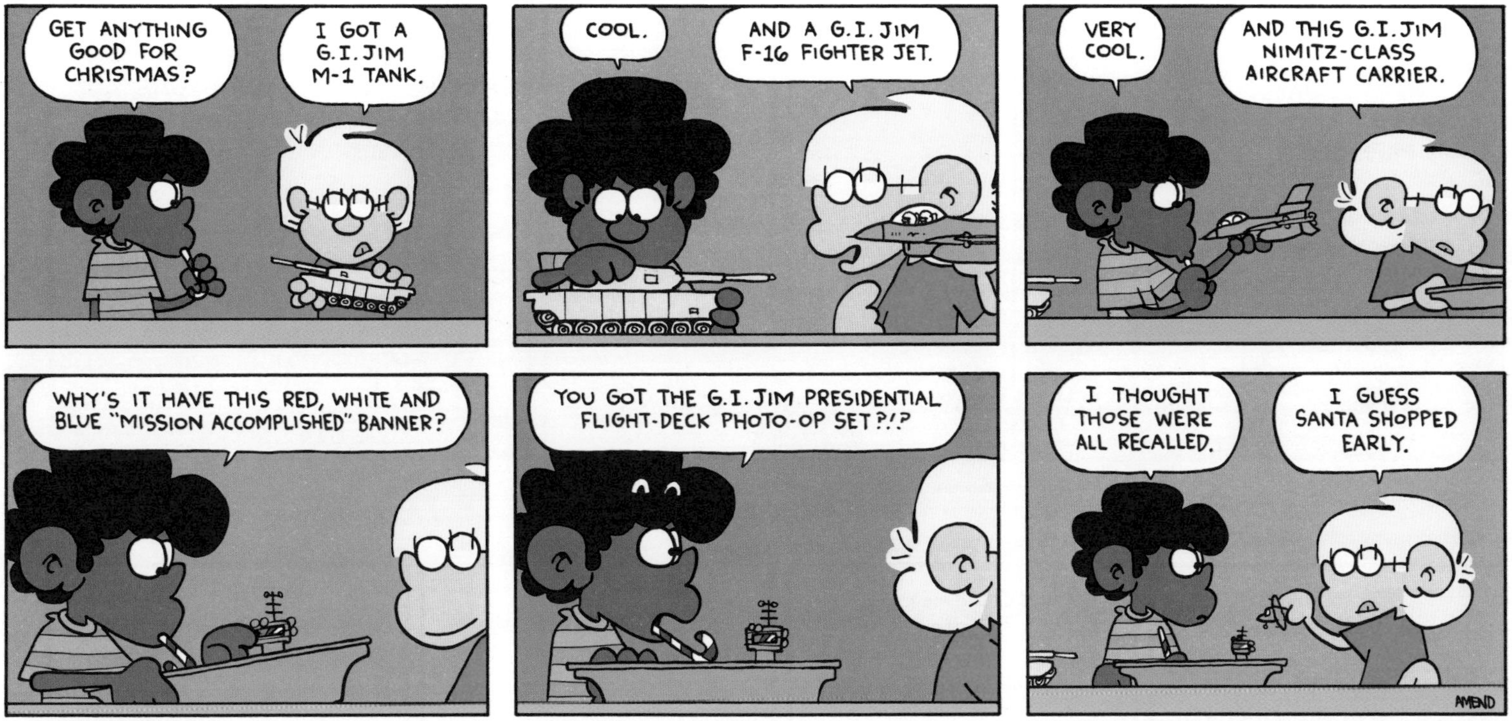
GET ANYTHING GOOD FOR CHRISTMAS?
I GOT A G.I. JIM M-1 TANK.
COOL.
AND A G.I. JIM F-16 FIGHTER JET.
VERY COOL.
AND THIS G.I. JIM NIMITZ-CLASS AIRCRAFT CARRIER.
WHY'S IT HAVE THIS RED, WHITE AND BLUE "MISSION ACCOMPLISHED" BANNER?
YOU GOT THE G.I. JIM PRESIDENTIAL FLIGHT-DECK PHOTO-OP SET?!?
I THOUGHT THOSE WERE ALL RECALLED.
I GUESS SANTA SHOPPED EARLY.
AMEND

December 28, 2003

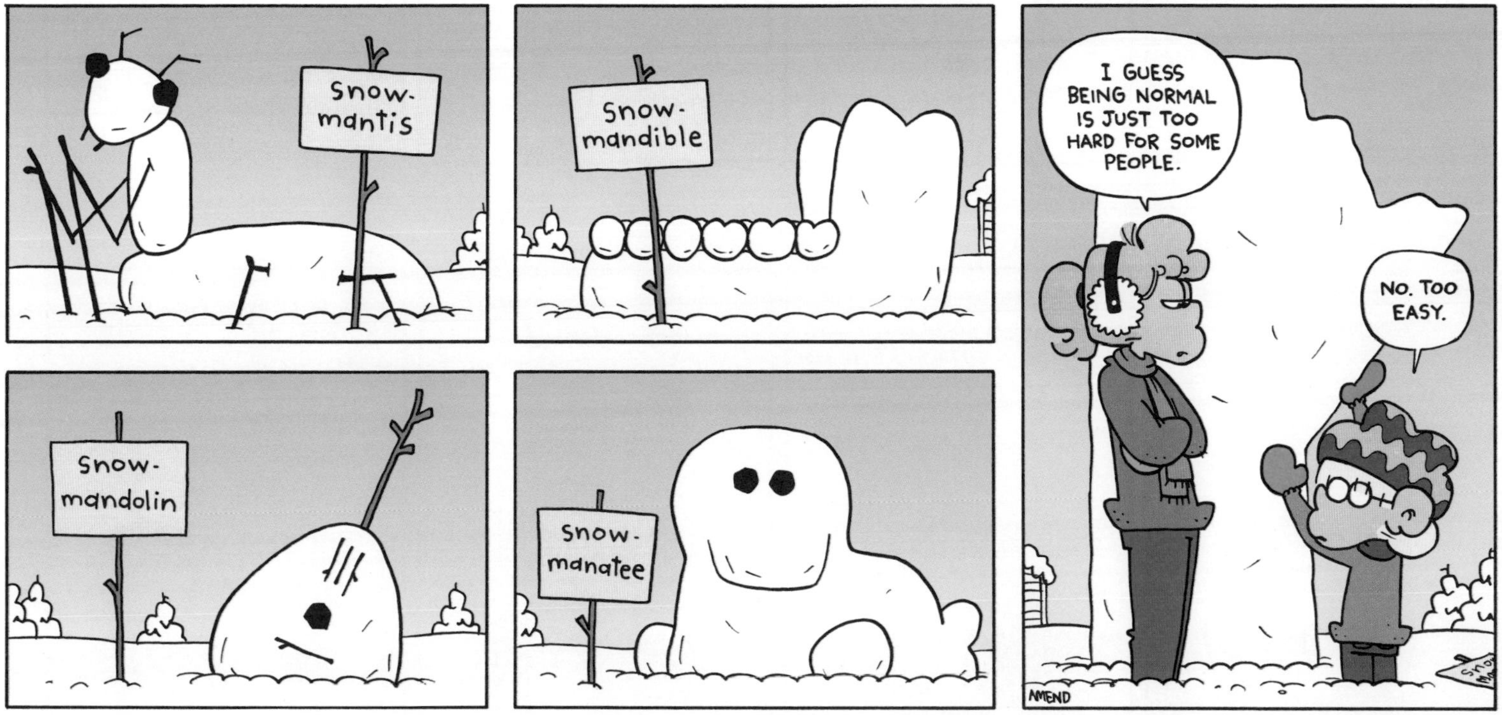
Snow-mantis
Snow-mandible
I GUESS BEING NORMAL IS JUST TOO HARD FOR SOME PEOPLE.
NO. TOO EASY.
Snow-mandolin
Snow-manatee
AMEND

January 4, 2004

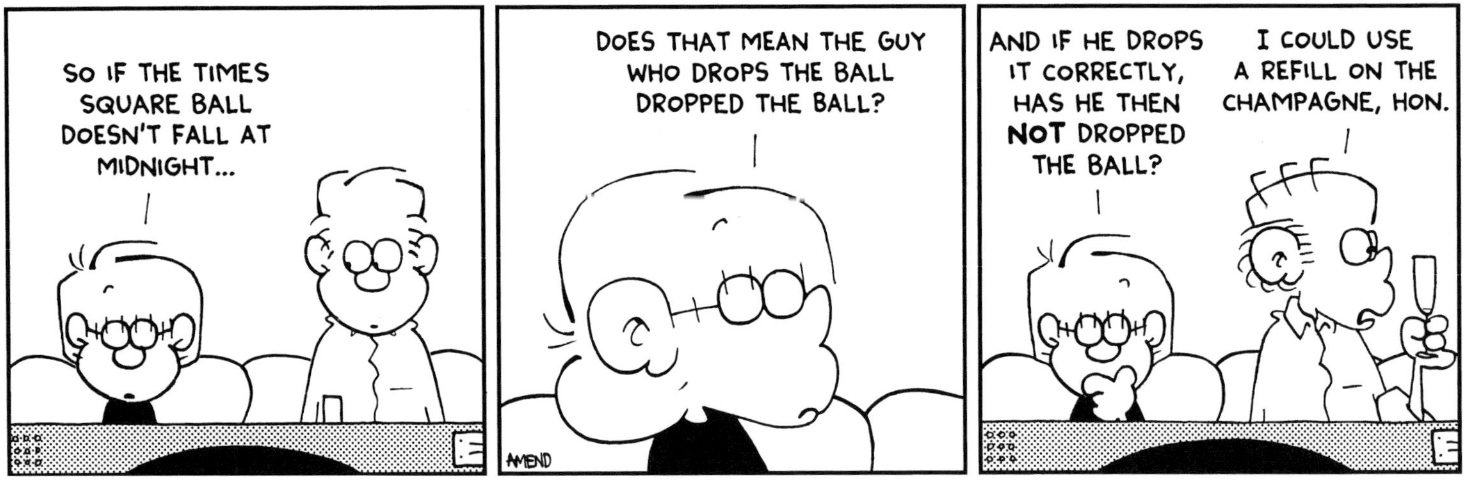
SO IF THE TIMES SQUARE BALL DOESN'T FALL AT MIDNIGHT...
DOES THAT MEAN THE GUY WHO DROPS THE BALL DROPPED THE BALL?
AND IF HE DROPS IT CORRECTLY, HAS HE THEN **NOT** DROPPED THE BALL?
I COULD USE A REFILL ON THE CHAMPAGNE, HON.
AMEND

December 31, 2003

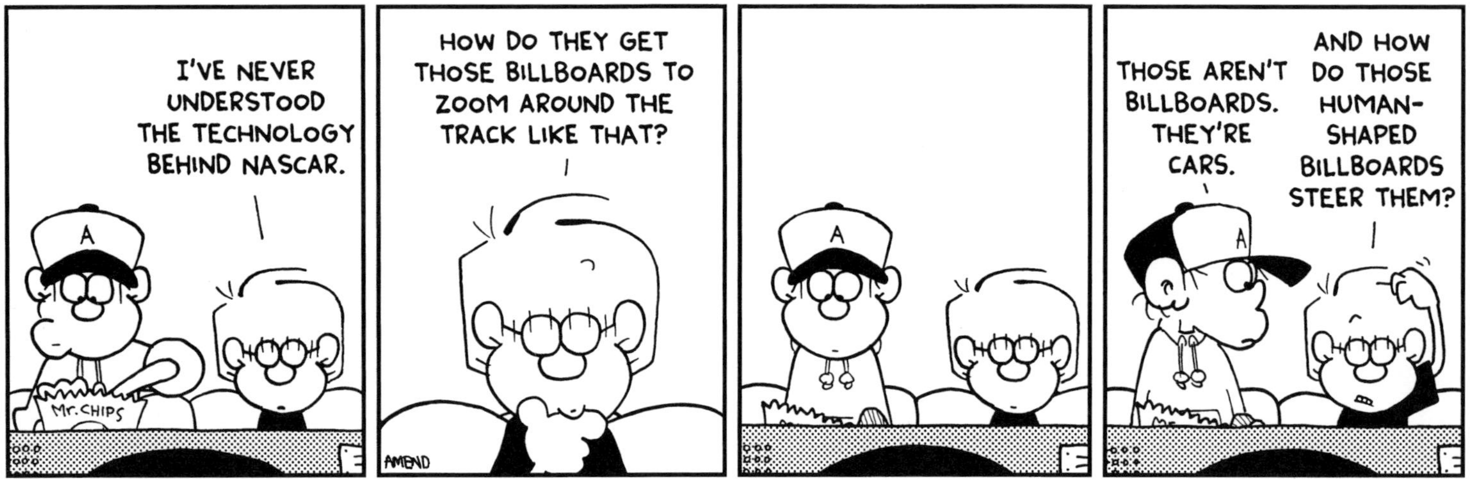
I'VE NEVER UNDERSTOOD THE TECHNOLOGY BEHIND NASCAR.
Mr. CHIPS
HOW DO THEY GET THOSE BILLBOARDS TO ZOOM AROUND THE TRACK LIKE THAT?
AMEND
THOSE AREN'T BILLBOARDS. THEY'RE CARS.
AND HOW DO THOSE HUMAN-SHAPED BILLBOARDS STEER THEM?

May 11, 2004

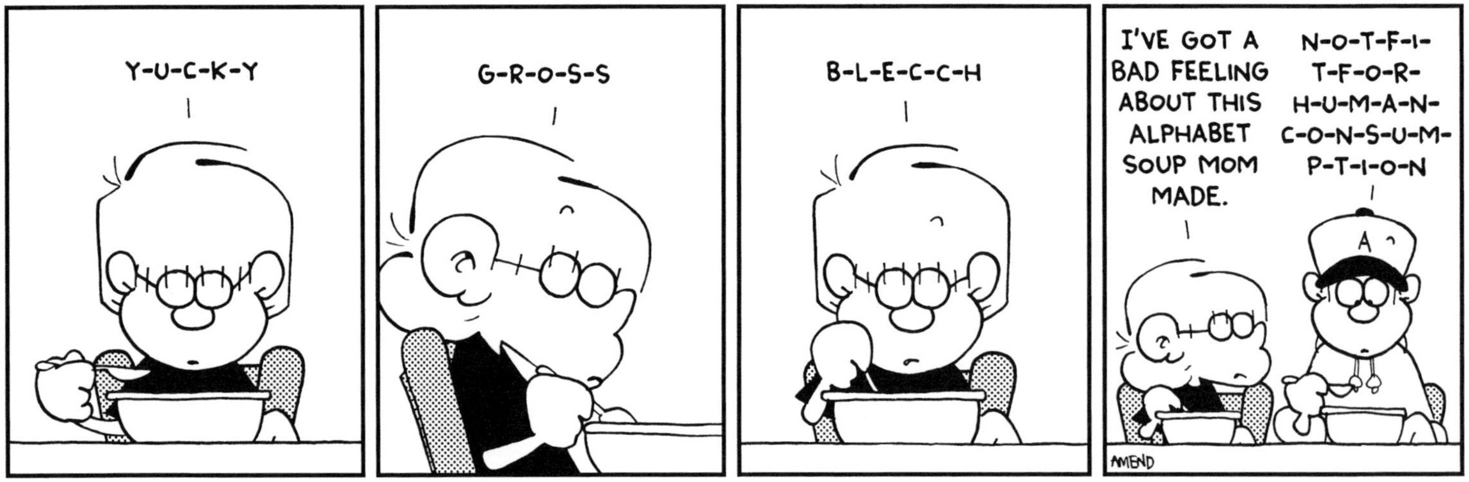
Y-U-C-K-Y
G-R-O-S-S
B-L-E-C-C-H
I'VE GOT A BAD FEELING ABOUT THIS ALPHABET SOUP MOM MADE.
N-O-T-F-I-T-F-O-R-H-U-M-A-N-C-O-N-S-U-M-P-T-I-O-N
AMEND

June 16, 2004

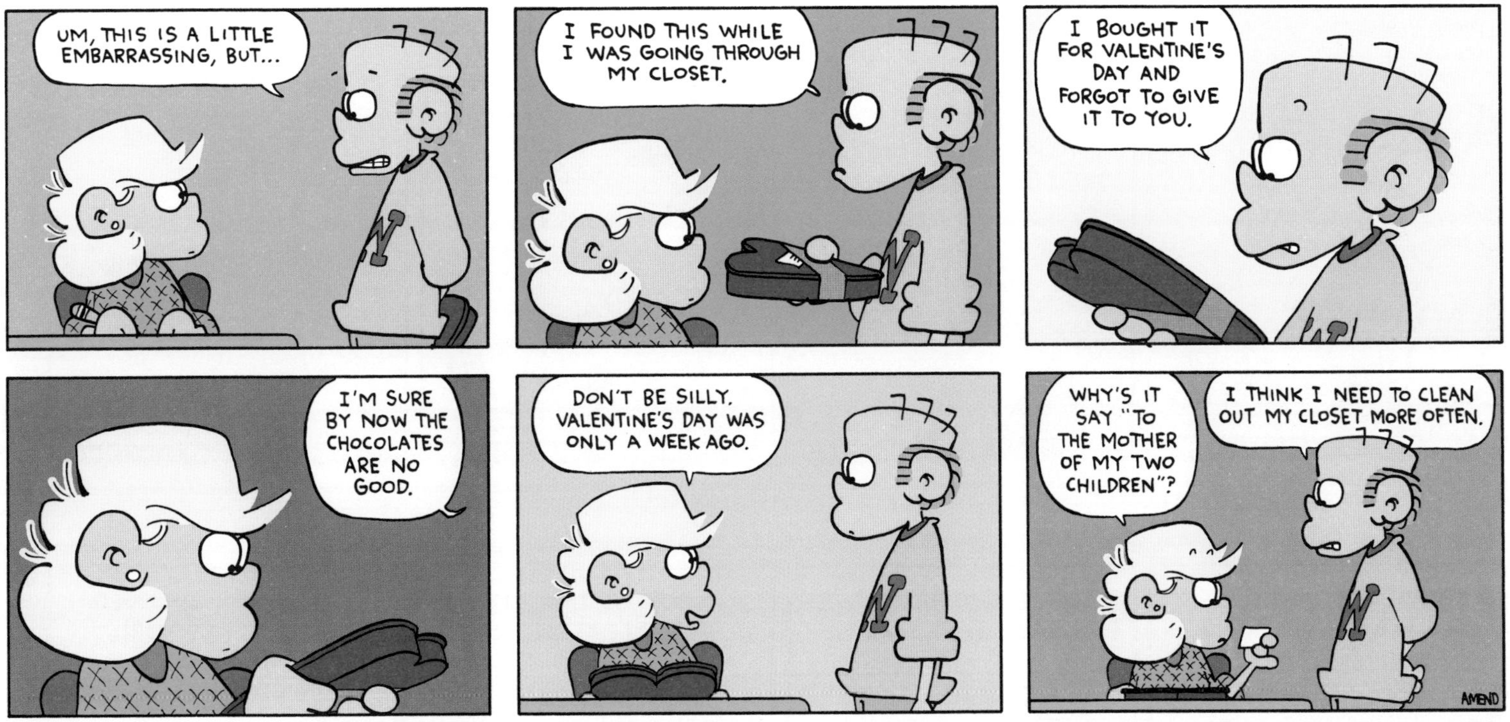
UM, THIS IS A LITTLE EMBARRASSING, BUT...
I FOUND THIS WHILE I WAS GOING THROUGH MY CLOSET.
I BOUGHT IT FOR VALENTINE'S DAY AND FORGOT TO GIVE IT TO YOU.
I'M SURE BY NOW THE CHOCOLATES ARE NO GOOD.
DON'T BE SILLY. VALENTINE'S DAY WAS ONLY A WEEK AGO.
WHY'S IT SAY "TO THE MOTHER OF MY TWO CHILDREN"?
I THINK I NEED TO CLEAN OUT MY CLOSET MORE OFTEN.
AMEND

February 22, 2004

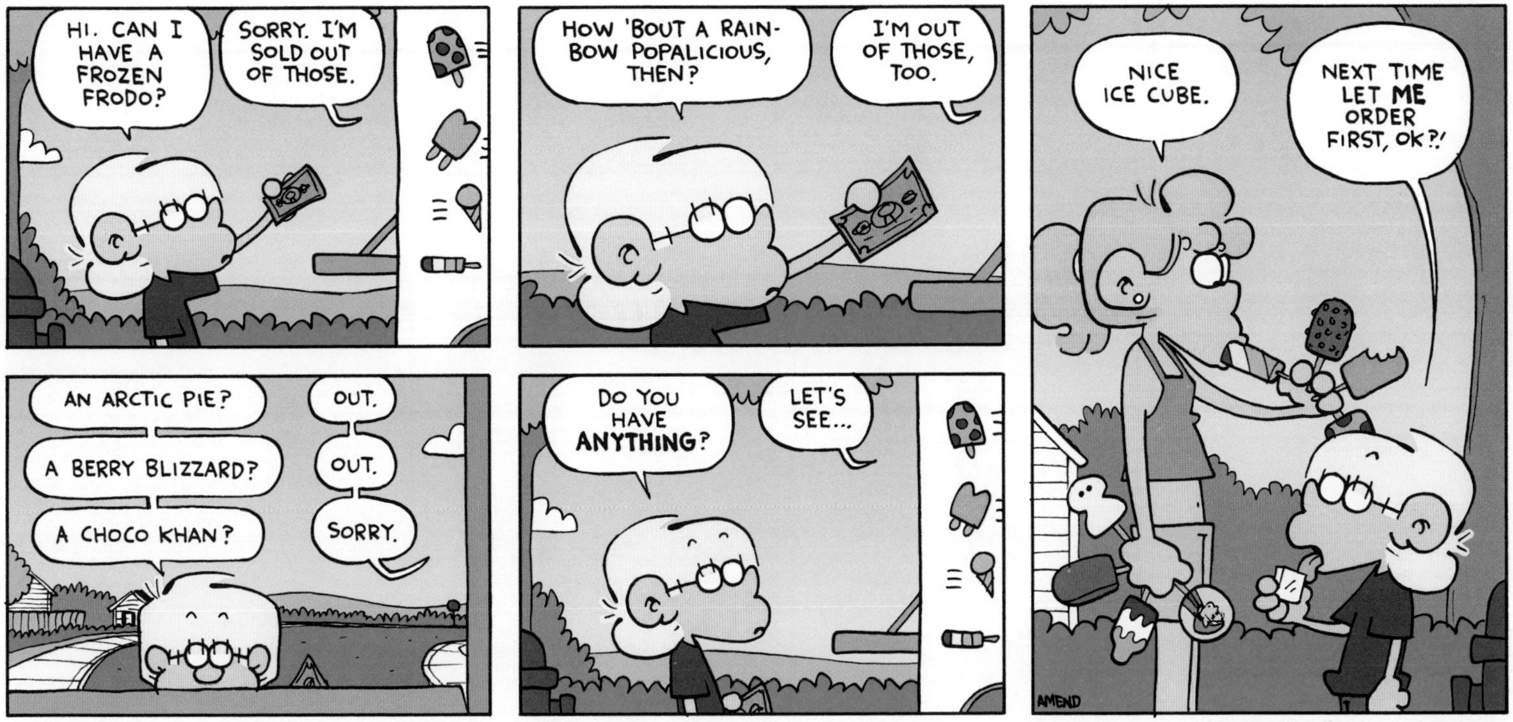
HI. CAN I HAVE A FROZEN FRODO?
SORRY. I'M SOLD OUT OF THOSE.
HOW 'BOUT A RAINBOW POPALICIOUS, THEN?
I'M OUT OF THOSE, TOO.
AN ARCTIC PIE?
OUT.
A BERRY BLIZZARD?
OUT.
A CHOCO KHAN?
SORRY.
DO YOU HAVE **ANYTHING**?
LET'S SEE...
NICE ICE CUBE.
NEXT TIME LET **ME** ORDER FIRST, OK?!
AMEND

July 11, 2004

Having fun with Microsoft is too easy sometimes. It's still fun though.

WHAT ARE YOU DOING?

READING ABOUT THE BIG WINDOWS SOURCE CODE LEAK.

IT'S LIKE 600-PLUS MEGS OF TOP-SECRET MICROSOFT PROGRAMMING, AND NOW IT'S ALL OVER THE INTERNET. BILL GATES MUST BE GOING BONKERS.

NOT THAT PEOPLE COULDN'T PROBABLY ALREADY GUESS SOME OF WHAT'S IN IT.

```
BEGIN
 IF browser_type =
    "Internet_Explorer"
 THEN smooth_sailing
 ELSE
    IF (browser_type =
       "Netscape") AND
    (justice_department
       NOT looking)
 THEN
    REPEAT
       crash (random)
```

March 1, 2004

SO HAVE YOU LOOKED AT THIS LEAKED WINDOWS SOURCE CODE?

NOT YET.

REALLY? I WOULD HAVE THOUGHT A GEEK LIKE YOU WOULD BE ALL OVER IT.

MICROSOFT IS THREATENING STIFF LEGAL ACTION AGAINST ANYONE WHO DOWNLOADS IT.

AH, AND PAIGE CHANGED HER LOGIN PASSWORD.

I'LL FIGURE IT OUT EVENTUALLY.

March 2, 2004

WHY IS THIS A BIG DEAL?

WE'RE TALKING ABOUT THE BLUEPRINT TO WINDOWS, PETER.

WHO KNOWS WHAT VULNERABILITIES THE HACKING COMMUNITY MIGHT FIND NOW THAT WE HAVE ACCESS TO CHUNKS OF THE SOURCE CODE?

BIG VULNERABILITIES?

ANYTHING'S POSSIBLE.

```
get_remote_login
   (user, password);
BEGIN
 IF (user = "BGates")
 AND (password =
       "applesux")
 THEN
    BEGIN
       sound ("trumpet_
          fanfare.wma");
       godmode (on);
```

196

March 3, 2004

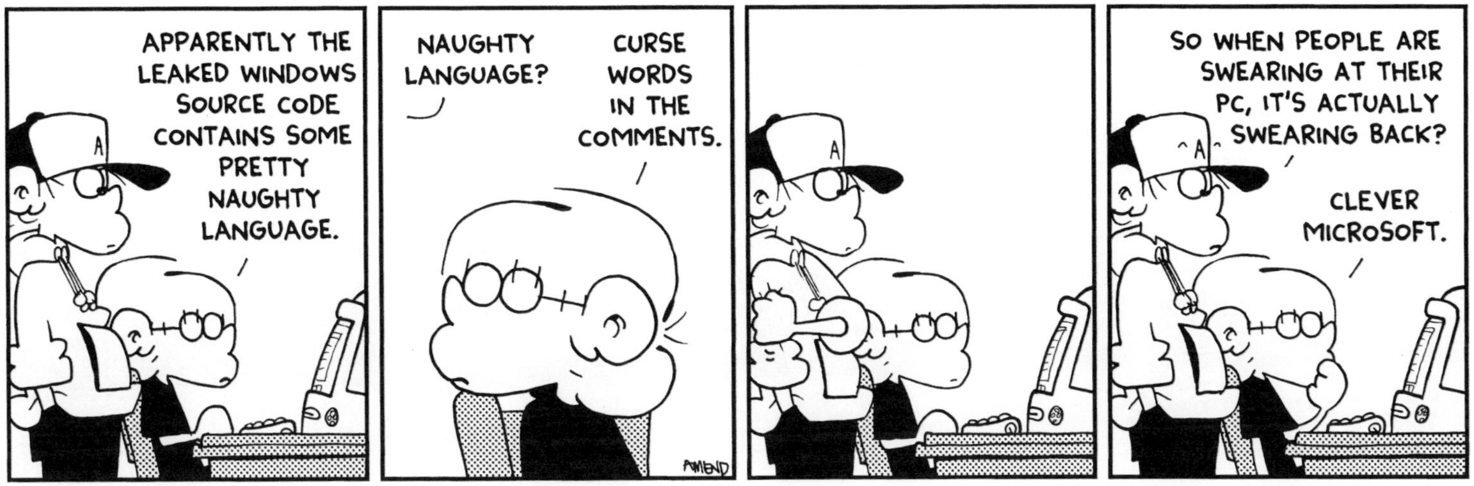
APPARENTLY THE LEAKED WINDOWS SOURCE CODE CONTAINS SOME PRETTY NAUGHTY LANGUAGE.
NAUGHTY LANGUAGE?
CURSE WORDS IN THE COMMENTS.
SO WHEN PEOPLE ARE SWEARING AT THEIR PC, IT'S ACTUALLY SWEARING BACK?
CLEVER MICROSOFT.
AMEND

March 4, 2004

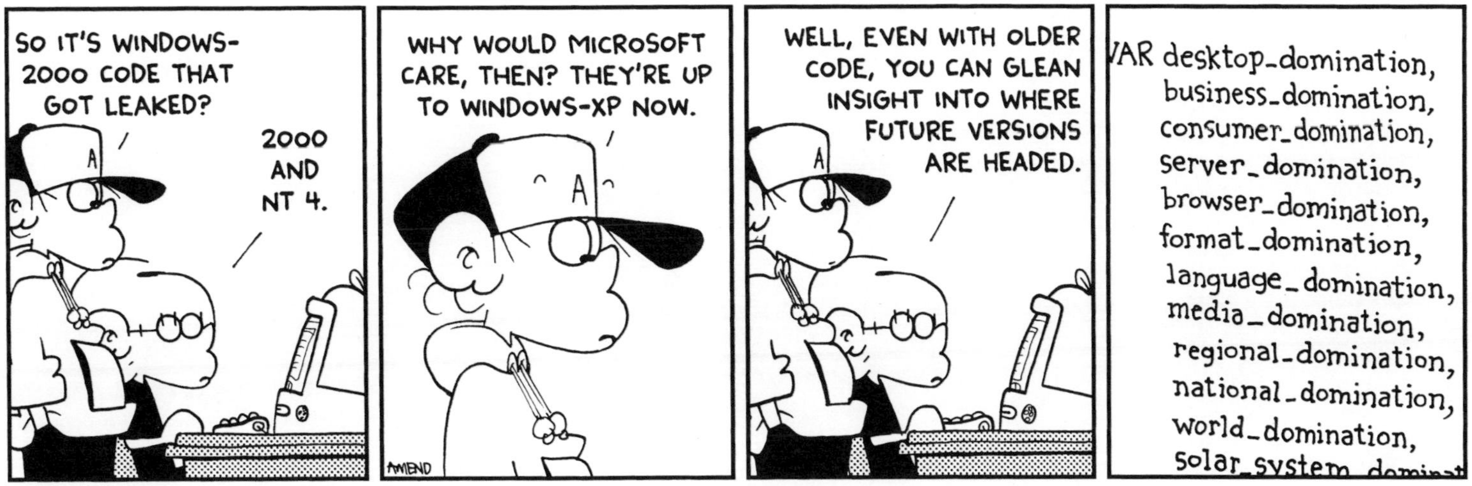
SO IT'S WINDOWS-2000 CODE THAT GOT LEAKED?
2000 AND NT 4.
WHY WOULD MICROSOFT CARE, THEN? THEY'RE UP TO WINDOWS-XP NOW.
AMEND
WELL, EVEN WITH OLDER CODE, YOU CAN GLEAN INSIGHT INTO WHERE FUTURE VERSIONS ARE HEADED.
VAR desktop_domination,
business_domination,
consumer_domination,
server_domination,
browser_domination,
format_domination,
language_domination,
media_domination,
regional_domination,
national_domination,
world_domination,
solar_system

March 5, 2004

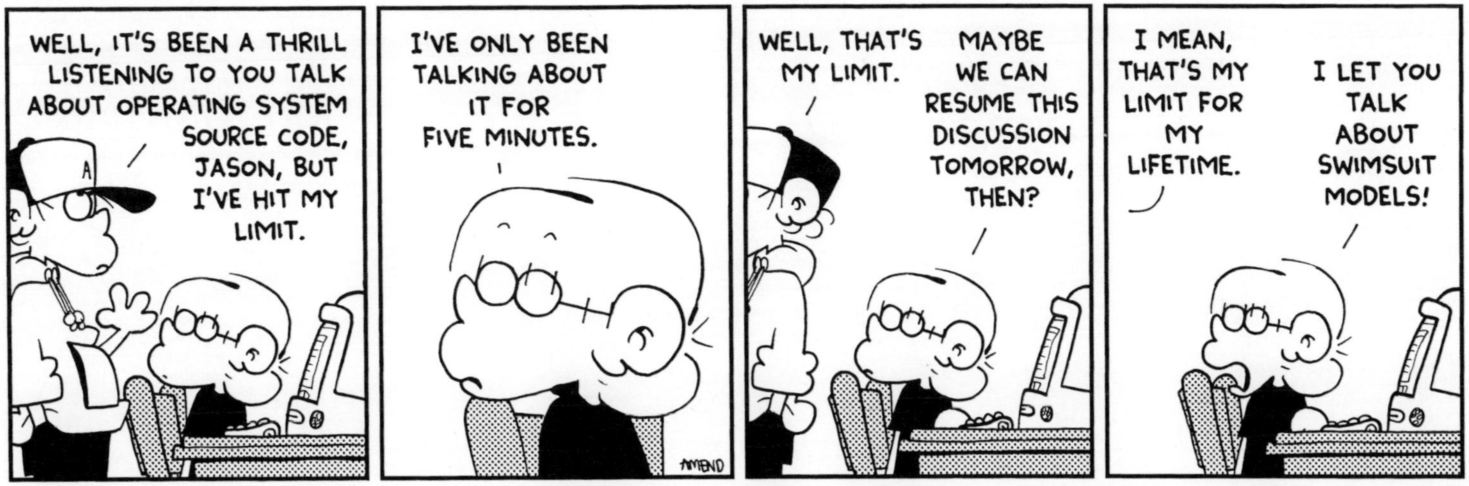
WELL, IT'S BEEN A THRILL LISTENING TO YOU TALK ABOUT OPERATING SYSTEM SOURCE CODE, JASON, BUT I'VE HIT MY LIMIT.
I'VE ONLY BEEN TALKING ABOUT IT FOR FIVE MINUTES.
AMEND
WELL, THAT'S MY LIMIT.
MAYBE WE CAN RESUME THIS DISCUSSION TOMORROW, THEN?
I MEAN, THAT'S MY LIMIT FOR MY LIFETIME.
I LET YOU TALK ABOUT SWIMSUIT MODELS!

March 6, 2004

WHERE'S JASON?

AT THE POST OFFICE MAILING HIS RESUME.

TO WHOM?!

HE'S DECIDED TO APPLY FOR THE CEO JOB AT DISNEY, JUST IN CASE MICHAEL EISNER GETS THE BOOT.

YOU'VE GOT TO BE KIDDING ME.

HE CLAIMS HE'S COME UP WITH SOME INNOVATIVE WAYS TO IMPROVE THINGS.

I SAID I WANT **REAL** GHOSTS IN THE HAUNTED MANSION!

YES, SIR, MR. FOX, SIR!

March 22, 2004

SO JASON HAS GOOD IDEAS FOR THE DISNEY COMPANY?

I NEVER SAID THE WORD "GOOD."

WE DIG, DIG, DIG, DIG, DIG, DIG, DIG IN OUR MINE, THE WHOLE DAY THROUGH...

BALROG!

March 23, 2004

DARE I ASK WHAT OTHER CHANGES JASON WOULD BRING TO DISNEY?

HE MENTIONED UPDATING SOME OF THE MOVIES.

March 24, 2004

I ALWAYS THOUGHT JASON PREFERRED JAPANESE ANIMATION.

MAYBE HE FIGURES AS DISNEY CEO, HE CAN CHANGE THINGS.

THAT MUSIC YOU ARE PLAYING SOUNDS LIKE "TURKEY IN THE STRAW"! I MUST SAY IT IS CATCHY!

IT IS "TURKEY IN THE STRAW"! WHO KNEW THAT GOATS MADE SUCH GOOD VICTROLAS?! I CERTAINLY DIDN'T!

This was a tough one to draw.

March 25, 2004

JASON ISN'T EVEN OLD ENOUGH TO SEE SOME DISNEY-OWNED MOVIES!

MAYBE AS CEO HE'LL HAVE THEM TAMED DOWN.

YOU KNOW WHAT THEY CALL A WATER BUFFALO WITH CHEESE IN THE PRIDELANDS?

THEY DON'T CALL IT A WATER BUFFALO WITH CHEESE?

March 26, 2004

YOU DIDN'T MAIL YOUR RESUME?

I DECIDED AGAINST IT AT THE LAST MINUTE.

DISNEY IS A HUGE CORPORATION. I GOT SCARED THAT RUNNING THE COMPANY MIGHT REQUIRE A LOT OF WORK.

DUH. WHAT'D YOU EXPECT?!

WELL...

I DON'T HAVE TO GET OFF! I'M THE CEO!

BUT SIR, YOU'VE BEEN RIDING IT FOR A WEEK...

SPACE MOUNTAIN

March 27, 2004

199

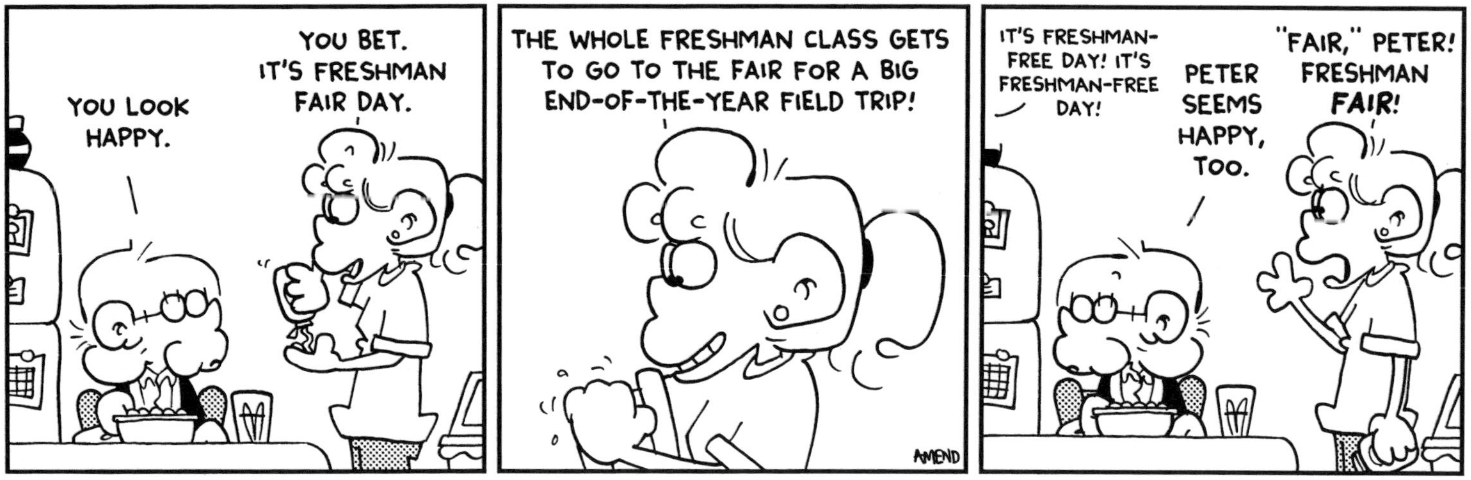
YOU LOOK HAPPY.
YOU BET. IT'S FRESHMAN FAIR DAY.
THE WHOLE FRESHMAN CLASS GETS TO GO TO THE FAIR FOR A BIG END-OF-THE-YEAR FIELD TRIP!
IT'S FRESHMAN-FREE DAY! IT'S FRESHMAN-FREE DAY!
PETER SEEMS HAPPY, TOO.
"FAIR," PETER! FRESHMAN **FAIR**!
AMEND

May 17, 2004

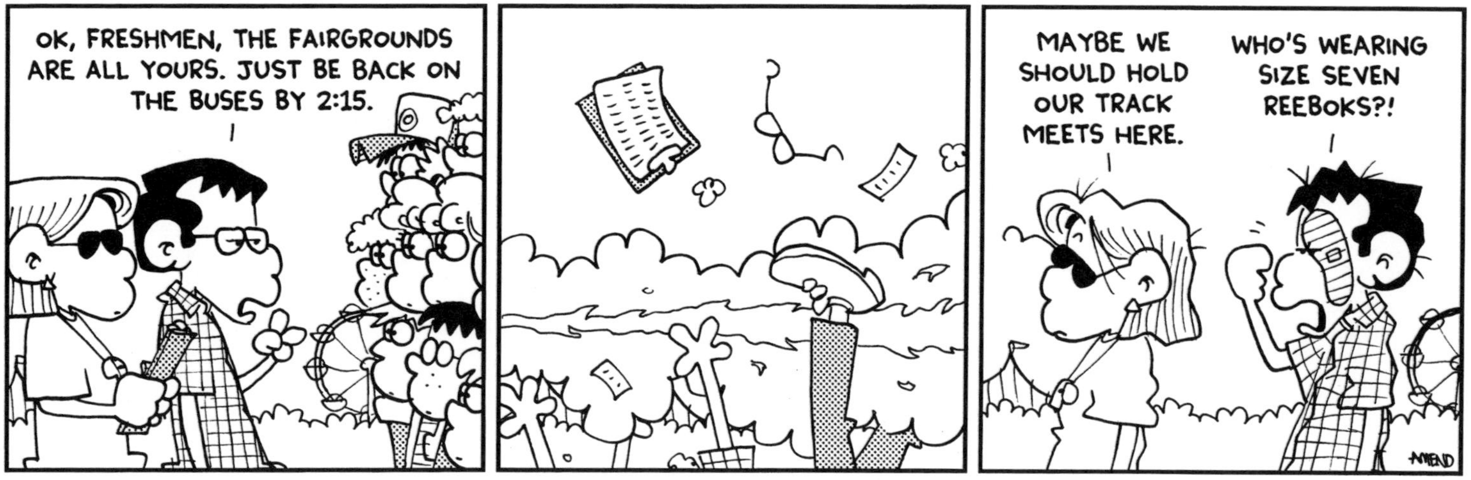
OK, FRESHMEN, THE FAIRGROUNDS ARE ALL YOURS. JUST BE BACK ON THE BUSES BY 2:15.
MAYBE WE SHOULD HOLD OUR TRACK MEETS HERE.
WHO'S WEARING SIZE SEVEN REEBOKS?!
AMEND

May 18, 2004

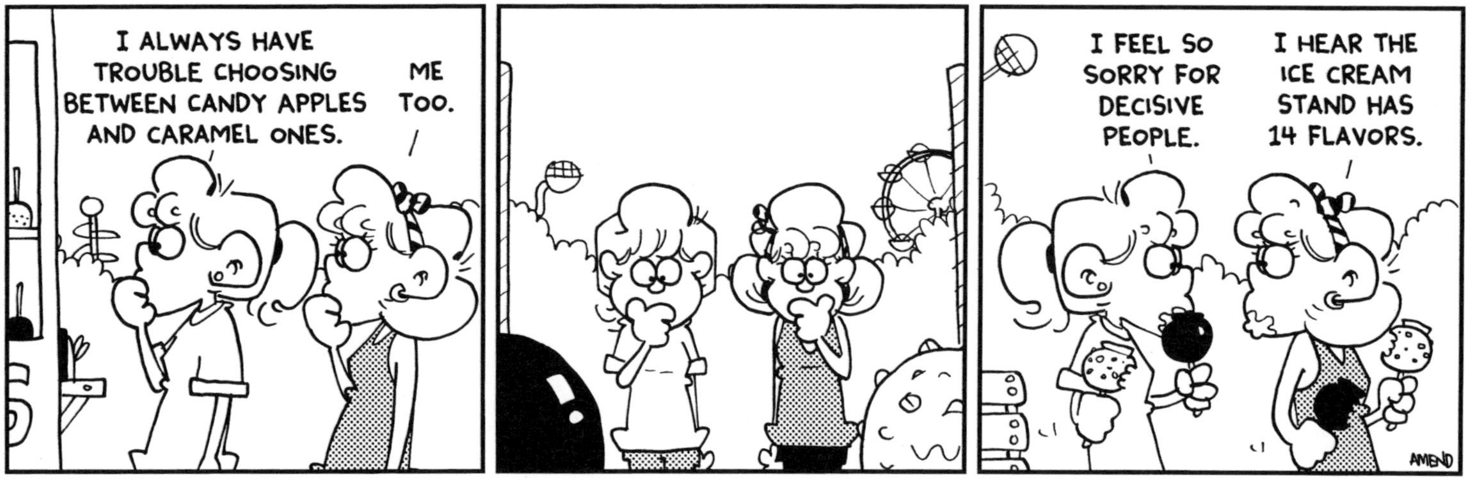
I ALWAYS HAVE TROUBLE CHOOSING BETWEEN CANDY APPLES AND CARAMEL ONES.
ME TOO.
I FEEL SO SORRY FOR DECISIVE PEOPLE.
I HEAR THE ICE CREAM STAND HAS 14 FLAVORS.
AMEND

May 19, 2004

May 20, 2004

May 21, 2004

Bob Romer was one of my college physics professors. He had a merry-go-round device in the classroom that would routinely induce nausea.

May 22, 2004

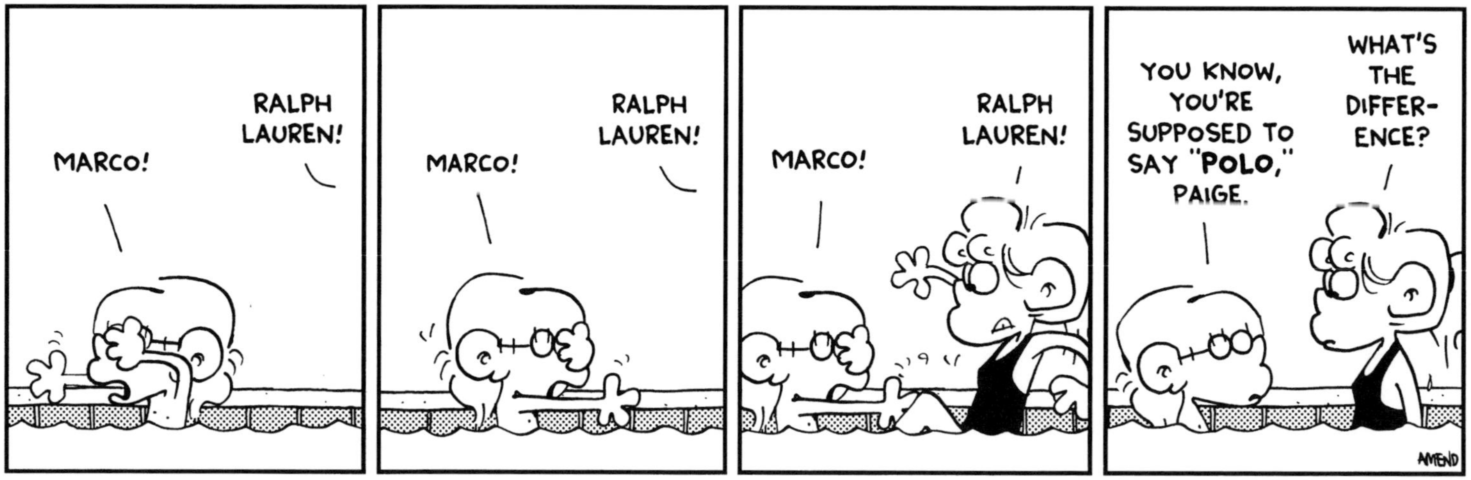
MARCO!
RALPH LAUREN!
MARCO!
RALPH LAUREN!
MARCO!
RALPH LAUREN!
YOU KNOW, YOU'RE SUPPOSED TO SAY "POLO," PAIGE.
WHAT'S THE DIFFER-ENCE?
AMEND

June 2, 2004

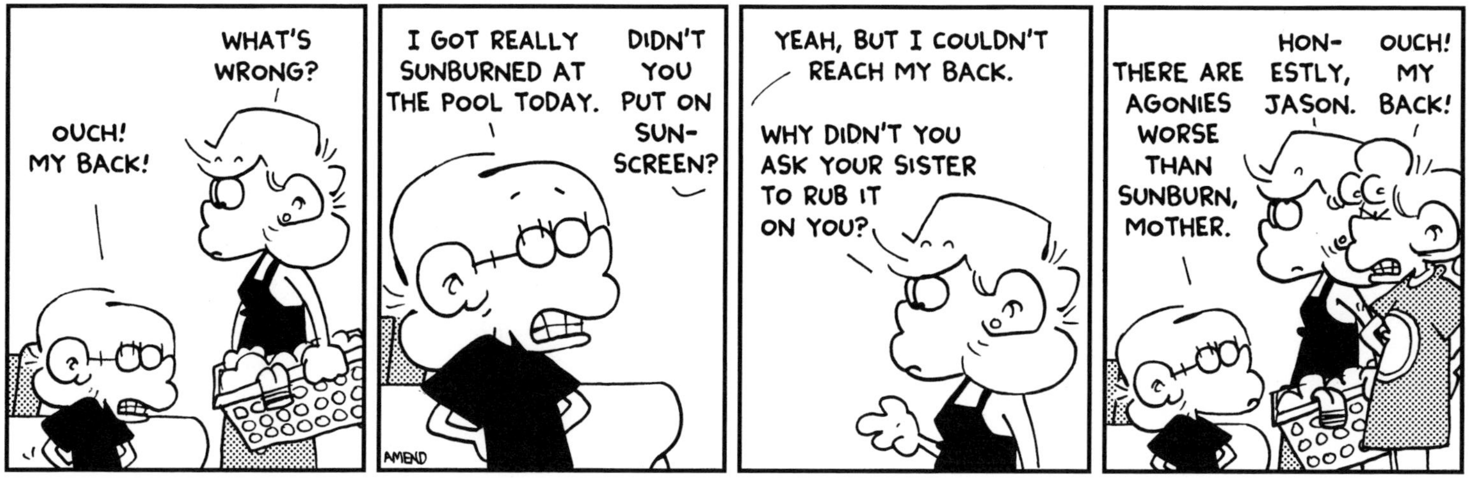
OUCH! MY BACK!
WHAT'S WRONG?
I GOT REALLY SUNBURNED AT THE POOL TODAY.
DIDN'T YOU PUT ON SUN-SCREEN?
AMEND
YEAH, BUT I COULDN'T REACH MY BACK.
WHY DIDN'T YOU ASK YOUR SISTER TO RUB IT ON YOU?
THERE ARE AGONIES WORSE THAN SUNBURN, MOTHER.
HON-ESTLY, JASON.
OUCH! MY BACK!

June 5, 2004

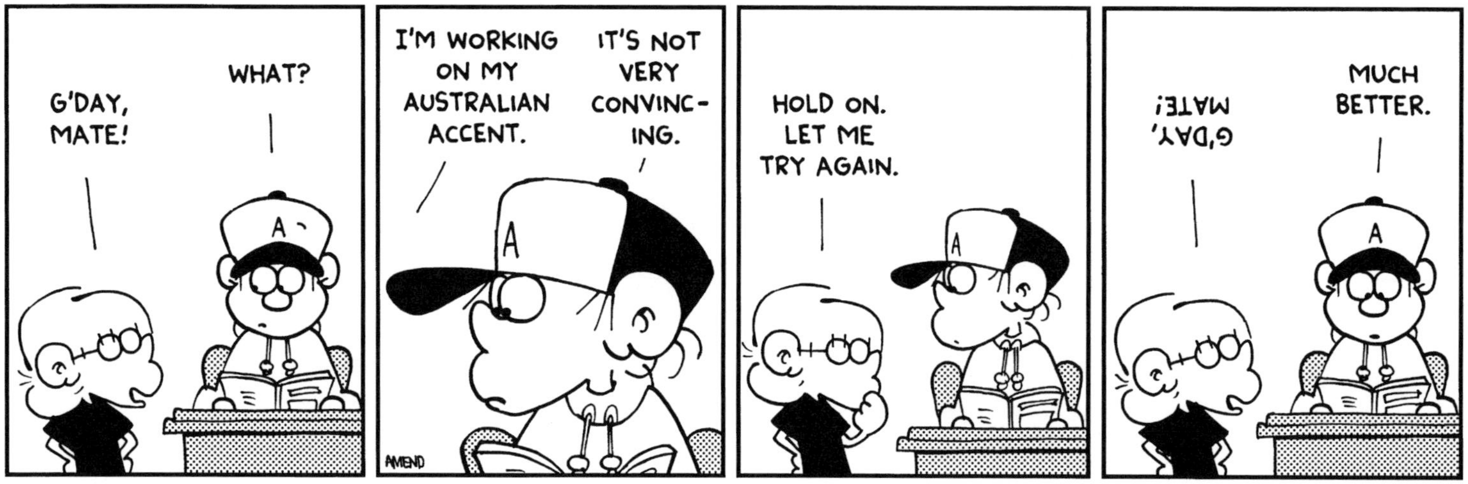
G'DAY, MATE!
WHAT?
I'M WORKING ON MY AUSTRALIAN ACCENT.
IT'S NOT VERY CONVINC-ING.
AMEND
HOLD ON. LET ME TRY AGAIN.
G'DAY, MATE!
MUCH BETTER.

September 27, 2004

July 18, 2004

Some of the executives at my syndicate were on this diet at the time. The line about the crouton is only a mild exaggeration.

August 8, 2004

July 26, 2004

Just drawing "fat" Peter didn't seem as funny to me as drawing him as though he had pizzas stacked up inside him.

July 27, 2004

204

July 28, 2004

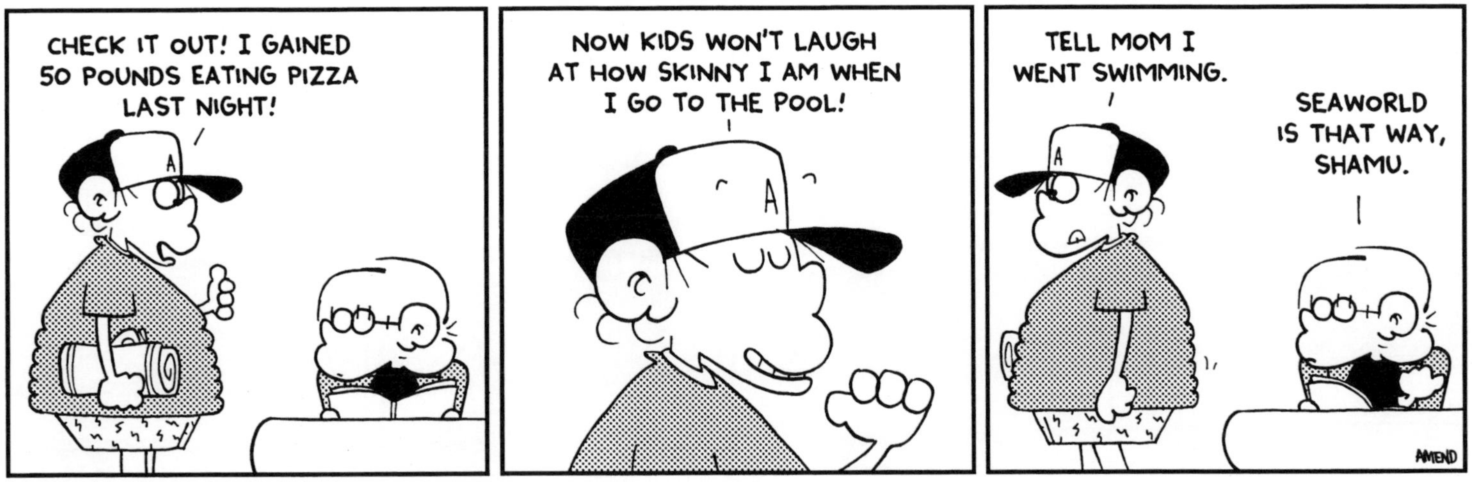
CHECK IT OUT! I GAINED 50 POUNDS EATING PIZZA LAST NIGHT!
NOW KIDS WON'T LAUGH AT HOW SKINNY I AM WHEN I GO TO THE POOL!
TELL MOM I WENT SWIMMING.
SEAWORLD IS THAT WAY, SHAMU.
AMEND

July 29, 2004

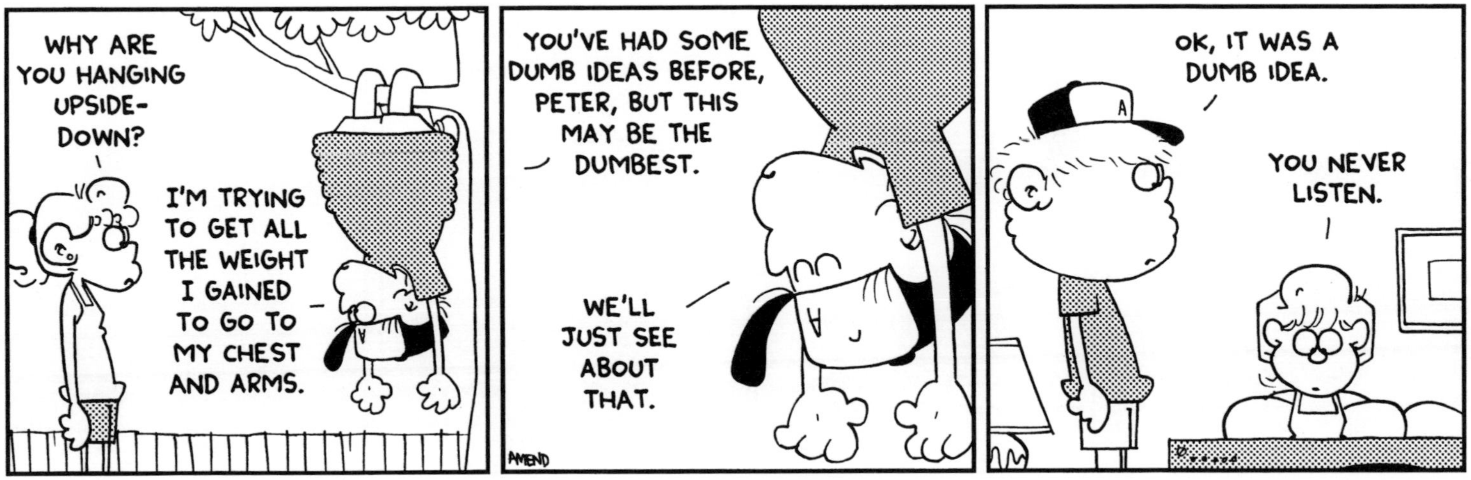
WHY ARE YOU HANGING UPSIDE-DOWN?
I'M TRYING TO GET ALL THE WEIGHT I GAINED TO GO TO MY CHEST AND ARMS.
AMEND
YOU'VE HAD SOME DUMB IDEAS BEFORE, PETER, BUT THIS MAY BE THE DUMBEST.
WE'LL JUST SEE ABOUT THAT.
OK, IT WAS A DUMB IDEA.
YOU NEVER LISTEN.

July 30, 2004

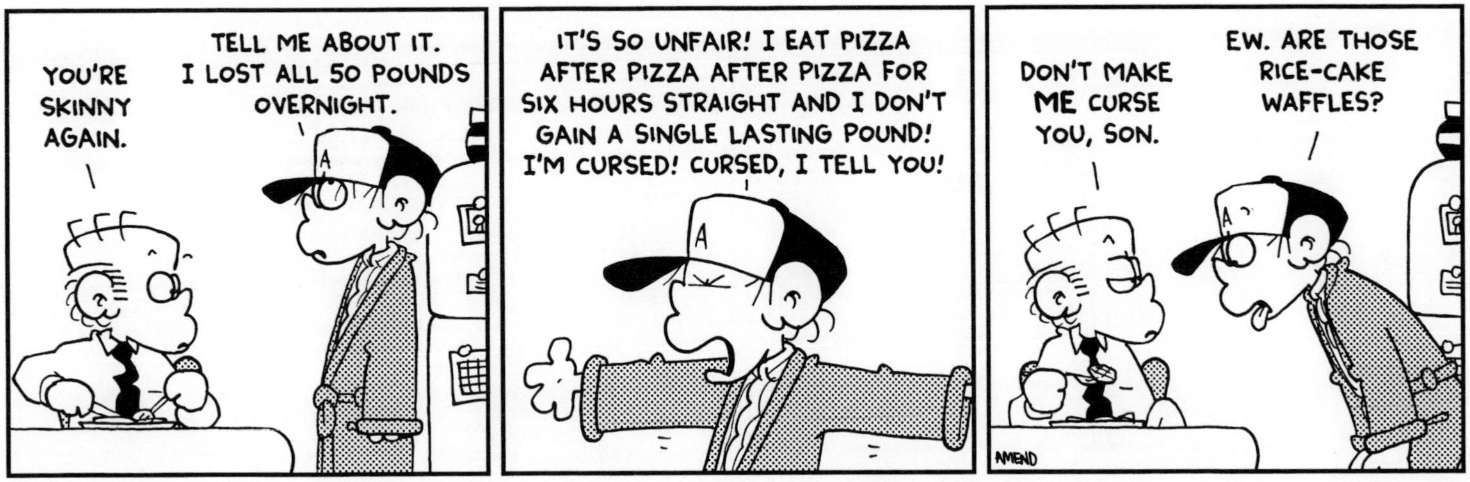
YOU'RE SKINNY AGAIN.
TELL ME ABOUT IT. I LOST ALL 50 POUNDS OVERNIGHT.
IT'S SO UNFAIR! I EAT PIZZA AFTER PIZZA AFTER PIZZA FOR SIX HOURS STRAIGHT AND I DON'T GAIN A SINGLE LASTING POUND! I'M CURSED! CURSED, I TELL YOU!
DON'T MAKE ME CURSE YOU, SON.
EW. ARE THOSE RICE-CAKE WAFFLES?
AMEND

July 31, 2004

August 2, 2004

This is totally how I was
when I first created FoxTrot.

August 3, 2004

206

August 4, 2004

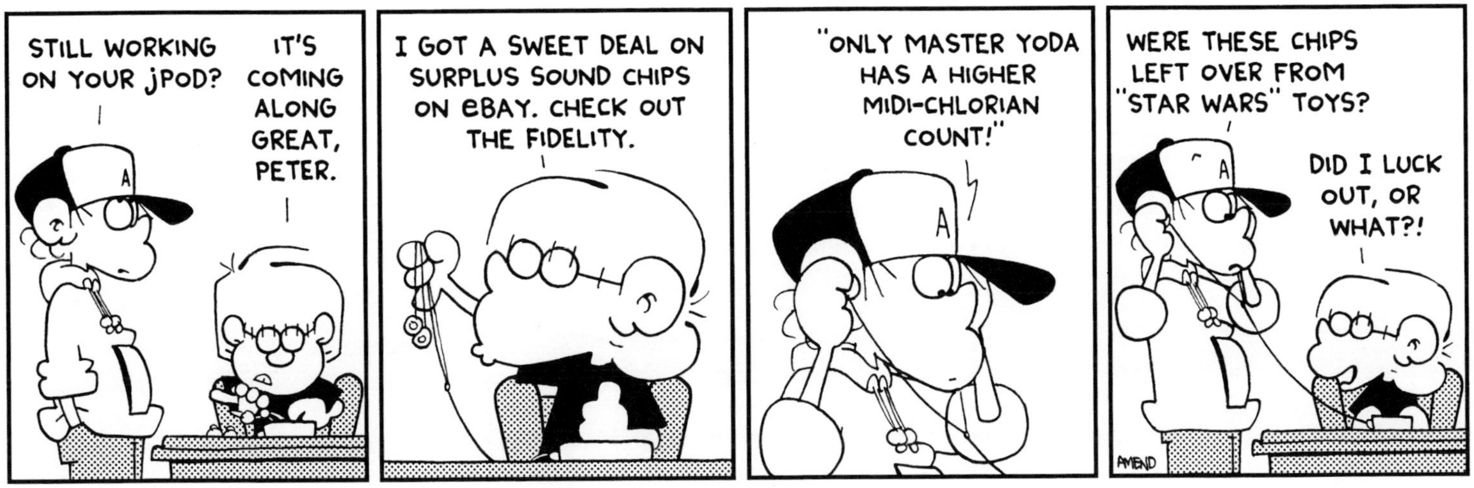
STILL WORKING ON YOUR jPOD?
IT'S COMING ALONG GREAT, PETER.
I GOT A SWEET DEAL ON SURPLUS SOUND CHIPS ON eBAY. CHECK OUT THE FIDELITY.
"ONLY MASTER YODA HAS A HIGHER MIDI-CHLORIAN COUNT!"
WERE THESE CHIPS LEFT OVER FROM "STAR WARS" TOYS?
DID I LUCK OUT, OR WHAT?!
AMEND
August 5, 2004

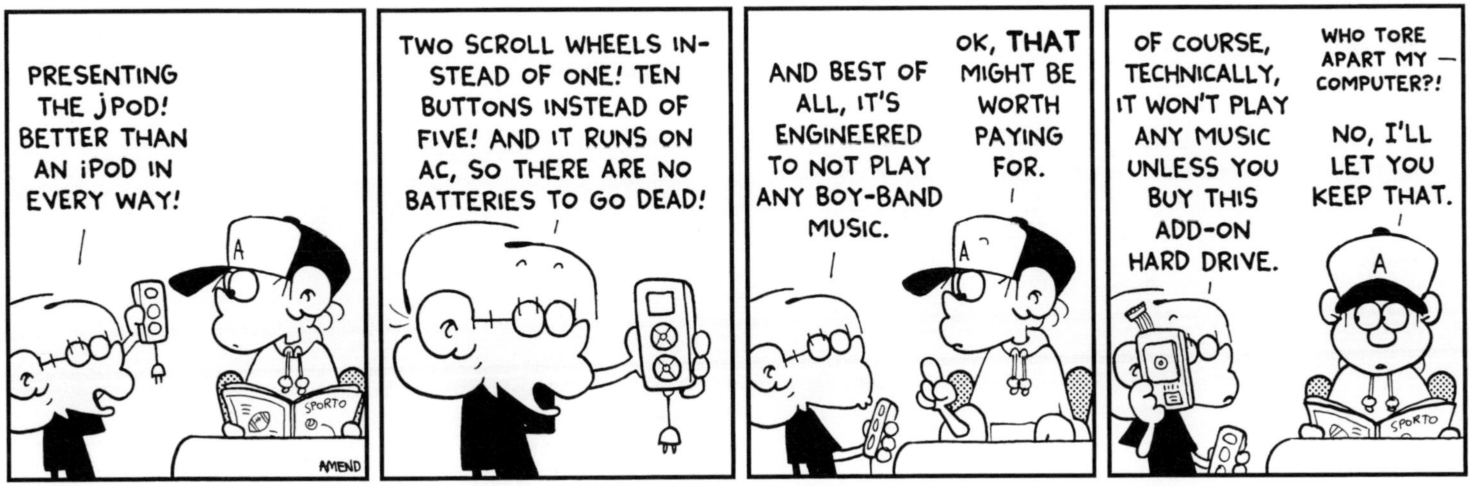
PRESENTING THE jPOD! BETTER THAN AN iPOD IN EVERY WAY!
SPORTO
AMEND
TWO SCROLL WHEELS IN-STEAD OF ONE! TEN BUTTONS INSTEAD OF FIVE! AND IT RUNS ON AC, SO THERE ARE NO BATTERIES TO GO DEAD!
AND BEST OF ALL, IT'S ENGINEERED TO NOT PLAY ANY BOY-BAND MUSIC.
OK, **THAT** MIGHT BE WORTH PAYING FOR.
OF COURSE, TECHNICALLY, IT WON'T PLAY ANY MUSIC UNLESS YOU BUY THIS ADD-ON HARD DRIVE.
WHO TORE APART MY COMPUTER?!
NO, I'LL LET YOU KEEP THAT.
SPORTO
August 6, 2004

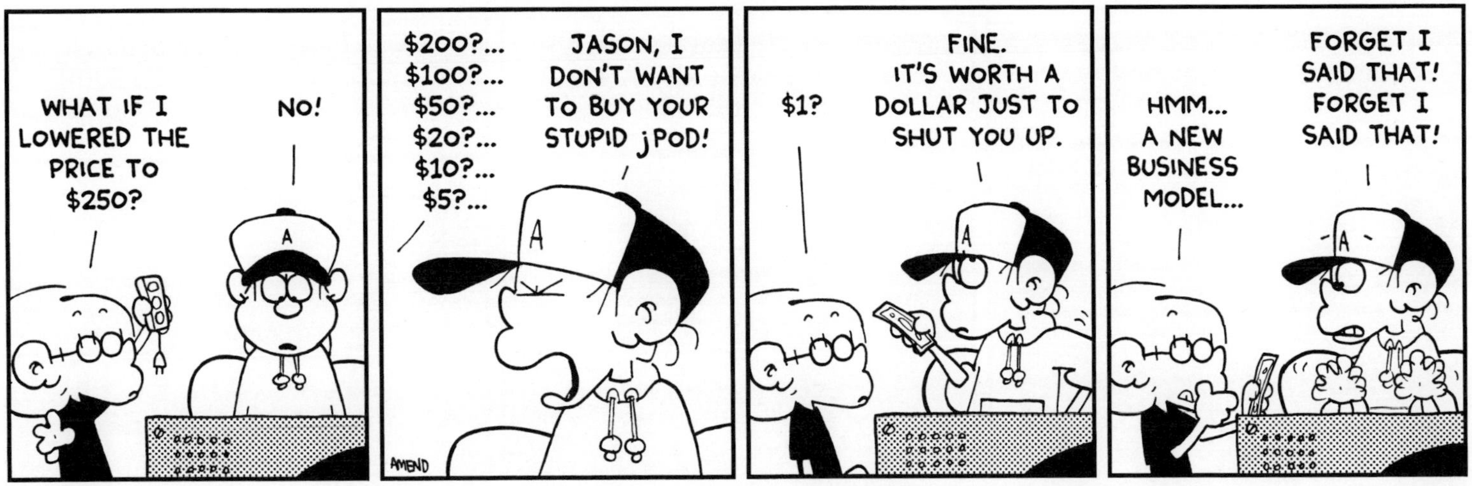
WHAT IF I LOWERED THE PRICE TO $250?
NO!
$200?... $100?... $50?... $20?... $10?... $5?...
JASON, I DON'T WANT TO BUY YOUR STUPID jPOD!
AMEND
$1?
FINE. IT'S WORTH A DOLLAR JUST TO SHUT YOU UP.
HMM... A NEW BUSINESS MODEL...
FORGET I SAID THAT! FORGET I SAID THAT!
August 7, 2004

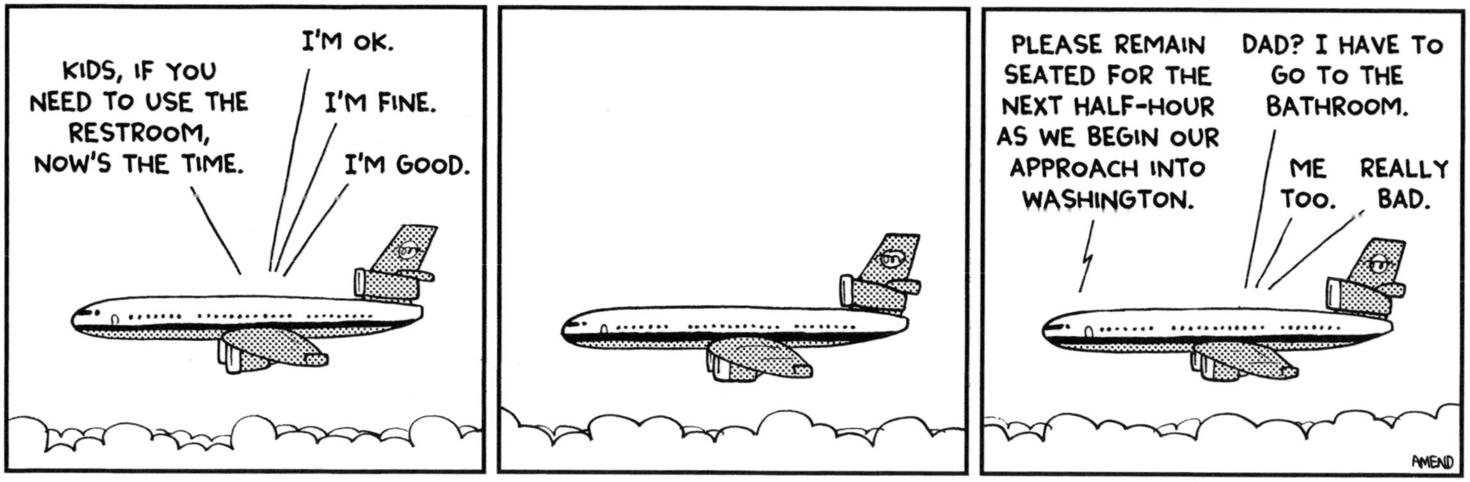
KIDS, IF YOU NEED TO USE THE RESTROOM, NOW'S THE TIME.
I'M OK.
I'M FINE.
I'M GOOD.
PLEASE REMAIN SEATED FOR THE NEXT HALF-HOUR AS WE BEGIN OUR APPROACH INTO WASHINGTON.
DAD? I HAVE TO GO TO THE BATHROOM.
ME TOO.
REALLY BAD.
AMEND

August 16, 2004

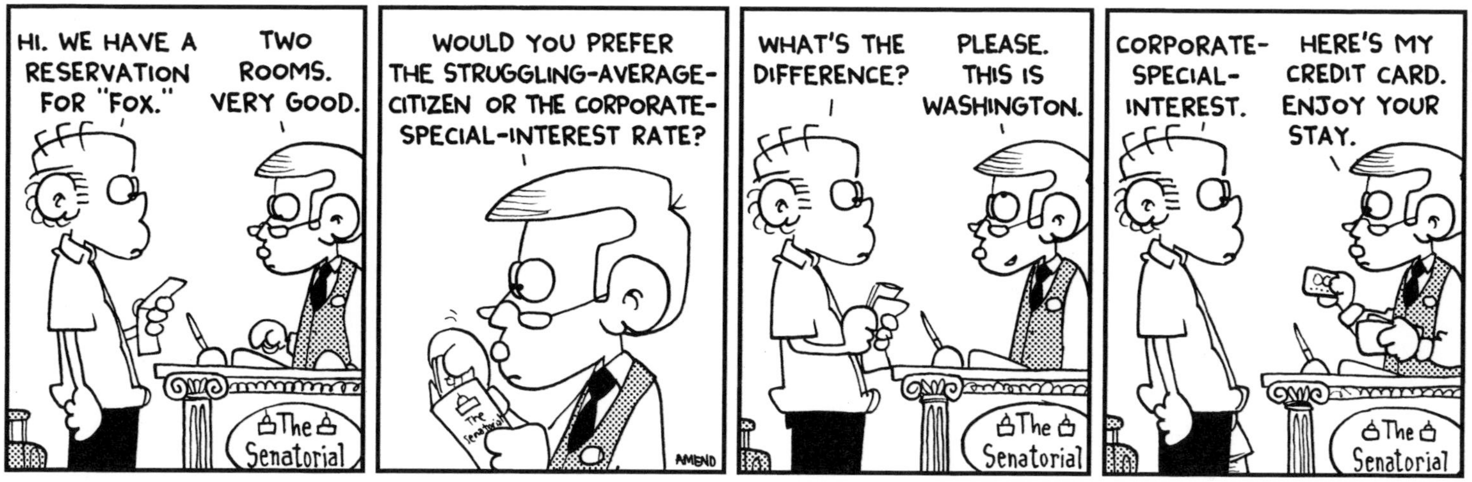
HI. WE HAVE A RESERVATION FOR "FOX."
TWO ROOMS. VERY GOOD.
The Senatorial
WOULD YOU PREFER THE STRUGGLING-AVERAGE-CITIZEN OR THE CORPORATE-SPECIAL-INTEREST RATE?
AMEND
WHAT'S THE DIFFERENCE?
PLEASE. THIS IS WASHINGTON.
The Senatorial
CORPORATE-SPECIAL-INTEREST.
HERE'S MY CREDIT CARD. ENJOY YOUR STAY.
The Senatorial

August 17, 2004

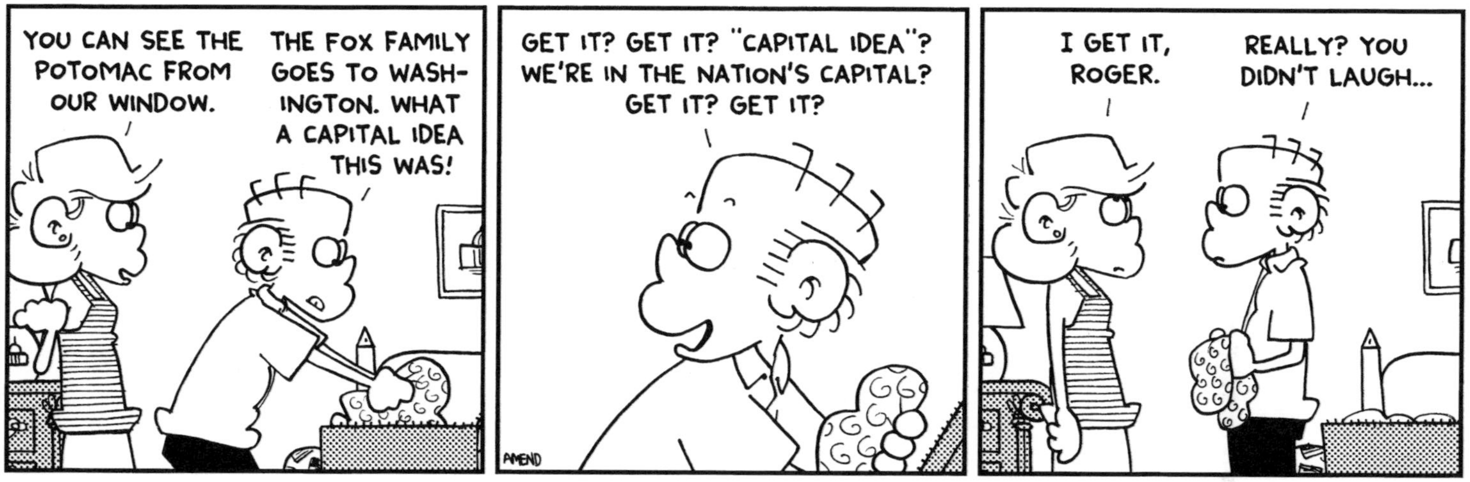
YOU CAN SEE THE POTOMAC FROM OUR WINDOW.
THE FOX FAMILY GOES TO WASH-INGTON. WHAT A CAPITAL IDEA THIS WAS!
GET IT? GET IT? "CAPITAL IDEA"? WE'RE IN THE NATION'S CAPITAL? GET IT? GET IT?
AMEND
I GET IT, ROGER.
REALLY? YOU DIDN'T LAUGH...

August 18, 2004

WAAAAA!

PAIGE, CALM DOWN.

WAAAAA!

PAIGE, YOU'RE MAKING A SCENE.

WAAAAA!

WHAT DID YOU **EXPECT** THE NATIONAL MALL TO BE LIKE??

August 19, 2004

SEE THAT BIG, DOMED BUILDING OVER THERE?

THAT'S THE CAPITOL BUILDING. IT'S WHERE CONGRESS MEETS TO PASS LAWS.

IT LOOKS EXACTLY LIKE THE BACK OF A $50 BILL.

I'D HEARD POLITICIANS LIKED MONEY, BUT WHOA.

NOW THAT YOU MENTION IT...

August 20, 2004

LOOK! IT'S WOLF BLITZER!

LOOK! IT'S TED KOPPEL!

LOOK! IT'S THAT BRIT HUME GUY!

LOOK! IT'S OUR CONGRESSMAN!

WHO?

August 21, 2004

209

August 23, 2004

Having to draw the Capitol and the White House frantically while on deadline this week made me feel sorry for Garry Trudeau, who has to do it all the time.

August 24, 2004

When I was eleven I had my mom sew a secret knife sheath in the back of my sport coat so I could play James West at church.

August 25, 2004

It's tempting to do strips like this more often.

August 26, 2004

August 27, 2004

August 28, 2004

211

I think any connection we can find to the cost of war is a good thing.

August 22, 2004

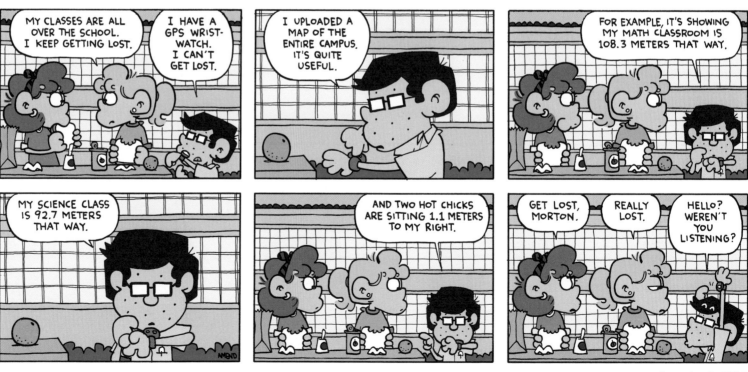

September 5, 2004

So this is why my teams always lose . . .

September 26, 2004

October 3, 2004

Which is larger? A liter of Pepsi or a quart of Pepsi?

"Carbonation" refers to the process by which what is added to a soda?
a. Carbon monoxide, b. Carbon fibers, c. Carbon dioxide

SIR, ABOUT THIS POP QUIZ...

QUESTION SEVEN HAS A TYPO, PEOPLE. IT SHOULD SAY — "DIET COKE."

September 10, 2005

I ALWAYS FORGET MY LOCKER COMBINATION.

DO WHAT I DO.

I ASSOCIATE EACH NUMBER WITH SOMETHING EASY TO REMEMBER.

MINE IS THE ATOMIC NUMBER OF CARBON LEFT, THE ATOMIC NUMBER OF PHOSPHORUS RIGHT, AND THE ATOMIC NUMBER OF MANGANESE LEFT.

I ALSO ALWAYS FORGET NOT TO DISCUSS THESE THINGS WITH YOU.

LAST YEAR I HAD KRYPTON.

October 1, 2004

SWEET.

HEY, PETER, I LIKE HOW YOUR PUMPKIN TURNED OUT. NICE JOB!

I HAVEN'T CARVED MINE YET. THAT'S PAIGE'S PUMPKIN.

YOUR PUMPKIN IS PATHETIC.

MY PUMPKIN IS?

October 25, 2004

I think Jason's actually doing better than I would be.

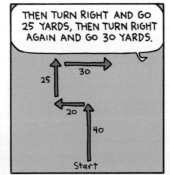

THE POOR KID IS TRICK-OR-TREATING AND EVERYONE KEEPS GIVING HIM ROCKS!

YOU KNOW WHAT HE SHOULD DO? HE SHOULD EAT THE ROCKS AND SAY HE NATURALLY ASSUMED THEY WERE CANDY.

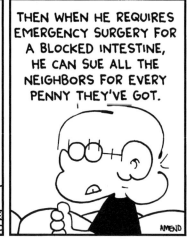
THEN WHEN HE REQUIRES EMERGENCY SURGERY FOR A BLOCKED INTESTINE, HE CAN SUE ALL THE NEIGHBORS FOR EVERY PENNY THEY'VE GOT.

FORTUNATELY, CARTOON CHARACTERS DON'T THINK THE WAY YOU DO.

"IT'S THE GREAT LAWSUIT, CHARLIE BROWN!"

October 29, 2004

BONK! —
OW!—

I CAN'T UNDERSTAND WHY PEOPLE THINK THROWING PLAYING CARDS IS DIFFICULT.

YOU'RE SUPPOSED TO TAKE THEM OUT OF THE BOX FIRST!

November 8, 2004

HERE YOU GO, PAIGE.

WHAT'S THIS?

I HEARD YOU SAY YOU WERE OUT OF PIMPLE CREAM.

THIS IS A 128-OUNCE TUBE! DO YOU REALLY THINK MY SKIN IS THAT BAD?!

WAAAAAAA!

SOME THINGS SHOULDN'T BE PURCHASED AT COSTCLUB, DEAR.

I GOT YOU THAT GRAY-AWAY HAIR DYE YOU LIKE.

216

February 11, 2005

I like Phoebe's Hobbes with a Calvin doll idea.

October 31, 2004

February 27, 2005

IT'S SO UTTERLY FRUSTRATING!

"HALF-LIFE 2" COMES OUT THIS MONTH AND IT WON'T RUN ON OUR iFRUIT! IT WAS THE SAME THING WITH "DOOM 3"!

WHY DO WE HAVE TO HAVE A COMPUTER THAT'S INCOMPATIBLE WITH 90 PERCENT OF THE GAMES I WANT?!

BECAUSE NONE WERE INCOMPATIBLE WITH 100 PERCENT. YOU'RE UTTERLY FRUSTRATING, TOO, BY THE WAY.

November 1, 2004

SINCE I CAN'T PLAY ANY OF THE "HALF-LIFE" GAMES ON OUR iFRUIT, I'VE DECIDED TO PROGRAM MY OWN.

ONLY MINE WILL BE 1,000 TIMES HARDER.

I'M CALLING IT "0.0005-LIFE."

I'D SUGGEST "JASON-GET-A-LIFE." IF player= "Peter" THEN death(player):= extra_gory

November 2, 2004

SO IS THIS GAME OF YOURS ONLY GOING TO WORK ON iFRUITS?

ABSO-LUTELY.

EVER SINCE WE GOT THIS COMPUTER, I'VE HAD TO WATCH COOL GAME AFTER COOL GAME COME OUT ONLY FOR WINDOWS. IT'S ABOUT TIME SOMEONE LIKE ME TURNED THE TABLES.

WHAT DO YOU HAVE TO SAY TO THAT, ALL YOU GLOATING PC USERS!

I JUST HEAR A CRICKET.

THAT'S PROBABLY BILL GATES CRYING. HE'S PRETTY FAR AWAY.

November 3, 2004

218

November 4, 2004

November 5, 2004

November 6, 2004

Stephan Pastis, Darby Conley, and I all used the same joke as an April Fool's prank. If the joke seems lame, blame Pastis.

WHAT'S THAT?

IT'S A OUIJA BOARD. SPIRITS FROM THE AFTER-LIFE GUIDE YOUR HANDS OVER A SERIES OF LETTERS, SPELLING OUT MESSAGES TO YOU FROM THE GREAT BEYOND. CHECK IT OUT...

P-A-I-G-E... I-S... A... B-I-G... F-A-T... M-o-R-O-N... P-L-E-A-S-E... K-I-C-K... H-E-R... I-N... T-H-E... S-H-I-N...

SOMEHOW I IMAGINED THE AFTERLIFE TO BE A MORE PEACEFUL PLACE.

T-H-E... G-O-D-S... A-R-E... M-O-S-T... P-L-E-A-S-E-D...

April 1, 2005

WHAT ARE YOU WATCHING?

"24."

THEY'RE INTO THE 2-3 A.M. PART NOW. I FIND IT HARD TO BELIEVE THAT THESE PEOPLE CAN STILL FUNCTION AT THAT HOUR.

MAYBE THEY USED TO BE CARTOONISTS.

HMM. I HADN'T CONSIDERED THAT.

May 2, 2005

As I recall, someone briefly uploaded a picture of Paige onto the Wikipedia "Wart-hog" page after this ran.

WHAT ARE YOU LOOKING AT?

WIKIPEDIA.

IT'S THIS TOTALLY COOL ONLINE ENCYCLOPEDIA THAT LETS USERS UPDATE AND EDIT ITS INFORMATION. IT'S THE GREATEST THING.

WATCH. PRETEND YOU WANT TO KNOW ABOUT WARTHOGS.

IS THAT A PICTURE OF OUR SISTER?

NOW LET'S PRETEND YOU WANT TO KNOW ABOUT RABIES...

May 7, 2005

220

February 20, 2005

March 27, 2005

I taught Sunday school for a year or two after college. No Jasons in the class, fortunately.

221

November 15, 2004

November 16, 2004

"Horsepower" just seemed inadequate.

November 17, 2004

November 18, 2004

November 19, 2004

November 20, 2004

November 29, 2004

November 30, 2004

Since $\sqrt{x^2}$ could be $\pm x$, pretend it says $\sqrt[3]{x^3}$.

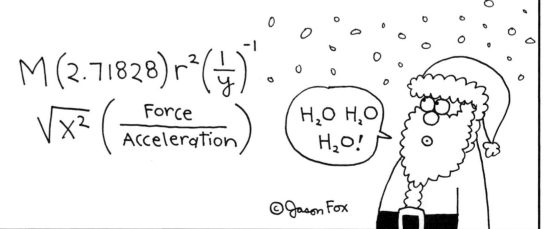

December 1, 2004

December 2, 2004

December 3, 2004

December 4, 2004

225

January 3, 2005

January 4, 2005

January 5, 2005

January 6, 2005

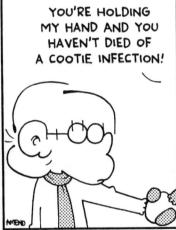

January 7, 2005

January 8, 2005

227

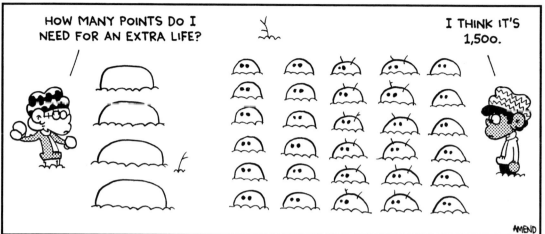

January 31, 2005

February 1, 2005

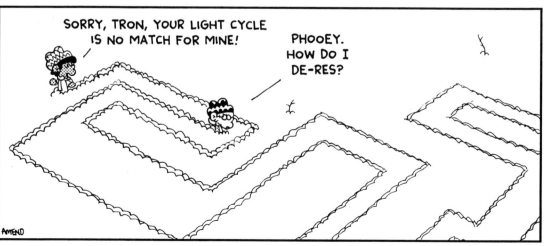

February 2, 2005

February 3, 2005

February 4, 2005

I was a little surprised that my syndicate let this go through.

February 5, 2005

229

February 21, 2005

February 22, 2005

February 23, 2005

February 24, 2005

February 25, 2005

February 26, 2005

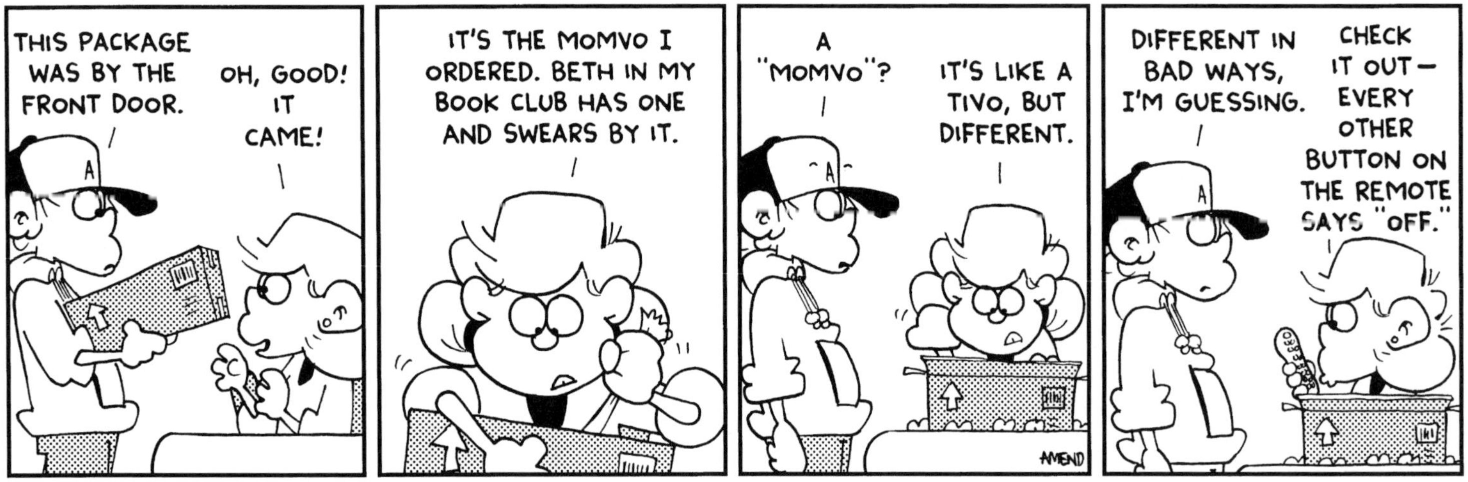

THIS PACKAGE WAS BY THE FRONT DOOR.
OH, GOOD! IT CAME!
IT'S THE MOMVO I ORDERED. BETH IN MY BOOK CLUB HAS ONE AND SWEARS BY IT.
A "MOMVO"?
IT'S LIKE A TIVO, BUT DIFFERENT.
DIFFERENT IN BAD WAYS, I'M GUESSING.
CHECK IT OUT— EVERY OTHER BUTTON ON THE REMOTE SAYS "OFF."

March 7, 2005

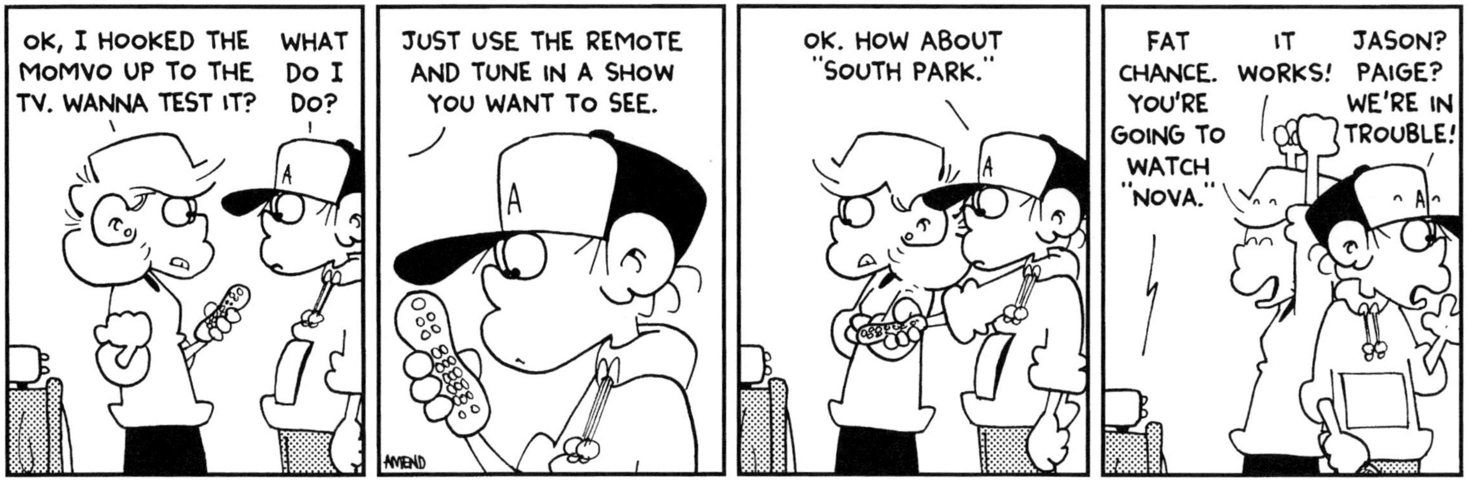

OK, I HOOKED THE MOMVO UP TO THE TV. WANNA TEST IT?
WHAT DO I DO?
JUST USE THE REMOTE AND TUNE IN A SHOW YOU WANT TO SEE.
OK. HOW ABOUT "SOUTH PARK."
FAT CHANCE. YOU'RE GOING TO WATCH "NOVA."
IT WORKS!
JASON? PAIGE? WE'RE IN TROUBLE!

March 8, 2005

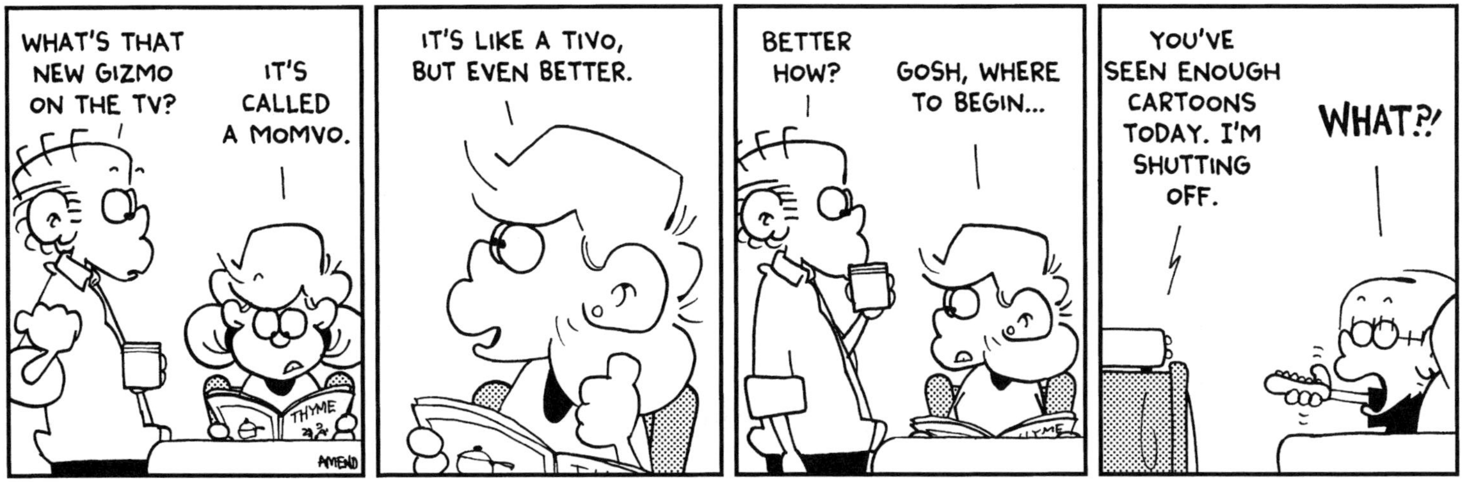

WHAT'S THAT NEW GIZMO ON THE TV?
IT'S CALLED A MOMVO.
THYME
IT'S LIKE A TIVO, BUT EVEN BETTER.
BETTER HOW?
GOSH, WHERE TO BEGIN...
YOU'VE SEEN ENOUGH CARTOONS TODAY. I'M SHUTTING OFF.
WHAT?!

March 9, 2005

HEY, I TOLD YOU TO RECORD "NEWLYWEDS"! IT'S THE ONE WHERE JESSICA TRIES TO MAKE TOAST!

SORRY. THAT CONFLICTED WITH MORE WORTHWHILE PROGRAMMING.

I HAVE SEVERAL EPISODES OF "MASTERPIECE THEATRE" YOU CAN WATCH.

AAAAAAAA!

AND THE GREAT THING IS, I CAN TELL WHEN THE MOMVO IS WORKING.

March 10, 2005

WE HAVE TO DO SOMETHING ABOUT THIS MOMVO! IT'S RUINING OUR LIVES!

IT WON'T LET US WATCH ANYTHING BUT "MOTHER-APPROVED" TELEVISION!

ANY WAY YOU COULD HACK IT?

ITS INSTRUCTIONS COME FROM A CENTRAL SERVER. I'D BE RISKING MAJOR JAIL TIME.

IT'S RECORDING "THE BEST OF FULL HOUSE."

I'LL GET RIGHT ON IT.

March 11, 2005

WHAT HAPPENED TO THE MOMVO?

MOM RETURNED IT.

SHE SAID SHE REALIZED IT WAS A MISTAKE TO DELEGATE PARENTAL CONTROL OF THE TV TO A MACHINE.

SHE SAID THAT EVEN THOUGH IT'S HARD WORK, IT'S HER JOB, AND NOT SOME OUTSIDER'S, TO GAUGE WHAT CONSTITUTES SUITABLE CONTENT FOR THIS FAMILY.

IT WOULDN'T LET HER RECORD HER SOAPS, IN OTHER WORDS.

YOU SHOULD HAVE SEEN HOW FAST SHE YANKED THE WIRES.

March 12, 2005

Yes, yes, I know that in the real world, Google uses static images often taken years prior. In the FoxTrot world, however, Google has more advanced tech.

WHAT ARE YOU DOING? GOOGLE NOW LETS YOU VIEW SATELLITE PHOTOS.

YOU CAN ZOOM IN ON JUST ABOUT ANYWHERE YOU WANT.

INTERESTING. IT'S REALLY FUN. I COULD DO THIS ALL DAY.

LITTLE BROTHER AS BIG BROTHER. IS THAT PETER'S CAR AT MAKE-OUT POINT I SEE?

April 18, 2005

SO YOU CAN SEE SATELLITE PICTURES OF THE WHOLE U.S.? YUP.

HOW FAR CAN YOU ZOOM IN? PRETTY FAR. YOU CAN SEE INDIVIDUAL HOUSES AND CARS.

WHAT ABOUT PEOPLE? WELL, THEY'D HAVE TO BE REALLY, REALLY, REALLY FAT.

IS DAD OUTSIDE? NAH. I ALREADY CHECKED.

April 19, 2005

WHAT ARE YOU LOOKING AT NOW? IT'S A SATELLITE PHOTO OF SKYWALKER RANCH.

I WAS HOPING TO GLEAN CLUES AS TO WHAT COOL THINGS ARE GOING TO BE IN THE NEXT "STAR WARS" MOVIE.

UNFORTUNATELY, IT'S TOO FUZZY TO REALLY TELL WHAT'S WHAT.

NONSENSE. THERE'S A GUY IN A JAR-JAR COSTUME. I SAID IT'S TOO FUZZY TO TELL WHAT'S WHAT!

April 20, 2005

SO YOU CAN VIEW SATELLITE PHOTOS OF ANYTHING?

JUST ABOUT.

THEY'VE OBVIOUSLY HAD TO RESTRICT SOME THINGS FOR SECURITY REASONS.

LIKE IF YOU ZOOM IN ON WASHINGTON, D.C., CONGRESS APPEARS AS A BIG, UNFOCUSED MESS.

ARE YOU SURE THAT'S NOT JUST HOW IT IS?

OK, BAD EXAMPLE...

April 21, 2005

THESE SATELLITE IMAGES ARE SO COOL!

NOT ALL OF THEM.

TAKE THIS ONE OF OUR NEIGHBORHOOD. IT MAKES IT LOOK LIKE EILEEN JACOBSON LIVES A MERE TWO INCHES AWAY FROM US.

AND IF I ZOOM OUT, IT'S AS IF WE'RE ON TOP OF EACH OTHER! BLECCH!

OOO — CAN YOU FIND JUSTIN TIMBERLAKE'S HOUSE?

HOW 'BOUT I FIND THE QUIT KEY INSTEAD?

April 22, 2005

WHAT ARE YOU LOOKING AT NOW?

THE GOOGLE HEAD-QUARTERS.

I'M A LITTLE DISAPPOINTED, SEEING AS THESE SATEL-LITE PHOTO SEARCHES ARE THEIR DOING.

I EXPECTED THEM TO HAVE A GIANT BANNER OUTSIDE SAYING "STOP SPYING ON US" OR SOMETHING.

THAT WOULD BE PRETTY FUNNY. LET'S HOPE MOM AGREES.

WHY ARE THERE BED-SHEETS ON OUR ROOF?!

April 23, 2005

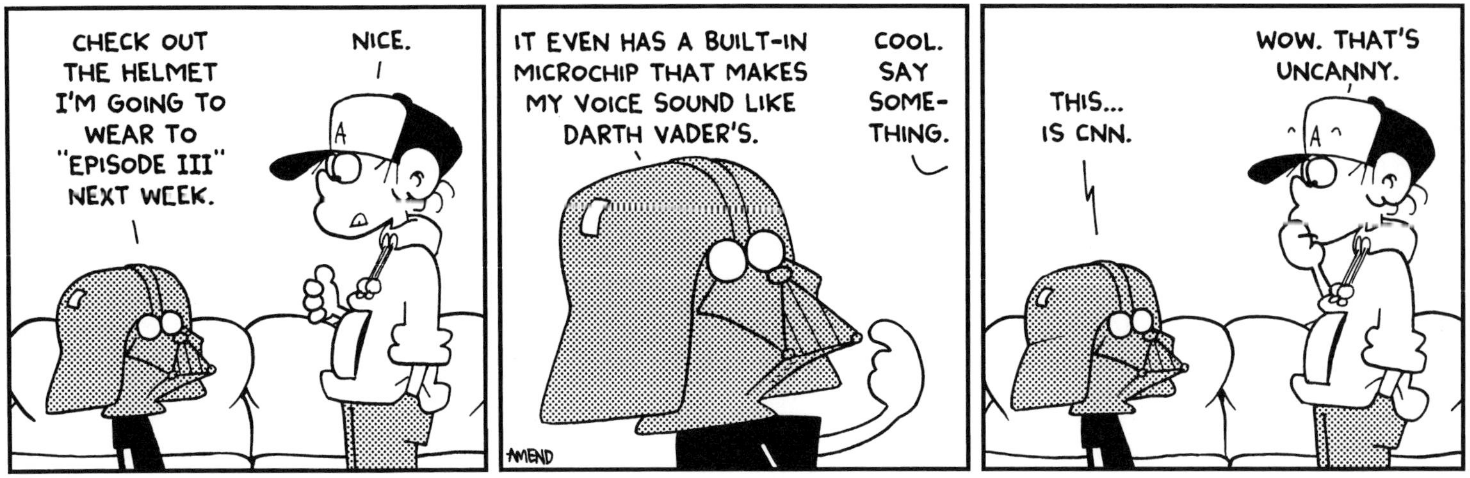
CHECK OUT THE HELMET I'M GOING TO WEAR TO "EPISODE III" NEXT WEEK.
NICE.
IT EVEN HAS A BUILT-IN MICROCHIP THAT MAKES MY VOICE SOUND LIKE DARTH VADER'S.
COOL. SAY SOME-THING.
AMEND
THIS... IS CNN.
WOW. THAT'S UNCANNY.

May 9, 2005

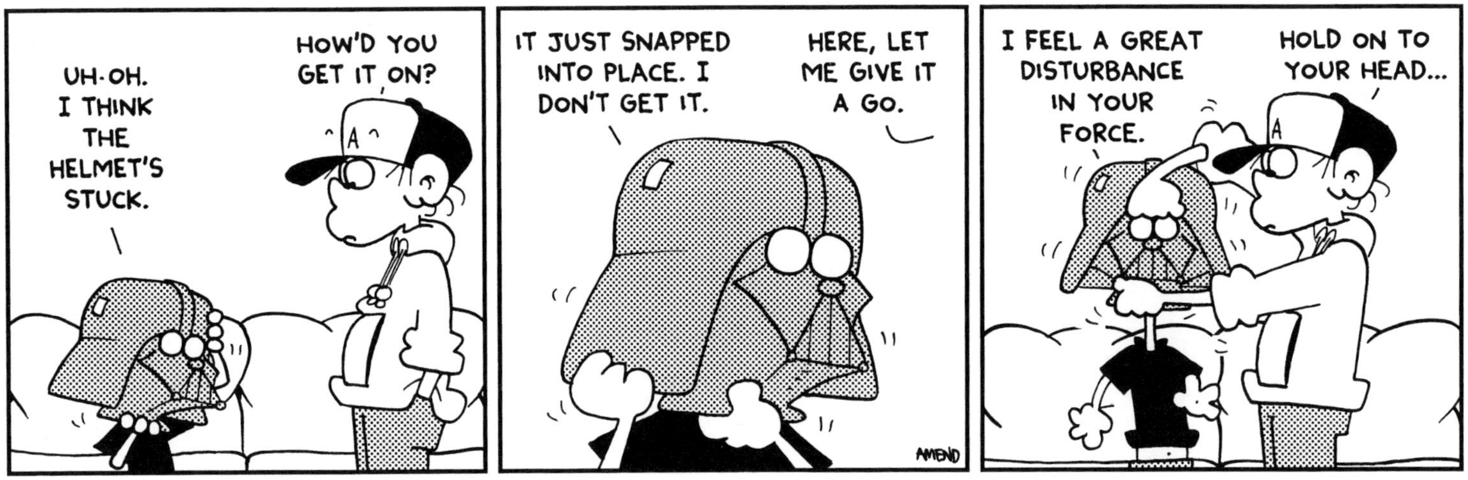
UH-OH. I THINK THE HELMET'S STUCK.
HOW'D YOU GET IT ON?
IT JUST SNAPPED INTO PLACE. I DON'T GET IT.
HERE, LET ME GIVE IT A GO.
AMEND
I FEEL A GREAT DISTURBANCE IN YOUR FORCE.
HOLD ON TO YOUR HEAD...

May 10, 2005

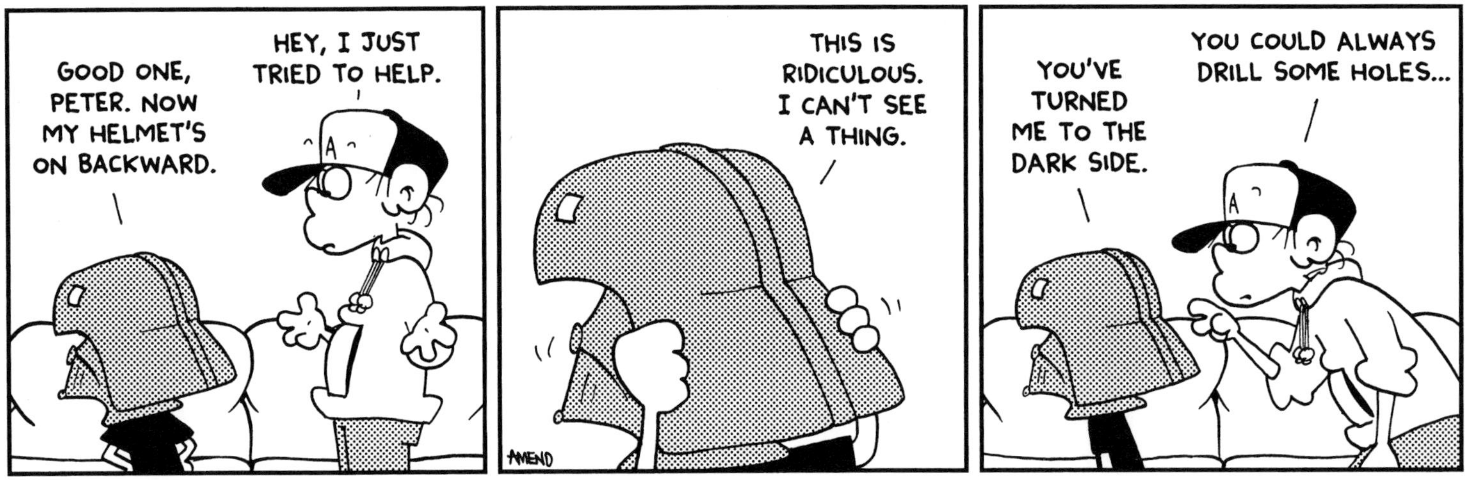
GOOD ONE, PETER. NOW MY HELMET'S ON BACKWARD.
HEY, I JUST TRIED TO HELP.
THIS IS RIDICULOUS. I CAN'T SEE A THING.
AMEND
YOU'VE TURNED ME TO THE DARK SIDE.
YOU COULD ALWAYS DRILL SOME HOLES...

May 11, 2005

Hard to argue with Peter's logic here.

IS JASON STILL TYING UP THE COMPUTER?

I'M NOT SURE. WHY?

SOME GUYS AT WORK TOLD ME ABOUT THIS GREAT ONLINE POKER SITE THEY GO TO. YOU GET TO PLAY FOR REAL MONEY.

I THOUGHT I'D GIVE IT A TRY.

I'LL GO CHECK.

GET BACK ON THE COMPUTER! NOW!

THIS IS A FIRST.

June 6, 2005

Roger wanted to wear those Greg Raymer glasses with the holographic eyes, but these were easier to draw.

WELCOME TO MEGA-POTS-OF-GOLD-SUPERSTAR-INTERNET POKER!!!!!!

PLEASE DESCRIBE YOUR LEVEL OF GAMEPLAY:

☐ EXPERT

☐ SEMI-EXPERT

☐ FOOL WHO **THINKS** HE'S AN EXPERT, BUT IS ABOUT TO LEARN A CRUEL LESSON

ARE YOU SURE YOU WANT TO DO THIS, DAD?

EXPERT!

June 7, 2005

I HEAR YOU'RE PLAYING ONLINE POKER.

I HAVEN'T STARTED YET.

I'M TRYING TO THINK UP A GOOD SCREEN NAME.

WHAT'S THAT, MOM?

MOM SUGGESTS "IDIOTHUSBAND."

DO ME A FAVOR AND CLOSE THE DOOR.

June 8, 2005

238

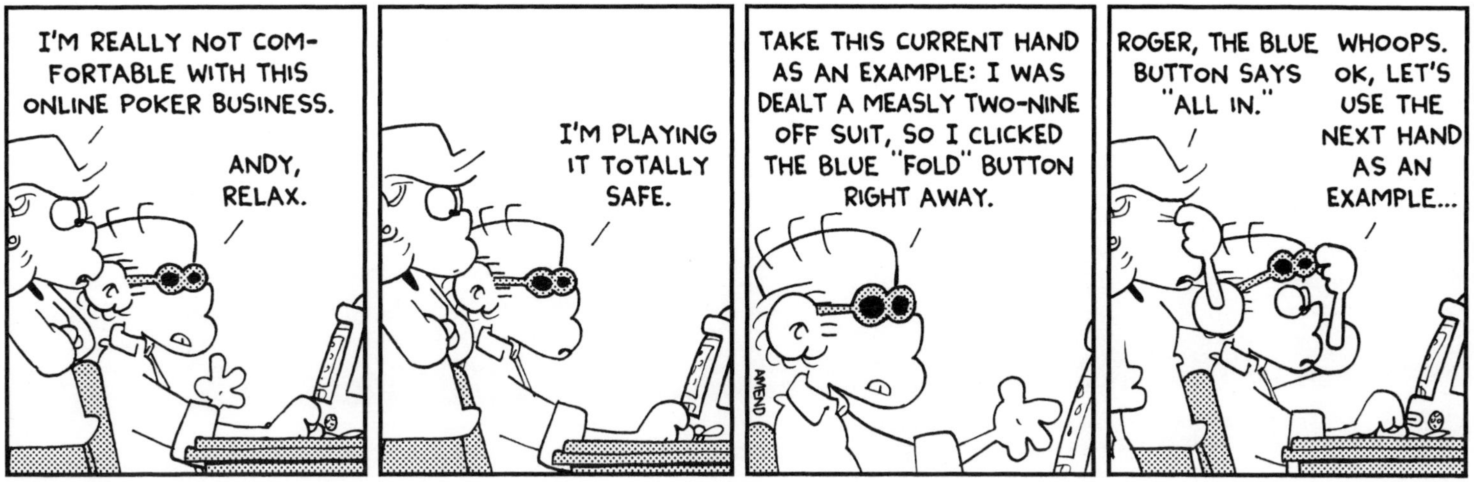
I'M REALLY NOT COMFORTABLE WITH THIS ONLINE POKER BUSINESS.
ANDY, RELAX.
I'M PLAYING IT TOTALLY SAFE.
TAKE THIS CURRENT HAND AS AN EXAMPLE: I WAS DEALT A MEASLY TWO-NINE OFF SUIT, SO I CLICKED THE BLUE "FOLD" BUTTON RIGHT AWAY.
ROGER, THE BLUE BUTTON SAYS "ALL IN."
WHOOPS. OK, LET'S USE THE NEXT HAND AS AN EXAMPLE...
AMEND
June 9, 2005

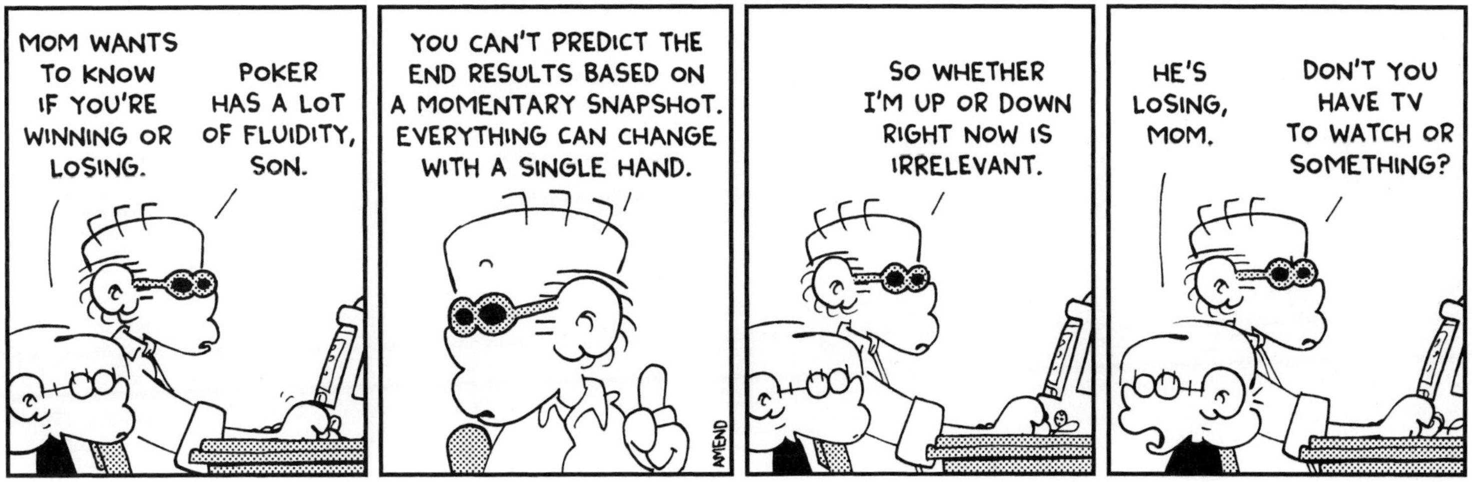
MOM WANTS TO KNOW IF YOU'RE WINNING OR LOSING.
POKER HAS A LOT OF FLUIDITY, SON.
YOU CAN'T PREDICT THE END RESULTS BASED ON A MOMENTARY SNAPSHOT. EVERYTHING CAN CHANGE WITH A SINGLE HAND.
AMEND
SO WHETHER I'M UP OR DOWN RIGHT NOW IS IRRELEVANT.
HE'S LOSING, MOM.
DON'T YOU HAVE TV TO WATCH OR SOMETHING?
June 10, 2005

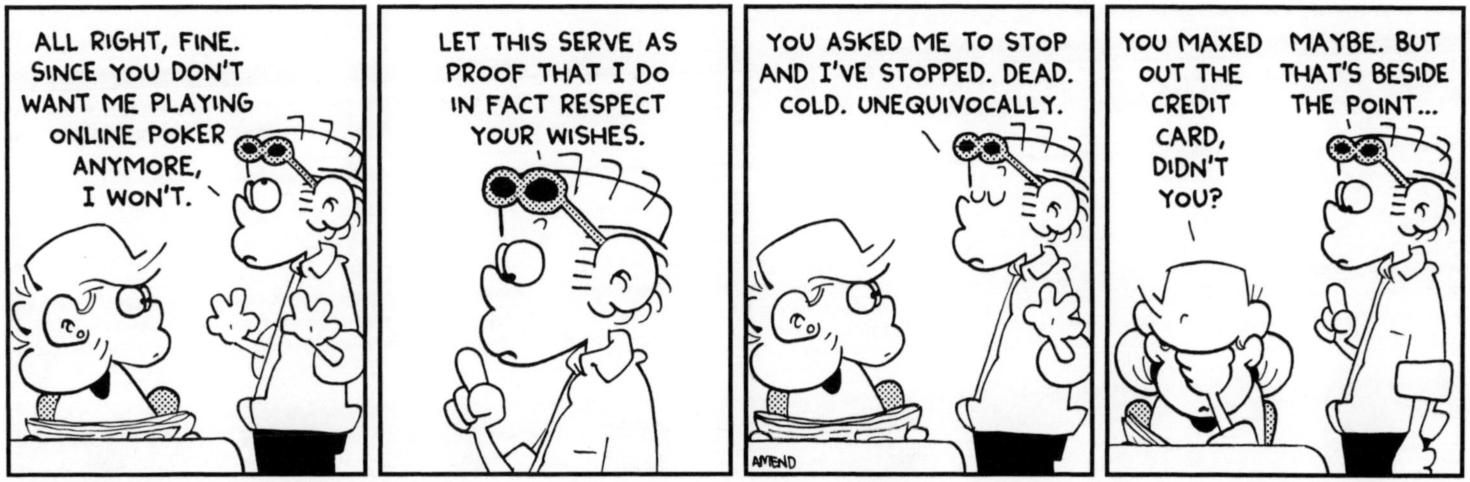
ALL RIGHT, FINE. SINCE YOU DON'T WANT ME PLAYING ONLINE POKER ANYMORE, I WON'T.
LET THIS SERVE AS PROOF THAT I DO IN FACT RESPECT YOUR WISHES.
YOU ASKED ME TO STOP AND I'VE STOPPED. DEAD. COLD. UNEQUIVOCALLY.
AMEND
YOU MAXED OUT THE CREDIT CARD, DIDN'T YOU?
MAYBE. BUT THAT'S BESIDE THE POINT...
June 11, 2005

My college roommates and I drove the PCH in a Winnebago once. I'm amazed we lived.

June 20, 2005

June 21, 2005

June 22, 2005

HOW'S THE DE-NERD-IFICATION PROCESS GOING?

PRETTY WELL.

PETER'S OFFERED TO TEACH ME ALL ABOUT SPORTS.

AFTER LUNCH WE'RE GOING TO THROW THIS BASE-BALL AROUND AT THE PARK.

THAT'S A FOOTBALL.

MAYBE WE SHOULD START SOONER, PETER.

June 23, 2005

MY TRANSITION FROM GEEKDOM IS NEARLY COMPLETE.

I'VE SAID GOODBYE TO COMPUTERS, VIDEO GAMES, COMIC BOOKS, SCIENCE FICTION... EVERY NERDY THING YOU CAN THINK OF.

AS OF RIGHT NOW, I'M 99.865 PERCENT REGULAR JOE.

WHAT'S LEFT?

BESIDES THAT YOU SAY THINGS LIKE 99.865?

WELL, THAT'S 0.0675 OF IT.

June 24, 2005

A BATMAN MASK? YOU'RE BACK TO BEING GEEKY?

YEAH, BEING NORMAL WAS JUST TOO UN-NATURAL.

IF GIRLS REALLY DO FIND NERDS SEXY, WELL, I'LL JUST HAVE TO LEARN TO AVOID THEM.

BESIDES, THAT ARTICLE PETER AND I READ COULD HAVE BEEN WRONG.

PETER READ THE ARTICLE, ALSO?

YEAH, WHY?

JASON, LET'S GO! THE MOVIE STARTS IN TWO HOURS!

June 25, 2005

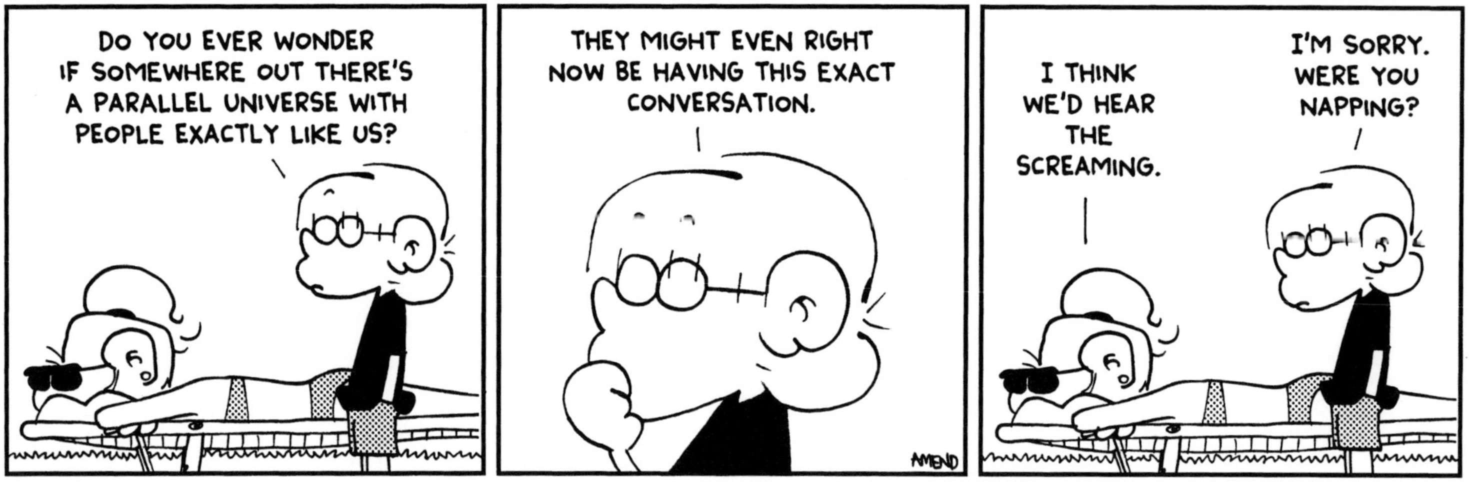
DO YOU EVER WONDER IF SOMEWHERE OUT THERE'S A PARALLEL UNIVERSE WITH PEOPLE EXACTLY LIKE US?
THEY MIGHT EVEN RIGHT NOW BE HAVING THIS EXACT CONVERSATION.
AMEND
I THINK WE'D HEAR THE SCREAMING.
I'M SORRY. WERE YOU NAPPING?

June 1, 2005

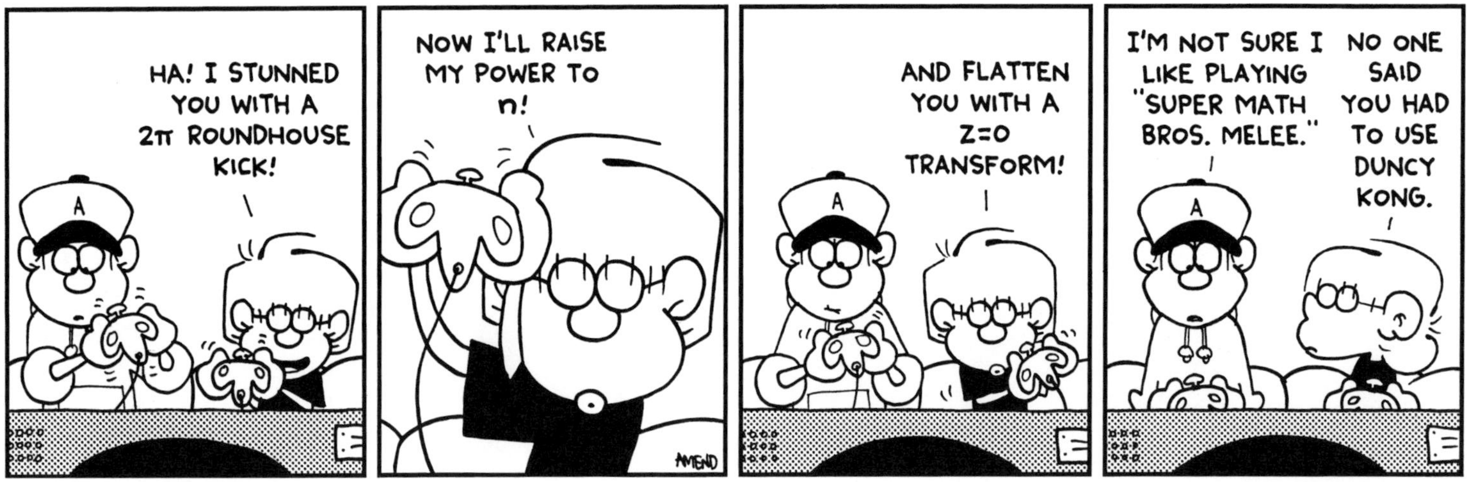
HA! I STUNNED YOU WITH A 2π ROUNDHOUSE KICK!
NOW I'LL RAISE MY POWER TO n!
AMEND
AND FLATTEN YOU WITH A Z=0 TRANSFORM!
I'M NOT SURE I LIKE PLAYING "SUPER MATH BROS. MELEE."
NO ONE SAID YOU HAD TO USE DUNCY KONG.

August 19, 2005

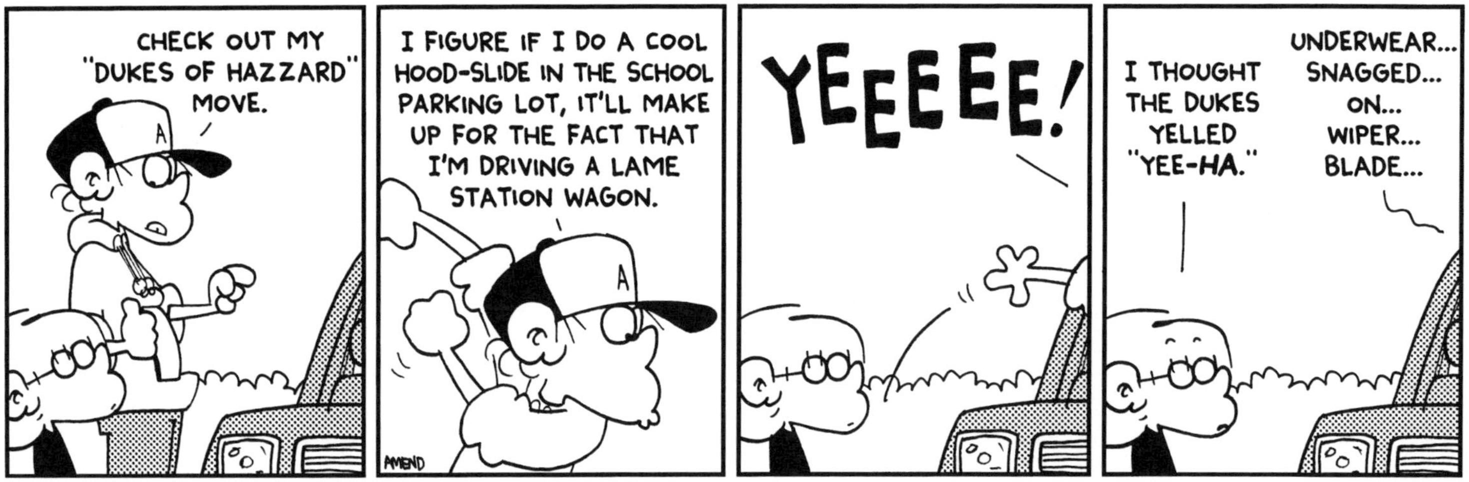
CHECK OUT MY "DUKES OF HAZZARD" MOVE.
I FIGURE IF I DO A COOL HOOD-SLIDE IN THE SCHOOL PARKING LOT, IT'LL MAKE UP FOR THE FACT THAT I'M DRIVING A LAME STATION WAGON.
AMEND
YEEEEEE!
I THOUGHT THE DUKES YELLED "YEE-HA."
UNDERWEAR... SNAGGED... ON... WIPER... BLADE...

August 25, 2005

This is my golf game in a nutshell.

April 10, 2005

June 12, 2005

243

I was new to MMORPGs, so it took me about six months of playing WoW to realize not everyone in these games is who or what they claim to be. Seemed like a good curveball to throw at Jason.

HOW GOES "WORLD OF WARQUEST"?

GOOD. I JUST GOT THROUGH THE CAVES OF CARNAGE.

I THOUGHT YOU ALWAYS DIED IN THERE.

I'VE MADE FRIENDS WITH ANOTHER PLAYER, AND HE'S HELPING ME OUT.

A FRIEND? DOES HE KNOW WHO YOU ARE IN REAL LIFE?

NAH. HE JUST KNOWS ME AS AN ORC.

CLOSE ENOUGH.

I GOT A NEW MACE. WANNA SEE IT?

July 25, 2005

SO WHO'S THIS NEW FRIEND OF YOURS?

SGT. NEELIE. HE'S A LEVEL 50 ROGUE.

HE CAN TURN INVISIBLE AND ATTACK MONSTERS FROM BEHIND. HE'S TOTALLY COOL.

THERE HE IS NOW. HE JUST KILLED THE OGRE KING AND IS DOING HIS VICTORY DANCE.

IS THAT THE ELECTRIC SLIDE?

OK, HE'S MOSTLY COOL.

July 26, 2005

CAN I BE EX-CUSED?

JASON, YOU'VE BARELY TOUCHED YOUR DINNER!

I KNOW, BUT I PROMISED SGT. NEELIE THAT I'D HELP HIM FIGHT THE HARPY QUEEN IN WARQUEST TONIGHT. IF I DON'T LOG ON SOON, HE'LL THINK I BLEW HIM OFF.

PLEASE? HE'S DEPENDING ON ME!

FINE. GO.

ARE YOU SURE IT ISN'T THE OTHER WAY AROUND?

EGG-PLANT TACOS. WHAT WAS MOM THINKING?!

244

July 27, 2005

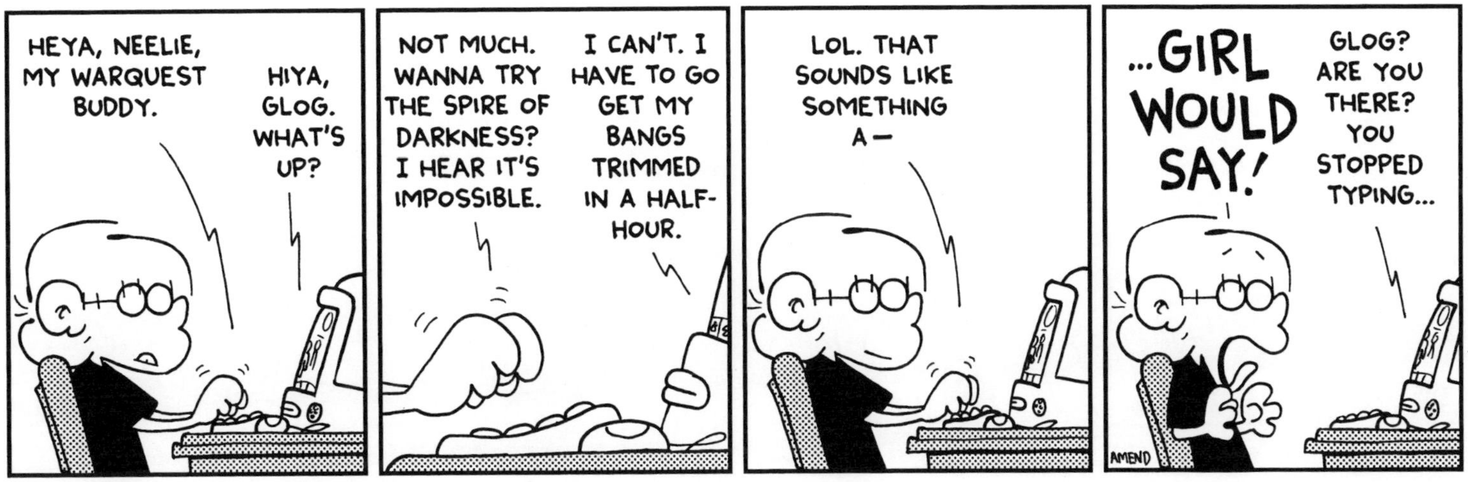
HEYA, NEELIE, MY WARQUEST BUDDY.
HIYA, GLOG. WHAT'S UP?
NOT MUCH. WANNA TRY THE SPIRE OF DARKNESS? I HEAR IT'S IMPOSSIBLE.
I CAN'T. I HAVE TO GO GET MY BANGS TRIMMED IN A HALF-HOUR.
LOL. THAT SOUNDS LIKE SOMETHING A—
...GIRL WOULD SAY!
GLOG? ARE YOU THERE? YOU STOPPED TYPING...
AMEND
July 28, 2005

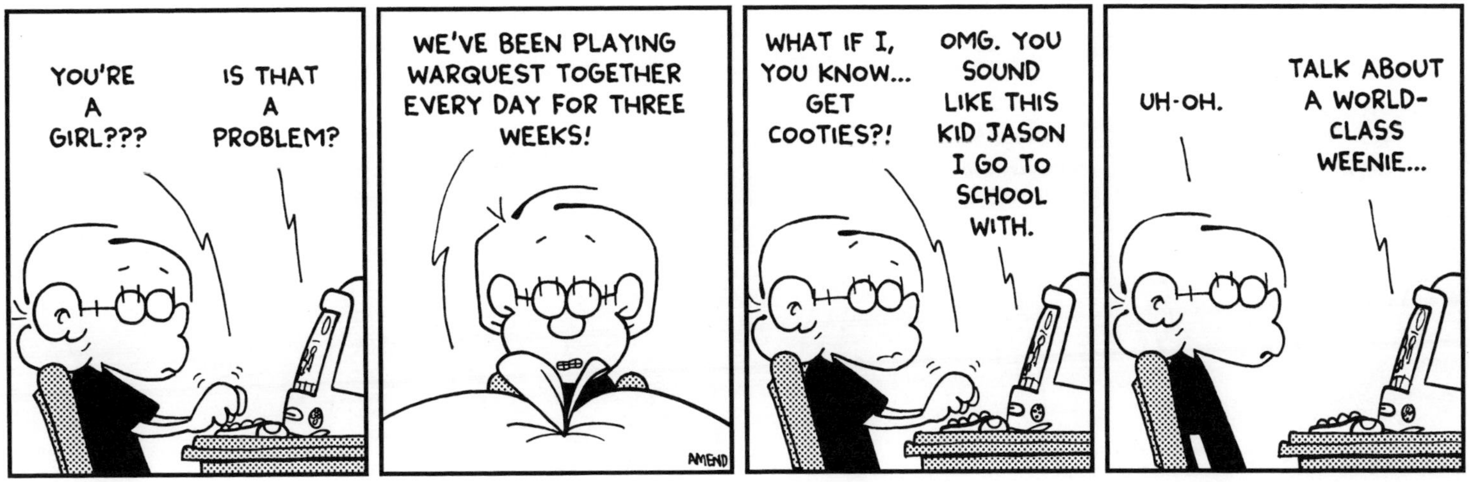
YOU'RE A GIRL???
IS THAT A PROBLEM?
WE'VE BEEN PLAYING WARQUEST TOGETHER EVERY DAY FOR THREE WEEKS!
AMEND
WHAT IF I, YOU KNOW... GET COOTIES?!
OMG. YOU SOUND LIKE THIS KID JASON I GO TO SCHOOL WITH.
UH-OH.
TALK ABOUT A WORLD-CLASS WEENIE...
July 29, 2005

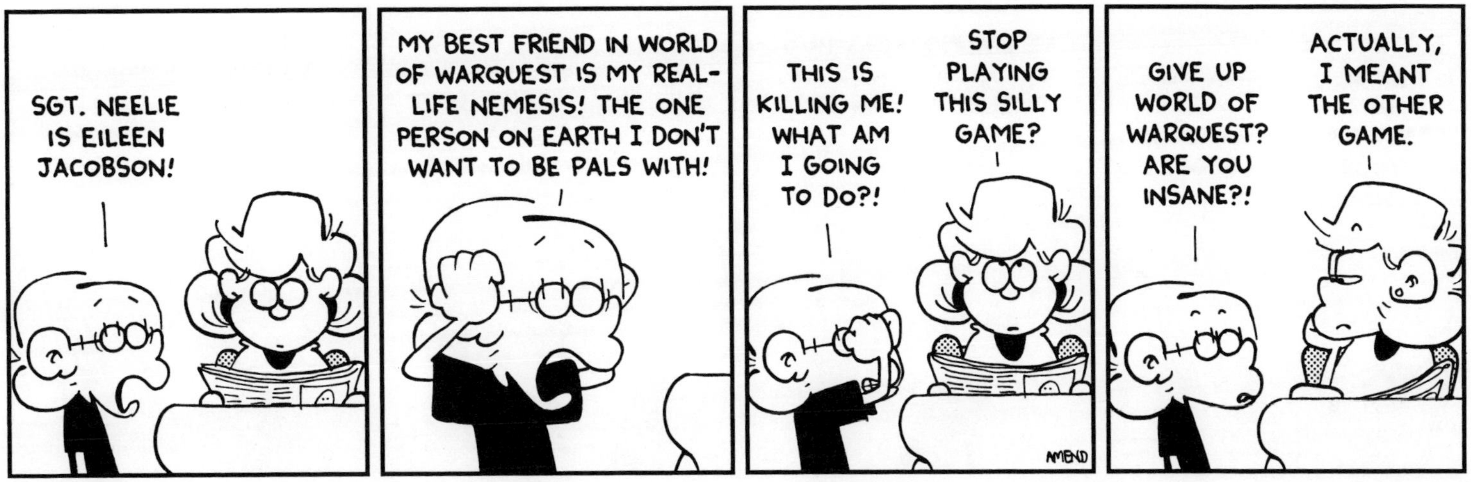
SGT. NEELIE IS EILEEN JACOBSON!
MY BEST FRIEND IN WORLD OF WARQUEST IS MY REAL-LIFE NEMESIS! THE ONE PERSON ON EARTH I DON'T WANT TO BE PALS WITH!
THIS IS KILLING ME! WHAT AM I GOING TO DO?!
STOP PLAYING THIS SILLY GAME?
AMEND
GIVE UP WORLD OF WARQUEST? ARE YOU INSANE?!
ACTUALLY, I MEANT THE OTHER GAME.
July 30, 2005

SO HAVE YOU TOLD EILEEN THAT GLOG MALBLOOD IS YOU?

ARE YOU CRAZY??

IF SHE WERE TO FIND OUT WE'VE BEEN ACCIDENTAL WORLD OF WARQUEST BUDDIES FOR THREE WEEKS, I'D NEVER HEAR THE END OF IT!

SHE'D SAY IT WAS KISMET AND WE SHOULD GET MARRIED!

MARRIED?

I HAVE AN AMULET OF +18 INTUITION. I CAN SENSE THESE THINGS.

August 1, 2005

SO, NEELIE, I WAS THINKING MAYBE I'D PLAY SOLO FOR A WHILE.

SOLO??

BUT YOU NEED MY HELP TO GET THROUGH THE ALPS OF ARCANERY. YOU WANT TO GET THE THORNY STAFF OF GODLY POWER, DON'T YOU?

DON'T YOU?

YES.

WHY'S YOUR HEALTH BAR DROPPING? IS SOMETHING KILLING YOU?

August 2, 2005

SO TELL ME MORE ABOUT THIS JASON AT YOUR SCHOOL.

GOSH, WHERE TO BEGIN...

HE'S ANNOYING... HE'S IMMATURE... HE'S AS DWEEBY AS CAN BE...

WHY WOULD YOU WANT TO HEAR ABOUT SUCH A PAIN-FUL LITTLE TWIT?

ER, JUST A MASOCHIST, I GUESS.

IMAGINE GOLLUM WITH GLASSES...

August 3, 2005

OK, ENOUGH ABOUT THIS JASON GUY.

BUT YOU HAVEN'T HEARD THE WORST PART.

NOT ONLY IS JASON THE BIGGEST DWEEB IN OUR CLASS, BUT HE HAS A MAJOR CRUSH ON ME. HE TRIES TO HIDE IT, BUT IT'S TOTALLY OBVIOUS.

EVERYONE AT SCHOOL KNOWS.

HOLD ON. I NEED TO CLOSE MY WINDOW. SOME NEIGHBOR'S DOG IS HOWLING.

NOOO-OOOO-OOOO...

August 4, 2005

LIFE... RUINED... MUST... FLEE... COUNTRY...

GOTCHA, JASON!

HUH??

I'VE JUST BEEN MESSING WITH YOU. MARCUS TOLD ME YOUR WARQUEST USERNAME.

WAIT UNTIL HE HEARS YOU AND I BECAME BUDDIES!

LIFE... REALLY... RUINED... MUST... REALLY... FLEE... COUNTRY...

GOTCHA AGAIN, JASON!

August 5, 2005

I CAN'T BELIEVE EILEEN TRICKED ME LIKE THAT!

SHE MADE ME THINK SHE WAS A GUY, JUST TO PROVE WE COULD BE FRIENDS IF IT WEREN'T FOR MY LITTLE "HANG-UPS"!

I'M SO MAD I COULD SPIT ACID.

MAD THAT SHE TRICKED YOU, OR MAD THAT SHE PROVED HER POINT?

NO COMMENT.

August 6, 2005

247

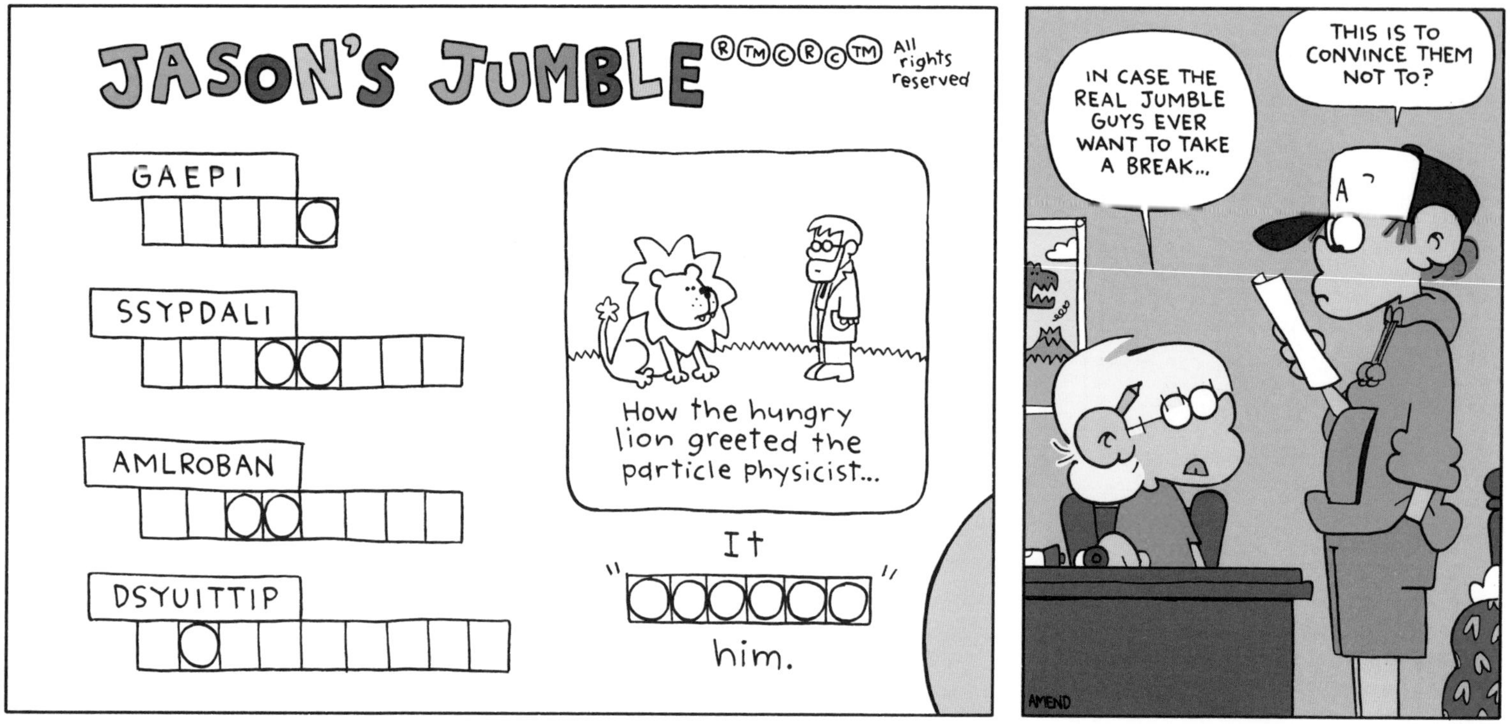

JASON'S JUMBLE ®™©®©™ All rights reserved
GAEPI
SSYPDALI
AMLROBAN
DSYUITTIP
How the hungry lion greeted the particle physicist...
It " " him.
IN CASE THE REAL JUMBLE GUYS EVER WANT TO TAKE A BREAK...
THIS IS TO CONVINCE THEM NOT TO?

July 3, 2005

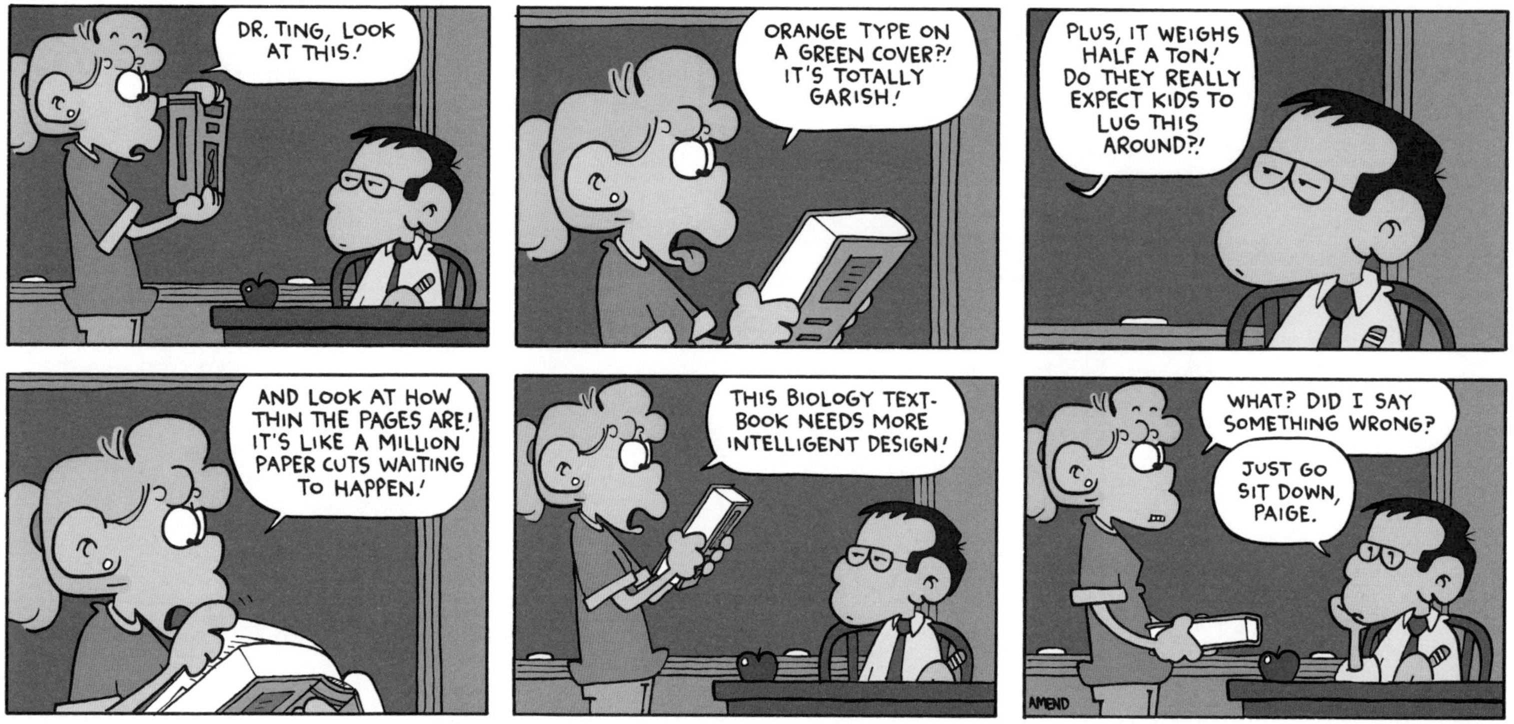

DR. TING, LOOK AT THIS!
ORANGE TYPE ON A GREEN COVER?! IT'S TOTALLY GARISH!
PLUS, IT WEIGHS HALF A TON! DO THEY REALLY EXPECT KIDS TO LUG THIS AROUND?!
AND LOOK AT HOW THIN THE PAGES ARE! IT'S LIKE A MILLION PAPER CUTS WAITING TO HAPPEN!
THIS BIOLOGY TEXT-BOOK NEEDS MORE INTELLIGENT DESIGN!
WHAT? DID I SAY SOMETHING WRONG?
JUST GO SIT DOWN, PAIGE.

September 4, 2005

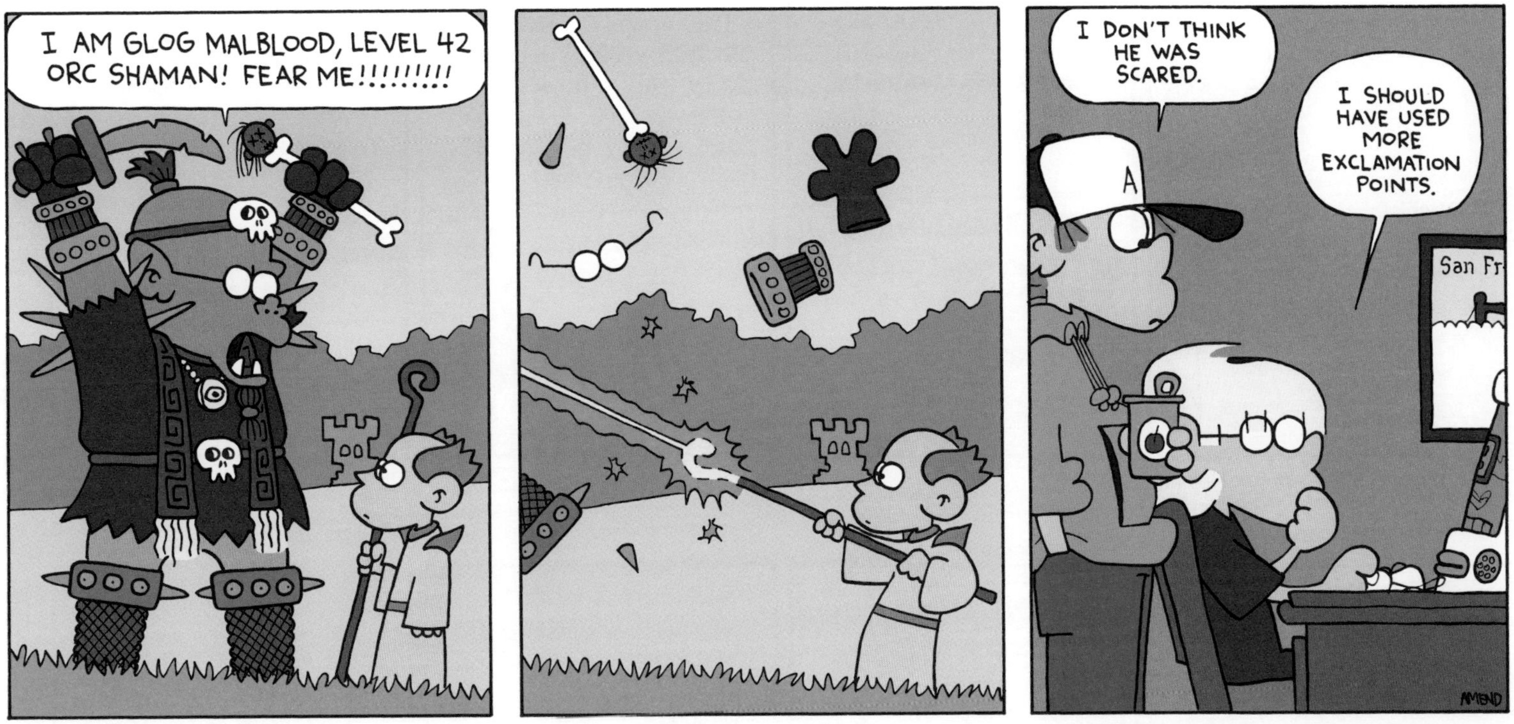
I AM GLOG MALBLOOD, LEVEL 42 ORC SHAMAN! FEAR ME!!!!!!!!!!
I DON'T THINK HE WAS SCARED.
I SHOULD HAVE USED MORE EXCLAMATION POINTS.
San Fr
AMEND

October 9, 2005

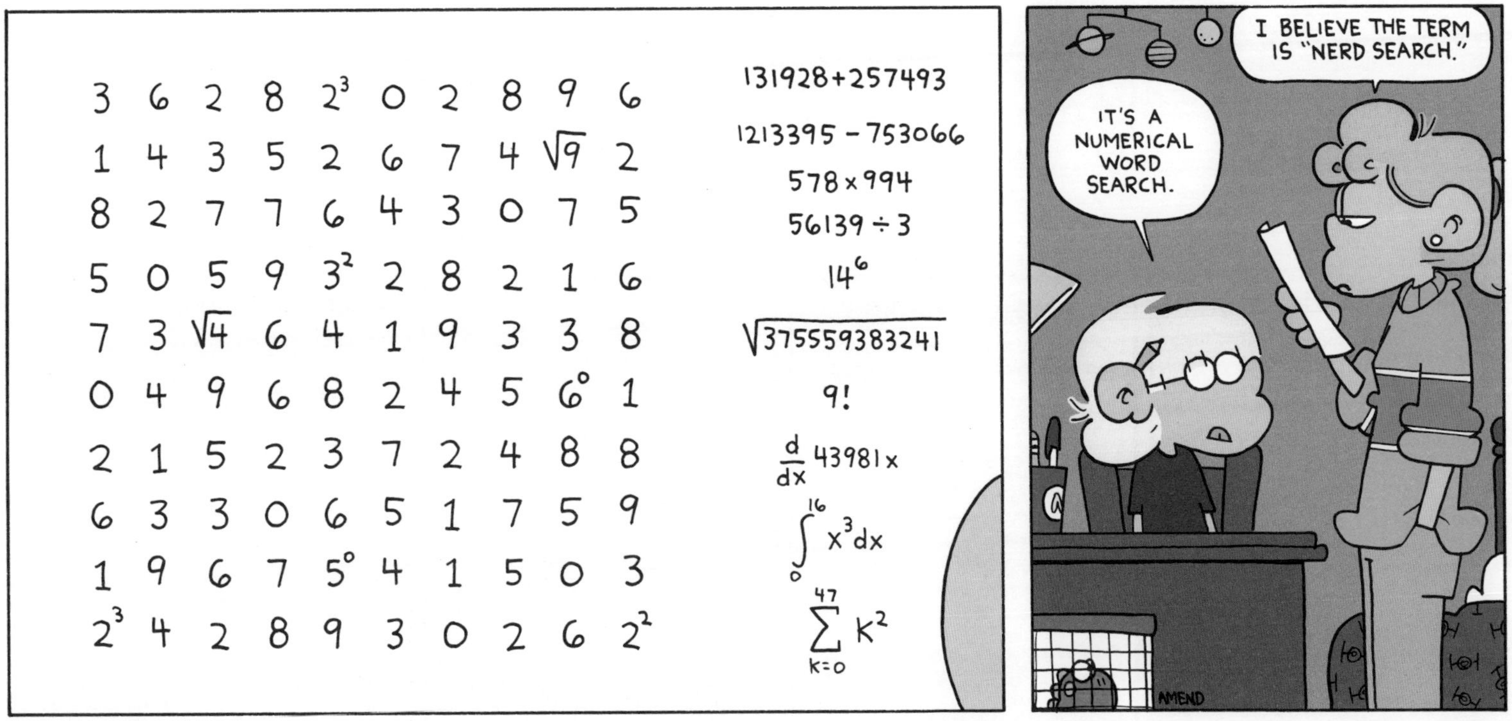
3 6 2 8 2^3 0 2 8 9 6
1 4 3 5 2 6 7 4 $\sqrt{9}$ 2
8 2 7 7 6 4 3 0 7 5
5 0 5 9 3^2 2 8 2 1 6
7 3 $\sqrt{4}$ 6 4 1 9 3 3 8
0 4 9 6 8 2 4 5 6^0 1
2 1 5 2 3 7 2 4 8 8
6 3 3 0 6 5 1 7 5 9
1 9 6 7 5^0 4 1 5 0 3
2^3 4 2 8 9 3 0 2 6 2^2
131928+257493
1213395 − 753066
578 × 994
56139 ÷ 3
14^6
$\sqrt{375559383241}$
9!
$\frac{d}{dx} 43981x$
$\int_0^{16} x^3 dx$
$\sum_{k=0}^{47} K^2$
I BELIEVE THE TERM IS "NERD SEARCH."
IT'S A NUMERICAL WORD SEARCH.
AMEND

November 6, 2005

September 19, 2005

September 20, 2005

250

September 21, 2005

September 22, 2005

September 23, 2005

September 24, 2005

WHO ARE YOU SUPPOSED TO BE?

I'M THE GREAT PUMPKIN FROM "PEANUTS."

I'M THE LEGENDARY CREATURE THAT LINUS SO PATIENTLY WAITED FOR ON HALLOWEEN.

ARE THOSE BITS OF A SECURITY BLANKET IN YOUR TEETH?

I ADDED A TOUCH OF IRONY.

October 25, 2005

HELP ME DECIDE WHICH COMIC BOOK CHARACTER TO TRICK-OR-TREAT AS.

IF I GO AS THE FLASH, I CAN HIT EVERY HOUSE IN THE COUNTRY, BUT IF I GO AS THE HULK, I CAN CARRY MORE CANDY.

OR I COULD GO AS SUPER-MAN, AND GET THE BEST OF BOTH WORLDS, BUT IF SOMEONE DRESSED LIKE KRYPTONITE, I'D BE DOOMED.

WHY DON'T YOU GO AS THE JOKER SO WE CAN LOCK YOU IN AN ASYLUM?

THAT'S WEIRD. PETER SAID THE SAME THING.

October 27, 2005

WHAT ABOUT THIS FOR A HALLOWEEN COSTUME?

A LEMON?

MAYBE PEOPLE WILL SEE ME AS BEING SO SOUR, THEY'LL WANT TO SWEETEN ME UP WITH EXTRA CANDY.

OR MAYBE THEY'LL START CRAVING LEMONADE AND WILL STICK YOU IN A JUICER.

I GUESS IT'S BACK TO THE DRAWING BOARD.

NO, DON'T! I LIKE THIS IDEA!

October 28, 2005

October 11, 2005

November 14, 2005

December 21, 2005

I did get to see a Steve Jobs keynote in person back in 2003. A highpoint of my nerd life.

WELCOME TO THE APPLE STORE.

SPARE ME THE PLEAS-ANTRIES, PEON. I'M YOUR BOSS, STEVE JOBS.

I'M GIVING MY BIG MACWORLD KEYNOTE TOMORROW AND I'VE FORGOTTEN EXACTLY WHAT ULTRA-TOP-SECRET NEW PRODUCTS I'LL BE INTRODUCING.

I NEED YOU TO SHOW THEM TO ME. AND BE DISCREET... THE INTERNET'S SPIES ARE EVERYWHERE.

I COULD START BY SHOWING YOU THE DOOR.

EXCEL-LENT. WOULD THIS BE AN iDOOR OR A POWER-DOOR?

January 9, 2006

ALPHA-BITS?

ALPHA-BYTES.

January 11, 2006

YIKES! I ALMOST HIT THAT TRUCK!

EEK! I ALMOST HIT THAT TREE!

YAAA! I ALMOST FLIPPED THE CAR OVER!

WOW. IT'S LIKE DRIVING WITH YOU IN REAL LIFE.

WHEN DID I ALMOST HIT A TREE?

February 1, 2006

January 22, 2006

January 29, 2006

Blizzard actually went and added a Doomulus Prime weapon to World of Warcraft a few months later. How cool is that?

I had a really bad cold when I did these. Considering how lousy I felt, I think they turned out pretty well.

EVER WONDER WHAT CARTOONISTS DO WHEN THEY GET SICK?

NOT REALLY. WHY?

WELL, IT'S NOT LIKE THEY CAN JUST SUSPEND THEIR DEADLINES UNTIL THEY FEEL BETTER.

I'M SURE THEY HAVE A STASH OF UNUSED JOKES SET ASIDE TO USE IN A PINCH.

I GUESS, SO LONG AS THEY KEEP IT UPDATED...

HEE HEE. DID YOU HEAR WHAT DAN QUAYLE SAID ON "CARSON" LAST NIGHT?

February 13, 2006

I STILL DON'T SEE HOW A CARTOONIST CAN MAKE HIS DEADLINE IF HE'S SICK.

I TOLD YOU, THEY KEEP EXTRA JOKES ON HAND FOR EMERGENCIES.

YEAH, BUT THEY STILL HAVE TO DRAW THE THINGS. HOW DO YOU MANAGE THAT WITH WADS OF KLEENEX IN YOUR HANDS?

THEY CAN JUST DRAW STICK FIGURES. IT'S NOT LIKE PAPERS PRINT STRIPS BIG ENOUGH TO NOTICE.

GOOD POINT.

MOM, WHEN'S DINNER? I'M STARVING.

February 14, 2006

SOMEHOW I DON'T SEE EVEN A SICK CARTOONIST REVERTING TO STICK FIGURES.

HOW ELSE WOULD THEY GET THE STRIPS DONE, THEN?

THEY COULD JUST USE A COMPUTER TO CUT AND PASTE EXISTING ART. THAT'D BE THE EASIEST WAY.

ASSUMING THEY KNOW HOW TO DO THAT.

OH, PLEASE. IT'S LIKE PHOTOSHOP 101.

WE'RE TALKING ABOUT CARTOONISTS, REMEMBER.

February 15, 2006

ANOTHER THING A SICK CARTOONIST COULD DO IF HE'S IN A REAL TIME CRUNCH IS USE THE OL' SNOWSTORM GAG.

WHAT'S THAT?

IT'S WHERE THE CARTOONIST LEAVES EVERYTHING WHITE, WITH THE JOKE BEING THAT A BLINDING BLIZZARD HAS HIT.

WHAT IF THE CHARACTERS ARE INDOORS?

WELL, I'M SURE THEY COULD THINK OF SOMETHING.

DID I SHOW YOU MY NEW 50,000-WATT FLASHLIGHT?

February 16, 2006

I GUESS IF A SICK CARTOONIST REALLY NEEDED TO, HE COULD ALWAYS FIND A SUBSTITUTE ARTIST.

WHAT DO YOU MEAN?

YOU KNOW, GET ONE OF HIS CARTOONING BUDDIES TO FILL IN FOR HIM WHILE HE'S LAID UP.

OF COURSE, THERE'D HAVE TO BE RIGID GUIDELINES.

I HEAR "PEARLS BEFORE SWINE" HAS A NEW BOOK COMING OUT.

February 17, 2006

Stephan Pastis did, in fact, draw that last panel for me.

I DON'T KNOW WHY I'M EVEN WORRYING ABOUT CARTOONISTS GETTING SICK, NOW THAT I THINK ABOUT IT.

AFTER ALL, THESE ARE SUPERIOR BEINGS WITH POWERS AND ABILITIES WELL BEYOND OUR FEEBLE COMPREHENSION... DESCENDANTS OF VISITORS FROM A MORE ADVANCED PLANET... GOD-LIKE IN NEARLY EVERY WAY...

I'M SURE THEY'RE RARELY UNDER THE WEATHER.

GOOD THING. THE MEDICINE MIGHT MESS WITH THEIR MINDS.

February 18, 2006

February 27, 2006

February 28, 2006

March 1, 2006

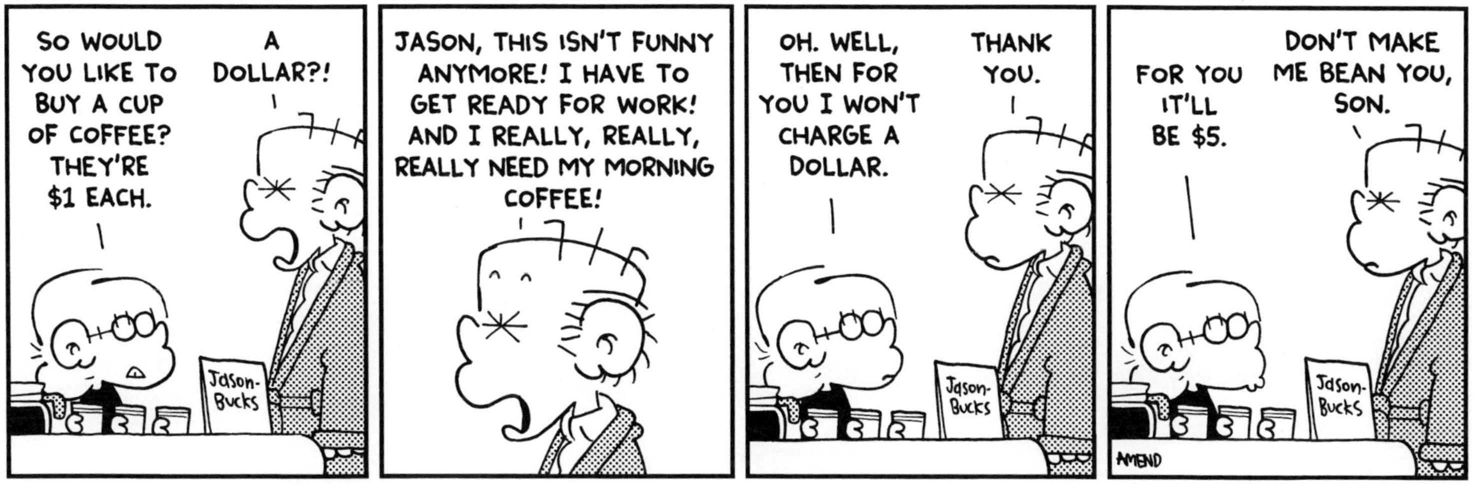
SO WOULD YOU LIKE TO BUY A CUP OF COFFEE? THEY'RE $1 EACH.
A DOLLAR?!
JASON, THIS ISN'T FUNNY ANYMORE! I HAVE TO GET READY FOR WORK! AND I REALLY, REALLY, REALLY NEED MY MORNING COFFEE!
OH. WELL, THEN FOR YOU I WON'T CHARGE A DOLLAR.
THANK YOU.
FOR YOU IT'LL BE $5.
DON'T MAKE ME BEAN YOU, SON.

March 2, 2006

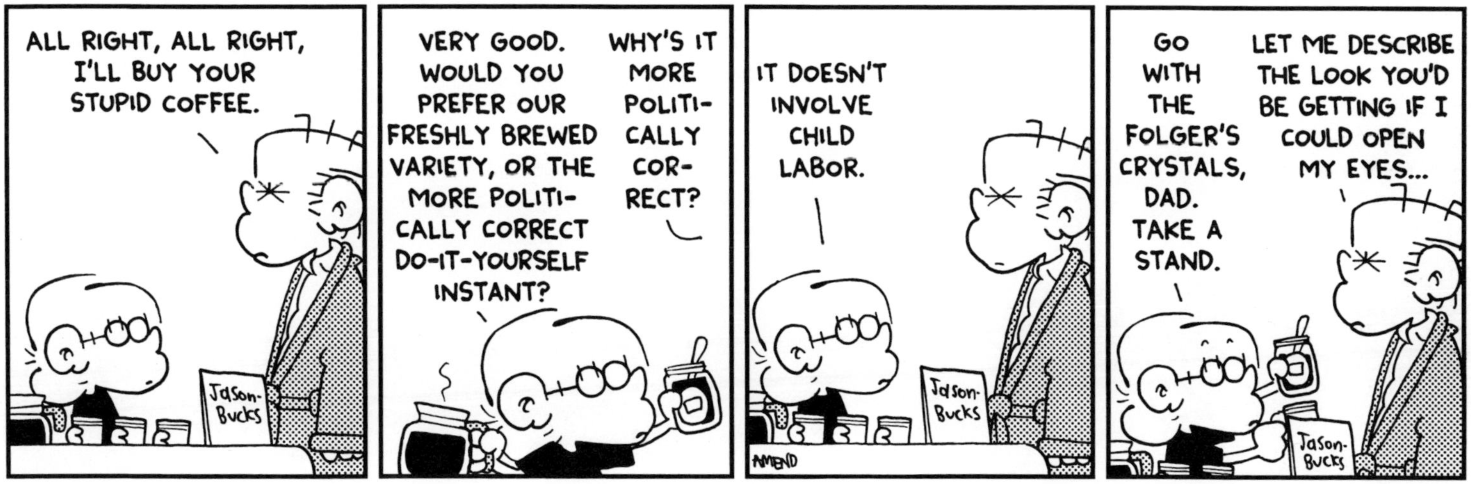
ALL RIGHT, ALL RIGHT, I'LL BUY YOUR STUPID COFFEE.
VERY GOOD. WOULD YOU PREFER OUR FRESHLY BREWED VARIETY, OR THE MORE POLITICALLY CORRECT DO-IT-YOURSELF INSTANT?
WHY'S IT MORE POLITICALLY CORRECT?
IT DOESN'T INVOLVE CHILD LABOR.
GO WITH THE FOLGER'S CRYSTALS, DAD. TAKE A STAND.
LET ME DESCRIBE THE LOOK YOU'D BE GETTING IF I COULD OPEN MY EYES...

March 3, 2006

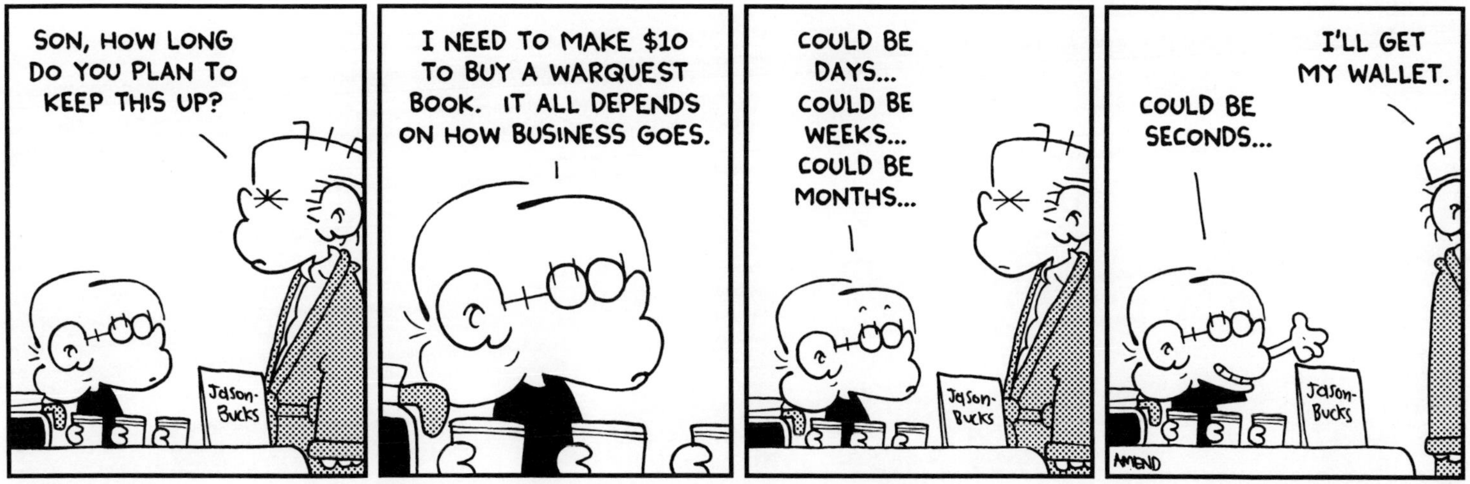
SON, HOW LONG DO YOU PLAN TO KEEP THIS UP?
I NEED TO MAKE $10 TO BUY A WARQUEST BOOK. IT ALL DEPENDS ON HOW BUSINESS GOES.
COULD BE DAYS... COULD BE WEEKS... COULD BE MONTHS...
COULD BE SECONDS...
I'LL GET MY WALLET.

March 4, 2006

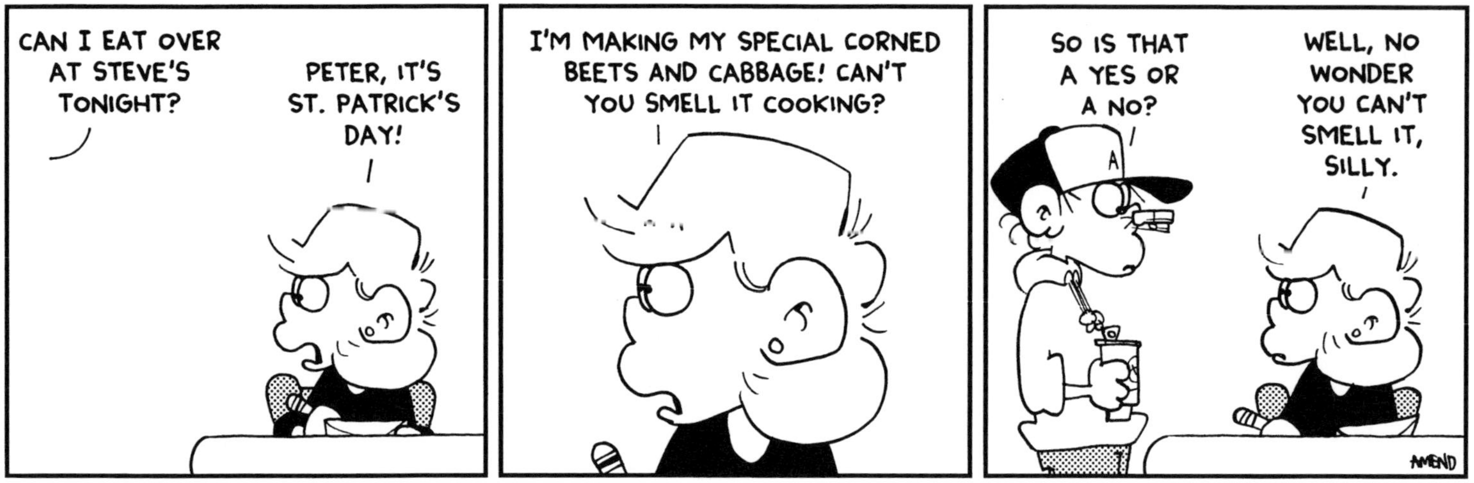
CAN I EAT OVER AT STEVE'S TONIGHT?
PETER, IT'S ST. PATRICK'S DAY!
I'M MAKING MY SPECIAL CORNED BEETS AND CABBAGE! CAN'T YOU SMELL IT COOKING?
SO IS THAT A YES OR A NO?
WELL, NO WONDER YOU CAN'T SMELL IT, SILLY.
AMEND

March 17, 2006

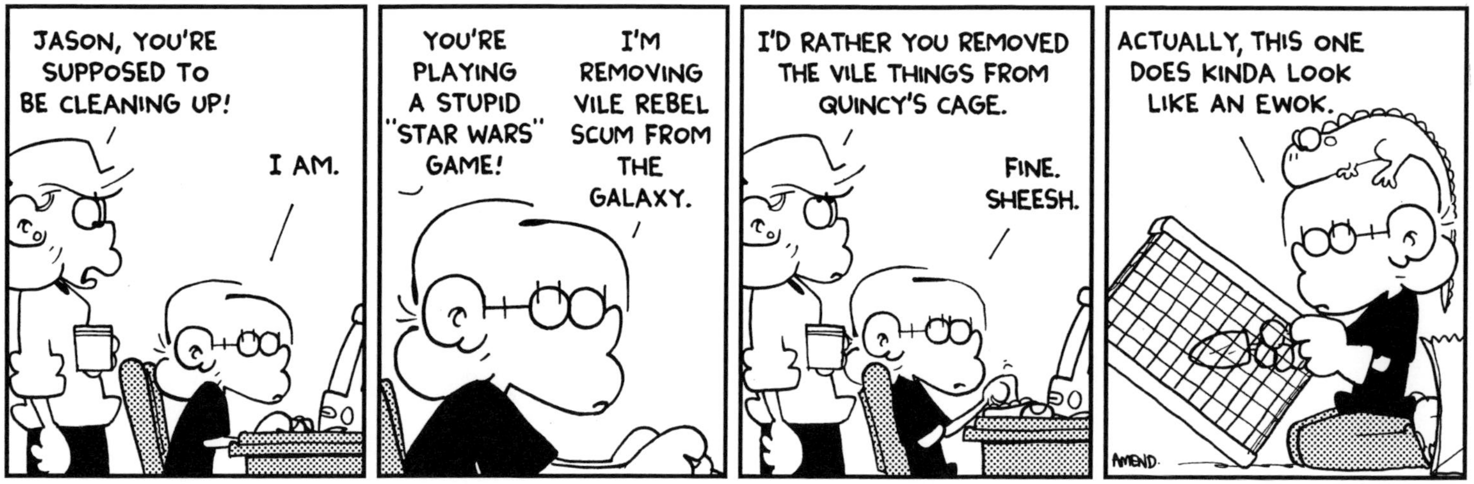
JASON, YOU'RE SUPPOSED TO BE CLEANING UP!
I AM.
YOU'RE PLAYING A STUPID "STAR WARS" GAME!
I'M REMOVING VILE REBEL SCUM FROM THE GALAXY.
I'D RATHER YOU REMOVED THE VILE THINGS FROM QUINCY'S CAGE.
FINE. SHEESH.
ACTUALLY, THIS ONE DOES KINDA LOOK LIKE AN EWOK.
AMEND

March 24, 2006

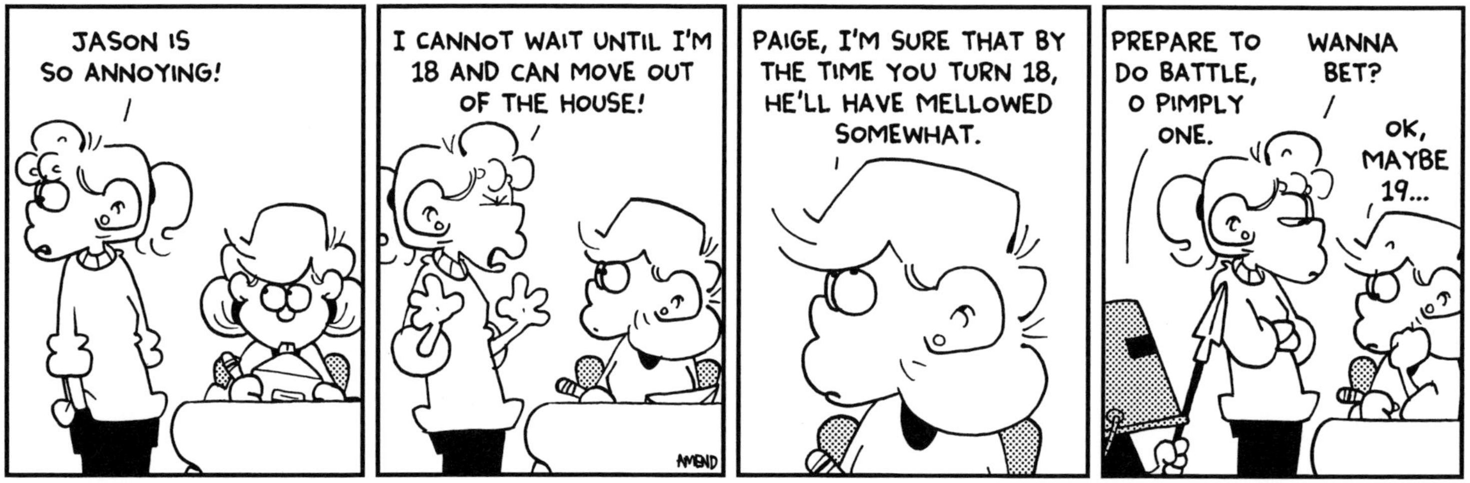
JASON IS SO ANNOYING!
I CANNOT WAIT UNTIL I'M 18 AND CAN MOVE OUT OF THE HOUSE!
AMEND
PAIGE, I'M SURE THAT BY THE TIME YOU TURN 18, HE'LL HAVE MELLOWED SOMEWHAT.
PREPARE TO DO BATTLE, O PIMPLY ONE.
WANNA BET?
OK, MAYBE 19...

April 10, 2006

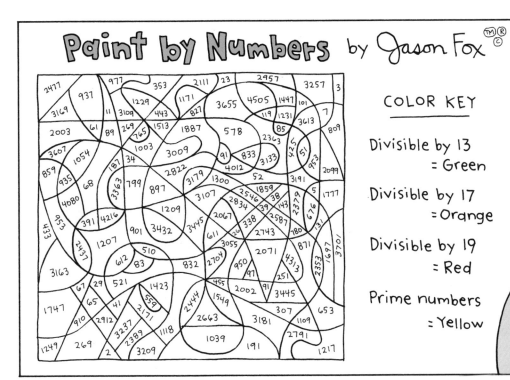

April 9, 2006

Trying to make the shapes on the left look like gibberish was a lot harder than I expected.

As you might guess, Jason's tap dance spells out a message in Morse Code.

May 21, 2006

261

EZEKIEL 25:17...

"...AND YOU WILL KNOW MY NAME IS THE **LORD**, WHEN I LAY MY VENGEANCE UPON THEE!"

SQUIRT! SQUIRT! SQUIRT! SQUIRT!

HOW ABOUT **I** WATER THE TULIPS FROM NOW ON?

"BULB FICTION."

April 22, 2006

YOU'RE NAPPING AGAIN?! PAIGE, YOU TOOK A NAP AN HOUR AGO!

THAT WAS A PRE-NAP.

I LIKE TO TAKE A PRE-NAP NAP TO UNWIND BEFORE MY REAL NAP. I FIND IT EASES THE TRANSITION INTO DREAMLAND.

NOW I'M TAKING MY ACTUAL NAP.

YOU'RE A PIECE OF WORK.

I'M TRYING TO SLEEP. CAN WE HAVE THIS CONVERSATION AFTER MY POST-NAP?

April 30, 2006

NEXT TIME LET ME TRIM THE BUSHES.

WHAT'S WRONG WITH IT?

262

July 5, 2006

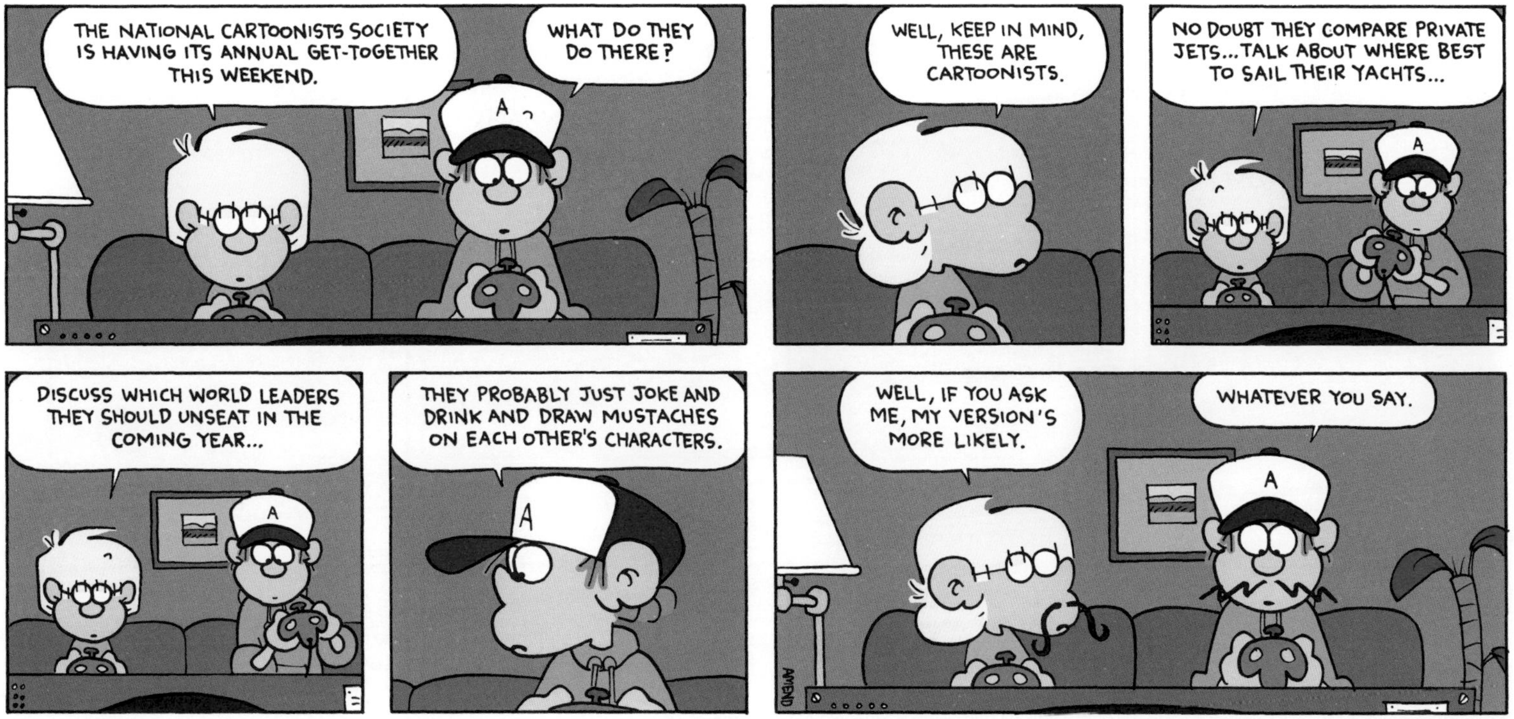
THE NATIONAL CARTOONISTS SOCIETY IS HAVING ITS ANNUAL GET-TOGETHER THIS WEEKEND.
WHAT DO THEY DO THERE?
WELL, KEEP IN MIND, THESE ARE CARTOONISTS.
NO DOUBT THEY COMPARE PRIVATE JETS... TALK ABOUT WHERE BEST TO SAIL THEIR YACHTS...
DISCUSS WHICH WORLD LEADERS THEY SHOULD UNSEAT IN THE COMING YEAR...
THEY PROBABLY JUST JOKE AND DRINK AND DRAW MUSTACHES ON EACH OTHER'S CHARACTERS.
WELL, IF YOU ASK ME, MY VERSION'S MORE LIKELY.
WHATEVER YOU SAY.

May 28, 2006

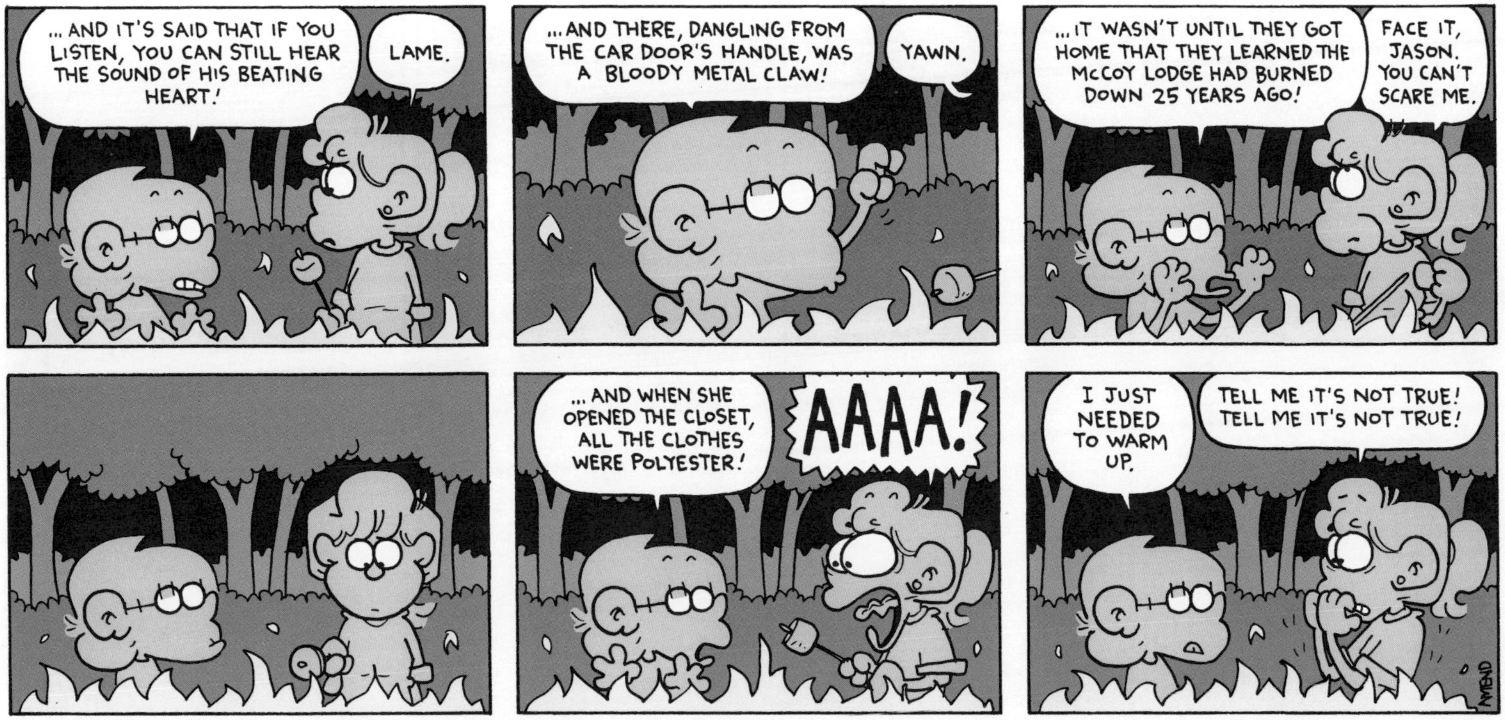
... AND IT'S SAID THAT IF YOU LISTEN, YOU CAN STILL HEAR THE SOUND OF HIS BEATING HEART!
LAME.
... AND THERE, DANGLING FROM THE CAR DOOR'S HANDLE, WAS A BLOODY METAL CLAW!
YAWN.
... IT WASN'T UNTIL THEY GOT HOME THAT THEY LEARNED THE McCOY LODGE HAD BURNED DOWN 25 YEARS AGO!
FACE IT, JASON. YOU CAN'T SCARE ME.
... AND WHEN SHE OPENED THE CLOSET, ALL THE CLOTHES WERE POLYESTER!
AAAA!
I JUST NEEDED TO WARM UP.
TELL ME IT'S NOT TRUE! TELL ME IT'S NOT TRUE!

August 13, 2006

In high school I did this to all the computers in the local Radio Shack. Ah, the simple pleasures.

June 5, 2006

June 6, 2006

264

June 7, 2006

CHECK IT OUT. THESE COMPUTERS HAVE BUILT-IN CAMERAS.

YOU CAN EVEN APPLY ALL SORTS OF COOL DISTORTION EFFECTS IF YOU WANT.

NOW I'LL SHOW IT **WITH** DISTORTION.

HA HA.

June 8, 2006

HOW DOES "WORLD OF WARQUEST" PERFORM ON THESE MACHINES?

LET ME PUT IT THIS WAY...

YOU KNOW WHEN YOU'RE IN CROWDED AREAS AND THE GAME TENDS TO SLOW TO A STUTTERY CRAWL?

WITH THESE BABIES IT ONLY SLOWS TO HALF A STUTTERY CRAWL.

/DROOL.

I HAD THE SAME REACTION.

June 9, 2006

SO HOW WAS YOUR TRIP TO THE iFRUIT STORE?

OK.

NOTHING AGAINST PETER, BUT I WOULD HAVE RATHER GONE WITH SOMEONE ELSE.

PETER'S NOT THAT INTO COMPUTERS?

PETER CAN'T BUY ME ONE.

REMIND ME TO CANCEL OUR CREDIT CARDS.

HEY, DAD, ARE YOU BUSY?

June 10, 2006

HAVE YOU SEEN PETER?!

WHY?

HE'S SUPPOSED TO DRIVE ME TO SEE "SUPERMAN RETURNS" AND THE MOVIE STARTS IN 45 MINUTES!

I'M GOING TO BE LATE!

YOU'RE SUPERMAN. CAN'T YOU FLY THERE?

PETER DRIVES FASTER.

GOOD POINT.

June 28, 2006

HMM.

WHAT'S WRONG?

I CAN'T SEEM TO RIP YOUR TICKET IN HALF. IT'S LIKE IT'S MADE FROM SOME SORT OF INDESTRUCTIBLE MATERIAL. YOU TRY.

RIP!

THANKS, SUPERMAN.

YOU DID THAT ON PURPOSE, DIDN'T YOU.

June 29, 2006

I DON'T FEEL SO GOOD.

WHAT'S WRONG?

MY STOMACH IS ALL QUEASY... MY HEAD IS ACHING... THIS THEATER MUST HAVE KRYPTONITE IN IT.

OR IT MIGHT BE THE LARGE POPCORN AND SIX BAGS OF SOUR PATCH KIDS YOU'VE EATEN.

I'VE ONLY HAD FIVE BAGS. IT'S GOTTA BE KRYPTONITE.

SAY, IS THAT EILEEN JACOBSON OVER THERE IN THE GREEN SHIRT?

June 30, 2006

OH, JOY. ANOTHER CARTOONIST RUNNING RERUNS WHILE ON VACATION.

SO?

SO? I SENT THEM ALL LETTERS EXPLAINING HOW I'D BE HAPPY TO FILL IN FOR THEM! I HAD SOME REALLY GREAT IDEAS, TOO!

AACK! This bathing suit makes me look hideous!!!

July 24, 2006

YOU REALLY SEND IDEAS TO CARTOONISTS?

ALL THE TIME. MY IDEAS ARE TOO GOOD TO KEEP THEM BOTTLED UP.

DOES ANYONE EVER WRITE BACK?

THE "FAMILY CIRCUS" GUY DOES. HE'S GOOD THAT WAY.

WHAT'S HE SAY?

USUALLY A LOT OF LEGALESE MUMBO-JUMBO. "CEASE AND DESIST"... THAT SORT OF THING.

July 25, 2006

I SENT A LOT OF IDEAS TO THE "PEARLS BEFORE SWINE" CARTOONIST. I HEARD HE'S PRETTY DESPERATE.

WHAT KIND OF IDEAS?

MOSTLY COSMETIC. LIKE SUBTLE WAYS TO MAKE THE CROCODILES LOOK EVEN LESS INTELLIGENT.

Hulloooo, zeeba neighba!

I'm a pig.

July 26, 2006

267

HERE'S ONE OF THE CARTOON IDEAS I HAD FOR "ZITS."

Hi! I'm Paige Fox!

OR WAS THAT MY IDEA FOR "MUTTS"?...

I'M SENSING A RECURRING THEME HERE.

July 27, 2006

I SENT SOME GREAT IDEAS TO THE "FOR BETTER OR FOR WORSE" CARTOONIST.

SUCH AS?

LIKE THE NEXT TIME SHE OFFS A DOG, SHE SHOULD DO IT IN A WAY THAT WON'T OFFEND READERS.

Good news! It was just Paige Fox dressed up like Farley!

July 28, 2006

You really don't know e-mail fury until you make fun of the death of Farley in your comic strip.

JASON, NO OFFENSE, BUT YOUR COMIC STRIP IDEAS ARE LAME.

WHY DO YOU SAY THAT?

THEY'RE JUST ONE DUMB JAB AT OUR SISTER AFTER ANOTHER. I MEAN, YOU COULD AT LEAST SHOW A LITTLE VARIETY.

I GUESS I COULD RETOOL A FEW OF THEM, MISTER CARTOON EXPERT.

I hate Mondays and Paige Fox.
Peter

268

July 29, 2006

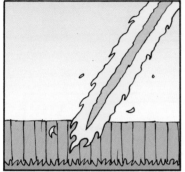

August 20, 2006

I got a lot of e-mails asking about FF-F8. Those are hexadecimal numbers. FF is 255 and F8 is 248.

October 15, 2006

August 29, 2006

September 14, 2006

October 9, 2006

LIKE MY HALLOWEEN COSTUME?

WHAT IS IT?

I'M A TOUCH-SCREEN ELECTRONIC VOTING MACHINE.

COMPUTER EXPERTS HAVE BEEN WARNING FOR YEARS THAT THESE THINGS CAN BE EASILY HACKED, AND WITHOUT A PAPER TRAIL, THERE'S NO WAY TO VERIFY THE VOTE COUNTS WEREN'T TAMPERED WITH.

NOW, HERE WE ARE NINE DAYS BEFORE ELECTIONS, AND REPORTEDLY ONE-THIRD OF ALL JURISDICTIONS WILL USE THEM.

SERIOUSLY, CAN YOU THINK OF ANYTHING SCARIER?

JASON, MOST PEOPLE DON'T CARE ABOUT THIS STUFF.

HMM. THAT WAS A PRETTY GOOD ANSWER.

October 29, 2006

"SOLD."

"SOLD."

"SOLD"... "SOLD"...

"SOLD"... "SOLD"...

AARG! I JUST **KNEW** I SHOULD HAVE DONE THIS **LAST** WEEKEND!

OH, WAIT! THAT LITTLE TREE OVER THERE ISN'T SOLD YET...

NOOOOOOOOO!...

SORRY, MISTER.

YOU SNOOZE, YOU LOSE!

December 10, 2006

I know, I know, Jason's about thirty years too young to have any idea who Grizzly Adams was.

40x MAGNIFICATION... NOTHING.

100x MAGNIFICATION... NOTHING.

400x MAGNIFI— WAIT! I SEE SOMETHING!

IS IT FACIAL HAIR?! IS IT FACIAL HAIR?!

STOP JIGGLING THE MICROSCOPE, GRIZZLY ADAMS!

October 14, 2006

GREETINGS, COMRADE.

"COMRADE"?

I FIGURE WITH THE LEFTY-PINKO DEMOCRATS TAKING OVER CONGRESS, THAT'S THE SORT OF LANGUAGE WE'LL ALL BE SPEAKING SOON.

DIDN'T YOU CALL THE REPUBLICAN CONGRESS "A BUNCH OF LOONY NEANDERTHALS"?

SO?

I'M JUST TRYING TO FIGURE OUT YOUR POLITICS.

POLITICS-SCHMOLITICS. I JUST LIKE MOCKING AUTHORITY.

SPEAKING OF WHICH, I GOT A CALL FROM YOUR PRINCIPAL...

November 27, 2006

WHAT ARE YOU DOING??

DRAWING TATTOOS ALL OVER MY BODY WITH A SHARPIE.

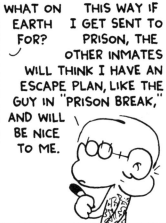

WHAT ON EARTH FOR?

THIS WAY IF I GET SENT TO PRISON, THE OTHER INMATES WILL THINK I HAVE AN ESCAPE PLAN, LIKE THE GUY IN "PRISON BREAK," AND WILL BE NICE TO ME.

IS THERE SOMETHING I SHOULD KNOW ABOUT?

THE CIA'S COMPUTERS ARE PUBLIC PROPERTY! AM I WRONG?!

DING DONG!

November 29, 2006

272

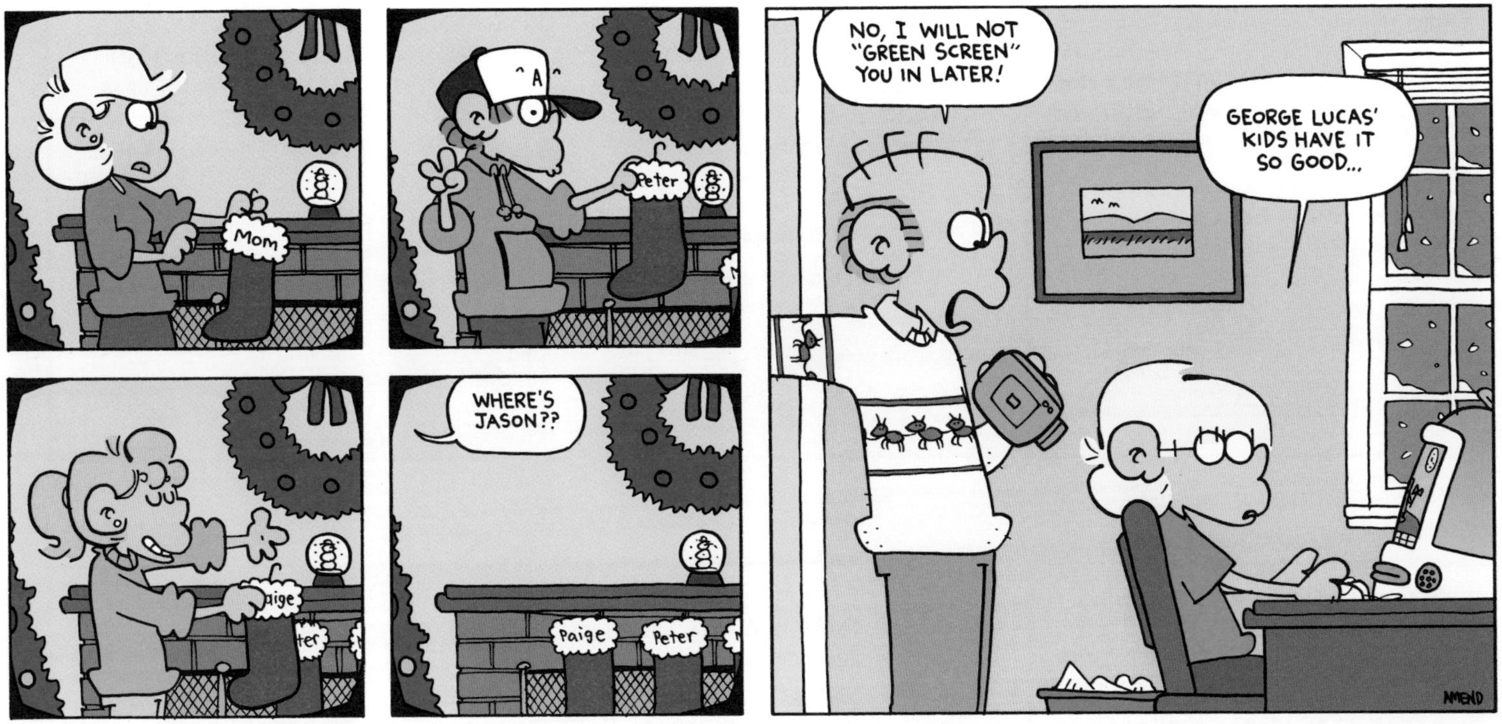
Mom
Peter
Paige
WHERE'S JASON??
Paige
Peter
NO, I WILL NOT "GREEN SCREEN" YOU IN LATER!
GEORGE LUCAS' KIDS HAVE IT SO GOOD...

December 24, 2006

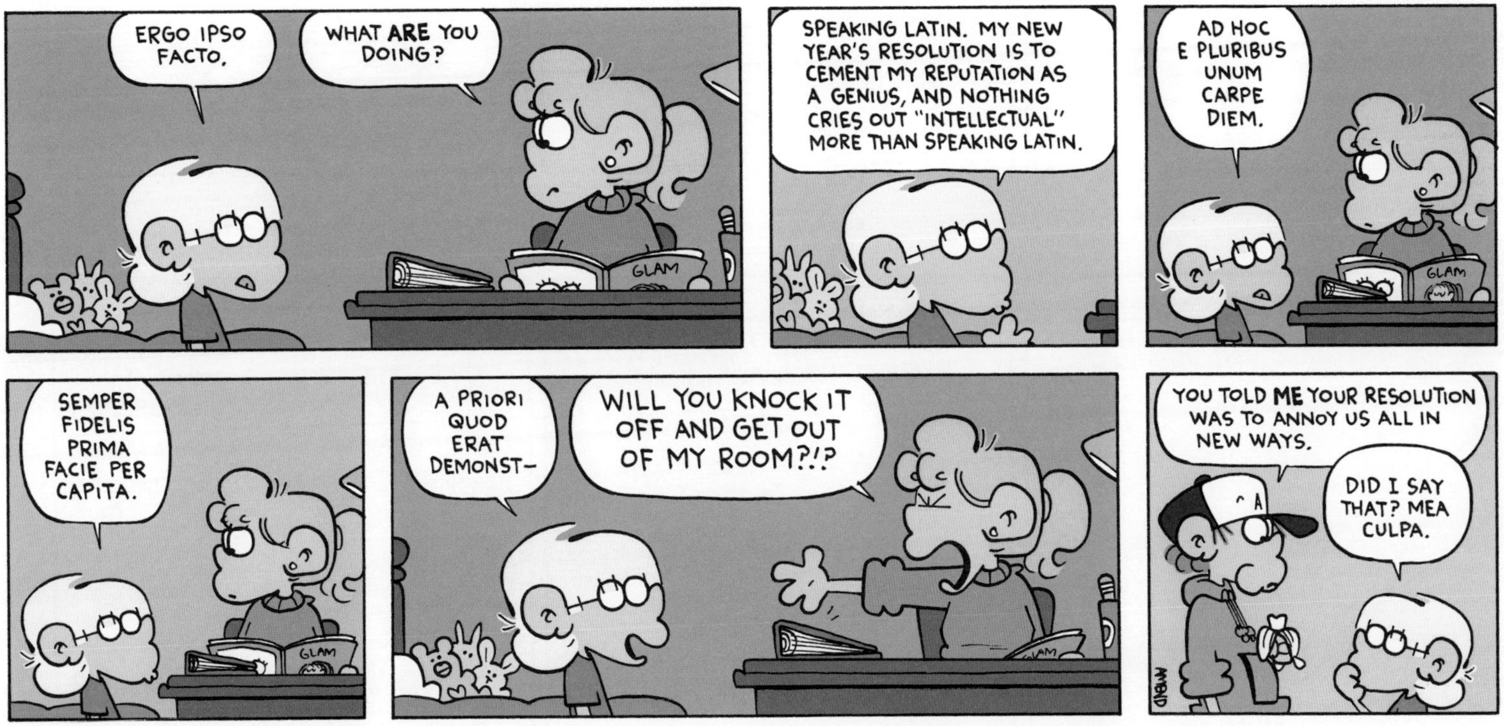
ERGO IPSO FACTO.
WHAT ARE YOU DOING?
GLAM
SPEAKING LATIN. MY NEW YEAR'S RESOLUTION IS TO CEMENT MY REPUTATION AS A GENIUS, AND NOTHING CRIES OUT "INTELLECTUAL" MORE THAN SPEAKING LATIN.
AD HOC E PLURIBUS UNUM CARPE DIEM.
GLAM
SEMPER FIDELIS PRIMA FACIE PER CAPITA.
GLAM
A PRIORI QUOD ERAT DEMONST–
WILL YOU KNOCK IT OFF AND GET OUT OF MY ROOM?!?
YOU TOLD ME YOUR RESOLUTION WAS TO ANNOY US ALL IN NEW WAYS.
DID I SAY THAT? MEA CULPA.

December 31, 2006

My last week of dailies. These were tough to do, both on a personal level and on a tonal one. I was sort of saying "half good-bye." How do you do that?

ANYTHING NOTEWORTHY IN THE NEWS?

LET'S SEE... A CARTOONIST IS SWITCHING HIS COMIC STRIP TO SUNDAYS ONLY...

HE SAYS THAT AFTER ALMOST 19 YEARS ON THE JOB HE WANTS TO "GET OUT OF THE HOUSE AND TRY SOME NEW THINGS."

I ASKED IF THERE WAS ANYTHING NOTEWORTHY IN THE NEWS.

LET'S SEE... BRAD AND ANGELINA WENT GROCERY SHOPPING...

December 25, 2006

WHY WOULD A CARTOONIST WANT TO DO FEWER CARTOONS?

MAYBE HE WANTS TO FREE UP TIME FOR OTHER PURSUITS.

LIKE WHAT?

I DON'T KNOW. I'M SURE THERE ARE ALL KINDS OF WORTHWHILE TASKS HE COULD CHOOSE FROM.

I SUPPOSE.

HE COULD WRITE NEW THINGS... HE COULD DO VOLUNTEER WORK...

WHOA! SOME GUY IN WORLD OF WARQUEST WENT FROM LEVEL 1 TO LEVEL 60 IN TWO DAYS!

December 26, 2006

IF A CARTOONIST WANTS TIME TO DO OTHER THINGS, COULDN'T HE JUST HIRE PEOPLE?

TO DO WHAT?

YOU KNOW, TAKE OVER THE ART OR WRITING. I'M SURE READERS WOULDN'T NOTICE.

PASS THE SUGAR.

GET IT YOURSELF.

December 27, 2006

Panel 1:
SO IS THIS SEMI-RETIRING CARTOONIST GOING TO FIND A NEW JOB?

I GUESS WE'LL JUST HAVE TO WAIT AND SEE.

Panel 2:
THEN AGAIN, WHAT KIND OF JOB DOES A CAREER IN CARTOONING PREPARE YOU FOR? PROFESSIONAL GOOF-OFF? PROFESSIONAL NAP-TAKER?

Panel 3:
PROFESSIONAL DEADLINE-MISSER?

I THINK YOU'RE BEING A LITTLE HARSH.

THERE'S SOME GUY AT THE DOOR WHO SAYS HE'LL EAT POTATO CHIPS IF WE PAY HIM.

December 28, 2006

Panel 1:
IT'LL BE INTERESTING TO SEE WHAT THIS GUY'S LAST DAILY STRIP IS LIKE.

I AGREE.

Panel 2:
I MEAN, THIS'LL BE A SIGNIFICANT MOMENT IN HIS STRIP'S LIFE. I WOULD THINK HE'D WANT TO END THE DAILIES WITH A BANG.

Panel 3:
MOM! JASON'S MIXING UP SOMETHING WEIRD WITH HIS CHEMISTRY SET!

FIGURATIVELY, OF COURSE.

OF COURSE.

December 29, 2006

Panel 1:
I JUST HOPE THIS CARTOONIST FELLOW REALIZES JUST HOW LUCKY HE'S BEEN THESE PAST 19 YEARS.

I'M SURE HE DOES.

Panel 2:
THE OPPORTUNITY TO DO A COMIC STRIP THAT MILLIONS OF PEOPLE READ EVERY DAY IS A RARE AND SPECIAL PRIVILEGE. THIS GUY HAD SURE BETTER THANK ALL THE NEWSPAPERS AND READERS WHO STUCK WITH HIM AND MADE IT POSSIBLE.

Panel 3:
MAYBE HE'LL SAY SOMETHING LIKE THAT IN THE STRIP.

AND BREAK THE FOURTH WALL? NOT LIKELY.

December 30, 2006

A DADDY BEAR, A MOMMY BEAR, AND A DAUGHTER BEAR.

THE DADDY BEAR **CLAIMED** TO LOVE THE DAUGHTER BEAR.

THE MOMMY BEAR **CLAIMED** TO LOVE THE DAUGHTER BEAR.

BUT WHEN THE DAUGHTER BEAR ASKED IF SHE COULD HAVE A MERE $319 FOR A PAIR OF DESIGNER SHOES, THE MOMMY AND DADDY BEARS SHOWED THEIR TRUE COLORS.

THEY TOLD THE DAUGHTER BEAR SHE'D HAVE TO EARN THE MONEY HERSELF.

January 28, 2007

February 11, 2007

276

April 29, 2007

I wrote this after a day pool-side with a bunch of cartoonists. It was blinding.

June 24, 2007

277

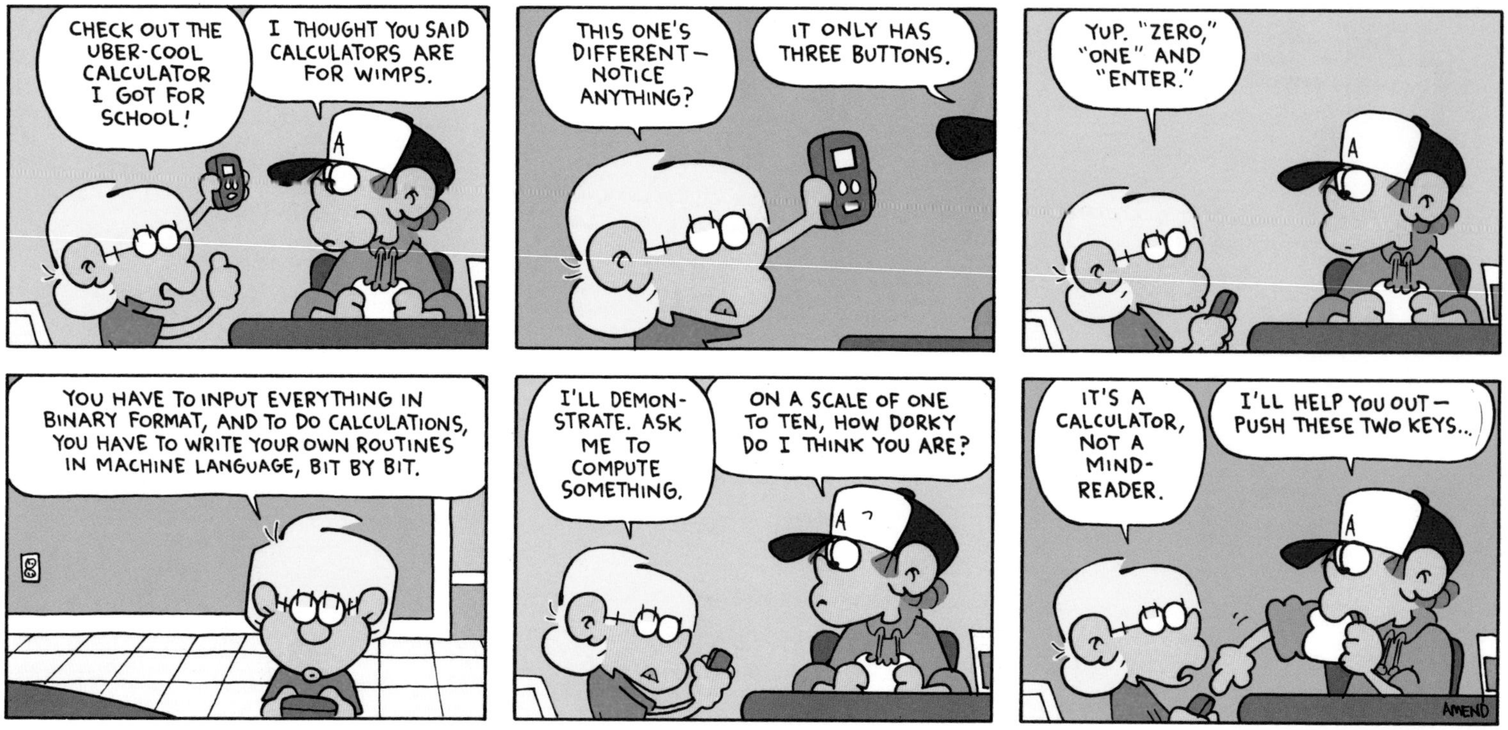
CHECK OUT THE UBER-COOL CALCULATOR I GOT FOR SCHOOL!
I THOUGHT YOU SAID CALCULATORS ARE FOR WIMPS.
THIS ONE'S DIFFERENT— NOTICE ANYTHING?
IT ONLY HAS THREE BUTTONS.
YUP. "ZERO," "ONE" AND "ENTER."
YOU HAVE TO INPUT EVERYTHING IN BINARY FORMAT, AND TO DO CALCULATIONS, YOU HAVE TO WRITE YOUR OWN ROUTINES IN MACHINE LANGUAGE, BIT BY BIT.
I'LL DEMONSTRATE. ASK ME TO COMPUTE SOMETHING.
ON A SCALE OF ONE TO TEN, HOW DORKY DO I THINK YOU ARE?
IT'S A CALCULATOR, NOT A MIND-READER.
I'LL HELP YOU OUT— PUSH THESE TWO KEYS...
AMEND

August 26, 2007

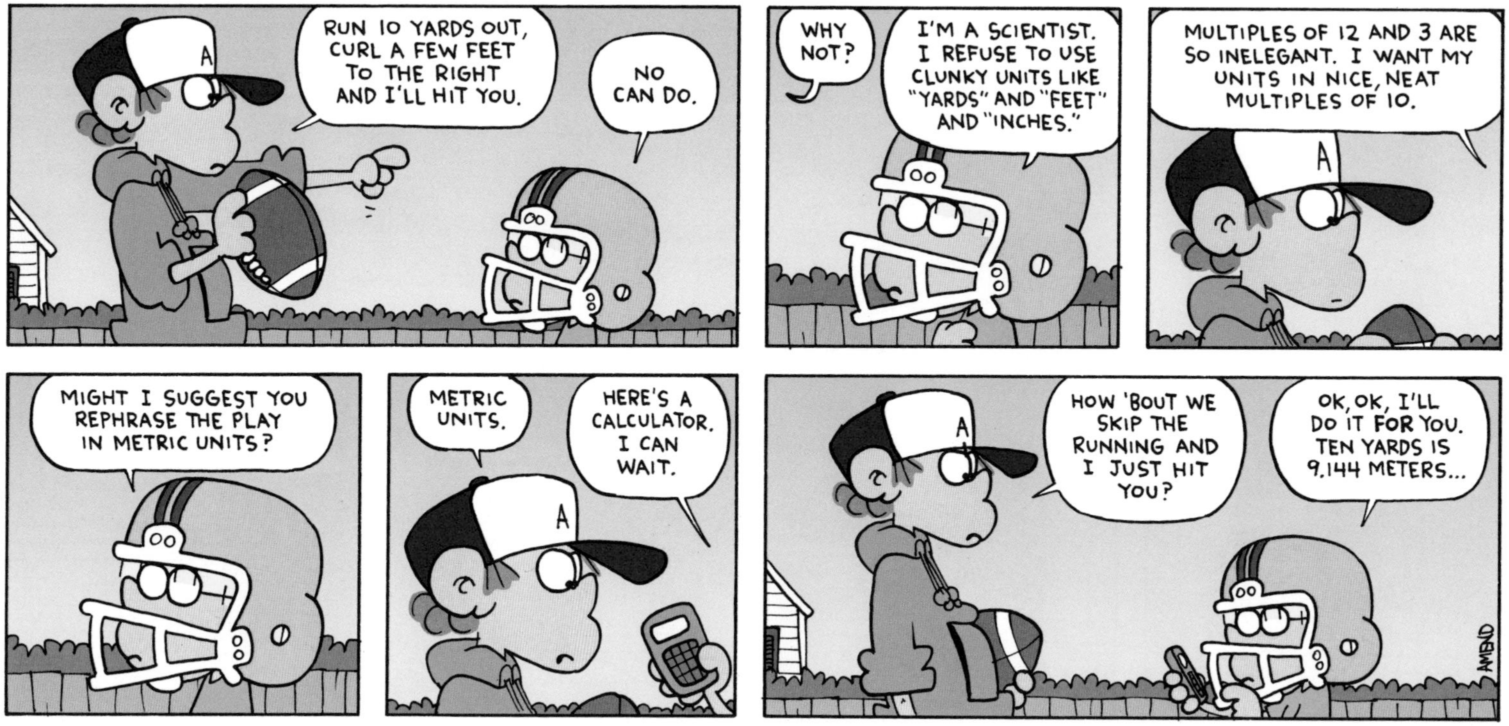
RUN 10 YARDS OUT, CURL A FEW FEET TO THE RIGHT AND I'LL HIT YOU.
NO CAN DO.
WHY NOT?
I'M A SCIENTIST. I REFUSE TO USE CLUNKY UNITS LIKE "YARDS" AND "FEET" AND "INCHES."
MULTIPLES OF 12 AND 3 ARE SO INELEGANT. I WANT MY UNITS IN NICE, NEAT MULTIPLES OF 10.
MIGHT I SUGGEST YOU REPHRASE THE PLAY IN METRIC UNITS?
METRIC UNITS.
HERE'S A CALCULATOR. I CAN WAIT.
HOW 'BOUT WE SKIP THE RUNNING AND I JUST HIT YOU?
OK, OK, I'LL DO IT FOR YOU. TEN YARDS IS 9.144 METERS...
AMEND

September 30, 2007

October 28, 2007

December 30, 2007

Sometimes I think there should be a maximum age as well as the current minimum age to serve in Congress.

February 10, 2008

If this game ever gets made, I hope I at least get a free copy.

February 17, 2008